WHY NOT?

Daring To Live The Challenge Of Christ

WHY NOT?
Daring To Live
The Challenge Of Christ

William J. O'Malley, S.J.

"Whom shall I send?
Who will be our messenger?"
And I said,
"Here I am.
Send me."
— Isaiah 6:8

ALBA · HOUSE NEW · YORK

SOCIETY OF ST. PAUL, 2187 VICTORY BLVD., STATEN ISLAND, NEW YORK 10314

Library of Congress Cataloging-in-Publication Data

O'Malley, William J.
  Why not?

  1. Meditations.   I. Title.
BX2182.2.043   1986   242   86-14059
ISBN 0-8189-0504-2

*Designed, printed and bound in the United States of
America by the Fathers and Brothers of the
Society of St. Paul, 2187 Victory Boulevard,
Staten Island, New York 10314, as part of their
communications apostolate.*

2 3 4 5 6 7 8 9 (Current Printing: first digit)

This book is for
Concetta Gioia, and
John and Ailene Glavin, and
Jeanne Teddy,
who dared to say,
"Why not?"

CONTENTS

Calling

1. Calling 3
2. Ungilding the Lily 5
3. The Model Disciple 9
4. Running Away 11
5. Un-Pride 13

Someone's Coming

6. The Absence of Heroism 19
7. The Disguises of God 21
8. Repent! Repent! 23
9. Pregnancy 26
10. All Souls Day 28
11. The Immaculate Conception .31
12. The Big, Bad, Beautiful Balancing Rock 33
13. Christmas and Xmas 36
14. The Never-Ending Story 39
15. The Star-Gazers 42
16. The Holy Family 45

Starting Over

17. The Perpetual January First .49
18. The Baptism of Jesus 52
19. I Can Get It For You Cut-Rate 54

The Mission of Christ is Ours

20. Jesus' Inaugural Address 59
21. Anti-Beatitudes 62
22. The First Miracle 64
23. Being Spoiled 67
24. Forgiving God 69
25. Back to Basics 71
26. Time is Money (Only Better) 75
27. The Burden of Astonishment 77
28. The Only Two Commandments 79
29. Conflicts of Interest 82
30. Turning Sheep Into Shepherds 85
31. St. Francis of Assisi 87
32. For Love or Money 90
33. Gratitude 92
34. Hanging in There 94
35. The Widow's Mite 96
36. Love > Justice 98
37. Jesus, the Naif 101
38. Apparently Barren Fig Trees 103
39. Sheep and Shepherds 106
40. Talents 107

The Week That Changed the World

41. Pomp and Circumstance 113
42. Grimless Sacrifice 115
43. The Ill-Mannered Jesus 118
44. The Power of Darkness 120
45. The Heart of Darkness 122
46. The *Tao* 124
47. The Eucharist of Our Lives .126
48. I Am 128
49. The Anguish of God 130

All Things New

50. The Rebirth 135
51. Spring 137
52. Doubting Thomas 139
53. Ascension Morning 141
54. Ascension Evening 145
55. Pentecost 147

Loving

56. Overdosing on Love 153
57. Love and Death 155
58. The Nefarious Velveteen Rabbit 158
59. Deserving Love 161
60. Tough Love 162
61. Love of Things 165
62. The Intoxicating Commonplace 167

INTRODUCTION

This is a very dangerous book. At least I hope it will be dangerous, in the same way the gospels are surely dangerous. It asks you to entertain the possibility that God is asking you to live your life more intensely than you'd planned—which is itself unsettling for starters. The price may be a lot of comfortable and protective habits and attitudes. Further, it asks (at least as an experiment) that you surrender for a quarter-hour a day your dependence on the discursive intelligence which balances budgets, works through assignments, figures things out. Instead, it asks you to open up unsuspected reservoirs of your spirit, and to allow the Spirit of God to take over.

The discursive intelligence is the power that analyzes, appraises, objectively judges. Most of our education tries to strengthen it, including the discursive study of theology. I surely don't mean to denigrate the discursive intelligence. But in my experience it's taken over and dominates almost all of what is called religious education. *Knowing about* God has replaced *knowing* God.

For the most part, we don't know persons analytically. And God—who, we are told even in the most analytic theology class, is a person—gets treated as little more than a character in a novel or a figure in history. Therefore, if he is to be known in any way other than the strictly and coldly academic mode, we have to approach him as we would approach any other person we want to know: as a friend.

But we are great talkers and rather poor listeners. Even in

prayer, we want to dominate, to tell God something he doesn't know, and then be sure that the conversation is productive. What I am suggesting in these pages is that we give God a chance, too. So, for a few minutes a day, I'm asking you to check your discursive intelligence at the door (preferably along with your shoes)—all that itching to come up with answers, to capture everything in words and formulas. I'm asking you to take the risk of being vulnerable to God.

The scriptures can do that, and they *are* the voice of God. I'm only a whisper in the wilderness. But the kind of reader I envision has already become perhaps too accustomed to the scriptures. He or she is looking for something different for awhile to prime the pump.

One day a friend of mine was grading *Macbeth* tests at his desk when his little daughter came up and said, "Daddy, Daddy! Come quick! The roof! The birds!" But he was up against a deadline; he'd promised his students he'd have the papers back the following day. With hardly a look at her he said, as many parents do, "Not now, honey. Daddy's busy." He went on with his work, hardly remembering that she'd even bothered him, when suddenly he was aware of her standing next to his desk, a big fat tear running down her cheek. In that moment he really saw her.

Wisely, he got up and let her lead him by the hand to the apartment window, and for ten minutes or so they looked out at the birds on the adjoining roof. They weren't "accomplishing" anything, but something was happening. In that moment of non-logical vision, things had fallen into their true perspective for him again. The murderous Macbeth has lasted for 350 years, but his daughter would be filled with wonder for only a few.

I know you have lots of important things to do, promises to keep, and miles to go before you sleep. But I have a Friend I'd like you to meet.

Take my hand. Come to the window.

CALLING

1. Calling

> *"Rabbi, where do you live?" they asked.*
> *And he said, "Come and see."*   — John 1:38-39

Habit tends to erode the richness of things, especially of words. "Vocation" has become a scary word, because it's been isolated into meaning only a call to the priesthood or religious life. And yet each of us, in acknowledging our baptism, accepts a vocation—a calling—to be a prophet of the liberating Good News of Jesus Christ. I suspect that every verse of each of the gospels is just one more variation on that one central theme: *we are called forth.*

Nor is it merely in the New Testament. The Old Testament is filled with calling as well. Adam and Eve were called, and Abraham and Sarah, and Joseph and Mary—to come out of their calm security, out into wider horizons than they had planned to enjoy. And, lest we forget, they were all lay people.

Why all these calls? Because our human nature itself is a call—to grow, to splinter our secure certitudes and see with a wider lens than the one our parents gave us. The very nature of the human mind and heart is to be hungry for more. At times, that hunger can be perverted and assuaged merely by more money, more "things," more lines in the newspaper. But at its core, it's the hunger to know, to see what's just beyond the hill. It's the call that drew Neanderthals from their caves, and Columbus from Europe, and astronauts out among the stars, and all human souls even beyond that. The very word "education" means "to lead out"; the word "vocation" is a call. Nor is that hungry urge laid to rest when we finish our formal education or make our definitive choice of profession or career. We are sons and daughters of an itinerant and never-contented God, who calls us always further. Growing is in our blood.

I confess the call of the Twelve kind of pulls me up short.

Jesus merely says, "Come and see," and they drop everything and come. In my more altruistic moments, I say, "My God, what faith!" They just chucked everything over and went out on the road with him. But in my more critical moments, I find myself saying, "Now *wait* a minute." Of the twelve of them, odds are that at least a few of them were married; they all seemed to have had jobs, and people depended on them. What was it? They were fed to the teeth with the wife's nagging, and the kids squalling, and the stink of fish? And surely it couldn't have been *both* instantaneous *and* reasoned. The tall, dark stranger comes loping into town and whispers, "Psst! Hey, babe. C'mon," and off they trot.

When my own vocation to the priesthood was pursuing me, let me tell you, it was a helluva lot more complicated and protracted duel than that. I dodged, I threw up smoke screens, I hid behind every one of the seven deadly sins—consecutively and concurrently. Finally, of course, and to my great joy, I surrendered to my destiny. It was, after all, inevitable. My Antagonist has infinite patience and a bag of tricks that makes my own look empty.

Trouble is: he's still using them on me. Just when I get everything all arranged and comfy and working smoothly, he delivers a curve or a screwball or a spitter. He drops in my path a book that's really too thick and too deep and too time-consuming. "Psst! Hey, babe. C'mon." He calls me up on the phone, disguising his voice, of course, and asks me to give a talk on something I don't really know much about. Yet. "Psst! Hey, babe. C'mon." In the 60's, he disguised himself as a hot-eyed radical who saw phoniness even in sincerity; in the 80's, he splits himself up and pretends to be a whole passel of students headed blissfully for MBA's with a complacency that would make Pollyanna blanch. "Psst! Hey, babe. C'mon. Change up. Switch gears." Worst of all his tricks, he makes me bored with the tried-and-true. "Psst!"

Of course, he does the same to you. One of the kids is chauffeured home from practice with a broken leg. The Market does a barrel-roll and Daddy comes home with a pink slip in his pay envelope. Mommy discovers to her chagrin that she's harboring a new little guest she hadn't quite expected. Wars, plague, pestilence, riots, "and the thousand natural shocks that flesh is heir to."

"Psst! Hey, babe. C'mon."

Something in us craves peace—not the peace of someone dancing serenely on a high wire without a net, but the peace of inertia, the peace of not being bothered, the peace which, under all its disguises, is a kind of death. But we were not born for that kind of peace. We were born for the hungry mind, the high wire, the open road. And in the going we're already there.

He may not be the God we want, but he's the God we've got.

"Psst! Hey, babe. C'mon."

* * * * *

2. Ungilding the Lily

When Simon Peter saw this, he fell at Jesus' knees
and said, "Lord, depart from me. I am a sinful man."
—Luke 5:8

When I went to Lourdes, I'd planned to spend the whole day there. Instead, I spent about four hours in the railroad station itching to get the first available train out of there.

The first problem was the town. Every inch of street right up to the gates of the shrine was crammed with shops hawking religious rip-offs: gold-plated rosaries, and John XXIII dinner plates, and plastic madonna rosary cases that lit up in the dark and played the Lourdes Hymn. Going inside was like snapping off a hurricane. The grounds were lovely and peaceful; the basilica was a mountainous pile of marble curves and spires; the forest of crutches at the grotto was awesome.

But even there, a mutant strain of that same get-rich-quick infection from the town had gotten past the gates and rooted itself inside. On the one hand, there was a bus caravan of a thousand pilgrims from Italy. It was like a Fellini movie. I saw one old lady entirely in black gorging down Lourdes water without pausing for breath. Crowds of people were filling up plastic jerry-cans, like the gas cans on jeeps, with Lourdes water to take home. On the other hand, at a bit of a distance, leaning silently against a balustrade, were other hawk-eyed visitors who seemed—at least to someone as disillusioned as I'd become—to be just *waiting* to see someone leap miraculously off a gurney cart and justify the observer's travel expenses.

I fled. But in Spain I encountered the same thing at Loyola, the birthplace of St. Ignatius, the founder of the Jesuits. Everything was marbled over; everybody in the town was trying to wangle a few pesos out of the visitors, trying to profiteer on the life of an ascetic. They'd missed the whole point. And yet, pictures of the Holy Land also seem to say that missing the point is a world-wide plague—marble and gold where once there was just the dirt and the manger, which God had chosen *instead* of marble and gold.

I was reminded of the no-doubt apocryphal story about a visitor to the Vatican during the Renaissance. The pope was showing him through the breathtaking basilica and the gardens and the treasuries of art. "See," the pope reputedly said, "Peter need no longer say, 'Silver and gold I have none.'" And the visitor replied, "No, Holiness. And neither can he say, 'Take up thy bed and walk.'"

I was reminded, too, of Peter after the overwhelming experience of the Transfiguration, saying to Jesus, "Let us build three tabernacles here, one for you, one for Moses, and one for Elijah." The Lord must have sighed and shaken his head and wondered if it were really worth all the bother—just as he must have done seconds before the Ascension when, after three years with him, after the shattering experiences of the crucifixion and the resurrection, his Eleven best students stood around him, eager-eyed, and asked, "Okay. *Now* you're going to restore the Kingdom to Israel, right?" I wonder if at that moment Jesus couldn't wait to get to the train station, too.

Our Lady and Bernadette were just little peasant girls. They'd probably be embarrassed to be trussed up in cloth of gold, intimidated by all the marble, willfully turned into something they were not. They were more at home with rough clothes and rough hands and rough work. But we would rather see them as heroines "should" look: like Faye Dunaway and Cheryl Tiegs. Why do we even believe Our Lady had to be beautiful—much less blue-eyed and white-skinned?

What's worst is that the opulence of Lourdes misses the whole point of the message that God has been sending since the beginning of time, namely: God doesn't look for messengers in marble palaces; he goes to the ash heaps. If there's anything one discovers about the personality of God from the scriptures, it's his embarrassing penchant for nobodies. God is an incorrigible sucker for the Cinderellas of this world.

Consider just a few. If you were looking for a man and woman to be the parents of the whole Hebrew race, would you pick Abraham and Sarah, who were both in their 70's and barren as a pair of bricks? If you were looking for a likely contender against Goliath, would you even consider a spindly little shepherd kid like David? The prophet Jeremiah was a stammerer; the general Gideon was a coward; the Moses you find in the Bible was far more like Don Knotts than like the Charlton Heston you find on the screen. When God went calling for the mother of his Son, he didn't go to Rome or Athens or Alexandria; he went to a no-name village, in a backwater province, to a little girl who very likely could neither read nor write. When

God chose his first pope, he chose a man who realized full well that he was a sinner and therefore "unworthy" of his calling. When God chose the Redeemer of all humankind, it wasn't a silver-sheathed commander at the head of a glittering host; it was the greatest Loser of them all—a battered carpenter gasping his last with spikes through his wrists and a crown of thorns on his head.

Surely, if *that* didn't get his point across, nothing could. And yet, apparently, nothing can subvert our demand that real winners *look* like real winners. We're distracted by all the advertisements for life as it "really" is.

That same helplessness haunts me every time my students or their parents or my colleagues say, "Oh, I could never do anything like that. I'm just a nobody. What difference could I make?" Can you imagine the noise if *all* the little nobodies raised their voices? And don't you realize how dangerous it is to think you're just a nobody? God's on the prowl for nobodies! Claiming to be a nobody is worse than spilling salt, or stepping on a crack, or walking under a ladder. Claiming to be a nobody is tempting lightning from heaven.

What's more, claiming to be a nobody is in defiance of your birth; *you* were called by God from "the no of all nothing" to exist, to come alive. And claiming to be a nobody is also in defiance of your baptism, when you were anointed a prophet of the Good News to anyone you meet.

Don't miss the point of the callings which took place in Lourdes, and Nazareth, and of every message God has sent us since the beginning of humankind. Don't say, "I'm a nobody." On the one hand, it's highly dangerous. On the other hand, it's a self-starving—and therefore self-defeating—lie.

*   *   *   *   *

3. The Model Disciple

"You are Peter. And on this rock I will build my Church."
—Matthew 16:18

One reason people read the gospel so rarely is that it's so very dangerous. We'd prefer not to know what it really asks of us, thank you very much. I mean, it says, "If you want to be my disciple, sell all you have and give it to the poor." It says, if you want to enter the Kingdom, you have to become as gullible as a child, ready to give to anyone—especially to those who don't deserve your gift. It says, if you want to find yourself, you've got to forget yourself. It says, if you want to be first, put everybody else ahead of you.

Well, now. The Miami Dolphins wouldn't get very far on that advice, would they? And the Miami Dolphins draw bigger crowds than Jesus any day. The whole thing's impossible. All this giving, and loving, and vulnerability. Best to settle for nice, comfortable mediocrity and leave the rest to the priests and nuns. That's what they get paid for. The gospel-all-the-way is just too much for ordinary Christians.

It's in order to subvert that falsehood, I think, that the gospels give Peter so much more space than the other apostles: because he's so much like all the rest of us. That's why he's the first called, always the first named. That's why he's at the Transfiguration, and the Agony in the Garden, and Jesus' trial. He's eager; he's protective of Jesus; he tries so hard. But, oh God, how he bumbles! Peter gets all that space not because he's the ideal apostle, but because he's the usual apostle.

He leaps eagerly onto the water to get to Jesus—and then begins thinking about the danger to himself, instead of about Jesus. When the apostles ask dumb questions, most often it's Peter. Impulsively, he tries to defend Jesus from the soldiers, and all he can do is lop off an earlobe. And when he tries to get Jesus to walk away from the crucifixion, Jesus snarls at him, "Get out of my way, you Satan!" He wants so badly to do the right thing, but he's always chickening out halfway through.

That's why Peter is such a great consolation to me when I sin—remembering that, within a couple of hours of his ordination as a priest, his first Mass, his first Communion, the first pope denied Christ. Not to a soldier with a knife at his throat. To a waitress. And not once. Three times, with plenty of time in between to think it over. And Jesus not only forgave him, but he made him the head of all the others.

That's what Peter's *for*, I think: to show us that even bumblers like ourselves can be not only loved but called to the first place—at the end of the line. It shows—as all the Cinderella stories in the scriptures show—that God can make miracles even with mud and spit.

But there's one very important difference between Peter and most of us: he tried, might and main—tried to live the whole thing to the hilt. Even if he did deny Christ, he was the only one there at the trial. He was, after all, the one who did leap from the boat. He was the one who tried, wrong-headedly but ardently, to protect Jesus. He was the one, for all his faults, who said, "Lord, to whom shall we go? You have the words of eternal life." If he failed, he failed in trying greatly. Beyond doubt, he was the last of the apostles in understanding, in keeping faith, in succeeding —and yet Jesus chose him to be the first of them.

Why? Because he had the guts to fail. He knew only too well the dangers of really listening to his intimidating call of Jesus. But he plunged into it, heart and soul. Yes, he botched, lost confidence, fell to thinking of the cost to himself. But he always came back, just as eager to try again.

Peter thought best with his heart and very badly with his head. That's why Jesus made him the first over all of them— because Jesus knew that it was not philosophy, or politics, or business that would save the world from its endless stupidities. It

was blind, naive, generous love. That's what Jesus had come for,
to spread that fire on the earth.

How about you? Taken any risks lately? Spread any fire
lately?

"Lord, depart from me. I am a sinful man."

But Jesus didn't.

*   *   *   *   *

4. Running away

> *The call of Yahweh came to Jonah, son of Amittai:*
> *"Up! Go to Nineveh, the great metropolis, and tell them*
> *that I know their wickedness."*
> *So, Jonah decided to flee to Tarshish away from*
> *Yahweh.*
>   —Jonah 1:1-3

Assyria was Israel's traditional enemy. Assyrian armies had
occupied Israel and deported many people—the "Ten Lost
Tribes."

Now, in that situation, no less a personage than the Lord
God Yahweh suddenly appears to little Jonah with an interesting
suggestion. "I want you to go and evangelize Nineveh"—which
just happened to be the capital of Assyria. All those bazaars, and
belly dancers, and caliphs. Name your perversion, and we've got
it for you. And we're inventing new ones every day.

Therefore, this call was like saying to a little French tailor—
with the pounding of Nazi jackboots on the cobbles outside his
shop: "Jonah, *mon vieux!* What's say we go and convert Berlin?"

"*Zut alors!*" gasps Jonah, and takes the only intelligent
option open to him: he runs in the other direction. If Nineveh is
in the east, then westward, ho! He sets out to sea. But—of
course—a storm comes up. The superstitious sailors look
around for the jinx. And Jonah shrugs and says, "*Helas, c'est*

moi!" So, somewhat ungallantly, they pitch him overboard. But Yahweh has this big fish, just waiting, see? And the big fish gulps up little Jonah, finds his way to Haifa, and spews him—pffft!— right back where he started.

There's no escaping the plans of God. I doubt Jonah converted all of Nineveh, no matter what the story says. Just getting Jonah to try is miracle enough for me. He stopped resisting his destiny; he stopped resisting God's call; he stopped resisting a life larger than the one he'd intended to live. He forgot his own shortcomings, and got on with the job.

So, today the Lord God Yahweh pays a visit to your kitchen, or your office, or your classroom. "Hi!" he says. "Let's go change the world. Of course, we're not going to win. But the enormity of evil will be less because of you. You game?"

Well, now . . . uh . . . .

We live in a nation not unlike Assyria, where anyone with a hard message can't be heard above the beat of "Go ahead with your life, this is *my* life." Anyone with the unlikely combination of principles and guts looks suspiciously like a fascist. Who mentions temperance to the chap who just inherited the still?

We live in the land of the free and the home of the brave. Everything's free because you only have to show them a little plastic card and walk off with anything that takes your fancy. We're free to believe in everything at once—even contradictory ideas, like the loathsomeness of battering babies, but the expediency of aborting them. We style ourselves free-thinkers, and yet freedom means making choices and sticking by them. Paradoxically, freedom limits us. Freedom costs.

And the home of the brave has electronic surveillance, with four locks, and electric can openers, and washers, and recorders so we needn't suffer even the inconvenience of missing "Dallas" while we're out at the hair stylist.

Abraham Lincoln, one suspects, would have wept. He was a nobody, a farm boy and rail-splitter from Illinois, but a man of flinty integrity, who wasn't afraid to look at things in their true perspective. He wasn't afraid to challenge Nineveh. He knew that human decency for the exploited demanded sacrifice from the comfortable. There are realities—most of them intangible, and surely not marketable—which are more important than comfort, or convenience, or even peace. Or even death.

Who wants to stand up against the orgies of Nineveh, or the vested interests of Jerusalem, or the injustices of your neighborhood or office or school? Shrewder to run in the other direction.

But if you do, you find nothing but storms. And that big fish will always be lurking in the waters around you, just waiting to gobble you up and escort you back to your destiny.

"Hi! Let's start with your neighborhood. Let's start with your office. Let's start with the 30 kids in your classroom. Oh, no, no, no! I'm not looking for a world-beater. I'm looking for you."

*   *   *   *   *

5. Un-pride

"No kingdom can be at war with itself without being
brought to desolation."   —Luke 11:17

I believe in God, the Father, the Almighty Creator. And I believe in humankind, created in God's image—and never more like the heavenly Father than when we ourselves create. God's given each of us a staggering gift: our incomplete selves. And he's offered us the freedom to help him complete that creation. Each of us has a unique potential to create something no other creature ever has or ever will create: a kingdom, with battlements and turrets and flags, like none other of God's dwellings.

But so often, like the Israelites, we are a kingdom at war with itself. And we spend forty years—or perhaps forever—grumbling around wildernesses of indecision, while our kingdom awaits creation. We chafe against God that he didn't create us like this one or that one, longing for a kingdom ready-made by God alone, fearing our daily freedom to create ourselves with him. There is, deep inside each of us, an inescapable conviction of our own unique value, and yet the devil of fear—who is a mute—wrestles against that conviction, every day, in darkness. And it is only by an inflexible act of faith in our own value that the devil of fear can be cast out.

But, isn't it gross pride to exult in my own goodness, to unflinchingly affirm my own value? Isn't it by Beelzebub, the devil-prince of pride, that I cast out the devil of fear and create a kingdom with myself as king-god?

Here, as in so many cases, the core problem is years of inept choice of words. For years, we've been told that "pride" and "self-love" and "ambition" are sins, devils if you will—when what the foolish speaker really meant was "arrogance" and "conceit" and "disdain." But the vices—and the virtues—were condemned and avoided under the same univocal label.

Pride is not our sin. Our devil is rather un-pride: the inability to see and rejoice at the fact that God has made us worthy of his life, that no matter what we might think of our worth he finds us pretty nifty.

Grace works through nature, and nature is all we have.

Until I was nearly 32, I listened to warped interpretations of the gospel from well-intentioned teachers and preachers. With admirable docility — even with masochistic eagerness — I grasped to my bosom their flinty doctrine that I was an "unprofitable servant." Being unprofitable, of course, and able to list every one of my manifold shortcomings, I was quite effectively paralyzed out of service—even unprofitable service.

I believed them when they said that pride was a sin. Consequently, I apologized for anything that I was good at. Anytime I did anything praiseworthy, I was the first one to spike all the praise by pointing out every single place where what I'd done fell short of perfection. I became quite adept at sneering at my own feeble efforts at anything: schoolwork, writing, conversation, chopping down a tree . . . breathing. It took me till I was over 30 to realize that all that self-inflicted pain had been not only useless but paralyzing, that it was the result of something as stupidly simple as sloppy use of language.

Pride is, ironically, humble. It's an honest acceptance of the fact that nothing we do can be perfect, but what we've done is our best. We've given with both hands and without reserve, and if our Father in heaven is proud of us, who the hell are we not to be proud of ourselves? Arrogance is something far different. It's the sin of Adam, of Oedipus, of the Prodigal Son: I can do it on my own—without my Father.

Few of us, I think, are in danger of arrogance. We have built-in governors against it: all those years of nit-picking, all those years of staring into the mirror at our warts and zits, all those years of report cards and races and credit ratings that always "proved" how mediocre we are. Our sin is the sin of the man in the parable who was given only a thousand talents—so he went out and buried them, so they wouldn't be lost.

Honest pride says: "Okay. I'm not the most talented, but by God I'm gonna use what I've got." There's the key: by God. I don't take pride in my miserable store of talents; I do take pride in the fact that, no matter what my imperfections, I've been *chosen*—by God! It doesn't matter that I'm a spindly shepherd kid; God can make me a king! He's done it before! It doesn't matter that I'm only an ordinary housewife in a kitchen; God can make me his bride! He's done it before!

By myself, I am an unprofitable servant, but God can take *stones* and turn them into sons of Abraham. He made a universe out of nothing. Surely he can use me, warts and all. I know that parts of my personality will actually be *obstacles* for some people to find the Kingdom of God. But there are some people who do have warts just like mine, and I can help them. As for the others, well, it just proves that God doesn't need me. That's humility. But he wants to use me. That's pride.

*   *   *   *   *

SOMEONE'S COMING

6. The Absence of Heroism

"A man came, sent by God. His name was John."

—John 1:6

When I was a kid, John the Baptist was inescapable. First of all, our parish was St. John the Baptist. Second, and worst perhaps, whenever the nun told us to write an essay on our patron saint, I couldn't exactly write on St. William, could I? That would have taken considerable research so, since my middle name is John, I always scored Brownie points by claiming my patron saint was John the Baptist (even though I was really just named after my Dad—who, now, really is my patron saint).

I kinda liked ol' John, though. To me, he always looked like Robert Ryan—or to the non-Trivia buffs, Clint Eastwood. I could picture him emerging from the heat-haze of the desert, raw-boned, fiery-eyed, single-minded. His chest was like a washboard, with tufts of mismatched hair curling up here and there, and hanks of smelly camelskin draped across his loins. John Wayne-tough, that was our ol' John. He appealed to me, as I suppose John Wayne did, because he was everything I wanted to be and wasn't, and never could be.

In my more recent conflicts with the truth—with the way things are (or at least with the way *I* am), I've wanted to be Mother Teresa of Calcutta. Somebody who chucked it all over, cleanly, surely, and went off to the devil-may-care, stubbly world of pure righteousness. Somebody who said, "I'm going where I never have to smile at equine efflatus again. I'll never have to compromise again. I'll call 'em the way I see 'em, and if they don't like it, they can osculate my fundament."

I never seriously wanted to be a fireman, you understand. Or a policeman. Or a doctor. I never did. But I always wanted to be a hero. Like John the Baptist. Those nuns (God bless 'em!) were pretty smart. They taught me at least to *want* to do something purely, honorably, righteously, and the devil—literally—take the hindmost.

I almost said, "They were wrong, too, of course." I almost said that they should have told me that there are needs right here, too, at home—where it's so mortifyingly undramatic. The pain inside the guts of an affluent boy or girl whose parents are contemplating divorce is, surely, pain. And who can quantify pain? Who can say that that pain isn't as excruciating as the pain in the bellies of the children Mother Teresa picks up and brings home? Who's to say that the pain within the girl who eats her lunch alone every day, or within the hatefully picky curmudgeon in your office, or within the recent widow down the block is any less than the anguish of any other leper?

All the nuns, and retreat givers, and homilists didn't want to engender in me a feeling of guilt for not achieving heroism. But they succeeded. And, in a sense, I'm glad they did. They gave me the courage never to stand silent in the face of injustice, even though a lot of people call me fool for it. I'm no hero. Neither, most likely, are you. No one is pondering whether to offer us a Nobel Prize. Nobody is trying to outbid anybody else for the rights to our life stories.

I don't mind that. As long as my Big Friend is willing to buy each chapter as it comes out, I'm content. And, with him fiddling with the plot-line as he consistently does, I'm reasonably sure he won't find each successive episode as boring as I've always been afraid it would be for him.

In Advent, I think a lot not only about John but about Our Lady. Now there's real Nobel Prize stuff. They've made a lot of movies about her. But do you want to bet she never suspected they would? What did she do? She made a home. She took care of a carpenter; she raised a son; she washed dishes, and swept, and took a pot of stew over to a neighbor who'd lost his wife. She set her son free to be what he was called to be—even though it wasn't what she'd expected for him. He was, after all, hanged.

And John was doing just what he'd been called, by name, to do. So is Mother Teresa.

So are we.

*   *   *   *   *

7. The Disguises of God

> *"Then they will ask, 'Lord, when did we see you hungry or thirsty, a stranger or naked, sick or in prison, and refused you help?' "*
> —Matthew 25:44

It's a cliché that God's ways aren't man's ways. And clichés become clichés because they're so true they keep getting repeated over and over. But despite the repetition—or maybe precisely because of it—we don't hear clichés any more. No matter how often God surprises us, we keep expecting him to be predictable, almost like a genie in a bottle we can uncork any time we need him—as if God depended on us in order to be . . . well, you know . . . useful.

The Old Testament evolution of the idea of what the Messiah would be like is a case in point. It's the story of a people's resolute, stubborn clinging to false expectations—despite all the evidence to the contrary. Over the course of their history, whenever Yahweh had sent them a small-m messiah, it had always been an improbable nobody: dried-up Abraham, stammering Moses, clutzy Gideon, sour-pussed Ecclesiastes.

You can't blame them of course for expecting a kind of Paul Bunyan messiah. They took the biggest heroes they'd ever known about—men like the mature David and the wise Solomon—stretched them to the nth degree, and thought they had a pretty good picture of The One Who Was To Come. The thunder of his stride would make mountains tremble; at his mere gaze the wicked would shrivel to puddles of ash. What's more,

Israel itself was a theocracy, not just a religion but a nation as well, so their expectations of the Messiah were all concretized in a political savior—who very often overshadowed even the spiritual savior. Like David, his ancestor, he'd be a superb warrior-king who'd drive into the sea whatever occupying force had the Hebrews currently under its heel.

With his eternal addiction to irony, God subverted their expectations. They got their warrior-king, all right. But he was a battler for peace, at the head of a ragtag army of pariahs and untouchables, crowned with thorns and enthroned on a gibbet. He bestowed riches on his subjects. But they were like the Emperor's Clothes: invisible except to those with eyes to see and appraise them. He worked miracles. But the greatest miracles were turning hearts from stone to life. Too bad, really. Because that's not what they wanted from him. It's not what we really want, either.

What did they go out into the desert to see when they went out to see the Baptist? What does a prophet and a man of God look like? Is he swathed up in luxurious garments? No, such men are in the palaces of princes. Too bad, really. In our image-conscious society, who would ever tout it around the neighborhood that John the Baptist was coming home for brunch after Mass? Clad in burlap, stinking of sweat, rawboned, unkempt. We all have to admit that, years ago, Fulton Sheen's wide appeal as a preacher wasn't undercut by the fact that he was draped in purple satin. That's what a man of God *should* look like.

And yet if false expectations kept sensible people from seeing a man of God in John, what would make those same misfocused eyes see God himself in a crucified carpenter? Or messengers from God in the lepers and whores and grafters for whom he had such a perverse predilection?

I once gave an Advent homily in the Oakland Cathedral. Having warned the ushers and the celebrant, I came from the back of the church while the celebrant was reading the gospel.

But I was all dressed up as Emmett Kelly—raggedy clothes, white face, red bulb nose, with a bottle in my hand. I came up the aisle and whispered, "Could you gimme a quarter for cuppa coffee?" Some were mildly amused, others mildly embarrassed. I heard one woman say, "Harry, stop him! He's going right up on the altar!"

The celebrant pretended to protest, but I jostled him out of the way, set down the bottle, peeled off my nose, and said, "In the name of the Father, and of the Son, and of the Holy Spirit, Amen. . . . If you came to church this morning looking for Jesus Christ, you just missed him. He came up that aisle a minute ago, trying to cadge a quarter for a cup of coffee. And you want to know something? He didn't get a nickel."

We're all honestly trying to find Jesus Christ, I think. But perhaps at least some of us are looking for him in the wrong direction, as the Jews were in the time of John and Jesus. We look for him in the clouds; we expect him to have a heavenly glow, the way he does on Christmas cards and in the movies. But the real Jesus, when he came the first time, looked just like any other ordinary man. Today, he looks just like you.

So, if you're looking for Jesus Christ, try the mirror. But if that's too difficult a place to start, guess who sits around your dining room table? Guess who sits at the next desk in your office? Guess who eats his lunch alone in your cafeteria?

Surprise!

* * * * *

8. Repent! Repent!

"The chaff he will burn with unquenchable fire!"
—Matthew 3:12

Those "Repent! Repent!" passages in the gospels aren't on my list of all-time Hit Parade favorites. I usually dodge them whenever I can.

The first reason is an honest one. I had the hell scared out of me by fiery retreat givers and preachers so often when I was a kid that I used to go and confess sins I hadn't even committed. Just for insurance. In fact, that was pretty much all I used confession for: anti-hell coverage. Like going to confess to my Dad about the crumpled fender. It was agony, but nowhere near the controlled volcano I'd face if I tried to cover it up and *then* he found out.

But then I finally got around really to understand the story of the Prodigal Son, whose Father runs to the repentant and won't even let us get our prepared speeches out—because we are his sons and daughters, and we were dead, and we've come to life and come home.

Still, those "Repent! Repent!" passages were so misused, at least in my own past, that even till recently I'd pick another gospel passage and fake out the congregation with some alibi like: "Oops! I read the wrong gospel, but might's well preach on this new one, okay?" Nobody seemed to object.

The basic reason I skirt those passages (to be perfectly honest) is that—like everyone else, I don't *like* to sit down and reassess my comfortable-if-imperfect habits of life. Not that I don't admit I've got faults. It's just that I don't like to *specify* them. There's such a danger of getting paranoid about them. As long as I admit I'm . . . you know . . . imperfect . . . human, I can say I'm honest and humble. And as long as I leave them vague, I really never have to get down to *doing* anything about them, right? I mean, we're *all* human, right?

Of course, that's why so few go to confession any more. Getting out of the confession habit is, I can only suspect, somewhat like getting out of a girdle. Whew! None of that constriction. None of that old inner eye assessing whether this action is just a bit too nasty to pass over. No more need to spend a half-hour trying to find words vague enough to con the confessor.

A lot of people ask me, "Why can't you just confess your sins to God directly?" I usually answer, "Terrific. When's the last time you did it?" Most of them just like talking about doing it. The very few who do take God for a walk and say, "Oh, God, I really kicked it around," or "Oh, God, I'm really such a general jerk." No need to specify. Nobody there to ask you to specify. No need to face squarely the times I've cheated on quizzes, or *which* people I've consistently ignored, or the times I've treated my children like millstones. No need, either, to find out that—no matter what I've done—I'm really not as irredeemable as I'd thought.

Just wriggle out of the girdle, sigh, let it gather dust, and just get nice and fat.

Finally, there's the defense against those "Repent!" passages which is humble self-righteousness. "Repent? Of what? Only trivial things, little petty meannesses? Insignificant little forays against others' reputations—just to make a little gossip, fill the empty air? Good God! I don't want to get scrupulous."

And there—right there—I'd hooked myself. It was the sheer pettiness of my "crimes" that was so shaming.

I'm like Gulliver, immobilized by a thousand tiny threads. I'm not a mass-murderer, or an orgiast, or a rapist. I'm just a well-meaning sneak. And that hurts. The guy who embezzles millions and the guy who can cheat a pay phone are in the same game. It's just that the embezzler has a larger vision and more guts.

Not that God expects me to be perfect—flawless. But he does expect me to be honest, and he expects me to keep growing. That's what he made me for.

And yet, that's what I avoid when I avoid an honest confrontation with my specific pettinesses: growth. If you were to ask me for a definition of sin, it would be simply this: sin is any action or attitude that makes me less able to grow. The easy lie that protects Old Number One, the flashes of anger that mask my shame at being caught doing something small, the shortcuts that get me finished early but leave loose ends for someone else to gather up—all these things say: "My comfort is more important than their comfort," and, beneath that, "I'm more important than they are." That is, in a nutshell, the opposite of love, because love—real love—says, "They're more important than I am."

Repentance which says only, "Oh, God! I'm scum!" isn't repentance at all. It's mere masochism, taking delight in lacerating oneself. Repentance worth the name says, calmly, "Well, I've failed most to grow in these three or four specific ways. Now, I'm going to do this, this, and this, in order to change that, at least a bit."

True repentance happens only when I say, "They're more important than I am—and I'm going to take concrete steps to keep reminding myself of that. I'm going to find imaginative ways to make their lives easier."

We're so used to depending on repairmen: doctors, plumbers, psychiatrists, priests, cleaning ladies.

In this instance, the only repairman is me.

* * * * *

9. Pregnancy

> *When Elizabeth heard what Mary said, the babe leaped in her womb. Elizabeth was filled with the Holy Spirit and she cried out, "Blessed are you among women! And blessed is the fruit of your womb."* —Luke 1:41-42

There are two things the Visitation makes me think of: one, Mary went to visit Elizabeth; and two, Elizabeth recognized who her guests were.

It will surprise no one that I've never been pregnant. It's

always seemed to me one of the many arguments for the existence of God: the fact that one-half of the human race has to go through menstruation, pregnancy and childbirth, while the other half is blissfully free of those burdens. There has to be a God, just in order to make it up to the ladies. But I tried—admittedly in a very removed way—to imagine what it cost Mary to leave Nazareth and travel to her old cousin Elizabeth to . . . well . . . just sort of help around the house.

When I was a kid, that was a common thing: if somebody in the neighborhood had a rough time, the neighbors just instinctively pitched in and got ready casseroles and pans of beans and got the kids out of the house. I suppose that doesn't happen as much nowadays. One hardly knows the names of the neighbors who live only a few yards away. But there was also, in those old days, almost always a maiden aunt who went around from house to house to take care of the kids while Mom was off having a baby, or to nurse the dying, or to stay unmarried so that someone could ease the aging of parents.

My Aunt Marion was the one in our family. She was the one who got the ". . . and we just don't know what we're going to do" letters. She'd just pack her bag, and off she went. Marion was something like God; she was the first one everybody called when they were in need, but when things were going okay, she was kind of the shy skunk at the garden party, always needing one of the relatives to give her a room and meals. She was like Our Lady in a way, too. One always thought that Marion had never seen a man naked. And yet she'd washed all her brothers day after day when they were dying. I remember once when I fell off the stationary tubs in the basement and caught the steel edge in my groin. I was devoured by embarrassment, but it was Marion who doctored it. When she was dying, I said to her, "Marion, you've had a rich life." And she said to me, only half-conscious of what she was saying, "Then where are my husband and my children?" And I said one of the few wise things I've said in my life. I said,

"I'm your son, Marion." And she was happy.

Like Our Lady, my Aunt Marion flew in the face of all the things we think are important, even at Christmas: the Super Bowl, the number of presents, the parties they forgot to invite one to. Old Marion, like Our Lady, was just there to be used. The only thing she needed was to be needed.

The second thing the Visitation story says to me is that Elizabeth knew who her guests were. When her cousin came to visit—and to help out—she saw not just a generous young peasant girl, but the Christ she had growing inside her belly. That tells us something too, surely. As with Our Lady, the Father comes to us every day and asks us to conceive his Son within us, and we carry him, like Our Lady, out to meet whomever we meet.

What would happen, I wonder, if each of us were transfigured as Jesus was at the Transfiguration, and all the godliness in us burned through the surfaces? How thunderstruck we'd be! How the saintliness in each of us would leap up, as John leaped within Elizabeth, to reach out to the holiness with which we are truly surrounded!

A Buddhist monk wrote to me once and ended his letter, instead of something vapid like "Very truly yours," with: "I bow to the divine in you."

And so I do. I bow to the divine in you.

*   *   *   *   *

10. All Souls Day

The souls of the just are in the hands of God.
—Wisdom 3:1

If you've never been to a funeral, the feast of All Souls is about as much cause for celebration as the feast of St.

Cunegonde. Unless you've knelt by the coffin of someone you've truly loved and allowed yourself to comprehend that this person will never speak again, never touch you again, then the feast which celebrates *cheating* death has no meaning at all. And, oddly, if you've never personally experienced death, you've never really experienced the value of life. If you've never truly understood that the number of your days is finite, you've never understood, for that very reason, that those days are too precious to waste. Those who have not felt realization of death can't possibly understand what Christianity is all about, because the whole message of the gospel is simply that: death has been vanquished.

Our culture insulates us from death. News reports of war deaths and traffic deaths are so censored that they're hard to distinguish from the deaths in a cowboy movie. People don't grow old or die at home any more, where we could see them. Death "happens" when we're not there, at some hospital or nursing home. We've become as prudish about death as Victorians were about sex: mustn't talk about it in front of the children, mustn't risk traumatizing them with such an unpleasant reality. And, strangely, it's precisely that sheltering of American children that makes them so impervious to religious education.

If "science is going to eliminate illness in my lifetime, and famine and war are on the other side of the globe, and death is something I don't have to consider for another 60 years," is it any wonder that young people find the obligatory visit to Whatshisname on Sunday morning an unbearable drag? "What the hell did He ever do for me?"

Most of the time—let's be honest about it—heaven is a rather boring idea. Life is here, now. At cocktail parties or in religion classes, we can sit around and rather dispassionately discuss whether there's a heaven or not. Even at the death of someone old, we can content ourselves with pious pacifiers like,

"Well, she lived a long life. She's better off now." But when the person in the coffin is young and never had a chance, the idea of death is infuriatingly unjust. Then, when I contemplate the unarguable fact that *I* will one day die, the idea of death is unthinkable.

If the people we know who have died are *not* in a better life—really, truly—then death is no more than an accident of evolution, a witless conspiracy of chemicals and cells which dumps us here, lets us struggle awhile, and then eliminates us—completely. All the dreams, all the risks taken and fulfilled, all the hard-won wisdom are simply . . . gone. And the "I" who dreamt and risked and won is . . . no longer real.

Either heaven is a pious and nearly obscene myth of self-deception, or it is a most shattering and humbling—and liberating—truth. The reality of death throws us up against what Christianity is all about. It hauls us up short from our daily, numb routines, from our weekly anesthetized presence at Mass. It forces us to see that Christianity and the Mass banquet focus, unerringly, on the fact that Jesus Christ walked through death and came back to show us that *we* can do it, too. As he yielded himself unto death, Jesus said to the repentant thief, *"Today* you will be with me in Paradise."

Somehow, we get the idea that Heaven—Paradise—the Kingdom of God—begins only when *we* get there. But if it exists, people are in that way of existing *now.* And whatever heaven may be like, it's unlimited by the barriers of time and space. But if that's true, then *we* are in it now! It's all around us, lurking under the surfaces of time and space, and we're like blind people, touching only the surfaces, beneath which lurks a reality so real that it would burn us if we could see it with unblinded eyes.

When we go to Mass, and acknowledge that fact, our blindness is momentarily lessened. But one day, in death, it will be permanently cured.

If that isn't something worth celebrating, I don't know what is.

* * * * *

11. The Immaculate Conception

"He has pulled the mighty off their thrones and raised up the lowly."   —Luke 1:52

Like so much of the gospel, Our Lady's Magnificat could have been written by a Communist. And I sometimes wonder if the gospel wasn't intended to be just as threatening, just as subversive to all we hold dear, as Marxism is.

For that reason, I get a bit irritated at what theologians and artists have done to Our Lady—burdening her with titles and crowns, endowing her with uncountable foot-candles of grace and foreknowledge of the crucifixion, insisting that she was transported miraculously into and out of human life. As if they were trying to redo the job as God would have done, had he known better.

I confess that I don't really understand the need for the Immaculate Conception. Or for the Assumption, for that matter. I don't deny them. I just don't see the need for them. In a way, I suppose I rather resent them—for what they say about ordinary human life and sinfulness and sexuality.

The one thing they miss—ruinously, I think—is that, if Mary had all that foreknowledge, she wouldn't have been human, since the very root of humanity and love and faith is doubt, vulnerability, *not* having foreknowledge of the outcomes. But she surely was human. It's perfectly obvious, looking at her Son. In trying to set Our Lady on a literal pedestal—even before she was born, they denied her her real greatness: that she *didn't* have a map of what was going to happen, any more than any of us does. But she did what she was asked to do.

Many of us think that what gets into the newspapers is really important. But the first time my Dad got his name in the paper was the day after he died. Most of us think winning is important, breaking the record, winning the crown. But the Man we claim was the Best of Us, won no awards but a mock crown of thorns, a lifting-above-the-crowd nailed to two pieces of wood. That's what a true winner looks like!

On January 10, 1978, on the evening news, I saw a true triumph. I was so moved by it that I sat down and wrote out what I'd seen, to capture it and keep it. I saw a young man of 23 receive his Eagle Scout Award. Not much newsworthy about that, but he was five years over-age. He couldn't even give his acceptance speech. His father had to read it for him as he spelled it out from letters on a board across the arms of his wheelchair. He had cerebral palsy. For his merit badge in hiking, he'd pushed himself the first nine miles in his wheelchair. And he'd crawled the rest of the way on his hands and knees.

To me, that's what human greatness looks like. It has nothing to do with beauty. Or with physical strength. Or with brains. And surely it has nothing to do with money or manipulative power. The truth is in the heart. The truth is in the human spirit that cries out, "I *can't*! . . . But I'll try."

I fear we've lost all sense of awe at the *truly* great. I fear the *TV Guide* and *Sports Illustrated* and "The Tonight Show with Johnny Carson" are so easily accessible to the lowest level of the human spirit that we really believe notoriety makes one important, worthy of attention, or—far worse—worthy of envy. Who remembers Sonia Henie, or Eleanor Holm, or Vera Hurba Ralston anymore? Yesterday, the great heroine was Marilyn Monroe; people still mourn her, a good-hearted kid who just happened to get caught up in the whirligig and died tragically. Today, heroines are born and fade within a year, not even a decade. One sees their flaws too quickly; they're not demigoddesses at all, as we'd mistakenly thought.

If you're looking for the real heroines, don't look where a *National Enquirer* reporter would look—Vegas, Hollywood, Miami, Wimbeldon. Look in the kitchen of your own home. Look in the nursing homes, and the schools for the retarded, and the Inner City schools. There they are, like Our Lady and Cinderella in the kitchen, sweeping up the ashes of society. All those Mother Teresas, who will never win a Nobel Prize, and who will get their names in the paper only the day after they die.

If you want to seek out true heroines, don't go to the Miss America Pageant or the Academy Awards. Go to Nazareth. There you'll find what the Ultimate Judge of Greatness considers great: "Be it done unto me according to your word."

I *can't* . . . but I'll try.

* * * * *

12. The Big, Bad, Beautiful Balancing Rock

Rejoice always.

—1 Thessalonians 5:16

Spang in the middle of Advent and Lent, the Church for some reason interrupts all the dolorous calls to repentance with a call to rejoice. Hmm. . . .

Chesterton once compared the Kingdom of God to an enormous ugly rock balanced precariously, like a child's top, on a single, improbably tiny point. The rock is covered with unsightly knobs, and ungainly extrusions, and ridiculous lumps that— somehow—manage to balance one another. In one and the same Church, we have fanatic liberals—but equally fanatic conservatives to compensate for them. We have men and women cloistered in monasteries who are blissfully content to speak only to God. And yet the selfsame Church can still accommodate someone like myself, whose mouth is the closest thing in human history to a perpetual motion machine. I talk even in my sleep. We have the majestic stillness of cathedrals and the bloody fury of crusades. We have rich and poor, beggars and burghers, puritans and pranksters. At one end of the gospel spectrum we have the lovely peace of the stable at Bethlehem, and at the other the raw brutality of the hill of Calvary.

We have Paul shouting "Rejoice!" and John ranting with equal vigor, "Repent!" On the one hand, in the world we share with Muhamar Qaddaffi and muggers and the President's Council of Economic Advisers, it's often hard to heed Paul's advice and muster up a sincere "whoopee." On the other hand, John is not quite the ideal guest for a cocktail party with all that "watch your step, you guys" talk.

Perhaps the reason for this uncomfortable profusion of paradoxes in the gospel and in the Church is that they are undeviatingly dedicated to the truth, which always balances between extremes. It's the same reason God gave us two eyes so we could see in three dimensions, so that we could respond not merely to the surfaces of things but to their depths as well. "There is a season for everything, a time for every occupation under heaven . . . a time for mourning, a time for dancing." And in every act of our Christian lives, there is that illogical fusion of mourning and dancing, darkness and light, Christmas and Calvary.

In our moments of greatest buoyancy, there's the deep leaden conviction of death—which, paradoxically, makes the joy all the sweeter, knowing that our times are limited and therefore irretrievably precious. Every time we choose, we surrender all the other options; every time we give away love, we are enriched. In birth there is pain, and in death there is joy. We Christians are an unremittingly paradoxical bunch.

But there is the key. We are people of binocular vision; we steadfastly refuse to be monochromatic. The world we live in is neither hell-hole nor heaven. We hate the world enough to want it changed, and we love the world enough to pitch in and help to nudge it toward salvation and rebirth. We're infuriated by pigheaded stupidity and selfishness, and yet just as pigheadedly patient in our conviction that stupidity and selfishness—though they can never be uprooted—can at least be eroded. We are infinitesimally tiny, and yet infinitely loved.

It's all wrapped up in a story about a psychiatrist and his two sons: one was an incurable pessimist, and the other was an incurable optimist. One Christmas he resolved to cure them once and for all. So, while they slept, he crept into the pessimist's room and filled it with toys, and then into the optimist's room and filled it with . . . well . . . horse manure. Christmas morning, he went into the pessimist's room and the boy was sitting, surrounded by the toys and terrified. "Son," the father said, "don't you realize all these toys are for you?" The little boy sniffled and said, "Yes, but if I move, I'll break them." When the father went into the optimist's room, the kid was laughing and singing and throwing the horse manure in the air. "Uh, son," the father said, "don't you realize what this stuff is?" And the boy giggled and said, "Sure, Daddy, but with all this horse-poop, there *must* be a pony!"

If we're off-balance and cockeyed at all, it's in our stubborn assurance that, no matter how dismal things get, at the heart of things there's a pony. Perhaps even a steed as lovely and mystical as a unicorn. One dark night, when the world was un-characteristically at peace, he crept into our world and trans-formed it right down to its roots. He changed things so radically that no story, no matter how tragic or tormented, would be without its happy ending.

And that's the truth.

*   *   *   *   *

13. Christmas and Xmas

> *She gave birth to her first-born son and wrapped him*
> *in swaddling clothes and laid him in a manger, because*
> *there was no room for them in the inn.*   —Luke 2:7

Christmas is a time for symbols. A symbol is a way we attempt to concretize something that's real, but not tangible. We act "as if" a non-physical reality really were physical. We can't see or touch or weigh an immaterial reality like love, so we physicalize it into valentine hearts and bunches of flowers and boxes of candy. And the symbol says, "Here. You can't see my love, but let this stand for it."

And every year, beginning even before Thanksgiving, people try to fabricate symbols that will embody the invisible spirit of Christmas: what it means. Christmas cards and TV spots embody that spirit in apple-cheeked carolers in the snow singing how Coca-Cola has really been embodying that spirit all along. Store windows blossom with elegant kings bringing the Baby Jesus gold, frankincense, and Chanel #5. And greeting cards try to capture that intangible spirit with cherubic Dickens characters, frosty pine cones, cheery firesides, and a chunky little man with a twinkle in his eye—coming improbably out of a fireplace with not a speck of soot on his red velvet suit.

It's called the willing suspension of disbelief.

Who can resist the omnipresence of all those voices crying in the wilderness of Madison Avenue: "Christmas is coming! Make straight the way of the Barbie Doll and the Parker Brothers Games! Clear a path through the desert for the gift-wrapped scotch and the hair driers! We have something for the man who has everything!"

And in the background, the Enemy sniggers and wrings his hands in Scroogian triumph. He's taken the best *his* Enemy had to offer—the birth of Christ in a cowstall—and deftly, subtly, with endless patience, metamorphosed it into a time of false hopes, of greed, of hollow generosity in so many cases. He's made us forget that Jesus was *the* Man who had everything, and that Christmas is the celebration of his giving it all up.

So when you look at the symbols we use for Christmas and try to distill out of them what the Christmas spirit really does mean to us, it is, on the one hand, a yearly opportunity for the genial rip-off which will be "good for the Economy," and on the other hand a happy time to get together with friends and relatives and people we find appealing. At least that's what our symbols say.

But from what I read in the New Testament, the God-Man whose birth began it all had something else entirely in mind. I'd imagine that, if he were to come back and try to find symbols for our Christmas cards and store windows, his symbols would be far less cheery than ours. He didn't come to bring happiness (which can be bought for awhile with money); he came to bring joy (which can be bought only by forgetting oneself). His Christmas cards, I fear, would look more like Bread for the World posters, with the children with their great hungry eyes and great distended bellies. He'd concretize the spirit of Christmas in pictures of retarded children struggling to be understood, old people in nursing homes waiting for a death that comes too slowly, the homeless, the pock-marked, the seemingly unlovable.

It was those people, after all, to whom he first revealed himself—not to friends and relatives and people who were appealing, but to illiterate shepherds, whose clothes were doubtless ridden with lice and whose bodies and breath stank.

That's what we celebrate at Christmas: that we were enriched by the presence of God in our midst, that the almighty God impoverished himself—emptied himself to assume the condition of a slave. He became an outcast, like us—for us.

"Joy to the world," we sing, "the Lord is come!" And he is

still here, lurking behind the unlikeliest faces. We can no longer—like the shepherds and wise men—bring gifts to the Baby Jesus. He grew up, and died, and rose again. But he embodied himself in every man and woman we meet. And in giving gifts to them, the least of his brethren, we give them to him.

Does this mean that we shouldn't enjoy the electric shavers and the new ice skates and the Butterball turkeys? No. He made them, and saw that they were very good, and he gave them to us to use. But let us not forget: in the middle of all the tinsel and tissue and tankards of Christmas cheer, at the core of the Christ-Mass spirit is Jesus Christ—a Man filled with the aliveness of God, who became an outcast among the outcasts.

If you seek him, seek him in a stable—or some such unlikely place. A nursing home, or an orphanage, or a ghetto. But you needn't even look that far. In every room you enter, right at your elbows, there are people no one notices, people you know are never invited anywhere, people who leave every day without looking back.

One needn't rise and go to Bethlehem to find Christ, about to be born. We're there already. He's here in our midst, waiting to be recognized. And he'll look no more almighty than a baby wrapped in swaddling clothes and lying in a manger. But if, unlike the shepherds, you're unwilling to look beneath the surfaces, you'll never find him.

If you want to embody the true spirit of Christmas in symbols, you'll be less than adequate if you use pine cones and fireplaces and Santa Clauses. You'll be less than adequate even if you embody the Christmas spirit in families and friends enjoying a holiday meal and one another's love. You'll find the embodiment of the true Christmas spirit where it was in the first place: in a dirty stable, in the bitter cold, where a young couple who'd been refused shelter everywhere gave the little they had—the warmth of their bodies—to the almighty God who had focused his entire aliveness into the most helpless thing there is: a newborn baby.

"He who has eyes to see, let him see. He who has ears to hear, let him hear."

* * * * *

14. The Never-Ending Story

> *An angel of the Lord appeared to Joseph in a dream and said, "Rise. Take the child and his mother, and flee into Egypt."*
> —Matthew 2:13

Christmas wasn't the only time God interfered with the goings-on of our planet. Nor would it be the last. But it was the greatest and the central interference, toward which all those events before it were building, and from which all those after it have flowed and taken life. It's the "ways of God" to interfere. If he didn't, at every instant of our lives, we'd cease to breathe.

I grow weary of preachers who drone on about "the ways of God" and fed up with bothersome people sighing disinterestedly at my pain and heartache with, "Ah, it's the ways of God!" Dumb. They make me feel that God actually *is* "interfering." As if "the ways of God" are there for the sole purpose of messing up things when they're going too well. It's as if bright-eyed children with runny noses and the flush of Autumn afternoons on their cheeks—and migrating birds—and Christmas—were not also "the ways of God."

The way of God is growth, ever returning through the same cycles of rain to sun to frost to snow; seeding, death, opening, maturing, harvest; pain, reflection, wisdom; sin, repentance, rebirth. But even if the pattern repeats itself, no two cycles are the same. It isn't just the static order of a circle, like a squirrel-cage. It's a spiral, repeating the order but moving forward. Order and surprise.

The pattern of salvation began with creation, when the Spirit of God hovered over the primeval waters, as he would over the Virgin Mary, and said, "Be it done!" From out of that first baptism, God drew life, a new earth, a new people. They were his adopted children, and he dwelt with them in the Garden. And the pattern had begun.

But Adam and Eve decided—as all his children would do—that being human was not enough. It was not enough that they be God's beloved, his stewards. They would be God. Then the shame, the forgiveness, and God called Adam and Eve out on the road, to begin again. We all know that first of stories. It is our story, too.

Once again humankind went against the will of God, the inbuilt nature of things, and God called the savior Noah, and made a new alliance with him. "Take the loyal few who love me into the ark, and I will deliver you." And Noah arose, grumbling, and went. Once again, out of the waters of rebirth, God made a new beginning. The faithful few of the old were the seed of the new generation. And He dwelt with them.

Still again, the people forgot the ways of God, and out of Ur of the Chaldees God called another savior, Abraham. The Lord promised that his sons would outnumber the stars, in another newborn land. But Abraham was a wanderer without roots, and his wife, Sarah, was as barren as the desert. Yet—like Noah before him and Joseph after him—Abraham rose and followed. To begin the story again.

With predictable consistency, the people again sold themselves to slavery in Egypt. But God raised up another messiah, Moses, to lead them again through the waters of rebirth in the Red Sea, out into the wilderness of trial and penitence, back to their home.

Always, there were messiahs to call the people back to the

truth. There were warriors like Joshua, Gideon, Samson, the Maccabees; kings like David and Solomon. But always the idols of Canaan seduced them away. It was the age-old fall into slavery. And yet Yahweh, the ever-faithful partner of the alliance, never left them. He never tired of sending them prophets—Isaiah, Jeremiah, Hosea—to be the living conscience of the people and to lure them back to rebirth, to a new alliance, to a new Kingdom.

Over and over, the same story. But never the same.

For centuries, the people relied on the faithfulness of God and dreamed of The One Who Would Come. "Behold, a young girl will conceive and bear a Son, and his name will be Emmanuel—God-With-Us" (Is 7:14). "For unto us a child is born. A son is given. And the government shall be upon his shoulders. And his name shall be called: Wonderful! Counselor! The Mighty God! The Everlasting Power! The Prince of Peace!" (Is 9:5). He would be the Servant of God, who would take upon himself the sin and suffering of all humankind, who would write a new alliance, no longer in tablets of stone, but in our hearts. "See! Your king is coming to you. He is just. He is victorious, humble, and riding upon a colt, the foal of an ass" (Zc 9:9). "And behold, with the clouds of heaven comes one like a son of man . . . and his dominion is an everlasting dominion which shall not pass away" (Dn 7:13-14).

And they waited.

Suddenly, in the dead of night, when all the earth was at peace, "Jesus Christ, eternal God and son of the eternal Father, desiring to sanctify the world by his most merciful coming, is born in Bethlehem of Judah."

He had come. It was the invasion. An Alien from beyond space and time had pitched his tent among us, to begin the story afresh.

He was all they had prayed for—not what they'd asked, but better than they'd hoped. Here was one to fulfill Adam's foolish boast: he would make men and women like God. Here was the son of Abraham to make all men his sons. Here was the savior to lead us, once for all, through the waters of rebirth, through the wilderness of penitence and conversion, into the promised Kingdom.

In Christ, heaven and earth, God and humankind, have become inextricably enmeshed.

Advent isn't a preparation for the actual birth of the Baby Jesus. That was the task of the whole story of Israel. We're missing the whole point if we wait till the end of December.

Since the great and agonizing triumph of that once-for-all Savior, every morning is Christmas—and Good Friday, and Easter, all together.

Every day, the story begins again. Every day, the Lord says to you—as he did to Adam and Eve, Abraham and Sarah, Joseph and Mary: "Arise and come. I will make you a spokesman to my people, a savior, a Christ." But who are we? Isn't that the job of the priests? Even Moses cried out, "O Lord! I beg you! Send someone else!" And Peter, "Lord! Depart from me. I am a sinful man."

That goes without saying. Whom else do I have but you? Enough of you. Arise and come. We have a story to begin again.

*   *   *   *   *

15. The Star-Gazers

> *Going into the house, they saw the child with Mary, his mother. And they fell to their knees and worshipped him.*
> —Matthew 2:11

Like typical absent-minded professors, the Wise Men turned up late. They were busy fussing—choosing the right gifts, taking incessant readings of the stars, pursuing variant readings in dusty texts. They were rich and educated and Gentiles, so the poor, simple, Jewish shepherds got to the stable first.

If you accept the Christian gospel, it certainly seems a drawback to be both rich and educated. Either factor alone is bad enough, but the two together—wealth and learning—seem lethal. And reading *The Imitation of Christ* makes one want to apologize to God for getting past kindergarten.

It's so much easier, in the long run, to be poor and dumb. After all, the more you know, the more questions and doubts arise. The Kingdom was promised to the simple, but the rich man has to squirm his ungainly hump through the eye of a needle, and the wise of this world must become servants to the simple. The whole inequity of the thing reminds me of Chesterton's saying about the biblical promise that, in the Kingdom, the lion will lie down with the lamb. If in this paradoxical menage, the lion must pare his claws and surrender all his leonine qualities to become lamb-like, it looks like rank imperialism on the part of the lamb. Selling all and giving it to the poor is a laudable thing—I've done it myself—but, if all rich Christians did that, whom would we make the victims of all our forms of genial extortion—our bazaars and next-to-new sales and fund drives? Without the fat cats, the poor couldn't survive.

I doubt that Jesus was extolling poverty as a goal to be sought by all with Kamikaze dedication—although many saints achieved greatness by that route. But a visit to any ghetto is evidence enough that poverty isn't automatically liberating and creative. True, there is a cliché about artists doing their best work on empty stomachs in garrets even the rats had deserted. But they were hungry with a hunger beyond the cravings of the belly. Like the Wise Men—and like the "poor" of the Beatitudes—they had a hunger of the spirit, which goes on craving even when the belly is full.

It was the hunger that drew the rich Magi across the sterile deserts of Asia Minor: the hunger to confront the Truth Himself, no matter how harassing the route or how unpromising his abode. They did, after all, find nothing more than a baby in a hovel, when they'd expected the King of the Universe. But both the poor, uneducated shepherds and the rich, learned Magi recognized Christ when they saw him. The complexity or the simplicity of their minds had nothing to do with it. It was the simplicity of their hearts that enabled their eyes to see beneath the surface to the Truth.

Anyone with the mind of Christ knows that in the Kingdom, where our Brother assured us there is a reality beyond time and space, money and education make no real difference, one way or the other. Whether one has plenty or nothing, whether one has a Ph.D. or never finished grade school, whether one is handsome or ugly, spry or crippled, it doesn't *really* matter. What matters is to know Christ Jesus who has saved us from death, and to know him is to be truly free of all seeming limitations—or advantages.

Wealth can corrupt, but so can poverty—as every pimp and pusher proves. But possessing Christ makes one willing to walk away from his wealth or from his poverty—with a free heart—when it's Christ who calls. If I can serve him better from my wealth, or if I can serve him better by divesting myself of it, I come.

In Evelyn Waugh's novel, *Helena*, the Empress-mother of Constantine addresses a prayer to the Wise Men who, like her, came to Christ only laboriously, taking sights and calculating, and yet still found him, and were accepted. She finishes her prayer: "Dear cousins, pray for me, for his sake who did not reject your curious gifts. Pray always for the learned, the oblique, the delicate. Let them not be quite forgotten at the throne of God, when the simple come into their Kingdom."

*   *   *   *   *

16. The Holy Family

And he went down with them to Nazareth and was
obedient to them. And his mother kept all of these things
in her heart. And Jesus grew in wisdom and in stature,
and in favor with God and man.   —Luke 2:51-52

The Church gives twelve days of each year to commemorate
Christ's birth, seven days to commemorate the revelation of
Jesus to the Gentile Wise Men. She gives a week to the events of
Our Lord's Passion. But she gives only one day to commemorate
the thirty years of Our Lord's life in Nazareth.

Why? Certainly not because those years were unimportant.
During those years, Jesus and his parents lived as we live. They
didn't have running water or central heating or television, but
they did live like ordinary middle-class people of their day, just
as we do. Their problems weren't the problems of statesmen or
movie stars or priests—or even those of Jesus' public life. They
had ordinary people's problems: taxes, the price of flour, the
death of friends, the warmth of summer and the dampness of
winter, backache at the end of the day—the things that gave
Jesus the metaphors in which to wrap his message.

We tend to think of Mary and Joseph as involved in heroic
deeds on a level far above our own ordinary kind of existence.
But when you consider what the gospels tell us, what did they
do? They did become refugees to save their Son's life. They
sought him, worried sick, when they feared he was lost. Mary
stood nearby, strong and helpless, while her Son was executed.
That's all the gospel tells.

Why were the events of those thirty so-called Hidden Years
not written down? Simple: because they weren't newsworthy.
After all, does the *New York Times* call up to get the complete
details when you have a birthday party or when your child cuts
her first tooth? Does some historian write to find the facts when

she has her first date? It's not newsworthy. But "newsworthy" isn't the same as "important."

Mary and Joseph didn't sanctify themselves only by allowing the Son of God to enter intimately into their lives at the Annunciation or at his birth. That was only how it began. And, really, it's how we began too: allowing him to enter into our lives by accepting our baptism. With Mary and Joseph, and with us, sanctity comes from the years of ordinariness—but ordinariness with Christ. And that makes all the difference.

The gospels tell us that whatever we do to the least of Christ's brethren, we do for Christ. It doesn't say "whatever *difficult* things you do." It says *anything* you do, even if it's just giving someone thirsty a cup of water. Even if that someone is someone you love. When you bandage your child's knee, or stir a pot, or wash the dishes, how are you different from Our Lady? You have different things to work with, but you're doing it for Christ—to Christ—who exists in a unique way in this particular child, who is yours. When you teach your kid brother how to tie his shoes, or repair the toaster cord, or drive the car, how different are you from St. Joseph? You're teaching Christ, who dwells in your brother. When a husband and wife sit together in the evening, maybe knitting and reading the paper, and occasionally looking up at one another, how are they different from Mary and Joseph?

The ordinariness of your lives is staggeringly beautiful, because it's the same life God thought important enough to live for thirty years. And he lives it over and over again, today, in you.

*   *   *   *   *

STARTING OVER

17. The Perpetual January First

At the end of eight days, when he was circumcised,
they called him Jesus.

—Luke 2:21

So why all the fuss? It's just another day. Like April 22 or August 18. The old earth keeps spinning a thousand miles an hour, rolling around the sun. My watch ticks past twelve, and in the little window a 1 replaces the 31. And yet it's cause for noisemakers and boozy good cheer and back-thumpings. This is gonna be the year, right? This year all the bills are going to be paid on time, and this year I'm going to start the job the day it's assigned, and this year the Cubs are gonna come home with the pennant.

It's a day of beginnings. The day we take down the old calendar that's a little dustier and more curled at the edges than when we put it on the wall. Somewhat like ourselves—a little older, a little dustier, a little more frayed by the passage of time. But we put up a new one—because time helps us situate ourselves. Time is, after all, the material God gave us to create new life with him. He doesn't want us to concentrate so hard on the end of life that we forget the importance of life itself. Time isn't just the vestibule of eternity. It's meant to be lived. And to prove that point, Our Lord focused himself into time from beyond it, and lived that life himself.

Life's created from a series of moments. Fully or half-heartedly, with the sense of ultimate worth or with a sense of being defeated before we begin. It can be tiny accretions on a shining gift, or a grudging drudgery. And, as a wise old lady once told me, "They ain't nobody gonna decide whether your livin' was worth somethin', honey, but you."

The first day of the year is a day we joke about New Year's resolutions, and it's also what used to be the feast of the Circumcision—which has been changed to merely "The Octave of Christmas." (I don't know why, but I can make a shrewd anti-puritan guess.) So how are resolutions and the naming of Jesus connected?

Well, circumcision for a Jew was and is very like what baptism is for us: the beginning of a new life, a new relation with God. When we're born, we're God's creatures, but in circumcision, the Jew becomes part of the nation of Israel and one of God's chosen people—just as, at baptism, we become part of the Body of Christ and one of God's adopted children.

In this act of circumcision, though, Jesus proved something else. It was the first time God had shed blood, the first time he'd shared our common pain. He began the journey we all begin, step by step, moment by moment, to achieve through our effort and cooperation with God the creation of a human life. It was a day of beginning. At baptism, we joined him on the journey not just as fellow human beings but as Christians.

For twenty years, I've been asking high school seniors (after what they think is twelve years of religious brainwashing) what being Christian really means. In about 99.9% of the responses, "Christian" boils down to "being nice, not hurting anybody." After all that Nazi indoctrination, being Christian turns out to be little more than good manners.

That's pretty insulting to Jews and Moslems and atheists, I think. Most of the ones I've met also want to be "nice, not hurting anybody," but they'd get a little hot under the collar if you called them Christians for it. Surely, Christians have no monopoly on wanting not only to live honorable lives but to live generously. Being nice and not hurting anybody are requirements of our basic *humanity*. Being Christian means something far more. It means being a prophet of the Good News. It means being an apostle, especially to the outcasts. It means living our lives, choosing our careers, making our decisions just as Christ would if he were standing in our loafers.

If the gospel doesn't unnerve you, very likely you haven't

even heard it yet. It asks you to forget yourself—your talents, your shortcomings, your due—and serve. That's pretty intimidating, no?

If the gospel doesn't give you joy almost too big to hold, very likely you haven't heard it yet. Jesus said that finding the Kingdom is like finding a treasure in a field. Think of it. There you are bopping along in a field, minding your own business, when all of a sudden your toe hits something. Hm. It looks like a box. You pull back the dirt and, whatddya know? It is, indeed, a box. You snap it open and—gasp!—it's brimming with diamonds and rubies and gold! And it's all *yours*! Well? What do you say? Avoiding coarser words, I know what I'd say: "Holy guacamole!!!" So, if you haven't heard your call to be a Christian apostle and gasped something like "Holy guacamole!" then you haven't heard your call to be a Christian apostle, kiddo.

Christ has no human voice on earth but yours and mine, no hands but our hands. Yours are the eyes through which he now looks with compassion on the crowds. He is the head, and we are the parts of his body. Without us, Christ is helpless. Wrap your head around that one.

We are the sons and daughters of the Most High God! When are we going to start acting like princes and princesses? When do we begin to understand that *noblesse oblige*?

The day you read this will quite likely not be January First. But it's still a day for beginnings and resolutions. It's a time when Christ begins again to live in our world—through you. Dr. Martin Luther King, Jr., said once, "If your job is to sweep streets, sweep those streets the way Michelangelo would have swept them." He might have said, sweep them the way Jesus of Nazareth would sweep them. Who can imagine a son or daughter of the Most High doing anything half-heartedly?

Perhaps the best resolution of all might be to resolve to take ten minutes a day to just sit quietly, feet up, relaxed, and ask yourself how your Brother would have handled that snotty

salesman, how Jesus would deal with the boring teacher, what he
would say to the friend who'd betrayed his trust.

*   *   *   *   *

18. The Baptism of Jesus

"You are my beloved Son. I am well pleased with you."
—Luke 3:22

When I was in the seminary, I was very prudent. I kept my
mouth shut. Don't ask questions, and they won't find out how
dumb you are. But I always wondered why, if Jesus knew he was
God, he bothered to get himself baptized. It was a very humble
gesture, of course, but surely it wasn't needed. I was troubled,
too, wondering whether, when Joseph was teaching Jesus how to
make a chair, Jesus just politely shut up and refrained from
telling Joseph a thousand better ways of making a chair. I
wondered, too, how anyone who had the fullness of the divine
knowledge could cry out in the Garden of Olives, "I can't do it!"
And on the cross, "My God! My God! Why have you abandoned
me?" If he'd had the full use of the divine knowledge, he'd have
known he could make it. He'd have known he wasn't abandoned.
Was he just, huh, well . . . faking terror and despair?

Disturbing.

And the doubts went deeper still. How could anyone be fully
human—and the dogma says he was fully God and fully man—
if he knew the future? How could one say that Jesus bore the full
burden of humanity if he never knew doubt? In a sense, doubt's
what makes us human: Who am I? Where am I going? What's it
all about? Am I kidding myself? But if Jesus had the full use of
the divine knowledge, he could never have known doubt.

And—at rock bottom—I had to admit that Jesus' possession
of divine foreknowledge made it a lot more difficult to admire
and to imitate him. It was easy for him. He was God.

Then I found the answer in St. Paul: "He was always divine,

but he didn't grasp at his equality with God. Instead, he emptied himself, to become a slave, a man as all men are" (Ph 2:6-7).

He emptied himself. He gave it all up to become fully human. He didn't stop *being* fully God, but he stopped *knowing*, with divine certitude, that he was God. In a sense, he freely chose to become, well, "amnesiac" about the divine knowledge. He became a baby, just like us, and learned just as we do, step-by-step, trial-and-error: Who am I? Where am I going? What's it all about? Am I kidding myself? As the passage on the Holy Family showed, "Jesus *grew* in wisdom." In the Garden, he truly felt terror of the unknown. On the cross, he was truly tormented by the fear that he'd been wrong about himself, that God had abandoned him to his folly. He wasn't abandoned—any more than we're abandoned when we feel loneliness and frustration and despair. But he *felt* it—to the depths of his soul.

Be clear about one thing: he didn't stop being God at the Incarnation, and gradually grew back more and more divine every day. He just discovered—as we do—who he was, more and more every year. Surely he knew he was special. Even if you allow for the Steven Spielberg "special effects" in the infancy narratives, there was certainly something different about his birth. At twelve, when he was left in the Temple and discussed scripture with the priests, it was evident that he was destined for some great vocation. He must have been tempted, as all bright, devout Jewish boys must be tempted, to wonder if perhaps he were being called. But that was unthinkable—just as it is to you or me—that God is calling one to greatness.

Then, at his baptism, it happened: the thunderous realization, the overwhelming confirmation by his Father: "You are my Son." Immediately after, he went out into the desert, and his temptations were precisely on that point: "If you *are* the Son of God, prove it: turn these stones into bread, leap from the Temple."

He was always God, but, as a human being, he found out

who he was and to what he was called, just as we do: slowly, until all the hints build themselves into a conviction. Take a clumsy comparison: at birth, each of us was male or female. We didn't know it, but we were. Then, much later, we found out little boys and little girls are, uh, different. It came as no small surprise: somehow I'm different. Even in biology classes, although we had some vague, notional knowledge of our sexuality, it was really paltry compared to the thunderous realizations that come with puberty. Still, even then, when we thought we "knew all about it," we knew so blessed little. Now, over fifty, way more than halfway through my days, I am still—thank God—discovering more about myself, my sexuality, my humanity. And God humbled himself to do the same thing: learn, slowly.

If you find it difficult to believe that *you* have been called to be a prophet in your own neighborhood, your school, your business, Our Lord shared the same intimidated feeling in the face of his calling. If you find it unthinkable that God would choose *you* to be his son or daughter, Our Lord was there first. If you feel doubt or frustration or abandonment, you have Someone to talk to who has plumbed those depths even more profoundly than you have—and he knows the way back.

You may not feel it, but it's true.

* * * * *

19. I Can Get It For You Cut-Rate

"If you worship me, the whole world will be yours."
—Luke 4:7

Jesus' temptations in the desert were a peak moment in the greatest ad campaign in history. It began in the Garden of Eden, and it continued to the Garden of Gethsemane, and it continues today—albeit in more pedestrian terms.

In the Garden, the Tempter used the grand-daddy of all salesmen's pitches: eat this and you'll become like God. And they fell for it. And so do we: drink this, drive this, smear this on, and you'll look and feel and act—if not like God, at least like those gorgeous American Dreams in the ads.

But it never really works, does it? At least not for long. Why not? Because only God is God. We are his sons and daughters, to be sure, but we're not God. The job's too big for any of us, or for all of us together. The promises of the Tempter always fall flat because they're lies. Or at least they were, until Jesus at the Last Supper paradoxically fulfilled that first false promise. He took bread and wine, blessed them, and gave them to his friends saying, "Now, eat this and you will become like God." It's funny, though. The salesmen we believe, and Jesus we hesitate about.

All the literature of humankind—Hebrew, Greek, African, Asian—records endless variations on that temptation: for us to push God aside and take his place; the creation myths of Micronesians, Incas, Mongolians all record our susceptibility to primal fraud. The stories of Job, Oedipus, Macbeth, Faust all tell the same story: human beings living a lie, acting as if they were born for center stage. As Orwell says, "When men stop worshipping God, they begin worshipping man—with disastrous results."

Jesus' temptations were the same temptation—with a heavily ironic twist. It wasn't a temptation to be divine; he already had that. It was, in a very real sense, a temptation for God to reject his new-found humanity. It was the lure of the quick sale, the easy conversion, bought faith.

The first temptation was to turn stones to bread. As Dostoevsky's Grand Inquisitor put it: "Feed them first. Then demand virtue of them." The second temptation was to cast himself from the pinnacle of the Temple: "What humankind seeks is not God but miracles." The third temptation was to join forces with Caesar and herd men and women toward virtue.

But Jesus refused. Because he knew the truth.

That's infuriating, isn't it? Because that's what we *want* from

Jesus, isn't it? The cheap miracle, the flashy magician's trick? Then we'll believe. We want him to rape away our freedom, to buy away the need for insecure trust by offering us bread and circuses and peace. And he fails us. Nowhere in the entire New Testament does Jesus perform a miracle in order to *secure* faith in him; he performs them only in *response* to faith already given: "Lord, I believe. Help my unbelief."

So often I find myself brooding over God's failure to live up to my expectations. Why didn't he make a world where at least all the children would be fed? It would be easy to love him then. Why doesn't he step in and miraculously end all the wars? It would be so easy to accept him then. Why doesn't God take all the heads of all the factions and beat them into sensibility and cooperation and concern for one another? Why doesn't he make everyone see the truth? Then I'd believe, without reserve.

It's at those times that he does pull a miracle: he brings me back to my senses. I realize I've turned reality topsy-turvy once again. I've forgotten that I was made in his image, not the other way around. I've forgotten that, for some almighty perversity, he values love above all other realities, and love must be free, or it's enslavement, not love. Neither faith nor love can be bought with bread, or with miracles, or with worldly might.

When we think of "strange gods," we think of Baal or Moloch or the idols of Easter Island, stained with the blood of sacrificial virgins. Today, they're hardly so dramatically bestial and clumsy. They are, in fact, most often very "cozy" idols: my car, my flat belly, my home, my children's SAT scores, my reputation, my Dun and Bradstreet report—any of the myriad objects that promise me a sense of power and control, a measure of security and autonomy, a momentary and ersatz divinity.

"You shall worship only the Lord your God. Him alone shall you serve."

*   *   *   *   *

THE MISSION
OF CHRIST IS OURS

20. Jesus' Inaugural Address

> *"The spirit of the Lord is upon me, because he anointed me. He has sent me to preach the Good News to the poor, to announce freedom to the captive and sight for the blind, to give liberty to the oppressed, to proclaim the Lord's year of jubilee."*
> —Luke 4:18-19

And there you have precisely what being a follower of Jesus Christ entails.

Jesus had heard the call of his mission, and had his vocation tested in the wilderness. Then he comes to the synagogue in his home town and gives his inaugural—the touchstone against which all Christians base their values, their priorities, their decisions, their very lives.

He says, "The Spirit of the Lord is upon me," and, although he rests so lightly on us most of the time that we're unaware of his presence, the Spirit of the Lord is indeed upon each of us, too. "Because he anointed me," that is: God officially installed him as an apostle, as "one sent forth," by anointing with the oil of chrism—which is why he is called The *Christos*. And each of us was anointed as an apostle with chrism at our baptism, and we were reanointed at confirmation—which is why we are called Christians: "The Anointed Ones." We are missioned to carry on the apostolate of Christ: "to preach the Good News to the poor, to announce freedom to the captive and sight for the blind, to give liberty to the oppressed, to proclaim the Lord's year of jubilee."

But, uh, that was just for Jesus, no? Or, maybe, nowadays, for priests and nuns, right? I mean, we're just lay people, housewives, students, doctors, businessmen. We don't have either the talent or the temerity to take all that on. I mean, they never really told us that in religious ed classes.

Unfortunately, that's all too often true. Too frequently,

religious education focuses on elements that are, of course, important—morality, religious practice, the sacraments—but are peripheral to the core of the Christian call voiced by Jesus in his inaugural. Even study of Christ himself too often centers on his cherishing and not enough on his challenging. But, at least as far as the Founder understood what Christians are for, it was to do the same jobs as his: preaching, freeing, giving sight, uplifting the oppressed.

Not to worry, however. On the one hand, I imagine Jesus knew that most Christians couldn't give themselves full time to those jobs. You have to make a living. Most of his disciples didn't leave home and families to follow him out on the road as the capital-A apostles did. On the other hand, though, we can't dust our hands of being small-a apostles and go about our lives like any other good, law-abiding, non-Christians.

With a perverse kind of irony, some of the most deeply *spiritual* people I know interpret Jesus' apostolic inaugural—and his mission—in the most rankly *materialistic* ways. They seem to be very literalist, and very univocal—as if Jesus were so one-sided, so narrow-minded, that he thought the only real poverty were material need, the only real imprisonment were actual incarceration, the only real blindness were physical.

Jesus knew—and you and I have known—wealthy people wretchedly impoverished of spirit, imprisoned in the de-humanizing rat race, blind to the needs even of their own families, to the purpose of human life. What's more, those literalist interpreters of scripture tend to forget that it was not merely the poor and illiterate shepherds who were invited to witness to the coming of the Savior. He was also careful to invite the rich and learned astrologers as well. Neither wealth nor poverty can exclude any man or woman from our apostolic concern.

Let's face up to the intimidating truth: we were anointed apostles, and we confirmed our acceptance of that vocation. And there is no lack of poor, imprisoned, blind people right at our elbows, right in our offices and classrooms and suburban tracts: the lonely, the surly, the reclusive, the embittered, the bereaved, the nerds and wimps and hamheads. We can't withdraw into comfortable anonymity and the solace that we're untalented nobodies. Our Father thinks more of our power than we do ourselves.

There's no one of us who can't say, "Hey, why not join us for lunch?" Not for a lifetime. Just for lunch.

In his first letter to the Corinthians, Paul refines and subdivides that apostolic vocation we've all agreed to assume: some are called to preach, others to explain; some are healers, some are fund-raisers, some are administrators. (I take a certain unhealthy delight in the fact that he put administrators second last.) But then he says, "Are all apostles? Are all prophets?" That looks like a very appealing way off the hook. See? Somebody else has that job. Sorry.

When Paul implied that we are not all "apostles," he was using a capital-A apostle. But the word "*apostolos*" means anyone who is "sent," not just to the foreign missions but to the supermarket. When he implied that we are not all "prophets," he was capitalizing again: Martin Luther King and Mother Teresa kind of prophets. But the word "*prophetes*" doesn't mean one who sees the future, nor is it restricted to that foolhardy few called to sass back to Pharaohs and Caesars. The word means "one who speaks for another, a messenger," and we're all anointed messengers sent to the poor, the imprisoned, the blind—in our offices and classrooms and suburban tracts.

I'm tempted to believe that the worst thing that happened to the apostolic Church wasn't the Protestant Reformation. Rather, I think it was the rhapsodically acclaimed conversion of the Emperor Constantine, when we stopped being persecuted and became the official religion. It was not a blessing without thorns. Ecclesiastical administrators began to pattern their dress and living accommodations and self-importance after those of their civil counterparts. The apostles were divided between the Church teaching (the clergy, "them") and the Church taught (the laity, "us") and offered a new way off the apostolic hook. "Just keep the contributions coming, friends. We'll take care of the rest." Sorry, again. They were wrong. The very Greek word for "Church" — "*ekklesia*"—means "those who are called forth."

But that does show you that you needn't be afraid of making blunders in your own apostolate. The first pope made more than a couple gaffes, both before and after his ordination. A few of his Renaissance successors might have given even Hugh Hefner a moment's hesitation. The official Church missed the point on money lending and slavery and the Galileo case.

Let us rejoice in our imperfection, then. I myself often feel like the court jester to the Czar who made infelicitous jokes about hemophiliacs. There are people who flee me—and in so doing flee the healing message I'd like to bring them. No difficulty. There are plenty more who are needful of healing and not as fastidious about the healer.

The only real failure is not to try, not to be what we've been called to be.

And if the almighty and omniscient God thinks we're up to the challenge, who the hell are we to say we're not?

*   *   *   *   *

21. Anti-Beatitudes

> *Seeing the crowds, he went up on the mountain, and*
> *after he had sat down his disciples gathered around him,*
> *and he taught them.*   —Matthew 5:1-2

We're so used to hearing the beatitudes that they become like old coins whose value has been rubbed off by over-use. So, I got out my thesaurus and found antonyms for all of them, as if Jesus were cursing the people who did exactly the opposite of what he was saying would fulfill them.

The first beatitude is "Blessed are the poor in spirit." Positively, a Hebrew would have heard those words saying, "How lucky are those who have no possibility of 'arriving,' of 'having it made.'" And its opposite would be, "How cursed are those who can afford to sneer." I imagine him saying, how awful it is for those who can say, "Well, I made something of myself, by God. Why the hell can't 'they'?" Their curse is their own smugness.

"Blessed are the sorrowing"—and cursed are those who have never known sorrow, who have never invested enough of themselves in another human being that that person can cause them grief. Cursed are the self-centered, who judge all goods and all evils solely by what is good or evil for me and mine. Their curse is their own cramped asbestos souls.

"Blessed are the gentle"—and cursed are the macho men, the cool, the invulnerable. Cursed are they with their impregnable security within their empty selves. Cursed are the world-beaters who never give themselves away, who are never taken in—and therefore never see the inside of anything. Their curse is their own empty eyes.

"Blessed are those who hunger and seek for the right"—and cursed are those who show no hunger, who have nothing left to learn. Cursed are those who live their lives in pieces, who have no wholeness, no center, no inner peace to unify every insignificant act of their lives into a self. Cursed are those who have no time for walking in the woods alone with God. Cursed are the sated. Their curse is their own bloated emptiness.

"Blessed are those who show mercy"—and cursed are those so sure of themselves that they can cast the first stone—at the pocky, the unathletic, the redneck, the homosexual, the tramp, the family on relief. Cursed are those who don't realize "a cup of cold water in my name" can mean nothing more demanding than a smile. Cursed are those who cannot realize that simple justice is not enough. Their curse is their own iron hearts.

"Blessed are the pure of heart"—and cursed are those whose pharisaism is a mask. Cursed are those whose puritanism is a strangulation of the human spirit. Cursed are the judgmental, the nit-pickers, the envious, the backbiters, the scandal mongers. Cursed are those who make us prove ourselves first. Their curse is their own passionless self-righteousness.

"Blessed are the peacemakers"—and cursed are those who nurse grudges, who find their hurt feelings too inflated to swallow, who will not forgive or give a second chance—even to their own. Cursed are those who, at the first mistake, wipe out that name from those worthy to be loved. Cursed are those who take offense when none was intended. Their curse is their own snarling edginess.

"Blessed are the persecuted"—and cursed are those so lukewarm that they stand for nothing. Cursed are those afraid to stand up and be counted—and persecuted. Cursed are those who judge those who do take a stand as "do-gooders" and "halo-seekers" and "show-offs." Cursed are those whose security is more important than the truth. Their curse is their own milky insipidity.

"Blessed are you when they insult you"—and cursed are those so "safe" that they have no enemies, that no one calls them "fool."

There needs to be no hell for such people. They already carry their hell within them.

* * * * *

22. The First Miracle

On the third day there was a wedding at Cana in Galilee. The mother of Jesus was there, and Jesus and his disciples had also been invited to the celebration.—John 2:1-2

In "The Skin of Our Teeth," the truculent and unsinkable earth-mother, Maggie Antrobus, gives about as good a description of marriage as I've ever heard: "I didn't marry you," she says to her husband, "because you were perfect. I didn't even marry you because I loved you. I married you because you gave me a promise. That promise made up for your faults. And the promise I gave you made up for mine. Two imperfect people got married, and it was the promise that made the marriage. And when our children were growing up, it wasn't a house that protected them; and it wasn't our love that protected them. It was that promise."

In all cultures, why are weddings done so . . . publicly? Why endure all the candles and the dressing up and the pocketbooks full of soppy Kleenex? They loved one another long before they dared come into that intimidating assemblage. Why not just have a trial marriage for a year or so and, if it works out, fine. If it doesn't, the two of them are a bit wiser, and they've avoided an idiotically naive gamble. Because, after all, the two of them aren't certain that this promise is going to work out "till death do us part." They're *betting* it will. It's an act of faith, backed by their whole selves.

The reason a trial marriage isn't enough is that there's no such thing. There's trial cohabitation, perhaps—where two people discover whether he can live with the pantyhose over the shower curtain, and she can tolerate his nights out with the boys. But that's as much like marriage as practicing to swim the English Channel by spluttering around your bathtub. Only a marriage—that promise, forever—can survive the crises that would make trial cohabitation fall to pieces.

All right, then: it takes a promise. But why so publicly? Why not roust out the Justice of the Peace at midnight (which is very romantic and adventurous), or get the whole thing over quick and clean at city hall (which is indisputably legal)? The reason is, I think, that at city hall the real thing just doesn't "happen."

These two people aren't giving their promise—in both senses of that word—just in order to civilly legitimate their children, or in order to bind one another to alimony. Nor are they asking the rather cold and indifferent State to witness their promise. They're asking us—their brothers and sisters, the Church, and they're presenting their promise to one another in the presence of the Father we all share.

Their promise is too big, too important for a J.P.'s parlor or an office in a municipal building. It's something that has to be shouted, something that has to be *celebrated*. Both the Mass and the marriage are the celebration of love, the celebration of life. At that moment, two celebrations—sacrifice and sex, the two perfect ways of showing love—fuse into one moment. And that's what makes a marriage: the self-surrender of sacrifice and the self-surrender of sexuality—and every self-surrender in between.

A wedding is a moment too big for legalisms, a moment that bursts the barriers of time and space, free of clocks and efficiency reports and who owes what in justice. It's a sacred moment: two people so certain they love one another that they're betting their lives on it. It's not a trial; it's a commitment. It's not just a promise which binds, but a promise which liberates.

"Promise" means you give your word—your name. But "promise" also means you show great expectations, a potential for growth. And marriage is that kind of promise, too. For in that moment we celebrate not only the promise that two people give but the promise that they show—to enrich one another and to enrich us, with their newfound self and with their children.

The opening of two whole selves which we celebrate at a wedding, that mingling of two vulnerabilities, is of its very nature explosively creative. It makes things happen. When God at the beginning gave his Word over the chaos, everything lined up and smiled back at him—ready to start growing. He gave his

Promise so that everything could become promising. A wedding does the same.

At your wedding, Our Father didn't promise you a ready-made Kingdom. Nor did he offer magic words or sure-fire instructions on how to build it. All he offered was a road—the assurance that your promise shows promise—which is all he gave Abraham and Sarah or Joseph and Mary: a road. And it was all he could offer his Son. Along your road, too, you've found the unavoidable hills of Golgotha which, we have on the best of testimony, is the only route to coming alive again. But it's your promise that carries you through them.

At that moment, Our Father said to the two of you no more than, "Come! Come out on the road with me, and together the three of us will create . . . we-know-not-what . . . but together. And together, we're already there."

* * * * *

23. Being Spoiled

> *"In your prayers, do not bibble-babble as the pagans do. They think that using a lot of words will make them heard."*
> —Matthew 6:7

Have you ever noticed that most of us pray only when we feel small? We pray in thunderstorms, in foxholes, or near the ocean, when the sky's ablaze with stars, and the enormity of the whole thing puts us in our places. We pray when we've sinned, when we've made fools of ourselves, when we're in need. Then we're hungry. Then we head for home.

But who prays when he's "up"? When everything's peaceful and serene? When we're sick we beg God to make us well, but when we're in tip-top shape, who remembers to thank him for *not* being sick? When I'm down and out, it's God's fault; he's in charge. When I'm lucky, I'm in charge; who needs him?

A very wise stand-up comic once said to me, "D'ya know what's wrong with us today, Father? We've forgot the taste of bread." And that's true. Unless we're really desperately hungry—and which of us has been that lately?—we can't taste the bread through the butter and jelly and ham and mayo and onions. While half the people on earth would lick the bottoms of your shoes for a piece of bread, we're so well-off that we throw out the end-pieces. Most Americans are the spoiled brats of the universe.

It's only the hungry who know the taste of bread, who savor the nuances of flavor, the textures, the way it fills up the emptiness in the belly. And it's only the hungry who know the taste of the Bread of Life.

Until we honestly admit who God really is, and what he's given us, and how indebted we are, we'll never know who *we* really are. Until we feel a hunger within us for something more, for some deeper relationship to God than panhandlers to Sugar Daddy, we'll leave the old fool doddering at home and come around only when we're hungry again.

If "I'm doing very well, thank you very much," who needs the Eucharist? "I go because my parents force me . . . I go because I think it's good for the kids . . . I don't go because I'm, like, hungry, but, well, you know . . . it's 'time.' "

If God gave us existence, he gave us everything. Without the gift of existence, no other gift would have been possible. Without that essential gift, I'd never have known the people I love, or sunshiny days, or beer, or books, or babies. How do I thank him for all that? Just the obligatory, routine visit every Sunday morning? Like the visit to the rich old-maid aunt, just in case she might kick off and remember me in her will?

People say they have no time to pray; they're too busy. But I often wonder how many days they're too busy to take a shower. Other people say they forget to pray in the morning and at night.

But I wonder how many mornings and evenings they forget to brush their teeth. It's important to smell clean and have a nice smile. More important than being grateful? More important than acknowledging who God is and who I really am before him?

Why does God allow suffering? One reason might be to show us that being spoiled isn't an incurable disease.

Gone for any walks with God recently? He's a good companion. He might even convince you that you were hungrier than you'd thought.

* * * * *

24. Forgiving God

When Jesus came to the gate of the town, a dead boy
was being carried out to be buried, the only son of his
mother, who was a widow. —Luke 7:12

We can face the death of someone old with a great sense of loss, but placidly. But the death of someone young, who's never had a chance, is somehow obscene. And I've been to too many funerals of young people not to have had more than a few chats with my Big Friend about his callousness.

There's a French legend called *"Le Jongleur de Dieu,"* God's Juggler. All the peasants of the village bring gifts at Christmas and leave them at the crib for the newborn Savior. But the tattered traveling juggler has nothing—no lamb, no apples, no bread. So, late at night, all alone, he comes before the Madonna and her Child and offers them the only thing he has: he juggles for them.

I've always had a fellow-feeling for that helpless little man. I'm a clown, too; I juggle words. It's all I have to offer; it's what I do. But where do I look for words to encompass the meaning of a child's death? The only thing I'm sure of is that, if I were God, I'd have handled things far better.

And yet, if I were God, I'd be a very poor one—the over-intrusive parent, eyes always clamped on my children, making all their decisions for them, hovering and smothering and paralyzing any possibility of their ever growing up and being free of me. They'd never hurt. I'd never have to say, "If only I'd . . ." Because I'd be God, wouldn't I?

There perhaps is a key: we're not God. We're Job—ravaged with pain, troubling the heavens with our need for explanation, our need at least to see some kind of justice in it all. And the heavens are confoundingly silent. When God finally did appear to Job, he shouted from the whirlwind, "Where were you when I laid the foundations of the earth?" Who are you to question what I do?

It's an infuriatingly humbling answer: God is God, and he's not answerable to us. We find ourselves before the ultimate and crucial mystery, before which we can no longer consider the question of God an academic inquiry, sitting around a cocktail party or a college dorm, assessing the pros and cons. Either there must be a God—who has his reasons, however impermeable they are to us, or there are no reasons at all—for anything. If there is no God, there isn't even anyone to blame. And that possibility makes a mockery of our minds and turns hope into a curse.

So, at the death of someone young, we're brought to our knees. We're reminded that, every time we've said the Our Father, we've said "*Thy* will be done."

But to say merely that such an obscenity is "the will of God," that the only meaning to it is to remind us of our place compared to God, is cold comfort indeed. It may be the truth, but what we are in need of at such moments is not lessons. We're in need of light, compassion, hope. I've had too much experience of God's goodness to think that the face of the God of Job is the only face of God. I've seen him in sun-dappled mountainsides; I've seen him in the faces of children, scrubbed and full of life; I've seen him in Jesus Christ, whose first word was always "Peace," who spent himself to the last drop of blood to heal and forgive and give life, who rose triumphant from the tomb to prove that life is too strong to bow before death.

God is my Father. But there are times when I've been angry with him, as I sometimes was with my own father and my other dearest friends. Terribly angry, angry enough to forget all the mountains and the children and the healing. Whether we are able to admit it or not, a great deal of our grief is really anger. And that needs healing. At those times, what I honestly believe we need is to take a walk with God; tell him how we feel; berate him, denounce him.

And then forgive him. For the good times.

$$* \quad * \quad * \quad * \quad *$$

25. Back to Basics

> *Jesus sent out the Twelve, charging them: "Preach as you go, 'The Kingdom of God is near.' Heal the sick, raise the dead, cleanse the lepers, cast out demons. You received freely; give freely."* — Matthew 10:5, 8

Being a prophet isn't very profitable. When the prophet Amos tried to speak, even the priests of his own religion said to him, "Go away. Do your prophesying somewhere else." I've felt just like ol' Amos sometimes. A couple of times I thought it was going to be terminal.

A priest who has a column in the local Catholic paper frequently writes articles asserting, in so many words, that the products of Catholic schools are so religiously illiterate and uncommitted to the Church that the schools themselves are undermining the faith. Since teaching religious education is my bag, I've several times tried to set him straight—since, I thought, we were both on the same side. So I sat down and wrote a series of articles telling parents (and the columnist) just what we were trying to teach.

Gasp! The letters to the editor were just short of lynching threats: "Modernist! Apostate! Perverter of youth!" Equivalently: "Go do your (devilish) prophesying somewhere else!" A lot of the less virulent letters demanded that religious education get "back to basics." At first, I thought they meant things like the Apostles' Creed, and I agreed with them wholeheartedly. But when they began to specify, I was dumbfounded. What they meant by basics was things like priests not handing out communion after the greeting of peace without washing their hands first. Really basic stuff like that.

Or they wanted to get back at least to the solid stuff about hell, and sin, and the Virgin Birth, and the infallibility of the pope, and how pernicious Communists are. As a teacher, I really haven't got time for secondary matters when a great many of the kids I teach have grave doubts about even the existence of God (what difference does it make?), about having any personal need for salvation (from what?), about feeling any empathic desire to help the outcasts or any sense of being apostles (you don't expect me to be a priest, do you?).

Those four questions are what I'd call "the basics." If students aren't even aware those questions exist—and have no felt need to answer them, then all the rest is sheerly academic. They'll endure religious education, as they do history and French, but there's nothing in any of them that has to do with "the real world."

It might help parents troubled by their children's ignorance—and ignoring—of the faith to make a few distinctions. *Theology* is what we *know* about God; *belief* is what we *accept* of what we know; *religion* is what we *do* about our belief. They're very definitely separable. For one thing, I can know that something is asserted by the Church without accepting it, and I can know and accept a doctrine of the Church without necessarily acting on my belief.

Theology is what you know about God. It can be taught, and it can be tested. Atheists can get A+ in theology without accepting a word of it, while the Cure of Ars flunked it with embarrassing regularity. Theology is the only thing we can teach.

Belief is what you accept of what you know. Only the individual, freely and in the silence of his or her own soul, can make that decision. Acceptance of the *gift* of faith can't be taught, it can't be forced, it can only be offered.

Religion is what you do about God. You can force your children to attend Mass each Sunday while they're at home, but you can't force them once they've gone away to college or after they're married. They've got to see a value in the Mass for themselves. And telling them they *should* want to go to Mass won't work, any more than telling them they should like the spouses you've chosen for them.

Whenever parents—or our local columnist—express concerns about the failure of their children's religious courses, I have several retorts. One, come in any time; listen to what we're saying; read the textbooks—they all have an Imprimatur. The theology is sound. But I can't make them accept it, any more than you can make them accept broccoli.

Two, if religious education is so important, have you gotten any yourself lately? Are your grammar school catechism or your college courses enough for a faith that has to keep growing? Can you help them with their theology homework, the same way you help them with their math?

Three, at the end of high school, when I get them, it's too late to change a kid's values dramatically except in a few cases. When I get them, they've had seventeen years of brainwashing from the Tube, which promises that the more things they have, the happier they'll be—whereas the gospel I'm trying to lure them to accept says the *fewer* things they have, the happier they'll be. Thus, everything I say is automatically a contradiction.

Also, in far too many cases, the students I teach have been told by their parents for the same seventeen years that they have to get good marks—but only so they'll get a good college, a good job, and "the good life." What does "the good life" really mean, concretely: a split-level in Miami or a grass hut in Molokai? When a boy tells his Dad he wants to be a social worker, and the father says, "How the hell much can you make doing that?" don't come to me and say, "What am I laying out all this good money for a Catholic education for? He doesn't even want to go to Mass!"

Far more basic than acceptance of—belief in—hell and the Virgin Birth and papal infallibility, there is the core message of Jesus Christ: first, Jesus Christ is the embodiment of God; second, you're going to die someday, but Jesus-God went through death in order to rise from it and share immortality with us; third, to be embodied in the Body of Christ, you have to give up the values of "The World" (Me first!), and take on the values of the Kingdom (Them first!)—and "them" is God and the neighbor, especially the outcasts: the sick, the "dead," the "lepers," the bedeviled; and finally, we celebrate our liberation from the fear of death and our mission to the needy every week.

The message of salvation from fear, from selfishness, from ultimate meaninglessness, is 180° away from the message of all those hypnotic commercials. It's a total reversal of what so many of us accept as the only way to survive in this dog-eat-dog world.

I don't think kids ignore the gospel or religion because it's so boring—even if that's what they say. I think they ignore it because accepting it is too scary. Accepting it would cost more than they're ready to pay.

When Jesus sent out the Twelve, he wasn't sending twelve bishops, or twelve priests and nuns. They hadn't been ordained yet. He was sending out twelve ordinary Christians. Like you. What you were freely given, freely give. Cast out the devils—like insane competitiveness, materialism, fear, self-protectiveness, greed.

"Well, uh, come on now. I'm not some kind of fanatic."

Jesus wasn't looking for fanatics. He was looking for fishers—people who, like him, were willing to set the earth on fire. He wanted people who submitted not just to a pouring of water but to a total reversal of all that The World says is essential.

That's pretty hot stuff. It's subversive.

You could get crucified for it.

*   *   *   *   *

26. Time is Money (Only Better)

> *"If you want to walk with me, give up your self, take up your cross every day, and follow me."* — Luke 9:23

A few unkind souls say I'm an extremist. On the one hand, my impatience with witless servitude would warm the embalmed heart of Vladimir Ulyanov Lenin. But on the other hand, my position on abortion would warm the cardiac cockles of Senator Jesse Helms. But I do tend to talk in extremes. I like to pose the ultimate oversimplifications at each end of any spectrum—which are, almost by definition, absurd.

I have three reasons for doing that. First, it shows up simple-mindedness for what it is. Second, everyone who's listening—including occasionally even myself—must have taken a stance on the question which is somewhere between those extremes. Third, I most often find the truth balanced precariously somewhere between the extremes.

When Jesus declared the conditions for Christian discipleship, he very forthrightly said you've got to put your concrete daily actions where your mouth is; don't say you're a Christian unless it shows, unless you take up your daily cross—with good humor and without playing to the grandstands or the college scouts. If being a Christian were a capital offense, could a grand jury find enough concrete evidence against you even to indict you—not as someone "nice, trying not to hurt anybody," but specifically as an apostolic, "World"-subversive Christian?

Well, now there's a thorny question. At one extreme, the guilt mongers and masochists are biting the tips of their fingers, and at the other extreme, the self-justified and narcissists are yawning and buffing their nails. And, I fear, too often our preachers pander either to our pain or to our pomposity.

"Oh, God!" the guilt-mongers and masochists and unprofitable servants moan, "there are so many people starving in the world, and what am I doing about them?" Well, I think you give what you can, and then just a touch more, for the pot—just to be sure. But I don't think you reduce your family to rice and beans and cholesterol just because most of the world eats too much starch. St. Paul says, "the collection should not impoverish you." I keep thinking that, no matter how Jesus praised her, the widow who threw her last two mites into the Temple poor box was going to be banging that night on the door of her daughter-in-law, who hadn't been so open-handedly generous.

Think of the pain-in-the-neck things you do right now, not only without complaint but without even the slightest thought of reward: the diapers; unloading the dishwasher; bringing the paycheck home instead of to OTB; writing an essay to be proud of, when you could squeeze a 70 out of ten minutes of swamp gas.

At the other extreme, the self-justified and the narcissists and the crypto-pharisees sigh, "Ah! I threw five scoots into the collection and pledged a hundred-each to Jerry Lewis and PBS." I'm not knocking that; keep those cards and checks comin', folks!

But it's not enough—even if it's a thousand each. Don't get me wrong. There's honest sacrifice there; there's a lot of nice things you could have bought for yourself or for your family. But—and I say this with a touch of trepidation—it's a stage-prop cross, with a velvet shoulderpad. There's no stink of sweat in writing a check so someone else can help the needy. There's no clutch at the heart because the people you're trying to help—in a hands-on situation—are so beyond your help, so terminally ill or terminally old, so smug, so slow, so afraid.

I risk blind-siding myself here. If you're reading a book like this, you very likely give a couple hours—or even more—of your week for working with retarded children, reading to blind people, acting as a literacy volunteer. I risk being like the preacher who rants against being late for Mass—to people who have obviously arrived at least before the homily. I'm taking the 99 sheep for granted, while I go snuffling around the bushes for one or two strays.

But I think each of us, no matter how cluttered and chaotic our weeks, can carve out a couple of hours to give of our selves rather than of our surplus. But it's like getting exercise. Or finding time to relax alone with God.

We do have the time. That's what time was given to us for.

*   *   *   *   *

27. The Burden of Astonishment

And Jesus was transfigured before them, and his face
shone like the sun, and his clothes were white as light.
— Matthew 17:2

It might seem that the Transfiguration was a startlingly unique experience. I mean, you and the two other apostles are ambling up this hill, nattering away about the crumby prices you can get for your fish, when suddenly Jesus just starts . . . well, blazing away! All the God-ness in him just starts burning through the human-ness of him. That's just about enough to tip you in the direction of a friendly psychiatrist, no? Fortunately— we console ourselves—we're folks too insignificant ever to bear the burden of such humbling astonishment.

Aha! Don't be too sure!

I doubt there's any one of us who hasn't gone outside on a clear summer night and been assaulted by the immensity of the sky, ablaze with stars. What do we say? "Oh, my God!" And that instinctive, defenseless response is precisely correct. That's exactly the One we've encountered.

When I walked into the Michelangelo museum in Florence, I suddenly found myself in an enormous room with nothing in it at all except me and his heroic-sized sculpture of David. Guess what I said? Right. "Oh, my God!" And I just stood there, for nearly an hour, dumbfounded, awe-stricken. Humbled.

Very likely every one of us has been stunned into a state of defenseless awe when—beyond any hoping—he or she said, very quietly, "And I love you, too." "Oh, my God!" And that's just whom we've encountered, the restless "freshness deep-down things," lurking below all the surfaces, waiting to catch us with our defenses down, ready to blaze us into a dimension of reality freed of time and space. Into God.

Ordinarily, we shield ourselves from the stars, with skylines and with lesser lights of our own devising. Ordinarily, we shield ourselves from art, with the far more pressing business that infests our days. Ordinarily, we shield ourselves from love, with our fear of being hurt, our fear of giving ourselves away, being caught outside, naked and vulnerable and ashamed.

Ordinarily we shield ourselves, then, from God.

Here, at this moment, radio waves and gamma rays and neutrinos are lancing through your body—and you aren't the least aware of them. We're nested in fields of forces we are as oblivious to as the blinking of our eyes, and the pulsing of our blood, and the digestion of our breakfasts. We're not aware of them—but they're there. So is God.

Asking why we never see God is like asking Helen Keller why she can't see the stars. The difference between the two, though, lies in another old cliché (where so many truths lie undetected): "There are none so blind as those who *will* not see."

At the end of the vision of the Transfiguration, the apostles "looked up, but they saw only Jesus." Imagine that: only Jesus. Which of us wouldn't like to do that? And yet we can. "I looked up, but I saw only the salt-scented surf; I looked up, but I saw only the Sistine Ceiling; I looked up, but I saw only my son."

At death, our busy self-blindedness will be cured. We'll look at him, no longer in a glass—darkly—but face to face. And we'll say, "Oh, my God! It was you, all the time."

Wouldn't it be a pity if we had to wait so long?

*   *   *   *   *

28. The Only Two Commandments

> *"You must love the Lord your God with all your heart, with all your soul, with all your strength, and with all your mind, and your neighbor as yourself." — Luke 10:27*

In capsule, that one sentence sums it all up. The trouble with it for us is twofold. First, we've heard it so often that the words have become as whispy as the words of the Our Father; we don't hear them any more, even when we're saying them ourselves. And second, it *is* in capsule form and, like $e = mc^2$, the components seem at one time too overly compressed and too irritatingly vague. Perhaps I can remind you of what you already know.

Apparently, loving is the best thing in the world, the door to joy, the reason for humans' living. We know that. But we forget.

And we know what love is, too. We know that quickening of the heart at the sight of the beloved, when the joy in us is fit to burst, when time and space are meaningless. But we also know, deep down, below the level of words, that love exists in its purest form when there are no kickbacks.

When I was born, my mother told me, she was so badly torn by a breech-birth that the doctor told my father to sleep somewhere else for three months. To avoid the slightest risk of hurting her, he slept somewhere else for a whole year. And I ask myself, how did he show more love for her—by going to bed with her, or by staying out? I think of that, too, when the girl tells me her boyfriend says, "If you really loved me, you'd let me do it." I tell her she ought to say to him, "If you really loved me, you wouldn't ask me to 'prove' it."

We all know that, but we forget. A small voice near the core of us occasionally whispers, "But what about *me*? After all I've done for them?" We know. But we forget.

There are three objects of love mentioned in those only two commandments: the neighbor, ourselves, and God.

We know that "the neighbor" is a word which covers all human beings—not just my cherished friends who've proved their way into my love, and not just the attractive people, but all those alien and broken bodies that lie along our road to Jericho: the poor, the lonely, the churlish, the crippled, the arrogant, the liars, the sneaks. Christ died for them all and, like it or not, being Christ's apostle means joining a family which includes "them." Christ was notoriously unselective in his choice of friends. After all, despite all the nastinesses about me that only he and I know about, he still chose me. That sort of obligates me to do the same thing. (Anyone who finds Christianity boring, hasn't wrapped his or her head around *that* one yet!)

The second person in there is one's self. Notice that it doesn't say we should love our neighbors "more than" or "in spite of" or "instead of" ourselves. It says "as"—and that means "as much as" or "in the same ways as." That means one must love his or her self, even when the chips are down. But when I see so many people who knock themselves, and demean themselves in order to be accepted, and lacerate themselves for being themselves, I begin to wonder if that isn't one of the big reasons why there's so precious little love of the neighbor going around.

Which of us is not more understanding about the shortcomings of those we really love than we are about our own shortcomings? If someone you really love isn't a genius, not the most beautiful person in the world, occasionally weak—don't you make allowances? Doesn't your love accept them the way they are, and love them all the more? And if the Almighty Creator forgives not only your imperfection (which is, after all, the way he made you) but also your blatant idiocies (which isn't the way he made you), who are you not to forgive yourself, once he has? We know that, but we forget.

And finally, there's God. The same two requirements of love are due to him, too: forgiveness and risk.

Robert Frost has a little verse that sums up the first: "Oh, God. Forgive my little jokes on thee, and I'll forgive your great big Joke on me." We have to forgive our Big Friend, too—for giving us the free will that mucks things up all the time, for creating cerebral palsy, and hurricanes, and the indignities of old age—without so much as a by-your-leave, and with a damnable lack of explanation. We have to forgive him for death. Because—like the people who are our friends, like the people we tolerate, like ourselves—God is a Person.

And we have to risk with him, too. Risk the effort and the shy tribute of becoming aware of his presence, risk speaking to him when heaven knows he remains so often silent, risk finding him beyond death—because, very truly, without him beyond death, there is nothing. We know that, but we forget.

Something in us, something shrewd, can't help asking,

"Well, it's nothing but give, give, give, then. What's in it for me?" That seems like an eminently sensible question to me. After all, it'd be mere blind whim to wager one's whole heart and soul and mind, one's whole life, without some value in return. Not to ask that question would be an admission that one's life is a valueless risk.

I can merely say that loving—with all it entails: joy, pride, growth—is its own reward. Oh, it'll cost, all right. The loveless are rarely hurt, merely discomforted. The loveless need never compromise, never lose, never lie awake worrying, never yearn or repent or shed tears.

Because the loveless are always alone.

*   *   *   *   *

29. Conflicts of Interest

> "Unless you hate your father, mother, wife, children, brothers, sisters—yes, even your own life, too, you cannot be my disciple."
>
> — Luke 14:26

To my mind, Luke is the gentlest of gospel writers. And yet he's got that . . . well, to put it at its lowest reading . . . bothersome word, "hate." Even Matthew, who doesn't hesitate to pull out the howitzers, softens it down to "If you *prefer* father," etc. I don't really like Luke's choice of words at all. I've really done all that Matthew asks: I've "preferred" Christ to all those people he mentions, and I'm a man for whom hyperbole is more habitual than shaving, but all the commentaries I've read don't help me at all with Luke's choice of the word "hate."

Over the years, many men and women have gotten low-to-high-grade guilt complexes over that gospel passage and passages like it. To our 20th century American ears, Jesus is saying that, if you have money, or if you love anyone *other* than God, you have no place with him in the Kingdom. If you're not close to destitution, if you haven't given up everything—and everybody, left them all behind to become a priest or a nun, you're a borderline Christian.

Obviously, Jesus isn't saying that. It contradicts so many things he says and does elsewhere in the gospels. He surely loved his own mother. His endless work and travel showed his love for his friends, concretely and visibly. He wept unashamedly at the tomb of his friend, Lazarus. He himself was accused of enjoying food and wine too much. No. He can't have meant that loving people and material goods was even a weakness—much less a sin—since he himself loved people and material goods. And love was his one commandment to us.

To read this passage (and so many others like it) with Puritan eyes is to make Jesus contradict himself. To ask if Jesus loves clerics better than lay people flies in the face of the evidence. The only people—in the whole gospel—he ever bawled out were clerics.

It is true that he gave special invitations to some people to become servants of the Church: the apostles, the women who followed him, the Rich Young Man. While all members of the Mystical Body are called to serve the growth of the Kingdom by bringing the message into the marketplace and raising up the downtrodden, a smaller number were called to minister to—to *serve*—the others. They were summoned from their fishing nets and tax booths and families, asked to leave it all behind, and invited to be the servants of the servants of God.

But that was a *special* invitation, as we see in the story of the Rich Young Man. He came to Jesus asking how he could serve God more fully. He'd kept the commandments all his life— which is certainly saying more than a little—and the gospel says "Jesus loved him" for that. But the young man was asking how he could do *more*. And Jesus told him, "sell all you have; give it to the poor; and come with us." It was a priestly vocation, a special call within the Kingdom: to be a capital-A apostle. But the young man couldn't do it, because he had great wealth. Somehow, he was pulled more strongly by his possessions than by God. And yet Jesus still loved him.

Jesus doesn't ask all of us to reject—much less to despise—our families and our material goods. The only problems arise, as they did with the Rich Young Man, when there's a *conflict* between our attachments to the people and the things we love and our attachments to the calls of God. He does *not* say, "No one can love material goods and love God at the same time." He says, "No one can be a *slave* of material goods and love God at the same time."

You know the old truism that what you do shouts so loudly that I can't hear what you say. When it comes to the crunch—as it did when God asked Abraham to sacrifice his son Isaac: do you love your family or your possessions *more* than you love God? When Jesus was busy preaching, and they told him his mother was outside, he gestured to the people he was serving and said, "At this moment, *these* are my mother and my brothers."

If your sons or daughters came to you and said they wanted to be priests or nuns, would your first reaction be disappointment?

Our Lord doesn't expect to win very time, in every one of our choices. If anyone knows we're human and weak, he does. His model disciple was Peter, and, for a long time, he lost with Peter far more than he won. What he's asking is: does my voice intrude on *any* of your choices? Buying an extra car, choosing a career, using your spare time? When you have a decision to make—large or small—do you ever say, "Now what would Jesus do, right now, in my place?"

That's a pretty nifty question.

* * * * *

30. Turning Sheep Into Shepherds

> *"Rejoice with me, I've found my sheep which was lost."*
> —Luke 15:6

When I was a lot younger, and a lot more romantic, and fancied myself a remarkable sinner, I doted on that gospel passage about forsaking the hypocritical, line-toeing 99 to come and look for me. What a joy to know that Jesus had an extra-soft place in his heart for us sinners. And me? Wow, boy. I was really, like, you know, his *pet* sinner, like Mickey Rooney was to Spencer Tracy in "Boys' Town."

But after spending far more than half my life as a religious, toiling loyally up and down the rows of the vineyard every day, I began to wonder if, for all those years—besides overdramatizing my own penny-ante sinfulness—I hadn't been just a touch smug about it as well. As if I were really the prodigal son, coming home the umpteenth time and causing all that joy all over again, sneering at the Elder Brother and saying, "Nyah-nyah-na-nyah-nyah! I'm a *sin*-ner, and you *are*-n't, and Daddy like me *be*-est!"

Silly, isn't it? The arrogance we develop in the name of humility? After all, the Good Shepherd never really did have to leave the 99 too often to track *me* down, and he never had to search too far. Hell, the only time I ever ran away from home when I was a kid, I stopped four blocks away because I was forbidden to cross the street at a light alone. I would guess the same was pretty much true of you, too, or else you wouldn't be turning these pages right now.

I don't know why that insight should have eluded me so long, what with all the plays I've put on. It never fails that, when we start reading for parts, *everybody* wants the lead—whether they have the talent or not, whether they're the right size and girth and personality or not. Despite those 55 plays, whenever I've played the story of the lost sheep or the prodigal son in my mind, I sure didn't want to play one of those dull old 99; I didn't want just a walk-on, for heaven's sake. I wanted to be the tragic hero! Let me play the sinner! Even though I was laughably unsuited for the part.

But then, as he usually does, my Big Friend pulled the rug from under my feet. "You dope, O'Malley," he chuckled, "I don't want you to play the lost sheep; I want you to play the *shepherd*. I don't want you to play the runaway boy; I want you to play the *father!*"

How many times do we say or sing that prayer of St. Francis that starts, "Make me a channel of your peace," that goes on to say that we really want more to give than to receive? I wonder if I really want more to be forgiven than to forgive.

I'm pretty sure that, if you cracked open the innermost kernel of the gospel, you'd find that word "forgiveness." Surely, you find it in nearly every episode of the gospel. You find it at the heart of the Mass, when the priest consecrates the chalice and says, "it shall be shed for you and for all, *so that* sins may be forgiven." But isn't it true that we usually think of that only as our own trespasses *being* forgiven? Don't we forget that, just after those words, the priest says, "Do *this*"—not just shed my blood, but forgive sins—"in memory of me"?

Maybe we've all misread the casting sheet. But, I know, it's easier to give someone God's forgiveness than it is to give him or her *my* forgiveness. I'm pretty sure that, at this moment, you can think of one person—just one—who really needs the healing of your forgiveness. Who?

And when do you forgive, if not right now?

* * * * *

31. St. Francis of Assisi

*"I tell you, anyone who does not welcome the
Kingdom of God like a little child, will never enter it."*
— Mark 10:15

Mentioning St. Francis' prayer in the last segment made me
think of the man who composed it. Till the day he died, Francis
was a child in his heart. But people like that are bound to raise
the eyebrows of the wise, the shrewd, the sophisticated. People
like Francis look not only child-like in their hearts, but childish in
their heads.

Francis was a very rich young man, who gave away everything he had to feed the poor—which is pretty stupid just for
openers. They were right out there in the streets starving the
next day, right? And he went roving through the towns and
hamlets of Italy, singing (right out loud), and laughing and
joking with all kinds of people from popes to pimps—which, for
a man of God, is at best "inappropriate" and at worst sheer
lunacy.

What did people *think* of a man of God who acted like such a
. . . such a *clown*? And he befriended every stray broken-winged
bird and cur and jackass he found in the streets. What's worse,
he *talked* to them! Animals! He preached to them! He called
them his brothers and sisters. Run *that* through the computers
that pick next year's college freshman class.

He was also, predictably, more than a whiff ripe, too—which
you might suspect, given all those birds and dogs and fish. The
sophisticated found him an embarrassment; God, on the contrary (which he usually is), apparently found him just fine.
Which argues a certain incompatibility between an excess of
sophistication and godliness.

Francis of Assisi had a wisdom which the learned and the
shrewd and the "cool" regard as idiocy. But Francis had a firm

grasp on the ultimate truth: who God really was, and who Francis really was. And that was far more than enough.

Francis reminds me of Holden Caulfield. He was "a catcher in the rye." Something in him rebelled (as it does in most of us, for awhile) against leaving behind the wonder and joy and unself-consciousness of childhood, in order to harness himself into the cynicism and paranoia and caution of false adulthood. He saw that the natural things, like dogs and the lilies of the field, never put on airs, never try to impress, never try to be what they aren't, never feel even a twinge of jealousy or hatred or arrogance. Dumbly, without question or rebellion, they are unashamedly themselves. They do what God set them to do. So did Francis.

Jesus says that, unlike the harness of the rat-race, his yoke is easy. Jesus doesn't deny that it *is* a yoke, that it is a burden. Unlike the voices of the modern media and magazines and songs, Jesus doesn't say that human fulfillment comes as easily as falling into bed. He's unnervingly honest that way. The yoke of Christ is the truth, plain and simple. And when you acknowledge the truth, you can work easily in the harness.

The harness—the truth—is constricting. It does limit your freedom, the way a lineman's shoulder pads do. But it also sets you free—free from comforting self-delusions. For instance, acknowledging the truth of the force of gravity restricts my freedom to walk off the roof; but it also sets me free to stay alive. Acknowledging that I'm most definitely not Robert Redford, nor Albert Einstein, nor Kareem Abdul Jabbar severely restricts my aspirations and plans. But it also sets me free, at last, to be only Bill O'Malley—but the only Bill O'Malley there's ever been. Which is the only real option I had in the first place.

Acknowledging that I'm not God, not in charge, not perfect, not guilty of everything that goes wrong—comes as a rather crushing restriction on my utopian expectations—to say nothing of my parents'. But it sets me free to be what I am—not God, but a human being; not the Boss, but the Boss's Sancho Panza; not perfectible, but indefinitely improvable.

St. Francis of Assisi called everybody his brother and sister—even jackasses, poor childish fool. But maybe he saw a truth for which there are no Nobel Prizes and no National Merit Scholarships: God is God, and *he* passes out the parts. If my role is to be an ox, then let me be the best ox I can be. Not an ox-god, not even a golden calf, just an admirably damn good ox.

Last night on HBO, I saw a very disturbing program called "Sex and the American Teenager." Those kids talked with such enviable and frightening certitude about sex. They were only fourteen and fifteen years old, but they were so "cool," so "with-it," so . . . pseudo-grown-up, like little kids dressed up in their Mommy's old hats and high heels. Like the butterfly Nikos Kazantzakis tried to hurry out of the cocoon too quickly, and it emerged a twisted mutant. Somehow they seemed, at least to me, to have skipped adolescence. They were violating the natures of things, and my heart went out to them. Because sooner or later the natures of things rise up and take their revenge.

Francis of Assisi had another insight into the truth which many people whose names appear in *The Congressional Record* and *People* magazine may not see, burdened as they are with pseudo-greatness. He acknowledged the yoke of his limitations, and therefore the yoke rested easy. Because he was serving his Father, and his Brother, Jesus Christ, who is a prince. The burden of imperfection was not really a yoke after all.

It was a crown.

*   *   *   *   *

32. For Love or Money

"For the sons of this world are wiser in their own generation than the sons of light. And I tell you, make friends with the mammon of iniquity, so that—when it fails—they will welcome you into their eternal habitation."
— Luke 16:8-9

There's an irony in Jesus' words here, bordering on cynicism. The little steward in question had been caught out cooking his master's accounts. He didn't have a chance. So, shrewdly, he called in all his master's debtors and made a deal with them: how about paying half and getting off the hook? Then, when he's fired, they'll be grateful to take him in.

I've always hated the homilies I've heard on that one: "See!" the preacher always intoned, "what happens to the shrewd businessmen of this world!" I'd walk out of the church feeling a bit . . . uneasy. Because I sort of admired that little chap. I mean, he cut his master's losses, and he made a lot of friends. What made me more uneasy was that the preacher had preached that money was the root of all evil—and then the instant he'd finished took up a collection of the root of all evil.

I don't really think that's the point of the parable: don't be shrewd with your money. Our Lord wasn't stupid. Telling Jews not to be shrewd about money is like telling the Irish not to like sentimental songs, or Negroes not to have rhythm in their hands and feet. It's not the shrewdness or the sentimentality or the rhythm that counts; it's how you use it, the place it has in your heart. Our Lord's saying that money and shrewdness aren't the end of this life. Love is. Money is only a means—a good means—but like all good means it can be overdone. It can get in the way.

The little steward was taking the too-simple way out. Our Lord admonished us, after all, to be shrewd as serpents and simple as doves. The trouble is we're too shrewd about some things—like getting stung, and too gullible about other things— like advertising.

There's no more pervasive and penetrating influence in our lives than advertising and the media. John Lennon was speaking the truth when he said, perhaps unguardedly, that kids knew more—and cared more—about the Beatles than they did about Jesus Christ. I don't think even anyone with a one-watt wit could deny that.

In the evenings, we don't look at one another; we're all looking in one direction, at the one-eyed idol. Where can you go that there isn't some ad trying to influence your thinking and your sense of values? Even charity has become more synonymous with dollar bills and checks than with the suckerhood of the Good Samaritan or the Good Shepherd who risked the 99 to save the one. (Where's the percentage in that one?)

Money and love. We come to a point where, without our realizing, making money—and even giving it—has become a way of expressing love. Money to take care of the family we love becomes more important than talking to them. Getting into the country club to improve my children's job possibilities becomes more important than training them to be intelligent, self-sacrificing human beings—than preparing them for a life where everything is not "given." A father said to me last year, "What do you think are the best ways I can market my son to the colleges?" I blanched. As if the kid were a new line of fashion underwear someone had to be cajoled to take off his hands.

We struggle to give our kids all they "need," all we never had—and in that very act deprive them of the one thing we got from going-without: spine.

What do most kids—and others—think is the key to human fulfillment: love or money? What they do shouts so loudly it's hard for me to hear what they claim.

* * * * *

33. Gratitude

> *"Were not ten made clean? Where are the other*
> *nine? Why did no one return to praise God except this*
> *foreigner?"*
> — Luke 17:17-18

First of all, there's gratitude to God. Mass is usually the way
we show that. But it can get pretty much the same old pro-forma
thing, no? Roll out of bed, roll into the car, roll into the pew.
Kind of like the weekly dutiful letter from college or from the
army: "Nothin' much to say, Ma. Thanks for the cookies. Is my
laundry done yet? Love. . . ." Then once you're rolled into the
pew, there are two hopes: first, that it's over quickly (like a visit to
the dentist), and second, that the homily is halfway interesting.
Otherwise, you get nothing out of it.

Maybe it'd be a livelier hour if we went to Mass each Sunday
to thank God that the sun came up seven times since we were
there last. It doesn't *have* to, you know. There'll be one day when
we stop the earth dead in its tracks. Thank God it didn't come
this week. We could also thank God for letting us see those seven
new days. There are thousands who were at Mass last Sunday
who won't be here this week and will never see another sunrise.
It'd be nice—not for God, but for us—to say thanks also for all
the other things we take for granted which many don't have:
sight, hearing, sanity.

It's funny. As kids, we were grateful to the tooth fairy for the
dimes (with inflation, dollars) under our pillows, but I wonder
how many ever thank Anybody for the teeth—old or new. We
were grateful to Santa Claus for putting oranges and walnuts and
toys in our Christmas stockings, but who ever felt the need to say
thanks to Anyone for putting legs into our everyday stockings?

We ask God for peace in Central America, and the Middle
East, and Northern Ireland, without thanking him for the peace

we've had in the United States since 1865. We beg for the end of someone's sickness, without thanking him for our own health. Maybe God's feeding us with the Body of his Son would be more meaningful if we could summon up a little gratitude for our own bodies. In my smug youth, I really sneered at those nine ingrate lepers who never troubled to come back and say thanks for being cured—and yet I'd never said thanks for never having had leprosy in the first place. Oddly, enough, my health never seemed a miracle to me. How spoiled I was.

It's strange how prodigal God is with his miraculous gifts—so prodigal that we end up taking his prodigality for granted, until he gets "tight-fisted" or throws us a curve.

But I think we can also thank God by thanking one another. How often do we do that? Oh, we do it on Christmas, and birthdays, and maybe Mother's and Father's days—at least partly because Madison Avenue reminds us it's time to release a little more cash into the Economy. And those can become as more-of-the-same as weekly Mass, done because . . . well, one really should.

How many husbands blow ten bucks on a bunch of flowers, just for the hell of it, for no special reason, just for . . . everything? How many youngsters who have a little extra cash buy a present on their *own* birthdays to give to their parents—without whom they wouldn't be having a birthday? How many parents are noticeably grateful to their children, not for being good, but just for *being*? For their crazy ideas that keep us jumping, keep us thinking, keep us growing—when we'd really like to curl up in front of the fire and doze our days away like a pair of old calico cats?

You know—when you take so many, many things for granted, life can be very, very boring.

* * * * *

34. Hanging in There

> *"Well, maybe I don't fear God or man, but this widow keeps pestering me. So, I'll give judgment in her favor. If I don't, she'll weary me to death with her incessant coming."*
> — Luke 18:4-5

For fifteen years, I rehearsed three plays a year in the school cafeteria—with sixty very healthy wrestlers grunting on the other end of the room. Like the importunate widow in the parable, I went back again, month after month, year after year, to four different rectors and six different principals. At the end of their terms, they moved blissfully on to some less thorny challenge, but—tenacious as kiss-proof lipstick and relentless as time—I kept coming back, and back, and back. And now the wrestlers have a home of their own.

I'd be the last one to quibble about pulling that same ploy on God. But I think I'd quibble about one's motives. Or maybe the better word is one's "expectations" in playing the gadfly with God.

By all means, keep going back and back, but remember what you're asking. You're asking God to change his mind; you're asking God to change his plans.

Remember Job, "the perfect and the upright man," nonetheless battered and baffled on his dunghill, demanding justice from God—as if he and God were equals in some "Higher" Court, as if—after the unutterable gift of life—God somehow still owed him something. And Job got his answer: "Where were you when I laid the foundations of the earth?" Rather humbling, but the truth.

Remember Peter, too, that time when Jesus said that he was going up to Jerusalem to fulfill his mission—even if the high priests killed him for trying. Peter tried to dissuade him; he tried to get the Son of God to change his mind. And Jesus said, "Get out of my way, you devil!" Rather humbling, but the truth.

My mother took 30 years to die. She had her first heart attack when I was a freshman in college and even though there were occasional brief upswings, it was pretty much an agonizingly slow downward spiral for the next three decades: broken legs, broken arms, near amputations, more heart attacks, glaucoma, cataracts, a long bout with "The Creature," internal operations. Then she broke her hip. Then the other hip. Then the nursing home. Then the strokes.

Every day at Mass for 25 years, I prayed she'd get better, that she'd be like other people's mothers. But she didn't. Then, in the final years, when her wonderful wit and her fine mind began to desert her, and she suffered both physically and mentally, when she got panicky and disoriented, I prayed every day at Mass that she'd die.

I went back to the Judge for six years of days. And I couldn't change his mind.

But it taught me something, something I imagine he wanted me to see all along, but something I was too obtuse to see, too determined as I was to misread all those promises about the efficacy of prayer.

Coming back the hour and a half every week in the car from the nursing home, I pleaded with him. I cajoled. I wheedled. I bargained. A few times I even cried. Finally, I played my ace of trump: his debts to me—for all I'd done for him. But all the while his refusals were trying to send me a message I wasn't open to receive. The message went along the line of that old and, to me, greatest of prayers: "There are some things I want you to change." I could accept that. I liked it, in fact; I like to fight when there's a chance.

"But there are some things you can't change—and I want you to accept that, too."

My mother's long dying was one of the things in my life I couldn't change. And there was the bitter, bitter lesson—the ultimate truth: you are not God.

And in coming to terms with that bitter truth, I was set a little more free. There are some judgments the Judge will not reverse, no matter how persistent the widow—God knows why. Oh, I go on knocking, even in all those quite obviously irreversible cases. Not to change God's mind. To change my own.

* * * * *

35. The Widow's Mite

"I tell you, this poor widow put in more than all the rest of them. They gave of their abundance. She put in all the living she had."
— Luke 21:3-4

When you look at the evening news any night of the week, and see whole cities blasted to graveyards, when buildings and cities and gridlocks get bigger and more dense and more impersonal, it's pretty easy to feel—like Alice in Wonderland— that you're shrinking to the point where you could look a rabbit in the eye.

As the space race hurtles onward, our minds are forced out of their parochial arrogance to see that the star on which we live is really only a tiny cinder in a vast whirlwind of galaxies and nebulae. Before such an immense background, someone as small as me doesn't cast a very long shadow.

In times like that—when I start feeling that nothing I can do can make any real difference—I'm glad someone introduced me to Christianity. Because Christianity tells me that, despite my apparent negligibility, a Person from beyond the deceptive limits of time and space came onto this tiny cinder to become like me.

There's a lesson there, surely.

Why would an infinite God smallen himself into time and

space? Why would he-who-is-limitless limit himself to six-feet, by two-feet, by one-foot? Why should he settle for a paltry 33 years, and die a shameful death, "before his time"?

Why, indeed?

I suspect a clue might be in that story of the widow. In the really real world where God exists, size is completely relative, in fact utterly unimportant—in fact meaningless. Nor is time important. Only who you are and what you do with who-you-are is important. If we're loved by a Love that transcends both size and centuries—despite our smallness, our pettinesses, our ineptitudes, then there must be a value to us which the dimensions of this life blind us to. If an infinite God still comes begging to us, if he even sends his Son—and we kill him—and he *still* dotes on us, we must have some strange importance, surely.

In the hurly-burly of trivia which swarm through our days and weeks, we tend to forget that. With the order forms, the P.T.A. meetings, the diapers, the homework, we forget that these dull Cinderella chores are being done with the handsome Prince already on his way with the glass slipper and the wedding license.

That isn't what the American Dream tries so convincingly to sell us. They're trying to sweet-talk Cinderella into stocking up on what she *really* needs: pine cleaners, acrylic waxes, and a microwave. She'll be able to get all her jobs done faster, so she can sit and watch even more television, like the Lady of Leisure she was born to be. They feed our visceral and stupid conviction that we are nothing without long life, large pectorals, and languorous vacations. It's their bedrock promise to turn all of us Lilliputians into Brobdingnagians.

How dumb. When the Architect of time and space desires us, when he's blessed our physical littleness with the immensity of his presence, his caring, his infectious loving, we are already giants in a world without end. Amen.

*   *   *   *   *

36. Love > Justice

> *"A man had two sons. He went to the first and said,*
> *'Son, go work the vineyard today.' And he answered, 'I'm*
> *on my way, sir.' But he didn't go. The father went to the*
> *second son and said the same, and the son answered, 'I*
> *won't.' But later, he repented and went. Which of the two*
> *did his father's will?"*
>
> —Matthew 21:28-31

Our first practical, concrete contact with responsibility begins with the garbage. "Billy, will you take the garbage out for
me, please?" . . . "Yeah. Uh, right away, Mom." But the kid's five,
right? And he's on his belly in the living room with the comics, or
his fire truck, or the Racing Form. So, about five minutes later,
it's: "Bill, how about the garbage?" . . . "I'm *coming!*" But he's not
coming; he's not moving a muscle. He likes Mommy, of course.
She's there to do nice things for him. But right now, her plans
and priorities don't exactly mesh with his plans and priorities.
And it's a real test whether she's a good Mommy or not: if she
avoids a hassle and takes out the garbage herself, or if she stands
over him and says, "Will*iam!*" and he jackknifes up and says,
"You *got* it, Mama!"

Then comes school, and Sr. Concepta or Mrs. McChokum-
child or Professor Gradgrind says, "We're going to have a test
two weeks from today." Yeah. Sure. I'll get to it right away this
time. I really mean it. And thirteen days later it's a dithering,
stupefying all-night cram session. Their priorities and my
priorities don't mesh—until Time inexorably starts to crack the
whip on my hindquarters. But, sooner or later, their priorities are
going to prevail.

Finally, it's the boss, who has the whip *all* the time. It's called
the paycheck. For the first two weeks, the boss is there even
when he *isn't* there, thwapping that ol' whip in his palm, watching for every false move. Ah, but after a while, when he's out of

sight, it's back to the comics, or the fire engine, or the Racing Form.

Believe it or not, I think all that has an effect on our image of God. And our *image* of God, the way we actually picture him, has a far more profound effect on our actions than, say, any textbook explanations of him. Somehow, the image of God gets all mixed up with other images. God is Mommy, who can be put off—because, after all, he's stuck with us, right? God is also the teacher you can safely set aside till the last minute—because, after all, even Dutch Schultz squeezed in a death-bed confession, right? But God is also like the boss, who calls the shots and cracks the whip, even sometimes when he's not really visible—because, after all, sooner or later he's going to show up for that final showdown, right?

Yeah, right. I guess. But also very wrong, too.

Like mothers, God gave us life. Like our teachers, he's trying to make us grow—sometimes when we feel we have no more growing to do. Like our bosses, he gives a job and a paycheck: a chance at a fulfilled life. For that, they can lay legitimate claims on us—in justice.

The Old Testament is about justice: the *lex talionis*, which says "an eye for an eye, a tooth for a tooth." On the one hand, if you borrow money from somebody, you're obligated to repay it. On the other hand, when you do repay it, in justice, your debt is cancelled. If you have two coats and your brother has none, your brother deserves one of your coats. In justice. Justice is the core of human society. Do unto others as you'd have others do unto you.

The New Testament goes far beyond justice. The New Testament is about love. Love doesn't play fair; love plays the fool. If somebody borrowed money from you three times, and three times in a row welched on you, you'd be a damned fool if you hadn't learned your lesson by then. But Jesus says in the gospel that if someone harms you 70 times seven times—that's

490 times—you've still got to forgive him or her. And not just after they've begged your forgiveness or made restitution. That'd be only justice. No. We have to forgive *before* they deserve it.

As I've said before, if the gospel doesn't unnerve you, you haven't really heard it yet.

There's a story about justice in the gospel in which a king forgives one of his officials an enormous debt. That's love. Then when the official goes out he finds someone who owes *him* only a fraction of the amount the king's just forgiven him. He's got a perfect right to it. Maybe he's too harsh on his debtor, but—in justice—he's got a right to slap his debtor in the slammer if he doesn't pay up. Just as Mommy and teacher and the boss have a right—in justice—to have certain demands met.

But what Christ asks is that we be like the king: he forgives the man his debt for no other reason than sheer magnanimity and open-heartedness. And the king doesn't punish the official for being unjust; he punishes him for having been loved and remained himself unloving.

When I was a kid, my Dad was in the food business, what they used to call a "jobber." He'd buy in bulk and break food-stuffs down into small packages to sell to Mom-and-Pop stores. He was doing pretty well, so he took a partner. But, alas, one black Sunday, he decamped with his wife and two daughters, and the entire business bank balance.

And my Dad wouldn't prosecute.

I hated him for it. It meant we all had to work, to pay off all those bills, while the ex-partner and his family went free. Dad had every right—in justice—to sic the cops on them and do what he could to get what was ours back. But Dad was adamant. He said, "I don't want those two girls growing up knowing their father is a convict."

In the eyes of the world—including the eyes of his son, who fancied himself a model Christian boy—my Dad was a damn fool. In justice, that money was ours. But in the eyes of Jesus Christ—and, however belatedly, in the eyes of his son—my Dad was very likely a saint. He chose love over justice, to sacrifice the money—and the justice—for a value more important than either money or justice.

When you love, you're going to look like a sap to many people—as my father looked to me when I was a boy. But consider the entire Old Testament: how many times Our Father was willing to forgive the Jews and start over. The picture you get so often is Yahweh, the husband, standing outside the whorehouse, waiting for Israel, his spouse to come home to him. That's far more than justice, surely.

Consider the entire New Testament, too. The same old story. The prodigal son, the woman taken in adultery, and Simon Peter: the biggest screw-up of them all.

Love never brings out the scales. Love never says, "There. We're even." Love never goes on strike.

Justice pays its bills. Love hands out blank checks.

*   *   *   *   *

37. Jesus, the Naif

"Good teacher, what must I do to share in everlasting life?"
—Luke 18:18

And Jesus answered the rich young man, "You shall buy low and sell high. You shall not borrow needlessly, but when you do, see HFC. You shall not drive last year's car or wear last year's clothes or play last year's records, as losers do. You shall get the better of the other guy before he gets the better of you. You shall take care of old Number One. You shall avoid perspiration odor, ring around the collar, yellowed linoleum and teeth, work, niggers, spicks, queers, and the lame, the halt and the blind. And one more thing: don't get involved unless you have to, and make sure you're covered by insurance before you do. Do this, and you may not have everlasting life, but you will have the illusion of everlasting youth. 'Cause that's where it's *at* baby."

Isn't it too bad Jesus was so naive? If he'd taken a few cues from the modern wisdom, he could have knocked the Beatles off the charts. They'd have liked him then—or at least been wary of him, and he could have avoided a quite nasty death. But what could he expect, peddling that pap about the lilies of the field and not worrying about your clothes? Just think: if everybody swallowed that stuff, what the hell'd become of the Economy? And when it comes to "sell all and give to the poor," why that's Communism, for God's sake!

That's right. It's (small-c) communism . . . for God's sake. This Jesus was a pretty subversive cat.

"Well, come on. When he said give everything to the poor, he meant . . . well, if you want to be *perfect*, right? But . . . (Man-to-man chuckle and a nudge with the elbow) . . . we're only human, right? That's just fine for the kids in their religion classes. Keeps 'em in line. But, I mean, I know the *score*. And the object of the game is to win, win, win, bubba!"

If that's all we are—only human—then baptism was just a nice afternoon to please the grandparents, an excuse to dress up, a party (and presents). The ad man's right: "Grab for all the gusto you can get," while you can still grab.

I think Jesus was trying to sell the rich young man, not poverty but freedom. I don't think he was saying that possessing material goods was bad, but rather that being possessed by material goods is bad. Because it makes a man or woman less than human.

How many people are almost literally enslaved to mortgages, interest payments, credit cards? I've known high school kids to work two jobs, thirty or forty hours a week, and sleep all day in school—in order to purchase, insure, support, nourish and pamper a car: a machine. A human being working for a machine.

Isn't it about time we say, "Whoa!"? Isn't it about time we took a few moments to step outside the rat-race and take a good, hard look at what our possessions are doing to our lives? "Wait a minute. Do I really need all this stuff? Is the stuff I'm working my tail off for really *essential*—or is it just what everybody's *told* me is essential?"

One quite practical thing to do is, one day a year, go through all your drawers and closets. Pull out everything you haven't worn in a year. You've already proved you don't need it. Give it away. Two people will benefit. Someone else will be warmer, and you'll travel lighter.

"Yeah. That's nice an' all. But, I mean, what'd happen to my . . . uh . . . you know . . . life?"

*   *   *   *   *

38. Apparently Barren Fig Trees

> *The mother of the sons of Zebedee came up to Jesus . . . and said, "Promise that these two sons of mine will sit, one at your right hand and the other at your left hand in your kingdom."*
>   —Matthew 20:20-21

This little whimsy is directed at the guys who sit on the bench, and other similar types: wallflowers, wimps, has-beens, and never-was's. I think they have some idea of how the barren fig tree felt when Jesus came along, saw there was no fruit, laid a curse on it, and it—zoop!—withered up on the spot.

But it's also for their parents.

One Friday morning, right after the opening night of a production we'd done of "Our Town," a senior came up to me and said, "When you gonna put on a play with some action? Nothing happened in that dumb play." Which showed that, no matter how hard we'd tried, he'd missed the whole point—and not just of the play.

What "Our Town" says is that, even on the dullest day of your life, there are so many miracles happening that it'd make your heart stop with the sheer wonder of it, if you could ever slip the protective lenses from your eyes. Your mother, all by herself is a miracle. Your Dad, your nasty siblings: all miracles. Being able to walk and tussle and laugh and cry. But we take them so for granted that they become dull. Like "Our Town."

Besides that, there are always people who live what seem to be so much more exciting lives that our envy also dulls the shine of what we have. We're always brooding on what we don't have, and thus become stupidly unaware of how blessed we are.

Which brings me to the bench.

Having been all my life the absolute last one summoned into any athletic fray, I think I can feel more than a bit for them. It's always the flashy ones who get in there, and here I sit, after all those punishing drills and perimeters, no better than a spectator with a closer seat.

But what about the guys who were cut? What about the guys who were too shy even to try out? What about the little freshman who's legally blind, who'll never even suit up? My God, the guys on the bench are lucky. Just to be part of it, to care so intensely, to sacrifice yourself for the others, even as the hamburger squad.

A few years ago, at a cast Mass after a play, a senior who'd been a football player and had been in the show (as a dancer, in fact) came up to me at the greeting of peace and said, "I don't believe it. In a play, everybody wins!" He was right. Not because we beat somebody else, not because we got a trophy, not because everybody had the same filled dance cards. Because we forgot ourselves and shared, even if it was only moving around flats.

Before the curtain opens, before the first kickoff, you've already won. You've beaten the toughest opposition there is: "But what about me?"

If winning is the only thing, there are damn few winners in this world. Because there can be only one Number One, and all the rest are merely various shades of losers. Even the Silver Medalist is a loser. And in four years, even the Gold Medalist's record is going to fall to someone else.

You learn all that—one hopes—as you grow older. The texture goes from your taut skin, your hair thins and greys, you don't have the same old Kamikaze get-up-and-go. And wisdom sometimes sets in. You say to yourself, "Well, it's gone, and life goes on, so those things couldn't have been as important as I thought they were for so long."

The same thing happens—one hopes—with objects we always used to think gave a certitude to things we liked to think about ourselves: trophies, filled dance cards, medals. The wise find that what they recall as truly precious were the people they knew, the sacrifices they shared, the love that happened.

But some grow up without becoming adults. Like the mother of the sons of Zebedee. It wasn't enough that she had, not one, but two sons picked for the team. She wanted to make sure one was captain and the other was quarterback. Like the fathers who buttonhole coaches and say, "What the hell's goin' on here? You haven't played my kid in two weeks." Or the mother who sidles up to the harried director and whispers, "I know she doesn't have all that much talent, but she's been in the chorus for four years."

We'd be so much happier—we'd "win" far more often—if we only had the eyes to see what we have, instead of only the eyes to see what we haven't.

*   *   *   *   *

39. Sheep and Shepherds

> *"The good shepherd is the one who lays down his life*
> *for his sheep."*
> — John 10:11

"Sheep" is one metaphor I'm not too keen on to explain what being a Christian means. (I'm not too keen on being "stones" to build the New Jerusalem, either, and for pretty much the same reasons.)

Sheep always seemed a bit too docile, too passive, too . . . dumb. After all, the more docile, passive, and dumb you are, the easier it is for some *other* sheep herder, with baser motives and better propaganda, to come into the sheepfold and lure you off. I wouldn't doubt that there's a major reason why daily television gets a considerable number more patrons than daily Mass.

I think the ones who will leave the Church will be precisely the ones we've most successfully convinced that obedience is the greatest of virtues. They rebel, they tell me, from that very conformity they've felt the Church has demanded—only to run pell-mell into conformity with what everybody else is doing. Passively, docilely, dumbly, they follow the Pied Pipers of Materialism, Relativism, Hedonism, right out the fold. And too many of the ones who remain, I fear, will also be marching in the direction they're marching only because most people around them are marching that way.

The hymns we sing don't help either, methinks. There, too, the Lamb of God has devoured the Lion of Judah.

Those who follow the unnerving Jesus we find in the New Testament may well disturb the sheep who prefer incuriously to crop the grass in the same comfortable old pens and stare without resentment through the bars of the gate. In fact, in a sheepfold, anyone who seems to have either confidence or the courage of his convictions is going to look absolutely arrogant. More like a wolf.

Those Christians who prefer to be relentlessly curious (in both senses of that word) are going to be more like Paul and Barnabas upsetting all kinds of orthodox applecarts, rejecting centuries-hallowed traditions like the Jewish dietary laws and muddying up everything by inviting in all kinds of un-circumcised former pagans. What's worse, they broke out of the Palestinian sheep-fold. They hit the road with the Good News—to Rome, Corinth, Athens. And to their separate, individual crucifixions. Because the Good News was too good to keep to themselves.

Jesus may ask us to come to the Kingdom like children and like sheep, but I rather suspect—from the effects of Pentecost—that he wanted children and sheep who were *intoxicated*! Reeling with the joy and hope and love of discovery. Running straight into the arms of strangers, eager to break down their gates, too. Eager to free them from their mannerly uptightness, their mannered sophistication, their fear of tomorrow.

Think of it. If we could only convince ourselves—and then everyone else we meet—that the Church is *not* about rules and conformity and sheephood. If we could convince them that the Church is a gathering of people who *hope*—not just to survive our worries, but to survive our deaths. Think of it!

That kind of news will not be spread by sheep. Only by shepherds. It's a job for lions and tigers and griffins—and martyrs. We can survive even that! And that discovery is far too good to keep to oneself!

*   *   *   *   *

40. Talents

> *To one he gave five talents. To another two. To a*
> *third, one—each according to his ability.* — Matthew 25:15

I was always afraid God had given me only one talent, and I

really took very cautious care of that. Then, I suspected, he might have given me three; so I took a risk. And then, when people responded to me as if I weren't a total fool, I wondered if he might have given me more. My God! Don't ask that of me. I'm really terrible at the stock market stuff. — So, I pray, is God.

The parable of the talents is another one of those sounds like Muzak; you know it's there, but it doesn't penetrate or irritate too much—unless you're a purist.

The parable is really about people who prefer sterility to risk. It's about people who always do the "right" thing.

The One-Talent-Person knows nowadays that the Lord (read: peer pressure) is a hard taskmaster. Let sleeping dogs lie; don't go out on a limb; don't rock the boat; don't stick your neck out; don't make waves. You've heard that; perhaps you've even said it. It's better to die a safe nobody than to be a trouble-maker—like Abe Lincoln or Mohandas Gandhi, or those Kennedys, or Martin Luther King. People willing to hazard their talents in order to make a difference, in order to make a world better for their having been in it, are more honored at their tombs than at their rallies, right? I mean, they get shot, right? They wagered their lives. And every wager's a bet you can lose, right?

Further, the parable of the talents tells us the reward for risk: even if one wins, it's no prize package. "Because you've been faithful in small things, I'll place you over greater things." Great! In other words, the reward for a job well done is: five more jobs. It seems a thankless wager. And yet, it's the core of the gospel message (repeated again in different words): I come not to be served, but to serve.

(I'm *really* getting sick of typing that. Aren't you really getting sick of reading it? And yet . . . it's the only message I was given when I was sent.)

A Christian has to find his or her fulfillment not in a larger bank account, or in closetsful of clothes, or in a deeper tan, or in a scrapbook of clippings. The critical proof of Christian value is that you haven't time for yourself. And that, paradoxically, is truly a gift. Because when you honestly give and don't count the cost, you have no time for loneliness, or self-pity, or frustrated lust, or any of the other mirrors which paralyze the human spirit.

We find no paradox in the cliché that says: "you've got to spend money to make money." But we balk at the apparent contradiction of the gospel: "the more you give yourself away, the more you have left to give." Oddly, the powers of the human spirit seem to grow with use and wither with disuse. The more prodigally you give love away, the more able you are to love. Like the flour bin the prophet Elijah gave to the widow who shared her last loaf of bread with him, love fills back up to the very top, every time you try to empty it.

One final note in the parable that I never saw before: the sin of pious security is treated exactly as are more positive sins— pride, covetousness, lust, anger, gluttony, envy and sloth. The reward of pious security is to be cast into outer darkness. The parable says, then, that those who refuse to risk have already lost.

It says don't worry that your life will have an end. Worry that it will never have a beginning.

*   *   *   *   *

THE WEEK
THAT CHANGED
THE WORLD

41. Pomp and Circumstance

> *The crowd spread their garments on the road. Some*
> *cut branches from the trees and spread them in his path.*
> *"Hosanna to the Son of David!" they cried. "Blessed is he*
> *who comes in the name of the Lord!"*
> — Matthew 21:8-9

I used to love Holy Week Tenebrae, when a full-throated choir sang the penitential psalms and the *Improperium*, and at the last psalm, in almost total darkness, the final candle was taken, flickering, behind the altar and then snuffed out. And we all filed silently out of a church which had become a tomb. Then, on Easter, at the Gloria, all the lights leaped on again, and all the bells rang out! There was a majesty about it which was thrilling. But, since the liturgical reforms, at least in the places I've found myself during Holy Week, we've swung the other direction: banal hymnlets sung listlessly by a clutch of well-meaning singers to the thrum of a solitary guitar.

Now, I'm uncomfortable with elements of both extremes. The gold and brocade of the old days were profoundly impressive, but they seem to run counter to the poverty Christ so indisputably stood for. But the music. Ah, the music! Now the liturgical celebration of great feasts is indeed plain and humble, but it is also artless, humdrum, unmoving. Since the liturgy is the only place in the week when the life of the laity intersects with the visible Church, I wish the bishops would do something about that. The liturgy should be an act of faith, not a test of it.

I wonder how embarrassed Jesus must have been when they led him into Jerusalem on the donkey. He'd always resisted showmanship before. In the temptations in the desert, all the temptations were to go for the tricks, to bring the audience to its feet, begging for baptism. And he rejected them. I've no way to be certain, of course, but my gut tells me they put Jesus on that donkey by force. The Jesus I find in the New Testament didn't go in for shows.

Dorothy Sayers, one of my gurus, makes a very good case that Palm Sunday was what turned Judas. According to her scenario, Judas had been a Zealot—a guerrilla fighter who wanted to bring down power with power. But Jesus had converted him. Then, when Judas saw Palm Sunday, he said, "He's sold out. He's going for the power." And the Pharisees certainly said the same thing: "He's not just a nice moral teacher anymore. We have to make plans."

With Palm Sunday—and all the other feasts—the liturgists over the years seemed and seem to be in a headlong rush to cover up Jesus' mistakes. The same's true of Ash Wednesday. Jesus said, very clearly, "When you fast, don't put ashes on your head. Hide it." And we've gone and institutionalized what he forbade.

But it's hard to avoid, isn't it? We *like* hoopla, at least when it's done well. I miss the sonorous chants of Tenebrae. I confess, too, God forgive me, I miss the Latin. I suspect I'd rather have the Mass arcane than inane. I wonder if it might have been the same thing that caught the soul of Henry James when he stood, open-mouthed, looking at the windows of Chartres. He was awe-stricken at the artistry, but had no way through to the One who had called forth the art from the artisans. He was so overcome by the beauty of the signposts that he didn't realize they were pointing to Someone beyond themselves.

I wonder if the pomp of the liturgy in the days when I was far younger didn't take the place of faith. The Roman Catholic Church just has to be "right." Nobody could put on a show like that unless there was something behind it. And yet P.T. Barnum put on pretty good shows, too, and he was the one who said, "There's a sucker born every minute." Adolf Hitler's minions put on breathtaking shows: the liturgies of the Antichrist. And they, too, were enormously successful at gilding the lie.

The great cathedrals and the grandiosities of the liturgy were a support to the faith of the simple. But I wonder. Weren't they also a support to the faith of the complex, the oblique, the learned, the doubting? Who could resist the lure of God when God had Bach and Handel and Mozart to do his bidding? I have no trouble with it in support of faith. I have trouble with it when it's a substitute for faith.

I think of the first Mass. If I'm to trust the scriptures, there were no choirs—angelic or otherwise. There was no organ and no rugs—new or otherwise. No one wore a costume. There were only thirteen friends around a table. They ate; they argued; one of them left, to do what he felt he had to do. And Jesus broke bread and shared a cup of wine with them. Most likely on earthenware. Surely not gold. The containers were not more important than what—than Whom—they contained. And, like ourselves, the men around the table weren't quite sure what was happening.

But our faith is weak. At least, God knows, mine is. And yet, one of the most moving Masses I ever offered was one summer, at a lake. I was all alone. I had nothing on but a pair of shorts. I was sitting at a slate coffee table. But when I broke the Bread, he was so incandescently *there* that I started to cry for the joy of it.

Kids tell me they don't go to Mass because they don't get anything out of it. Like a dull rock concert. That's odd, too. I go to Mass for a completely different reason: because I'm so damn grateful—for having been so damn spoiled.

Paradoxically, what undergirds my flagging middle-aged faith is that, with all the resources at his disposal, Jesus could have put on *such* a good show. But he didn't.

* * * * *

42. Grimless Sacrifice

> *Let each one give what he has decided in his own mind— not grudgingly or because he's been forced to. God loves a cheerful giver.*
> — 2 Corinthians 9:7

"Sacrifice" is a word with multi-colored connotations. In "historical" movies, the lovely virgin, daughter of the king, is led in triumph to the rock, smothered in flowers, and then hurled to her death in order to placate the rumbling god. The similarity to the events of Holy Week isn't lost on our subconscious. Here is the Son—not merely of the king, but of God himself—led in triumph through the streets of the capital to what will turn into a sacrificial slaughter. And, we suspect, for the same reason: to placate an angry and capricious God.

"Sacrifice" calls up grim pictures for most of us, ranging from little Billy taking out the garbage all the way to "the ultimate sacrifice for one's country." Because of these pictures from our subconscious, we get the idea that sacrifice *must* be grim. Obviously, no one can deny that sacrifice can be costly, but I'd like to deny that it has to be grim.

Consider the mother in childbirth. She's enduring agony almost to the point of death, and yet we hate to call her labor "sacrifice" because, though it's painful, it's also a labor of joy, the fruit of her marriage-love, the birth of a new being for her to love. Consider the man who has to hold down two jobs to care for his family. It's surely a sacrifice. He may find it grim, but if his love—not merely his duty in justice—is uppermost, it can be a joyful gift. Love's hard to put into mere words, but it becomes undeniably visible in deeds, in un*self*conscious sacrifice. And the love somehow short-circuits the pain.

We find it difficult to call it sacrifice when someone doesn't find the gift "grimly tolerable." If someone disregards the pain—and him- or herself—because of the loved one for whom he or she sacrifices, we tend to think of it as less valuable, less costly, less sacrificial. But isn't it even far *more* valuable—simply because the cost is less important than the love?

My second problem with much I've heard about sacrifice and Holy Week is that part about placating the angry God. It gives a picture—which we crowd into the back of our minds—of

God turning his back on humankind, in an almighty huff over Adam and Eve's dumb mistake. For centuries he went on nursing his bruised feelings, no matter what man tried to do to make things up. Then one day his Son sneaked down, got himself crucified, and God suddenly looked over his shoulder and said, "Ah! Now that's more like it. Finally, a gift worthy of Me."

That, of course, is blasphemously untrue. Part of the reason for its persistence, even in otherwise quite sophisticated people, is that the redemption is couched in terms children could understand—the terms of the catechism. And, because most adults haven't had much time since their catechism days to mull over such things, there the explanation has stayed.

In trying to stress God's great gift of redemption, we were seduced into making him a monster of demanding justice, a sadistic man-eater who refused to settle for anything less than total restitution. Of course, that picture is totally contradictory to the picture of God we find even in the Old Testament. Yahweh is incessantly faithful to his People, no matter what further variations they invented on Adam and Eve's initial stupidity.

It seems we forget that God didn't cease to love humankind, no matter what we had done. It wasn't God who had to be changed. It was us.

God hadn't been "hurt" by Adam and Eve; it was *they* who had hurt themselves. In convincing themselves that they could get along without God, they found themselves in a world with no explanation beyond its own ongoing, accidental existence. When they found how bewilderingly enormous and ancient the universe was, and how infinitesimally small and temporary they themselves were by comparison, they began to wonder if they were, ultimately, meaningless.

So, God entered our world—not to exact punishment, but to reassure us. He'd sent prophets to tell us that we were far more important and meaningful than even we ourselves believed, that our self-indulgences were less an insult to him than to ourselves, that they degraded and demeaned us. The sinner does not love himself too much; he loves himself too little. But we are nothing if not impervious to true praise. So, God himself came to offer healing to the sickness of human nature, to assure us of our meaningfulness beyond time and space, to adopt us as his sons and daughters.

Calvary wasn't a grim sacrifice to Justice. It was a sacrifice of Love.

For ourselves, if the gift of self is grimly formal, merely because we can't avoid it, then the sacrifice will be one that—in the very giving—makes us smaller, because it is counted as loss. But if it is given unselfconsciously, without our even realizing it, it's a gift not only to the one who receives but also to the one who gives.

Nor is it the size of the sacrifice that counts. God himself asks only for bits of bread and a cup of wine. But love and joy turn them into an infinite gift—to him and to us: Jesus Christ. No matter what we give, love and joy can turn the gift into a gift of Christ.

* * * * *

43. The Ill-Mannered Jesus

> *Jesus made a whip of some cord and drove them all out of the Temple, along with their sheep and cattle. He scattered the money-changers' coins and knocked over their tables.* — John 2:15

I truly love that section of the gospel, where Jesus blows his stack. For me, it balances off the picture that I thought was the *only* Jesus—the "other-cheek" Jesus, the Jesus of biblical movies, with those glistening what-am-I-doing-among-these-unkempt-people eyes. The distant Jesus. The unflappable Jesus.

But here he is in all his spiky manhood. You can smell his sweat. You can hear the squawking of all those caged pigeons and the squealing of all those incontinent sheep. You can sense the rage and terror in the exploiters, as this hot-eyed young man bears down on their stalls, fed to the teeth with their leeching. The Good Shepherd may be very gentle with his sheep, but let the wolves beware.

The Jesus who is so blasphemously and effeminately captured in holy cards—especially the ones with the thin edge of gilt paint that they give you in funeral parlors—may be the Jesus of the popular imagination, but he's not the Jesus of the gospels. And yet I fear he's too often the Jesus who's offered to children, perhaps to becalm their savage and even warlike tendencies, until they're drafted. But that image stays on, until it seems that, to be a Christian, one must be gutless.

At that point, religion truly does become what Karl Marx called it: the opiate of the people. The pacifier, the one hour a week when we return to childhood and become dewy-eyed and pious.

But, to give them their due, the people who hanged Christ didn't do it because of his spinelessness, his adaptability, his piosity. They hanged him for a firebrand. They executed him because he stood for something, and he by God wouldn't shut up about it.

We all like to pride ourselves on open minds, forgetting that the most open mind is an empty head, that to stand for everything is to stand for nothing. We don't want to overturn tables; we don't want to raise our voices; we don't want—surely—to upset righteous businessmen who are making a tidy living off the Temple. At the root of it, we don't want to take the chance even of being noticed, much less of being wrong.

To stand up and shout against injustice is too much like the mad prophet in the movie, "Network," who wanted everybody to go to the window and stick out their heads and shout, "I'm mad as hell! And I'm not going to take it any longer!" There's something ill-mannered in acting that way, something ill-bred. It upsets people. It makes the rest of the sheepfold skittery and uneasy. It's just not . . . well, it's just not *done*.

There's the key, I think, to our prisons: the gag of good manners, the shackles of propriety, the emasculating legacy of our Puritan founders and the good Queen Victoria. Lord Acton said that the only thing needed for the triumph of evil was that good men and women remain silent. That's the reason they can vacuum fetuses out of wombs in New York, and burn copies of *Catcher in the Rye* in California, and brainwash greed into children every ten minutes on the Tube, and send gunships to kill peasants in Central America, and spend billions to come up with a thrilling new bomb that will kill only people and leave buildings intact.

Because the people who do those things know only a few cranks will write letters to the newspaper. Only a few unwashed hippie-types will carry crude placards and disrupt the street traffic of legitimate businesses and upright citizens. Such people should be put in jail. As Jesus was.

You can't crusade for everything, but I'm pretty sure that— unless you carry the Christian label under false pretenses—you have to crusade for something or you stop being Christ-like. Even if you have to disrupt things to get people's attention. Even if you offend sober and serious-minded people. Even if you get crucified for it. As Jesus was.

There are lots of crusades available. Which one'll it be?

* * * * *

44. The Power of Darkness

"This is your hour," Jesus said. "The power of darkness."
— Luke 22:53

Why do we gather every year to remember a week of events which took place nearly 2,000 years ago? We don't gather every year to celebrate other crucial encounters in our story: the Battles of Lepanto, Waterloo, Gettysburg, The Bulge, Danang. And yet, year after year, something draws us to celebrate this pivotal battle—of a sinewy young Jewish carpenter—deserted by his friends, reviled by the priests of his own religion, tortured by indifferent soldiers—all alone, holding out against the reign of darkness.

Part of it, of course, is our heritage; it's part of the legends of our tribe, bred into our fibres as children, which makes "us" different from "them." We wear different feathers; we dance to a different drum; our feasts are not the same as their feasts. Even without our realizing, what we commemorate this week is the foundation of who we are: Thursday, the Day of the Eucharist; Friday, the Day of the End; Sunday, the Day of the Beginning.

To understand the importance of this week, we must understand the powers of darkness against which he struggled, so long ago. To understand what he saved us from—to understand what "salvation" means—we have to understand what death means. Without Jesus Christ, death is the ultimate darkness.

We've always associated the power of darkness with some bestial devil, a devious and serpentine personage who crept about in shadows and laid snares for the incautious. Again, the images picked up in childhood and never replaced with more sophisticated understanding. All the devils out of Dante and "Faust" and "The Exorcist," no matter how colorfully dramatic, couldn't be as frightening as the ultimate darkness: nothingness, meaninglessness, the struggle unto futility, the eviscerating myth of Sisyphus. There is the ultimate waste: to struggle a lifetime against what one thought were his shortcomings and cowardice, only to find that the heroes and the cowards are undifferentiable, that sanctity and sin—both of them—are equally absurd. Annulled by death, as if we had never been.

There is the one shining hope we cling to during Holy Week, hemmed round as we are by the tides of skepticism and cynicism and paranoia: one of us has broken through to the Light, and, like Prometheus, he's come back to spread the fire of the gods on the earth. He's come from his Father to offer us the light which the darkness can neither comprehend nor overwhelm.

Isaiah says, "It was not enough that you be my servant. I will make you a light to the nations." But if Yahweh said that of his Christ, he said it also of all Christians. You are not dungheaps. You are not sheep. You are not even servants. You are his light against the darkness.

Perhaps we think we keep betraying our calling, that we are the petty Judases of our generation, with our sexual peccadillos, our trivial temper tantrums, our passionless submission to the ways of the World. And so, indeed, we are. But not because our sins are scarlet and dramatic, but by the fact that they are so petty, because they so sell short the light we carry within us.

There is only one way you can sell short what we celebrate every Holy Week: by making these events seem trivial— compared to the NHL Playoffs, compared to the American Economy, compared to the flight of the Space Shuttle. There is only one way to revivify Judas: to say "I am insignificant"— when the Son of God was spat upon and shamed and crucified to prove to us otherwise.

That was the sin of Judas: that his self-centeredness blinded him to how much he was loved.

*   *   *   *   *

45. The Heart of Darkness

"I am the vine. You are the branches."

— John 15:5

You probably have seen the film "Apocalypse Now." It deals with the search for an American colonel in Vietnam who's been cut off from the main bodies of American troops, and he's "gone native," escalating the Viet Cong's cruelty back against them, using a savage band of Vietnamese natives and renegade Americans who, literally, worship him. He's like a rogue elephant, cut off from the security of the herd, wary, vicious, elementally cruel. The movie is based on Joseph Conrad's novel, *The Heart of Darkness*, and I believe that that really is the heart of darkness, the root of evil: man alone.

In the very beginning of Genesis, God himself says it: "It is not good for the man to be alone." The cruelest torture of all—crueler even than death—is solitary confinement. And yet, with a perverse kind of attraction/repulsion, we seek it: to be left alone, to be unbothered, to be secure.

Whenever we withdraw all reality into the limits of our own skins, something wicked begins to fester. Not "you and me against the world"; just me against the world. The individualist binds all meaning around himself, wrapping it more and more tightly, till his soul is hard and pitted, like the seed of a peach.

What evil can't you trace to that root of isolation and insulation? Paranoia. Me-first. Self-protectiveness, self-aggrandizement, self-hatred. To say nothing of pride, covetousness, lust, anger, gluttony, envy and sloth. As Viktor Frankl says, in the concentration camps it was the individualists who cracked first. Because they were alone.

My job as a teacher is to fight that infection every day of my life, trying to draw signs in kids' hands, trying to bring them to Helen Keller's triumphant and liberating discovery at that pump handle: that she was not alone.

What, then, keeps even the best of us on our guard against that discovery—our steel cocoons zipped up, wary, defensive, paranoid? Fear, of course. If I admit I was wrong, I'll lose face. If I commit myself to some new enterprise, if I open myself to strangers, if I dare crack open my horizons and see the whole human family, what will it cost? Always, the fear of what I will lose blinds me to the glory of what I might gain. It's only when we shed ourselves of self that we're able to love in deed and in truth. "I" is the narrowest of words, and the narrowest of worlds.

Nor are we alone even out in the wilderness. We're not alone in the universe. Even if we're physically isolated from the herd, even if we're locked into solitary confinement, even if we're in the solitude of a hermitage, we're not alone. He is with us. Because of our incorporation into the Body of Christ, we are grafted into God. Through the meal around the table of the Eucharist, we ingest into ourselves the living presence of Jesus Christ; we are enlivened with the aliveness of God; we are infected with the light that the darkness cannot overcome.

In order to fly, bright-winged, as we were always told angels were, butterflies have to leave the secure confinement of the cocoon. It's no different with us. To see the light, all we have to lose, all we have to leave behind, is the heart of darkness: me, alone.

*   *   *   *   *

46. The TAO

"I am the Way, the Truth, and the Life."
— John 14:6

The ancient Chinese had a comprehensive, focused philosophy of human life called The *Tao*—which means "The Way." It was the concentration of the wisdom of centuries into one small book (the *Tao Te Ching*) which told men (and sometimes even women) how to find fulfillment as human beings. Now we know that the Way is focused into one Person: Jesus Christ. All that human beings are or can become is embodied in that one Jewish carpenter.

He was, as we learned in the catechism but perhaps forgot

along with quadratic equations, the perfect human being. One could study him—how he acted, how he treated people, how he aligned his scale of values—like the definitive message of God on how to be fully human. He was God's last Word on the subject.

He was also the physical embodiment of the infinite God. You remember how, when we were kids, we held a magnifying glass over a dry leaf and focused the immeasurable power of the sun into a pinpoint—which burst into fire? That's what happened at the Incarnation—when the immeasurable aliveness of God was focused into the fiery aliveness of this one man.

If you want to understand the personality of God, all you have to study is the personality of this man.

But who has the courage to throw off the uptightness, the fear of our peers' expectations? Who dares risk the secure spot in the pecking order to rock the boat the way he did? Who has time—or perhaps more precisely, the courage—to comprehend that "through Jesus Christ our Lord" that fiery aliveness of God is within *us*, just waiting to be tapped, just waiting to be unleashed on the world in which we live?

No. Far better to concentrate on the Baby Jesus, who will solace all our woes, and forget that the Baby Jesus grew up to be that fiery Galilean, who said he had come to bring not peace, but a sword, who had come to spread fire on the earth, who had come to give us more abundant life than we had planned on.

Far easier to endure the boring hour each Sunday morning, mooing the responses dully back at a "celebration" which is less celebratory than a Kiwanis luncheon. One hour a week out of 168 is reasonable for insurance. Besides, it's the priest's job to enliven the Mass. I keep my nose clean.

"I am the Way, the Truth, and the Life." Without him, then, we are lost; we live a lie; we are the living dead.

We say we have the truth. Well, the truth should set you free, give you joy.

Can I see your freedom? Can I feel your joy?

*   *   *   *   *

47. The Eucharist of Our Lives

*He took bread into his hands, and he blessed it. He
broke the bread and gave it to them, saying "Take this. It
is my body."*
                                                    — Mark 14:22

"He took bread into his hands." Because it's so commonplace
and therefore forgettable, we rarely give bread the respect its
complexity and importance deserve. I suspect that's why the
wise Jesus took it to himself—because, like his Father, he exults
in the romance of the ordinary.

The seemingly simple pearl is no more than a fleck of grit,
but wrapped endlessly in the slow, immeasurably complex in-
crustation of time. The simple atom is really aswarm with firefly
particles, strained to bursting with their burden of energy. So,
too, with bread. It carries within itself the complexity of seed and
sun, rain and dust, harvester and baker. There is life in it. So, too,
with each of us. At the inner focus of each is a self, like no other
of God's dwelling places, and around this center are woven and
coiled the accretions of the years—reaching, grasping, assimilating, growing.

Somehow, in this seemingly uncomplicated, seemingly commonplace person, is an insoluble labyrinth of darkness and light,
arrogance and fear, child and adult. To a very large extent, what
has formed this pearl of great price, what has energized this
small universe of nearly limitless power, has been the abrasion
against all those people in our lives—not just parents and
teachers and friends, but all the bullies and boors and battleaxes
as well. It's this bread we offer at Mass, to be transformed into
the Body of Christ.

"And he blessed it." Of course, each of us has been blessed—with life, with health, with talent. But what we celebrate at the Eucharist is a new consecration, a new life. "When I was a child, my speech, my feelings and my thinking were all childlike; now that I am an adult, I have no more use for childish ways." What hallows the gift of life at the Eucharist is the bestowal of freedom to create a life-within-life. But it's a paradoxical inheritance, because it's a gift we have to pay for. And the price is the responsibility, risk, uncertainty of accepting the calling to be apostles.

"He broke the bread." The Eucharist is about the breaking of bread. And in the Eucharist of our lives there are many breakings within our selves—doubts, misunderstandings, confusions, goals striven for and not achieved. But it's these rendings, these splittings of the simple cell—however painful—which are the price of growth, the release of power.

The result is too good, too vibrant to keep to ourselves. We have to break ourselves up and pass around the pieces, to spread the fire within us. We can multiply ourselves only by dividing ourselves.

"He gave it to them." Something happens when bread is broken and wine is shared. Somehow they become assimilated. They take on a greater life than they had before, and in their turn enliven the bodies they enter. Bread gives life, and wine gives joy, and this is what life in Jesus Christ is all about: giving life, giving joy.

We put ourselves into Christ's hands when we put ourselves into one another's hands—to be taken advantage of, to be used, to share life and joy instead of keeping it to ourselves. And by that very giving, we grow. We are no longer merely ourselves. We are bread taken into the Body of Christ. All that we are is transformed by the electrifying aliveness of God.

Take me. Use me. I am the Body of Christ. For you.

*   *   *   *   *

48. I Am

> The high priest put another question to him. "Are you the Christ," he asked, "the son of the Most High?"
>
> "I am," Jesus said, "and you will see the Son of Man seated at the right hand of the Power, coming on the clouds of heaven."
>
> The high priest ripped his robe. "What need have we of testimony? You have heard his blasphemy. What is your verdict?"
>
> And they said, "Let him die."   — Mark 14:61-64

Earlier in the gospel, Jesus said, "Before Abraham was, I am." And they all took up stones to kill him.

Why? Perhaps the statement was curious, confusing, convoluted, but hardly worth stoning a man for. More a matter for puzzlement, if it came from one who'd always made good—if unnerving—sense before.

The reason for the murderous response of Jesus' listeners was that, to their minds, he had just uttered the unutterable. He had blasphemed.

In the Garden of Olives, after his agony, the soldiers arrived and asked, "Which one is Jesus of Nazareth?" And Jesus came forward and said, "I am." And all the Jews present fell on their faces in terror. In the trial before the high priests and elders, in response to the high priest's question, Jesus simply says, "I am," and those two words are enough to throw the assembly into consternation. The high priest rips his robe in revulsion. Those two simple words were enough to seal Jesus' doom.

Why the seemingly melodramatic reaction to such a simple —to us—statement? For years, I thought it was that he had claimed to be the Messiah. Smugly, I condemned the priests; after all, the Messiah was going to come. How could they be so iron-minded that they wouldn't investigate his claims? But when you begin to understand the mind of a Jew, their response was not only understandable; it was very likely what I would have done myself in their place. Or laughed.

With those two words, Jesus wasn't merely claiming to be the Messiah. He was claiming to be God.

When Yahweh sent Moses to the Pharaoh to demand the release of the Jews from Egypt, Moses very wisely asked, "Well, who shall I say sends me? What's your name?" And Yahweh gave his name: "I am, who am."

Thereafter, no pious Hebrew dared use those words. There were circumlocutions: the Lord, the Holy One, He Who Is, but no one could say, "I am." Even today, when an orthodox Jew has to refer to God in writing, he or she will write "G-d." When someone asked, "Are you Baruch, son of Jacob?" the only affirmative answer was another circumlocution: "You have said it," or "As you said." In the versions of the Sanhedrin trial in Matthew and Luke, they guard themselves with just such words. But not the forthright Mark, and it's very likely that his is the better reading of Jesus' response. The high priest was far less likely to rip his garment at a circumlocution. No. Jesus had said, "My name is the name of Yahweh."

What would I do, today, if a young carpenter from Appalachia claimed he was God—not once, but several times? I suppose I'd chuckle and turn to the funny papers. Why should it have been any easier for the high priests and elders of Jerusalem—especially when their reverence for such questions was far greater than our own?

There are only three open-minded responses to Jesus' claim: either he was out of his mind, or he was a charlatan, or he was telling the truth.

But everything he says elsewhere has such a ring of authenticity to it. It may be a very difficult message, but it hardly seems like the ravings of a madman. And everything he said and did gave the lie to his being a charlatan, out to aggrandize himself: he divested himself of everything. There is only one conclusion left, then. He was "I Am."

Whatever the truth, let no one claim that Jesus was a fine moral teacher—like Buddha, or Gandhi, or Martin Luther King. He didn't leave that option open. He said "I Am." And, to give credit to the men who slaughtered him, they may not have accepted his claim, but they sure as hell knew what he was claiming.

And so, out of profound reverence for "I Am," they slew him.

* * * * *

49. The Anguish of God

"My God! My God! Why have you abandoned me?"
— Mark 15:34

I have little patience with simplicism. I become restive, too, with adults—even with religious educators—who persist in understanding the ways of God still in the simplicities they learned as children. They continue to speak as if our sins "hurt" God. They may insult God. They may hurt our relationship with him. They may hurt ourselves. But our sins cannot "hurt" One who is by his very nature perfect.

There was a time, though, when God was truly hurt. He suffered what we suffer: hunger, laceration, loneliness, fatigue, sexual desire, being misunderstood, and—in the end—doubt that plunged him just short of despair.

It's hard to understand how the All-Just, All-Merciful, All-Loving God could allow anyone he loved to suffer. And yet, very obviously, he did. He did not spare his own Son.

That tangle of thorns has worried the minds of humankind since the beginning of thought—and not just the great thinkers, but also the little men and women keening over a dead child: "How could a good God let this happen?"

As the cynic Nickles says in the play "J.B.": "If God is God, he is not good. If God is good, he is not God." If the Mind Behind It All really is the one who allows the just and the innocent to suffer, he is not good; he is a sadist who derives some perverse satisfaction from the unthinkable. But if the One we've always called "God" is good, then he cannot be the Mind Behind the unjustifiable suffering which confronts us everywhere we turn; he is simply a sweet and consoling irrelevance.

To call it merely a riddle would be obscene. To pose it merely as "the problem of pain" would be to demean the question to the level of "the problem of urban crowding." No. It is the ultimate enigma.

On the hill of Calvary, and along the road to it, our Father posed it to us at its most unavoidable. Job, "the perfect and the upright man," had suffered. The innocent since the birth of humankind have suffered: plague, pestilence, pogrom. But here is the All-Just, the All-Merciful, the All-Loving suffering himself.

Why does God offer even his Most Beloved the strange privilege of pain?

The Old Testament pictures the Lord as a silversmith who sits down, for it will take a long time, to refine us. He applies the bellows to the fire and, in the crucible, the ore cracks and melts. Slowly, the dross scums to the top. Carefully, he skims it off, and works the bellows again. Again, and again, until he knows the silver is pure, when he can lean over the cauldron and, in the metal, see his own face.

There is no one more alone than the person in pain. There is no machine that can measure it, no words that can allow the sufferer to share it, no empathy outside it sensitive enough to comprehend. It is the barren wilderness where God is inescapable.

It is in this darkness, when nothing is left in us to please or comfort our minds, when we seem useless and worthy of nothing but contempt, when we seem destroyed and devoured—it is then that the deep and secret selfishness that is too close to us to identify can be stripped from our souls.

It is in this darkness that we are set free even of ourselves. It is in this apparent rejection even by God that we find out who we are, and who he is. This is the night that empties us, so that we can be filled with him.

"Unless a grain of wheat fall into the ground and die, it can never live."

God asked it of his Son. He asks it of us.

*   *   *   *   *

ALL THINGS NEW

50. The Rebirth

"For behold, I come—to make all things new."
— Revelation 21:5

You've heard that, one day, there will come a great Kingdom where God's people will dwell with him, forever. We keep waiting for fiery signs in the air to signal the beginning of the end. Or for our own deaths to release us into the Kingdom of Heaven. No. Here, today, the Kingdom is come. It is us.

You've heard that, one day, there will be a great banquet, with Abraham, and Isaac, and Jacob, and all the saints sitting down together. This prophecy has been fulfilled in your midst. The banquet is the Eucharist. It's ours for the taking.

If you're still waiting for "thy Kingdom come," you're 2,000 years behind the times.

It's unfinished, of course. But it's begun. Because of Jesus Christ, you're immortal—right now!

Jesus' rebirth from death isn't just an edifying story from the gospels. Nor is it merely a Christian doctrine in a book. It's *the* calling, to be lived: a new life, a conversion, a recreation of humankind, a great springtime in the history of the human race. It happened, once for all, when that great womb of the sepulchre burst open, and New Life came striding forth, never to die again. And that new life is also ours for the taking. It will never be forced on us. We're still free, but "all those who did welcome him, he empowered to become children of God."

We can never say again, "Well, I'm only human." We're now far more than that.

Just as Adam was "all of us," so too this Carpenter was "all of us"—and God. Jesus was a man, so that he could represent all of us in the sacrifice which assured that we are all meaningful, beyond our wildest hopes. Jesus was God, so that all suffering would be fruitful, now and forever. He didn't merely "atone for sin," the wild and dehumanizing boast of Adam and Eve—and each of us—that they would be perfect, "like God." He granted their wish. In taking us into himself, he made us not only human again, he made us his brothers and sisters and, like himself, children of God.

We've all heard that the result of the cross and resurrection was our ability once again to receive sanctifying grace. And that means as much to most of us as a six-months' free supply of air. And "sanctifying grace" means little more than "*not* being in mortal sin." God help us!

Such tragic ignorance of our greatness results, I suppose, from all those facile descriptions of baptism and confession as spiritual laundromats for dirty souls. It's so much more than that!

As the father of the prodigal son said, "My son who was dead is alive again!" God has performed a miracle. What was sick is now vibrant, what was weak is now robust, what was flaccid is now energizing. "The world is charged with the grandeur of God. It will flame out, like shining, from shook foil." Down to our fingertips, we are renewed, not just wiped clean but alive with the aliveness of God. That is what grace is: the aliveness of God, in us.

Just as the New Life burst from the tomb, so that same New Life of God bursts into our whole being, when we share with one another, when we give love to those who have little or none, when we meet at the Eucharist to share his triumph.

"For behold, I come—to make all things new." *All* things. Even you.

Who can keep quiet about that kind of news?

*   *   *   *   *

51. Spring

> *"Come away to a lonely place, by yourselves, and rest awhile."*
> — Mark 6:31

Spring kind of does the old heart good, doesn't it? All the cornmealy yellow-and-green dustings along the arms of the trees, and the grass deepening into green, firming up for walking-on. You hear the crickets at night, like all the old men in all the rockers in the world chattering away. It makes the redeemed part of me, the child part of me, want to throw up the window and say, "Amen, to that, brothers! Welcome back!" Then, mornings, kids in red and yellow boots come sloshing to the big yellow buses, and the world is suddenly "mud-luscious" and "puddle-wonderful." It's happening all over again.

Rather than just take Spring for granted, like the spoiled ingrate I've been too much of my life, I'd like to make a small donation to Those In Charge for the privilege of witnessing all this coming-alive. And I imagine the best means of payment is to fall in line and do just what everything else is doing in Spring: shivering the winter cold out of our souls, shucking off the cocoons, and coming alive again.

Our lives move in cycles, just like the seasons. And it's not just the progression from childhood Spring, to adolescent Summer, middle-aged Autumn, aged Winter. If we're wise, and susceptible to the signals, it ought to happen every year of our lives.

First, there's the new conversion; something cracks open our horizons to an even larger world than we'd expected. It could be triggered by just about anything: a book, a movie, a person— anything that makes us say, "Oh, my God!" It's a bit mucky at first, finding our feet in a strange landscape, coming-back-to-life, the Spring cleaning of our year, the resolutions to be someone worthy of human life and divine life.

Then comes the warm, summery exuberance of fervor—loving God, serving our fellow human beings with honeymoon-vigor and creativity. But then, inevitably, by the nature of things, routine sets in again. Innocence and candor and verve begin to look, well, a bit unsophisticated, perhaps even childish, and surely not appreciated by the recipients. Burn-out strikes our resolve as it does our fields and lawns. Then, the winter-world, alone, huddled around ourselves. And the desultory search for any momentary warmth or escape, and the brassy pretense that we've found a formula for getting by. Why change things? Living, and partly-living.

Spring hits our backyards without so much as a by-your-leave, regular and automatic as sunrise and sunset, and we're carried along with it as we're carried around by the planet. Not so with our souls.

The Sower of the parable scattered good seed. The rest was up to the places it landed: the path, rock, thorns, good ground. Even when it takes root, we can't just walk away from it. There's weeding and hoeing and burning away. Being a full time person is even harder than being a full time farmer.

But there are also so many other more important . . . well, at least more *pressing* things to be done: the ironing, reorganizing the checkbook, the game next week, making a living. And all the while, Spring eludes our lives; the rebirth Christ came to offer has to wait until there's time to sit down and mull it over, to own it. And, of course, there's never time. So, living and making a living keep us from discovering what living is for.

Whenever mothers come to confession to me, they almost invariably confess they've lost their tempers with the kids. As a penance, I usually tell them that every afternoon—a half-hour before the school bus is due—they have to kick off their shoes, make themselves a cup of tea, put up their feet, and entertain Christ in their homes. Very often, they get kind of weepy. I guess because it makes so much sense—just to take time to get back a hold on perspective, to renew, to shed the jitters and the feelings that the whole world is on your shoulders alone.

The same could be said of fathers—and daughters, and sons, which pretty well includes us all, I think. There's a time every day when there's a bit of slack—just before dinner, just before starting homework, just before the time we all evacuate our brains at the TV and settle them down for sleep. Take a walk alone, let the pieces fall back into place and the nerves untangle, realize—peacefully—that the world got along without you for about eight billion years, that there are, indeed, "things you cannot change," that you have been very, very lucky.

In Spring, the trees and the grass are shouting a lesson to us, but we've turned off the sound. We're too frenetic and frantic to hear what they're singing at us: "You can be young again!" It's not the pastes and the powders and the potions, it's not the clothes and the car and the career, it's not the golf and the racquetball and *Thirty Days to Thinner Thighs*. It's something *inside* that's gotta be spruced up, decked out, slimmed down.

Remember, too, according to Jesus, that God's always had a special spot for wildflowers and weeds. They're the hardy ones that don't give up, who've come to recognize that they're not really meant to be roses, but they're by-God alive. And every time they come back, God blesses them with growing. That's the one condition for growth: coming back. That's what we were made for. If only we had time to find that out.

* * * * *

52. Doubting Thomas

> *"Unless I see the nail holes in his hands and put my finger into the holes . . . I won't believe."* — John 20:25

I'd get no arguments over the fact that I tend to be a mite

persnickety. Some might even say downright perverse. Well, if that's true—and I have no doubt it is—I guess my now-wait-just-a-minute habit of mind is about as unchangeable as the other areas in the vicinity of my face, like the wrinkles and the freckles and the daily-wider part in my daily-whiter hair.

Therefore, I find myself really liking some of the people in the gospels whom most of my retreat directors for the last 34 years have been going, "Tsk-tsk," about. You remember the man whom our Lord told to keep quiet about his cure—and yet the man went trumpeting it all over the place? Those retreat directors tsk-tsked that poor guy up and down from Lake Genesereth to the Red Sea. But I sort of sympathize with him. I mean, how do you keep quiet when you've just been cured of *leprosy*?

I also have a soft spot in my heart for Martha. Jesus said that her sister, Mary, had chosen the better part by sitting at his feet listening to him and leaving Martha out in the kitchen. I've always had the irksome (and perhaps heretical) suspicion that line was slipped in by some scripture scholar—since most of the scripture scholars I've known personally never seemed in danger of dishpan hands. But after 12 years of monastic silence and the relentless pursuit of interior recollection, I still feel a bit guilty that I'd rather work than pray, getting in there and mixing it up, and having the confidence that God is watching, without my having to remind him of what a good boy I am.

And after all, man may not live by bread alone, but he sure gets pretty wobbly without it—Our Lord included. I have a rather strong notion that, had I been there, I'd have been out there walloping pots with Martha. God forgive me, Mary always seemed a bit too goo-goo-eyed and kittenish to me.

I feel the same way about Doubting Thomas, whose Easter came a week later than the others'. He got tsk-tsked by the retreat directors, too. "Oh, he of little faith!" they moaned. Maybe Thomas was just a bit smarter than the other ten; maybe he was just a bit less gullible. Jesus did tell us to be simple as doves, but he also told us to be shrewd as serpents. I have a strong notion that, if I'd been in Thomas' sandals, my fingers would have itched to probe those nail holes, too.

It's easier for us. We've believed that death isn't the end since we were babies. But what would you say if someone—even ten people—told you they'd just had an afternoon's chat with John Kennedy? Or Marilyn Monroe? Hey, that's UFO talk, guys.

For some stupid reason, we've been taught to fear doubt, to go for the securities and the certitudes, to put our tushes in a tub of butter and leave them there, unperturbed. On the contrary, just as guilt is a very good and natural and life-giving hunger—as long as it turns into responsibility, so also doubt is a very good and natural and life-giving hunger—as long as it leads us to search for answers better than the ones we contented ourselves with before. Without doubt, there is no learning.

Let's hear it for pot-walloping Martha! Let's hear it for doubting Thomas! Because without people willing to wallop pots, what you get is dewy-eyed utopianism. And without people willing to doubt, what you get is Auschwitz.

*　*　*　*　*

53. Ascension Morning

> *He was lifted up while they looked on, and a cloud*
> *took him from their sight.* — Acts 1:9

My first difficulty with the whole idea of the Ascension came very late in life. I had to give a homily on it in the first year I was ordained. Now I hate to give the same old stuff, so I sat down and tried to find something new about it, some new angle that'd bring the congregation right out of their socks. So I read the passage in Acts over and tried to focus myself into the scene as if I were really there.

I saw them—us—going out to that hill, talking together like old friends out for a stroll after lunch. I mean it was so real, I could feel the soft dust between my toes. Then suddenly he got us together and said goodbye. Then, just as suddenly, he wasn't there anymore. And yet we were convinced that he still was there, even though we couldn't see him.

So, when we described that indescribable moment, we had nothing but the primitive elements a group of upcountry fishermen had 2,000 years ago. He started to rise, and then he was gone.

All right for them, perhaps, but there I was at the back of the crowd—Joe Sophisticate, with 28 years of formal education, not least painful of which were two and a half years of physics.

All right, perhaps, for the first fifteen or twenty yards or so—to the place most painters freeze-frame the event. But after that? It began to look a bit . . . well, silly. Like a missile going up in slow gear. I mean, did he go through the stratosphere? Through the Van Allen Belt? Was he radioactive? Then did he move slowly out past the galaxies and planets and endless, endless cold of space—till he suddenly came up against the thin membrane that separates the material universe from heaven and then—Zoop!—like a nail into a self-sealing tire, he was in the place God lives, in heaven?

I say this in no way to be mocking of the scriptures nor of the faith of the simple, but if you are able to have read this far, surely the simplicities of the catechism and the primitiveness of the explanations available to the apostles are not enough to anyone who's had even the most rudimentary science.

Symbols are concretizations of the non-concrete, attempts to explain the radically unexplainable. And symbols are always inadequate—the box of candy to the love it embodies, the flag to the American spirit it physicalizes, the New Jerusalem to the heaven it tries to explain.

First of all, heaven is not a place—not in any way in which we mean the word "place." It's a dimension to reality which is *impervious* to space and time; it has nothing to do with the spatial or the temporal. And there's no need to "travel there," as one would have to travel from New York to San Francisco, or from earth to the moon. We're already *in* it. To describe the Ascension of Jesus as going "up" is as inadequate as describing love as "a trip to the moon on gossamer wings."

Second, in the universe Einstein opened to us, the word "up" has no meaning, except relative to where I am at the particular moment. When I'm in Rochester, New York, "up" is in one direction; when I'm in the hills of Palestine, "up" is in almost entirely the opposite direction.

Don't get me wrong. I'm in no way impugning the *event*. Jesus really did go into another way of existing. What I'm quibbling with is trying to *understand* that event—and with it the whole concept of heaven—restricting myself to the severely limited terms and cosmology available to men 2,000 years ago, as if nothing had been discovered since then.

Then, paradoxically, an answer came to me from precisely the quadrant of my knowledge that had provoked the doubt: modern science. Note carefully, though, that I say "an" answer, and not "the" answer. My symbols are incredibly inadequate, too. But, for me, a man of the twentieth century, they are just a bit less inadequate than limiting myself to the understandings available to a world which believed—almost universally—that the earth was flat, that it was at the center of the universe, and that heaven lay just above the crystal blue firmament of the sky.

Maybe it's easier—or less difficult, anyway—for those of us whose imaginations have been liberated not only by science but by science fiction. In both, humans can slip into time-warps and end up in some other time and space. Carl Sagan (who is surely no religious believer) says that it's conceivable that a space craft, sucked into a black hole, could negotiate the gravitational tides and get through to the other side. Where would it end up, the less knowledgeable ask. And without batting a lash, Sagan says, "In another universe." Whenever a skeptic says, "Where do you get your heaven?" I answer, "The same place Carl Sagan gets his other universe."

Here we are, thinking that *our* solid space-time reality is the *only* reality, when actually we're surrounded by and thoroughly penetrated by a transcendent reality—just as we are by neutrinos and gamma rays and muons, even though we can't see *them* either. We'll never see an electron, not because it isn't there, but because of the limitations of our eyes. Within the transcendent dimension, we're like Helen Keller in the sunshine or the prisoners in Plato's Cave. Our blindness must take the word of someone who's seen the light that it is truly there. But our blindness doesn't make the light exist—or cease to exist.

What I'm driving at is that Jesus did not go beyond the farthest star. He didn't go any *spatial distance*. He went into another way of existence—and yet remained *here*, not "out there." When we pray, we don't pray across the infinite cold of space to heaven, where God lives. We pray to Someone closer to us than our own heartbeats.

That's what the "Ascension" tells us: not that God is "out there," beyond our reach. He is here. And, if so, then we are already "in heaven" here and now.

At death, we don't "go" anywhere.

At death our blindness is cured.

*   *   *   *

54. Ascension Evening

> *Peter said to the crowd, "God raised this man Jesus to*
> *life, and all of us are witnesses to that. Now he has been*
> *exalted at God's right hand."* — Acts 2:14, 32-33

What must it have been like for the Eleven to go back to Jerusalem that evening and tell what had happened to those who hadn't been there? People like us. Like the people to whom we are sent.

Okay, so they get back to the city, and they sit there in the Upper Room, sort of stunned, I'd imagine. It isn't every day one witnesses a friend just . . . not being there. Especially a friend they've seen as a corpse. And then fully alive. It takes a bit of getting used to.

So, the others start drifting in.

"Oy, vay! That boss of mine. Thick-headed as a battering ram."

"The prices! Look at the prices! We'll all starve! Take my word."

"Jesus . . . Jesus rose into heaven today. We saw it."

"I'm telling you, she's headed for trouble that one. Not just a flirt. Worse. Trouble is what she's headed for."

"Jesus. . . ."

"Hear about that race yesterday? Nobody can beat that kid. But nobody. Never seen anything like him. Never."

"Jesus . . . left."

"What are you talking about?"

"Jesus . . . disappeared. Right in front of us. It was as if . . . it was as if he was . . . taken back into heaven."

"You're crazy, all of you. Wear a hat in such sun."

"Drunk. Drunk is what they are. You are drunk, yes?"

"No, he . . . it's hard to explain."

"Nobody disappears into thin air."

"But he did! Remember, nobody rises from the dead either. You saw him!"

"Of course they don't rise from the dead. Not usually. But we saw that! You can touch somebody who's there; you can see him. But you can't *not* see somebody who's not . . . this whole thing's ridiculous. He probably just slipped away to pray for awhile. He's done it before. Why don't you lie down and rest?"

It must have been awfully lonely. And awfully frustrating. To have the majority of the people you know and love pooh-pooh your experience. Just because they haven't experienced it themselves and can't even imagine experiencing it. But the apostles were, after all, talking about something as palpably impossible as UFO's appearing and disappearing. It was as foolish as saying the earth wasn't flat, and tomatoes weren't poisonous, and the sea wasn't full of dragons.

The truth is a lonely possession.

Perhaps that first Ascension evening was like Holden Caulfield trying to make his baby sister, Phoebe, understand how painful it is to grow up. She thought he was crazy, and in a sense he was, but he was reporting a pain he'd experienced, and she hadn't. And we, who have been through it, know that a lot of what Holden said makes very good sense. Well, *The Catcher in the Rye* was written a long time ago. Today, Phoebe would probably be about fifty. I guess she understands now a little better.

Teachers and parents know what the apostles felt that day, and so many days after. We spend our whole lives, really, trying to explain—first to ourselves and then to the young. But, to refer again to one from my pantheon of patrons, Annie Sullivan. Understanding was only her first gift; her real gift was patience. Day after day, she drew signs in those infuriatingly uncomprehending hands, trusting that one day the light would crack into that stubborn darkness.

Their intransigence used to trouble me. But it doesn't any

longer—at least not as deeply or as painfully. St. Paul, the teacher, wisely recognized that *he* didn't open the eyes of the people he spoke to or wrote for. "Paul planted. Apollos watered. God gives the increase."

We're merely matchmakers. But the Bridegroom—as each of us knows—is persistent. And, unlike ourselves, he is infinitely patient.

*   *   *   *   *

55. Pentecost

Suddenly they heard what sounded like a great wind from the heavens. The noise filled the entire house where they sat. And something like tongues of fire separated and came to rest on the head of each of them. — Acts 2:2-3

The Church has many birthdays. Christmas, of course. Easter. You could say that a milestone on the way to the Church's coming alive was the appearance of Adam and Eve, or crossing out of Egypt, or the Annunciation. But, to me, this is the day for which all other days were preparing. All of the other days said, "Yes!" But Pentecost said, "Now!"

Pentecost is a feast we "borrowed" from Israel. For the Hebrew, Pentecost celebrates the fiftieth day after their forefathers left Egypt, when Moses came down from Sinai, his face radiant from having encountered Yahweh again. The Exodus was the event celebrated at Passover; it was the call of the Hebrews to be the New People of God. The Covenant of Sinai was the event celebrated at Pentecost; it was the official inauguration of the Hebrew mission to act as the privileged channel of communication between Yahweh and humankind.

The New Covenant was sealed in the events of the Last Supper, the crucifixion, and the resurrection, when Jesus went fearlessly through the desert of death and emerged from it more real and alive than any human being could have ever hoped to be. It was our Passover, our call. But the moment when that Covenant was ratified—from our side, the moment we *accepted* our mission, was the moment when the apostles emerged from the Upper Room, ablaze with the enlivening Spirit of God. Just as that Spirit, the divine energy of God, had been embodied in Jesus for 33 years, henceforward, it would now be embodied in us.

The Spirit appeared to them in "what sounded like" a great wind and "something like" tongues of fire.

Anyone who could consult the meteorological statistics of Palestine in about 33 A.D. to see whether there was a tornado that Sunday and a mysterious outbreak of St. Elmo's fire, has missed the whole point. The description Luke gives in Acts has nothing to do with a literal disruption on that eruptive morning. The fire and wind are symbols of a great, enlivening, unstoppable power—which had always been offered, but on this morning was accepted.

It is the same "whirlwind" which brooded over the initial waters at the creation of the world, the same "storm" out of which Yahweh spoke to Job. It is the same "fire" which inflamed the burning bush out of which Yahweh spoke to Moses. And the fire hovered not only over Peter, the pope, nor over those first priests. It divided itself and hovered over "each of the disciples"—empowering even the nameless with the mission of Jesus. It was the calling to all who bore the name of Christ to exercise that cauterizing, healing power of Jesus.

The disciples—and that includes each of us—were sent out to teach all nations. But none of them went a'sailing. They brought the calling to those nearest them. Here, on this first of Pentecosts, we see them standing up to be counted, the cowards of Calvary, fearlessly proclaiming that Jesus is Lord, that we are freed from the fear of death, that the Kingdom is come.

Despite the fact that these men knew only Aramaic and a kind of pidgin Greek, their listeners understood them, each in his own tongue. Again, if one tries to find a literal method behind this first of simultaneous translations, he or she is missing the whole point. What this event is trying to communicate, all inadequately, is that the fragmentation of Babel had begun to be healed; the message of Jesus transcends all differences of language or color or nation or economic status. From now on, there is neither Jew nor Greek, male nor female. There is only the one Body of Christ, with its many and diverse members.

This new People of God which has been invaded by the Spirit is united, but richly multifaceted. A unity of diversities. There is a place for liberal and conservative, the raucous and the timid, the young and the old, the lax and the scrupulous. As long as each of us grasps and accepts the core truths, we will compensate for one another's shortcomings and biases. The hand will not say to the eye, "I don't need you." The eye will not say to the foot, "I am more noble than you." We need our diversity, for the ears that are closed to one voice are opened to another's.

Your voice can speak to ears which can hear no other.

*   *   *   *   *

LOVING

56. Overdosing on Love

"This is my commandment: love one another, as I have loved you."
— John 15:12

I wish John the Evangelist had had an editor. I mean "I am in you, and you are in me, and we are in them, and they are in us." Especially in the discourses at the Last Supper, he keeps repeating and repeating till, after awhile, it's like meeting yourself in a revolving door. C'mon, Johnny baby, lighten up a bit; send in the clowns; give 'em the ol' razzle-dazzle for a bit of a change-up. And enough of the love talk; give us a little action—like scourging the money-changers out of the Temple. Now that sells tickets!

I'm not entirely facetious there. And it's not just in John's gospel that we get love-glut; it's all around us. In a given day, you hear the word "love" so often that it becomes as insipid and empty as, "You have a nice day now!" I mean, think about it: "I *love* that dress . . . I'd love to buy a new stereo." The word "love"—and I think also the reality—has become like paper money in the Depression: you have to bring somebody a whole wheelbarrow of it before you can even get their attention.

In our narcissistic culture, love isn't just trivialized; it's debased. Consider the Rod Stewart lyric: "I don't want to challenge you, marry you, or remember you. I just wanna make love to you." There are far more accurate words to describe what ol' Rod wants, but we're too fastidious to use them.

Consider about eight hours of daily television programming, where if the Carringtons and their various clones haven't fallen into the sack at least fives times an hour—in any one of a dozen permutations—there's something wrong with the way the world turns.

The word "love" now stands in for envy, greed, lust, sexual blackmail—and just about any other feeling of acquisitiveness.

Yet, I'm convinced, the real thing has very little—if anything—to do with the feelings, and surely nothing to do with acquisitiveness.

What's worse, we often balk at using the word "love" when that's what we're actually talking about. For instance, I ask the boys I teach to think of their best male friend, somebody they'd sacrifice just about anything for. And I ask if, even in the secrecy of their own minds, where nobody else would know, they can say, "I . . . love . . . him." First, they blanch; then they blush.

And yet the best definition of love I ever heard was from a seventeen-year-old boy. He was head over heels for a girl but, as will happen, she began to become interested in one of his best friends. He told me later, not without a few tears, that he'd told her, "If you honestly think he can make you happier than I can, that's what I want."

To me, that looks pretty much like the genuine article.

What troubles me about the debasement of love in the culture of narcissism is that it makes it look so easy. It makes it look as if, when it's not fun anymore, it isn't love anymore. It's time to head for Reno.

On the contrary, if it don't cost, it ain't lovin'. And if it becomes commonplace, it's as trivial as Confederate greenbacks.

Which sets up a conundrum. On the one hand, "love" is so watered down that you can use it about dresses and revenge and the casual coupling of two strangers. On the other hand, "love" is so restricted and scary that we can use it—in its purest sense—only for a handful of people. Often, even, only for one single person.

A disinterested observer might suspect we're avoiding something—something very important and very costly, in the middle of those two extremes: that we are called, slowly and painfully, to spread that intense love we hoard for only a restricted circle of trusted friends—out to more and more and more.

Hm. I wish that weren't true. Trouble is—it is.

* * * *

57. Love and Death

> *"Father, if it is your will, take this cup from me. But let your will be done, not mine."*
> — Luke 22:42

Theoretically at least, a priest stands between the people and God. On the one hand, his job is to offer the people's sacrifice to God and explain their needs to him, and on the other hand, to pass God's grace to the people and explain his ways to them.

In practice, though, we often feel like Maytag repairmen. When everything's serene (which, we forget, it usually is), nobody bothers us much. There's really no felt need for understanding God's ways when things are going well; God's ways are just jim-dandy. He's the good Father who keeps the sun shining and lets the good times roll. But in the bad times—as when someone young dies—you come to us with your lives broken. And, with rock-bottom honesty, we don't know how to mend them so they'll be good as new again. We don't know how to explain it all away, so that everything will make sense once again.

It's like the first time in a child's life when she's seen, incontestably, that Mommy can be unfair or that Daddy can be afraid. More profoundly, we also discover that the God we've trusted, the God whose benevolence we just took for granted, doesn't always do what we expect either. It's humbling for us—which is probably one of the major reasons why it happens—but, at first, it seems so manifestly unfair of him.

One of my worst fallings-out with God happened over Fraser MacKenzie. I'd taught him as a senior, in those days when the way kids tested their newfound adulthood was with long hair. Fraser had long, honey-colored hair of which he was as proud as Samson probably was of his. When he was told he either had to have it cut or have his senior portrait left out of the yearbook, that was no choice at all. He came from a family of thirteen, all of them hockey players, feisty, Celtic-handsome, with eyes that could melt granite. When he married his wife, Mimi, I was the priest who received their vows.

Two years later, I heard that Fraser had cancer. The night I found out, I went up to my room, and closed the door, and sat there for about an hour in the dark, *daring* God to make it make sense to me. I'm supposed to be the expert on that, you see.

I'm wise enough to realize God didn't "select" Fraser, like some capricious deity picking pieces off a board at whim, in defiance of "the rules." But God *did* create a world where that—and so many other incomprehensibles—could happen. He did have to answer to me for that.

Oh, the clichés come rolling trippingly to the tongue when you're sent to heal someone else's pain: "God always takes the best . . . God has plans we're not invited into . . . God's ways are not man's ways." But this was *my* pain, not someone else's, and the clichés just wouldn't do. Those answers were not coming from God; they were coming from the recesses of my own memory where I store placebos.

So, as I had done with him over my mother, I tried to bargain with God. I'm not ashamed of that. Abraham wheedled with him. In the Agony in the Garden, Jesus himself tried to argue his way out of the crucifixion. I said to him, "Why not some poor old derelict, or someone languishing in a cancer hospital, who'd be *glad* to die?" Finally, truly, I said to him, "Take me instead." And he didn't.

So then, as I've had to do many times before, I got mad at God—fiercely, forthrightly, cleanly. And then I forgave him.

Why? Not just because he's God, and I'm not. Not just because the only other alternative is the world of Camus, where nothing has a reason and all is meaningless. Not just because

God invented the Game and can play it without giving reasons for his moves. I forgave him because he's my Friend.

In the cocoon of helplessness and grief, we forget that, if God created a universe in which the good can die young, he also created a universe in which the good can be born in the first place. I forgave him because the God who invented the irrationality of death also invented the irrationality of loving.

When Fraser died, it came to me for the first time in my life: without love, death wouldn't hurt; death would be meaningless. A stranger was there, and then he was not. But—far more importantly—without death, we would take love for granted. It wouldn't be limited. It wouldn't be precious.

Earth and water and air are seemingly limitless, and so we pay them no heed. Gold and diamonds and oil will run out some day, and so we hold them precious. Whatever God's reasons for taking a young man whose life had scarcely begun, I think I had found at least a lesson for myself in it. I would never take anyone I loved for granted again. Shyness or the fear of being misunderstood would never again stand between me and saying, "I love you." Because, one day, the "right moment" for saying it will have passed, irretrievably.

The God who called Fraser MacKenzie into my life called him out of my life. If he invites him out of this "great happening illimitably earth," into the Great Dance of the Universe, who am I to tell God it isn't time yet? And who am I to deny my friend that scope for his goodness? Who am I not to let him go—to a peace and a joy and a loving which is endlessly precious only *because* we have known a life which ends?

To ask why this enviable young man lived so few years is equivalently to deny that he is still alive. To ask why I had so little time to know him is to act as if I deserved to know him at all. Am I that spoiled? At the moment Fraser died, all that filled my mind was how unfortunate his wife and his family—and I—were at that moment. Didn't I know how fortunate we'd been? Didn't I know how fortunate we still are?

Although it's difficult to see it from the cramped perspective of this life, those who have died young are surely busy about more important things right now than the things we busy ourselves with. But each of them has left a message: look at all the loving we made happen. It's been here all the time, of course. But at moments when we are bereft, we are reminded to treasure it. To forget the shyness that holds it in. To resolve never again to take it for granted, because it becomes precious again because of our pain.

If you don't want to be hurt deeply, then never love deeply again. And you'll be safe. You'll already be dead.

* * * * *

58. The Nefarious Velveteen Rabbit

"Whoever dotes on himself destroys himself."
— John 12:25

There was a time when brides asked to have readings other than the scriptures at their weddings. Which says something, I think, of the meaningfulness of the scriptures to them. But they'd choose something that had spoken to their hearts—you know, Kahlil Gibran or Paul McCartney or Robert Frost. But, as I enter my curmudgeon years, I've dug in my heels. Nix on that. Sing anything you want that isn't directly immoral, but the readings'll be from the Book which is the reason for having a church wedding in the first place.

Foolishly or not, I've given my life away on the basis of those scriptures, and although they aren't quite "in," and although they often use a tone that's uncomfortably challenging, I'd rather "my" readings have a bit of spine than a great deal of molasses.

One of the readings that surfaced comes from a pernicious

little book for children called *The Velveteen Rabbit*. The principal thesis of this tome is this: if a child loves a toy strongly enough, eventually, when the toy falls into the shabby days of old age, it will become "really real." That's why, in the story, the Velveteen Rabbit ends up as a live bunny in a lettuce patch. When you are loved, the story claims, you become real. It's a lovely little story, tenderly told, but I'd hate my children to grow up or my friends to get married basing their lives on that lie. Some people would like to burn *The Catcher in the Rye* and *Huckleberry Finn*. I'd like to burn *The Velveteen Rabbit*.

That seemingly innocuous little book is a lie on three counts. First, one doesn't become real when he or she is loved. If the author and her devotees meant that people become real when *God* starts loving them, I'd be willing to go along. Somehow, though, I suspect they mean one becomes real only when other people start loving him or her.

If that were true, though, how could the rabbit even have been found—much less known and loved—if he weren't real *before* he was discovered? Love might make him feel *more* real, but it doesn't give him his fundamental existence and worth. Yet, tragically at times, too many people honestly believe that, until they're loved, they're not even "there." You'll find them hiding in the nooks and carrels of any school during recess, trying to avoid being negated again.

Others who feel like "nothings" scrabble for approval, and the price cannot be too high. They load themselves with Clearasil and Aim and Secret and Head-and-Shoulders, as if that would somehow attract the love-laser and make them real, worth attention. Poor wretches. They so yearn to be someone else, as if other people are more real than they are. They fear to stand up to bullies, lest they be disapproved and disappear. They fear to give themselves away because no one has loved them first. Unloved, they're unreal, and therefore a thin gift indeed.

The second reason why the Pernicious Rabbit is a lie is that it negates the unloved—and seemingly unlovable: the boors, the fearfully anonymous, the outcasts. If they are, by their own admission, unloved, they disappear into thin air, and we have no need to deal with them—much less reach out to their pain as we've been missioned to do. They may be unpleasant, but they aren't unreal. Neither is their pain. They are in fact—unnerving as it is to admit—Christ himself in disguise, silently begging us to reach out to *his* need, in the needy, and thus to grow ourselves.

There's a third reason why I find the Velveteen Rabbit a rather meretricious little bunny. The thesis of the story is that one must *be* loved—which is, of course, why the damned book is so popular: because, underneath all the cutesy-poo, it panders to our own selfishness. It's precisely opposite to the truth of the scriptures (which those brides-to-be wanted to substitute it for): if you love somebody strongly enough, it is not the object of your love who becomes more real; it's *you*. It's loving that gives life. Being loved is the whipped cream and the cherry.

The moment two people in love start to analyze their love, the moment they start thinking of *being* insufficiently loved, they are on the grim and greasy chute to Mine and Thine, His and Hers, whose needs are more real, and who gets the children.

Rather than hearken to the saccharine Rabbit, I would hope two people in love would listen to the Lion of Judah, who says that one becomes real—finds his or her true self—by forgetting the self. True, the Lion of Judah is also the Lamb of God, but he's not a Cuddly-Warm Fuzzy. He came to lay down his own life so that we might come truly alive—not at death; here and now.

There's a lesson there somewhere, surely.

*   *   *   *   *

59. Deserving Love

Love, then, consists in this: not that we have loved
God, but that he has loved us. — 1 John 4:10

How often in our lives have we felt that the price of love was success? We had to bring home a gold star, or Mommy would be silently disappointed. We had to make the first team in the Little League, or Dad would be sad and his son would be nothing to brag about. If we brought home a dismal report card—even though the teacher were an idiot, even though the matter were way over even the eggheads, even though we were in the throes of some *affaire du coeur* and couldn't concentrate—we weren't going to be loved anymore by the people who really counted.

And it goes on and on: pleasing the girl or boy we go out with, pleasing the boss, pleasing the kids, the husband, the neighbors, the relatives. Then, multiply that by about eight billion, and try to please an infinite God, what chance have we? After all, he's seen real pros like Our Lady and St. Teresa and Thomas More and John XXIII. They're the long-ball hitters. They're the ones the Daddy-of-Us-All must love more. How can simple, fumbly tiddly-squats like ourselves ever even compete for his attention?

If you make even a cursory study of the gospels, you see that Jesus' model disciple was Peter—a simple, fumbly tiddly-squat. What had Our Lady done to be chosen the Mother of God? Had she led any crusades, changed the world? What had Joan of Arc done to be chosen to lead the armies of France? What had Bernadette done? Or the Cure of Ars, who had flunked almost every exam he'd ever taken? What had Cinderella done to merit an invitation to the ball? Nothing. She was chosen simply because the Fairy Godmother had a soft spot for tiddly-squats.

Think of the person you love best in the world. Could that person do anything that would make you annul your love? Could

he or she commit some crime so awful that you wouldn't stick by
them in court and in prison? If they could, then perhaps you
don't really love them—not in the real sense of the word "love."
When we love, we love not because people succeed, or because
they share some kind of glory with us, or because they repay our
investment in them. We love them simply because . . . well,
because we do, that's all. They're ours. Thick and thin, fail or
succeed, difficult or easy.

   And if *we* treat those we love that way—without reference to
profit-loss margins—who says God needs something from us to
go on loving us? He gave us the gift *sine qua non*: existence—
before we had done anything capable of "earning" existence. He
forgives us our sins even before we commit them; all he asks is
that we accept the forgiveness he offers. He gives us the gift of
eternal life when, sometimes, we act as if we don't even deserve
the gift of temporary life.

   Surely this mystifying love is something worthy of dancing!
But we, blinded by what we haven't, sit moping in the corner
over our inadequacies—when the greatest of Lovers is there
beckoning us out into the greatest of parties, the liveliest of
circuses, the profoundest of loves. And in denying we are
lovable, we call the Truth a liar.

   Odd, isn't it?

                *   *   *   *   *

60. Tough Love

> *"It is not peace I've come to bring. I bring a sword."*
> — Matthew 10:34

   I confess I get irritated with people who moan to me that
they're checking out of a Church that doesn't fit their needs,
makes egregious claims, and is, generally, irrelevant. The reason

I get angry is that, if they check out, most of them haven't the slightest idea of what they're leaving behind.

One of the roots of that ignorance, I think, is that they're leaving behind the Jesus of the holy pictures—that tall, slim, erect man with the soft, gentle, feminine face, looking halfway between yearning love and hurt feelings. Like the Baptist, but for opposite reasons, he's surely not the kind of guy you'd want to invite home for brunch after Mass on Sunday.

In a way, their disaffection becomes understandable. All they've had to go on is the catechism, sermons over their heads, and gooey (or gory) pictures of an easily dismissable irrelevance, who looks scarcely human, much less male. "Loving" to him seems to mean turning yourself into a doormat.

They've been "Christians" ever since the Sunday afternoon when they were hauled, all unknowing, to the baptismal font and committed to an organization for the rest of their lives. But the organization is meaningless without the Person whom it embodies. And if the Person appears to be wimpy, so does the Church.

Charles de Gaulle once said that, if you want to take command of a nation, don't look for help from its great thinkers, or its great statesmen, or its great saints. Go instead to the men and women who write its popular songs and create its popular art. One only has to look at the dramatic effect rock'n'roll and television have wrought on our mores in the last thirty years to see how right he was. The same is true of the Church. If people are leaving it, lay the blame not on the theologians or Vatican II or John Paul II, lay the blame squarely where it belongs, on the popular artists—the hymn writers, the holy-card painters, the liturgists, the teachers—and those who enlist, advise and support them.

We've all seen the insipid pictures and heard the treacly hymns—the ones that give rise to the belief that Jesus is only the Good Shepherd, who's gonna pat our woolly heads and make everything nice again. Like *The Velveteen Rabbit*, they're lies.

Consider the facts. Jesus was a Jew, living in the searing sun day after day. How could he be pale and white and blue-eyed? Long before he was ten, he began to work as a carpenter. Look at the calloused sausage fingers of a carpenter some time. His shoulders were muscled from years of hauling logs and raising roofbeams. After a night so terrifying that he sweat blood, after being scourged with leaded whips, crowned with thorns, dragged from one senseless trial to another, booted through the streets—fainting—he still had the raw physical strength to crawl onto a cross, have spikes driven through his wrists, and nonetheless held out, hanging there, for another three hours.

Call him anything, but you can't call him effeminate.

What's worse, the physical image we have of Jesus profoundly affects our ability even to judge his personality or his message. The only way to judge those fairly is to look at what he said and the way he acted.

He had guts. We've seen that. He wasn't just the dull, sweet, meek, boring man of the hymns and pictures. To give the Pharisees their due, they didn't railroad Jesus to his death because he was so boring. You don't crucify irrelevance. On the contrary, he was too dynamic to be safe. It's later generations of artists and preachers who muffled up that shattering personality and made him timid and tedious.

True, he was tender to the unfortunate, patient with slowness to learn. But he called the reigning king "that old fox." He went to parties with highly disreputable company—grafters and women who were no better than they had to be. He was accused of over-eating and drinking with too much enjoyment. He threw indignant businessmen out of church. He failed to give the deference due to men of position and pedigree. He called clergymen some pretty uncomplimentary names: "whited sepulchres, tangle of vipers, hypocrites," to name but a few. He asked the kind of questions that can't be answered out of a catechism.

Call him anything, but you can't call him dull.

And yet, he is also God. Totally divine, and yet totally one of us. He felt our pain, wrestled with our anguish, dreamed our dreams. King and peasant, God and man, and—hard as it might be to comprehend—our Brother. If he isn't all those things, Christianity is, in truth, irrelevant.

Perhaps if we preached that tough-love Jesus, even more people would leave the Church. But it wouldn't be for all the wrong reasons: boredom, irrelevance, doormat-passivity. It would be for the only comprehensible reason for walking away from Christ: fear of the cost.

*　*　*　*　*

61. Love of Things

> *I've learned to manage on whatever I have. I know how to be poor, and I know how to be rich. I've learned how to cope with every circumstance. I'm ready for anything, anywhere: full belly or empty, poverty or plenty. There's nothing I can't master with the help of him who strengthens me.*
> — Philippians 4:11-13

So often, the gospel stacks the cards in favor of the poor. They're the ones who will inherit the land, while the rich man drags the anchor of his goods through the eye of that needle. And yet, some of the really poor I've known have been more embittered, more greedy, than many of the really rich I've known, who have been almost embarrassingly generous, not only with their goods but with themselves.

What Paul is saying—and what Jesus says when he speaks of the lilies of the field—isn't that we ought to hate wealth and comfort, but that we ought to be independent of our wealth and comfort. They are very good servants; they are very wicked masters. We ought to be able to enjoy material goods; after all, Jesus himself was accused of enjoying eating and drinking more than a man of God should. But we can't become distraught when we don't have them, like an alcoholic who begins to get edgy around three in the afternoon. What Jesus and Paul offer is the aliveness that comes from freedom.

How much have we bought the competitive disease which strangles our freedom—and thus our aliveness? No matter how much money you've already got, you've gotta keep your eye on the main chance. We compete to define our worth with grades, money, prestige, all week long. And then, on the weekends, to relax, we get out on the links or the tennis court and do it all over again. Or we sit and watch 22 men do it for us.

For a compulsive, I consider myself pretty laid-back. But one Christmas, I was playing Trivial Pursuit with a family. At one point, the little girl, who was only ten, asked for help on a question. She was only ten, mind you. And yet, I heard my laid-back, hang-easy self nearly shouting. "Oh . . . no . . . you . . . don't!" It gives one uneasy pause.

Why do we compete? Isn't it because, no matter what we say, we still have to prove ourselves, to ourselves, despite ourselves? A bonus or an A+ is a crutch to a faltering self-image. We try to assure ourselves that we've got value by piling up more and more *things*—not because we honestly enjoy them, but because they define our worth. And no matter how high the pile gets, it's never enough to satisfy, never enough to give peace.

Paul says that having Christ makes having plenty or having nothing a matter of indifference. I think what "having Christ" means is that one realizes that having the Son of God as an adopted brother makes me a prince, in the only Kingdom that's really real.

How much is that really worth?
That's a very nifty question.

*   *   *   *   *

62. The Intoxicating Commonplace

Simon Peter said, "I'm going fishing."
— John 21:3

In the very last episode in John's gospel, the disciples are lying around the dark beach on the Sea of Tiberias. Typically, Peter's getting edgy. So, he huffs to his feet and says he's going fishing. Having nothing better to do, the others come along. As dawn comes up there's a man standing on the beach waiting for them as they pull toward shore in their empty boat. The stranger tells them to cast their nets on the other side, and they haul in a catch so enormous they can hardly pull it over the gunnels. John peers across the shallows and turns to Peter. "It's the Lord," he says.

Peter, who's been working practically naked, throws on some clothes and jumps overboard, sloshing toward Jesus. When the rest gather, they see Jesus has laid a fire and has fish cooking on it. "Come and have breakfast," he says. And in that simple place, as the sun is coming up, Jesus makes Peter the first pope.

It's a wonderfully unadorned story, and yet speckled with the same ordinary, everyday things Renaissance painters used to put into their pictures—the cat curled in the corner, the letter on the table, the flowers on the sunny windowsill. The nets hanging empty after a whole night's trying. Rambunctious Peter's shy propriety throwing *on* clothes in order to jump into the water, his impetuosity softened by a touching attempt to do the proper thing in the presence of the Lord. And Jesus himself, with his commonplace thoughtfulness, providing breakfast for them. His teasing but meaningful triple question to the Simon who had triply denied him.

And on this commonplace, early-morning beach, the Son of God confers the primacy on the man who had deserted him. He does it without the pomp of St. Peter's Square, without the swelling diapason of great organs and trumpets and choirs, without the scarlet and purple robes of office. The only adornments are sedge and pebbles, the only sound the wash of the lake on the shore, the pope and his priests are naked to the waist, their sweat chilling in the early morning air. The words are simple: feeding lambs and sheep.

I've said before that I feared we put barriers of ceremony and rank and pomposity between ourselves and the simple, commonplace ways in which Jesus spoke the enormous truths of our emancipation. We can no longer savor simple bread and wine. We've heroicized those twelve simple men into giants, and etherealized their Teacher into a being beyond the scope of our imitation.

Jesus was transfigured for them only once. The rest of the time he was merely their Friend, their Teacher. His sweat smelled no different from theirs, and he grew weary of the road just as they did. But they stumbled along beside him, never quite sure where they were going or why, only that he had the words of eternal life.

Like Peter and James and John, there are few moments of true transfiguration for us. Like them, we're ordinary men and women who have had an encounter with an extraordinary calling, to come out on the road with Christ. We fail and fall, in big ways and small, but when we do, it is a good man or woman who falls. We live days no more extraordinary than those first fishermen's days—balancing budgets, answering letters, jerry-rigging meals and schedules and lives. But there's a greatness in our commonplace lives—not in their extraordinary outcome, but in that extraordinary calling. That it should come to such Cinderellas.

In our commonplace fishing expeditions, in our wrestling with the petty inertias in ourselves and in the people we love and the people with whom we work, there is a greatness. Because, no matter how small our lakes, the Son of God is waiting by the side to give us rest and peace—if only we have the wisdom to pull ashore once in a while and share it with him.

It isn't marble that gives dignity to our work—nor titles, nor publicity, nor pomp. It's the presence of the limitless God, who—incomprehensibly—has chosen to share our commonplace lives.

* * * * *

PART I

MURDER

"If security and happiness are among your early companions, there's a good chance they'll continue to be so. But if despair and difficulty rock your cradle, they may show an unfortunate tendency to take up permanent residence in your household."

—Margo Livesey, "The Third Servant" (*Five Points,* fall 1998)

Chapter 1

December 1956

Our electricity had been turned off. Mama and I were cold and alone in our house in Trade Alley. She lit the oven and all four burners on our old gas range in the kitchen. We wrapped ourselves in blankets and sat near the oven's open door, talking. Mama smoked a cigarette. "You was nearly born in the cab of that big truck your daddy used to drive for F.M.," said Mama. "Bet you didn't know that."

Of course I knew. My mother told me the same stories over and over, and this was one of her favorites. But I didn't care. I just loved to hear her talk, so I always played along.

"What happened, Mama?" I asked.

"You was almost born in that truck, that's what happened."

"Why's that, Mama?"

"'Cause your daddy can't pay his bills and we had to drive all the way to Lauderdale County, that's why—almost forty miles away." Mama paused. She took a drag off her cigarette. "Let me tell you what happened. The day you was born, I worked like the devil washin' and dryin' every curtain in that house, then moppin' and waxin' all the floors. That's when we had our own house, you know, before your daddy lost it." Mama took another drag off her cigarette, then wiped a fleck of tobacco from her bottom lip with the tip of her little finger. She examined it briefly, then flicked it away. "Honey, that was a nice house, not like this dump here." Mama shook her head, a disgusted look on her face.

"Anyway, I guess it was all the work I did that day 'cause labor pains started that night. And I couldn't call nobody 'cause we didn't have a phone, and I couldn't walk over to your

3

pawpaw and granny's 'cause it was too far. Besides, I had your sister Dianne to look after; she was just two.

"It was 10:00 at night. I remember 'cause I kept starin' at a little clock I kept on the mantelpiece and thinkin', Where's Chuck? Ten o'clock and I ain't seen him since 5:00 this mornin'. I couldn't take it no more, so I just balled up on the sofa with your sister, closed my eyes, and tried to sleep, but I couldn't."

"'Cause you was hurtin', huh, Mama?"

"That's right, honey. Mama was hurtin'—hurtin' real bad.

"So here comes your daddy, staggerin' in the front door at 2:00 in the mornin'. Honey, he just stood there in the doorway lookin' at me and Dianne lyin' there on the sofa. You know what he said?"

"What, Mama?"

"He said, 'Irene, what's wrong? How come you and Dianne ain't in bed?'

"'What the hell you think's wrong, Chuck,' I yelled at him. 'I'm about to have this here baby, while you been out all night gallivantin', doin' Lord knows what!'

"'Just tryin' to make a livin', Irene, that's all.'

"'You call hangin' out at the Moose Club all night makin' a livin', Chuck? You smell like a whiskey bottle,' I told him.

"'I had a coupla drinks with the fellas down at the Moose Club, that's all.'

"'Till 2:00 in the mornin', Chuck! I can't believe what a sorry excuse for a man you are!'" Mama took another drag off her cigarette, then a sip from a coffee cup near her right hand.

"Then your daddy carried me and your sister out to F.M.'s truck. He put us in the cab and off we went. Honey, it was a rough ride. I bounced up and down like a rubber ball every time your daddy shifted gears. I ain't never hurt so much in my life. I thought I was gonna die. Then I looked out the window and realized that we weren't goin' to the hospital in Shelby at all.

4

"'Chuck, where you goin'?' I said. 'The hospital's that way.'
'I'm takin' you to the hospital to have this baby,' he said. 'But
the hospital's in Shelby,' I told him. 'I know, Irene, but I'm takin'
you to this clinic in Lauderdale County.' 'But, Chuck, that's forty
miles away.'"

Mama paused, shook her head.

"Well, honey, when your daddy didn't answer, it dawned on
me what I'd been suspectin' for a long time."

"What's that, Mama?"

"Your daddy never did pay the hospital bill in Shelby for
your sister Dianne, and that's why we had to drive all the way to
Lauderdale County so I could have you.

"That was a long, painful trip, honey, and I almost didn't
make it. My water broke right there as soon as we pulled into
the parking lot of that clinic," said Mama. "You know what your
daddy said when he first laid eyes on you, honey?"

"What, Mama?"

"He said, 'Damn, Irene! That's the ugliest baby I ever saw!
All red and wrinkled, bald as an onion! Damn, if he ain't the
spittin' image of F.M.! Just my luck!'"

"I was ugly, Mama?" I asked, my feelings hurt.

"Just till your skin cleared up and you grew some hair, then
you turned out to be the prettiest baby ever. Just look how
handsome you are now."

Mama tousled my hair. I grinned.

My father hated his father, F.M., although he worked for
him off and on for years. Of Scottish descent, F.M., whose real
name was Frederick Martin, was a stern, tightfisted, but
successful businessman. He often operated two or three small
businesses simultaneously and always had at least one small
grocery store where he charged high prices for extending credit
to the poor. He also supplied moonshine and illegal whiskey to

most of the bootleggers in shantytown. F.M. himself drank moonshine his entire life but only a half glass at night before bed. My mother once told me that the ill will between my father and F.M. started because of an incident that occurred during World War II.

"Your daddy didn't fight in the war," Mama told me, "'cause he only had that one eye. So F.M. put your daddy in charge of this service station he owned in downtown Shelby, right across from the high school." Mama took a drag off her cigarette.

"Honey, during the war, you couldn't just buy all the gasoline you wanted, you know. Gas was rationed—and not just gas but all kinds of products needed for the war effort, stuff like tires and batteries. So the government issued these little stamps, kinda like postage stamps, that you had to have to buy products that was rationed. Every adult got a certain number of ration stamps every month, that is, unless you had a job, like a truck driver, taxi driver, or a farmer. Then you got extra stamps and could buy extra gas and tires.

"Everybody wanted more stamps so they could buy more products, especially gas. So, somehow your daddy got his hands on these counterfeit stamps and started givin' them to his customers so they could buy more gas.

"Pretty soon your daddy's sellin' more gas than anybody in Shelby. I don't know if F.M. knew anything about it. Maybe he did and just looked the other way, I don't know. But I do know that F.M.'s always been smart enough to get somebody else to do his dirt for him. Anyway, somehow the government finds out about the fake stamps and they sent two agents over to the station. Your daddy recognized the government car as soon as it pulled up."

"What did daddy do, Mama?"

Mama laughed. "Honey, your daddy's always been a damn fool. He grabbed up all those fake stamps and ran to the storeroom. He locked the door, then your daddy ate all them fake stamps, except for a couple he dropped on the floor. But that was enough evidence for the government to shut down F.M.'s station and to fine F.M. They let your daddy off with probation. F.M. ain't trusted your daddy with any real responsibility since. Sure, he still lets your daddy work for him, but he won't put him in charge of nothin'."

My father was tall, lean, brooding, and handsome. He had brown eyes and black hair, his Native American lineage evident. He took great pride in being a hard worker and showed a lively sense of humor with his peers but seldom at home. He could also be charming, particularly with a debtor or employer and, at times, even with my mother.

I remember once watching my father make my mother smile even though she was angry with him. He crooned the old ballad "Goodnight, Irene" and refused to stop until she smiled.

My father was intelligent but had little formal education. I often heard him say that school was unimportant and that learning to work hard was what mattered most. More than once I heard him brag about how he had jumped out of the school window when he was nine and never returned.

Years later, I learned that my father's disdain for education really had to do with a tragedy that occurred when he was very young.

"Your daddy lost his right eye when he was only six years old," Mama told me. "He was playing hide-and-seek with his older brothers when he was accidentally hit in the eye by a branch with long thorns on it.

"The doctor had to remove your daddy's right eye, and he had to wear a black eye patch until he was old enough to be

7

fitted with an artificial eye. At school, your daddy was teased by the other kids. They called him One-Eye and Patch. Your daddy often came home from school cryin'. He got to where he hated to go. It was around this time that your daddy started smokin'," said Mama.

"Every mornin' on his way to school, your daddy would stop off at the cotton mill and pick up cigarette butts the mill workers threw away. When Mama Bridges found out, it broke her heart. Even though she knew smokin' wasn't good for him, she just couldn't deny her youngest son, a little boy who had already suffered so much, so she struck a bargain. She told your daddy that she would buy him a carton of cigarettes every week if he would go to school every day and quit pickin' up cigarette butts.

"Mama Bridges kept her part of the bargain until your daddy quit school at nine and went to work. Then your daddy bought his own cigarettes."

My paternal grandmother was a tall, quiet, attractive woman with long black hair that she always kept neatly pinned and coiled. Native American, she was born and raised on the Cherokee reservation in the nearby Smoky Mountains. How she and F.M. met, I don't know.

All of her grandchildren called her Mama Bridges. She carried herself with great dignity and humility. Mama Bridges was one of those rare people that quietly separated herself from the normal chaos and concerns of ordinary people yet stayed connected and was always present to encourage and guide others with a smile, kind words, and, most importantly, by making her life a living example.

Always busy, Mama Bridges still found time to devote to her church, community, and family—cleaning, cooking, and working at her sewing machine or in her vegetable garden.

Whenever I visited her home as a boy, I always felt a sense of awe. Her quiet presence always seemed to soothe the barbarian growing inside me. Without prompting, I would lower my voice and speak in hushed tones, as if I had just walked into a museum or a cathedral.

When it became obvious how harmful was my parents' lifestyle, Mama Bridges saved my older sister, Dianne. She convinced first F.M., then my parents, that it would be best for Dianne to come live with them.

My mother was a preacher's daughter. When she met my father, she was a beautiful teenage girl standing five-four, with long golden hair. Her nose wrinkled when she smiled and her laughter was contagious. But her most beautiful and dominant feature were her intense blue-green eyes, eyes that she inherited from her father and then passed on to me.

As a girl, my mother was precocious and popular, always the center of attention. When all my aunts and uncles and cousins gathered on major holidays, she was the golden girl who played the piano and sang with the voice of an angel.

"Honey, I met your daddy during the war when he managed that service station for F.M.," Mama told me. "That station was right across the street from Shelby High. Me and my friends used to stop there after school for a Coke. Lord, he was good lookin' then."

"Daddy!" I was shocked.

"Yes, honey, your daddy was good lookin' when I met him. He had an artificial eye, but you couldn't tell it. I'd stop at the station after school and your daddy would flirt like crazy with me. He was always askin' me to go out with him. But I couldn't. Your pawpaw wouldn't let me date. But that didn't stop your daddy; he just kept on askin'.

9

"I finally gave in and we started sneakin' around seein' each other. After a coupla months, we decided to elope one night. We was just crazy, like most teenagers. You'll see what I mean one day, honey. Anyway, we drove to South Carolina and got married by a justice of the peace. Your daddy was nineteen and I was fifteen. When your pawpaw found out, he was fit to be tied."

Growing up, I often wondered why my mother had chosen to marry my father, a man I saw as inferior in intelligence and appearance. When I was older, I asked her.

"Honey, the reason I married your daddy," she said, "was because he just kept askin' me, wouldn't take no for an answer. And your daddy made me laugh."

Years later, after I had been bitten by the love bug myself and had learned a little about human nature, I came up with my own theory. I believe that as a young teen, my mother had felt trapped in a household of ten siblings dominated by a religious zealot and had seen marriage as a way out—a doorway to freedom and adventure. But there was a problem; because of the war, there were few eligible young men, and those that had been left were all flawed. I believe that my mother had simply chosen the best of those left behind—my father.

When my mother got home from Morganton, she looked brand new, like a doll just taken out of the box. Her hair was lustrous and she wore just a hint of makeup. Her beautiful eyes were clear and free of fear. Dressed in a blue linen summer dress and white sandals, she smiled when she saw me. I ran to her.

Everything was perfect for about six weeks. My father came home every night instead of going to the Moose Club, and every night my mother had a carefully prepared supper on the table. During the day, she scrubbed and cleaned. She taught me to play

solitaire and gin rummy (games she had learned in Morganton) and we talked. Then one night my father failed to come home directly after work. Supper grew cold on the table. My mother smoked cigarette after cigarette. She paced the small apartment and kept staring out the window.

My father didn't come home until after midnight, and my parents argued for the first time since my mother had gotten out of Morganton.

During the next few days, I watched my mother wind down like a toy with a weak battery. Every day she cleaned, cooked, talked, and smiled less until finally all she could do was sit in her ladder-back chair and stare out the window.

After school, I opened the door and shouted, "Mama, I'm home!"

There was no response, so I walked into the living room and looked around. My mother was sitting in a chair in front of the window, staring out while slowly rubbing the base of the third finger of her left hand with the pad of her left thumb.

"I'm home," I told her, but she ignored me and continued to stare out the window as if in a trance. I walked up behind her and put my right hand on her right shoulder. She turned her head, looked up at me, and covered my hand with her own. She squeezed weakly, dropped her hand, then turned back to the window.

Looking over her shoulder, I strained to see what had captured her attention, but all I saw was the red dirt road out front, the drainage ditch alongside, and the grassy ridge that led to shantytown. Beyond the ridge was a cornfield. Months before, the corn had been vibrant and bursting with life, shimmering in the sun like regimented rows of green soldiers at attention, but with the change of season all that remained was a

field of brown rotten cornstalks, randomly scattered about like a child's plastic pick-up sticks.

I walked over to the sofa and sat down. Picking up a schoolbook, I began to read, every page or two looking over at Mama, who continued to stare out the window. I wondered why she kept rubbing her finger with her thumb. Then, all of a sudden, she stood and said, "Mama's okay now, honey." She walked past me and down the short hall to her bedroom. I heard her shut and lock the door.

My father almost never made considered choices but rather acted impulsively then struggled to live with the consequences. Trade Alley was the worst possible location that he could have chosen for my mother after her suicide attempt because of its proximity to shantytown. On the other hand, it was great for the bootleggers in shantytown. They treated my mother like royalty. It was the Deep South in the 1950s and she was a white woman but, more importantly, she was F.M.'s daughter-in-law, so they allowed her to drink on credit (one bill my father always paid).

The next day, when I got home from school my mother was gone and I knew where. I grabbed my bag of marbles and walked the grassy ridge to shantytown.

A couple hours later, hot and sweaty, standing on the porch of a bare-wood shack, drinking a glass of cold water given me by a playmate's mother, I casually looked through the window into the living room. There, curled up on a sofa asleep, was my mother. I couldn't believe my eyes. Finally, with great effort I looked away, then slowly looked around to see if anyone had seen my reaction. Embarrassed, I felt myself blush. I finished the water and handed the glass to my friend's mother while pretending that I hadn't just seen my own.

My father's old Pontiac bounced to a stop in front of where I sat on the front porch steps. He opened the door and walked toward me, smelling of burnt grease, the black lubricant smeared across the front of his dark-blue uniform shirt. I felt guilty when my father looked at me, sensing that he not only knew that she was gone but that I knew where she was.

Shaking his head in frustration, my father rubbed his face with a stained hand, his broken fingernails caked with black grease, and without a word brushed past me, hurrying through the front door. Cautiously I followed, stopping just inside. I watched my father search the bedroom first, then the bathroom. He walked back into the living room and, hands on his hips, stared at me, his good eye accusatory, his glass eye cloudy, a thin film of mucus strung across it like yellow taffy. In a quiet but strained voice he asked, "Where is she? How long's she been gone? Was she drinkin'?"

I wanted to tell him the truth, that I had just seen her in shantytown and could even tell him which house, but for some reason I couldn't. I lied. "I don't know Da … Daddy," I stammered, staring at the floor. "She was here this mornin' when I went to school."

"You don't know!" yelled my father, moving toward me. I stepped back. "Hell, you're the one here with her all the time— her little pet! She tells you everything! And you say you don't know! How many times have I told you don't let her leave this house!"

"But, Daddy, I … I was …"

"Shut up! Just shut up!" He drew back his hand and I flinched. My father grabbed my arm and shook me. I fell to the floor and whimpered. He looked down at me and, as if examining roadkill on the highway, nudged my arm with his boot. "Shut up that cryin'!"

Without washing his hands or changing his clothes, my father left, slamming the screen door behind him so hard it rocked back and forth on its rusty hinges for what seemed a long time.

When I heard my father's car crank, I got up, walked to the screen door, and watched the old Pontiac drive away. A cloud of red dust arose, then settled onto the front porch.

Chapter 2

"Damnit, Irene!" shouted my father, shocking me awake. I sat up and watched him shove my mother through the front door. She stumbled and like a blind woman caught the wall with both hands.

My mother's once beautiful hair was now stringy and greasy, plastered to the side of her head. Her once pleasing voice was now raspy and slurred, painful to listen to. My mother's once intensely alive eyes were now dull and glazed, difficult to look into.

Instead of her usually charming self, she was now mordant and mean and aggressive, screaming and cursing until out of breath, then calmly pretending that she hadn't said an ill word to anyone.

"You son of a bitch!" she yelled. Turning, she beat my father in the chest with her fists.

My father grabbed her wrist and shook her. "Damnit, Irene! Go to bed!"

"You one-eyed bastard!" screamed my mother.

My father slapped her, the sound so sudden I jumped. She stumbled sideways, hit her head against the wall, and slid to the floor. My father stood over her. "Irene, I'm tired of chasin' you all over Shelby! I can't work all day and chase you all night. I'm goin' to bed. You can come with me or sleep on the floor, I don't care."

I walked over and got down on my knees beside my mother, cradled her head while she whimpered. She squinted at me through swollen eyes. Her lips were split and bleeding. "My baby," she slurred. "You're the only one that understands." She reached up and hugged me in a tight grip, her foul breath causing me to turn my head.

I pried myself free and rushed to the bathroom where I wet a washcloth with warm water. After wiping the blood from my mother's face, I helped her to the bedroom.

The bedroom reeked of whiskey, cigarettes, grease, and dirty feet. Still in his uniform, my father lay on his back, already asleep, his artificial eye open and staring blankly at the ceiling. When my mother saw him sleeping peacefully, the sight enraged her and gave her new life. She charged the bed and climbed him like a rock face. Straddling him, she beat him with her clenched fists. "You bastard!" she screamed. "You one-eyed bastard!"

I grabbed her from behind and tried to restrain her, but when she pulled back to hit him again, she caught me with a backhand in the face. I let go of her and cupped my nose. Tears filled my eyes and blood trickled onto my upper lip.

My mother hit my father a hard blow high on the right cheek, dislodging his glass eye. It flew through the air, bounced off the wall, and landed on the floor at my feet. My father sat up, let out a grunt, then flopped back onto the bed. My mother's eyes rolled back in her head. She fell forward, passing out atop my father.

Quiet now, I stood at the foot of the bed and looked at my parents entwined. Their posture reminded me of an engraving I had seen in a *National Geographic* magazine at school; it was of petrified Pompeians after the eruption of Vesuvius.

Bending down, I picked up my father's glass eye and rubbed it with my thumb. It felt smooth and cool like a marble. Turning, I placed it on the dresser next to a chipped black lacquer music box my father had given my mother years before on her birthday. On top of the music box was a tiny, painted ballerina, the head and one arm missing. I turned a recessed key on the bottom of the box and opened the lid. Music played and the disfigured dancer twirled. I placed my father's glass eye inside and closed the lid.

Our electricity disconnected, night found the three of us sitting at the small table in the kitchen, two candles for light. We ate Spam and mayonnaise sandwiches.

Suddenly, there was a loud knock at the door. We froze, looked at each other. My father leaned forward and blew out the candles. The scent of candle wax filled the air.

Again there was a loud knock, this one more insistent. My father carefully parted the blinds and looked out.

"Who is it, Chuck?" asked my mother.

"Shhh," he whispered. "Keep quiet, Irene. It's Old Man Stuart."

"Well, Chuck, just answer the door. He's gotta know you're in here; the car's parked out front. Tell him you'll pay the rent Friday when you get paid."

"Just hush up, Irene," hissed my father. "Just be quiet and wait. The old bastard'll get tired and leave."

Sure enough, a few minutes later we heard a car door slam, then the sound of a car driving away. "He's gone," said my father, relighting the candles.

"Chuck, I hate this not havin' electricity and hidin' out in our own house. I can't even fix a decent meal. Why don't you just pay your bills like a man!" My mother puffed her cigarette, the tip flaring in the dim light. "What kinda man lets his family live like this!"

"What kinda woman runs off and leaves her family for two or three days at a time. Irene, I could probably pay the rent and the power bill if I didn't have to give all my money to the bootleggers!"

My mother glared at my father and after a moment stubbed out her cigarette. She stood and picked up one of the lit candles. "Chuck, you quit stayin' out all night, gamblin' away all your money at the Moose Club, and I'll stay at home too! But as long

17

as you go out, I'm goin' out!" She turned and walked to the bedroom. I followed.

Sitting on the bed, her arms crossed, my mother nervously tapped her foot. I sat down beside her. We heard the screen door slam, then the sound of my father's old Pontiac.

"Is Daddy leavin'?" I asked.

"Guess so, honey."

My mother got up, walked into the living room. She looked out the window.

A week later, sitting at the kitchen table doing my homework, I heard a car stop out front. Looking out the window, I saw Mr. Stuart and another man get out of Mr. Stuart's car. Running into the bedroom, I awakened my mother. "Mama, Mr. Stuart's outside, him and another man." We then heard a knock on the door.

I followed my mother to the front door and stood behind her. "Mr. Stuart," she said.

"Mrs. Bridges," said the landlord. He turned to the man beside him. "This here's Constable Evans." The Constable carried a small hammer and a sheet of printed paper.

"Chuck's not home," she said.

"I'm afraid it's too late for that, Mrs. Bridges. You just tell your husband that I came by."

"Too late?"

"Afraid so. You see, Constable Evans is here to serve you an eviction notice."

"Eviction notice!"

"Yes, ma'am!"

"I don't understand, Mr. Stuart. Chuck told me he paid you last Friday."

"No, ma'am. I ain't seen your husband in weeks, and I've given him plenty of chances to catch up on the rent. He ain't paid me in two months."

"Two months! But Chuck told me he paid you!"

"Mrs. Bridges, you'll have to take that up with your husband. All I know is he ain't paid a dime in two months. I don't like puttin' folks out, especially with young children, but your husband ain't left me no choice." Mr. Stuart stretched his hands wide, then shrugged his shoulders. He turned to the constable beside him and nodded his head.

"I see," said my mother, resigned.

The constable nailed an eviction notice onto the screen door's center brace. "You got twenty-four hours to vacate the premises," he said, turning to my mother. "By law, you can't remove this notice. I suggest you read it."

Mama shut the door, walked into the kitchen, and sat at the table. I followed.

"Mama, does that mean we gotta move?" I asked her.

"Yes, sweetheart," she said in a quiet voice. Tilting her head back, she exhaled smoke from her cigarette.

"Where we gonna move to?"

"I don't know, honey. I don't know," she said, her voice weary.

That evening when my father got home from work, he and my mother argued. I grabbed my marbles and headed for shantytown.

When I got home, it was dark. My mother was in the kitchen wrapping dishes in newspaper and putting them in cardboard boxes. Daddy was carrying the boxes out to the car.

I looked inside the old Pontiac. It was packed with boxes of pots and pans and dishes. On top, almost level with the windows, were clothes. When the back seat was full, my father loaded the trunk and I helped, the old Pontiac groaning with every armload we squeezed inside.

"Okay, that's it," said my father, forcing the trunk lid closed. Looking around, he saw a large bundle of clothes wrapped in a

sheet sitting on the front porch. "Shit," he said. "I thought we had everything."

My father picked up the large bundle of clothes and sat them on top of the car. When he opened the trunk, it popped open like a jack-in-the-box. My father forced the forgotten bundle inside but now couldn't get the lid closed. Frustrated, he climbed on top of the trunk and, using his body weight, forced it shut.

"Look, Daddy," I said, standing just behind him. "The sheet's hangin' out." A corner of the white bedsheet hung from the trunk, partially covering the left taillight.

"Well, it'll just have to hang out," said my father, "'cause I'll be damned if I'm gonna open that trunk again till I get where I'm goin'!"

My mother walked onto the porch. "That's it, Chuck. That's everything."

"Just one more thing," said my father, stepping onto the porch. He snatched the eviction notice off the screen door and ripped it in half, then he grabbed the screen door and jerked it back and forth, breaking the frame. "Now that's everything," he said.

"Chuck!" yelled my mother. "That's illegal! They'll put you in jail for that!"

"Gotta catch me first, and I plan on being near the Florida line by first light!"

"We're movin' to Florida!" I shouted with excitement.

My parents looked at each other, then my mother turned to me. "Honey, you're gonna have to stay at your pawpaw and granny's till we get settled," she said.

"Nooo, Mama!" I wailed. "I don't wanna stay with Pawpaw and Granny. I wanna go to Florida with you and Daddy!"

"I'm sorry, sweetheart. You gotta stay here. It won't be long, I promise."

"No, Mama, don't leave me here, please!" I cried.

"Damnit, Rickey! Shut up that cryin'. My nerves are already shot! I can't take much more!" My mother turned to my father. "Chuck, do something!"

"Boy," yelled my father, "you heard your mama! Now get in this car and stop that bawlin'!"

We drove three blocks to my grandparents' house. Daddy stayed in the car while my mother and I climbed the front porch. When my mother knocked on the door, the porch light came on and the front door opened.

My grandmother, dressed in a flannel nightgown, stood in the open door. "Irene, what in the world?"

"Mother, sorry to wake you up."

"What's wrong, Irene? It's almost 1:00 in the morning."

"I know, I'm sorry, but me and Chuck's movin' to Florida."

"Florida! In the middle of the night!" said my grandmother.

"Yes, Mama. See, we got evicted from our house. We gotta move."

"Lord, I declare. I knew something like this was gonna happen. Irene, it's all that drinkin' you and Chuck do, that's the problem. I ain't surprised you can't pay your bills."

"I know, Mama, you're right. I promise when me and Chuck get to Florida, we're both gonna quit drinkin'. I promise. We're gonna make a new start, but right now I need you and Daddy to do me a favor."

"Irene, if it's money you need, you know me and Elmer's livin' off Social Security. We ain't got no money to spare."

"No, it ain't money, Mama. We ain't got much, but I reckon we got enough to get us to Florida."

"What is it then, Irene?"

"We need you and Daddy to keep Rickey for us till we get settled."

A long silence followed. Finally, my grandmother said, "Irene, we can't keep that boy while you and Chuck go traipsin' off to God knows where."

"Florida, Mama. We're goin' to Florida."

"I'm sorry, Irene, me and Elmer's just too old to be chasin' after a young'un. We done raised our kids."

"But, Mama, we just need to leave Rickey with you for a couple weeks, that's all. Just till when we get settled, then we'll come get him, I promise. Just two weeks."

My grandfather, dressed in pajamas, appeared beside my grandmother. He placed his hand on her shoulder.

"What's goin' on, Dearie?" he asked.

"It's Irene, Elmer. Her and Chuck's moving to Florida and they want us to keep this here young'un."

"For just two weeks, Daddy. Just till we get settled," said my mother.

My grandparents looked at each other, and my grandfather nodded his head. My grandmother said, "Okay, Irene, we'll keep him—but for two weeks, that's all. But you gotta promise me that you and Chuck's gonna stop drinkin'!"

"We will, Mama, I promise."

"And, Irene, you gotta start payin' your bills. I mean, you already got one child livin' with Mrs. Bridges and another with your sister Bibby. You got to learn some responsibility."

"I will, Mama, I will. I promise." My mother hugged her parents. "Oh, thank you."

She bent down and hugged me. "Now, you be a good boy, you hear. Mind your pawpaw and granny."

"Yes, ma'am," I mumbled.

Holding a brown paper bag in my arms, I stood and watched my mother walk toward the old Pontiac.

My grandmother shouted, "Two weeks, Irene! Two weeks!" My mother didn't even break stride, she just lifted her hand and kept walking. Climbing into the Pontiac, she shut the door.

The old Pontiac, low to the ground, one hubcap missing, bounced up and down on worn-out shocks and moved down Gardner Street on threadbare tires. When it passed under a streetlight, the triangle-shaped corner of sheet hanging from the trunk seemed to wave goodbye.

Chapter 3

Carrying my paper bag, I followed my grandmother down a long, narrow hall to a door on the right. "This here used to be your aunt Dolly's room," she said. "You can sleep here, but don't make a mess and don't break nothin'." She looked at the bag I cradled. "That all you got?" I nodded my head. "Well, just go ahead and put your sack on the dresser. In the mornin' I'll find you some drawer space."

I looked around. There were two windows, both with venetian blinds and lace curtains, and the walls were covered in floral wallpaper. A large four-poster bed and two matching night tables with lamps took up most of the floor space. Neatly folded across the bottom of the bed were two patchwork quilts. A red cedar hope chest sat on the floor at the foot of the bed. Against one wall stood a dresser in dark wood, with a large oval mirror. Along another wall stood a tall chiffonier and next to it was a treadle sewing machine and a chair. I removed my shoes, turned out the light, and climbed onto the soft bed.

My grandmother's name was Dearie but her grandchildren called her Granny. Short and stout, she had faded blue eyes and steel-gray hair. During the day she always kept her hair braided and pinned up but took it down at night. I remember how surprised I was the first time I saw how long and beautiful it was. I had gone to her bedroom as she was preparing for bed and had surprised her at her dressing table, brushing her waist-length hair.

As a boy, I never had a conversation with my grandmother about her past, so all I knew about her I learned from my mother and from listening to the conversations of others.

24

Born and raised in the mountains of western North Carolina, not too far from Asheville, my grandmother, I was told, taught school barefoot, something I've always found hard to believe—not that she had been barefoot, but that she had taught school, because I never thought of her as "educated," although I suppose she could have been and I was just too young to realize it. I do remember, however, that she was a prolific letter writer and that her entire life she actively corresponded with all six of her daughters, including my mother.

My grandmother worked alongside my grandfather in the cotton mill for over thirty years, while giving birth to and caring for ten children. Not given to sentimentality or open displays of affection, she was kind but seldom smiled, and if she had a sense of humor, I never saw it.

She knew a lot about home remedies. For a bee sting or an insect bite, she dabbed the wounded area with tobacco juice. (My grandmother dipped snuff her entire life—a point of contention early in her marriage until one day my grandfather refused to allow it in the house and saw firsthand what life was like when his bride didn't have her snuff. Grudgingly, he learned to accept this one bad habit of hers.) For boils or "risins," as my grandmother called them, she applied a poultice of raw potato to draw out the poison. She once treated a wart on the base of my thumb by tying a piece of thread tightly around it, then telling me to leave it there for three days. And three days later, the wart came off with the string. My grandmother then told me to hide the string under a rock to prevent the wart returning. For most other ailments, she just gave a liberal dose of castor oil, which always made me gag.

There was no doubt in anyone's mind that my grandmother was in charge, although she often allowed my grandfather the illusion that he was. She had learned early in their marriage that

when dealing with a man as egocentric as her husband, it was sometimes wiser to appear to lose.

My grandfather's name was Elmer Sellinger Davis. He was born and raised in Cincinnati, Ohio, but during the Great Depression moved south looking for work. Eventually he found a job at the cotton mill in Shelby. It was there that he met my grandmother, who had also moved to Shelby seeking employment.

Called Pawpaw by his grandchildren, my grandfather was short, muscular, and handsome, with a strong nose and a wide mouth. He had thick, jet-black curly hair, with just a little gray at the temples. His eyes were green and shined with the intensity of either a madman or a prophet, and during his life he had been both. As a young man, he had been a brawler, a bit of a scoundrel, and, I suspect, a ladies' man. But a short time after moving to Shelby, he became a born-again Christian and eventually a deacon of the local Church of God.

Charismatic, my grandfather was a great storyteller. He once told me that his own mother had been Jewish and claimed that his father had been a direct descendant of Confederate president Jefferson Davis, but this I doubted even when young.

He was the only person, other than my mother, who took the time to talk to me about our family's history. I spent hours sitting on the floor at his feet, listening to him spin the same yarns over and over. But what I really enjoyed was watching him act out these stories.

Pawpaw flexed his bicep, then held up his fist. "Boy, you see this here?" he asked me.

"I see it, Pawpaw. I see it."

"Well, I'll tell you what. If I hit a man with this left and he don't fall, then I can understand it; he must be a purty stout fella." Then he held up his right fist. "But you see this one here?"

"I see it, Pawpaw."

"Well, if I hit him with this one and he don't fall, then I'm gonna walk around behind him and see what he's propped up against!"

My grandparents were total opposites, yet often complemented each other. My grandmother had her feet firmly on the ground, making all the practical decisions regarding their lives, while my grandfather had his head in the "clouds," free to contemplate loftier matters, such as how to get to heaven.

Breakfast the next morning was a feast for a skinny boy used to cold cereal or stolen candy on the best of mornings. I was astounded by the variety and amount of food my grandmother put on the table. Like a spectator at a tennis match, my eyes shifted back and forth as I watched her sprint from the kitchen to the dining table with a large platter of fried eggs, a bowl of steaming grits, fried fatback, fried livermush, homemade biscuits, butter, three kinds of jam, a pitcher of cold milk, a bowl of sugar, a pot of coffee, and a can of condensed milk. She then stood and considered the table like an artist at her easel. Satisfied, she wiped her hands on her apron, shouted, "Elmer, breakfast is ready!" I heard the toilet flush, then a few seconds later Pawpaw appeared in the doorway, resplendent in starched white shirt and black dress pants. His curly hair was neatly combed, his freshly shaved face smelled of aftershave. Standing, he studied the table like an art critic, then looked over at Granny and said, "Dearie, this looks fine, real fine." Granny glowed. She almost smiled.

"Come on, Dearie. Let's sit down and give thanks."

Granny at one end, Pawpaw at the other, and me in the middle, we bowed our heads as one.

"Lord," prayed Pawpaw, "we humbly thank you for another day and for this young man that has joined our table." I felt pride when I heard him mention me to God. "We thank you for this food we are about to receive and ask that it be nourishment to our bodies. In Jesus's name, amen."

"Boy, do you know what day it is?" asked my grandfather.

"Yes, Pawpaw," I said, "it's Saturday. I know 'cause I don't have to go to school."

"Well, tomorrow you'll be goin' to church with me and your granny. You live in my house, you go to church. Is that clear?"

"Yes, Pawpaw."

"Well, good. You have Sunday clothes?"

"No, just my school clothes."

"No church clothes. Hmmm."

"I ain't never been to church."

My grandfather raised his eyebrows, looked at my grandmother. "Never been to church. Well, we'll have to do something about that. After breakfast, I'll take you and your granny to town. She can outfit you."

The next morning, the three of us were a grand sight as we left for church. Pawpaw led the way in shoes shined to a high luster, his dark-blue suit perfectly pressed, his blindingly white shirt starched stiff, and his beautiful necktie knotted just right. In his right hand he carried a black leather zip-up Bible. Granny wore a blue satin dress imprinted with light-pink roses. On her head sat a dark-blue straw hat with half veil. A corsage was pinned over her heart. She wore patent leather pumps with two-inch heels.

I was dressed in a light-blue linen suit, a white shirt, and a dark-blue bow tie with white polka dots. I had a fresh haircut and my snow-white hair was slicked into place with Pawpaw's

Wildroot Cream-Oil. On my feet were new black-and-white oxfords.

I was amazed at how much the congregation loved my grandfather, as it seems God loves the reformed sinner more. They shook his hand, patted him on the back, called him Brother Davis.

"Well, Brother Davis," said a church member, "what a fine lookin' young man. Is that your grandson? I know he loves Jesus." He bent at the waist to look me in the eye. His breath smelled like peppermint. "Don't you love Jesus, son?" he asked.

Embarrassed and afraid I'd say the wrong thing, yet not wanting to admit that I didn't even know Jesus, therefore couldn't possibly love him, I lied. "Yes sir." That satisfied him. He moved on to the next group.

Then I recognized a familiar face—Mr. Stuart, our landlord from Trade Alley. He was standing with a group of men near the altar and didn't see me.

The women of the congregation, in all their finery, surged forward like peacocks to greet my grandmother. They called her Sister Davis. A large, effusive woman in a lavender dress fluttered forth. "Oh, Sister Davis, it's so good to see you. Don't you look pretty this mornin'." She then looked down at me. "Which one of your daughters is the mother of this fine lookin' young man?" When Granny told her that I was Irene's son, the lady's eyes narrowed slightly but her smile remained frozen in place. I heard a chill in her voice. "And how *is* Irene ... doin' these days?"

We sat in the front row near the altar and listened to the preacher warn us against adultery, drinking, and taking the Lord's name in vain. He told us that no one was perfect except Jesus and that we were all sinners and had fallen short of God's glory.

The preacher described in detail a burning inferno where all sinners would eventually go. He scared me. I was convinced I was going there, but then I felt comforted by the thought that I wouldn't be alone; my parents would be there too. For the first time, I saw and heard people speaking in tongues. My grandfather, sitting next to me, joined a chorus of others babbling in what sounded like Chinese and Arabic. One man left his seat and started spinning in circles, finally collapsing in front of the altar. There, on his back, he writhed, repeating the same unintelligible phrase over and over. The scene was as frightening to me as the horror movies I sometimes saw on Saturday mornings at the Webb Theatre in downtown Shelby.

I discovered that life with my grandparents was very different from life with my parents. My grandparents' lives were all about routine, structured and safe, whereas life with my parents had been spontaneous, haphazard, and sometimes dangerous.

Every other Saturday morning, my grandfather and I would climb into his shiny black Ford and drive to Mrs. Patrick's farm.
It always seemed as if we were on holiday. Pawpaw would sing gospel songs and I'd join in as we drove up and down hilly two-lane blacktops, the sun beaming through the windshield, warming my face, and a cool breeze blowing through the open window, making my hair stand straight up. Out the window, I'd watch trees zip by at what seemed a hundred miles an hour.
At Mrs. Patrick's farm, we would always buy two dozen brown eggs, carefully stacked in a brown paper bag (later, we often discovered that some had two yolks), two cakes of beautiful, dark-yellow butter, the tops molded with the design of lovebirds, and a gallon of pungent, rich, creamy buttermilk, the

top of the glass jar covered with wax paper and held in place with a wide red rubber band.

When we would return with our purchases, my grandmother would carefully examine every egg, trace the raised lovebirds on the cakes of butter with her forefinger, and remove the wax paper from the gallon jar of buttermilk so that she could smell it. She would then grace my grandfather with a Mona Lisa smile.

One Saturday my grandfather took me swimming at the Jumping Off Place. The Jumping Off Place was a rushing mountain stream high in the foothills, about ten miles outside Shelby. There, hidden in the woods, large granite boulders stood in a narrow stream, creating a series of small waterfalls. While I jumped off the rocks and swam, my grandfather, his old gray fedora tilted on his head, shirtsleeves rolled up, sat on a rock in the shade and read his small New Testament, looking up often to make sure I was safe.

After swimming, my grandfather took me to his "special place." To get there, we walked a little-used path that meandered through thick woods until we came to a clearing twenty feet square. In the center of the clearing stood a mound of rocks four feet high. Most were softball-sized but some were much larger, especially those at the base.

"What's that, Pawpaw?" I asked.

"It's an altar, son, a special place to pray. It's been here for years but only a few people know about it.

"Now, son, this is what I want you to do. I want you to find a nice-sized rock, one that suits you."

I walked around the edge of the clearing and searched until I found a rock the shape and size of a pine cone. I took it back to show my grandfather. "How's this one?" I asked.

"It's just fine," he said, "just fine." I watched my grandfather reverently approach the altar, then go to his knees. He looked over his shoulder at me. "Come on over here, son, next to me."

Still holding my rock, I got down on my knees next to my grandfather.

"Now, son, here's what we're gonna do. We're gonna pray and ask the Lord to deliver us from our sins."

"I don't know what to say, Pawpaw."

"It'll come to you. Don't worry about it, just speak from the heart. You don't have to speak out loud. The Lord can hear you just fine; he knows what's in your heart. Just ask the Lord for forgiveness. Ask him for guidance. Now, let's bow our heads."

I couldn't resist squinting my eyes and turning my head slightly so that I could look at my grandfather. He was silent but I could see his lips were moving, his brow furrowed in concentration. I turned back, closed my eyes tightly, and spoke to Jesus. But I didn't ask for forgiveness or guidance. Instead, I secretly asked, "Lord, please take care of Mama and Daddy down there in Florida, especially Mama. Daddy can take care of himself purty good, but Mama needs special help. Lord, make her feel happy instead of sad all the time. And, Lord, help them both to stop drinkin' and fightin' all the time. Lord, make them come and get me and take me back to Florida and give us a nice house to live in, a place where nobody can make us leave. I guess that's all. Amen."

I opened my eyes to see my grandfather smiling down at me.

"Did you ask for forgiveness, son?"

"Yeah, Pawpaw, just like you told me to," I lied.

We stacked our rocks on the altar and left.

My parents didn't return in two weeks as promised. And as the weeks turned to months, even my grandmother, in her way, began to show me affection. But my world revolved around my grandfather. I had never had anyone treat me so kindly, and wherever he went, I was his shadow. He didn't seem to mind the adoration.

One day I was sitting on the front porch steps, watching the traffic on Gardner Street, when a skinny golden-brown dog walked to the edge of the yard. The dog stopped and stared at me.

I got up and walked toward the dog, but when I got within three feet, it turned and loped away. I walked into the house and filled one of Granny's pie pans with water, then found two biscuits left over from breakfast.

When I got back outside, the dog was standing in the yard again.

Patiently, using the water and biscuits as bait and speaking softly, I coaxed the dog closer. It slowly inched up to the pie pan, all the while watching me carefully, then lowered its snout and greedily lapped at the water. The dog sniffed at the biscuit and cautiously ate it.

After the dog had eaten the last bite, I said, "Look, I have another one." I held up the biscuit for the dog to see. "Come on. Come get it. I ain't gonna hurt you."

The dog took cautious steps, stopped, then stretched its neck, quickly taking the biscuit from my hand. I reached up and scratched the dog under the neck. The dog stopped eating, stepped back.

"Come on, I ain't gonna hurt you."

The dog moved toward me again and allowed me to rub its head while it ate the rest of the biscuit. Then a floodgate opened.

The dog leaned into me, whimpered, then happily licked my hands and face.

"Whoa! Whoa there!" I laughed. "Looks like to me you was as hungry for some lovin' as you was for them biscuits!"

At that moment my grandfather drove up and parked. When he slammed the car door, the dog disengaged and ran to the middle of the yard.

"You feed that dog, you'll never get rid of it," he said. Then he saw the pie pan. "Your granny catches you with one of her pie pans, she'll take a switch to you."

"I'll take it back inside, Pawpaw. Can I keep him?" I begged. "He's starvin'."

"You'll have to ask your granny. And that dog ain't a *he*, it's a *she*. And I doubt your granny's gonna want a dog in the house."

"I ain't gotta keep him—her—in the house. I can fix up a place in the coal shed. Please!"

"I told you, you gotta ask your granny, and you better get that pie pan back inside 'fore she gets home or you'll be livin' in the coal shed yourself."

After much pleading, my grandmother reluctantly agreed to let me keep the dog, with the following provisions: That I never bring the dog inside the house and that the dog never create any problems in the neighborhood.

I named the dog Lady. And after finding some cardboard, a couple burlap sacks, and begging an old blanket from my grandmother, I made her a comfortable place in a corner of the coal shed, shutting the door at night so that she couldn't get out.

Lady and I were inseparable except when I went to school. And even then she waited for me in the woods nearby until school let out.

34

One Sunday, we came home from church to find Lady and a male dog mating in the front yard. My grandmother was furious. "Elmer! Do something!" She rushed into the house. The dogs were stuck together back-to-back and neither seemed able to break loose. I didn't understand what was happening, thought they were fighting, and so grabbed Lady and tried to pull her loose. Meanwhile my grandfather rushed to the side of the house, grabbed the water hose, and turned it on full force. He brought the hose to the front yard and sprayed the dogs until they separated. The male dog ran down Gardner Street. Lady stood wet and trembling. I ran and hugged her, then checked to see if she was hurt.

That evening at supper, my grandfather told me, "Son, we need to talk about that dog of yours."

"She's okay, Pawpaw. I checked her all over. She ain't hurt."

"That's not what I mean," he said. "She's not okay."

"Why, Pawpaw? What's wrong?"

"Son, your granny allowed you to keep that dog long as it didn't cause no problems. Now we got a problem."

"Lady wasn't no problem, Pawpaw. She was in her own yard. That other dog was trying to fight her."

"They wasn't fightin', son," said Pawpaw. "They was matin'—makin' puppies."

"Puppies, Pawpaw! I wouldn't mind some puppies. I could take care of 'em."

"Well, maybe you wouldn't mind, but me and your granny would. We got enough to take care of without a passel of puppies too. I'm afraid we're gonna have to get rid of that dog of yours, take her out to the country and turn her loose."

My heart sank. I couldn't believe what I had just heard. "Turn her loose! But, Pawpaw, I don't want to turn her loose! Who's gonna take care of her?"

"Son, it's the best thing for everybody."

35

"It ain't the best thing for Lady!" I whined. "She's gonna be all by herself. She needs me to take care of her! Please, Pawpaw! Please!" I cried.

"Now you stop that cryin', you hear!"

"But, Pawpaw ... ," I wailed.

"Stop, you hear! Stop right this minute!"

That night, after my grandparents had gone to bed, I sneaked out to the coal shed. When I opened the door, Lady's eyes shone up at me like twin moons. She ran to me, stood on her hind legs, and pawed my chest. She whimpered and I wrapped my arms around her.

"Pawpaw said he's gonna take you out to the country and turn you loose. He said it's 'cause you're gonna have puppies and that we can't take care of 'em. But I could. I know I could. But they won't let me. Oh, Lady, I don't want you to go, but they say it's best. Now you ain't gonna have no place to live either—not really, not a place of your own. I wish it was just me and you and the puppies and we had our own house."

The next morning at breakfast my grandparents didn't mention Lady, and I allowed myself to believe that they had either forgotten or had changed their minds. But after lunch my grandfather said, "Go get that dog of yours and put her in the car."

"Nooo, Pawpaw!" I wailed. "Please don't take Lady to the country!" I refused to go get her. Pawpaw grabbed a length of rope and went to the coal shed. A few minutes later he returned, dragging Lady, the rope around her neck choking her.

"Pawpaw, stop! You're chokin' her! Let me, Pawpaw. I'll put her in the car."

He handed me the rope and I removed it from Lady's neck. Picking her up, I carried her to the car and put her in the back seat. When I climbed in with her, her shaking and whimpering

36

made me sick to my stomach. As we rode, I tried to comfort her.

We drove the same highway that led to Mrs. Patrick's farm, and the day was like all the others; the sun shone just as brightly and the breeze just as refreshing, except there were no songs of joy, no glad hearts, no smiles, no laughter, and only a deep sadness, accompanied by the sound of tires on the asphalt and the whimpering of Lady, as if she knew her fate.

Right before we got to Mrs. Patrick's farm, my grandfather drove onto a dirt road. "This oughta be far enough," he said. "We'll put her out here."

He pulled over and stopped the car.

"No, Pawpaw, please!" I cried. "Let's take Lady back! Not here, Pawpaw! She won't get stuck to no more dogs, I promise!"

"Now, son, we agreed this was the best thing to do."

"I didn't agree, Pawpaw! I didn't agree!"

"Look, son, some nice family will find her and take her in. Now, let's put her out."

I wrapped both arms around Lady. "No, Pawpaw! Please don't leave Lady here! Just take her back home! I promise I won't ask for nothin' else! Please! I promise!"

Pawpaw finally lost his patience. "Boy, I'm tired of your foolishness! You let go of that dog or I'm gonna take my belt to you!"

He got out of the car, jerked the rear door open, reached in, and forced my arms from around Lady. He grabbed the dog by the scruff of her neck and pulled. Lady dug in. Her hind legs skidded on the vinyl seat. She yelped, then snapped at my grandfather. He jerked his hand back.

"I'll get her out! I'll do it, Pawpaw!" I yelled, tears running down my cheeks.

I picked up Lady, slid across the seat, and got out, putting her down beside a ditch that ran alongside the dirt road.

"Get back in the car," said my grandfather. I climbed onto the back seat and Lady tried to climb in behind me. My grandfather blocked her with his foot, then slammed the door shut. He rushed around to the driver's side, opened the door, and got in. He started the engine, put the car in gear, and slammed down on the accelerator, kicking up dirt and gravel.

I stood on the back seat, head pressed against the rear window, tears blurring my vision, and saw Lady chase the car through a cloud of dust. *Run! Run!* I silently cheered, hoping she'd be able to keep up with the car and follow us home, but when my grandfather shifted into third gear, Lady grew smaller and smaller until she vanished completely.

I curled up on the back seat and cried.

Chapter 4

A couple weeks later, while sitting in the chinaberry tree in the front yard, I watched as a white Chevrolet pulled into the driveway. The passenger door opened, and my mother got out. She was wearing shorts and sandals and had a deep tan. Her hair had been permed. I climbed from the tree and ran to her. She hugged me, then kissed the top of my head.

"You been a good boy?" she asked.

Before I could answer, she turned to my grandparents, who had just stepped onto the porch. My grandmother reached into her apron pocket, removed a lace handkerchief, and delicately wiped tobacco juice from the corner of her mouth.

"What happened to two weeks, Irene?" she asked.

"Mother, I tried. I really did. It just took us longer to get settled than I figured."

"Humph. You shoulda called, Irene. It's been six months."

"I know, Mother. I know."

My father got out of the car carrying a suitcase and a bag of oranges.

Later, my parents and grandparents sat at the dining room table, drinking coffee. I stood beside my mother's chair and listened to her tell my grandmother, "That's right, Mama, me and Chuck quit drinkin'. Chuck's got a real good job. He's workin' as a mechanic at a big garage and we got a nice place to live."

Every time I tried to get my mother's attention, she pushed me away. Finally, she said, "Honey, why don't you go outside and play. Me and you can talk later. Right now, Mama's tryin' to talk to your granny."

My feelings hurt, I walked outside and climbed the chinaberry tree. A short time later, hidden from sight, I watched my father leave the house and walk to the car. He opened the door, bent down, reached under the seat, and pulled out a pint of vodka. He looked around, then unscrewed the cap and tipped the bottle back.

I climbed down and walked up behind him. "Mama told Granny you and her quit drinkin'," I said.

Startled, he jumped. "Boy, don't walk up on me like that! And you better learn to mind your own business! Ain't no harm in a little drink! Helps me put up with your pawpaw's preachin'!"

"But Mama said …"

"Boy, I know what your mama said! She says a lot of things, but that don't make 'em so! Damn, if you ain't gettin' as bad as your pawpaw. One preacher in the family's all I can stand. You just keep your trap shut or you'll wish you had."

Early the next morning we left, and as soon as we crossed the state line into South Carolina we stopped for gas. I accompanied my mother to a restaurant next door. There she bought me a sausage and egg biscuit.

While the attendant filled the car with gas, my father went inside a store next to the service station. When we got back, my father was sitting behind the wheel. On the seat next to him was a paper bag.

"Irene, reach in that bag and open us a beer."

Mama searched through the glove compartment until she found a beer opener. She opened a beer for my father, then one for herself.

"Mama," I said.

"Yes, sweetheart," she said, blowing out a cloud of cigarette smoke, then taking a sip of her beer.

"You told Granny you wasn't drinkin' no more."

"Honey, it's just a beer."

"But I heard you! You said … "

"Rickey! Just shut up!" she interrupted. "You just sit there, eat your sandwich, and shut up!"

"Boy" shouted my father over his shoulder, "I'm about up to here with your shit! Your pawpaw done ruint you with all that religious crap! Me and your mama's gonna drink a beer when we get good and goddamn ready and we ain't gotta answer to nobody! You hear!"

"But that's not what Mama told … "

Before I could finish, my father twisted around, reached over the seat, and slapped the sandwich out of my hand. It landed on the floorboard at my feet. The car swerved onto the shoulder, but my father quickly muscled it back onto the highway.

"Chuck!" shouted my mother. "Watch it! You're gonna kill us all!"

"Irene, I'm tired of that boy's shit!"

When we reached Georgia, we stopped for gas again and another six-pack. As soon as we got back onto the road, my mother opened two beers. When she handed my father his, she said, "Chuck, I saw the way you looked at that woman back there. I ain't blind."

"Irene, you're crazy as hell. I was just gettin' change for cigarettes!"

"You bastard! You was tryin' to get more than change!"

My parents drank and smoked and argued all the way across the state of Georgia. By the time we reached Jacksonville, Florida, my mother had passed out, her head wedged between the window and the front seat. It was quiet now, the only sound the rhythmic drone of the tires on the blacktop, and I too drifted off to sleep.

Several hours later, sensing that we were no longer moving, I opened my eyes, sat up, and looked out the window. The sky was just beginning to lighten. In stark relief against the red sky of morning, I saw in the distance a row of what I would later learn were royal palms. The thick, straight tree trunks looked as if they had been made of concrete. Then I saw my new home; it was a long beige stucco building with a monotonous row of blue windows and doors.

I opened the car door and stepped onto sand and crushed oyster shells. Here and there were a few stubborn patches of wiry grass.

"Daddy, look at those trees," I said, pointing at the royal palms.

"This is Miami. They're all over down here. Go wake up your mama, tell her we're home. I gotta get ready for work."

After awakening my mother, I followed her inside a small apartment that looked a lot like our old duplex in Trade Alley. It had one bedroom, a living room, a small kitchen, and a bathroom.

"Mama, where am I gonna sleep?" I asked.

"On the daybed in the livin' room. It folds down to make a bed," she said.

"But I had my own room at Pawpaw and Granny's."

"Well, you ain't at Pawpaw and Granny's now, are you! Rickey, don't start on me! I'm tired! Now, just stop your whinin' and go get on that daybed."

My mother walked into the bedroom and shut the door.

I sat down on a burnt-orange daybed covered with a frayed white bedspread. On the floor in front of the daybed was an oval multicolored braided rug, tattered around the edges and water stained. Sitting on the rug was a dark-brown coffee-table with cigarette burns on top. Climbing one of the legs of the coffee-table was the biggest cockroach I'd ever seen. It was at least an

inch and a half in length. My father, now wearing his mechanic's uniform, walked into the living room carrying a cup of coffee and smoking a cigarette. "Where's your mama?" he asked.

"She went to bed," I said. "Look, Daddy, look at that giant bug."

"That's a palmetto bug. They won't hurt you."

He walked over and brushed the bug from the coffee-table with the side of his hand. It landed upside down, righted itself, then ran for freedom. My father walked over and stomped it with his heavy work boot.

After my father left for work, I lay down on the daybed, covered myself with the bedspread, and stared at the dead palmetto bug on the floor a few feet away. Greenish-yellow guts squished out the sides of the bug's hard dark-brown body, reminding me of lemon pie filling. Then, miraculously, one of the giant bug's antennae moved back and forth. It gathered its mangled legs under its smashed body and slowly dragged itself across the floor, leaving behind a trail of body fluids. Finally, the bug disappeared through a crack in the baseboard.

A couple days later, I walked four blocks to my new school. There I gave the teacher a note from my mother stating that we had just moved to Miami from North Carolina and asking that I be enrolled in the fourth grade.

I didn't like being the new kid in school and the center of attention. When the teacher asked me to stand, introduce myself, and tell the class where I was from, I mumbled my name and told them I was from Shelby, North Carolina. A couple kids in the back of the class snickered. I heard them mimic my accent when I sat down, saw them giggling behind their hand-covered mouths.

When I got home after school, my mother was at the stove stirring a large pot with a spoon. "Chili," she said without my

asking. On the table was a can of beer and a lit cigarette in an ashtray. She turned. "How did you like your first day of school?"

"The teacher was nice, but some of the kids made fun of how I talk. They called me a hillbilly."

"They'll get used to you. Just takes time."

Later, during supper, my father bragged to my mother about a set of tools he had stolen from the garage where he worked.

"Chuck, they find out you're stealin', they'll fire you," warned my mother.

"Irene, that's a big garage, probably the biggest in Miami. They ain't gonna miss one set of wrenches. Besides, hard as I work, they owe me somethin' extra."

"That still don't make it right."

"I'll tell you what's right, Irene! What puts food on this table! That's what's right!"

I soon became friends with a Cuban American boy who lived in the apartment next to ours. His name was Carlos and he was two years older than me. Every Sunday Carlos sold newspapers in downtown Miami, and he asked if I wanted to work with him. Always eager to make money, I agreed. Carlos told me that the *Miami Herald* paid him a few pennies for every Sunday newspaper that he sold but that he made most of his money from tips.

The next Sunday I dressed in my best school clothes and went with Carlos to downtown Miami. There he gave me a stack of newspapers, then led me to a busy intersection. "Now, all you gotta do," said Carlos, "is stand right here on this median under the stoplight and hold up a newspaper. When the cars stop for the light, if they want a paper, they'll call you over. When they pay you, most times they'll give you a tip. Then at the end of the day you pay me for every paper you sell and you keep the tips."

I worked all day and only made a dollar and a half. When I complained to Carlos, he told me, "Look, if you wanna hustle in Miami, you gotta find a gimmick."

"A gimmick?" I asked

"Yeah, a gimmick. You wanna sell more newspapers and get more tips, you gotta dress in old, ragged clothes, and when someone buys a paper, you gotta take your time makin' change. Let the red light turn to green. And with all them cars honkin' their horns, most of the time the driver will just drive off and leave you with all the change."

The next Sunday I dressed in old jeans with holes in the knees and a shirt with a torn collar and two buttons missing. I took my time making change and earned almost $5 in tips.

The first couple months in Miami all seemed to go well, then an old pattern repeated itself. My father began to stay out most nights drinking and gambling and my mother began to hang out at the bars. And every time my father came home and found her gone, he would leave to find her. But Miami wasn't like Shelby; there were hundreds of bars and nightclubs. So more often than not, my father would come home alone, drunk himself.

Somehow my mother always found her way home. Usually, after a couple days, I'd come home from school and find her on the daybed or in her bed, unkempt and passed out, more often than not suffering a black eye or swollen lip.

When my father got home, they'd fight.

One day after school I came home to find the apartment dark and quiet. My mother had been gone for three days and my father had been out every night looking for her.

When I walked into my parents' bedroom, the blinds and curtains had been drawn, but there was still enough light for me to see that someone was in the bed asleep. I smelled whiskey, stale cigarettes, and something I didn't recognize. An old clock

radio on the dresser was turned low. A country singer crooned about lost love. On the nightstand beside the bed was an overturned whiskey bottle and a blue plastic tumbler. Next to the tumbler was an ashtray overflowing with cigarette butts.

I walked closer to the bed, stopped, and stared. My mother was covered with a sheet wet with dark stains.

"Mama," I said.

She didn't respond, so I moved closer, touched her on the shoulder. I shook her gently.

"Mama, wake up."

She still didn't move. I shook her harder, and her head flopped side to side.

"Wake up, Mama! Wake up!"

I stepped back. My feet seemed stuck to the floor. I looked down. I was standing in a baseball-sized pool of blood. Next to the blood was a razor blade. I bent down and touched the small puddle. It was cold and sticky. Holding my finger to my nose, I smelled it, then wiped my finger on my jeans.

Slowly I backed from the room, unable to take my eyes off my mother's blood-soaked body. At the door I turned and ran from our apartment.

I banged on Carlos's door. His mother answered.

Two days later, my father put me on a Greyhound bus to Shelby. My grandfather met me at the bus station.

For the second time that year, I enrolled in the same elementary school in Shelby. There no one made fun of my hillbilly accent because I sounded like everyone else, and I wasn't the new kid in school—I was the interesting kid. I had been to, and had successfully returned from, a faraway and exciting land and had interacted with other cultures. The kids at Shelby Elementary stood on the playground open-mouthed when I told them about living in exotic and exciting Miami.

46

Of course, I didn't tell them about the real Miami that I kept hidden—the Miami not of dreams but of nightmares, the Miami forever embedded in my psyche, where it would fester like an open wound and influence my thoughts and actions for years.

The Miami experience cost me greatly. For whatever small measure of sophistication I gained, I lost twice as much in innocence. Now I got into fights at school and often came home with a black eye or bloody nose, my clothes torn.

My grandfather secretly liked that I fought at school. When we were alone, he would ask for the details of every encounter, but my grandmother didn't like it at all; she was tired of repairing my torn clothes.

One day I came home from school with all the buttons ripped from my shirt, and my grandmother was furious. That evening she sewed large rhinestone-studded buttons onto my shirt—buttons salvaged from an old dress—and made me wear it to school the next day. All that morning I suffered giggles and stares, and during recess I ripped the buttons off myself.

Four months later my parents showed up, and what a surprise—my two sisters were with them. When my mother reached to hug me, I couldn't stop my eyes travelling to the ugly scars on her wrists.

Chapter 5

Summer 1959

While I was in Shelby, my mother was in a psychiatric hospital in Florida. When she got out, the five of us moved into a ramshackle frame house on Sullivan's Island, a small coastal community near Charleston, South Carolina. There my father went to work for a contractor building new homes on the adjacent island of Isle of Palms.

Unlike Trade Alley or Miami, Sullivan's Island was isolated. There were no bars, nightclubs, liquor stores, or bootleggers within walking distance, and my mother didn't drive. What Sullivan's Island did have was an abundance of fresh air and sunshine, making it the perfect place for my mother to heal after her second suicide attempt and for me to experience a happy childhood for the first time. And having my sisters Dianne, now thirteen, and Tonda, five, gave me hope that we would now have a normal family.

In the short time that we lived there, I developed a love for the ocean that would stay with me my entire life. I liked the smell of suntan oil, seaweed, and decaying marine life. I loved the sound of roaring breakers and screeching seagulls and the days when the sun was so hot it burned the soles of my feet. I found the fierce thunderheads that turned a midday sky black, exciting, and marveled at the neat holes, like buckshot, left in the sand by a pelting wind and rain. I spent every day of that summer fishing, crabbing, swimming, and exploring the island's old forts.

My mother loved it too. She walked the shoreline early in the mornings and evenings, and often I'd go with her. But she didn't love the water itself. Since early childhood, she had developed an irrational fear of drowning and wouldn't even walk in the surf.

Sullivan's Island was perfect for my father too. He now had my mother safely tucked away on an isolated island while he was free to come and go as he pleased. And he did. More and more often, my father drove across the Ashley River Bridge to Charleston to drink and gamble after work. My mother complained, and they argued. To try to appease her, my father brought home whiskey and beer, but that only made the situation worse and they argued and fought even more.

Once again my father didn't pay his debts. The electricity was disconnected and another eviction notice tacked to the door. We packed in the middle of the night and fled to the next island, Isle of Palms. There the five of us moved to an unfinished house that my father had been helping to build near the ocean.

Approaching the house, my father turned off the headlights and like a thief pulled the car around to the back of the house to hide it from view while we unpacked only what we needed for the night. The foundation, floors, framework, and roof were completed, but the house didn't yet have solid walls. By the light of the moon, I could look through the framework and see the ocean a hundred yards away.

The entire experience was tense. We were all aware that the police could arrive at any moment and arrest the entire family for trespassing. Like refugees, we huddled with our possessions in what would be a living room and ate potted meat and mayonnaise sandwiches by flashlight. Afterward, Dianne swept the floor free of sawdust and we spread blankets and retired for the night.

We awakened before dawn so that we could pack and leave before my father's boss and fellow workmen arrived. While my father and I finished packing the car, my mother and sisters walked to a nearby store where they bought coffee and a newspaper. While my father worked that day, my mother read

the classified ads, looking for a cheap apartment in Charleston. My sisters and I played on the beach one last time.

That evening my sisters and I sat atop a mountain of pots and pans and clothes in the back seat while my father drove and my mother called out directions.

The apartment wasn't hard to find. It was on the second floor, above a jewelry store on King Street in downtown Charleston. While we all stayed in the car, my father walked inside the jewelry store to talk to our new landlord.

It took numerous trips to get the several cardboard boxes filled with pots, pans, and dishes and the bulky bundles of clothes wrapped in bedsheets up the steep stairs.

At the top of the stairs was a long, narrow hallway. The left side of the hallway had three large windows that afforded a view of the brick wall of the adjacent building. The right side of the hallway had five doors; each was the entrance to a very small apartment. At the far end of the hall were two doors. One led to a communal bathroom and the other to a tar and gravel roof.

Our apartment was the third door down. It had a long, narrow entranceway that served as a kitchen and dining area. The kitchen had a long counter against one wall, with cabinets above. On the counter was a two-burner hot plate. Sitting on the floor, under the counter, was a small refrigerator. Next to the refrigerator were a small table and two chairs.

The kitchen opened into the only other room, a bedroom. A large bed took up most of the floor space. Next to the bed was a floor-to-ceiling bay window with a window seat that looked out onto busy King Street.

The only other furniture was a large bureau. It had four drawers, with most of the pulls missing. Next to the bureau was a shallow closet with a thin orange curtain for a door.

My parents slept on the large bed, and my sisters and I slept on pallets on the floor.

The apartment had electricity but no running water. Whenever my mother cooked on the hot plate, my sister Dianne and I washed and dried the dishes, which required carrying two large pans down the hall to the bathroom and filling them from the bathtub faucet. We then carried them back to our apartment, and no matter how careful I tried to be, I always left a trail of water in the hall.

While Dianne used one pan of water to wash the dishes, I rinsed them in the other, then dried them. Afterword, we carried the pans back down the hall and emptied them in the bathtub.

It was all too much for Dianne, who had grown accustomed to much better living conditions. Shortly after moving to the cramped apartment, she called Mama Bridges, who arranged bus fare for her back to Shelby.

Initially, when I passed other tenants in the hall, I politely acknowledged them with a nod or a simple "hello," but when most ignored me and walked past, their heads down as if embarrassed by their squalid lives, I started doing the same.

One day, I passed a man and a woman in the hall. Both appeared to be in their mid-forties. The woman was toothless and wore a loose, wrinkled dress with white socks and tennis shoes. Wisps of stringy blond hair stuck out of a blue kerchief tied around her head. The man wore gray pants with an old suit coat over a denim shirt. On his head was a red sweat-stained baseball cap pulled low, forcing his ears parallel to the floor. Both their faces were heavily creased and bronzed from working outside. *What a shame,* I thought. *Just look at those poor people.* I walked on down the hall to the bathroom. There, after using the toilet, I stood and stared at myself in the mirror over the sink. My wrinkled plaid shirt had three white buttons and one blue. I

51

needed a haircut. I looked down at my jeans; they had holes in the knees and were dirty. My shoes were scuffed and overrun. I suddenly and sadly realized that I looked as if I could have been the son of the people I had just pitied. It was a depressing thought.

My backyard was a tar and gravel roof. From there, all I could see were the sides and backs of several businesses and a small patch of bare ground where a scraggy tree had taken root. It had grown to a height of about twenty feet. Near the back door of the jewelry store, I found a rope about ten feet long. Tying it to the tree's thickest limb, I made myself a swing from the roof to the ground.

I enrolled in Memminger Elementary, an inner-city school about ten blocks from our apartment. The school, surrounded by a six-foot concrete wall, was in a tough neighborhood, directly across the street from a large housing project.

At my new school I made friends with a boy my age, nicknamed Poochie. Poochie told me that he had a job after school selling peanuts for an old lady who had a junk shop on King Street near Charleston Harbor. Eager to make money, I asked Poochie to help me get a job there too and he agreed.

After school I accompanied Poochie to the junk shop, located in an old dilapidated building next to an antique shop. When we entered, a bell over the door announced our arrival. It was a large room filled floor to ceiling with curios, paintings, frames, candlesticks, tables, chairs, a wrought iron bed frame, dishware, electrical appliances, garden tools, and numerous unidentifiable objects. A long, glass-topped counter, trimmed in dark wood, ran the length of the back of the shop.

Suddenly, from behind the counter, a door opened and steam billowed out along with a tall, thin, stooped woman with long, frizzy, white hair.

"That's Mama Demarest," said Poochie, nudging my arm. "She's the peanut lady."

"Looks like a witch to me!" I whispered back.

"She is," laughed Poochie, "but she's a good witch."

Poochie introduced me to Mama Demarest and told her that I wanted a job. She looked at me through small glasses with wire-rimmed frames.

"Rickey, is it?"

"Yes, ma'am," I said.

"Well, I might be able to give you a job. Step over here in the light and let me get a good look at you."

I moved to the counter.

"Now, Rickey, did Poochie tell you the rules?"

"No, ma'am."

"Polite, I like that," she said. "All my boys gotta follow the rules. They don't follow the rules, they can't work for me."

Mama Demarest told me that I was expected to sell her peanuts for twenty cents a bag and that for every bag I sold, I got to keep seven cents, giving her thirteen. She then told me that she would give me twenty bags of peanuts to sell and that if I sold all twenty, I'd make $1.40.

"Rickey, do you know what 'responsibility' means?" asked Mama Demarest.

"No, ma'am, but I can learn."

"That's a good answer. I 'spect you will. Well, 'responsibility' means takin' care of your business like a man's supposed to. It means always doing the right thing. It means always payin' your bills on time and never, never takin' nothin' you don't rightfully earn, never takin' nothin' that don't rightfully belong to you. You understand?"

53

"Yes, ma'am."

Mama Demarest wiped a stray hair from her face with a blue-veined hand, then turned and opened the door behind the counter. A cloud of steam and the smell of roasted peanuts escaped, teasing my appetite. When the peanut lady returned, she carried two woven picnic baskets with sturdy handles. Inside the baskets were neatly stacked small brown paper bags.

"Now, boys, you each have twenty bags—ten boiled and ten parched. Remember, I close up at 7:00, so if I'm gone when you finish for the day, come in tomorrow and we'll settle up."

Excited, I followed Poochie to the Battery, an old Civil War artillery emplacement, now a memorial and park in Charleston Harbor, overlooking Fort Sumter. There we split up.

I sat on a park bench and examined the contents of my basket. The tops of the paper bags were rolled and stapled but it was easy to distinguish the parched from the boiled; the boiled were much heavier and the bottoms slightly damp. The peanuts smelled so good that I wanted to eat a bag of each immediately, but the word "responsibility" sounded in my mind, so I decided to wait until I had sold several bags.

Being shy, I only sold six bags, which barely covered the cost of the two I ate. I returned to Mama Demarest's shop around 6:30 with twelve unsold bags.

The second day I was more aggressive and hawked, "Peanuts! Get your fresh peanuts!" I sold fourteen bags but still only made seventy-two cents because once again I ate two bags.

A few days later, I discovered a group of large office buildings not far from the Battery and walked inside the lobby of one of the buildings. Riding the elevator to the top floor, I worked my way to the bottom, calling on secretaries and receptionists at their desks. It was surprising to discover how eager the office workers were to relieve their monotony by enjoying an afternoon snack. By the time that I reached the

lobby, I had sold out. Rushing back to the junk shop, I refilled my basket.

Within a month, I was selling thirty to forty bags a day, making $2 or $3, and now had money to buy new clothes, go swimming at the YMCA, and buy lunch at school.

One weekend I worked until dark both Saturday and Sunday, determined not to stop until I had sold forty bags both days. That Sunday evening when I got back to the shop it was closed, so I continued up King Street until I reached our apartment.

When I walked in, my mother was sitting in the window seat looking out onto King Street. My younger sister was asleep on a pallet of blankets on the floor. My father wasn't home yet.

I emptied my pockets of over $10 in change, putting the money in the top drawer of the bureau. After grabbing a towel, washcloth, and soap, I walked to the bathroom at the end of the hall.

When I returned, my mother was gone. I walked back down the hall and onto the roof, but there was no sign of her. Tired, I made a pallet on the floor next to my sister and, listening to the faint sound of traffic on King Street, drifted off to sleep.

A couple hours later, my father awakened me.

"Where's your mama?" he asked.

"Daddy, I don't know. She was here when I got home, but when I came back from takin' a bath, she was gone."

My father, furious, left without another word.

The next morning when I searched through the bureau, I discovered my peanut money missing and realized that my mother must have taken it while I was bathing.

All day at school I worried about the missing peanut money and hurried home that afternoon, hoping to find that my mother had returned, along with the missing money. Walking into the empty apartment, I again searched the bureau drawers, praying

that I had missed the money during my search that morning, but found nothing.

While my little sister sat at the small table in the kitchen with crayons and a coloring book, I sat in the window seat and stared out at the people and traffic below, thinking, *Maybe if I just go to Mama Demarest and tell her what happened, she'll understand. But I can't do that. I can't tell her that my mother stoled my peanut money to go drinkin'. Maybe I could tell her I lost it. I did kinda lose it. No, she said I got to be responsible.*

I couldn't decide what to do, so I did nothing.

When my father came home from work, he stood at the entrance to the bedroom, his hands on his hips, looking tired and disgusted. Removing his glass eye, he slowly cleaned it with a dingy handkerchief, then said, "How come you ain't out sellin' peanuts?" When I told him about the missing money, he exploded, "Damn that woman! Damn her!" He turned and left.

I rushed to the bay window and watched him get into his car and drive off.

I walked out onto the roof and my sister followed me. While she played in an old cardboard box, I sat and tried to find the courage to face Mama Demarest but couldn't. The shame was just too great and the word "responsibility" again sounded loudly in my head.

Two days later, while sitting in the window seat watching the traffic on King Street, I heard a loud knock on the door and cringed, fearing it was the landlord looking for my father again. Instead, it was a tall, heavyset Black man with the stub of a fat unlit cigar clenched between his teeth. Beside him, swaying, was my mother, her eyes barely open.

"Boy, this your mother?" he asked in a quiet voice.

Embarrassed, I nodded my head.

56

"I drive a yella cab. This man paid me to drive her to this address, said this was where she lived. You want me to help you get her inside?"

"No, no, I can do it."

I wrapped my arms around my mother's waist, then slowly guided her through the narrow kitchen and into the bedroom.

A couple months later, I found a new job delivering newspapers, which I did on foot until I saved enough money (that I hid from my mother) to buy a used bicycle for $8.

My father found a new job too—and a new profession—as a sandblaster and painter on the bridge that linked Charleston to Mt. Pleasant. We moved to a larger apartment, one with a real kitchen, running water, and our own bathroom.

Chapter 6

A year later, the Charleston bridge finished, my father's company moved on to Jacksonville, Florida, and another bridge. There we moved into a duplex in a neighborhood near the Gator Bowl and close to the bridge where my father worked.

My older sister, Dianne, joined us for a short time, but again our parents' sordid lifestyle quickly forced her to return to Shelby and a safer, quieter life with Mama Bridges.

During the year we spent in Jacksonville, we lived in three different locations, finally ending up in yet another housing project.

After Jacksonville, we moved to New Orleans and my father got a job working on the Mississippi River bridge. There we rented a mobile home in a park with a grand name—Oak Manor. The small mobile home park wasn't grand but it was clean, with wide white oyster-shell streets and several newer, well-maintained mobile homes.

But the mobile home we rented was older and smaller and had only two bedrooms. Again Dianne came to live with us, and she and my younger sister shared one bedroom, while my parents shared the other. I slept on the sofa in the living room.

I had forgotten much about the two years we lived in New Orleans. Then in 2017, when my sisters Dianne, now seventy, and Tonda, sixty-two, visited me here in prison, they refreshed my memory.

It was the first time that we'd seen each other in over thirty years. The last time had been the summer of 1986. I had visited for two days, then had driven to Corpus Christi, Texas, where I

had robbed yet another bank and had embarked on my coast-to-coast crime spree.

"Remember that little turtle you had?" asked Tonda.

"Yeah," I laughed. "I'd almost forgotten about that. I kept him in a round fishbowl. His name was Herman. Remember that?" I asked.

"Herman, that's right," laughed Tonda.

"I kept the bottom of the bowl filled with small pebbles and just a little water. Every day I fed Herman these little flakes of turtle food that came in a small box. But what I remember most," I told Tonda, "is that you used to think that Herman ate the rocks on the bottom of the bowl. Remember that?"

"No," said Tonda.

"Well, you did and that was the funniest thing. You used to walk around telling anyone that would listen, 'Herman eats rocks! Herman eats rocks!'"

We all laughed.

"I don't remember that, but I do remember when Herman died," said Tonda.

"Me too," I said. "We dug him a grave under the edge of the trailer and had a little ceremony for him."

"Oak Manor's where I got my first babysittin' job," said Dianne. "It was 1961, so I must have been fifteen or sixteen—anyway, old enough to babysit.

"So I got this job babysittin' two small children for a woman who worked as a dancer in a club in the French Quarter. She lived in a big mobile home at the far end of the trailer park. And she always paid me at the end of the week, on Saturday. And a lot of times I'd spend part of my money on groceries."

"I didn't know that," I said.

"Often, during the middle of the week, Mama and Daddy would be out drinkin', leavin' us kids at home with nothing to eat. That was rough. I remember this one time we didn't have

anything in the trailer to eat, and I had to leave you and Tonda to go babysit. I was so worried the whole time I was there, all I could think about was where I could get some money to buy groceries. I prayed and prayed, asking God to help me get some food.

"Then, while walking back to our trailer after babysittin' all night, a voice told me to stop and look down at the ground and I did. And there on the ground was a $20 bill. I couldn't believe it! A $20 bill! Back then you could buy a lot of groceries for $20, and that's just what I did."

On school days, I rode the city bus to a junior high in an area in downtown New Orleans called the Irish Channel and, unlike my sister, when I got hungry I didn't pray for a miracle but shoplifted my lunch at Schwegmann's, a giant supermarket on St. Claude not far from the school.

It was in this tough urban school that I discovered a talent for drawing and painting, and under the guidance of a kind and dedicated art teacher, named Dennis Piatolly, I was taught the fundamentals of painting in oil. At fourteen, I completed my first oil painting, a still life on canvas, and won an honorable mention in a citywide art show for middle school students.

Two years later we moved to Baton Rouge. There I worked after school alongside my father as a painter's helper on the bridge his company was painting.

Dianne, after graduating high school, married a young man seven or eight years older who also worked as a painter/sandblaster on the same bridge. His name was George. A quiet, kind man with an easygoing manner, he was just what my sister needed. Raised in Lake Charles, a city in southwestern Louisiana, George had moved to Baton Rouge after being honorably discharged from the army, and it was there he met my sister.

60

In 1966, America's involvement in the conflict in Southeast Asia intensified, and the Pentagon needed young strong bodies with malleable minds to train and send to confront the communist aggression there. And I was the perfect candidate. I wanted adventure, I wanted to get away from my parents, and I had no sense of my own mortality, knowing nothing of the horrors of war or the frailty of the spirit.

One day I visited the Marine Corps recruiting office in downtown Baton Rouge and was told that if I signed up for four years I would be guaranteed a job in Marine Aviation. Naïve, I assumed I'd be assigned to a flight crew. The recruiter also told me that because I was just seventeen, my parents would have to sign a consent form before I could enlist.

First I talked to my mother, but her only comment was, "Talk to your father."

My father, not having experienced the horrors of war himself, was eager to sign the consent form. He told me, "Maybe the Marines will make a man outta ya."

Now that I think about it, my father probably was eager to get rid of the last of his responsibilities. Tonda, now eleven, had gone to live with Dianne and her new husband, and with me gone, my parents would now be free to continue the gypsy lifestyle they loved.

I dropped out of high school and the week after that was sent to New Orleans for induction. Two weeks later I flew to San Diego, California, to begin boot camp.

When I arrived in San Diego, I was herded onto a bus with seventy other recruits for the ride to the Marine Corps Recruit Depot. All of us fearful, we masked our fear by laughing and joking during the bus ride. But as soon as we reached the front gate, saw actual armed Marines in uniform, and witnessed how

solemn their demeanor, the mood on the bus quickly changed. Like frightened children—and many of us were—we now sat quietly and stared wide-eyed out the windows.

The bus pulled past the front gate and stopped a quarter mile away. The door opened and two drill instructors—a sergeant and a corporal, recently returned from the jungles of Vietnam—boarded the bus. Dressed in starched summer uniforms and wearing "Smokey Bear" hats, they didn't say a word, just stood very still and studied us as if ranchers assessing cattle at an auction. Then the sergeant turned to the corporal and said, "You see what kind of shit they send us to work with. We'd be better off if they had just stopped at the zoo and picked up a bunch of monkeys. Probably be easier to train."

"Civilians!" said the corporal. "Puke-ass civilians! I hate civilians!"

"All right!" yelled the sergeant. "From now until you graduate boot camp—and some of you assholes ain't gonna make it—you're mine! Is that clear! I am the final word! When I say jump, you jump! And when I give the word, you will exit this military conveyance—that means bus for you uneducated shitheads—and you will exit quickly!"

Two men in the back of the bus stood.

The sergeant's eyes got big. "Why the fuck you two idiots standin'."

The two men looked around.

"I'm talking to you!" shouted the sergeant. "Both you pieces of shit! Sit down!"

The men, clearly embarrassed, sat down.

"Did you hear me give the word! No! Because I *did not* give the word. I said, *when* I give the word!"

The sergeant was silent for a full minute. We sat, poised to move in an instant.

"Now! When I *do* give the word, you will grab your shit and exit quickly! Is that understood?"

A few men mumbled, "Yes sir."

"What! What was that! You sound like a bunch of girls! From this day forward, whenever I ask you a question, you will respond clearly and loudly with, 'Sir, yes sir!'" He paused. "Now do you understand!"

"Sir, yes sir!" we responded a little louder.

"I can't hear you! Do you understand!"

"Sir, yes sir!" we roared.

Again we endured a minute, maybe two, of silence, all of us staring at the D.I.s like expectant dogs. The D.I.s moved to the front of the bus. At the door, the sergeant yelled, "Move! Move! Move! Move!"

We had waited so long that we were now momentarily stunned to finally hear, without a doubt, the word. We panicked and pushed and tripped over each other like frightened patrons trying to get out of a burning movie theater. When we finally spilled onto the tarmac, the D.I.s were waiting.

"That was pitiful!" shouted the corporal. "You idiots line up! Stand on those yellow feet!"

I looked down and, sure enough, pairs of yellow shoe prints had been painted on the asphalt next to the bus. I stepped onto a pair.

Most found the yellow shoe prints, but a few had no idea what the corporal was talking about. They stood and looked to the left and right, everywhere but down. The D.I.s, frustrated, ran to the confused men and dragged each of the recruits to a set of shoe prints.

Finally, when everyone was standing on a set of shoe prints, the sergeant shouted, "Put all your shit on the deck!"

I dropped my small bag like everyone else, and the D.I.s went from man to man, opening each bag and rifling through

every suitcase. They threw clothes onto the tarmac and shattered bottles of aftershave.

"You don't need this! You don't need that! The Marine Corps will issue what you need. If the Corps don't issue it, you don't need it!" they shouted.

It didn't take long to learn to blend in with the crowd, to never be first and to never be last but to seek safety in the middle. And I learned the usual way, by observing the mistakes of others and by making mistakes myself, then suffering the consequences afterward.

Once, while on the rifle range, I complained of a soreness in my arms and shoulders and the D.I. calmly listened to my complaints. Then, instead of sending me to the infirmary, which is what I had hoped for, he made me stand at attention and hit me in the solar plexus three times with the butt of my rifle, knocking me to the ground.

"Now, get your ass back to the rifle range!" he yelled.

And another time I was caught looking around when I was supposed to be standing at attention. The D.I. choked me, then picked me up and hung me on a wall hook by my shirt collar, my feet dangling in air.

But the most embarrassing moment occurred on my eighteenth birthday.

"Sir, Private Bridges reporting as ordered," I said, while standing stiffly at attention in front of the D.I.'s desk.

"At ease, Private Bridges," said the D.I.

Spreading my feet wide and locking my arms behind me, I stood at parade rest and looked straight ahead. Directly behind the D.I.'s desk sat three Black recruits.

"Today your birthday?" asked the D.I.

"Sir, yes sir," I replied cautiously.

"How old are you?"

"Sir, eighteen, sir."

"Eighteen … um." He turned to one of the recruits sitting against the wall. "You. Go get Private Bridges a chair."

The recruit brought me a chair.

"Sit," ordered the D.I.

Warily I sat.

The D.I. reached into a shirt pocket and removed a pack of Camel unfiltered cigarettes. He shook one loose and reached it toward me. "Here," he said. "Smoke."

"Sir, the private don't smoke, sir."

"I said smoke it!" he demanded.

I took the cigarette and put it in my mouth. The D.I. lit it. I drew on the cigarette and felt the harshness of it burning deep into my lungs. Coughing violently, my eyes teared. I turned red in the face.

The three recruits and the D.I. roared with laughter. The D.I. then turned to a recruit he called Private White. He was heavy, probably over three hundred pounds, and his skin was black as onyx.

"Private White," said the D.I.

"Sir, yes sir."

"I want you to sing 'Happy Birthday' to Private Bridges."

"Sir, the private don't know that song," said Private White.

"Come on, you're bullshittin'. Everybody knows 'Happy Birthday'!"

"Sir, the private don't know it," insisted Private White.

"Okay, okay. Well, what song do you know?"

"Sir, the private knows 'Blueberry Hill.'"

"'Blueberry Hill'! Okay, sing 'Blueberry Hill' to Private Bridges."

While I sat choking on a cigarette, the three recruits stood in a circle around me and sang "Blueberry Hill."

The D.I. laughed uncontrollably.

I'll never forget the instructor that taught us the basic handling and use of hand grenades. The entire platoon, all seventy of us, sat on bleachers listening to an instructor explain the proper method of arming and throwing a grenade. As usual, I sat in the middle.

The instructor reached into a wooden box sitting on the ground at his feet and picked up the grenade. "A hand grenade is an effective and powerful weapon when handled and used properly," he said.

He held the grenade above his head and turned it so we could all see.

"See this pin? As long as this pin is in place, the grenade is safe, but when you remove the pin, the grenade is armed but it still won't explode as long as you have the spoon depressed. In fact," he removed the pin, held the grenade in his left hand and the pin in his right, our eyes glued to the grenade and the pin he held, "you can replace the pin," he inserted the pin into the top of the grenade, "and now you can release the spoon and it's safe to handle again."

He tossed the grenade from hand to hand like a baseball. There was a collective sigh.

"Here's another point to remember," said the instructor. Again he held the grenade high above his head and again he removed the pin. "Remember, when you remove the pin and let go of the spoon, you have about six or seven seconds until the grenade explodes."

The instructor then casually threw the grenade underhanded into the middle of the bleachers. A thought flashed through my mind as I watched the grenade arc toward me in what seemed slow motion. *This is it! There goes my theory of safety in the middle.* The grenade hit the bleacher next to me with a thud. *Six seconds. I got six seconds,* also resounded in my head. Turning, I scrambled like

a lizard to the top of the bleachers and dove off, landing on top of those who had been quicker. Covering my head with my arms, I waited for the explosion. But six, seven, ten, fifteen seconds passed and nothing happened. The only sound was the instructor laughing.

We slowly untangled and climbed back onto the bleachers.

"Of course," said the instructor, "that one was a dummy. But I'll be happy to report to your D.I. that you guys can move pretty quick."

He started laughing again. Several in the platoon joined him. I wasn't one of them.

After three months, fully indoctrinated, I graduated boot camp with a sense of accomplishment, proud to be a trained warrior and part of an elite fighting force. As customary, I was granted thirty days' leave time before I had to report to my new post, the Naval Air Station in Millington, Tennessee. I looked forward to going home and seeing my family and friends and having them see me in uniform. But that wasn't to be.

I flew from San Diego to Baton Rouge. At the airport, I took a cab to West Baton Rouge, where I had lived in a mobile home in a small trailer park with my parents before leaving for boot camp. When I knocked on the door, a stranger answered, and I discovered that soon after I left for San Diego, my parents had moved.

Telephoning my sister Dianne, who still lived in Baton Rouge with her husband George, I was told that soon after I left, our parents had moved to Shelby and were now living with my mother's parents. My sister graciously invited me to stay with her and her new husband during my thirty days' leave and I accepted, having no other place to go. They were kind and accommodating but I was seldom there, spending most of my time drinking and partying with high school friends.

When my leave time was up, I reported to the Naval Air Station in Millington, just outside Memphis. There I learned the ugly truth; I would not be flying but instead would be sent to school to be a hydraulic mechanic on jet aircraft. When I was told that I was going to be a mechanic, my enthusiasm for the Marines plummeted. The image of my father, stinking of black grease, the lubricant caked under his broken fingernails, played over and over in my head.

At the Naval Air Station, while waiting to attend school, I was assigned menial tasks—unloading trucks, cleaning the base bowling alley, and picking up cigarette butts. I lived for the weekends when several of us would take the bus fifty miles south to Clarksdale, Mississippi, where the legal age to drink was eighteen. There we'd party until Sunday night, then take the bus back to Memphis.

I passed a couple months this way, then a week before Christmas I learned that I would be given a three-day pass Christmas Eve. I telephoned my grandparents' house in Shelby and my mother answered the telephone.

"Mama, this is Rickey."

"Rickey! We've been waitin' to hear from you. I talked to Dianne. She told me you stayed there. Where are you?"

"I'm in Memphis, Mama. I'm here waitin' to go to school to become a mechanic on jet airplanes."

"Oh, like your daddy."

"No, not like Daddy, Mama! I'm gonna work on jets. Mama, why didn't you answer my letters? I wrote you twice from boot camp."

"Honey, I didn't get any mail from you."

"Why didn't you tell me you and Daddy was movin'?" I asked.

"I didn't know how to get in touch with you. But that's all in the past now, honey. I know where you are now. When you comin' to see us?"

"Mama, I can't just go where I want, when I want. I'm in the United States Marine Corps now."

"But me and your daddy wanna see you."

"I wanna see you too and I got a three-day pass for Christmas, but it's five hundred miles from Memphis to Shelby."

"You can fly and be here in a couple of hours," said my mother.

"I don't have enough money for air fare, Mama. I don't make that much."

"Do you have enough for a ticket one way?"

"Barely, I guess."

"Well, I'll tell you what," she said. "I'll talk to your daddy. You pay for your ticket here and we'll buy you a ticket back."

"You sure, Mama?"

"Sure, honey. Your daddy's makin' good money roofin' with your uncle Grady."

That settled, I spent most of my pay on an airline ticket to Charlotte, the only big airport near Shelby. Arriving Christmas Eve morning, I took a Greyhound bus to Shelby. There I telephoned and my grandfather answered. He agreed to pick me up at the bus station.

My mother looked so much healthier than the last time I had seen her, with one big difference: her hands shook when she picked up a cup of coffee or lit a cigarette. She told me that my father was working and would be home around 5:00.

At 9:00 that night, my mother and I sat at the kitchen table, drank coffee, and talked. My father still hadn't gotten home from work, so every time the headlights of a passing car flashed on the windows, my mother got up and looked out.

69

"I don't know what's keepin' your daddy. He knows it's Christmas Eve. He knows you was comin' today," she said forlornly.

I gave voice to what we both feared. "Maybe he stopped off at the Moose Lodge for a drink."

"Oh no, honey! Your daddy's been real good since we moved up here. He's been comin' home right after work. Ain't been drinkin'. Neither of us have."

Finally, around midnight my mother gave up and went to bed, and I lay down on the sofa in the living room. A couple hours later, I awakened when the front door opened and my father staggered through. He looked at me.

"So you made it," he said.

"Yeah, been here since this mornin'," I said.

My mother, dressed in one of my grandmother's flannel nightgowns, walked in.

"Chuck, where the hell you been!" she yelled. "It's Christmas Eve and you knew Rickey was comin' in today!"

"That's right, Irene! It's Christmas Eve and a man needs a drink on Christmas Eve! I just stopped off for a coupla, that's all!"

"Irene, what's goin' on in there?" shouted my grandmother from her bedroom.

"Nothing, Mama," said my mother. "Go back to sleep. Everything's okay."

My parents took their argument to their room and shut the door.

I lay back down on the sofa but couldn't go back to sleep. I kept tossing and turning, my mind racing. *I shoulda stayed in Memphis. Ain't nothin' changed. Nothin' at all.*

After breakfast Christmas morning, my mother and I talked while my father slept.

"Mama, I need to get back to Memphis," I told her. "If you could just get the money from Daddy for my airfare, then I'll ask Pawpaw to drive me to the bus station."

"You said you didn't have to be back until tomorrow night," she said.

"That's true, but it's probably best to just get on back."

"Well, if that's what you want, I'll talk to your daddy when he wakes up."

After lunch, my mother said, "Honey, I got some bad news to tell you."

"What's that?"

"Your daddy lost his whole paycheck, plus the Christmas bonus your uncle Grady gave him, playin' poker. Honey, I'm so sorry. I'm so mad at him I could kill 'im."

"Mama, you got to be kiddin'! What am I supposed to do now! If I don't get back by tomorrow night, I'll be AWOL, Mama! AWOL! You know what that means!"

"Shhh! Keep your voice down. Your pawpaw's takin' a nap. Look, honey, I'm sorry. Your daddy said that in a couple days, he'd try to borrow the money from your uncle Grady."

"A couple days! Mama, I ain't got a couple days!"

"Honey, don't yell."

"Mama, I gotta be back tomorrow. This is the Marine Corps, Mama. They don't play about stuff like this."

"Well, I'm sure they'll understand. Things like this happen all the time."

"No, Mama, things like this *don't* happen all the time! Not to normal people!"

"Hold your voice down."

I leaned closer. "Mama, understand. The Marine Corps has strict rules. I had a three-day pass. Three days, Mama, not four and not five. Three days."

"Rickey, I don't know what to tell you. You can't get blood out of a turnip."

Disgusted, I turned away and didn't speak to either of my parents the rest of the day. Instead, I sat outside in a lawn chair and stared at the highway, brooding. My grandfather noticed and asked me if I wanted to ride to the store with him. In the car, he said, "Son, I know what happened. Your mother told me."

"Well, what am I supposed to do now, Pawpaw? I gotta be back tomorrow night and it's five hundred miles to Memphis. I could hitchhike, but there's no way I can make it back in time unless I get lucky and catch a ride straight through."

"Son, you know me and your granny would buy you a ticket if we had it, but we don't."

"I know, Pawpaw. I know."

"I'll tell you what I can do."

"What's that?"

"In the mornin', first light, I'll drive you up to the main highway west. There you can try to catch a ride. That's the best I can do."

The next morning, dressed in my heavy green winter uniform and overcoat, I put my seabag in the back of Pawpaw's old Ford, the very same car that nine years earlier had taken us to Mrs. Patrick's farm, the Jumping Off Place, and Lady for her last ride. Thirty miles west of Shelby, in the foothills of the Smoky Mountains, my grandfather pulled onto the shoulder of a two-lane blacktop and turned to me.

"Son, I'll be prayin' for you. If you just trust in the Lord, everything will work out."

"I appreciate it, Pawpaw," I said with little enthusiasm.

My grandfather reached in his hip pocket, pulled out his wallet, and handed me a $5 bill.

"Son, this is the best I can do. Maybe you can get something to eat along the way."

Reluctantly, I took the $5 bill and put it in my pocket.

"Thanks, Pawpaw. I appreciate it."

I opened the door and my grandfather reached out his hand. I grasped it firmly, the last time I'd ever be able to do so. Standing on the shoulder of the highway, my duffel bag beside me, I watched my grandfather make a U-turn, then drive away.

As soon as his old Ford disappeared, it started snowing. I raised the collar of my overcoat and adjusted my cap, looked left and right, but there was no traffic at all, so I sat on my duffel bag and waited.

Several minutes later a lone car approached. I stood, raised my thumb, and smiled. *What kind of fool stands alongside a highway in a snowstorm, smiling?* I asked myself. The car passed without slowing. I sat back down on the duffel bag.

The snow came down harder, the snowflakes as big as quarters. Standing, I stomped my feet to warm them, twisted back and forth, and did some jumping jacks. Another car approached. *Okay, showtime!* I told myself. Again, I held my thumb high, but the car blew past like a freight train, spraying me with snow. "Son of a bitch!" I yelled at the car, shaking my fist.

I looked at my watch and walked back and forth. *Eight o'clock. It's 8:00. In nine more hours, I'll be AWOL. No way I can make five hundred miles in nine hours, even if I catch a ride straight through right now. May as well start walking. At least I can keep warm.*

Hoisting the duffel bag onto my shoulder, I struggled up the slippery highway. But after about a hundred yards, I dropped the duffel bag and sat atop it to rest. My hands and feet were numb and my face, particularly my ears and nose, stung. Another car approached, but I was now so dispirited that I didn't even stand, I just lazily raised my thumb as if I didn't give a damn. The car

passed and the cold wind buffeted me. I yelled, "That's right, you bastard, just keep goin'!"

I turned and started walking again. Then I changed my mind, stopped, and again sat down on the duffel bag.

"I can't believe this shit!" I said out loud. "What kinda damn fool am I?" I shook my head in disgust. "I should know better by now. Every time I get around them, it's the same old shit. Why even try! Why! If they don't care about me, why should I care about myself?"

I felt my will disappearing, like a spoon of instant coffee in a gallon of hot water, and I hated myself for my weakness. I tried to find a reason to continue but couldn't. I felt totally drained and empty inside. Self-pity filled the void. *Nobody's dependin' on me. Nobody cares, not really. They say they do, but their actions say they don't. Nobody cares—not Mama, not Daddy, not even Pawpaw. And I know the Marines don't care. I'm just another stupid young fool they tricked, another mind and body for them to control.*

"Fuck this!" I leaned my head back and yelled into the falling snow. "You hear me! Fuck this! From now on, Rickey Troy Bridges is gonna do *exactly* what he wants to do, when he wants to do it! I'll show 'em! I'll show 'em all! They can all kiss my ass!"

I dragged the duffel bag into the trees, opened it, and rummaged through until I found civilian clothes, shoes, and my shaving kit. Shivering, I took off my uniform and put on jeans, a shirt, sweater, and jacket, then dry socks. After stuffing my uniform and topcoat in the duffel bag, I lifted it over my head and heaved it as far as I could. Picking up my shaving kit, I crossed to the other side of the slushy highway and started walking back down the mountain.

Unencumbered, I felt light and free and wicked. Then a nagging hopelessness gripped me again.

What am I gonna do now? I pushed that thought away.

One foot in front of the other, I told myself. *One foot in front of the other, that's all. Just stop thinking.*

A few minutes later, I looked over my shoulder and saw the headlights of a vehicle coming down the mountain. Turning around, I walked backward, my thumb out. A pickup truck passed me, then stopped a few feet ahead. I couldn't believe it. The driver motioned for me to hurry. I ran to the truck, opened the passenger door, and got in.

Behind the wheel was a heavyset man wearing a sheepskin coat and a baseball cap. "What in the world you doin' out here in the middle of nowhere?" he asked.

"I just left Memphis day before yesterday," I lied. "I'm tryin' to make it to Miami. I got family there."

"I can take you as far as Charleston, if that'll help."

"That'll help a lot," I said. "I know Charleston."

Yeah, I know Charleston real good, I told myself. *Real good.*

It wasn't until many years later that I realized just how damaging my decision to desert the Marine Corps would be and how that decision would change the course of my life. It also took many years to realize that most people's course in life is often determined by as little as four or five important choices they make. Choose wisely and your life is often smooth and happy. Choose foolishly and your life is often difficult and sad.

I honestly thought that I had but one choice, either get back to Memphis before my three-day pass expired or suffer the ruination of my career in the Marine Corps, when in truth I had not just one choice, but many. I could have called the Naval Air Station in Millington, talked to the Officer of the Day, told him—for whatever reason—that I would be a day late reporting in, and at worse would have suffered a mild reprimand. But being immature, I didn't realize that I had that option.

Since, I've often wondered why none of the adults involved (particularly my grandparents) didn't advise me to call or make that call themselves.

Chapter 7

I reached Charleston a little after dark and walked down King Street. When I got to the jewelry store we had lived above, I stood and stared up at the dimly lit window my mother and I used to share. In my mind, I clearly saw our cramped squalid apartment and remembered how I used to sit at that window for hours and look at the people and traffic below, envying them their lives. And now here I was, looking up at the window and envying those enjoying the relative comfort and safety of those two cramped rooms.

Continuing on down King Street, I stopped at Mama Demarest's old junk shop and looked in the window. The shop looked as if nothing had changed in the seven years since I'd been there.

That night I slept on a bench in the park near the old Battery and the next morning walked back up King Street until I found the highway south. After catching several short rides, I spent the night sleeping under an overpass just south of Jacksonville.

I stood alongside the highway three hours the next morning before finally catching a ride south, then west. I spent the night sleeping under a pier on Clearwater Beach.

The next morning I caught a ride south with a kind elderly couple in a Winnebago. They fed me lunch, then dropped me off several hours later at a truck stop near the Everglades. The elderly lady, who reminded me of Mama Bridges, pressed two crumpled $1 bills into my palm. It was a timely gift; I had spent the last of the $5 my grandfather had given me the day before.

That night, seeking refuge from a horde of mosquitoes in a phone booth along a stretch of highway called Alligator Alley, I was miserable. At first light, I caught a ride all the way to Miami. The driver let me out near a small park on Biscayne Boulevard.

There, on a bench, I found a copy of the *Miami Herald* and while reading the classified section came across the following ad: "Dishwashers Needed. Daily pay for a twelve-hour shift. Junior's Seafood Restaurant."

Spending the last of my $2, I caught a crosstown bus and arrived at the restaurant around 2:00. It was easy to get the job and the work wasn't hard, but still, after standing on my feet for twelve hours, I was exhausted at the end of my shift. Later, when I got off the bus near the park on Biscayne Boulevard, I had $10 in my pocket, a full stomach, and a large bag of leftovers.

In the park, I crawled under an oleander bush and, using my jacket for a pillow, quickly fell asleep.

A few hours later, I felt the warmth of the sun on my face and a burning sensation on my legs. I sat up. Red ants covered both legs from the knees down and had formed a trail to the bag of leftovers on the ground beside me.

Quickly removing my shoes and socks, I shook them out, then stood and opened the bag of leftovers. Grabbing a large piece of steak, I brushed the ants off and, still barefoot, walked over to a bench and sat down. There I ate the food and watched the people and traffic on busy Biscayne Boulevard.

For a week I worked at the restaurant, bathed in the restaurant's restroom, slept in the park, and saved most of my earnings. I then rented a room in a shabby hotel and found a better job, parking cars in a high-rise apartment building on the Bay. The tips were good and enabled me to buy new clothes and rent a better room.

I discovered that I was okay as long as I stayed busy, but when I was idle, especially when I was alone in my room at night, my thoughts were a torturous merry-go-round of what ifs and whys. With no one to talk to, I often felt helpless and sank into a depression.

Inexplicably, two weeks into my new job a familiar self-destructive voice spoke to me while I was parking a new Buick Riviera. *What does it matter whether you park this car or drive it into the Bay? Who cares? Just keep driving. It don't matter!*

As if hypnotized, I exited the parking lot and drove north, not even stopping at my hotel room to get my few possessions. Driving and sleeping in the back seat when tired, I continued north and west until I ran out of gas and money near Chattanooga, Tennessee. There I traded the Buick's spare tire to a service station attendant for a tank of gasoline.

It was still cold in Tennessee, so when I left the service station I reversed direction and headed south again, with no destination in mind and no plan of any sort other than escape the cold.

Several hours later, just outside Meridian, Mississippi, and again low on gas, I pulled up to a gas pump at a country store. Keeping the engine running while the proprietor, an older man dressed in denim overalls, filled the tank, I nervously watched in the rearview mirror while also keeping an eye on the fuel gauge. When the needle registered full, I eased the shifter into drive and stomped the gas pedal. The car lurched like a wild bronco out of the chute, ripping the gas nozzle from the attendant's hands and whipping around, spraying gasoline.

The Buick fishtailed when I hit the gravel on the shoulder of the road and I almost lost control, but when the tires grabbed blacktop, I straightened and flew down the highway. Pushing eighty-five a few miles from the country store, I passed a state trooper in the opposite lane. I eased off the accelerator, but it was too late.

The trooper slowed, made a U-turn, then hit his lights and siren. Automatically, I let off the gas, but just as I reached my foot toward the brake, I again heard that familiar voice. *Go for it!*

Who cares! Go for it! I stomped down on the gas pedal and the Buick's front end dipped, then raised up as the passing gear kicked in. The speedometer quickly climbed to 90, 100, 110. Every cell in my body screamed in terror.

Glancing in the rearview mirror, I saw that the gap between the Buick and the trooper's car had widened. I felt the car swerve to the right and looked up to see a steel pole bounce off the hood. A stop sign hit the windshield, creating a spiderweb. I muscled the car back onto the highway.

In the distance, I saw the flashing lights of three more police cars and a fully loaded log truck blocking the highway. To the right was a canal and to my left a guardrail. Behind me, the trooper's car had now closed the gap between us.

I stomped the brake, turned the steering wheel to the right, and the Buick flipped, rolling onto its side and sliding into the log truck. On impact, the windows imploded, covering me in glass and flinging me into the back seat.

I regained consciousness when rough hands pulled me through the rear window and dropped me onto the asphalt. I felt gravel dig into the side of my face, a knee pressed against the center of my back, and handcuffs pinching my wrists.

Chapter 8

I was taken to the courthouse in downtown Meridian. It was an old, three-story, brick-and-concrete structure with steep steps out front. Inside we took an elevator to the jail on the second floor. There we entered a large room with several desks scattered about. To one side was a small alcove for photographing and fingerprinting. Next to the alcove were three doors, one marked "Sheriff's Office." We passed a trustee in a blue jumpsuit. He stopped and stared for a moment, then continued sweeping the floor.

The jail was operated and maintained by a husband-and-wife team, he the jailer and she the cook as well as matron to a small population of female prisoners. They lived on the third floor.

After being photographed and fingerprinted, I was led down a short corridor to a heavy iron door with round, half-dollar-size rivets along the edges. The jailer removed a large brass key from his waistband and opened the door. I looked through a grille of steel bars to see a large dayroom. The jailer pulled a heavy lever built into the wall and the grille gate slid open with a solid thump. He turned to me.

"In you go."

I stepped through into the dayroom and the steel bars slid shut, the heavy iron door slamming closed with a frightening finality. Everyone in the dayroom stopped what they had been doing to look at me. I stared back, unsure what to do.

The dayroom had a long steel table painted gray and securely bolted to the floor. Sitting on benches attached to the table were two prisoners playing dominoes while three others watched and talked. Two prisoners paced back and forth from one end of the dayroom to the other, passing six four-man cells

along each side. Along the back wall was a one-man shower stall, the front covered by a mildewed piece of canvas.

A man I recognized as the trustee who had been sweeping out front when I came in two hours earlier said to me, "I'm Clyde, the bull here. I run this tank. You need somethin', come through me. Understand?" I nodded. "That second cell's empty. You can bunk there."

"Thanks," I mumbled, then entered the cell. I lay down on the bottom bunk, rolled over, and stared at the wall, my mind racing and my body sore from the car crash.

The next day I got a cell partner nicknamed Trigger. He was a thirty-year-old local who had already been to prison twice and was headed there for a third time after being convicted of shooting a man in a nightclub in a dispute over a woman.

Trigger stood six feet and was lean and muscular. He had jet black hair that he combed constantly, a square jaw, and piercing blue eyes. He bragged often of his exploits—gambling, fighting, and with women. Trigger welcomed confrontation and liked being the center of attention. He was at times brooding, defiant, dishonest, manipulative, and brutal. He imagined himself superior and thought that everyone else had been put on the planet to serve his needs.

Because I was young and impressionable, Trigger quickly became my role model and I hung on his every word.

At night when we were all locked in our cells, one man, Clyde, the trustee and self-proclaimed bull, was allowed to move freely. It was his job to sweep and mop the dayroom and to pass objects between cells. Clyde also ran the black market, and the hottest item was confiscated moonshine. The potent whiskey was stored in a large five-hundred-gallon vat under a shed on the second-floor roof. At night when the jailer and his wife retired for the evening, Clyde would sneak out onto the roof and lower a mop bucket tied to a rope into the vat of illegal whiskey.

He then poured the moonshine into quart-size plastic bleach bottles and sold them for $3 each.

One night, Trigger and I pooled our money and bought a quart of white lightnin' from Clyde. We stood near the front of the cell drinking booze out of small Styrofoam cups and talking. "It's all about respect," said Trigger. "If somebody disrespects you, you gotta straighten 'em out quick." Trigger reached in his back pocket, removed a black plastic comb, and carefully combed his hair. "You'll see what I mean when you get to the joint. Game. They all got game, all of 'em tryin' to beat you out of somethin'. You gotta learn to recognize game when you see it comin', know what I mean?"

"Yeah, I got it," I said, not really sure that I did. I took a drink of moonshine and choked back a gag.

"Don't let nobody disrespect you," said Trigger. "Set them straight from the git-go."

"Damn straight. I ain't letting nobody disrespect me!" I took another drink. "Nobody!"

"Let me tell you about somethin' that happened up in Parchman when I was up there a few years ago," said Trigger.

"What's that?"

"Well, I saw a man get killed for steppin' on another dude's bed."

"No shit?"

"I ain't shittin' ya." Trigger emptied his cup. He grabbed the bleach bottle and refilled it. "I ain't jokin'." Trigger walked back and forth. "This old Indian dude kilt his bunk partner for steppin' on his bed."

"How'd that happen?"

"Well, the dorm we lived in had double bunks, you know, like bunk beds. And this old Indian dude slept on the bottom bunk. Real quiet dude, been in Parchman for years. And on the top bunk slept this new man, just got to Parchman. Now,

usually, in order to get on the top bunk, you got to step on the bottom bunk, but most people just step on the railing, then pull themself up. Course, most people take off their shoes.

"Well, this new man, he worked out in the field hoein' cotton, diggin' ditches, that kind of thing. One day they quit early because it started raining. This new guy comes into the dorm and he's too tired, or maybe too lazy, to take off his brogans. So he just stepped on the bottom bunk, pulled himself up, and went to sleep.

"About an hour later, this old Indian dude comes in from work. He worked in the upholstery shop and, like I said, was a quiet guy, minded his own business, didn't bother nobody, but kind of a peculiar guy too. He liked all his stuff real neat—bed made up perfect, everything all neat and in its place. You know guys like that."

"Like a neat freak."

"Yeah, like a neat freak. Anyway, he comes in from work and the first thing he sees is this muddy boot print on his clean sheets. He looked up at the new dude asleep on the top bunk. He didn't yell, he didn't say a word. He just stood there with his hands on his hips, looking at the man like he was trying to make up his mind on somethin'.

"Then this old Indian dude bent down and opened his locker box. He fumbled around inside until he found a razor blade. He walked over to the dude sleepin' on the top bunk, grabbed his hair, pulled his head back, and slit his throat from ear to ear. The dude sat up in bed, grabbed his throat, and started chokin' on his own blood. Then he flopped over dead, and that's all she wrote."

"Damn! What did the Indian dude do then?"

"He didn't do nothing. He just sat down on his bunk and calm as you please rolled himself a cigarette. He was still

smoking it when four guards rushed into the dorm, handcuffed him, and hauled him off to lockup."

I refilled my cup, then joined Trigger at the front of the cell.

"I learned the first time I went to the joint," said Trigger, "you can't show no weakness. You gotta be strong. Prison is like livin' in a big ocean and you're either a shark or a fish, one or the other. You know what happens when a shark comes face-to-face with a fish, don't you?"

"Hell, yeah," I said. "The shark eats the shit out of 'em!"

I took a drink, then set my cup on the flat horizontal piece of steel that held the vertical bars in place. Clyde walked up, stood on the other side of the steel bars, looking in. Trigger and I looked at each other but didn't acknowledge Clyde. Without asking permission, Clyde grabbed my cup and took a drink.

"What the fuck you doing!" yelled Trigger.

"That's my fucking cup!" I yelled.

"Fuck you!" yelled Clyde. "I just took one sip!"

I grabbed Clyde's shirt and pulled him to me. He struggled to free himself, but before he could, Trigger reached through the steel bars and yelled, "Look at your heart, motherfucker!"

I let go of Clyde's shirt, not sure what had happened. Clyde staggered back a couple steps, his ripped shirt covered in blood. I then saw that he had a horizontal gash about eight inches long just above his navel. Turning, I saw that Trigger held a large pocketknife. Clyde's back hit the steel table and he sat down hard on the concrete floor, his arms now wrapped around his midsection to staunch the blood and hold in his intestines.

Trigger calmly wiped his prints from the Barlow knife with the hem of his shirt and said, "Hey, big man! Look, we're going to shake down and make some noise, try to get somebody back here to help you! When they get back here you tell 'em you cut yourself. You hear! Or next time I'll cut your fucking head off!"

85

Clyde shook his head but didn't answer. Trigger reached through the bars and threw the Barlow knife at the trustee. It bounced off his outstretched legs and landed next to him.

Trigger looked at me. "Come on, let's get this disrespectful motherfucker some help back here before he dies on us." He grabbed the steel bars, shook them, and I joined in. Soon the entire cellblock was awake and shaking the steel bars. Trigger walked over to a small mirror above the sink and started combing his hair.

The heavy iron door swung open, the grille gate slid to the side, and the jailer, accompanied by a sheriff's deputy and a trustee, stepped into the dayroom. "What the hell's goin' on in here?"

He saw Clyde sitting in a pool of blood and rushed over. "What in the world happened to you?"

"I ... ," Clyde looked over at Trigger, who was standing at the front of the cell staring at him. "I cut myself," he said weakly.

The jailer shook his head. "Now, Clyde, I seriously doubt you cut yourself. I seriously do." The jailer picked up the knife and handed it to the deputy. "But never mind that now, Clyde. You just sit there and keep still. I'll get you some help." The jailer turned to the trustee. "Go to the storeroom and get that stretcher." The trustee left and the jailer yelled after him, "And bring a mop back with you!"

They put Clyde on a stretcher and left.

A couple hours later the jailer returned and this time he had three sheriff's deputies with him. They entered our cell and handcuffed us. I was taken to the third floor and locked in a solitary cell. I don't know where they took Trigger, but I never saw or heard from him again.

The rusted, heavy iron door was trimmed in bands of steel held in place by large rivets. The cell was older and much larger

86

than those on the second floor. The plaster on the wall was cracked, exposing red brick underneath. All four walls were covered in graffiti. I looked up at the twelve-foot ceiling and to my amazement saw that it was also covered in graffiti. But the graffiti on the ceiling hadn't been scratched into the surface or written on with pen and pencil, like on the walls; it had been drawn with what appeared to be smoke. And directly in the center of the ceiling was a trapdoor three feet square.

I found the graffiti on the ceiling puzzling and the trapdoor even more so. Bolted to the floor along the far wall was a steel bunk, and on it was an old lumpy mattress covered in ticking. On the mattress was an old, green army blanket. Directly above the steel bunk, about five feet above the concrete floor, was a small window with iron bars. To the side of the window was a toilet, with a small sink above. I looked up at the ceiling again and wondered how previous occupants had been able to draw the smoke graffiti. I wondered about the trapdoor.

Walking over to the bunk, I lay down and covered myself with the blanket. It smelled of urine and sweat. I tried to sleep but tossed and turned, my head throbbing and my stomach queasy. I thought about what had happened. *I gotta be careful. If I hadn't grabbed Clyde, none of this would've happened. All he did was drink from my cup, but I made a big deal of it. I think I just reacted 'cause I felt Trigger wanted me to. I gotta be careful, watch what I do, watch what I say from now on.*

Hours later the jailer opened the door and I jumped up, not knowing what to expect. "Here's your breakfast," said the jailer. A trustee put the tray on the floor. "Shouldn't even feed you after what you boys did to Clyde."

"I didn't do nothin' to him," I said.

"Well, somebody did, that's for sure." The jailer slammed the door shut.

I picked up the tray and walked over to my bunk, sat down, and hungrily ate the watery grits, biscuits, and molasses. That evening, when the trustee handed me my supper tray, I asked him about the trapdoor in the ceiling. He said, "You're in the old death cell. In the old days, every county jail had one. Back then they executed murderers instead of sending them to Parchman, like they do now. Hung 'em from that trapdoor up there."

To help relieve the boredom and tire myself so I could sleep, I did push-ups and sit-ups, then walked back and forth in the cell for hours. At least twice daily, usually in the morning and in the evening, I reached up and grabbed the steel bars covering the window and, by bracing my feet against the wall, was able to climb until I could see the edge of the roof and a slice of sky. It wasn't much but just enough to remind me there was still a world beyond my dismal dungeon.

After almost forty days in solitary confinement, two military policemen showed up one morning and took me back to the Naval Air Station at Millington.

There I was confined to barracks to await a court-martial. At the first opportunity I escaped. Fleeing to New Orleans, I spent my nineteenth birthday living with hippies in the attic of an old house in the French Quarter.

Recaptured a few months later, I was again escorted to the Naval Air Station, but this time I was locked in a cell in solitary confinement in the brig. There I refused to cooperate and was repeatedly punished.

Two months later, the Marine Corps washed their hands of me and I was delivered into the custody of U.S. marshals. They put me in the Shelby County Jail in downtown Memphis and a few weeks later escorted me south to Biloxi, Mississippi, where I pled guilty to interstate transportation of a stolen motor vehicle in federal court and was sentenced to two years in federal prison.

A few weeks later, I was sent to the Federal Correctional Institution (FCI) just east of Tallahassee, Florida.

Chapter 9

Entrance to the Federal Correctional Institution was an illusion created to fool an unsuspecting public and first-timers like me.

The golf-course-green lawn and circular drive leading to the three-story, red-brick administration building was bordered by colorful, well-tended flower beds and was so idyllic that at first glance I almost expected to see sheep grazing.

But the illusion fell apart the closer we got. From the back seat of the marshal's car I now saw two twelve-foot fences, topped with razor wire, and a tall gun tower, the guard inside tracking our car with his automatic weapon.

I may have been fooled initially by the peaceful illusion, but it didn't take long to realize that I had indeed been sent to a real prison. Three weeks into my first month, I witnessed a murder at breakfast.

Almost all prisons now use plastic tableware and food trays, but when I got to FCI Tallahassee in 1968, federal prisons still used stainless steel trays, spoons, forks, and even butter knives.

During breakfast one morning, an argument erupted between two men at a nearby table. One was tall and slim, and the other muscular and medium height. They yelled so loudly that all talk in the small dining room stopped while everyone listened and watched.

Abruptly, they stopped yelling and both stood at the same time, glaring at each other—the sudden silence ominous, the tension palpable. His arm a blur, the shorter man reached across the small table and stabbed the taller in the chest with a butter knife.

The taller, shock in his eyes and an "O" on his lips, took a step back, bent, and grabbed a chair. He hit the shorter man hard in the head, then both men fell to the tile floor at the same time. The shorter quickly got to his feet, but the taller lay still.

Guards rushed to the disturbance. The taller man was examined and pronounced dead from a single stab wound to the heart, and the shorter was handcuffed and led away.

Although I had unwittingly been part of the brutal attack on Clyde, the trustee, just a few months earlier, witnessing this murder had more of an effect on me than the tragedy in Meridian. I was now genuinely fearful, realizing for the first time that my life could end in an instant.

I wasn't the only one affected by the murder. For a week or two afterward the mood at the prison was somber, and the guards, as well as the prisoners, treated each other if not with more respect certainly with more caution.

Near the end of my first year at FCI Tallahassee, Dr. Martin Luther King Jr. was assassinated in Memphis and Black inmates rioted. The riot began on the recreation yard, spilled over into the living area. Normally, I would have been on the recreation yard and in the middle of it, but on that particular day I had been at the dental clinic, where I worked as a dental assistant, and so had been out of harm's way. No one was killed during the riot but several were stabbed and dozens seriously injured.

Having less than a year to serve, a few months after the riot my custody level was reduced to minimum and I was assigned to work outside the prison on a landscaping crew.

Illogically, after a month working outside the fences, the temptation was too much for me and I escaped. During the next six months I traveled all over the U.S., even spent a few days in Canada and San Francisco living in a crowded apartment there on Haight Street. But eventually I made my way south again to

New Orleans and after only a few weeks was arrested by local police. Turned over to the FBI, I was sent to Orleans Parish Prison to await extradition back to Tallahassee.

Orleans Parish Prison, located in downtown New Orleans, was built in the late 1800s, and when I was taken there in late 1968, it was still being used to house prisoners. The crumbling structure, with twenty-foot crenellated walls, could have been easily mistaken for an old castle had it not been for the rolls of heavy, sharp razor wire. The only way in and out of the old jail was through a heavy grille gate made of ornamental iron and guarded twenty-four hours a day by a guard tower.

After being photographed and fingerprinted, I was ushered down a short hall, then prodded through an old, heavy iron door with a TV camera incongruously mounted over it. I was then led past a large dayroom and down a long, dimly lit hall with no windows and only a few fluorescent lights.

There were five four-man cells on each side, and I was directed to the third cell on the left. As soon as I stepped inside, the barred door slid shut. I stood and looked around.

The cell was dark and dank, the air fetid, making it hard to breathe deeply without choking. Foot-thick unpainted walls sweated slime, like the inside of a cave, and were covered in decades of graffiti. My cellmate was a twenty-eight-year-old man from Georgia who had been in Orleans Parish Prison only a couple weeks, serving a ninety-day sentence for drunk and disorderly conduct. His name was Patrick.

"Watch out!" shouted Patrick when I entered the cell, carrying a torn mattress. He pointed to the floor. I looked down to see that I was standing in an inch of water. "It's that damn toilet. Floods every time you flush it."

I looked at the toilet; a large chunk of porcelain had been knocked out of the rim and a crack ran from the seat to the floor.

"How long has it been like that?" I asked, flopping my mattress onto an empty bottom bunk.

"Long as I've been here," said Patrick. "Couple weeks."

"Damn."

"You'll get used to it. At first I tried to keep it mopped up with an old t-shirt, then I just gave up. Now I just put up with it, only flush the toilet when I have to."

"Damn," I said again. "Stinks too."

"You'll get used to that too. Welcome to hell. Name is Patrick."

He reached out his hand. I took it.

I immediately liked Patrick because he didn't demand much of my attention, having withdrawn into his own space and developed a routine to help him cope. Patrick slept ten to twelve hours a day, and when he wasn't sleeping he read action novels. He counted his days and marked them off on a calendar he had drawn on the wall. It was obvious that he longed to get back to family and friends in Georgia.

It didn't take long for me to develop my own routine. I slept during the day when the cell doors were left open and it was chaotic and noisy, then stayed up at night when we were safely locked in our cells and it was quiet. And every morning at breakfast I saved a small Styrofoam cup of coffee and two slices of bread until that evening, then prepared myself a snack. After picking up a roll of toilet tissue and wrapping several feet around my free hand, I tucked in the ends to make a tube. Then I struck a match, reached inside the tube, and lit it. Balancing the burning toilet tissue tube, called a bomb, on the rim of the toilet, I heated up the coffee first, then made toast.

It was late Saturday night. All was quiet except for the sound of distant traffic on Tulane Avenue fading in and out like a weak AM radio station. I sat on my bunk slurping burnt coffee,

nibbling toast, and straining my eyes to read a two-week-old *Times-Picayune* when I heard, "Hey, amigo. Chowin' down, ain't ya?"

I looked up and recognized a short brown-skinned man named Carlos. He was one of two trustees who swept and mopped at night. The other was his cellmate, a large Black man named Roland. Occasionally Carlos stopped by at night and we talked for a few minutes.

Grabbing my coffee, I walked to the front of the cell. "This coffee tastes like burnt shit," I said, "but better than nothin'."

"Yeah, it ain't Community dark roast, that's for sure," said Carlos, leaning on the steel bars at the front of the cell. "Look, man, I need you to do me a favor."

"If I can," I said warily.

Carlos moved closer. I did too.

"Amigo," whispered Carlos, "can you hold this for me?" Carlos shoved a cigar box sideways through the steel bars.

"What's in it?" I asked, taking the box.

"Ain't much," said Carlos. "Just a deck of cards, two packs of rolling tobacco, a ballpoint pen, some stamps, some envelopes, and two candy bars—and, oh yeah, a picture of my little girl. But it's all I got that's worth anything."

"Sure, I'll hold it for you," I told him. "Going somewhere?"

"Might be. Probably. See, I gotta take care of some business and I'll get this from you later."

When Carlos turned his head and the dim hall light shone on his face, I saw that his right eye was red and swollen.

"What the hell happened to your eye?" I asked.

Carlos squatted and pulled up his left pant leg. Tied to his calf was a homemade ice pick with a six-inch blade. "I'm going to kill that motherfucker Roland," he hissed.

"Roland! Your cell partner! Why!"

"Shhh," said Carlos. He gently touched his swollen eye. "This. He punched me and stoled eighty-five cents, that's why. I'm gonna kill that big bastard."

"Damn," I said.

"That sack of shit jumped me while I was moppin' the dayroom. He sucker punched me and stoled my money." Carlos stroked the ice pick strapped to his leg. "That's okay. I've got somethin' for his big ass now."

I looked down at the weapon, then up at Carlos. It occurred to me to say something, but I didn't know what so I didn't say anything.

Carlos left. I put the cigar box on my bunk, leaned back, and finished my toast and coffee.

Almost twenty minutes later I heard what sounded like someone thumping a melon hard, followed by an "Ahhhh!" A shiver travelled from my toes to the top of my head. Pushing myself off the bunk, I rushed to the front of the cell, grabbed the bars, and strained to look up the hall.

"Here's eighty-five cents!" yelled Carlos in his familiar voice. And again I heard a thumping sound, followed by a scream and scuffling.

Roland scrambled down the hall on all fours with Carlos riding him like a bull and repeatedly stabbing him in the neck and upper back. Roland tried in vain to buck Carlos off, but when that didn't work, he rolled on the floor like a dog. Still Carlos hung on. Roland, gurgling blood, finally got one foot under his heavy body in an attempt to stand. Carlos slid off and took a step back as if finished. Patiently he waited. As soon as Roland got to an upright position and was balancing on shaky legs, Carlos rushed back in and viciously kicked Roland's legs out from under him. Roland hit the concrete floor on his face and slid, coming to rest just outside my cell door. Carlos ran over

and straddled Roland's prostrate body. Slowly he raised his ice pick and buried it deep in the base of Roland's neck. Roland jerked once, then was still.

Standing, Carlos took a step back and turned in my direction. He looked straight through me, then turned back and kicked Roland's head like a soccer ball. Blood and sweat sprayed me where I stood on the other side of the steel bars. I jumped back and wiped my face with the hem of my t-shirt.

Carlos, spit spewing from the corners of his mouth, screamed at Roland's body, "How you like that? That's eighty-five cents for ya! How you like that!"

The TV camera over the door recorded it all, and in just a few minutes the door banged open and in rushed three jail deputies, each carrying long batons. Carlos, covered in Roland's blood, was still holding the murder weapon. He slowly backed away from Roland's body, his hands in the air.

The first guard to reach Carlos swung his baton like a baseball bat, hitting Carlos on the elbow. Carlos screamed. The ice pick hit the floor with a "clang" and slid. Carlos fell to his knees, holding his broken arm and grimacing in pain. The second deputy rushed forward and, using his baton like a goad, struck Carlos in the solar plexus. Carlos collapsed, gasping for air.

Then all three deputies surrounded Carlos and, while he screamed in pain, they handcuffed him and ran a baton between his cuffed hands. Like a side of beef, two deputies dragged Carlos toward the door. The other picked up the ice pick, then bent over Roland. He examined Roland's eyes and checked his pulse. "He's dead," he announced.

Stunned, I stood in my cell and stared out at the trail of blood in the hall. Squatting, I looked closer at Roland's lifeless eyes, then stood and removed my shirt. I stepped to the small sink above the toilet and started washing my t-shirt.

"You washin' clothes this time of the mornin'? Is it time for breakfast yet?" I looked up to see Patrick sitting up, a blanket wrapped around him.

"We still got a couple hours till breakfast. And, yeah, I'm washin' clothes—my t-shirt, anyway. It got splattered with blood when Carlos killed Roland," I said in a casual voice intended to shock Patrick.

"Carlos did what! Killed Roland! What are you talkin' about?"

"I'm talkin' about Carlos killing Roland just a little while ago while you was sleeping!" I shouted, then pointed to Roland's body just outside the cell door.

"Damn!" shouted Patrick. He jumped off the top bunk. When he landed, his feet made a "splat" sound. He looked down. "Fuck! I hate that!" Patrick walked past me, stood and stared at Roland's body. "Man look at all that blood!" He turned to me. "Why'd he kill 'im?"

"Roland jumped him, stoled eighty-five cents. So Carlos waited till he went to sleep, then stabbed him."

"That's insane! For just eighty-five cents! I gotta get outta this crazy house!" said Patrick, sitting down on my bunk. He noticed the cigar box and opened it. When he saw the candy bars, he shouted, "Wow! Candy bars! I'm 'bout to starve! Can I have one?" Patrick picked up one of the candy bars, without waiting for an answer.

"Sure," I said, "I guess so. They ain't mine. They belong to Carlos, but he'll probably be lookin' for 'em when he gets outta the hole."

"Oh, hell no!" shouted Patrick. He threw the candy bar back in the box, shut it, and pushed it to the edge of my bunk with the tips of his fingers. "I gotta get outta this crazy house!" Patrick climbed on his bunk and covered his head with his blanket.

I paced back and forth in the cell, thinking about the murder I'd just witnessed. *And I gotta read people better than that,* I thought. *I really didn't think Carlos was serious, thought he was just blowin' off steam. I gotta be more aware what's goin' on around me.*

What I didn't know at the time, but do now, is that sometimes you just happen to be in the wrong place at the wrong time. And when that happens, all the awareness in the world won't help you avoid other people's insanity any more than defensive driving will help you avoid a drunk or crazed driver headed straight for you on a one-lane bridge, because no matter which way you turn, you still get hit.

Chapter 10

After almost two months in Orleans Parish Prison, two U.S. marshals showed up one morning, put me in handcuffs and leg-irons, and drove me to Marianna, Florida, where I went to federal court. There I pled guilty to simple escape from federal custody and was sentenced to an additional fifteen months. I was sent back to FCI Tallahassee.

I wasn't back long before the administration decided to round up the prison's troublemakers, and I found myself among them.

Twenty of us were taken to the receiving area and subjected to a thorough body search. Naked, we were crammed into a holding cell for almost three hours. Issued clothes, we were locked in handcuffs, belly chains, and leg-irons, then marched outside to a waiting bus.

Twelve of us were dropped off at the federal prison in Atlanta, Georgia. There we were given mattresses, escorted to a large holding cell, and told to find a spot on the floor to sleep.

Three weeks later, eight of us were again handcuffed, shackled, and marched to another waiting bus. Later that night, we arrived at the federal prison in Terre Haute, Indiana.

My arrival at the infamous federal prison was one of the most sobering experiences of my life. It was snowing heavily and near midnight when I stepped off the bus into a dark, wet, frozen, black-and-white world. Single file and very slowly, the leg-irons biting into my ankles with every step, I followed the other prisoners across a tarmac covered in crunching snow to stand under a tall guard tower built of stone. A cold wind whipped at the thin clothes I wore, causing me to shiver.

I stared up at the guard in the tower. Dressed in a fur-lined hooded parka, he pointed a fully automatic assault rifle at me.

This is real, I thought. *This ain't some old black-and-white prison movie or a nightmare that will go away when I wake up. This is real. One wrong move and he'll kill me.* Inexplicably, I felt a strong urge to run, just as a person standing on the ledge of a tall building may feel a strong urge to jump.

"All right, now!" shouted the guard to my right. "Single file! Let's move out!"

For six weeks, I was locked in an isolation cell at Terre Haute, then early one morning put on a bus headed west. It was during this ride that I heard for the first time the term "diesel therapy."

Sitting next to me was an older prisoner nicknamed Doc. He told me that he had been in federal prison for almost fifteen years and had been in diesel therapy for almost four.

"Diesel therapy?" I asked. "What's that?"

"You don't know what diesel therapy is?" asked Doc. "Man, you *are new* to the system, ain't you? Let me explain. Look, whenever the Feds get a problem prisoner like me—and obviously like you, 'cause you're here with me—they put 'em on a bus and ride 'em all over the country from prison to prison. And believe me, that usually solves the problem."

"Is that what happened to you? That the reason you've been ridin' buses for four years?"

"Yep. I was just a little too smart for my own good and I wanted to show 'em just how smart I was. You know what's worse than being *dumb* and in prison?"

"What?"

"Being *smart* and in prison," said Doc, "especially if you let 'em know just how smart you are. You see, I was a pretty good jailhouse lawyer—one of the best, if I do say so myself—and I filed several good legitimate lawsuits against the Federal Bureau of Prisons. So one day they put me on a bus and set me to ridin',

and I been ridin' around the country from prison to prison since. I no longer have access to the law library, nor am I able to get a visit from my family. Hell, I can't even get my mail or money sent to me so I can go to the canteen because by the time my mail or money gets to where I am, I been moved to another prison. And you know what? There's nothin' I can do about it."

"You mean I been in diesel therapy and didn't even know it?" I said.

"Yep," said Doc. "What'd you do?"

"All I did was escape."

"That'll do it."

That evening I was dropped off at Leavenworth federal prison, where I lived in an eight-man cell in population for the next few weeks.

Leavenworth was even more impressive and scarier than Atlanta or Terre Haute. The cellblocks were five stories high and housed thousands of prisoners. The dayroom was as large as an airport hangar.

One day I ran into a captain who had worked at FCI Tallahassee. He remembered me. "Bridges," he told me. "I figured you'd end up in a place like this. Did you know that at twenty years old you're officially the youngest prisoner in Leavenworth?"

A few weeks later I was sent to FCI El Reno in Oklahoma, where I lived for six weeks, then was sent to my final destination, FCI Texarkana, near the Texas-Arkansas line.

Twenty months later, in 1972, after serving three years and three months on an original sentence of two years, I was released.

When my sister Dianne learned that I had no place to go, she again came to my rescue, graciously inviting me to come live

with her family, which now included two small children and my younger sister, Tonda.

I took a bus to Lake Charles in southwest Louisiana where she and her family lived.

In retrospect, I now realize how difficult life must have been for my sister, working a full-time job at the telephone company while caring for a growing family, but she seldom complained. All her life had been given over to caring for others. She had always been the calm center of the hurricane that had been our dysfunctional family.

When I got out of federal prison, I was twenty-two and had spent the last two years working out, developing my body, but had done little to develop my mind. Consequently, I was physically strong but still angry, confused, and self-centered.

The next three years (1972–1975) were a whirlwind of anger and discontent and I made mistake after mistake, callously and deliberately stepping on or grinding down anyone or anything that tried to prevent my immediate gratification.

I got married and had a son but was a much worse parent than even my own parents had been, abandoning my young wife and son when it pleased me, often for a month at a time. I worked when I wanted, seldom paid my bills, and moved from house to house and state to state, just like my father. It was inevitable that I would become involved in some form of criminal activity. I burglarized businesses, stole their payroll checks, and cashed them. I got away with it for a while, then in 1975 I tripped a silent alarm while burglarizing a construction company in Plaquemines Parish, just south of New Orleans.

Caught inside the business, I was sent thirty miles south to the Plaquemines Parish jail, located in the small community of Pointe à La Hache near the mouth of the Mississippi River.

On one side of the long highway that led to Pointe à La Hache flowed the mighty Mississippi River, and on the other an earthen levee. In some places, the land was only a hundred yards wide. Beyond the levee were endless miles of marsh and swamp.

From the first day, convinced that I could escape (and ignoring the consequences), I examined every inch of the third-floor jail, trying to find a way out and failing time and again. First, I carefully made a key for the back door out of a folded aluminum tobacco can, but the key bent and wouldn't turn in the lock. Next, I tried to dig through a foot-thick concrete ceiling using only a large metal spoon but gave up after a week.

Then one day while sitting on the toilet, I noticed that the back wall of my cell, made of quarter-inch steel, was rusted in several places, exposing tiny holes the size of BBs. I quickly grabbed my large spoon and, using the handle, enlarged one of the holes to the size of a penny.

The next day I rented the use of a pipe wrench from a trustee in exchange for $20. Working at the wall for hours, I used the wrench to rip out an L-shaped area large enough for me to crawl into the pipe chase behind my cell.

That night I crawled through the hole into the pipe chase and from there was able to get to the catwalk and windows to the outside. After twisting out the window frame with the pipe wrench, I tied several sheets together to make a rope and climbed out the third-story window to the parking area below. Crossing the nearby highway, I reached the levee and headed north. Jogging, I quickly developed blisters and soon threw my shoes away, which I regretted later when I ran into large patches of stickers.

I made about eight or nine miles before daylight, then, certain that men with dogs would be out searching for me at first light, I started looking for a place to hide until dark. Seeing a

large bush near a small pond, I walked closer to investigate. After months of nothing but gray walls, dirty concrete, and steel bars, I stood at the edge of the marsh pond and truly appreciated the red, orange, and violet sky of early morning, the nearby cattails gently waving in the breeze, and, thirty yards away, a blue heron perched on one leg, fishing for breakfast. It was fascinating and achingly beautiful.

I heard a dog bark and dropped into a crouch. Trembling, I crawled inside the large bush and looked out to see two deputies with a dog on a leash, walking behind a slow-moving pickup truck. I burrowed deeper inside the bush, closed my eyes, and prayed.

After the deputies passed, I slept away the entire day, emerging at dusk to continue on stiff legs and tender feet my trek north to New Orleans.

I was hungry and covered in mud and mosquito bites but mostly I was thirsty. I needed fresh water but was afraid to get too close to the Mississippi River because of all the people living along its banks. So I continued to hobble along the base of the levee. Eventually I came across a mud puddle, three feet by two feet, and stopped. The water in the center was crystal clear, although around the edges it was cloudy and muddy. I straddled the puddle and bent until my face was an inch from the center. Careful not to stir the water on the bottom, I gently slurped the sweet rainwater until satisfied.

Refreshed, I continued north, walking again until first light, then stopping to fashion a hideout in the tall grass. But after a few hours of tossing and turning and battling mosquitoes, I grew impatient and left my hideout. It was early afternoon, the sun hot and bright, and there was almost no traffic on the lone highway, so I took a chance and started walking.

A couple hours later, exhausted, I sat down on an old railroad tie to rest and had been there only a few minutes when

I heard, "Don't move! Don't even think about it!" Slowly I turned my head, despite the warning, and two feet behind me stood two sheriff's deputies, both holding shotguns.

Covered in mud, stinking of swamp, red welts covering my shirtless torso, barefoot, and hobbling in leg-irons, the sheriff proudly paraded me past the other prisoners (including the trustee that had rented me the pipe wrench) to show them the end result should they decide to escape themselves.

I was locked in a padded cell. The walls were covered in heavy pads and the floor, except for a hole in the center, was covered with a black rubber mat. Exhausted, I slept as soundly as if in a hotel.

It seemed as if the sheriff and I shared a sense of the dramatic as well as the practical. The next morning, he showed up outside my cell with two trustees and a portable welding machine. He welded the cell door shut. It's strange, but I actually felt a sense of pride in knowing that the sheriff thought I was so dangerous that he needed to seal me inside the cell like a wild but clever animal.

Six weeks later, the welds sealing the door were cut, and that afternoon I was moved back to the general population.

A couple weeks later, after listening to the advice of my court-appointed lawyer, I pled guilty to all charges and was sentenced to five years for burglary and three years for escape.

Two weeks later, I was sent to the state penitentiary at Angola.

Chapter 11

The swift, muddy Mississippi River wraps itself around Angola horseshoe fashion, hugging the eighteen-thousand-acre prison farm like it is something precious that may get lost or something evil that may be loosed upon the world.

The open end of the horseshoe is protected by the Tunica Hills, treacherous cliffs that suddenly drop fifty feet in some places. And beyond the river and hills are snake- and alligator-infested swampland.

Shortly after the Civil War, Angola initiated the practice of convict leasing: renting its convicts to surrounding plantations to replace slave labor. During this sorrowful period, which lasted for decades, thousands of prisoners died from beatings, exposure, and malnutrition. Eventually the inhumane practice was abolished, but the cruelty and corruption at Angola continued.

In the fifties, Angola received national attention when prisoners on work gangs opted to slash the tendons of their ankles rather than to continue to work in the sugarcane fields. In the sixties, a nationally known magazine called Angola the "bloodiest prison in the South."

By the time I got to Angola in 1976, the National Guard and state police had been called in so often to deal with work strikes and riots that the mood, while not exactly peaceful, was certainly more subdued. Still, there was a lot of violence in Angola and I personally witnessed three murders and several assaults during my time there.

Angola was more than just a prison; it was a large prison complex. Home to more than five thousand inmates, Angola had its own chapel, cemetery, license tag plant, silk-screen shop,

blood bank, cannery, print shop, rodeo arena, and even a residential area for the families of employees.

Divided into two areas, Angola's main prison was called the Big Yard and housed about three thousand prisoners. Surrounding the Big Yard were several smaller prisons, called camps, each housing two to three hundred. These camps were where all new prisoners were sent the first six months to perform hard labor clearing fields, digging drainage ditches, and picking soybeans or cotton under the supervision of brutal shotgun guards on horseback.

I hated working in the fields and couldn't wait to complete my required six months. Finally, when my time was up, I asked to be transferred to the Big Yard and to be assigned to a job in the cannery. It was while working in the cannery that I witnessed my first murder.

That morning, when we reported to work, all seventy of us were given short paring knives and instructed to line up on both sides of a long conveyer stacked with okra. We were then told to cut the okra into half-inch pieces so that it could be processed further.

All morning I worked between two men who viciously argued. By afternoon, their argument escalated; one man reached over me and stabbed the other with his paring knife. Immediately I dropped to my knees and crawled under the conveyer. I watched the two men roll in the sawdust and stab each other repeatedly. When it was all over, one of the men was dead.

A couple months later I went to work in Angola's tag plant, silk-screening road signs, and at night volunteered as an illustrator and layout artist on the prison news magazine, *The Angolite*. After a year I quit working at the tag plant and went to work on the news magazine full-time.

During my third year in Angola I received a letter from Dianne telling me that our mother had been told by her doctor that she only had a couple months to live. A few weeks later I received a short note from my mother herself. She didn't say anything about her terminal illness, only that she and my father were coming to visit.

The last time that I had seen my parents I was eighteen, and now I was thirty-one. We had all aged, but when I walked into the visiting area I was shocked by my mother's physical appearance. Although she was still in her mid-fifties, she looked seventy years old. Her skinny arms were covered in large reddish-brown sores, some the size of quarters, and her stomach was distended. Her face was skeletal. My mother's once beautiful long blond hair was clipped and thin and stringy and looked like a clown's wig. She could barely sit up, and my father had to take her to the restroom four times during our three-hour visit.

During one trip to the restroom, I accompanied my father. While we waited he told me, "The doctor said your mama's only got about a month to live. He said she's got cirrhosis of the liver." He then took out his handkerchief and removed his glass eye. Embarrassed, I looked around to see if anyone was watching. My father wiped his eye carefully, then put it back in. "I'm getting me a new eye. This one's cracked. Just a couple weeks ago, out of the blue, your mama says, 'I wanna go see Rickey.' So here we are."

Back at the table, I asked her how she was feeling, hoping that she'd tell me of her illness, hoping that she'd tell me herself that she was dying, but instead she told me that she was okay. I wondered if I should just tell her that I knew. I kept hoping that my father would say something about her illness in her presence so that we could stop the charade and get it all out in the open, but neither of us had the courage to make such a bold, honest declaration. So the small talk continued. My mother talked about

the drive from Lake Charles, my father about his work, and I talked about the living conditions in prison.

When it was time for them to leave, I hugged my mother's frail body for the last time and shook my father's disinterested hand. As I watched them leave, I asked myself, *Who are they? Who am I?* I walked back to my dormitory on the Big Yard.

Three weeks later, the chaplain called me to his office and told me what I had been expecting to hear. "I'm sorry to tell you, but your mother has died."

I felt sadness but also relief. Life had never been kind to her and now she was finally free from her illness and the debilitating sadness that had always been so much a part of her life.

"The memorial service will be in five days," said the chaplain. "If you want to go, an officer will take you."

"Will I have to be handcuffed and wear leg-irons?" I asked.

"Yes, that's the normal policy. You'll be in restraints and escorted by an armed correctional officer."

"Well then, I don't wanna go."

"Are you sure? This is your mother."

Three days later, a guard told me that the warden wanted to see me. Handcuffed, I was escorted through the front gate to a transport van for a short drive to the administration building.

The administration building was only a quarter of a mile from the Big Yard, but it was a world away in appearance. The walkway, leading to a modern, one-story brick structure, was bordered in colorful flower beds, the grass emerald green. And inside the building the walls were painted white instead of the usual pale institutional green. Prints, posters, and paintings adorned the walls. Large plants in big red clay pots sat next to plush office furniture.

The guard and I stood outside the warden's office, waiting. Bored, the guard shuffled from foot to foot and kept looking at

his watch. Finally, the door opened and the warden's secretary, an attractive woman in her early thirties, stepped out. "Warden Blackburn will see you now," she said.

"Let's go," said the guard gruffly, nudging me toward the door.

We stepped into a large, well-lit office with carpeting on the floor and waist-high wooden wainscoting on the walls. It was apparent by the awards and photos that Warden Blackburn was a man of many accomplishments.

The warden was a short, heavy, swarthy man with a thick black mustache. He wore a dress shirt and tie and sat behind an ornate desk reading a file folder while chewing on an unlit cigar. He looked up when we entered.

"Remove the handcuffs and wait outside," he told the guard standing next to me.

After the office door had closed and we were alone, Warden Blackburn said, "Bridges, go ahead have a seat."

I sat in a chair to the right of his desk.

"I'm sorry to hear that your mother passed."

"Thank you. I was expecting it. She came to see me a few weeks ago."

"Well, I know it's never easy when a man loses his mother."

"Yes sir."

"The reason I asked to see you," said the warden, "is that the chaplain tells me you don't want to attend your mother's memorial service in Lake Charles. Is that right?"

"Not exactly, Warden. I *do* want to go; I just don't want to go in handcuffs like some kinda freak. That would be embarrassing not only for me, but for all my relatives."

"I understand that. But you *are* a prisoner and our policy is clear, especially when it comes to inmates with a history of escape. I've been looking at your file." He patted the folder he'd been reading when I first entered his office. "You're serving an

escape sentence right now—from Plaquemines Parish jail. Is that correct?"

"Yes sir."

"So tell me why I should take a chance and let you go to your mother's memorial service without restraints."

"I understand, Warden. And I'm not saying you should. I'm just saying that I don't want to go looking like a freak, that's all."

Warden Blackburn picked up my file. He flipped through it. "You've maintained a good record since you've been at Angola. You've done excellent work on *The Angolite*. You have what—about a year and a half left?"

"Twenty months, I think, Warden."

"You'd be a fool to escape again," said the warden. "It's almost over."

"I agree. I just want to finish my time, get out, and start a new life," I said.

"Well, I'll tell you what I'm going to do, Bridges. I'm going to take a chance on you. If you give me your word you won't try to escape, I'll let you go to your mother's memorial service without restraints."

"You've got it," I said. "There's no way that I'd dishonor my mama's memory by escaping. I promise. And, Warden, I appreciate the trust."

"Don't let me down, Bridges. You know if you do, we'll just catch you again and you'll get more time."

"I won't. You got my word."

Warden Blackburn sent for the correctional officer. When the guard fished in his Sam Browne belt for handcuffs, the warden said, "That's not necessary. Me and Bridges here have an understanding." He smiled. "Just take him on back to the Big Yard."

The next morning, after an early breakfast, I was hustled through three checkpoints and two metal detectors and just

outside the back gate got into a van with a lone, unarmed guard. We drove past several camps until we came to a ferry docked at a landing. The guard drove the van onto the ferry and parked.

"Let's get out and stretch our legs," he said.

I was wary, not used to a guard treating me as an equal. I stood at the railing, transfixed and silent, watching the swirling muddy river play at the bow of the ferry.

I turned, looked back at Angola. The early morning sun was just beginning to lighten the sky. In the distance, I saw the silhouette of a long line of prisoners carrying hoes on their shoulders like rifles and marching behind two guards on horseback. A water wagon, drawn by a mule, followed. I thought about the first day that I too had carried a hoe and had marched in that line. I remembered asking the man in front of me, "How long we work?"

He laughed, then said, "Man, in Angola, we work from can't see to can't see."

Chapter 12

When we docked on the opposite bank, it was as if the ferry had been a time machine and we had travelled back in time a thousand years. Stretched in front of us was a straight two-lane blacktop on a narrow strip of land bordered by water as black as oil and partially covered in green scum. Huge cypress, draped in moss and surrounded by cypress "knees"—seedlings three or four feet tall—were positioned like opposing pieces on some giant's chessboard.

Both the officer and I were quiet—he staring straight ahead and me out the passenger window as we drove to the small town of St. Francisville. There we turned south toward Baton Rouge.

Baton Rouge held a lot of memories. It was in Baton Rouge that I learned to drink in nightclubs, where the relaxed laws allowed sixteen- and seventeen-year-olds to do so with impunity. It was there, in the back seat of a '55 Chevy, that I experienced a crude and embarrassing form of sexual intercourse for the first time. And there in a recruiter's office that I joined the Marine Corps, leading to a spiral of pain and crime from which I would spend a lifetime trying to break free.

After Baton Rouge we travelled Interstate 10 west and forty miles later crossed the Atchafalaya Swamp to reach the small Cajun community of Breaux Bridge, Crawfish Capital of the World. Twenty-five miles past Breaux Bridge we passed the outskirts of Lafayette. I knew that ninety minutes more would bring us to our destination, Lake Charles. But what I didn't know, and couldn't have known, was that six years later I would rob a bank in Lafayette, one of many.

An hour and a half later I stood beside my mother's coffin and stared at her body. She was in a satin-lined casket, her hands

on her breast, left over right. On her ring finger was a small diamond engagement ring and a matching wedding band. On her face was a tight smile.

What a rough life she had, I thought, *but it's all over now. She can finally rest. I just regret that the last time we saw each other, we didn't say what a normal mother and son should when one of them is facing certain death.*

I wish my mother had told me, "Son, I'm dyin' and I just had to come see you once more so that I could tell you that I love you and say how sorry I am that you had such a terrible childhood. I really wanted life to be different for both of us, but I was just too weak and didn't have the strength to overcome all that life threw at me. I hope you'll forgive me. I'm sorry."

I wish I had told her, "Mama, I'm sorry too. I'm sorry that when you needed me most, I was in prison. I'm sorry that I wasn't a better son."

Not only did we waste our last chance to say a few simple words to ease the pain and validate our journey through life as mother and son, but we've both wasted the gifts that life has given us. Just look at her. It's hard to believe that just a few weeks ago, she had been a living, breathing human being and we had shared the same space, and now she's just an empty shell in a fancy box.

I felt someone lightly touch my arm and turned to see Dianne standing next to me. We hugged. "They did a good job, didn't they?" she whispered. "She looks so alive. I fixed her hair and makeup this morning."

Yeah, she looks more alive dead than she did alive, I thought.

"The doctor said that she drank so much that her liver hardened," continued my sister.

"Yeah, she looks real good," I said out loud. "You did a nice job on her hair and makeup." But inside I continued my bitter inner dialogue. *Don't you see! That's not our mother! And whatever it is, it don't look alive! It looks like something out of a wax museum. I don't know where our mother is, but she's not in that box.*

I looked beyond my sister to see my father walk into the chapel. He had always been a lean man, but now he looked shrunken, as if he had lost weight. The dark-blue suit he wore hung on him like the saggy jowls of a bloodhound. He wore glasses, the right lens darkened to hide his empty eye socket. His sparse, dark hair was still wet and the few strands left were carefully combed.

He stared across the room, saw me and Dianne standing by the casket, and walked over. Dianne hugged him. I shook his hand and patted his arm.

My father stepped closer to the casket. He leaned over and looked inside. "I'm gonna miss her," he said. "We been married thirty-five years." He looked at me. "Dianne came over this mornin' and fixed her hair. I bought her a new dress. Don't she look good?"

"Yeah, Daddy, she looks real good. Everybody did a nice job fixin' her up," I said. *Why didn't you buy her a new dress when she was alive? Why didn't somebody fix her hair and makeup while she could still appreciate it? This thing in a box don't know if it's wearing a ball gown or rags; it don't know if its lipstick's on right. New clothes and nice makeup and memorial services are for the living, not the dead.*

"Rickey," said my father, interrupting my thoughts. "I got her a nice burial plot [years later, I found out that Dianne had paid for everything] and I bought me one right next to her."

"That's nice, Dad." *Oh, just great! Now on Friday and Saturday nights you can crawl out of your grave and into hers and beat the hell out of her like you used to do when we lived in Trade Alley. Just great! And now you'll always know just exactly where she is. How convenient.*

After the short memorial service, in which no one gave a eulogy, my sister approached the guard standing next to me. "We're all planning to go across the street for lunch. Would it be okay for you and Rickey to join us?"

115

The guard looked at his watch. "We still got an hour and a half till we need to head back. I wanna get back to Angola before dark." He turned to me. "It's up to him. If he wants to."

I nodded my head, certainly not in a hurry to rush back to prison.

While crossing the street to a small neighborhood restaurant, the guard said, "I just wanna remind you that I'm trusting you. Don't do nothin' foolish and you'll be able to get yourself a good free-world meal before we head back."

"I gave the warden my word," I said. "I'll keep it." Even as the words left my lips, I wondered if I'd be able to control myself should the opportunity present itself.

Followed by the guard, I walked into the restaurant and sat down at a long table next to my uncle Blackie, a man I hadn't seen since I was a boy. Married to my mother's youngest sister, he had always been kind to me and my mother. He had taught me to shoot marbles when I was a young boy. I wasn't surprised that he and Aunt Dolly were the only members of my mother's family to travel to Lake Charles for her memorial service. The rest had given up on my parents years ago.

"How much longer until you get out?" asked Uncle Blackie.

"About a year and a half," I said, "that is, if north Louisiana drops some old charges they got against me. I've filed legal papers but haven't heard anything yet."

"Well, we're livin' in Greenville now," said Uncle Blackie. "I manage a car lot there. Come look me up when you do get out and I'll put you to work selling cars."

"I just might do that," I said. "Thanks," but thought, *I doubt you really want an ex-con working for you, but I appreciate you making the offer. I really do.*

I had witnessed death up close and personal but I had never been to a memorial service or a funeral, so my only model of

behavior for those attending was what I had seen on TV or in the movies. And there everybody talked about what a wonderful person the deceased had been. They spoke of the dead person's strength of character or their sense of humor, they spoke of the departed's honesty or generosity, but that wasn't what I was hearing at this gathering. Instead, the talk was about the food or the weather. I heard Uncle Blackie talking to the guard about pickup trucks. The only complimentary words that I had heard all day regarding my mother weren't how well she had lived her life but how good she looked dead.

What did I expect? I asked myself. Did I really expect the people gathered around this table to honestly describe my mother's life? Of course not! Because if they did, the only words they could honestly speak would be "extreme tragedy, long suffering, chronic alcoholism, frequent infidelity, severe mental illness," and "soul-wrenching pain."

There will be plenty of time later for raw honesty, probably during the drive home or later, while safe and snug behind their bedroom doors. Then they can speak truthfully of my mother and her life. But not today and not here.

Even though it had been years since I had eaten anything other than prison food, I had no appetite and only picked at the seafood platter in front of me, my stomach feeling queasy. I turned to the guard. "I think I'm gonna be sick. I need to go to the restroom."

"Go ahead," he said, holding my gaze longer than normal.

I excused myself, got up, and walked to the restroom. Inside I found a stall, closed the door, dropped my pants, and sat down. *I'm alone and free for the first time in years,* I thought. I looked around. Five feet above me was a window with a latch on the inside.

I pulled up my pants, stood on the toilet, reached over the stall, unlocked the window, opened it, and looked outside. All I

saw was an empty alley with a dumpster and the side of the building next door.

All I gotta do is crawl through, drop to the ground, and then I'm free, I thought. *Free to do what? Steal a car and head for the Texas line thirty miles away. Oh, that's just perfect! A perfect ending to my mother's sad life. I can see the headlines now: "Convict Escapes During Mother's Memorial Service."*

When I returned to the table and sat down, the look of relief in the eyes of the guard was unmistakable.

The guard and I spoke little during the drive back, and I was thankful that he was sensitive enough to leave me to my own thoughts.

Staring out the window at the flat, vivid-green Louisiana landscape zipping by, I thought about all that had happened since I had left Angola that morning. I specifically remembered what my sister Dianne had told me when we were alone and I had asked her, "When Mama came to visit me at Angola, she wasn't wearing a wedding band or engagement ring, but I saw rings on her finger. Where did they come from?"

"Oh, Daddy bought those rings for her on credit just two weeks before she died," said Dianne. "She was so proud. You should've seen her. She told me that those rings were the first ones she'd had in thirty years. You see, Daddy pawned her original rings when me and you were little. I don't think she ever got over it."

I conjured the image of my mother sitting in her ladder-back chair, staring out the window. I saw her slowly rubbing the base of her empty ring finger with the pad of her left thumb. In that moment, I discovered a small but important clue to the sadness that had been so much a part of my mother's life.

Chapter 13

Depressed, I grieved not just for the loss of my mother but for the way she had lived her life. And I was conflicted; while part of me felt foolish for voluntarily returning to a maximum-security prison, another part felt proud that I had kept my word to the warden. The first week back, all I did was sleep, watch TV, and, with a radio and headphones glued to my head, walk mile after mile on the recreation yard. Then one morning, languishing in bed, I told myself, *Enough! Get up and get your ass in gear!*

I took a shower and went to work in *The Angolite* office. The coeditors, Wilbert Rideau and Billy Sinclair, were busy working on the next issue and had plenty of projects to keep me busy. Rideau and Sinclair had met on Angola's death row in the sixties. There they had shared an interest in reading and writing and had become friends. When the death sentence was repealed, albeit briefly, in the seventies (and death row inmates all over the country had their sentences commuted to life), Rideau and Sinclair were released to live in Angola's general population, where they became coeditors of *The Angolite*.

I arrived in Angola a couple years after Rideau and Sinclair took over as coeditors. At first I worked as an illustrator, then as a layout artist and photographer. During the four years that I worked on *The Angolite*, I helped transform what had been a crude, black-and-white prison newspaper into a slick, two-color publication. But it was Rideau and Sinclair's probing articles and highly polished writing that made *The Angolite* the most celebrated prison publication ever printed. While I was on the newspaper staff, *The Angolite* won the Robert F. Kennedy Journalism Award and the George Polk Award and two of the issues I worked on in 1978 and 1979 are in the Smithsonian

National Museum of African American History and Culture. I personally won a national award for design and layout.

Eighteen months later, on the morning of my release, I said goodbye to the friends I had made the last five years and walked to receiving and discharge. There, after signing release papers and dressing in civilian clothes, I was escorted to a holding cell to, I assumed, await transportation to the bus station in downtown St. Francisville. Joyous and anxious at the same time, I walked back and forth in the holding cell, my mind a swirl of plans for the future, when I heard someone yell, "Bridges!" Then I heard another voice answer, "Yeah, we got him in a holding cell in the back!"

A prison guard, trailed by two sheriff's deputies carrying leg-irons, handcuffs, and a belly chain, entered the room. I felt sick to my stomach when I read the deputies' shoulder patches. And even though I knew the answer, I asked, "What's going on?"

"These two deputies are here to take you back to north Louisiana," said the correctional officer.

Heartbroken, I didn't have the strength to respond or complain. I quietly allowed myself to be trussed in chains, then escorted to Angola's parking area. There I was placed in the back of a patrol car for the two-hour trip to north Louisiana.

After being photographed and fingerprinted in the jail's booking room, a deputy escorted me to the sheriff's office. "Son, I understand that you just came here from Angola," said the sheriff.

"Yes sir," I responded. "I've been there five and a half years."

"That's what it says here," he said, holding up a sheet of paper.

"I thought the detainer against me had been dropped," I said. "A couple years ago, I filed legal papers but never heard anything, so I thought the charges had been dropped."

"Well, I don't know anything about that. That's not my department. The reason I wanted to talk to you is because I need someone your age and height to stand in a lineup for me. You don't have to worry; you won't be charged with nothing since you were in Angola when the crime occurred. It's just that I need a warm body fits the description. So how's about it?"

"I don't think so, Sheriff. I really don't feel much like standin' in a lineup."

"Ain't no harm gonna come of it. Hell, even if the witness picked you out, nothin's gonna happen. You got the world's greatest alibi. You were in prison. So how about it? I'd consider it a personal favor."

"Sheriff, ain't nothin' says I gotta stand in a lineup. I don't want to and don't have to! And I ain't doin' it!" I shouted, louder than I should have.

The sheriff's neck and face went from normally pale cream to a crimson. "Red!" he yelled to the deputy standing behind me. "Red!"

"Yes sir!" said the deputy, rushing to stand in front of me.

"Take this smart-ass back there to B-tank!"

"B-tank! You sure, Sheriff?"

"That's what I said, Red! You heard me! Take him back to B-tank and let those niggers fuck 'im in the ass! Let's see how he likes that! I bet he'll cooperate then!" The sheriff then looked me in the eye. "You just fucked up, boy!" He turned to Red. "Get him outta my sight!"

At that point, I probably should have fallen to my knees, begged the sheriff for forgiveness, and asked to be included in his lineup, but my pride wouldn't let me. And even though I had witnessed the sheriff's rage firsthand and had listened to his rant,

I didn't really understand how dangerous his threat was. I wouldn't fully grasp his evil intention until after I had been in B-tank for a while and had seen the cruelty firsthand.

Red, a tall, skinny, pasty-faced man in his early thirties who seemed to take a mean pleasure in his job, hummed a country tune while herding me past steel door after steel door. Finally, when we reached a door marked B-tank, he opened it and we stepped through into a short hall with steel bars floor to ceiling, I looked through to see about twenty Black faces staring back at me.

Red pulled a lever built into a control box on the wall behind me and a door in the steel bars slid open. "Go on, get in there," grinned Red. "Find yourself a bunk."

Even after all the prisons I'd been in and all the violence I'd seen, I had never been as scared as I was at that moment. Still, I knew that no matter what I felt on the inside, I dare not show it on the outside. Experience reminded me that to show fear was to invite an attack. I also knew that I had to appear calm and confident but not arrogant because showing arrogance was just as bad as showing fear.

I stepped through the door and stood for a moment. In a freeze-frame moment, every man in B-tank stopped what he had been doing to quickly take his measure of me. I looked around. In the middle of the hall that ran the length of the cellblock, six men played cards while sitting on blankets spread on the floor. Near the shower at the end of the hall, a man greased and plaited the hair of another who sat on an upturned mop bucket. Two prisoners walked back and forth, talking. A few stood just inside their cell doors, staring out.

Fully aware that I was being observed, I walked down the hall, looking for a cell with an empty bunk. When I sidestepped a man playing cards, I said, "Excuse me," but he didn't respect me enough to acknowledge me.

Finally, I found a cell with three empty beds. A large man reading a book was on one of the top bunks. I stuck my head just inside the door and said, "Excuse me, any of these bunks empty?"

"They all empty, except this one," he said, smiling. He laid the open book on his bare chest. "Just take your pick." He picked up his book again.

"Appreciate it," I said, ending our brief conversation.

Stretching out on one of the bottom bunks, I closed my eyes and pretended to sleep, but behind closed eyes my mind raced. *What do I do now? Can't show fear, no matter what happens. Got to just keep quiet and mind my own business for now. Got to stay humble and polite but strong. Can't show fear. No fear. No fear. No ...* I repeated my new mantra until I fell asleep.

Later that afternoon the big man on the top bunk—who was probably six-six, weighed three hundred pounds, and appeared even larger off the bunk—told me that his name was Calvin.

Now that he had decided to talk, Calvin spoke freely of his family, his work, his worries, and his dreams. In his mid-thirties, Calvin was married, with three children. He had lived in north Louisiana his entire life and had worked as a bricklayer since he was a teen. Calvin, who had never been in jail before, had been arrested for DUI. Understandably, he was worried about the welfare of his wife and children and showed me photos of his family. He bragged about how smart his children were. We talked until late that night.

A week later Calvin and I were sitting on an empty bottom bunk playing cards when the door banged open and in walked a short, powerfully built Black man, his right arm in a cast from the elbow to the wrist and supported by a sling. The man's nickname was Cannonball. He was in his early forties, stood about five-five, and weighed about 250 pounds.

Born and raised in Chicago, Cannonball was a career criminal and had been in and out of prison since a teenager. Recently, he had jumped parole and had fled south where, during the attempted robbery of a convenience store the day before, he had been shot by an off-duty policeman. After spending the night in the hospital under close guard, the next day he had been booked into the jail and promptly sent to B-tank.

Most men with Cannonball's history and recent bad luck would've been bitter and angry, but not him. He had a lively, if macabre, sense of humor (as do many who have served long periods in prison), and he smiled often behind a Pancho Villa–style mustache. His front teeth were capped in gold and flashed when he smiled.

Cannonball was a fatalist and didn't believe in *cause and effect*. He had somehow reasoned that to do so would require a measure of responsibility for his lot in life and so had decided that it was much easier to just do *what* he wanted, *when* he wanted, and *how* he wanted, then blame fate and accept the consequences, no matter how dire. In fact, my own outlook on life at the time was very similar to that of Cannonball's, and we got along great from the beginning.

Sharing what little we had, Cannonball, Calvin, and I spent the majority of our time in the cell reading, talking, and playing cards.

I soon realized that the population of B-tank could be divided into two factions: those under twenty-five and those older. The younger faction was suspicious of anyone older or different. Scared and insecure, they felt the need to prove they weren't and so looked for any excuse to argue or fight. The older faction, to which Cannonball, Calvin, and I belonged, still held dearly to a misunderstood sense of honor. Not feeling the need

to prove ourselves to anyone, we responded to violence only when our personal safety had been threatened or our sense of honor compromised.

After a month in B-tank with no problems, I began to relax but didn't forget that I was despised by many simply because of the color of my skin. I was particularly disliked by those younger and so continued to maintain a low profile, staying out of the hall where most arguments and fights started, keeping my emotions in check and my innermost thoughts to myself.

One day, the door banged open and everyone in B-tank turned toward the sound. Red pushed a tall, skinny white man through the door. Obviously drunk, he appeared to be in his late fifties and wore a red baseball cap with a Confederate flag on the front. Underneath the flag were written the words "Hell no! We ain't forgetting."

As soon as I read the front of the hat, I knew that the drunk was in trouble and wondered what *he* could have possibly done to anger the sheriff.

The barred door slammed shut. Startled, the drunk spun in a half circle, then stumbled. Regaining his balance, he shook his head slowly, like an animal trying to shake off the effects of a tranquilizer dart.

After a whispered discussion, three young prisoners stopped their card game and walked over to where the confused drunk stood. "Why they put you in here, Pop?" asked the first prisoner.

The drunk didn't answer.

"Where'd you get that cap?" asked the second. "You some kinda Klux or somethin'?"

"Yeah, I betcha that's what he is," said the third, giggling. "He's one of them Kluxers for sure."

The first prisoner reached up and slapped the old man hard on the side of the head. The drunk fell, landing on his back. His

125

cap slid down the hall. The drunk rubbed the side of his head and looked up.

"What'd you do that for?" he whined.

"'Cause you a racist old pig, that's why! I oughta stomp your ass!" shouted the first prisoner.

The drunk crawled over to retrieve his cap, but just as he reached for it, the second prisoner kicked him in the backside, sending him sprawling.

"Oh Lord! Oh Lord!" screamed the drunk. "They tryin' to kill me! Somebody help me! Help!" He crawled to the door, grabbed the steel bars, pulled himself to his feet, and yelled for help that didn't come. Finally, a coughing fit took his voice. He staggered over to an empty cell, found a bottom bunk, and passed out.

The three prisoners returned to their card game. The first prisoner, now wearing the drunk's baseball cap backwards like a trophy, said to the other two, "Let's give 'im a little while, then we'll wrap 'im." They all laughed.

About an hour later, standing in the doorway of my cell, I watched the three prisoners enter the drunk's cell. One of them carried a roll of toilet paper. Carefully, they wrapped the old man head to toe like a mummy.

Curious, I stepped just outside the cell to get a better look. *What the hell are they doing?* I asked myself. *Why wrap him in toilet paper? Surely when he wakes up he can get loose easily.*

Then I saw the prisoner wearing the drunk's cap smile at the other two. He struck a match. The flaming toilet paper quickly traced the drunk's body like a lit fuse and the three prisoners ran from the drunk's cell, their faces as excited as those of children at a fireworks display.

With no thought, I grabbed my blanket off my bunk and ran to the drunk's cell, passing the three prisoners standing in the hall. When I entered the cell, the toilet paper covering the

drunk's arms and legs was a flaming spiderweb. The man, now awake and realizing that he was on fire, beat at his body, screaming and thrashing about, trying to wipe off the burning toilet paper but only fanning the flames. He rolled off his bunk and hit the concrete floor. I threw the blanket onto him but he thought that I was attacking him and flailed his arms, striking me in the chest and shoulders. Finally, I pinned him to the floor and smothered the flames.

I backed out of the cell and into the hall. The drunk, his clothes burnt and still smoking, followed.

A smoke alarm in the hall went off. When Red finally responded to the smoke alarm, he found the drunk on his knees at the grille gate weeping, his hair singed. The drunk had screamed so loudly for so long that now the only sound he could make was an insane whimper.

Red looked at the drunk and shook his head in disgust. He turned to a trustee standing behind him. "Go open those windows on the catwalk and let some fresh air in here." Red opened the grille gate and the drunk crawled through. He locked the door.

"I ain't comin' up here every five minutes!" he announced. "Y'all gonna quit setting shit on fire too, else I'm gonna come and take all the matches!"

Red, followed by the drunk and trustee, left.

On the way back to my cell, I passed the three prisoners in the hall, and the tension between us was electric.

"You need to learn to mind your own business, white boy," said the first prisoner, still wearing the drunk's cap.

"Yeah," said the second. "We been lettin' you make it in here, but now you fuckin' with our thing."

I realized that anything I said would only make matters worse, so I didn't respond. I just kept walking.

127

When I entered the cell, Calvin and Cannonball were now awake and sitting on Cannonball's bunk.

"Them young dudes is some sorry shits," said Calvin. "They coulda killed that old man."

"Man, they pissed off at you for putting out that fire. Took all their fun," smiled Cannonball. "You ain't gonna win no popularity contests around here, tell you that."

"Yeah, I know," I said warily. I sat down on my bunk, facing Cannonball and Calvin. "What was I supposed to do, let 'em burn him up?"

"I'm just saying," said Cannonball, "them young dudes is pissed."

"Maybe it'll pass," said Calvin the optimist.

"Yeah, and maybe they'll serve ice cream and pizza for lunch instead of greens and cornbread," grinned Cannonball, "but don't count on it."

"I ain't countin' on nothin', Cannonball. Nothin'!" I said, shaking my head.

Chapter 14

My eyes covered with a t-shirt to block out the bright lights, I lay on my bunk and thought, *Well, so much for low profile. Now everybody will be watchin' to see what happens next. Damn! Why didn't I just mind my own business? As much time as I've done, I should know better. But no! I just had to help that drunk. Why? Was it because he was white? I wonder if I would have helped him had he been Black. Probably not, no matter how much I'd like to think so. The truth is, deep down we're all biased to some degree and we all gravitate toward what looks like us. We're tribal. And what I did wasn't done out of compassion but was simply one tribe member protecting another.*

Well, the why of it doesn't matter now, not really. The damage is done and I've got myself in a jam, just what I've been trying to avoid. Well, maybe Calvin's right and it'll all blow over, but I doubt it. More than likely, Cannonball's right and those young dudes ain't gonna forget me spoilin' their fun. The way they see it, I disrespected 'em and somehow they'll figure out how to get even.

In a high state of paranoia, several times during the day I sneaked a look at the three arsonists huddled in their cell next to the shower, certain they were discussing me and what had happened. When one of them caught me watching, he whispered to the other two, and all three, as if their heads were on a swivel, stared back simultaneously. Embarrassed and frightened, I quickly looked away.

Living in the cell next to me was a quiet, angry young man named Jerome. Twenty years old and in jail for burglarizing parked cars, he stood six-one and had a lean athletic build. Even though Jerome and I lived within feet of each other, we had never spoken, and I had never seen him talking to the three

arsonists either, so later that day, when I saw him in their cell for what seemed a long time, I grew even more paranoid.

That night, Jerome, as instructed, crawled under his bunk, which was level with mine, reached through the steel bars separating our cells, and stole two packs of cigarettes and several packs of hot chocolate out of a plastic bag I had stored there.

I didn't discover the theft until that afternoon. When I did, I didn't react, knowing that I was in no position to make accusations and that it would be safer to suffer the loss and pretend nothing had happened. I thought this a good strategy, not realizing that pretending the theft had never occurred may even make the situation worse: I would now be seen as a coward by the thief and anyone else who knew.

After lockdown that night, I noticed Jerome in his cell not five feet away, smoking a cigarette, something I had never seen him do. That made me suspicious, but still I didn't say anything, determined to stick to my plan. But my plan quickly went down the toilet when Jerome stepped closer to the steel bars, sucked his teeth (a sound that to this day makes my skin crawl), took a long drag on his cigarette, and deliberately blew smoke in my face. "Yeah, that's right, white boy!" he said, loud enough for all to hear. "I'm the one stoled your smokes and hot chocolate! And you know what! Ain't nothin' you can do 'bout it!"

I was so angry I was speechless. Turning, I saw Calvin and Cannonball both staring at me, and I felt so much shame that I was unable to meet their eyes. I lay down on my bunk and, with trembling hands, picked up a book I'd been reading earlier. But I couldn't concentrate. I kept reading the same paragraph over and over, understanding nothing. Finally, I quit trying and simply used the book as a prop to hide behind while I sorted through my feelings. I reached the conclusion that I'd rather die than continue to live in such shame and fear. With that decision made came relief.

I put the book away and slept until well after midnight. When I got up, everyone was asleep. As quietly as possible, I walked over to the toilet and, using it as a step, climbed up to stand on the lip of the attached sink. Reaching out, I grabbed an inch-wide strip of aluminum molding encircling the air filter. For an hour I patiently worked the strip of metal back and forth until I broke free a length eight inches long. Squatting next to the toilet, I scraped the strip of metal on the concrete floor until I had a rough dagger point. Then I melted two plastic spoons to fashion a handle and wrapped the handle with thin strips of torn bedsheet to improve the grip.

Turning to the knife's edge again, I further refined the blade by continuing to gently sharpen it on the concrete floor.

"What you doin' with that?" asked Calvin.

I looked up to see him sitting up in bed.

"Just puttin' an edge on it," I said.

Calvin got up and walked over to stand over me. "Well, I can see that. What I mean is, whatcha plannin' to do with it?"

I stood and faced Calvin, the knife in my hand. "I'm plannin' to stick that dude Jerome, that's what," I whispered.

"Man, you done lost your mind!"

"Shhh!" I hissed, but too late. Cannonball sat up in bed.

Calvin stepped closer. "You do that, you're really gonna mess yourself up," he whispered back. "It ain't that serious, not for just a few dollars."

"Calvin, it ain't the amount that matters, it's the principle."

"Man, you know how many times I heard that over the years?" said Cannonball. "And I gotta admit, sometimes it's true, but most times it ain't. It's just hurt pride. I've learned that we only get so many chances in life to make the right choice, so a man's gotta pick his battles. You gotta ask yourself, This a good battle? This worth my life?"

"I understand what you're sayin', Cannonball, but I gotta do somethin'. I gotta show Jerome and those dudes that put him up to it that I ain't nothin' to play with. I gotta get my respect."

"And you can, but you ain't gotta stab some young dude barely out of diapers to get it. You'll get a lot more respect if you fight him head up with your fists. Man, only a coward needs a knife when it's one-on-one. Fight 'im head up and you'll get plenty of respect, win or lose," said Cannonball.

"I'll think about it," I said, irritated that my resolve had been challenged.

"Do that. Think long and hard about it," said Cannonball. "I'm gonna get me some sleep. It's a long time till breakfast."

I slid the knife back under my mattress and lay down but couldn't sleep.

Man, I would've just let the whole thing go, I told myself, *but Jerome had to open his mouth and tell the whole cellblock he stoled my shit. What a mess. Now I'm left with little choice; either I make a stand or I won't be allowed to have nothin' as long as I'm in B-tank. It'll be worse than that. I'll be a punk or a slave, washin' socks and dirty drawers. Nah, I can't live like that. I'd rather die. Cannonball's right, though. I ain't gotta stick Jerome to get respect. He's just a dumb kid doin' what they told him to do. Still, I gotta teach him a lesson and I gotta make a stand.*

A short time later, I stood beside Cannonball's bunk. "Cannonball, you awake?" I whispered.

"Just barely. Mostly, I was just lying here thinkin'. What's up?"

"I've been thinkin' myself."

"Yeah?"

"You're right. I ain't gotta stab Jerome. I'm just scared that the rest of 'em, you know, those dudes that set that old man on fire, will gang up on me. Figured if I stabbed Jerome, they'd keep their distance."

132

"Yeah, I understand that. Tell you what—you fight Jerome with your fists, one-on-one, and if those other dudes try to crowd you, I got your back. You got my word on that."

"Man, you'd do that!"

"Just said I would."

"And I'll help him," said Calvin, who had been listening to the entire conversation.

I couldn't believe what I had just heard. "Man, you dudes are unbelievable," I said. "I appreciate it. Thanks, both of you."

I reached under the edge of the mattress, grabbed the knife, and handed it to Cannonball. He slid it into the underside of his cast, next to his forearm.

"Ah, that feels good," he said. "Just what I needed." Cannonball smiled, his gold tooth glinting in the dim light. "My arm itches like a bitch and I've been lookin' for somethin' to scratch it with."

We all laughed, releasing tension.

I lay down again. *Timin'*, I told myself. *It's all about timin'. When Red sends the trustees back with the breakfast trays and opens all the cell doors, then I'll get Jerome when he first gets up, while he's still half asleep. That way, if they gang up on me and Cannonball and Calvin can't get there in time, maybe Red'll stop them before they kill me, although I'd sure hate to depend on Red for help.*

When I could see a slit of early morning light out the window, I got up, put on my shoes, and pulled the laces tight. Walking to the sink, I washed my hands and face with cold water and shadowboxed my way to the front of the cell. There I did knee bends and loosened my arms and shoulders. In the distance I could hear cell doors in the adjacent cellblock banging open.

It won't be long now, I told myself. I no longer fretted over what would or would not happen; my mind was set and my resolve firm.

The sounds grew louder, more defined. I could now clearly hear the jingle of keys and the low rumbling sound the chow-cart wheels made on the concrete floor. I took a deep breath and sucked in the smell of freshly baked biscuits and molasses but had no appetite.

The outside door opened and two trustees pushed the chow cart through. Red followed, barking orders. He opened the grille gate to B-tank, and the trustees, each carrying two metal trays filled with biscuits, grits, and molasses, went from cell to cell putting trays on the floor in front of each. After the trustees had finished and left, Red closed the grille gate and locked it. He pulled a heavy steel lever and all the cell doors in B-tank opened simultaneously, the sound like a clap of thunder.

Wearing only shoes, cutoff jeans, and a wide leather belt, I rushed from my cell into Jerome's. He had just gotten up and was urinating in the toilet, one hand bracing the wall, the other holding his penis. I hit him hard on the side of the head with an overhand right. His head hit the steel wall with a loud *thunk*, then bounced like a rubber ball. Jerome's knees buckled and he pissed a half circle on the wall. I followed up with a left that caught him in the neck. Terrified, Jerome pushed me and I staggered, losing my balance. He rushed into the hall, holding his throat and choking. I regained my balance, turned, and ran after him.

When I reached Jerome, he was still stunned and not sure what had just happened. I windmilled punches at him. He threw up his arms to ward off my blows, backpedaling all the way down the hall to the showers. I chased him, not wanting to give him time to recover, but in my haste I stepped in a tray of warm grits and molasses and slid down the hall like a skateboarder, flailing my arms and legs and losing my balance. I landed on my butt in the hallway.

Jerome, now recovered, saw me slip and rushed toward me. Just as I got to my feet, he hit me in the upper shoulder with a

hard right and I staggered but stayed on my feet. Jerome rushed in again and I kicked out with my right foot as hard as I could, hitting him in the solar plexus. All the wind knocked out of him, he grunted and fell backward, grabbing the shower curtain and ripping it loose. Wrapped in the shower curtain, he landed in the corner of the shower stall.

I went in after him, even though I could see from the look in his eyes that all the fight had gone out of him. Putting him in a headlock, I pulled him to his feet and dragged him out of the shower stall. Circling in that position, we ended up in the cell of the three arsonists, the last place I wanted to be.

Someone grabbed me from behind and yelled, "Okay, Joe Louis, okay! That's enough! Let him go!"

Recognizing Red's voice, I let go of Jerome, straightened, and looked around. The three arsonists had surrounded me and were staring darts at me, but I was too pumped to feel fear. I just stared back.

Red pushed me from the cell. Gasping for breath, I walked back up the hall. Everybody was awake now and either standing in the hall or just inside their doors, staring. When I got to my cell, Cannonball and Calvin stepped aside to let me enter.

When I saw Red approaching my cell, I fully expected him to tell me that he was putting me in solitary for fighting, which is what I wanted, but he just walked past as if nothing had happened. He opened the door to B-tank and locked it behind him. Realizing that there would be no outside help, I turned to Cannonball. "Give me that knife." For just a moment he hesitated, then he reached inside his cast, removed the knife, and handed it to me.

I didn't try to hide the knife now. I was way past that. I wanted everyone in B-tank, especially Jerome and the arsonists, to see that I had it and was willing to use it. I slid the knife under

my belt like a pistol and sat down on the toilet, watching and waiting.

Chapter 15

Sitting on the toilet, hand on my knife, I thought about what just happened and made a connection between B-tank and Orleans Parish Prison fourteen years earlier.

Carlos hadn't just happened by that night and, seeing me awake, impulsively ask that I hold his personal possessions while he killed Roland. No, subconsciously he had been searching for someone to talk him out of committing murder, someone who would calmly use reason the way Cannonball and Calvin had with me. But instead, he had stumbled upon me, an inexperienced twenty-year-old who had no idea what to say or do. Then again, maybe I'm givin' Cannonball and Calvin too much credit. What if they hadn't been trying to save me from destroying my life further but had really been trying to protect a member of their own tribe, the way I'd been trying to protect mine?

I turned to look at Jerome in the cell next to me. Dejected and shamed by the others in B-tank for losing the fight, he lay on his bunk, arms covering his face. I felt sorry for him. It occurred to me that in a fashion he and I were brothers; we were collateral damage in a deadly game created by others.

Once, during the day, I thought an attack imminent when one of the arsonists, a homemade straight razor in his hand, positioned himself just outside my cell. He didn't say a word, just stared at me with hateful eyes while nervously shifting the razor from hand to hand. I didn't say anything either, just pretended that he didn't exist, yet I kept him in my peripheral vision and was aware of his every move. Eventually he left.

That night after the cell doors were locked for the night I lay down, and even though I was exhausted I was unable to sleep. Again I was up before the doors opened for breakfast and sat on the toilet with the knife in my belt.

By that afternoon there was little talk of the fight and I felt a considerable lessening of tension in B-tank. The hall once again filled with men playing cards and dominoes and pacing and talking and laughing.

Realizing that I couldn't spend the rest of my life sitting on the toilet I ventured into the hall, where I talked to several men I had never spoken to before, but I didn't let my guard down completely. Now, wherever I went I took the knife with me, even to the shower.

Two weeks after the fight, just when I was beginning to feel more relaxed, Red yelled from the other side of the grille gate, "Bridges, pack up! You're movin'!"

The news caught me totally unaware. "Where am I goin'?" I asked.

"Isolation cell," he said. "Sheriff's orders."

"What for?" I yelled back, feeling it necessary to pretend I didn't want to go even though I was one of the few prisoners who actually welcomed the peace and quiet and safety of isolation.

Red didn't respond.

The isolation cell was small, only seven-by-nine feet, with double bunks. I placed my mattress on the bottom bed and put my personal possessions on the top. Opening a book, I lay down to enjoy the safety and solitude of my new home. But my newfound peace didn't last long.

A few days later, I heard a disturbance in the hall, got up, and walked to the door to listen. The argument moved closer, then suddenly my cell door opened and Red pushed a short, stocky, young Black man into the cell with me.

The young man glared at me, threw his laundry bag onto the floor, and started beating on the door with his fists. "Let me

outta here!" he yelled. "I ain't livin' in a cell with no stinkin' white boy!"

"You'll live where I put you!" yelled Red from somewhere down the hall.

I lay back down and picked up my book, determined to ignore my new cellmate, but he wouldn't let me. Pacing the cell like a lion in a cage, he beat the door and yelled at the top of his lungs on every pass.

When I could stand it no longer, I threw my book down and stood. "Hey!" I shouted. "Hey, man!" The young man stopped. He turned to look at me. "Man, don't you understand, they're ignorin' you! You're just wastin' your breath! And you're disturbing my peace! So just chill out!"

"Fuck you!" he yelled. "Ain't no cracker piece of shit gonna tell me what to do!"

He stepped toward me. I slugged him with a right hand, then braced for a counterattack, but instead he grabbed his laundry bag and retreated to the far corner of the cell. There he searched through his bag until he found a toothbrush, matches, and a double-edge razor blade. Squatting in the corner, he lit a match, then held it under the toothbrush handle until it began to melt. When it was soft and pliable, he carefully inserted the razor blade and held it in place until the plastic cooled and hardened. He held the weapon in his fist and stared at me, a smile on his face. He stood.

Staring back, I reached into my pillowcase and found the knife I had made while in B-tank. Squatting, I sharpened the blade on the floor, never taking my eyes off him, then stood.

I was scared, but I saw fear in his eyes as well. I don't know what he was thinking, but I was thinking how insane the predicament—two men locked in a small cage, intent on killing one another for no reason other than they didn't know each other.

Our shared fear saved us both. I sat down on my bunk and he squatted in the corner. We settled into an uneasy truce.

When Red and a trustee brought the supper trays, my new cell partner politely asked to see the sheriff. Red led him away in handcuffs.

While Red and my cell partner were gone, I spoke to the trustee alone. "Man, that young dude's been drivin' me crazy. Where'd he come from?"

"B-tank," said the trustee, "but he was only there two days. The only reason the sheriff put him back here with you was to teach him a lesson."

"How's that?"

"Well, he was really cuttin' up, throwin' food trays and shit, breakin' brooms and mops, beatin' on the walls. Finally, Red told him that if he didn't quit showin' his ass, the sheriff was gonna put him in the isolation cell with that crazy white boy. So after he set his mattress on fire, the sheriff told Red to bring him back here."

I never saw the young man again, and after a couple uneventful weeks I pled guilty to an old charge of forgery and was sentenced to three years on the Parish Prison farm.

The Parish Prison farm, nicknamed the P-farm, was a small minimum-security compound surrounded by a ten-foot fence topped with a single strand of razor wire. Inside the compound was a dormitory, housing about eighty prisoners; a small recreation yard; and a two-story brick building with a kitchen and chow hall on the first floor and administration offices on the second.

Most of the prisoners at the P-farm were serving short sentences and worked in the surrounding communities, maintaining highway rights-of-way and state buildings. From the first day I intended to escape and watched the routine of the

guards. I walked every inch of the small compound. At night I lay awake, assimilating the day's information, plotting, and planning.

Finally, my opportunity came—not from within the prison, but from without. One evening a guard walked into the dormitory and asked for volunteers to do restoration work on a state school for the disabled. I raised my hand. The school was located about twenty miles north of the P-farm and only a few miles from the Arkansas state line.

The first week I worked with a crew of four men under the watchful eye of a guard, but as the work progressed, the guard relaxed. He sent men out unchaperoned to work on certain areas of the school.

"Tomorrow, I want you to paint that last empty classroom on the north side of the school," the guard told me. "Think you can handle it by yourself?"

"Sure," I told him. "No problem."

Early the next morning, while everyone was asleep, I got up and double dressed, putting civilian clothes under the prison denim I normally wore. When we got to the school I was dropped off at the classroom and given a five-gallon bucket of paint, a brush, and a paint roller.

"Start in here," the guard said. "I'll be back to check on you a little later."

"When you gonna be back?" I asked. "Just in case I run out of paint."

"Oh, I doubt you'll use all the paint before I get back," said the guard. "But if you do, take yourself a break. I gotta go to the other end of the school and get a crew started there."

The guard left. I gave him a few minutes, then walked over and looked out the front window to make sure that he had really left. Then I walked over to the back window and looked out at the thick woods, only about twenty feet away. Slowly I raised the

window, stuck my head out, and looked around. Cautiously I climbed out, listening and looking, ready to climb back in should I see anyone.

When my feet hit the ground, I felt as if I had been hit with an electric charge. I ran to the woods, knelt, and looked back at the building. My stomach nauseous, I was terrified and elated at the same time. Kneeling there, I remembered a similar feeling many years ago as a young boy in New Orleans. That day, I had been on the giant roller coaster at Pontchartrain Beach for the first time and could barely contain my excitement as I sat in the small car while it slowly chugged to the top. On top of the first steep grade, the car hung suspended for what seemed a long time, then jerked and went into a free fall at breakneck speed, tying my stomach in knots and stealing my breath.

I ran deeper into the woods, stopping a short distance from the school to take off my prison denim and hide the clothes in a clump of thick bushes. I worked my way through the thick underbrush until I came to a path and started jogging.

About half a mile from the school, I tripped over an exposed root, lost my balance, and tumbled down an incline, ending up on my back in a gully. Unharmed except for a skinned elbow, I climbed out and found the path again. Eventually I came to a narrow creek and walked across to find a more defined trail on the other side. Following the trail for perhaps a mile, I came to a clearing. Across the clearing I saw a winding two-lane blacktop.

Paranoid that the police may be out searching for me already, I cautiously approached the highway, stood in the bushes, and watched it for several minutes.

It's been at least forty-five minutes since I jumped out the window, I thought. *Wonder if that guard came back to check on me yet. Probably not. I still got time to run back to the school, climb back in the window. That won't work. I have no idea where I am. I'll never find my way back.*

No. This is it. I'm committed. May as well start walking, put as much distance between me and that school as possible.

Just as I turned to take a step, I caught a flash of light bouncing off something at the top of the hill two hundred yards away. Like a frightened animal I scampered for the bushes. On my hands and knees, I strained to see. It was just a plain car. I stood, stepped to the shoulder, and raised my thumb.

A shiny blue Pontiac stopped just ahead of where I stood. Hurrying to the passenger window, I looked inside to see a heavyset man dressed in a shirt and tie. He had neatly cut blue-black hair, a wide bulbous nose, red cheeks, and thick glasses. Smiling, he motioned for me to open the door and get in.

"Need a lift?" he asked.

"Yeah, thanks. My old truck broke down just up the road," I said, closing the door. "I was on my way home from work. I live in Little Rock but I've been workin' on an oil rig in the Gulf, mostly out of Houma, Louisiana."

"If you want, I can drive you back, take a look at your truck. I got a toolbox in the trunk. I'm a pretty fair mechanic."

"I appreciate the offer, I really do, but I'm sure I blew a rod. Been expectin' it for a while. She's been knocking like hell, blowing smoke, using oil. I just been too busy to get it fixed."

"You sure?"

"Yeah. Just drop me off the next town you come to. I'll call my wife to come get me, then come back in a few days and tow it home."

"Suit yourself," said the driver, pulling the big Pontiac onto the highway. "Name is Harry. Harry Shipman." He reached his right hand toward me.

"Glad to meet you," I said, taking his hand. "I'm Lee Harris. What kind of work you do?" I asked, anxious to talk about him rather than me.

Harry Shipman had no problem talking about himself. "I'm an insurance salesman," he told me. "Been workin' for the same company over twenty years. Travel the whole northern section of Louisiana. Matter fact, I gotta make a few calls out this way. Hope you don't mind. Won't take long."

"Sure, I ain't in no hurry," I lied, then told the truth, "I'm just glad to get a ride."

After a few miles Harry pulled onto a red dirt road, heavily wooded on both sides. Half a mile down the road, we stopped in front of a double-wide mobile home sitting in a field of cotton. Next to the mobile home was an old black pickup with no tires or windshield. Two small boys, both with snow-white hair, were playing in the back of the abandoned truck, but when they saw Harry's car they ran for the door, yelling, "Mama! It's the insurance man!"

A woman who appeared to be in her early thirties opened the door and stepped onto an attached wooden porch. She stared at the car while wiping her hands on her apron. One of the little boys hugged his mother's leg, the other peeked shyly from behind her hip.

Harry turned to me. "This won't take long." He left the car, climbed the porch, and shook the woman's hand.

After several minutes, the little boys, curious, approached the car. They stood next to the passenger door and stared at me. Anxious and paranoid, I ignored them, staring instead at Harry and the woman, willing them to hurry.

I looked at my watch. *Ten minutes,* I told myself. *He's been talking to her for ten minutes. How long does it take? Come on, Harry, let's wrap this up! I'm sure that guard's back at the classroom by now. They're probably settin' up roadblocks! And here I am in a cotton field only a few miles away.*

A few minutes later Harry got in the car. "Sorry that took so long."

"No problem," I lied.

We made one more stop, then crossed the Arkansas state line. There Harry and I shook hands. I got out near the edge of a small town, stood and watched Harry make a U-turn and head back south. Near the town center I crossed in front of the courthouse and city jail. Out front, two trustees, dressed in orange jumpsuits, were washing a police car. One of them nodded. Self-consciously, I looked down at the brogans I wore, wondering if he had noticed them. Uneasy, I crossed to the other side of the street and walked, looking behind me occasionally, until I was out of sight. Eventually I came across the Greyhound bus station on the outskirts.

It wasn't much of an operation, just a converted service station with a few bays outside for buses. I walked up and looked through a large window area to see a few chairs, a pay phone, and vending machines. Cautiously I walked inside. The small waiting area was deserted except for a clerk behind the ticket counter. I walked over to an arrival/departure schedule on the wall, stood and studied it. I looked at my watch. *It's almost 11:00. The next bus leaves at 2:30. It'll cost almost $40. That'll leave me about $100. I'll call soon as I get there—that is, if Charlie's still there.*

Too paranoid to sit in the bus station waiting area for three hours, I left and walked about a quarter mile until I came to a thick grove of pine trees. Looking around to see if anyone was watching and satisfied they weren't, I entered the grove. Hidden from view, I sat down with my back against a pine tree and took off my right brogan. Using a stick, I peeled back the boot's insole and carefully removed two folded and stained bills, a $100 and a $50—money that had been hidden there since Angola. I leaned back, closed my eyes, and rested.

At 2:20, I left the pine grove and walked to within fifty yards of the bus station. I stood for a moment and waited. Seeing

nothing out of the ordinary, I continued on to the bus station. Inside I purchased a ticket to Dallas.

Chapter 16

I arrived in Dallas at 9:00 that night and called the number that Charlie had given me a couple years earlier when we had lived in the same dormitory in Angola. The morning Charlie had left Angola, he had handed me a slip of paper and had told me, "This is my brother's name and number. He lives in Dallas. That's where I'm headed. I've had it with Louisiana. When you get out, come on out to Dallas and call this number. He'll tell you how to get in touch with me."

I knew full well that Charlie hadn't meant, "When you escape, come on out to Dallas and call me," but the fact was I had escaped and I wasn't going to tell him. I didn't like deceiving Charlie but I had nowhere else to go and I needed somewhere to hide until I could get money and identification, then I'd be gone.

Charlie showed up at the Dallas bus station driving a new white Chrysler. Sitting next to him was an attractive woman who appeared to be in her late twenties. He seemed genuinely pleased to see me, his girlfriend less so. After we left the bus station Charlie drove to the nightclub where he worked nights as a bartender. There we had a couple drinks and reminisced about our time together in Angola.

Charlie and his girlfriend lived in a nice two-bedroom apartment. And to his credit, he didn't ask me how long I planned to stay; he just led me to the spare bedroom and said, "Welcome to Dallas."

A few days later, Charlie introduced me to a home-improvement contractor who frequented the club where he worked, and the man offered me a job.

Besides the new Chrysler, Charlie also had an old Ford station wagon, and he let me borrow it to drive back and forth

to work even though he knew I didn't have a driver's license yet. I knew that getting a driver's license was imperative, but I was afraid to present myself at the Department of Public Safety, concerned they may discover I had escaped from a Louisiana prison.

But after a couple weeks I overcame my fear, took the day off work, and, with only a birth certificate that I had gotten in the mail from North Carolina, drove to the driver's license office. There I passed both the written and driving tests and was issued a temporary license. A couple weeks later, a permanent photo license was sent to Charlie's address.

A week after I received the license, two Dallas police detectives knocked on Charlie's front door. They showed him my photo, then told him that I had escaped from a prison farm in north Louisiana. Charlie denied that he had seen me even though the detective told him that they knew my driver's license had been mailed to his address. Frustrated, the detectives left but promised to return.

When I got back to the apartment that night, I found a note from Charlie telling me to call him at work. When I called, he told me about the visit from the two detectives and was understandably angry that I hadn't told him that I was an escapee. "Look," said Charlie, anxious to get rid of me, "I can't put up with the heat. Just take the station wagon and get outta the state of Texas. If you get caught in it, you tell 'em you stoled it. You got three weeks, then I'm going to report it stolen myself. Understand?"

With a little over $200 in my pocket and no destination in mind, I left Dallas and drove north. When I crossed into Oklahoma early the next morning, I parked the station wagon in a truck stop parking lot and slept until noon.

That afternoon I continued north until I crossed into Kansas. There, at a service station, I filled up with gas, then sat in the car, sipped a cup of coffee, and looked at a Kansas map.

Of course, Wichita, in larger print, stood out and I liked the sound of the name when I said it out loud; it reminded me of an old western movie. So I headed for Wichita, fascinated as I drove through a landscape that quickly changed from hilly and green to mostly flat and brown.

The first thing that I did in Wichita was buy a newspaper, then I drove around until I came to a narrow river near downtown. There I parked, sat at a picnic table, and read the classified section. I circled "Rooms by the Week. Reasonable Rates. Cottonwood Motel."

The Cottonwood Motel wasn't much to look at. Laid out in the shape of a horseshoe, the buildings enclosed a dusty courtyard. There, in a circle of crumbling bricks, stood one scraggly cottonwood tree, barely clinging to life. Scattered about, as if some giant had put them in a huge bucket then turned the bucket upside down, were several older model cars and trucks in various states of disrepair.

This old station wagon fits right in, I thought.

The building was a cracker-box structure of beige stucco, the window frames and doors painted a peeling olive green, reminding me of many of the places I'd lived as a child. I walked into the lobby, which looked like a junk shop. This too reminded me of an important part of my childhood: Mama Demarest's junk shop in Charleston.

Weaving my way to a cluttered registration desk, I hit a small, round bell. A door directly behind the counter opened and out walked a white-haired man dressed in gray work pants, a white shirt, and red suspenders.

"Can I help you?" he asked.

"Your ad says you rent rooms by the week," I said. "How much?"

"Seventy-five, plus tax, plus a $2 key deposit," said the clerk.

"Sounds good," I told him. "I'll take a room for the week."

When I walked into the shabby room, with water-stained, mint-green walls, my sinuses were assaulted by the strong smell of ammonia and urine. I rushed over to an old window-mounted air conditioner and turned it on. The ancient contraption groaned and sputtered, then spat out a weak stream of cool, damp air. Water dripped onto the matted, gold shag carpet.

Next to a sagging double bed covered with an old bedspread was a wobbly blond nightstand with long, dark cigarette burns on top. Emptying my pockets onto the nightstand, I counted $120 and some change. *That won't last long,* I told myself, sitting on the edge of the bed. *Seems it always comes down to the same thing— money. How to get it and how to keep it. Wonder what life would be like if I never had to worry about money.*

When I was young, I was sure of two things: we were poor and my mother was unhappy. It didn't take long to connect the two realities. In an attempt to make her happy, I often told her, usually when she was quietly sitting in her chair by the window, "Mama, when I grow up, I'm going to buy you a Cadillac and a mink coat." But for all her faults, my mother knew that the cause of her unhappiness was too deep and could never be healed by such foolish gifts. Still, rather than hurt my feelings, she always forced a thin smile and said, "Honey, Mama don't need no Cadillac car and, besides, what would I do with a mink coat?" She would then kiss the top of my head.

At the foot of the bed stood an old TV on a rusted metal stand, the antenna fashioned from a coat hanger wrapped in aluminum foil. I got up, walked over, and turned it on. The TV flickered, then showed a fuzzy black-and-white picture. I moved the coat hanger until the picture cleared, then tried to change the

channel but discovered the channel knob missing. Unable to change the channel, I turned it off. A short time later, searching the nightstand, I found an old rusted pair of pliers and made an instant connection. Walking over to the TV, I turned it on again and, using the pliers, easily scanned the channels.

A short time later, I drove to a nearby store where I bought a loaf of bread, a jar of peanut butter, jelly, a wedge of cheese, crackers, two six-packs of beer, and a bag of ice.

Back at the motel—propped up on pillows, eating cheese and crackers, drinking beer after beer, and watching an old movie on TV—I had a drunken thought, a thought more honest than I would have permitted myself sober: *All I'm doin' is tryin' to find distractions to keep myself from thinkin'. Think, dammit! What are you gonna do?*

I put away the food and beer, turned off the TV and light, and stretched out on the lumpy mattress. *You need to figure out how to get some money and you need to figure it out soon! I guess I can always get a job, like I did in Dallas; sleep in the car till I get paid. I ain't no stranger to work. That's one of the things my father taught me. He may have been an alcoholic, a cheat, and a gambler, but he was a hard worker and never missed a day's work, even after staying out all night drinkin'. Yeah, he taught me how to work, but he also taught me to lie and steal and not pay my debts.*

My mother also taught me a few lessons, I thought. *She taught me to ignore my problems and never face them directly. But the most important lesson has been the most harmful and has ruled my life: she taught me how to give up.*

Feeling the same deep pang of defeat I had felt almost twenty years earlier as an eighteen-year-old Marine stranded in the snow alongside a desolate mountain highway, I asked myself, *What's the point? Even if I get a job, sooner or later the fake name and Social Security number I'm using will be discovered, just like in Dallas, and I'll have to run again. And next time I may not have enough warning before*

the police show up. Forget goin' to work. But still I need money and I need to ditch this car before it's reported stolen. I've got to come up with a plan. I stayed up late that night thinking.

The next morning, my decision made, I got up early.

My first stop in Wichita was a thrift store. There, for less than $20, I bought an off-white linen suit, an old pair of dress shoes, a white shirt, a clip-on tie, a snap-brim cap, and a pair of mirrored sunglasses.

Next, I drove around until I found what I thought the ideal bank. It was close to the center of town and small, with only seven employees. Most importantly, there were no security guards. Forty feet from the rear of the bank was a six-foot wooden privacy fence. On the other side of the fence were the rear entrances to shops in a strip shopping center. Next to the strip shopping center, only a block from the bank, was a restaurant with a large parking lot.

I waited until the bank closed, parked in the restaurant parking lot, walked behind the shopping center, and when I reached the privacy fence loosened two of the boards.

Back at the motel, I wrote on a slip of paper: THIS IS A HOLDUP! I HAVE A GUN! DON'T GET HURT! I then dressed in my disguise, stood in front of the mirror, and practiced removing the note from my shirt pocket with my left hand while simultaneously reaching with my right for an imaginary gun inside my suit coat.

The next day, dressed in my disguise, the holdup note in my shirt pocket, I parked near the restaurant and watched the bank a block away but couldn't find the courage to walk inside. Finally, after about twenty minutes, afraid of arousing suspicion if I stayed longer and disgusted by my lack of courage, I drove back to the Cottonwood Motel.

152

There I soothed my ego by coming up with excuse after excuse. *There's no need to hurry; I still got a few days left on my rent, still got a few dollars in my pocket. Anyway, I must be crazy plannin' to rob a bank without a gun. What if an off-duty cop walks in? He won't ask questions, he'll just start shootin'.*

Despite the fear and doubt, I went back the next day, sat in the car, and watched the bank. But again, I couldn't find the courage to rob it.

I didn't go back the next day. Instead, I tried a new ploy to bolster my courage. I squandered what little money I had on beer and pizza, certain that my lack of money would lead to desperation, and desperation to action.

Friday night, broke and hungry, a quarter tank of gas in the stolen car, and with the rent due the next morning, I was the very definition of desperation. If a surveillance camera had been installed in my room, the monitor would have shown a fearful man sitting in a dark room, staring at the wall, and drowning in self-pity. And if that camera had been equipped with a futuristic device that could read a person's thoughts, it would have recorded, *Satisfied now! Your weak ass is totally broke and the car's almost outta gas! Your old man was right: you* are *a mistake, a sorry, fuckin' mistake! Either you rob the bank tomorrow or you'll be homeless and an escaped convict. Lots of luck with that.*

Reaching over, I picked up the jar of peanut butter on the nightstand and looked inside. It was empty. I had forgotten that I had scraped it clean hours ago. Frustrated, I threw the jar at a wastebasket in the corner. It bounced off the wall, spun half a turn on the ugly carpet, and stopped.

"Figures!" I yelled. "Can't even hit the damn trash can!"

The next morning, I checked out of the Cottonwood Motel.

The bank closed at noon. I walked in at three minutes before and it was just as I had hoped—there were no other

customers and all the tellers were busy tallying the day's receipts. One of the tellers looked up. I walked straight to her station.

"May I help you?" asked the teller.

"Yes, please," I said, reaching in my shirt pocket and sliding the note forward with my left hand while reaching under my coat for an imaginary gun with my right, just as I had practiced. The teller read the note, then looked up, fear and confusion in her eyes.

"Let's go," I said. "Put all the money on the counter."

The teller looked to the left, then to the right for help, but her coworkers were too busy to notice her alarm.

I leaned closer. "Hurry up—or else!" I said.

The teller opened the drawer, but her hands shook so badly that she couldn't manipulate the cash from the drawer to the counter. I was stunned. I had no idea something like that could happen, and I also felt like a monster for causing her such distress. Reaching across the counter, I touched her lightly on the arm. She looked me in the eyes.

"Look," I whispered, "just calm down and put the money on the counter."

She calmed. Her hands quit shaking. The teller quickly put the money on the counter. Reaching inside my coat pocket, I removed a folded plastic shopping bag and shook it open. I raked the money into it, then turned and headed for the door.

The bank manager stood by the first set of double glass doors, keys in her hand, oblivious that I had just robbed one of her tellers until the teller screamed, "He robbed the bank!" I turned. The teller pointed and screamed again, "He robbed the bank!"

The manager, still holding the keys, took a step back, terror in her eyes. I rushed forward and pushed on the door. It was locked! A flood of thoughts rushed through my head. *I'm locked inside a bank, I don't have a weapon, and I'm outnumbered seven to one.*

154

I ate my panic, stepped to the bank manager, reached inside my coat for my imaginary gun, and shouted in her face, "Open this fuckin' door now!"

The manager opened the door and I stepped through, hitting the second glass door so hard with my shoulder that I felt the glass give.

At the wooden privacy fence, I turned and looked back at the bank entrance. All seven employees were bunched together just outside the door. The teller that I had robbed pointed and yelled, "There he is! That's him by the fence! That's him! He robbed the bank!"

Turning back, I kicked the two fence boards loose, pulled them aside, and squeezed through.

After sprinting to the far end of the buildings, I sat down behind a large bush and, now out of sight, stripped down to cargo shorts and a t-shirt. Rolling the linen suit, cap, shirt, and tie in a ball, I hid them under the bush. Carrying the shopping bag, I stepped from behind the building to the restaurant parking lot, walked to the station wagon, got in, and stuffed the money under the driver's seat.

In the distance, I heard the sirens of police cars responding to the bank's alarm.

I started the car, and just as I eased toward the exit, out of nowhere two police cars in tandem, lights ablaze and sirens blaring, barreled into the exit. I slammed down hard on the brakes, almost broadsiding the lead police car and causing the bag of money to slide from under the seat. Cash covered the floorboard.

Like the frightened teller, my hands shook uncontrollably. My heart pounded. I sat for a moment and watched the police cars slide to a stop in front of the bank a block away. Then I bent over, put the money back into the shopping bag, and put it back under the seat.

I entered the flow of traffic.

Several blocks from the bank, I heard the unmistakable "whump, whump, whump" of a helicopter, and even though I felt confident no one had connected the car to the bank robbery, I played it safe, pulling into a service station with a canopy over the pumps. I filled the car while waiting for the helicopter to move on.

Ten miles east of Wichita, I turned onto a two-lane highway south, hoping that it would take me out of Wichita and eventually the state.

An hour later the paved highway turned to gravel and the only traffic I encountered was a tractor. Eventually the gravel turned to dirt, and for a moment I feared being lost. But then I quickly realized that with no destination I could hardly be lost, my only goal being to get as far from Wichita and the bank as possible. I continued driving south and was overjoyed when I crossed the state line into Oklahoma.

Reaching Oklahoma City that night, I checked into a motel, took a shower, lay in bed, ate fried chicken, drank scotch, watched TV, and counted money.

Before going to sleep, I reviewed the day's events. It all seemed surreal, as if I had just been a witness and the bank robbery committed by someone else. To confirm it was indeed me, I got up and dumped all of the cash onto the bed. By the glow of late-night television, I again counted the stolen money. I had over $7,000, mostly in small bills, which seemed like a fortune to a man who had awakened that morning with less than a dollar in his pocket. I didn't consider that I had risked my life for it.

The next morning, I drove to the airport and parked the station wagon in long-term parking, leaving the door unlocked and the keys in the ignition. Walking inside the terminal, I purchased a one-way ticket to Miami.

Josie Irene Davis

Married

Troy Andrew Bridges

Paternal grandparents
F.M. and Mama Bridges

Maternal grandparents
Pawpaw and Granny Davis

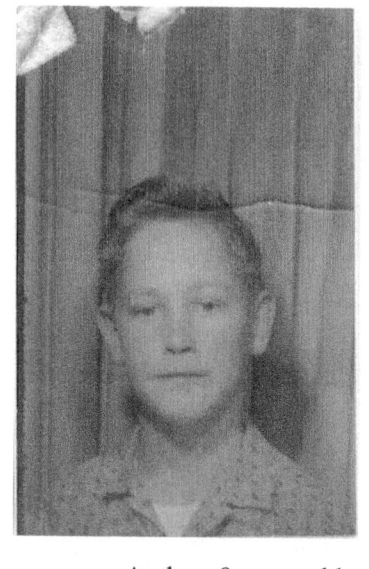

Author, 9 years old

Author, Mama Bridges, Dianne, and Tonda during Mama Bridges's visit to Sullivan's Island, S.C.

Author, Dianne, mother, and Tonda in apartment on King Street in Charleston, S.C.

Author and Tonda in Charleston

Tonda and author in
Charleston apartment

Author and Tonda at playground
in Charleston

Author in high school in
Baton Rouge, La.

Author at boot camp
graduation MCRD,
San Diego, Calif.

Author on leave at sister's
house in Baton Rouge,

Author and Dianne while
on leave

Last photo of mother
on her 50th birthday

Father at time of visit to
Angola

L-R: *Angolite* staff coeditors Billy Sinclair, Wilbert
Rideau, and author after workout in prison gym at Angola

Jacqueline and author during a
visit at Donaldson prison

Jacqueline and author during a visit at
Donaldson

Jacqueline and author married in prison chapel
June 17, 2002

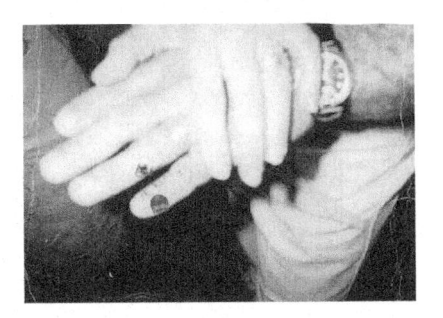

The bond still holds 18 years later.

PART II

MADNESS

"If only it were all so simple! If only there were evil people somewhere insidiously committing evil deeds, and it were necessary only to separate them from the rest of us and destroy them. But the line dividing good and evil cuts through the heart of every human being. And who is willing to destroy a piece of his own heart?"

—Aleksandr Solzhenitsyn, *The Gulag Archipelago*

Chapter 17

In Miami, I spent the first day in a motel room near the airport. There, lying in bed, gorging on rich food and drink, I watched old movies on cable TV.

The second day I spent riding the city bus, looking for a car. That afternoon, I bought a ten-year-old white Volvo station wagon for $1,500 and the next morning headed south for the 160-mile drive to Key West, a place where fortunes were made or lost with the rise and fall of the tide.

It was in Key Largo that the land narrowed considerably. I could turn my head left and see the Atlantic Ocean out the driver's window or turn my head right and see the Gulf of Mexico out the passenger window. After so many years of cages and fences and restricted views, it was thrilling to be able to see unobstructed for miles and to know that it was possible for me to get in a boat and go almost anywhere in the world.

The view wasn't just unobstructed, it was a fantasy land with clear blue-green water, azure skies, tropical plants and flowers, and an abundance of coconut-filled palms, my favorite tree. I was convinced that I had found the paradise I had dreamed about all those years in prison.

In Key West, I found a place to rent a block from the beach. It was a converted carriage house located behind a white two-story Colonial. The small apartment had a private entrance protected by a beautiful wrought iron fence and was reminiscent of those in the New Orleans French Quarter. Beyond the fence was a cobblestone path that passed through a small but lush tropical courtyard. The apartment was one large room with a kitchen, a small dining area, a full bath, and a large bed. Newly painted, it was furnished with everything, from bed linens to pots and pans.

After grocery shopping, I returned to the apartment, took a shower, turned the air conditioner on high, got under the cool, clean sheets, and didn't get up until I was awakened the next morning by the sun slanting through the window near my bed.

After making a cup of coffee, I walked outside and sat on a wrought iron bench, half in sunlight and half in shade. All around me were tropical plants and flowers. Songbirds sang overhead. I looked up to see them sitting in the thick canopy of the most unusual tree I'd ever seen. Thick roots dripped from its branches like stalactites, piercing the ground all around me and creating a maze. I later found out that the tree was called a banyan.

After finishing my coffee, I got dressed and left to explore Key West. I soon found out that Key West, a town of many cultures and choices, felt more like a foreign country than an American town. Having so many choices after years of suffering so few was intoxicating. It was like emerging from a cave to suddenly find myself in blinding sunlight.

I spent most afternoons on Smathers Beach, the hot sun and cool breezes soothing my skin and healing years of pain. There on the beach, time didn't just pass but rather evaporated like mist.

One afternoon, while lying on the beach, I heard music in the distance and sat up, searching for the source. Fifty yards away I saw a bearded, barefoot man sitting under a palm tree, softly playing a saxophone. A small crowd had gathered.

Inside my head, the word saxophone changed into sexophone, and no matter how much I fought it, I was transported to 1956 and Trade Alley.

Just home from school, I opened the screen door and stepped inside. The house was dark. Walking into the kitchen, I put my schoolbooks on the white enamel table, then walked to my parents' room. The door was slightly

ajar. Just as I started to enter, I heard voices and paused to listen. Through the partially opened door I saw that my mother was in bed with a man I recognized as the father of a girl in my third-grade class.

Propped on her left arm, my mother held a glass of whiskey in her right hand. Every time that she raised the glass to drink, her right breast exposed itself.

"Irene," said the man, "you know I play the saxophone, but I betcha didn't know how good I can play the sex-ophone." The man dove under the covers and my mother squealed with delight.

Not understanding, I pushed open the door. My mother grabbed the sheet and covered herself.

"Rickey!" she said. Then, "Harold! Stop! My son's here! Stop!"

"I'm sorry, Irene," said the man, emerging from the blanket.

"Mama, I'm hungry," I said.

"Go wait in the kitchen," she said, "and I'll fix you something. Go on now."

I walked into the kitchen, sat at the white enamel table, and waited. The toilet flushed, then a few minutes later my mother, wearing her blue housecoat, walked into the kitchen. She looked through the cupboards.

The saxophone player, now neatly dressed, walked to the front door, opened it, and without a word left.

"How about pancakes?" asked my mother. "I can make you some pancakes."

"With syrup?"

"Honey, we're out of syrup. How about jam? You like strawberry jam, I know."

"I want syrup!"

"Rickey, don't start with me! It's pancakes with jam or nothing! Now make up your mind, mister, or I'm going back to bed!"

Realizing that I was quickly running out of money, I came up with a foolish idea: I would live the life of an artist, painting Key West scenes and selling them to the tourists. I rushed out

and bought a cheap easel, several stretched canvases, oil paints, and brushes.

After completing several paintings, I half-heartedly tried to sell them but gave up after only a week. I rushed to find a job, completing several job applications and going for an interview. Questions about my past made me nervous, and when I was asked if I could be bonded, I felt so paranoid that I almost ran from the interview.

Then I saw a listing in the local newspaper for help in a marina store. The marina was in a resort in a small town called Islamorada, about halfway between Miami and Key West. With $300 left over from the Wichita bank robbery, I regretfully left Key West and drove north.

When I got to Islamorada, I went straight to the marina and applied for the job. The whole process was very informal. I didn't even have to complete a job application. The dockmaster and I just talked for a short while, then he hired me. Of course, I gave him a fake Social Security number, but I figured that I'd be long gone before that came into question.

After finding a room in a rundown but charming motel with a great name, Evening Shade, I paid for a week in advance and started to work at the marina the next morning.

She walked into the marina store the second week that I worked there. There are some people you encounter a hundred times in life yet barely remember anything about them, and then there are those rare few that you meet only once yet remember everything about them. She was one of those people.

It was early afternoon and extremely hot outside. Inside the empty marina store, the air conditioner was working hard to keep the place cool. Bored, I was standing behind the cash register when she sashayed through the door, her long straight hair to her waist. She wore thin translucent pants in a tropical

pattern, tied at the ankle and slit open to show bare leg, very similar to what Barbara Eden wore in the TV sitcom *I Dream of Jeannie*. She had on a red, stretchable halter top, without a bra, and wore several gold chains around her lovely neck.

Standing about five-seven, she had the well-developed arms and shoulders of a swimmer and the curves of a beauty queen. She had dark Asian eyes and high cheekbones.

Later, I would hear her beauty described as "exotic" and discover that she was bilingual, speaking fluent Spanish as well as precise English. She had a didactic intelligence and the charismatic energy of a shaman, commanding attention and attracting an entourage wherever she went. She was from a small island just off the coast of Belize and was descended from Spanish, African, and Arawak Indian. She had come to the United States when she was eighteen and was now in her mid-thirties. I watched her walk toward a rack of cloth beach bags imprinted with the resort's name. She picked a bag, then brought it to the counter.

"I get 20 percent off," she told me.

"Really," I said. "Why?"

"Because I work here and all employees get 20 percent off."

Trying to keep her in the store a little longer, I teased, "Well, nobody told me that employees get 20 percent off, and besides, how do I know you work here? I've never seen you before."

Even with all her other assets—her grace and beauty and intelligence—the one thing she didn't have was a well-developed sense of humor. Expressionless, she stared straight into my eyes for a moment, then abruptly turned, put the beach bag back on the rack, and walked out the door, leaving me stunned.

We encountered each other a few days later at a local bar called Smugglers Cove. The place was noisy and crowded, and I'd been sitting at a small table with a girl I'd met who was on

vacation from Ohio. The girl and I had been shooting shots of tequila when I just happened to look over her head and see the exotic beauty sitting at a table with friends. Our eyes met.

I disengaged myself and made my way across the crowded bar. The seat next to her was empty, so I sat down.

"Sold any beach bags lately?" she asked.

Looking into her dark eyes, I said, "As a matter of fact, I have—and at regular price."

She smiled.

I found out that her name was Ora and that she *did* indeed work at the resort and had for years, as a bartender at a small tiki bar. I also found out that she was obsessed with stopping the spread of communism, particularly in the Caribbean where she came from. She told me that when she was a young girl, communist soldiers from nearby Cuba had actually invaded the small island where she grew up and so her hatred for communism had begun.

After a while, tired of the noise, we stepped outside onto an attached deck. There Ora lit a joint and passed it to me. We both felt the effects of the marijuana immediately and it was the first time that I saw her smile.

Ora and I shared an unusual interest—painting. She told me that she had first learned to paint after coming to the United States and that she occasionally sold small seascapes to the tourists that flocked to the island during the winter. I told her that I had learned to paint as a young boy growing up in New Orleans, but what I didn't tell her was that I had greatly improved during my many years in prison.

We talked until well after midnight and when she had to leave I tried to kiss her but she pushed me away. When I asked to see her later in the week she was noncommittal and instead asked where I lived.

I worked at the marina seven days a week, from 1:00 P.M. until closing at 7:00. That left my mornings free to sleep, if I stayed out late, or to get up early and either go to the beach or paint before work.

A few days after Ora and I met at Smugglers Cove I was sitting just outside my door early one morning, painting, when an old, brown, rusted station wagon drove up and parked not ten feet away. Putting down my paintbrush, I stood. Ora opened the door and got out. Barefoot, she wore a silk paisley gown with long sleeves and in her hand she carried a bulging bread bag. Without a word of greeting, she walked over and stood behind me to look at the partially finished canvas on the easel.

"You *can* paint," she said.

"What! You thought I was lying!" I said, smiling.

She didn't respond. Instead, she thrust the bread bag at me. "Here, I brought you something."

"What is it, a loaf of bread?"

"Open it and find out."

Inside the bread bag was at least a quarter pound of marijuana. Shocked, I looked at Ora. "What do you want for all this?"

"Nothing. It's a gift."

"Wow! That's a hell of a gift! What can I say? Thank you."

I put away my painting and we sat at my small kitchen table, smoked a joint, and talked.

"You always get up so early?" I asked Ora.

"Most mornings," she said. "I don't sleep much. Sometimes I stay up and listen to the BBC on the radio to find out what's really going on in the world, but I like to get up just before dawn, when it's quiet and the rest of the world sleeps. That's a magical time for me."

Ora was unlike anyone I'd ever met. Free of guile, honest, and straightforward like a child, she was also wise, like only an

old soul can be. She refused to waste time on the trivial, but if what you said interested her she would spend all night helping you worry the topic, like a Chihuahua with a buffalo bone. If not, she would quickly get bored and move on.

"Do you ..." I started to say. Ora reached across the small table and placed a slender forefinger against my lips, silencing my nervous chatter.

She stood, took my hand, and pulled me to my feet. "Let's go in there," she said, pointing toward the bedroom, amusement in her dark eyes.

Standing beside the bed, I took Ora in my arms and kissed her for the first time. She eagerly responded and I picked her up and gently laid her on my bed. Side by side we kissed while exploring each other's bodies. Caressing Ora's right leg just below the knee, I felt a hard round object about the shape and size of a toothbrush holder. It was attached to her calf by an elastic band and felt like polished wood.

"What's that?" I asked, feeling Ora tense.

"Oh, that's my ice pick," she said.

"Ice pick!"

"Yeah," she said, sitting up. "I take it with me everywhere."

Chapter 18

Ora's live-in boyfriend had helped smuggle tons of marijuana into the Florida Keys during the seventies and was an island legend. Imposing and unforgettable, he stood six-four (the locals called him Big Jim) and looked like a character out of the book *Kidnapped*. He had long dark hair, a full black beard, and walked about on a steel prosthetic. (He had lost his right foot in an accident and, having been a welder before becoming a smuggler, had fashioned himself a steel peg to replace the missing foot.)

Naturally, after seeing Big Jim and hearing of his exploits I was wary of bedding his girlfriend, but I was more enchanted by Ora than I was afraid of Big Jim so I continued to see her. And if nothing else, I knew that I could always outrun him.

Ora and I spent part of every day together. I would either go to the tiki bar where she worked or she would come by the marina. Often, early in the morning just before dawn, she would slip out of Big Jim's bed and into mine at the Evening Shade. We would make love, talk, then make love again.

The last thing that I wanted was a showdown with Big Jim or any of his friends. I talked to Ora about that and she assured me that even though she and Big Jim had been together for years (they had met in Fort Lauderdale and had moved to the Keys together), their love for each other had changed, and now they were more friends than lovers. She also told me that she had told Big Jim about us and he had said that he was okay with it.

Once, while sitting at the tiki bar, someone had pointed out Big Jim. He was standing at a larger, outdoor bar about fifty yards away, drinking beer and surrounded by a large group of people. Judging by his demeanor, he didn't look like a man okay

with much in life. He looked like a man pissed off at the world and drowning his sorrow.

After only two months, I asked Ora to leave Big Jim and move in with me. She thought about it for a few days, and no doubt had a long talk with Big Jim, then agreed. Ora borrowed Big Jim's station wagon one last time to transport her few possessions from his house to mine.

When she drove up in the old station wagon, I witnessed one of the strangest sights I'd ever seen. In the back of the station wagon, surrounded by clothes, was a bale of hay, and sitting on the hay was the largest rooster I'd ever seen. His feathers were reddish-orange and bluish-black and they glistened as if they had been oiled. (Ora had never once mentioned that she had a rooster.)

The rooster was a Cuban fighting cock that Ora had raised from a chick and that had been given to her one Easter by an old Cuban man who frequented the tiki bar. Ora had taken the chick home, thinking it was just a regular chicken, and had named it Jennifer Chicken after a friend of hers. And when the bird grew into a very large rooster, she refused to change its name, continuing to call it Jennifer Chicken.

Also in the station wagon was a five-foot wooden perch and something else Ora had forgotten to mention—an assault rifle with two banana clips and a thousand rounds of ammunition. When I saw the assault rifle and all that ammunition, my first thought was, *Damn, I pity the communist that decides to snoop around the Evening Shade.*

Perhaps one of the reasons that Jennifer Chicken was so large was that Ora fed the bird raw hamburger every day. She would roll the hamburger into marble-sized balls, then throw them onto the floor. Jennifer Chicken would follow close behind her and snap them up as quickly as they hit the linoleum.

The first full night we spent together, Ora put the rooster on his perch in the living room, then joined me in bed. Around 4:30 I was awakened by a wall-shaking *cock-a-doodle-do*—the sound so loud and unexpected in the small apartment that I sat straight up in bed and shouted, "What the hell?"

Then Ora flung back the covers, rushed into the living room, grabbed the rooster off the perch, and put him in a dark closet. She shut the door and without a word came back to bed. The rooster didn't crow again until we let him out around 8:00 that morning. And so every morning, as soon as Jennifer Chicken flapped his wings, preparatory to crowing, Ora bounded from the bed and put him in the closet.

I grew quite fond of Jennifer Chicken and one day, while watching him grab a small stuffed bear with his beak and shake it, much like a dog would, I came up with an idea. Picking up the bear, I advanced it toward the rooster, who backed up, not understanding what was happening. I followed with the bear, rubbing it in his face until he reacted. He snatched it out of my hand with his beak, shook it, dropped it, then backed up. Jennifer Chicken rushed forward and raked the bear two or three times with his inch-and-a-half spurs. I was amazed at how fast he was.

I played with Jennifer Chicken in this manner every day, and soon he became so used to the daily game that all I had to do was pick up the stuffed bear and he'd fly from his perch and attack it.

When we went to the beach, I'd tuck Jennifer Chicken under my arm like a football and carry him across the highway. There he'd entertain himself by scratching for bugs and tiny crabs near the edge of a small mangrove while Ora and I walked the shoreline. We didn't have to worry about him getting lost because whenever we got too far ahead, he would race to catch up.

Sometimes a moment is so special that it will stand out in your memory when you think of a particular time, place, or person. Even now, after so many years, when I think of the Florida Keys I remember one particular day: I had left Ora and Jennifer Chicken near the shoreline and had walked off by myself to explore a group of small sand dunes, something unusual in the Keys.

On my way back, when I topped the highest dune and looked down, I saw a sight that gave me a great rush of pleasure and contentment. Ora, beautiful in a black string bikini, her skin golden, and her hair in a ponytail, walked the shoreline while Jennifer Chicken followed a few paces behind.

I thought, *I'm a happy man. If I die today, I won't feel cheated.*

Before I came along, Big Jim and Ora had been the ideal Keys couple. Almost royalty, they had been revered by the locals, society's outcasts, who saw their love as proof that in the Keys it was possible for even a one-legged smuggler to capture the heart of an exotic island girl.

And they saw me as the hated interloper who had destroyed everyone's dream. Some of Ora's friends couldn't wait to get me alone so they could tell me, "I've known Ora and Big Jim both for years. They're the *best*. You're one lucky man, you know that? You better treat her right—or *else*."

It was always that word, *else*, that drove me nuts. *Else what!* I would think, boiling inside. *You don't know me!* However, I did agree with part of what they said. I *was* a lucky man, but a man who didn't like to be threatened. Ora, realizing that some of her friends were giving me a hard time, decided to invite some of them over so they could see for themselves what a nice guy I was.

One Sunday, three of Ora's closest friends—two women and a man, all in their mid-thirties—showed up for a barbecue. Originally from New York, all three had been living in the Keys for four years, long enough to be considered "local" yet not so long that they had lost their sarcasm, especially the man. He clearly resented my relationship with Ora and all day looked for any way to put me down in front of her. An unhappy man, he was highly critical of everything and everyone, except Ora, whom he clearly adored.

After we had eaten, we all sat in the living room talking, the three guests on the sofa, Ora and me in chairs facing them, and Jennifer Chicken on his perch in between. We had been drinking beer and smoking pot all afternoon and were all stoned. The man, whose name was Ogden, started criticizing roosters, then Jennifer Chicken in particular.

"Roosters may actually be the dumbest creatures on the face of this planet," said Ogden. "Certainly the dumbest bird. I mean, what good are they? Brain about the size of a BB. They're not even good to eat—too tough and stringy. Just look at this one here." He pointed at Jennifer Chicken. "Just sitting there. Hasn't moved in hours."

I had forgiven Ogden's personal attacks, but when he started in on Jennifer Chicken, who had been sitting on his perch being the perfect host, I was duty bound to do something, Ora's friend or not.

"I agree that roosters may not be the smartest animals on the planet, but they're not as dumb as you might think. Every creature has its own unique form of intelligence," I said diplomatically.

"I beg to differ there, T-Roy," said Ogden.

"Name is Troy," I said.

"Whatever. Any fool can look at this creature and see that it barely knows it's alive."

"Oh, he knows he's alive, all right. And he knows his purpose in life. Right now he's just conserving his energy, just waitin' and watchin'."

"Waiting and watching? For what?" asked Ogden.

"That's a highly trained attack rooster you're looking at, mister. Trained him myself to guard the house and make sure Ora and I are safe."

"You're out of your mind! Don't be ridiculous! Whoever heard of an attack rooster? That's absurd."

I didn't respond. Instead, I waited several minutes and continued to listen to Ogden's criticism on another subject in which he thought himself an expert. Then I casually said to Ogden, "Would you do me a favor and hand me that stuffed bear right there beside you, wedged in between the sofa and the wall?"

Ogden picked up the stuffed bear and reached it toward me. Just as the bear passed in front of Jennifer Chicken, the rooster stiffened, flapped his wings once, then flew straight at the stuffed bear Ogden held, hitting it so hard that Ogden stumbled backwards and did a backflip over the sofa, landing on the floor. Jennifer Chicken followed the bear Ogden now held close to his chest. He grabbed it with his beak, shook it, then hit it with his sharp spurs, once, twice, three times. He stood on Ogden's stomach, waiting for the game to continue.

"Get him off!" screamed Ogden. "Please! Get him off! Oh God!"

I calmly walked to the other side of the sofa, bent down, and picked up Jennifer Chicken. "Down, boy," I said. "Down. He's had enough."

I told a frightened Ogden, "See, Oggie, I told you he was an attack rooster. You just didn't believe me. Now you can tell everybody you meet that you've seen a genuine attack rooster up close and personal."

On Sunday mornings, Ora and I enjoyed lying in bed naked, drinking beer, getting stoned, and watching the evangelists on TV, especially Kenneth Copeland and his wife.

We didn't do this to mock preachers or religion but to hear what they had to say regarding the big questions all thinking people eventually ask: "Who am I? Where did I come from?" and "What is the point of it all?"

This led us to church three times. The first time, we attended a Baptist church on Big Pine Key. The next, a Church of God in Key Largo. But our last church was our favorite—an Episcopal church in Tavernier. It was there we felt more welcomed and found the sermon more interesting. Perhaps another reason we preferred the Episcopal church was because of what happened the Sunday we attended.

While driving to church, Ora yelled for me to stop. I pulled over to the side of the highway and parked. Without a word she bolted from the car, and I followed. Thrashing about on a bed of oyster shells near the shoreline was an older man, his face almost in the water. Apparently, he had been fishing and had suffered an epileptic seizure.

We pulled him free of the water and while Ora held his head in her lap and consoled him, I ran to a nearby convenience store and called 911. We stayed until the paramedics arrived, then continued on to church.

Thrashing about, the man had cut his face and hands on the oyster shells, and by helping him Ora had gotten blood on the front of her blouse, which neither of us noticed until the drive back to the Evening Shade. And, I guess, the church congregation hadn't noticed either or else they had been too polite to comment. Another reason to prefer them.

Ora knew a great deal about many things most people know little about, yet she knew little about the American culture. She was like a child with no filter; to her, the truth was the truth and should always be told. There were no gray areas. She saw it as her right and duty to always speak her mind. Consequently, she and anyone with her often found themselves in difficult and dangerous predicaments.

A couple months after we started living together, Ora playfully followed me into the men's restroom in a shopping plaza. There she locked the door behind her and used the toilet while I used the urinal. Someone had tried to get in, had found the door locked, and had gone to the manager to complain. The manager had come to investigate. After using his key to open the door and finding Ora and me in the restroom, he was understandably upset. I apologized, but Ora argued. Her argument involved me in a shoving match with the manager. He called the police and we passed them leaving the parking lot.

Another time, we were in a bar in Key Largo. Near where we sat, an older and a younger man gambled on a game of pool. Whenever the older man turned his back or went to the bar for a drink, the younger moved his own cue balls so that he had an easier shot. He did this game after game.

Finally, Ora got up and walked over to the younger man. "Stop cheating," she told him. Then she turned to the older man and told him what the younger man had been doing. The older man demanded his money back, creating a three-way argument with Ora in the middle. I grabbed Ora and practically had to drag her from the bar.

Once, in another bar, I came back from the restroom to find Ora on top of a woman she had pinned between two barstools. She was choking the woman because the woman had made disparaging remarks about her hero—president and ardent anticommunist Ronald Reagan.

Again, we passed the sheriff's patrol car entering the parking lot just as we were leaving.

When we first moved in together, Ora made it clear that she didn't like to cook and I accepted that, but she decided to make an exception to celebrate our first Thanksgiving together. She told me that she would cook a Thanksgiving dinner with all the trimmings if I would find someone who otherwise wouldn't have a home-cooked meal to share it with us.

While Ora cooked, I drove around trolling for a homeless person, and it didn't take long to find him. After turning off the main highway, I followed a short shell road to a dead end and there, sitting in front of a small tent, I saw a man drinking from a bottle of wine wrapped in a brown paper bag. I pulled over and stopped.

The man welcomed me to this camp and offered me a drink out of his bottle. "Just call me Ohio Shorty," he said. "I was born in Ohio, that's true, but I ain't been back there in years. You see, I'm what's known in some circles as a travelin' man. Every winter when it gets cold, I come down here to warm up my bones and get a little sand in my shoes."

Ohio Shorty was about five-four. He was bald except for a rim of salt and pepper hair. He had a red, vein-streaked pug nose, bright blue eyes, and a round, acne-scarred face. Ohio Shorty had a slight build and was always hitching up his pants as if he had lost weight, had bought them too big, or they had belonged to someone else.

When I asked Ohio Shorty if he would like to come home with me for Thanksgiving dinner, he asked, "Why?"

"Because it's Thanksgiving and everyone oughta have a good meal on Thanksgiving," I said. "Besides, you'd be helping me out."

"How's that?" asked Ohio Shorty.

"Well, my girlfriend won't feed me unless I bring a guest to dinner."

"Well, in that case, I don't mind helping you out. Just let me get my good luck hat," he said.

Ohio Shorty crawled into his tent and popped out a moment later wearing a soft, white fisherman's hat, like the one Henry Fonda wore in the movie *On Golden Pond*. But instead of fishing lures, Ohio Shorty's hat had state pins attached, proving that he was indeed a travelling man. Later, I found out that every pin had a story to go with it.

As soon as we walked into the apartment, Ohio Shorty stopped in his tracks. He stood for a moment and studied Jennifer Chicken on his perch. "You gotta chicken!" he exclaimed. "Living in the house. I'll be. Hope that ain't dinner. If it is, it'll sure be fresh."

"No! That ain't what we're eatin'," I said. "That's our pet rooster, a Cuban fighting cock. We're eatin' turkey. My girlfriend's cookin' it now."

Ora had her faults but discrimination wasn't one of them; she greeted the rich or poor, the great or the most humble, equally. She shook Shorty's hand and welcomed him, then asked if he would like something to drink. Ohio Shorty's first choice was wine, which we didn't have, so he settled for a beer. He drank several before dinner, regaling us with tales of his travels.

The meal was delicious, and Ohio Shorty, while continuing to guzzle beer, ate like a man who hadn't eaten in several days and didn't expect to eat for another week. Ora was pleased that I had found such a worthy guest for Thanksgiving dinner, but I wasn't so sure after closer examination. Seemed to me that Ohio Shorty had slowed down and was starting to look extremely uncomfortable.

Ohio Shorty swallowed a couple times, his eyes bulged, then he heaved. He covered his mouth with his hand but couldn't

stop the volcanic eruption of turkey, beer, dressing, and sweet potatoes that shot from between his outstretched fingers. Ora and I quickly jumped to our feet and shared a quick look. But Ohio Shorty continued to sit, holding his head with vomit-covered hands, obviously embarrassed. "I'm sorry. I'm sorry," he wailed.

"I'll get a towel," said Ora.

"Shorty," I said, making light of the predicament, "I know in some cultures it's complimentary to belch or fart after a good meal, but this is a new one on me. Where'd you say you was from?"

Just before Christmas, ATF agents targeted the Florida Keys. They brought in seventeen-year-olds who looked twenty, paired them with agents, and made the rounds of the bars and restaurants in the Middle Keys. Ora, along with several of her bartender friends, were arrested for serving alcoholic drinks to minors.

When I found out that Ora had been arrested, I was too paranoid to show up at the sheriff's substation to bond her out, so I asked one of her close friends to do it for me, using the excuse that I had a couple unpaid traffic tickets. I waited in the parking lot—as close as I dared get—until Ora was released.

On the drive home, Ora insisted on stopping at a bar and restaurant where close friends worked. And while we were sitting at the bar, the same two ATF agents and the minor that had busted Ora earlier at the tiki bar walked in and sat down at the opposite end of the bar.

When Ora saw them, she stood and shouted, "Don't serve them! Those are the pigs that busted me! That girl's a minor!" Everyone in the crowded bar turned to stare. The bar got very quiet.

"We can arrest you right now for obstructing justice!" shouted one of the agents, standing to confront Ora.

"Go ahead!" yelled Ora. "I'd expect that! You're worse than communists! Go ahead! Arrest me!"

The bar patrons applauded.

I grabbed Ora's arm. "Please, just calm down," I said. "Let's get outta here before we get in more trouble." She resisted, enjoying all the attention, but I finally persuaded her to leave.

When we got back to the Evening Shade, I knew that it was time to finally tell Ora the truth. I told her why I couldn't afford to be arrested, fingerprinted, or investigated for some minor charge. She surprised me once again; she actually thought it exciting that I had escaped from prison and had robbed a bank. Ora promised to keep my secret and be more careful in the future.

Shortly after the incident with the ATF, we had an incident with Jennifer Chicken.

Every morning after Ora fed the rooster, she let him out to forage in the small yard outside our apartment. One day Jennifer Chicken encountered our landlady's dog. The dog attacked and Jennifer Chicken raked the dog with his spurs, almost blinding him. We were given an ultimatum: either get rid of the rooster or move.

With great sadness, we took Jennifer Chicken north to Homestead, where a Cuban family with lots of hens took him in. On the drive back, I told Ora, "He'll be happy there. They may not feed him hamburger or take him to the beach, but he's young and healthy and surrounded by dozens of adoring hens, and that's a pretty good life."

When we got back to the apartment, Ora was told that she was being charged with obstruction of justice and that a hearing date would be set. Because of the situation, we decided to flee the Keys after Christmas and before Ora's date in court.

With all the bad news, it was a dismal Christmas. I promised the next would be better, not realizing that next Christmas would find us in Tampa, sitting in an old pickup truck outside a bank, preparing to rob it.

Chapter 19

After the first of the year Ora and I fled the Florida Keys for Tampa, where I hoped to get a job as a sign painter. (The only experience I had was years earlier in Angola. There I had worked for a short time in the license tag plant, silk-screening and hand-painting signs for various state agencies.)

In Tampa, we rented a two-bedroom house just off Hillsborough Avenue, east of town. We had no furniture and for the first few weeks slept on a pallet of blankets on the floor.

I quickly found a job with a master sign painter who had a shop a few blocks off Dale Mabry Highway. An immigrant from Cuba, the sign painter understood that I had limited experience and was willing to train me.

It didn't take me long to learn the art of sign painting. I was used to handling a brush and had a good sense of color and composition.

In just a couple months, I was also making money on the side, painting signs on the weekends and in the evenings after work. Slowly we filled the house with furniture, and I bought an old pickup truck and some sign-painting equipment.

When I got a contract with a large grocery chain to paint all their signs and then another with a tire dealership with several locations, I quit the sign shop and went into business for myself. I set up a small sign shop in a shed in back of the house and used our concrete parking pad for storage and space to work on larger signs.

The future looked bright, with one major hitch: I didn't have a business license or insurance and didn't dare apply for either, realizing that I'd just have to keep my business small and hope to stay under the radar.

There were some who thought Ora a witch. She was aware of it and seemed to enjoy the mystique (and power) associated with the title. I saw her more as a shaman or a medicine woman with a deep belief in island superstitions. Once I caught her burning her fingernail clippings and hair she had taken from her hairbrush. When I asked her why, she told me matter-of-factly that if certain people were to get hold of her nail clippings or hair, they may be able to cast a spell on her. I didn't pursue the topic.

One Sunday after a long day at the beach, on the way home we passed a huge tent lit with hundreds of lights and surrounded by numerous cars and trucks. When Ora saw the tent, the lights, and the people, she shouted, "What's going on in that tent?"

"Oh, that's a tent revival," I said. "I went to one with my grandfather when I was a boy. You never seen a tent revival before?"

"No. What do they do there?"

"They have church. It's usually sponsored by the Church of God or one of the Pentecostal churches. Some people call 'em Holy Rollers."

"Holy Rollers? What's that mean?"

"Well, some of the congregation get so filled with spirit— or the Holy Ghost, as they call it—that they start speaking in tongues and rollin' around on the floor. The preacher's usually a faith healer."

"I saw something like that once in Honduras," said Ora, "but they didn't call it a tent revival. They called it something else. Can we go?"

I turned the Volvo around, and even though I felt uneasy I drove back to the tent revival, parked in the lot, and we walked inside. Ora insisted that we sit in the front row, only a few feet from the preacher, a large red-faced man who appeared to be in his mid-fifties. He had a crew cut and was dressed in a shirt with

his tie undone. His shirtsleeves were rolled to his elbows. Dozens of believers formed a line from the preacher to the back of the tent. One by one they marched forth to have the preacher lay his large hands on them. He helped a man, then later a woman, both get out of their wheelchairs and stand on shaky legs. Others, walking with canes, threw them away and walked normally; a man suffering back pain removed his brace; and a blind man was miraculously able to see again. Those spiritually infirmed were filled with the Holy Ghost and started speaking in tongues. One woman passed out and had to be carried away.

Mesmerized by all that was happening, I didn't notice when Ora left her seat. I was shocked when I saw her standing in line and waved for her to return to her seat, but she ignored me. When she moved forward in line, I saw the imprint of her bikini under the sheer *I Dream of Jeannie* pants she wore.

The preacher laid his hands on Ora's beautiful forehead and said, "Lord Jesus, I beg you to heal this woman of all her infirmities and this day to free her of sin. Cleanse her soul. Fill her with the Holy Ghost so that she may know your love, Jesus. In Jesus's name!" He jerked his huge hand away as if he had just touched a hot stove.

Ora didn't fall to the floor, she didn't speak in tongues. Instead, she stood perfectly still, looked the preacher in the eye, and said very slowly, "I didn't feel anything."

The preacher's whole head turned as red as Ora's nail polish. He started gasping, then stuttered into the microphone, "You're … You're … a… wit…witch!"

"And you're a fake!" shot back Ora.

"Harlot!" yelled the preacher.

I jumped up. "Now, hold on, mister. You can't talk to her like that!"

Suddenly, it was very quiet. The three of us stared at each other as if we were gunfighters, then the preacher broke the

spell. He said to Ora, "You're the devil's child! I rebuke the devil in the name of Jesus!"

I ran to the podium and grabbed Ora by the arm.

The congregation stood. They moved toward us.

I pushed my way to the exit. We jumped in the Volvo and sped away.

Feeling safe and settled after several months in Tampa, I called my older sister, Dianne, in Lake Charles. It was the first time we had spoken since our mother's death. She assumed that I had served my time and had gotten out and I didn't tell her differently.

When I asked about our father, she told me that he was unable to work and had been staying with her, her husband George, and their three small children. She also told me about his excessive drinking and how his behavior had created a lot of tension for her family. What she didn't tell me about (I learned years later) was an incident where my father nearly killed himself.

To protect her three children from their grandfather's drunkenness, my sister banished him from living in her house. Instead, he slept in his old station wagon parked in her driveway. One night Dianne just happened to get up and look out the front window to see his car engulfed in flames. She awakened her husband, who quickly ran outside and dragged his unconscious father-in-law free of the burning inferno. My sister called 911. The fire department extinguished the fire but not before the car had burned to a smoking shell. The next day a wrecker removed what was left of the old Rambler.

After that, my father went to live in the Salvation Army, where it was hoped that he would get treatment for his alcoholism.

When I telephoned, my father was sober and just happened to be visiting for the day. I spoke to him. During the course of

our conversation, without consulting Ora and without considering the consequences, I invited him to come to Tampa.

A couple days later my father arrived at the Tampa bus terminal and called me. When I searched the waiting area, I couldn't find him, so I stepped to an adjoining small coffee shop and there he sat on a stool at the counter, sipping a cup of coffee and smoking a cigarette. Typically, he was deep into a conversation with the man sitting next to him.

I stood for a minute and watched. He hadn't changed that much since my mother's funeral. His rim of black hair still had very little gray. He wore a plaid Western shirt and jeans and was still as lean at sixty-two as he had been at thirty-two, if just a little more stooped. From where I stood, the fact that he had a glass eye wasn't apparent.

When I got back to the house, Ora was gracious and welcomed my father warmly even though just the day before she had expressed her displeasure at my inviting him without first discussing it with her.

Probably part of Ora's displeasure was losing her communications room. Almost every night after I went to sleep, Ora retreated to our spare bedroom where she monitored the BBC on a broadband radio and studied the world maps on the wall. She also had a small TV tuned to an all-night news channel and numerous newspapers and news magazines that she searched for any mention of communist aggression. She kept a large scrapbook and even wrote political poetry.

In just a few short weeks, Ora's graciousness turned into resentment. "He won't clean up his room. Have you been in there? It smells like an ashtray and he leaves empty whiskey bottles on the nightstand. There's a trail of coffee from the kitchen to the living room on our new shag carpet."

"Oh, come on now. He can't be that bad," I said, even though, remembering Dianne's complaints, I knew he could.

192

"You have no idea; you're gone all day. I'm here with him. He's more manipulative than you think."

"Aw, come on."

"You think I'm joking! I'm not! He's unfit to live with. He's not even housebroken! Last night when I brushed my teeth and picked up the glass on the sink to rinse, I almost swallowed his glass eye."

"Yeah, he's done that since I was a kid. That's how he cleans it, lets it sit in a half glass of water overnight. I'll tell him to use another glass and to put it on his nightstand from now on."

After Thanksgiving passed the sign-painting business suddenly slumped, and I hadn't saved a dime. I worried how I would pay my rent and utilities and brooded because I knew that we wouldn't be able to celebrate Christmas.

The fact that my father was living with me reminded me of the "lean" Christmases we had when I was young. I remembered once, when we lived in Miami, that Dianne and I had gotten a single pair of skates and we were told to share them. We had our own idea of sharing, and rather than take turns using them we each wore one skate while balancing on one leg.

When we lived over the jewelry store in Charleston in 1959, my younger sister, Tonda, who was only five years old, was the only family member to get a present that Christmas, thanks to Dianne. Stored under our parents' bed was a shoebox. Inside was a doll, still in good condition, that Dianne had had for a few years. She wrapped the shoebox in Christmas paper, and that Christmas morning there was one solitary present under the small Christmas tree sitting on the small table in the kitchen.

A couple days after a Christmas without decorations, presents, or any kind of celebration, and worried about paying my rent and utilities, I decided to rob another bank.

Surprisingly, when I told Ora she neither discouraged nor encouraged me. She listened, then calmly said, "Well, if you've made up your mind, then I'm going with you."

"Look, I can do this by myself. No sense in us both taking a chance on getting locked up."

"You don't understand," she said. "If you get killed or locked up, I don't want to be out here by myself, so we may as well do it together. Besides, we can watch each other's back, and I can make us invisible."

"Invisible?"

"You'll see. Trust me."

Intent on staying with a formula that had worked before, I drove around Tampa until I found a bank location very much like the one in Wichita.

Rather than use the Volvo as my getaway vehicle, I decided to use my old work truck, even though it wasn't dependable and was conspicuously covered in splotches of red and gray primer. The morning of the bank robbery I mixed together a couple cans of leftover sign paint, making a dark gray-green. With a paint roller and a brush I painted the entire truck, and as soon as I finished it started raining.

Ora stepped onto the porch. "It's raining. I guess we'll have to put it off," she said.

"Rain ain't gonna stop nothin'," I said. "Actually, it'll work in our favor—keep the cops busy working more accidents. Slow down their response time."

"But the paint's still wet."

"That's no problem. Once we get rollin' down the highway, the wind'll dry it," I said, determined not to be put off.

It was still raining when we drove to the bank, only ten miles from our home. We parked behind a tall wooden fence in an

194

alley behind a dry cleaner and sat quietly for a moment, watching rivulets of gray-green paint run down the truck's windshield.

"This could be the end of our life," said Ora.

"Or it could be the beginning," I replied, kissing her lightly on the cheek. I opened the door and Ora slid behind the wheel.

The plan was simple, yet dangerous. I'd walk into the bank, give the teller a note, get the money, and leave. After going through the opening in the fence, I'd change clothes, then walk around to the front of the dry cleaner's, where Ora would be waiting with the truck.

The robbery went off without a problem, but when I squeezed through the opening in the fence, the truck, with Ora in it, was still sitting where I'd left it.

"What happened! You were supposed to drive out front!" I yelled.

"It won't start!" shouted Ora. "I tried and tried. It won't start!"

"Let me try," I said, turning the key in the ignition. Nothing. I looked at Ora. "Damn. Must be the battery."

We heard sirens in the distance. "What are we going to do?" asked Ora.

"I'll try to get it started," I said. "If not, we'll have to leave it. We've gotta get outta here. Hear those sirens?"

I stashed the bag of robbery money behind the seat, grabbed an old washcloth, and got out. Rushing to the front of the truck, I raised the hood and checked the battery connections. They were tight. The sound of the sirens was closer now. I held my panic in check and with both hands on the fender stared at the engine as if I expected it to tell me what was ailing it. And in a sense, it did. I saw rainwater dripping onto the distributor.

"The distributor!" I shouted. "That's what it is, I betcha!"

"Slide over, get behind the wheel!" I yelled to Ora.

195

Releasing the fasteners that held the distributor cap in place, I removed it to find condensation inside. Carefully I wiped the inside of the cap dry, then reattached it.

"Okay, give it a try!" I yelled. "Turn the key!"

The old truck coughed and sputtered, then came to life. I slammed the hood shut, got behind the wheel, and backed out of the alley. We passed the police just as we were leaving the parking lot.

"Don't worry," said Ora, now more confident. "We're invisible. We can drive right through them and they won't see us."

"Right," I said. "And a good thing too. They're all over the place."

Now isn't the time or place to debate the effectiveness of voodoo versus practical planning, I told myself. *She has her way and I have mine; mine is to make sure that no witnesses connect this truck to the robbery, and hers is to believe we're invisible.*

Five miles from the bank we stopped at a traffic light and the engine died. While Ora steered, I strained to push the truck to the side of the road. Again I raised the hood and dried the inside of the distributor cap. The truck started and we continued our bizarre getaway. At a stop sign, half a mile from our doorstep, the truck died once more.

Finally, we limped into our driveway and parked. When we walked into the house, my father was sitting in a chair in the living room smoking a cigarette, drinking a cup of coffee, and watching *The Price Is Right*.

I sat down on the sofa while Ora went into the bedroom and shut the door. When my father got up to go to the bathroom, I rushed out to the truck, grabbed the bag of money, took it to our bedroom, and shut the door.

I dumped the cash onto the bed and started counting it. The total take was $9,362. After putting a couple hundred in my

pocket, I put the rest in the closet and joined my father in the living room.

With some of the stolen money I bought a used Jeep Cherokee in excellent condition, scaffolding, and other equipment I needed to paint larger signs. And Ora and I spent a lot of time at the beach.

My father continued to irritate Ora and she finally gave me an ultimatum: either he left or she would. When I explained the situation to my father, his comment was, "Son, I never thought I'd see the day you'd let a woman henpeck you like that." I gave him $200 and dropped him at the bus station.

After my father left, so did tension at home. The sign business prospered, but Ora and I spent less time together. She often frequented Ybor City, the Cuban section of Tampa, where she had made new friends and there joined an anti-Castro group. When she wasn't in Ybor City, she was in her newly reclaimed communications room monitoring the news, obsessed with being the first in her new group to recognize a communist conspiracy or buildup.

I spent more time drinking at the bars after work and developed a whole new set of friends myself.

Then one day out of the blue my father called. He asked me to meet him downtown. There he told me that when I had dropped him at the bus station a year earlier, instead of going to Lake Charles he had gotten off the bus in New Orleans, where he had gone to live at the Salvation Army. Assigned as a driver of one of the large trucks that drove around picking up donated furniture, he and the man that worked with him had sold some of the furniture to a secondhand furniture dealer and had been caught. He said that he had been kicked out of the New Orleans Salvation Army and so had caught a bus back to Tampa and was currently living in the Salvation Army here.

I now spent a part of most weekends with my father. We'd go to a restaurant or to the beach where we'd sit and talk and I'd always give him a little money.

But then after a few short months, my father called and told me that he had gotten drunk and had been kicked out of the Tampa Salvation Army too. Once again I took him to the bus station, gave him some money, and put him on a bus to Lake Charles.

I didn't contact them, but I'm sure that my sisters weren't pleased to see him again.

Years later I found out that my younger sister, Tonda, came up with the perfect solution, one that provided our father with a safe, comfortable place to live while keeping him out of everybody's way. She bought a small travel trailer and put it in a pasture in back of her house. There my father, now drawing his Social Security check, was free to pursue his lifestyle unhindered.

I couldn't help but blame Ora for the growing disinterest in our relationship, for her new friends, and for her renewed interest in communist aggression. I even blamed her for my own drinking and cheating, even though the fault was my own and had deeper roots. The real damage had been done years before I had met Ora, even years before I had made that fateful decision while standing in the snow alongside a highway in the mountains of North Carolina.

I began to question myself: *Why was I still in Tampa? Why was I busting my ass painting signs when there was an easier way to make money? How can two people be so much in love in the beginning and in just a few short years seem not to care? What takes place that leads to such a complete change of heart? How does that happen?*

Perhaps my father's presence had been the initial crack in our relationship. Or it could have been that after the bank robbery, Ora realized that I was not the freedom fighter she thought me to be but just a common criminal.

198

Whatever, the chasm had grown so deep and wide that it had swallowed whatever love we had for each other. With nothing left to keep us together—no common interests, nothing financial, and certainly nothing moral—it was easy to walk away, something I had been doing my entire life.

Ora got a job as a bartender in Ybor City and decided to keep the house. I left her the Volvo and furniture, took the Cherokee, my clothes, and paintbrushes, and left.

I drove north, with no destination and only $400 in my pocket. When I got close to North Carolina, I decided to drive to Shelby, curious to see what it looked like after so many years and perhaps to also try to understand what part the small town had played in making me into a man I didn't like or respect very much.

Chapter 20

It had been twenty years since last I was in Shelby. Then I'd been an eighteen-year-old Marine on a three-day Christmas pass, arriving like a conquering hero and leaving like a defeated beggar.

Painfully, I drove the streets of my youth, stopping at the old cotton mill where my grandparents had labored for over thirty years. Now abandoned, it was an empty, red brick memorial to a different generation and way of life.

When I was young, every weekday at 4:30 I'd run down Gardner Street to meet my grandfather after his shift at the mill. Dressed in faded blue overalls, a blue chambray shirt, and carrying a scuffed, black metal lunch box, my grandfather, no matter how tired, would always smile when he saw me. He'd tousle my snow-white hair and hand me his lunch box to carry.

Next, I drove past my grandparents' old house on Gardner Street. Still standing, but ramshackle after the passing of so many years, it held many pleasant memories and, I would guess, a few dark secrets that died with my grandparents.

I remembered the Easter that my cousins and I had an egg fight in the hall. Egg yolk was stuck on the wallpaper, the polished wooden floor, and our best Sunday clothes. My grandmother had singled me out as the instigator and rightfully so. Dragging me by the arm to Aunt Dolly's old bedroom, she paddled me with a hairbrush, then confined me to the bedroom for the rest of that day and night.

But that was nothing compared to the paddling I watched my grandmother give my mother months earlier.

My father had been out of town driving a truck long-distance for F.M., and my mother had been gone for two days, so I had been staying at my grandparents' house when a

concerned citizen and member of the Church of God congregation had telephoned my grandfather and had told him that his daughter Irene had been seen in shantytown. My grandfather drove to get her.

I was sitting in the dining room when he escorted my mother through the back door and into the kitchen. My grandmother grabbed the first object she could find, a large spatula sitting on the kitchen counter, and, while holding my mother's arm with her free hand, she spanked her repeatedly on the butt with the spatula, all the while yelling at her.

Whack! "Irene, what in the world is wrong with you! [*whack!*] Leaving your kids for other folks to take care of! [*whack!*] While you run off to get drunk! [*whack! whack!*] You should be ashamed of yourself! [*whack!*] I never thought I would raise a young'un that would act like that!"

Whack! Whack! Whack!

The handle on the spatula broke.

My mother curled into a fetal position on the kitchen floor and whimpered like a puppy.

Sometimes my grandfather would give me a nickel, and to this day if I close my eyes I can see him reaching into his pants pocket and pulling out a little, red, plastic coin purse shaped like a deflated football with a slit in the side. He would squeeze the purse and like magic the slit would open to reveal various coins. My grandfather would finger through the coins until he found a buffalo nickel, the most beautifully designed coin ever minted. I'd hold it in the palm of my small hand, amazed at how big it seemed. In my pocket, I'd trace the design of the Indian on the front and the buffalo on the back with my forefinger.

I remember once how my desire to get a nickel caused me illness. After Thanksgiving dinner, I stood in the dining room and watched Aunt Dolly ferry plates and glasses and bowls to

the kitchen. When she picked up a large bowl, half full of green beans, she suffered a moment of indecision. She didn't want to throw them away and there wasn't room in the refrigerator to store them, so she turned to me and said, "I'll give you a nickel if you eat the rest of these green beans."

I would do almost anything for a nickel and I was always that kid who would accept a dare. I ate until sick but finished them and got my nickel. For years after I refused to eat green beans, even got nauseous at the smell.

Maybe Gardner Street and my grandparents' old house hadn't changed much, but Trade Alley had undergone drastic changes. The old duplex where I had lived was gone. In its place were neat brick apartments with a swimming pool, playground, and an asphalt parking area. The red dirt road was now paved, and everywhere I looked instead of poor white people I saw middle-class Black people.

I drove to my old elementary school, then on to City Park where I used to play baseball in the summer and football in the winter.

At a convenience store, I looked through the telephone book and was tempted to call an aunt, uncle, or cousin, but didn't. *What would I say? What would they expect of me? What would I expect of them? It's just too complicated,* I told myself.

After three hours in Shelby I felt no wiser for having stopped. Leaving town, I drove west on the same highway where two decades earlier as a young Marine my life had taken an errant turn. As I drove down that highway I couldn't help but think of my grandfather, the one person that I had held above all others—until he failed me. Not until I had made so many poor choices and mistakes myself did I begin to understand the complexities of adulthood and could finally forgive him.

I drove to Asheville, then over to Chattanooga where I spent the night in a motel. The next day I passed through Nashville, then on to Memphis.

In Memphis I stopped at a rest area just south of town, determined to make a decision before continuing. Running low on money, I realized that I could no longer afford to travel without direction or purpose. Not wanting to stray too far from the ocean, I headed back south. In Jackson, Mississippi, I caught the interstate west and spent the night in a rest area just outside Dallas. It had been years since I'd spoken to my friend Charlie who lived there, but I didn't dare call.

The next morning I again drove south, angling for the Gulf Coast. South of Galveston I discovered a little-known paradise called Matagorda. Sparsely populated, it was a shrimping village with a pristine beach of packed sand and blue-green water. At the time, it was one of the few places that permitted camping and allowed cars to drive directly onto the beach.

It was perfect. The week that I spent there I never once saw a cop or park ranger. I slept on the deserted beach at night, and during the day blended with the locals and tourists. A few days after my arrival I met an attractive secretary on holiday from Houston. We spent the afternoon swimming and that night in her motel room, only a few miles from the beach.

I spent a lot of time in thought. I had already decided what I had to do, I just wasn't sure where or exactly how.

When I decided to rob a bank in Corpus Christi, about seventy miles south, I drove there on Friday and spent the day casing banks. Spoiled after living on the beach for a week, I resented having to put on clothes, especially shoes and socks, and disliked having to spend my day hemmed in by traffic and people.

When I finally found the right bank location, I could hardly wait to get out of Corpus Christi and back to the nearest beach, ten miles east of town. There I parked the Cherokee near the sand dunes, about a hundred yards from the surf.

Determined to rob the bank on Monday, I played the spectator Saturday and Sunday, observing the beachgoers from atop a sand dune, much like a sports fan would enjoy a game from the bleachers. And like a fan who watches but doesn't participate, I was highly critical.

Just look at 'em, I told myself. *Packin' up their blankets and loadin' up their chairs and portable grills, goin' home to face the same old grind. But not me! Hell no. I ain't gotta go nowhere! Pretty soon I'll have this whole beach to myself. What suckers!*

I didn't realize it at the time but my criticisms were really an attempt to ease the pain of my loneliness. I actually envied them for their material possessions and familial closeness and for something much deeper, something priceless yet intangible, something I thought I would never have—meaning and purpose in their lives.

Meaning and purpose fostered responsibility and motivated them to get out of their comfortable beds on Monday morning to report to a job that they may not like but would report to nonetheless because it was their responsibility to make sure that the bills were paid, that their kids had braces on their teeth, and that money was saved for college and retirement.

I envied the beachgoers because they had found the secret to happiness: compromise. All I knew about life was that it was all or nothing—either I had money or I was broke, either my stomach was full or it was empty, either I was incredibly happy or miserably sad. There were no in-betweens.

Many years later I would again explore the words "responsibility" and "compromise" and this time would

understand the two words to be part of a larger word: conscience. And I would ask myself if it was possible through the proper regimen for me to develop a healthy conscience, or was I simply stuck with what I had learned in early childhood?

Afraid this may be the last night of my freedom, I couldn't sleep Sunday night, knowing that I was going to rob a bank in just a few hours. I lay on my back on the sand and stared at the heavenly panorama that was my ceiling. Sometime after midnight I covered my head, curled in a ball, clasped my hands between my legs, and finally fell asleep.

Not long after I was awakened by someone shaking my shoulder.

"Mister! Wake up, please! We need help!"

I sat up to stare into the face of a boy who appeared to be ten or eleven.

"Mister! Please! My dad and I need help, please!"

"Help? Help you do what?" I said, standing to shake the sand out of my blanket. "What's the problem?"

"It's our van. We're stuck in the ocean. The water is already up to the middle of the tires."

"I don't know if I can help or not. Your dad got a chain or rope?"

"I think he's got a rope. Hurry, please!"

I got in the Cherokee and drove to the water's edge to find a blue van with Illinois plates stuck in the surf. They had parked at the water's edge during low tide and had gone to sleep inside the van. High tide had caught them unaware and now threatened to wash the van out to sea.

After tying a rope to the front bumper of the van, then to the rear bumper of my Cherokee, I put the car in four-wheel-drive, slowly tightened the rope until it was taut, and towed the van well past the high-water mark.

The man was extremely grateful and offered to pay me. But even though I was down to a quarter of a tank of gas, hadn't eaten the previous day, and had only $3 in my pocket, I was too prideful to accept. I drove back to my spot at the base of the sand dunes and settled in to sleep.

The smell of salt in the air and the screeching sound of seagulls awakened me just after dawn. I sat up, looked around, sighed, then closed my eyes again, dreading the danger I'd face in a few hours.

Four hours later I robbed a branch bank in Corpus Christi and made my getaway across the bridge north. Safely on the other side, I stopped at a small rest area, pulled the sack of money from under the seat, and, while scanning the rearview mirror, quickly counted it. I had a little over $4,300. Not as much as I had hoped, but enough.

Driving north, then east, I stopped that evening at a restaurant in Lake Charles. While eating, I stared at the black hard-plastic payphone on the wall and resisted the urge to telephone one or both of my sisters and father who lived there.

Leaving Lake Charles I drove east to Lafayette, where I spent the night in a motel. The next morning I drove north to Jackson, Mississippi, and that afternoon checked into the Sheraton, just off Interstate 55, north of town.

There, enjoying room service, drinking scotch, and watching movies on cable TV, I thought a lot about what to do next. Inebriated, I came up with an idea that made perfect sense. I picked up the phone, called Delta Airlines, and reserved a seat on a flight leaving the next day for Honolulu. I got in the Cherokee and went shopping for luggage, shorts, sandals, and Hawaiian shirts.

Chapter 21

The next morning I awakened with a throbbing headache and looked at the half-empty bottle of scotch sitting on the nightstand. I shook my head when I saw the new suitcase, partially opened, on the nearby dresser. Colorful shirts and cargo shorts were scattered about, reminding me that I had booked a flight to Hawaii for that afternoon.

"I can't go to Hawaii!" I yelled, then to myself, *What am I going to do with my car? How about when I run outta money? I can't rob a bank! It's an island. There's nowhere to run!*

Picking up the telephone, I cancelled the reservation, packed, and left Jackson, driving I-20 west. That night in a motel in Dallas, realizing that all I was doing was circling, I decided that it was time for a completely new direction.

It took me five days to get to California. My first stop was the incredibly beautiful coastal community of Morro Bay. After parking the Cherokee I walked to the beach, stood, and stared at the Pacific Ocean, my first view in over twenty years—not since I had been a seventeen-year-old Marine stationed at Camp Pendleton.

The Atlantic Ocean is beautiful in many locations and even the Gulf of Mexico is pristine and clear in a few rare locations, but neither can compare to the majesty and wild beauty of the Pacific. Its grandeur will affect even the most insensitive, and humble even the most arrogant.

The hour that I spent at Morro Bay renewed and invigorated me. When I got back in the Cherokee I followed the coastal highway north, stopping in Big Sur. It was there at a bar and restaurant overlooking a clear mountain stream that I heard about a lively roadhouse nearby.

After an excellent dinner of fried calamari, I drove to the roadhouse. It was small but crowded, and the rock 'n' roll band was better than average. Finding a small table to myself, I sat down, drank a beer, and studied the people all around me.

It appeared that most were local. I could tell because, like in Key West, they dressed like leftover hippies that had been pushed to the fringe of society and so had created their own community—a place that was still a part of the world yet apart from it, a place where they could practice their own beliefs and customs.

Having experienced a similar mind-set in the Keys, I knew they were also a fiercely loyal group that wouldn't take kindly to an outsider intruding, so I reminded myself to tread carefully. Then I saw a tall girl with beautiful long blond hair sitting at a table on the opposite side of the dance floor. With her was a short, slim girl with dark curly hair. Hovering over her table was a tall, heavyset, surly looking man with long greasy hair tied in a ponytail. He wore jeans, boots, and a thick blue-plaid shirt.

The tall blonde appeared to be either in her late twenties or early thirties. She had a wide-set mouth that was very attractive, and when she smiled she glowed from head to foot. Wearing a tight black skirt that enhanced her figure and revealed the most beautiful legs I'd ever seen, I watched as she danced with the surly man, who had been standing nearby.

After the dance, the tall man escorted the girl to her table and sat down opposite her. When the music started again, I saw him take her hand and watched her pull away. The man stood and motioned for her to get up but she refused, shaking her head no. The man walked away.

I waited a moment, then walked over and asked her to dance. She flashed a lovely smile of acceptance. Taking her hand, I led her to the dance floor where the band had just begun a slow song, giving us an opportunity to talk. She told me that her

name was Laurie and that she lived and worked in Big Sur but had grown up in San Francisco. I told her my name, then lied and told her that I was a commercial artist on extended vacation from Florida.

"Is that your boyfriend, the big guy sitting at your table earlier?" I asked.

"No," said Laurie. "He's one of the locals. Works for the park service, like I do. He's always trying to get me to date him."

"Maybe you should give the guy a break," I said.

"Sorry," said Laurie, "he's just not my type."

"Yeah, what is your type?"

"That's a secret." She smiled flirtatiously.

We danced to two more songs before I escorted Laurie back to her table. She invited me to join her. When I sat down she introduced me to her friend, an English girl who was apparently on extended vacation herself. The girl smiled and offered her hand.

Looking around, I saw that the surly man was now sitting at a table with two other men and they were all staring in our direction. I looked away, directing my attention to Laurie.

"It's too crowded in here," said Laurie. "You wanna go outside and smoke a joint? You smoke pot, don't you?"

"I hate to think I don't!" I said. "My car's parked right by the front door."

In the Cherokee, while Laurie searched her purse for a baggie of pot and some rolling papers, I popped a Janis Joplin tape into the cassette player. Laurie quickly rolled a joint, lit it, then passed it to me. I inhaled deeply, the smoke burning my lungs and throat, and passed it back. Reaching over I turned the cassette player to full volume, causing the dashboard to vibrate.

I was totally lost in the effects of the pot, the loud music, and Laurie when a dull rap on the driver's window caught my

attention. Turning, I saw a man just outside, his mouth moving, but I couldn't hear what he said. Then I realized why.

"Oh shit!" I turned off the cassette player and rolled down the window. Smoke enveloped the man. He stepped back.

"Excuse me," he said politely, "but I'm the manager of this place. Would you mind turning your stereo down, you're drowning out the band."

"Sure," I said. "No problem."

When the manager left, I looked at Laurie. She rolled her eyes, then we both laughed uncontrollably.

"I know a turnout we can go to," said Laurie. "It's not far."

"What's a turnout?"

"It's a place alongside the highway where people park to look at the view. Sometimes people even camp there overnight. There are several along this stretch of the coast highway."

"That's what we call 'scenic overlooks' where I come from," I said, "but I like 'turnout' better. Show me the way."

The turnout was only half a mile from the roadhouse. No one else was parked there and it was dark and quiet. We got out of the car and walked toward the cliff's edge. Laurie put her hand in the center of my back.

"Be careful," she warned, "a lot of people have died falling off these cliffs. Sometimes the soft dirt along the edge crumbles and gives way. And it's a long drop, probably about a hundred feet to the rocks and ocean from here."

I stood near the edge and watched the waves crashing against the rocks. The sight and sound were hypnotic, pulling at me like a magnet. I shivered, stepped away from the cliff's edge. Laurie met me. Taking her in my arms I kissed her deeply. Hand in hand we walked back to the Cherokee.

Inside the car we held and kissed. "Do you want to get in the back?" I asked. Laurie nodded yes.

In the back, I released the latch to lay the seats flat and give us more space. Opening the tailgate, I hastily threw out whatever was in the way, then spread my open sleeping bag, blanket, and two pillows to make a bed. Laurie joined me.

In relative privacy, except for an occasional vehicle bathing us in a foggy light, we made love while Janis Joplin sang of her loneliness and despair. Entangled, we fell asleep.

Four events let me know that it was morning and reminded me of where I was and who I was with: a brilliant sun warmed the side of my face, the sound of occasional traffic, a tall naked girl wrapped around me like an overcoat, and Janis Joplin wailing, "Cry, cccrrryyy, ba-by!"

Rubbing sleep from my eyes, I carefully disentangled myself, sat up, and looked around. "What the … !" The tailgate was wide open, yawning at passing cars like a giant clown with a wide-open mouth. Curious adults stared as they drove by. Children waved and pointed.

My clothes and luggage surrounded the Cherokee like a magician's circle of protection. One boot lay a few feet from the highway, the other under a nearby scraggly bush, my pants and shirt were near the left tire, and my open suitcase near the right. Colorful Hawaiian shirts shined like butterflies in the early morning light.

Carefully I covered Laurie with the sleeping bag and wrapped the blanket around my waist and left shoulder, holding it there with my right hand. After climbing from the rear of the Cherokee, I reached out my left hand to pick up my pants, stumbled, and hit my head hard on the edge of the tailgate.

"Damn!" I yelled, reaching my right hand to my head and dropping the blanket!

There I stood for a brief moment alongside the Pacific Coast Highway, naked in the early morning light, holding my head with one hand and my pants with the other. Quickly I

picked up the blanket, wrapped it around me, and crawled back inside the Cherokee. After putting on my pants, I reached over the top of the front seat, pushed the off button on the cassette player, and put an end to Janis's suffering.

The silence awakened Laurie and she sat up, clutching the sleeping bag to her breast.

"Good morning," I said, smiling.

Confused and sleepy eyed, she smiled back. "Good morning. What's going on?"

"You wouldn't believe it," I said. "I just mooned a station wagon full of tourists from Indiana."

"You did what!"

"I'm serious," I said and told her what had happened. We both laughed, a good way to start any day.

Following Laurie's directions I took her to Pfeiffer Big Sur State Park, where she had a small room and bath above the store where she worked five days a week selling supplies to campers and tourists. It was Sunday and Laurie didn't have to work until the following day, so she showed me around Big Sur and the nearby communities of Carmel and Monterey. We had lunch at a restaurant on Cannery Row.

That night, after dropping Laurie at her room, I drove to the turnout, crawled in the back of the Cherokee, and slept. I still had a little money left and could have rented a motel room, but I enjoyed the isolation and solitude of the turnout so much that I started spending every night there.

Why, I asked myself, *would I voluntarily close myself in by four walls when I could have such a magical world for a room? Why would I walk on hardwood or carpet when I could walk on soft grass? Why would I turn on the stereo or watch television when I could hear the ocean or, on a clear night, watch it crash against the rocks?*

Most nights after work Laurie drove over in her car and joined me for a few hours. Sometimes I followed her back to her room, took a shower, and stayed until morning.

On the nights when I was alone and the fog so thick I could barely see the edge of the cliff, I played what I called the cliff game. I'd walk to the edge of the cliff, stop, then slowly drag one foot after another until just the toes of my shoes hung over the edge. Frozen in place, my heart racing, I'd slowly move each foot forward, making adjustments until I felt certain both feet were even and dead center of the cliff's edge. Balanced on the hundred-foot precipice in complete darkness, toes hanging free, salt spray in my face, and the wind buffeting me, I'd rock back and forth like a great sea captain at the wheel of his schooner during a fierce storm.

Then one night something happened that changed my view of life and death forever.

As usual, I stood in the dark in the thick fog playing the cliff game. When I dragged my left foot to align with my right, the soft dirt gave way and I slipped over the edge. Windmilling my arms and yelling, "Oh God! Oh God! Please ... " I turned in midair like a cat and clawed at the face of the cliff. Catching the ledge a few feet into my fall, I hung there, trembling so hard that I could barely hold on while the ocean below roared like a beast waiting to be fed. I gasped so hard I almost passed out.

Then, slowly, my breathing returned to normal, and like a centipede I carefully crawled back up the side of the cliff. When I reached the top I pulled myself over and lay flat on the ground, my chest heaving and my face and arms scraped and bleeding. Raising my head I spit out dirt, then turned and stared at the cliff as if at a lover that had betrayed me.

Lying there, my heart pounding into the ground, the vibration echoing in my head, I realized that just like the preacher at the tent revival in Tampa, I too was a hypocrite and

a fake. I had told myself that I wasn't afraid of dying and that life was unimportant to me, and now I knew that to be a lie else I would have just given up and allowed myself to slip into the ocean.

I never walked to the edge of the cliff in the fog again.

Two weeks later I left Big Sur and drove to Portland, Oregon. There I checked into a motel for the night. The next day I robbed another bank.

Chapter 22

The Portland bank robbery went smoothly enough, but all I got was a disappointing $1,400. Three weeks later I robbed another in Fresno and got even less—$1,200.

After the robberies I continued to return to Big Sur, its unique energy drawing me to it like matter to a black hole.

Although Key West and Big Sur were as distant geographically as any two locations in the continental U.S., they shared more similarities than differences. In both, the locals lived every day as if it were their last, squeezing all the joy out of life and ignoring all the sorrow. And in both there was an energy just below normal awareness. In Key West this unseen energy had given me the feeling that I was on the verge of a great discovery, while in Big Sur it had given me the feeling that I was standing near a door that may suddenly open to a larger understanding.

During the next couple weeks I spent a lot of time thinking and realized it was time to move on. I knew that I couldn't continue to live at the turnout. Sooner or later the highway patrol that drove by three or four times a day would grow suspicious seeing the white Cherokee with Florida plates parked there every night and come to investigate. And then, Laurie had recently told me that before we met she had been dating a doctor in nearby Carmel and that he had proposed. She said that she had accepted but since meeting me had decided to break off the engagement.

When Laurie revealed that, at first I felt flattered, then conflicted. I fantasized that I could give up crime and settle with her in Monterey or even San Francisco, but that idea quickly faded when I realized that it was just a matter of time before we

grew bored with each other and I left or robbed another bank. I knew that I was in a downward spiral and that there was only one way out for me now: capture or death. And when that happened, those closest to me would be collateral damage. I knew that the only decent thing to do—and the safest—was to leave.

The last night that Laurie and I spent together we talked of many things, most of them trivial. I couldn't find the courage to tell her that I was leaving in the morning, but it seemed to me that somehow she knew because later, in her room after making love, she clung to me like she was drowning.

Near dawn, I disentangled myself, carefully got out of bed, dressed, and walked to the door. There I stood for a moment, held the doorknob, and watched her, freezing her image in my mind. Easing the door open, I walked away.

While the Cherokee warmed up I stared hypnotically at the streaks of condensation on the windshield. A cool breeze blew through the partially opened driver's window, making me shiver. I turned on the windshield wipers, gripped the steering wheel firmly, took a deep breath, sighed heavily, then backed from the parking space.

Several miles south, I stopped at a general store, bought a cup of coffee, and filled the car with gas. While pumping gas with one hand and sipping coffee with the other, doubt crept in.

It's not too late. I can still turn around and go back. It'll be hard on her when she drives to the turnout after work and I'm not there. But in the long run, she'll be better off without me. She's too good to get involved with the likes of me. I'm doin' the right thing. Just keep going. Do the right thing for once.

After I left the general store, I drove with a new determination, afraid that I'd change my mind and turn around. While negotiating a curve on a steep decline, a ghostly image darted in front of the car. I slammed on the brakes, skidded onto

the shoulder, and stopped. Standing on the opposite side of the highway was a dirty golden-brown dog, so skinny that I could see the ridge of its backbone and the outline of its ribs. The dog had sagging tits, which told me that it had recently given birth.

"Go on, get outta the road before you get run over!" I shouted, reaching my arm out the window and beating my hand on the side of the car door. But the dog didn't flinch. She just stood there, staring straight through me with haunted eyes, too tired and too hungry and too desperate to be afraid. Taking her time, she turned, tucked her tail between her legs, and loped off into the brush.

By late afternoon I was traveling through *Bonanza* country, a land of clear lakes, rugged hills, and limitless Ponderosa pine. After crossing into Nevada, I spent the night in a motel in Reno. There, while washing my clothes at a laundromat, I played the slot machines, an activity which seemed harmless until I lost $40 before the rinse cycle was complete. After that I made a vow not to leave the motel for the rest of the night. I had less than $100 left from the Fresno robbery and couldn't afford to waste any more money until I knew definitely where I was going.

On Friday morning, a couple days later, I arrived in Denver. I was so out of touch with the mainstream that I had no idea that the following Monday would be Labor Day. Down to just a few dollars, my belly empty, and the Cherokee thirsting for gas, I was now in a hurry to find a bank and rob it.

I scouted a bank near a shopping center that morning and went back that afternoon to rob it, but just as I stepped to the teller's window, a man wearing a sports coat and tie entered the bank. He looked like a police detective or even the FBI, and that spooked me. When the teller asked if she could help, I patted my shirt pockets as if I'd forgotten something, then muttered that I must've left my check in the car. I hurried from the bank.

I wasn't too concerned about not robbing the bank that Friday. I knew that I could always do it tomorrow, on Saturday, before noon, just as I had done in Wichita, so I spent the last of my money on a couple gallons of gas and a hamburger. Finding a parking place downtown that night, I crawled in the back of the Cherokee and went to sleep.

The next morning I discovered that Denver banks weren't open on Saturday and that I'd have to wait until Monday. Then I found out that Monday was Labor Day and I'd have to wait until Tuesday, three days away.

Denver was celebrating the Labor Day weekend with a huge festival on the grounds of the state capitol, not far from where I had parked the Cherokee. With nothing else to do but wait until Tuesday, I spent the next three days wandering among the tents and stages set up for entertainment and cooking demonstrations.

The smell from the food tents drove me crazy, but I couldn't resist returning time after time to experience the sweet torture. Like a starving dog tied to a pole outside the window of the steakhouse, I salivated so much Saturday, Sunday, and Monday that my throat stayed dried and raw. Trying to replenish the liquid in my body and put something in my stomach, I made the water fountain near the steps of the capitol my base of operations. From there I ventured forth time and time again to sniff my way through the festival. That's when I sank to a new low.

On the steps of the capitol building, I looked down to see a large corn chip, about the size of a small pancake, that someone had taken a bite out of it before dropping. It was covered in ants. Standing over the corn chip I looked around. When I felt no one was watching I bent to one knee, as if to tie my shoe, and scooped it up. Wiping the ants off I ate it as I walked.

By Tuesday morning I was so hungry I was incoherent. If someone had asked me a direct question, all I would've been able to do was mumble.

After the long holiday weekend, the bank was packed with customers. There were four tellers and each had eight to ten people standing in front of them. Normally I would've waited until that afternoon when the bank was almost empty, but I was too tired and too hungry to give a damn anymore. Entering the bank around 9:15, I rudely elbowed my way to the teller nearest the door.

"Excuse me! Excuse me! Let me through here!" I said. Amazingly, no one said anything to me as I stepped to the head of the line.

The male bank teller read the note I handed him, looked up at me, and froze. When I reached inside my shirt for an imaginary gun, he quickly opened his cash drawer and stacked all the money on the counter. While dozens of witnesses watched, I raked the cash into a canvas bag and tucked it inside the waistband of my now too-loose pants. With my hands free, I headed for the door.

As soon as I stepped through, a sensor over the door tripped the trigger on a dye-pack bomb the teller had slipped in with the money. The loud explosion scared the hell out of me and actually lifted me off my feet. It blew a hole the size of a half-dollar in the side of the canvas bag stuffed inside my waistband. Red dye and tear gas exploded upward, hitting me in the chest, neck, and face, temporarily blinding me.

Recovering quickly, I removed my light jacket and wrapped the still-smoking canvas bag in it. Cradling the bomb and money in my arms, I ran for an alley across the street from the bank, red smoke trailing me like a Roman candle.

In the alley, hidden from view, I dropped the jacket and canvas bag onto the pavement and removed my hat, sunglasses, and brightly colored, blue-green Hawaiian shirt. Wrapping it all in a bundle I walked half a block to where the Cherokee was parked. As I drove, I hung my head out the driver's window to clear my eyes of tear gas.

Even though the car's gas gauge was resting firmly on empty, I made it to a fast food restaurant ten miles away. After parking near the rear entrance, I looked inside the canvas bag for the first time. The money was completely covered in red dye and in the center, where the bomb had been located, hard plastic and cash were fused into a knot as big as a baseball.

I removed a $20 that was smeared with red dye but still intact. Walking to the restaurant's rear entrance, I went straight for the restroom. Luckily, it was empty. Turning on the water in the sink closest to the door, I stretched out my leg so that I could prop my foot against the door to stop anyone that tried to open the door. Using the powdered soap in the dispenser above the sink. I scrubbed the $20 like a pair of socks until it turned light pink. I then held it under the hand dryer.

At the counter, I told the server, "Give me two large cheeseburgers with everything, two orders of french fries, an order of onion rings, two fried apple pies, and a large Coke to go."

A few minutes later, when the kid handed me my order, I gave him the pink $20. He turned it over and over, examining it. Before he could speak, I said, "Betcha never saw a pink $20 before. Me neither. I left that one in the watch pocket of my jeans and my wife washed 'em along with her new red blouse. Everything came out pink. You should see my jeans! They're ruined. It'll still spend, won't it?"

"Yeah … sure. I guess so," he said, putting it in the register and handing me my change.

In the Cherokee I unwrapped one of the cheeseburgers with trembling hands. After taking a deep breath I gobbled it down in a few bites. After that I slowly savored the rest of the meal.

I filled the car with gas and drove east on I-70.

That night, in Kansas, I stopped in a small town off the interstate. At a service station I pulled to the side and searched the canvas bag more thoroughly, finding about $300 unmarked. Putting the cash in my pocket, I thought about the best way to clean the rest of the money and finally decided on bleach. Inside the convenience store attached to the service station, I bought a gallon of bleach, a bottle of scotch, then found a motel and checked in.

In the room, I dumped all the stained and mangled cash into my ice chest, then poured the entire gallon of bleach on top, swirling it around with my hand. Immediately the bleach turned red. Closing the lid I slid the ice chest under the bed, removed my clothes and got in the shower. While washing between my legs, I felt an intense burning sensation, and discovered that the force of the dye-pack bomb had actually embedded the numeral "20" into the side of my scrotum and inner thigh.

The next morning I bounded from bed and opened the ice chest, anxious to count my newly cleaned money, but what I saw caused me to fall to the carpet on my knees. All the stolen money had turned to a green goo that looked like split pea soup. The pure bleach had totally disintegrated the paper bills. Reaching inside the ice chest, I picked up two handfuls of green slime, examined it closely, then let the gobs of ruined money fall back into the ice chest.

I dumped the contents in the toilet and flushed it.

I left, driving east, totally disillusioned by the events of the past week. While driving through Texas, Louisiana, Mississippi, Alabama, and, finally, the state of Georgia, I reflected, *In the past week, I've abandoned a woman who may have loved me, starved myself into*

recklessness, committed another bank robbery, been blown up by a bomb, and have flushed about $5,000 down the toilet. There's not much else that could happen.

As usual, I was wrong.

In Atlanta, with only about $100 left, I turned south, determined to return to Tampa, get a job, and give up bank robbery forever. Just south of Savannah, the Cherokee died and I coasted to the shoulder of the road. The gas gauge was half full but the engine light was on; I'd apparently been running hot and hadn't noticed.

When I raised the hood, steam boiled from the radiator and the engine gave off heat like a potbellied stove in midwinter. It emitted a strange *ping ping ping.* I tried to remember the last time I had checked the water level in the radiator and couldn't remember ever doing it. There wasn't much I could do but let it cool off, then hope it would start. Having no water, I wondered if I should find something to piss in and put the urine in the radiator when it cooled down.

Meanwhile, I knew that I shouldn't stay with the car. Afraid to draw the attention of the highway patrol, I walked into some thick pine trees fifty yards from the highway and waited about three hours. In all that time I saw only one highway patrol car pass, and he didn't even slow down.

I walked back to the Cherokee, removed the radiator cap, and using my shirt for a glove I poured a Coke can full of urine in the radiator. I got in the car and turned the key. Nothing.

"Damn!" I shouted, banging my hands on the steering wheel. I didn't have the money to get the Cherokee towed or fixed and couldn't stay with it. It had served me well but I had no choice but to abandon it.

Leaving my bulky suitcase, I packed a small travel bag with the absolute essentials: my shaving kit and three changes of

clothes. Walking until out of sight of the Cherokee, I raised my thumb.

The first ride I caught was in a fast red Camaro driven by a man who appeared to be in his late twenties. He was handsome, well dressed, talkative, and friendly. As I listened to him, it was obvious that we had lived very different lives. To this point, his had been a pleasant experience—popular in school, good at sports, and above average scholastically. He had succeeded at everything he had attempted so far and I was sure his parents were well educated and doted on him. And *my* life, well, you know what it's been like.

He told me that he was headed home to Jacksonville to visit his parents for two weeks. And I told him that I was headed to Miami to visit my brother, who owned a small construction business and had offered me a job. I also told him that I was recently divorced and the reason that I was hitchhiking was that my wife had gotten our only car in the settlement.

He told me that he had an interesting but demanding job and that he was looking forward to some time off. He said that he'd probably do a little fishing and may even take his sailboat out if the weather was nice.

"What kind of work do you do?" I asked.

"I work for the FBI," he said.

Chapter 23

I felt my face flush when the driver of the red Camaro told me that he worked for the FBI. I was thankful for the dark sunglasses I wore; otherwise, he would have surely seen the shock and fear in my eyes. Quickly regaining my composure, I turned and studied the young agent. He seemed relaxed; obviously had no idea that the hitchhiker he had just given a ride was a fugitive and bank robber.

Understandably, he was very proud of his profession and talked freely while speeding along the highway at ninety miles an hour, one hand on the steering wheel, the other fiddling with a dash-mounted radar detector.

All I have to do is act normal, I told myself, *and a normal person would be curious and ask questions.*

"Have you ever caught any kidnappers?" I asked, intent on working my way up to the subject I really wanted to ask about.

"I've worked on a couple kidnapping cases," he told me, "but I've never been directly involved in the apprehension of a suspect."

"Well, what about bank robberies? Ever worked on any bank robbery cases?"

"A couple," he said, not volunteering much information.

I continued to probe. "I was just wondering—do most bank robbers get caught?"

"Yeah, I'd say that 99 percent get caught eventually, although most do get away with the first robbery. After that, though, every time they rob another bank the odds of getting caught shift dramatically."

"So if they just robbed one or maybe two banks then stopped, they probably wouldn't get caught."

"Well, possibly," said the agent, "but they never just hit one or two then stop."

"Why?"

"The money's too easy and they can't help but tell someone about it, usually a wife or girlfriend. And, for whatever reason, she tells on him."

"Is that how most get caught?"

"A lot get caught because of informants, but most catch themselves."

"How's that?"

"Their lifestyle catches them—their addiction to drugs, alcohol, sex, even gambling."

When the FBI agent let me out just south of Jacksonville, his words stayed with me. I knew that he had spoken the truth and that sooner or later the law of averages would catch up with me. Standing alongside the interstate, I renewed my vow to stop.

Night found me standing on the interstate east of Orlando. I knew it was useless to try to hitchhike in the dark—and dangerous should the highway patrol stop to investigate—so I walked until I reached an overpass and climbed to the top of the slanted concrete to hide for the night.

I couldn't sleep; the mosquitoes were relentless. I covered my arms, head, and neck with extra clothes but they still found a way inside, buzzing my ears until I couldn't stand it. At one point I slapped at my ears until they rang, then sat up, feeling like an idiot for hitting myself. The next morning, even though exhausted, I was more than ready to hit the road.

With only a few dollars left in my pocket, I made it to Tampa that afternoon and my first thought was to call Ora and ask for help, but my pride wouldn't let me. Instead, I called the Cuban sign painter I'd worked for when I had first moved to Tampa and asked for a job, hoping that he would hire me and let me sleep at his sign shop until I earned enough to get a place of my

own. But he told me that business was slow and that he had more than enough help.

I spent my first night back in Tampa sleeping in the tall grass in an adjacent lot across from a large shopping center east of town. Again the mosquitoes worked me over.

The next day, dirty and exhausted, I spent money I should've spent on food, telephoning and riding the bus all over Tampa in a desperate attempt to find a job. I didn't have any luck and spent another miserable night in the tall grass.

My third day found me dead on my feet from hunger and lack of sleep. I only had $1.50 in my pocket. I made a decision I thought I'd never make. I decided to seek asylum in the Salvation Army.

Setting out early that morning, I headed for downtown Tampa, stopping often to rest. Not thinking much about it, I took a shortcut through a Black neighborhood, one I had driven through often. When I walked past the playground, where about twenty young people had congregated, two teens, probably seventeen and eighteen, left a basketball game and followed close behind me. When they fell in step, one on each side as if escorting me, they both hit me at the same time with their fists on the left and right sides of my head. I staggered and fell to one knee but kept my balance. The two teens turned and fled.

I jogged from the neighborhood.

At a convenience store and service station, I looked at my reflection in the glass storefront. Blood trickled down the left side of my face onto my neck, and I had a crescent-shaped cut about half an inch long on my left cheek. I walked over to the gas pumps and rinsed the cut with a water hose, then continued my journey.

A couple hours later I reached the Salvation Army in downtown Tampa, the very same facility where, with my pockets full of money, driving a nice car, and feeling superior, I

had visited my father. I remembered sitting in the Cherokee, looking at him and listening to him talk and wondering how anyone could ever allow themselves to sink so low as to live off charity. And now that I knew the answer to that question, I didn't feel any wiser. Just more hopeless and tired.

I stayed at the Salvation Army almost six weeks, long enough to regain my physical strength, reclaim my arrogance, and forget the desperate vow I had made when stranded. One morning I left the Salvation Army and spent the day riding the bus, casing banks. The next day I robbed a bank in North Tampa, and since I didn't have a car I made my getaway on a city bus.

Again, as in Denver, the bank teller slipped me a dye-pack bomb. And again it exploded just as I stepped outside, but this time I was surrounded by shoppers in a busy shopping plaza and they blocked the entrance to an alley where I intended to change clothes. Trailing red smoke and tear gas, I ran straight at a knot of shoppers. Stunned, they stared and pointed but got out of the way. None followed me into the alley.

A block from the bank, I entered a dimly lit restaurant and went straight to the restroom. There, to the faint sound of sirens outside, I scrubbed red dye from my hands and adjusted my clothes.

As soon as I left the restaurant and sat down on a bus bench, a bus pulled up and stopped. I got on and found a seat in the back and, like the other passengers, curiously looked out the window as more police cars raced past.

The bank robbery in Denver may have been a fiasco and failure but the experience had taught me how to clean badly stained money. I went shopping.

Hunched over a toilet bowl that night in a motel on Clearwater Beach, I stirred a hunk of cash about the size of a football. When the water turned bloodred, I held the money to

the side of the toilet bowl with one hand while flushing it with the other. When clean water filled the basin, I stirred it again, repeating the process over and over until the water was only slightly pink. I then dumped all the money into a bathtub of equal parts warm water and bleach.

While the money soaked, I returned to the bedroom and strung four clotheslines of kite string diagonally across the room, from the curtain rod on the front window to a clothes rod in the closet. On each line I clipped clothespins.

After about two hours I removed each bill from the bathtub and examined it. If it was clean, I rinsed it with water from the sink, then hung it on the clothesline to dry. If it was still stained, I scrubbed it with a toothbrush and fingernail polish remover, then rinsed it again and hung it on the clothesline.

A couple hours later, all four clotheslines were filled with money, creating a canopy of green in the bedroom. Whenever the room's central air-conditioning kicked on, the bills flapped madly, like Tibetan prayer flags in a stiff breeze.

After taking a shower I fixed myself a glass of scotch and ice, then lay down to watch a movie on TV, feeling satisfaction for the first time in a long while. The next morning I was awakened by the sound of a key opening my door. Sitting straight up in bed, I turned to see the doorknob rotate.

"Oh shit!" I yelled, leaping from the bed, and in three quick steps reached the door just as it opened about half an inch, slamming into it with my shoulder and closing it.

"It's the maid!" said a voice from the other side. "I'm here to clean your room!"

"Look, I'm naked in here!" I yelled back. "Can you come back in thirty minutes?"

"Sure," she said, "I'll be back later."

I heard her cleaning cart squeak on down to the next room.

Naked, I stood on a chair and removed all the cash from the clotheslines, then ripped down the lines and stuffed everything into my travel bag. Rushing to the bathroom, I scrubbed the red stains from the toilet, bathtub, and sink as best I could. I then dressed, sat on the bed, and counted the cleaned money. I had $3,600.

After leaving the motel I caught a trolley to the other end of the island. There I rented an efficiency room for a week. During the next week, using one of my forged driver's licenses and paying a $250 deposit, I rented an older model Buick.

Now that I had money and a car, I flirted with the idea of contacting Ora, and one night drove to a bar that she and I used to frequent. There the bartender, a woman Ora and I had known since moving to Tampa, told me that she had seen Ora only two nights earlier. She said that she had come in with her Cuban American boyfriend, a retired professional baseball player. She also told me that Ora now lived in Ybor City, and she gave me her new phone number.

Later, in my room, I stared at the phone number and even picked up the phone a couple times, but every time, after experiencing a tight, little, petty feeling inside, I couldn't make myself call. *I'm jealous*, I thought, *but I don't have a right to be. I'm the one that abandoned her.* Then I thought of Big Jim in the Keys and realized that what I was feeling must've been similar to what he had felt when I had replaced him. It wasn't a good feeling.

A few weeks later I robbed another bank, in Clearwater, the small town adjacent to Clearwater Beach. And for the third time in a row the bank teller slipped me a dye-pack bomb with the money. The device destroyed over half the cash and unnerved me. That night, while again cleaning money, I vowed to never let another teller hand me a dye-pack bomb.

The money from the Clearwater robbery lasted only three weeks. Beginning to feel extremely paranoid, I knew that it was

time to leave the Tampa Bay area and Florida itself. One morning I packed and drove a couple hundred miles north, stopping in the small town of Ocala. There I drove around until I found a branch bank that looked promising.

After parking the Buick in a shopping strip, I crossed a footbridge over a canal to an office complex where the bank was located, but instead of going inside I sat on a concrete bench and looked through the bank's windows. I saw three tellers but, more importantly, I didn't see any security guards. Returning to the Buick, I left the area, drove to a restaurant parking lot, sat for a while, and thought about the bank robbery.

Thirty minutes later I drove back to the shopping strip and parked. Dressed in a coat and tie and carrying a plastic shopping bag, I walked across the footbridge to the office complex where the bank was located.

Right before I walked inside, I put on an overcoat, a baseball cap, and sunglasses, concealing what I wore underneath. I gave the teller a holdup note as usual, leaned close, and whispered, "If you put a dye-pack bomb in there, I'm gonna come back and shoot everybody. You hear me?" She shook her head, then put all the money on the counter.

I stuffed the money inside the overcoat's large inside pockets, turned, and left.

As soon as I was out of view of the bank's windows, I removed the long coat, hat, and sunglasses and rolled it all into a ball. Bending down, I put the disguise under a row of hedges, straightened my sports coat and tie, and walked off.

Midway across the footbridge I realized that I had forgotten to take the money out of the pockets of the overcoat. Every nerve ending in my body came alive; I felt as if I had just jumped off a ten-story building. There was no question that I'd have to go back and get the money and that I'd have to hurry.

Turning, I quickly retraced my steps. When I got back to the office building with the hedges out front, I bent down and searched under the first hedge but found nothing. *Did somebody see me and get the money?* I asked myself, on the verge of panic. I got down on my knees and reached further under the hedges—nothing.

Then, finally, I felt the overcoat and a surge of joy. Unrolling it, I removed the money and quickly stuffed all of it in the inside and outside pockets of my sport coat. I put the overcoat back under the hedge and quickly headed for the footbridge.

Later, while driving the interstate north, I replayed the bank robbery in my mind, amazed at how close I had come to throwing the money away. I was reminded of a recurring dream I often had as a child:

I'm always in a clearing surrounded by an old growth forest. I leave the clearing and follow a narrow path until I'm deep in the woods. Tired, I sit down and rest my back against a large tree. When I look down, I see that mixed in with the multicolored leaves around the base of the tree are thousands of coins—silver dollars, half-dollars, quarters, dimes, nickels, and even pennies—sparkling in the dappled sunlight. I remove my shirt and, picking coins like mushrooms, quickly fill it. I button the shirt and tie the sleeves to make a carrying pouch, then follow the path back to the edge of the clearing. But as soon as I step out of the shelter of the trees, the coins disappear.

I return to the tree time and again, but every time that I get to the clearing the money disappears. Finally, I try throwing the shirt full of coins from the forest into the clearing, but as soon as the shirt reaches the perimeter the coins disappear and the shirt floats to the ground.

Perplexed, I return to the large tree and sit down, pick up the double handfuls of coins, and let them run through my

fingers. I wonder why I'm allowed to find all this money yet am never allowed to keep any of it, therefore rendering the money useless.

When I reached Tallahassee that evening, I checked into a motel, took a shower, then ate at a nice restaurant. The next day I drove west until I reached Biloxi, Mississippi.

That evening I checked into a hotel on Highway 90, across from the beach. After taking a shower and changing clothes, I walked across the highway to a large nightclub.

It was there that I met Melinda.

Chapter 24

As soon as I entered, the lights went out and the nightclub was plunged into darkness. I stopped in my tracks to let my eyes adjust. A single spotlight then popped on, highlighting a beautiful Spanish girl in a skimpy gold lamé bikini. She twirled a baton of fire and danced across the stage to the song "Burning Down the House," by the popular group Talking Heads.

I made my way to a table near the front and sat down. When a cocktail waitress took my drink order, I asked her to extend an invitation to the Spanish girl on stage to join me for a drink.

Melinda stood about five feet, three inches, had long jet-black hair and large brown eyes that still shined with innocence, something unusual for someone in her profession. I wondered how many more years of dancing and entertaining "clients" until that sparkle was replaced by a hard stare.

Shy, Melinda didn't talk much, which was okay with me. I didn't feel much like talking myself. I couldn't honestly talk about my past and it was a lot of effort to lie about my present. I just sat, saying a few words occasionally to prevent any awkward silences, and enjoyed Melinda's flirtations and mysterious smile, which was enough to keep me buying her drink after watered-down drink at highly inflated prices, well aware that it was her job to encourage customers to spend as much money as possible.

When Melinda did speak, it was with a distinctly Southern accent, which surprised me. I discovered that Melinda had been born in Panama and along with her mother and older brother had immigrated to America when she was five, living in Mississippi since.

Melinda and I spent the entire evening together. Around 2:00 A.M., tired and clearly intoxicated, I told Melinda that I was

calling it a night, and she surprised me by offering to come to my motel room when she got off at 3:00. I didn't really believe her, thought that she was just being nice because I had spent so much money on her, but I told her my room number anyway and left.

An hour later I was awakened by a knock on the door. Melinda stood there in tight jeans and a fur jacket. She looked at me with a shy smile.

We passionately made love, then slept until noon.

When she left, Melinda pressed a slip of paper into my palm. "That's my phone number," she said. "Call if you want."

Later that evening I called Melinda and we went out to dinner. Afterward, we went back to her apartment and spent the night. The next day she boldly asked me if I wanted to move in with her, and I did. Melinda never went back to work at the nightclub.

Time passed pleasantly and quickly. Melinda and I spent lazy days at the beach and long afternoons on the sofa wrapped in each other's arms, making love, talking, and watching old movies on TV.

My money passed quickly too. After only a couple weeks I was down to my last $100. I told Melinda that I had to leave on business and would be back in a couple days. Surprisingly, she didn't ask any questions.

I drove to Baton Rouge and robbed a branch bank in a subdivision north of town. I didn't count the money until I was safely back across the Mississippi state line. I had over $4,000. Satisfied, I drove until I reached Melinda's apartment, and there we resumed our lazy, sensuous life together.

What Melinda and I shared wasn't love, not in the traditional sense. It certainly wasn't what Ora and I had shared the first few years, but we enjoyed being together and we enjoyed the sex. And we each gave what we had. I gave Melinda an opportunity

to quit a life she hated and, I sensed, was ashamed of, and she gave me companionship, a legitimate place to hide, and an additional reason to continue my illegal lifestyle.

A few weeks later I robbed another bank in Baton Rouge, and then a month after that, one in Lafayette. In that robbery I got almost $7,000.

I knew that it was past time to get rid of the Buick I'd rented months earlier in Tampa and so, for a couple thousand dollars, bought a Datsun pickup truck with a camper shell and registered it in Melinda's name. She followed me in the Datsun while I drove the Buick to New Orleans and left it at the airport.

Melinda never once asked any questions regarding the Buick, my trips out of town, or where I seemed to come up with all the cash I spent so freely. Appreciating her discretion and seeing that as proof that I could trust her, I told her about my past and the bank robberies I had committed, even though afterward I worried when I remembered the FBI in the red Camaro telling me that most get caught because they tell someone.

Six weeks later I drove to Mobile, Alabama, robbed a bank there, and returned to Mississippi with over $5,000. Now, with every bank robbery I grew more and more paranoid, and rightly so. Since I had met Melinda, I had robbed five banks in less than five months. I decided that I'd rob one more bank, then use the money to start a small sign business, like I had in Tampa.

For my last bank robbery I picked the small university town of Hattiesburg, one hundred miles north. When I told Melinda my plans, she surprised me by asking to go with me.

"I can drive for you," said Melinda.

"I can drive myself. Besides, it's too dangerous."

"Please! Just let me go, okay? I can help out. It'll be exciting!"

"Melinda, this ain't no game. This is serious business. You can get shot or end up in prison for the rest of your life. You prepared for that?"

"I don't care! I wanna go!"

"I'd feel terrible if something bad happened to you," I told her.

"Not if it's my decision," said Melinda. "If it's my decision, then I'll be the one responsible."

"Not if I'm the one who knows better. That would make me responsible," I replied.

"Let me go. I'll just sit in the truck and wait for you. You won't even know I'm there."

"Oh, I'll know! Believe me, I'll know!"

We didn't speak anymore that night, and the next morning I drove to Hattiesburg to find the right bank. On the drive back, I stopped at a rest area and walked a well-worn path into the nearby woods, looking for a quiet spot to think. When I came to a narrow creek about a quarter of a mile from the rest area, I stopped.

The first thing I noticed was a small mountain of trash bags. There was even an old refrigerator ten yards off the path. Then the smell of sulfur hit me. I walked over. The water was a brown froth bubbling in swirling eddies, tumbling over rocks covered in green slime. It wasn't scenic, but at least it was quiet, so I sat down on a large rock and studied the contaminated creek and surrounding mudbank, convinced that nothing could live in such filth and pollution.

I was wrong. The longer that I sat there, the more movement I noticed—an army of red ants moving in precise orderly lines methodically dissected, section by tiny section, a grasshopper, while overhead a large spider weaved an intricate web between two large leaves. On the opposite bank, grotesque yet beautifully colored bottle flies cleaned the last of the meat

from a dead sparrow, leaving only a beak and an empty sack of feathers and bones.

Survival, I thought. *It's all about survival.*

When I got back, Melinda continued to give me the silent treatment. She didn't even say hello when I walked in the door.

The next morning I awakened early, quietly slipped out of bed, walked into the kitchen, and made a cup of coffee. Carrying it to the patio in the back of the apartment, I sat and watched the sun slowly gather itself, then pop up like a giant orange balloon. Dread filled me, overpowering the beauty of the moment and causing me to ask if this would be the last sunrise I saw.

Resigned, I walked back inside to get my gear and passed Melinda sitting at the table, drinking a cup of coffee. She looked at me with puffy eyes but didn't say anything.

In the bedroom, I put jacket, shirt, hat, and sunglasses in my travel bag, then carried it into the kitchen. I set it on the counter and made myself another cup of coffee. Sitting at the table opposite Melinda, I said, "Look, if you're goin' with me, you need to get dressed."

"What? Really!" grinned Melinda. She got up, ran around the table, hugged my neck, and kissed me.

"But you've got to promise you'll do exactly as I say, no questions asked."

"Yes sir! I promise!" she said. "I'll do exactly what you say and it'll be okay. You just wait and see." She ran to the bedroom to dress.

"I hope so," I said. "I certainly hope so."

When we got to Hattiesburg a couple hours later, I parked at a pizza restaurant a block from the bank.

"This is where I'll park the truck," I told Melinda. "All you gotta do is wait for me here. After the robbery I'll make my way

back here, get in the truck, and then we'll just calmly drive off. There's no need to drive fast or get in a hurry. Just drive normally, go with the flow of traffic. Got it?"

"I've got it," she said.

"Good. Now let me show you our backup plan."

"Backup plan?"

"Yeah, in case something goes wrong." I drove five blocks south to a movie theater parking lot. "If anything goes wrong at the pizza restaurant, drive here and wait for me. The main thing is we can't let anyone connect this vehicle to the bank robbery. If that happens we got a real problem."

"Why?" asked Melinda.

"Well, then the cops will have a description of the getaway vehicle, that's why, and all they gotta do is throw up a roadblock and wait. Understand?"

Melinda nodded her head yes, but I now saw doubt and fear in her eyes instead of the excitement and confidence she had shown back at the apartment. I knew quite well that it was one thing to speak bravely about doing something dangerous from a safe distance, and another to maintain that same attitude when the actual event was about to take place.

"Are you sure you want to wait in the truck?" I asked. "I can drop you off somewhere and pick you up after, if you want?"

"No, no. I'm okay, really."

"Okay then, let's do this," I said with false bravado myself, not wanting to undermine the courage we both hoped to find.

I drove back to the pizza restaurant, parked, reached under the seat, and pulled out a white plastic grocery bag. I turned and looked at Melinda.

"Remember what I told you. See you in about ten minutes." I left.

After crossing busy Hardy Street I entered a laundromat. Finding it empty, I walked into the restroom and locked the

door. Reaching in the plastic bag I took out a shirt, jacket, cap, and sunglasses. First, I put the shirt on over the top of the one I wore and buttoned it to the top. I put on the light jacket and zipped it halfway, then the sunglasses and baseball cap. I folded the plastic bag, put it in my back pocket, then the holdup note in my shirt pocket. I left the laundromat.

Directly across the street from the bank, I sat on a bus bench and watched the entrance, gathering courage. I said a prayer, something I'd done before. *God, just let me get through this one and I promise I'll quit. Just this one more.* But the prayer made me feel like a hypocrite.

"Fuck God!" I said. "I got this!"

I crossed the street and entered the bank and for some reason did something I'd never done before: I pulled my baseball cap low so that my ears stuck out and shuffled slowly into the bank as if mentally impaired. I walked to the teller closest to the door, but a teller (I would later find out that she was the head teller) three stations away said, "Sir!" I turned. "Sir, I'll take you here."

Easing to the counter, I handed her the note. She read it, then asked, "What do you want?"

"I want the money," I leaned forward and said just above a whisper. "Put it all on the counter and don't give me no dye packs—or else."

She opened the top drawer and nervously stacked the cash onto the counter. Reaching into my back pocket, I pulled out the plastic bag and shook it open. I swept the money into it and turned to leave but changed my mind. "Give me the money in that other drawer too," I said, having heard that some tellers had two drawers.

To my surprise, she reached down and opened a second drawer and stacked even more cash on the counter, so much that I filled the plastic grocery bag to overflowing. I had to lace

the handles to keep the money from falling out, leaving me with just one plastic handle to support the bag's weight. I turned and, now walking normally, hurried out the door.

About fifty yards from the bank, the handle on the plastic bag, stretched to its limit, broke, and the bag of money hit the pavement, spilling the top layer of cash. When I bent down to pick up the money, I looked over my shoulder and saw two men and three women step out of the bank. One of the men pointed at me. They started in my direction.

Hugging the grocery bag full of money like a baby, with my chin resting on top, I ran toward the pizza restaurant, the two men following but giving me space. When I reached the back of the restaurant and was out of sight, I set the bag of money on the pavement, then ripped off the jacket, top shirt, hat, and sunglasses, leaving them where they fell. Picking up the bag of money, I hurried around to the area where Melinda was parked.

When she saw me she panicked, put the truck in reverse, and stomped down on the accelerator. I tried to get out of the way but the bumper hit me in the hip and knocked me off my feet. The bag of money flew straight up, hit the pavement, and exploded. Money covered the parking lot, swirled in the wind like leaves. I lay on the pavement, surrounded by money, and watched the Datsun drive away.

Just then, the two men from the bank turned the corner and saw me lying there. One of them pointed and yelled, "There he is!"

Patrons in the pizza restaurant, having seen it all out the large windows, rushed outside. Most ignored me and busied themselves picking up money, but several joined the two men from the bank. They encircled me, intent on making a citizen's arrest.

Realizing their intention and having vowed not to go down without a fight even though I didn't have a gun, I struggled to

one knee, quickly pulled my shirt over my head, concealing my hands, and pointed my index fingers as if they were the barrel of a gun. I lunged at the nearest. "Back up, motherfuckers!" I yelled. "Back up or I'll shoot!"

Just at that moment I heard a vehicle squeal into the parking lot and turned to see Melinda in the Datsun, heading straight for me. The would-be vigilantes ran to get out of the way. The truck skidded to a stop in front of me. I opened the passenger door and crawled inside. Melinda gunned it, shifted into second, and jumped the curb, the rear tires catching the concrete embankment. The truck spun around in the middle of the four-lane street, stopping traffic in both directions. Melinda straightened it out and we headed for the highway south of town.

"Which way?" asked Melinda, eyes big as walnuts.

"Just stay on this highway here," I told her. "It'll take us to Mobile. I told you to wait at the movie theater if anything happened. Now they've got a description of the truck, probably got the tag number too."

"I left like you said but ran into a dead end. When I turned around and came back and saw you layin' there with all those people around you, I had to come get you."

"Yeah, you hit me with the truck when you backed out and I lost all the money. Shit! I wish we coulda kept some of it."

"What are we going to do now?" asked Melinda.

"Hopefully, we can make it back to the apartment. We'll try again tomorrow or the next day if my hip ain't too bad. Right now it hurts like hell."

"That wasn't anything like what I thought it would be," said Melinda.

"Never is," I said. "I've had some close calls, but that was the closest. We're lucky we got away."

Hearing a helicopter overhead, I looked out the window. At the same time, seemingly out of nowhere, two highway patrol cars pulled in behind us.

Melinda looked at me. "What do I do?" she asked.

"Nothing to do," I said. "Just act natural. Maybe they'll go around us."

When we reached the crest of a steep hill, I saw four police cars and an RV positioned under a caution light, creating a roadblock. We looked at each other. I shook my head but didn't say a word.

One of the highway patrol cars closed the gap, riding our bumper, while the other raced to our left to box us in. The driver motioned for us to pull over. Melinda pulled over and stopped a few feet from the roadblock.

Policemen, pointing their shotguns and pistols at us, rushed the truck. The doors were jerked open. I was forced facedown in the gravel on the shoulder of the highway. I didn't see what happened to Melinda. I can only assume they treated her the same. My arms were stretched behind me. A deputy stepped on the left side of my face, holding me there, while another handcuffed me.

Lamely, I struggled to look up at the deputy and said, "What's wrong, Officer? Were we speeding?"

"Shut up, asshole! You know exactly what you did!"

Two city police officers lifted me by my outstretched arms and escorted me to the back of a patrol car. As we drove away, I twisted in my seat to look out the back window. I saw a local TV newsman talking into a camera. *Where the hell did he come from?* I asked myself.

In Hattiesburg I was booked into the Forrest County jail. After being fingerprinted, photographed, and fitted with a jail jumpsuit. I was locked in an isolated holding cell near the front

desk. I heard later from a trustee that Melinda had been locked in the women's section. I tried to send her a message but wasn't successful.

Except for the heavy steel door, the cell was all reinforced concrete blocks with no windows and bare, except for a toilet. I sat in a corner, stretched out my leg, and massaged my hip, feeling like a dog licking its wounds after a fierce fight. *What went wrong?* I asked myself, a question I'd ponder for decades.

A short while later when the key turned in the heavy steel door, I struggled to my feet. Defiantly, I waited. A jailer held the door open while a trustee threw in one coarse sheet and a thin plastic mattress.

Chapter 25

After forty days in the isolation cell I was escorted to what I later learned was the district attorney's office. There I found Melinda, along with the court-appointed lawyer we shared, waiting for me. The attorney told me that he had arranged for us to have about twenty minutes alone.

When he left, Melinda told me that our attorney had made a deal with the D.A. She said that if I pled guilty to bank robbery and accepted the maximum sentence of fifteen years, day-for day without benefit of parole, then she would be released on five years' probation.

The next day I went to court and pled guilty and was sentenced to fifteen years. Melinda was released. A few days later I was sent to prison.

Parchman reminded me of Angola. It too was a huge, plantation-style prison complex made up of smaller prison camps spread over thousands of acres of farmland. And like Angola, it had a storied history of brutality and abuse, often employing guards who had grown up on prison land and had inherited their jobs from their fathers.

Parchman was isolated, with endless acres of treeless cotton fields giving their K-9 unit (expertly trained trackers with dogs) an unobstructed view for miles. Very few prisoners had ever successfully escaped from Parchman and I was determined to be one of the few.

Wanting to avoid working in the cotton fields, I quickly wrangled a job in the receiving and discharge area as a clerk. This allowed me to live in Camp 15-A, one of the best living areas at Parchman and closest to the main highway, less than a mile away.

Camp 15-A was small, with only fifty prisoners, yet it had its own kitchen, dining area, and a small recreation yard. The entire compound wasn't much larger than a football field but it was secure, surrounded by a twelve-foot fence topped with razor wire and two fifteen-foot guard towers positioned to protect the front and back gates.

As soon as I settled in I started looking for a way out. It didn't take me long to realize that I had only two options: I could either climb over the fence and get cut up by the razor wire and possibly shot by the tower guards, or I could try to get my hands on some wire cutters and cut through the fences and still possibly get shot by the tower guards. I didn't like either option so I kept looking, hoping to find a safer way out.

Meanwhile I kept in shape, lifting weights and jogging daily, and soon became friends with another clerk in receiving that also worked out. His name was Ned and he'd been at Parchman several years, serving a life sentence for a brutal murder in Tupelo. As our trust grew, Ned revealed that he too had been planning to escape and we bounced ideas off each other, but it always came back to either climbing the fence or cutting through it.

However, Ned brought an invaluable asset to the table. He had a girlfriend that lived in Memphis, only ninety miles away, and she had agreed to drive down and pick him up should he ever get to the other side of the fence.

Every day, after we worked out, Ned and I stood on the small back porch near the kitchen (from there we could see the traffic on the highway) and brainstormed but made little progress. Then one evening we watched a guard walk to the back gate, look up, and nod at the tower guard. The tower guard then pulled his shotgun inside the tower window. The guard pulled out a key, opened the lock on the gate, and stepped through. He

then reached back and snapped the lock shut. I recognized the significance of what I'd seen and started laughing.

"What the hell's so funny?" asked Ned, looking at me as if I had lost my senses.

"You ain't going to believe it! It's that simple!"

"What? What are you talking about?"

"That guard. Did you see what that guard just did?" I asked.

"No, not really. What?"

"Well, he opened the gate and just walked out, pretty as you please. That's exactly what we're gonna do."

"Yeah, but we ain't guards," said Ned.

"No, we ain't, but we can pretend to be guards," I said. "All we gotta do is make some uniforms and a key for the back gate."

"You've lost your mind. How we gonna do all that?"

"Don't worry, we'll figure it out. Then we'll just walk outta here."

"Yeah, and get our asses shot off in the process!"

"I don't think so," I smiled. "This'll work, and I'll tell you why."

It took me the rest of the evening to convince Ned that we could walk out the back gate without getting shot. The next afternoon we stood on the small back porch making plans.

"We can get a couple pairs of dark-blue pants outta the clothing room in receiving," said Ned, warming to the idea.

"Yeah, that'll work. Then all we gotta do is cut off four or five inches from the pant legs and use that material to make the dark-blue pocket flaps and epaulets on the shoulders of the shirts."

"The guard shirts are light blue," said Ned.

"Yeah, I know. We'll use faded light-blue denim shirts. Once I sew the pocket flaps and epaulets on 'em, nobody will know the difference—not from a distance, anyway."

"The dark-blue baseball caps will be easy to get," said Ned.

"Yeah, I already got one. I'll paint MDOC [Mississippi Department of Corrections] in white lettering on the front."

"We'll make the badges out of aluminum foil," said Ned. "I can also make some ID cards to hang on the front of the shirts."

"The only thing left is the hardest part."

"What's that?"

"The key. We gotta get somebody to make us a key."

"How 'bout Eddy? He used to be a locksmith on the streets," said Ned.

"Think he'll do it?" I asked.

"Sure, we pay him enough. But first we gotta get an impression of the master key, and I think I know how to do that."

"How?"

"From our boss in receiving."

"The Colonel?"

"Yeah, he's got a master key on that big key ring on his belt. I've watched him open the back gate lots of times when he leaves in the evening."

"Okay, you work on that and I'll talk to Eddy."

The next afternoon Ned handed me a piece of Styrofoam, about two inches square, from a small coffee cup. On the Styrofoam were stamped two clean key impressions.

"Have any trouble?"

"Nah, it was easy. I waited until the Colonel was settled at his desk with a cup of coffee, then told him that I needed to get a pen and some paper clips outta the supply cabinet. I figured he'd be too lazy to get up and I was right. He complained about 'you convicts' always wanting somethin', then, instead of getting up himself, he reached on his belt, pulled off his big ring of keys, and handed 'em to me. When I had my back to him, I made an impression of the master key on the Styrofoam, opened the

cabinet, got the pen and paper clips, then gave him his keys back."

It took the locksmith—who had been in Parchman over ten years for killing a wife he had caught cheating—two weeks to make a master key from the impressions I gave him. When he gave me the key, he assured me that it would work. I paid him the $100 he had asked for even though I wouldn't know for sure if it would work until I inserted it in the lock the morning of our escape.

While Eddy had been making the key, Ned and I stole two pairs of dark-blue pants from the clothing room in receiving. We then found two light-blue chambray shirts, and I went to work on the uniforms and baseball caps while Ned fashioned the badges and made the ID cards to attach to the shirt-pocket flaps. In less than three weeks we had everything ready and hid the uniforms in a five-gallon paint bucket that I kept under my bunk.

Ned telephoned his girlfriend to arrange the day and time for her to pick us up. The date, Sunday, April 10, was set for our escape. We planned to walk out the gate at around 5:20 A.M. while most were eating breakfast. Ned's girlfriend had agreed to pick us up between 5:30 and 5:50 A.M. at a predetermined point on the main highway, about a mile from Camp 15-A and the front gate.

The Friday afternoon before our escape, word came through the prison grapevine that there was to be a general shakedown of the entire prison. The news threw us into a momentary panic.

"Damn!" said Ned. "This couldn't have happened at a worse time. Do you think they know?"

"I don't think so; otherwise, they would've just shook *us* down. I think it's just bad timing, that's all. But man, I don't need to get caught with all that illegal shit under my bed."

"What do you think they'd do if they found all that stuff?" asked Ned.

"Well, to start with they'd beat the hell out of us both—probably put us in the hospital. Then if we survived that they'd throw us in the hole for years, plus give us more time for attempted escape," I said.

"Maybe we oughta dump all that shit before they get here," said Ned.

"I hate to do that. There's gotta be somewhere we can stash that bucket," I said.

"You're kidding? This is the K-9 unit. They search everywhere."

"Everywhere except the classification and captain's office," I said.

"You know, you're right! That's it! The captain's office! He's gone today, won't be back till Monday. All he's got on his door is one of them small padlocks. Shit, I can pick that. I just need to borrow a set of homemade lock picks from Eddy."

We picked the lock on the captain's office door, hid the bucket of contraband in the ceiling tiles, then locked the door back. On the way to our dorm, we heard K-9 yell, "Shakedown! Everyone to your assigned bed! Let's move!"

In all the Southern prisons that I've been in, the shakedown squad may be called by many different names: the goon squad, the tactical unit, the K-9 unit, etc. But they all dress the same—in black fatigues and combat boots—and carry the same equipment—long batons and pepper spray, and their mission is the same: to terrorize prisoners into submission through verbal and physical abuse.

The K-9 unit marched into Camp 15-A in a column of twos, yelling and screaming and shoving and punching and even slapping those too slow to get out of their way. They then forced

all of us to stand and strip naked. After we were searched we were made to lie facedown on the concrete floor and told to cross our legs at the ankles and lock our hands behind our heads.

We remained in this excruciating and humiliating position for over an hour while the K-9 unit rifled through our footlockers, throwing everything on the floor, mixing one man's property with another's, and stepping on photos of loved ones.

When they finished they left the way they had entered, marching in twos. Slowly we all got up off the floor and dressed. Like the rest, I felt as if I had been violated, but unlike them I also felt satisfaction knowing that in two days I'd exact my own form of retribution.

An hour later, we again burglarized the captain's office and retrieved the five-gallon bucket of contraband.

Sunday morning around 5:20 A.M., while the rest ate breakfast, Ned and I stood on the small back porch near the walkway that led to the back gate. Quickly we dressed in our uniforms and stepped onto the walkway. The guard in the tower noticed us and leaned forward, the barrel of his shotgun sticking out of the window. In my hand I carried the master key Eddy had made, and Ned carried a clipboard for a prop.

When we reached the gate we stopped. I looked up at the guard in the tower and nodded my head hello, the way I'd seen the real guard do. When the tower guard pulled his shotgun back inside the window, I grabbed the large, round American lock firmly with my left hand and inserted the key with my right.

In a millisecond the thought flashed through my mind, *What if it doesn't open?* But I pushed that thought away and twisted the key. The lock fell open easily. After Ned and I walked through, I snapped the lock shut.

Walking the fifty yards to the fence that surrounded the prison's farm offices, I expected to be shot at any moment. I

actually felt a tingling sensation in the center of my exposed back, as if a target had been painted on my shirt to help the aim of the tower guard. But nothing happened, and when we got to the farm offices I grabbed the heavy chain and lock and shook them, like I'd seen other guards do, while glancing over my shoulder at the tower guard, who seemed to have settled down to finish his shift.

When we reached the other side of the farm offices and were outside of the tower's view, we started jogging across an open cotton field toward the highway, almost a mile away. At the highway we crossed a deep, wide drainage ditch, then hid there to wait.

We didn't have to wait long. Within just a few minutes, Ned's girlfriend pulled up and stopped. We got in the car and headed east toward the state line.

Seven months and one week after the bungled bank robbery in Hattiesburg, I was free once again. When asked where I wanted to go, I directed Ned and his girlfriend to the nearest ocean and a place where I felt familiar and safe: Isle of Palms, South Carolina. The last time that I'd been there I had been an eleven-year-old spending the night with my family in a partially built house on the beach.

We got to Isle of Palms around 4:00 P.M., parked, and walked to the beach. I removed my shoes and shirts, rolled my jeans to my knees, ran to the surf, and dove into the ocean. The water was so cold I gasped.

We drove back to Charleston and spent our first night in a motel there.

Chapter 26

Escaping from prison and living life on the run is not as exciting and glamorous as some would think, especially without outside help. Even with help, getting away and staying away takes an extraordinary amount of stubbornness, a good measure of self-control, and lots of luck. Without help, most get caught within the first twenty-four hours, and it's a miracle to last thirty days.

Escaping is both an exhilarating and a terrifying experience. Initially you're thrilled that you got away, but then you find yourself paranoid and alone, often lost, without food, water, proper clothing, shelter, money, or identification. You have nowhere to turn for help and you're afraid to show your face in public. Your photo has been shown on TV and displayed in newspapers, even passed around in places frequented by the destitute and the desperate—homeless shelters, cheap motels and bars and restaurants, even grocery stores and laundromats.

Fortunately, unlike my previous escapes, this time I had help, and I was thankful to have a ride waiting, money for necessities, and someone willing to stay with me and shield me until I could care for myself. But getting away from a facility is only part of a successful escape. The most important part is what you do after the escape. A successful escape, like most endeavors, requires both short- and long-range planning.

My short-range plan was simple: I would quickly put two or three states between me and Mississippi, then find someplace to hide while I made driver's licenses good enough to pass a cursory examination. Unfortunately, I didn't have a long-range plan.

After Charleston, we drove to Charlotte, North Carolina. There Ned's girlfriend rented two rooms for a week, and that

night, alone in mine, I made a list of some of the things I needed to forge driver's licenses: a portable drafting board, various plastic triangles, Rapidograph (inking) pens, different colored inks, a Leroy lettering kit with templates, dry transfer lettering, an illustration board, a printer's ruler, rubber cement, tape, acetate, paper, lamination supplies, a tripod, a light, and two cameras, an SX-70 and a 35 mm. We spent all of the next day on a scavenger hunt for the materials and equipment.

I used the dresser in the motel room for a work space and Ned's girlfriend's Arkansas license as a template. After carefully measuring it, then doubling the measurements in pencil on the illustration board, I inked in the lines dark brown and let them dry, then used the dry transfer lettering for the smaller headings—name, address, height, weight, hair color, etc.—and the Leroy lettering kit to create the larger. I carefully duplicated the state seal.

Next, I put the enlarged license aside and concentrated on the photos. After taping a light-blue poster board to the wall for a backdrop, I had Ned photograph me with the 35 mm camera in three disguises, then I photographed him and his girlfriend in various disguises. We took these photos to be developed.

When the photos came back, I trimmed them to fit the space I'd drawn on the license, then attached the photo with rubber cement. After covering the license with a transparent sheet of acetate, I signed the name of the director of public safety on the acetate so that when photographed it would appear as a watermark.

Using the lettering kit, I inscribed a fictitious name, address, and physical description in the appropriate places on the overlay, then, near the bottom, signed a fictitious name with an ink pen. I taped the large reproduction of the license to the wall, attached the SX-70 camera to the tripod, and after marking with masking

tape the spot where the tripod's forward legs touched the floor, I photographed the license.

When the SX-70 film developed, I measured the image of the license and discovered that it was a quarter inch too small, so I moved the tripod forward about two inches and took another photo. When I measured again, the license size was perfect. I set the photo aside to let the inside dry so that I could separate the front and back later.

I then worked on the back of the license, which was a lot less complicated. When I finished the back, I took several photos, then also put those aside to dry.

When all the photos were dry, I carefully separated the image side from the black backing, giving me extremely thin photos of the fronts and backs of a driver's license. I glued the fronts to the backs with a thin spread of rubber cement, trimmed them to size, rounded the corners with sandpaper, then laminated them.

It took five days, working ten to twelve hours, to complete three sets of licenses for myself, Ned, and his girlfriend. And it took most of the money that Ned's girlfriend had brought with her, so before we could part ways we needed traveling money.

Picking up the Charlotte telephone book, I searched the yellow pages, looking for a local company with a nationally recognized name. Finally, I settled on a pest control company because the logo was easy to duplicate and the local business was closed on Saturday and Sunday.

Using watered-down ink to make a light gray, I drew parallel lines a sixteenth of an inch apart on good quality paper, creating what would pass for the safety paper used to print checks. Then, using dry transfer lettering, I put the local company's name and address at the top, then the words "Pay to the Order of" below. I drew in the lines with the black ink, then the company's logo on the top. On the bottom, I put in fake account numbers.

It took me two days to complete twenty-five checks.

While I worked on the checks, Ned and his girlfriend went to a flea market where for $35 they bought a check protector—a machine that stamps the check's amount and the words "Bonded and Insured" in red and blue ink. After stamping the checks with the machine, I signed them with a fancy but illegible signature.

Between Friday night and Sunday we drove from supermarket to supermarket, cashing all twenty-five checks. After we split the money, my take was almost $2,000.

Early Monday morning, using a fake license for proof of identification and posting a $250 cash deposit, I rented an older model Ford station wagon. Ned and his girlfriend headed north, and I drove south. I never heard from or saw them again.

On Clearwater Beach I rented a room in a clean but inexpensive motel and during the next few days eased into the role of a tourist on a budget vacation. I shopped in the local secondhand stores for clothes and occasionally spent an evening in one of the bars along the beach. Mostly I ate fast food, but every few days I'd splurge on a meal in a good restaurant.

I watched a lot of TV and spent most days at the beach, where I pondered my situation, trying to decide what to do next. Already, in just a few weeks, I was down to a few hundred dollars. I knew that I could probably make more checks or even rob a bank, but I had lost my nerve and was afraid to risk being locked up again after such a short period of freedom.

Instead, I searched the classified section of the newspaper looking for a job. When I came across an ad for a graphic artist/painter willing to travel throughout the South, I called the phone number listed. It was in Bradenton, not far away, and that afternoon I drove over for a personal interview.

The painting contractor, a large friendly man in his late forties, told me that his company had a contract with a major chain to repaint the inside of their drugstores. He said that the walls inside each store would be painted in bands of color, resembling a rainbow, and that he needed someone that could not only paint a straight line quickly but could read a blueprint and draft those lines. He also told me the job involved a great deal of travel and that his company paid travel expenses. Before he agreed to hire me, he asked that I meet him the next day in St. Petersburg where he would show me exactly what his company was doing and also find out if I could satisfactorily do the work.

I was hired.

It was the perfect job for a man on the run. We seldom stayed in any one town for more than two or three days, and during the next six weeks we worked our way up the coast of Florida to Jacksonville, where we stayed three days, painting two stores. Then, to my surprise, instead of continuing up the East Coast we turned west, spending two days in Tallahassee.

Continuing west, we painted a store in Pensacola, then arrived in Mobile, Alabama, the evening of June 20, 1988. It had been only seventy-one days since I had escaped from Parchman and I was extremely paranoid, being only twenty miles from the Mississippi state line.

But that evening after talking to the foreman I was relieved to find out that we would paint all the stores in Alabama before moving on to Mississippi, and that would give me a few weeks to decide whether to chance crossing into Mississippi or not.

That evening, while filling out the registration card at a motel in Mobile, I looked up to catch the clerk staring at me. Sensing danger, I felt a strong urge to turn, walk out the door, get in my old car, and head for the Florida state line. But I had worked all day and I was tired. I told myself that I was simply

256

paranoid. I completed the registration card, paid, got my key, and left to find my room.

The next morning I left the room at 5:20 A.M. to meet the paint crew at a coffee shop two blocks away. After opening the car door I slid behind the wheel, put the key in the ignition, and then, out of habit, adjusted the rearview mirror. I couldn't believe what I saw—at least six cars raced forward, blocking my exit. Out of them poured FBI, sheriff's deputies, and city police, all pointing guns at me.

Someone yelled, "Put both hands out the window! Now!"

Just as I got both hands out the window, someone else yelled, "Put your hands on the steering wheel! Do it! Now!"

When I reached my hands back inside the car to comply with the last command, an entirely different voice shouted, "Look out! He's going for a gun!"

I heard several weapons chambered, froze, hands half in and half out of the window, then yelled, "I ain't got a gun! I'm unarmed! Look, I can either put both hands out the window or on the steering wheel, but I can't do ... ."

The door jerked open and an officer, obviously anxious to later be recognized as the first to lay hands on me, dragged me from the car by my arm and pinned me to the pavement. Having captured me, the law officers were jubilant during the drive to the jail. Like a parade for them, it was like a funeral procession for me.

In the Mobile jail I was fingerprinted, photographed, then put in a solitary cell. That afternoon a detective came by and said, "I got a message for you from the warden at Parchman prison."

"Yeah, what is it?" I asked.

"The warden said to tell you that when he gets you back to Parchman, he's gonna put a loggin' chain on you and put your ass where you never see sunshine again."

I didn't respond, but the words sent a chill up my spine.

"Now, you can sign extradition papers to go back to Mississippi, or not; it's your choice."

"I don't think so," I said. "I ain't goin' back to Mississippi!"

"That's up to you," said the detective.

I sat down on the bunk. *Some choice*, I thought.

PART III

MEDITATION

"Recurrent moments of crisis or decision are growth points or points of self-initiation, which mark the possibility of movement from one level of Being to the next. It is no easy matter to transform Being; some brave souls take the direct path of surrender and illumination, while others make a gradual ascent, so that when they spiral round, they can see if anything has changed in them since a certain time ago or since a particular problem was last encountered."

—Bruce Thomas, *The Body of Time: And the Energies of Being*

Chapter 27

Because I had refused to sign extradition, Mississippi had 120 days in which to file for a warrant, allowing them to come get me. If they failed to do so within that time frame Alabama could release me. And even though I knew that almost never happened, I counted the days, hoping for a mistake or irregularity that would result in my being released.

On day 119, I was taken to court and charged with the Mobile bank robbery that I had committed months before the botched Hattiesburg robbery. A trial date was set for nine months later. I was transferred from the city jail to the newly opened Mobile County jail complex, located just off Interstate 10, east of the city.

The jail was divided into separate living areas called pods. Each pod had twelve two-man cells, with six cells upstairs and six down, and a large dayroom with a shower area. A glass enclosed cubicle was positioned so that a lone deputy could easily monitor two separate pods.

My cellmate was sixty-four years old. His name was George and he had never been in jail before. He had thin gray hair, a large potbelly, and stood five-ten. Born and raised in Mobile, he had worked for the railroad for thirty-five years. And now, when most his age were getting ready to retire, he found himself in jail facing a life sentence, accused of murdering a man that had raped his daughter.

Understandably, George was angry and depressed. He seldom spoke and lay in bed day and night, staring at the wall. Then one day he saw me working out and expressed an interest.

"Think I could get rid of this belly?" he asked, patting his large stomach.

"Sure," I told him. "If you exercise regularly, I guarantee you'll get rid of it. Just start slow, stay with it, and watch what you eat. If you want, you can work out with me."

George couldn't do much to begin with, but he stayed with it and gradually was able to do more. He even lost a few pounds and his attitude improved. He began to talk more and even joke on occasion.

George pushed himself harder and harder, and I repeatedly cautioned him to take it slow and easy but he ignored me. A man driven, George had found an activity that not only made him feel better, but helped him deal with his depression. We usually worked out together in the cell, but when we went outside to the recreation yard (a large concrete area the size of a full basketball court), we worked out separately; he would walk the perimeter and do push-ups, while I worked out on an old Universal machine.

One day, about ten minutes into my workout, I looked over to check on George and was surprised to see him jogging. *That's odd*, I thought. *He's never done that before. Must be feelin' pretty good.* When George passed and saw me watching, he smiled and waved. I waved back, then went back to the weight machine.

When I sat up again, I saw that a crowd of prisoners had gathered on the basketball court and, not seeing George, rushed over. Forcing my way through the crowd, I saw George lying facedown in a pool of his own urine and watched his face quickly change from vivid crimson to purple to sheet-white. He stopped breathing.

After carefully turning George onto his back, I saw that his face was covered in blood from a three-inch gash on his forehead. Removing my shirt, I placed it under George's head, tilted his head back, got down on both knees, and pumped his chest with cupped hands like I'd seen them do on TV. Pinching his nose, I blew into his mouth. He didn't respond. I tried again,

this time pushing harder on his chest and again blowing into his mouth.

Over and over I massaged his chest and blew air into his lungs, and just when I was about to give up, George miraculously kicked out with his right leg. His chest heaved and he gasped. He started breathing but didn't open his eyes.

Two guards rushed over. One ordered all of the prisoners from the recreation yard except for me. He asked, "Is he breathing?"

"He is now," I said. "He just started."

"Stay with him," he told me. "We called 911. They'll be here shortly."

Just before the paramedics arrived, George opened his eyes, blinked, and looked around. He tried to form words but couldn't.

"Hang in there," I said. "An ambulance is on the way."

After the paramedics arrived and put George in an ambulance, I was told to return to my pod. When I walked into the dayroom everyone stared, and I wondered why. A young man with tears in his eyes came up to me.

"Is that old man dead?" he asked.

"No," I told him. "They've taken him to the hospital, but I believe he's gonna make it."

Another prisoner walked up and handed me George's glasses. One of the lenses was cracked.

"Found 'em where he fell," he said.

Inside my cell I stood at the stainless steel mirror over the sink. I now understood why everyone had stared at me when I had entered the dayroom. My face was smeared with George's blood.

A couple days later, the chief deputy sent for me and a guard escorted me to his office. He spoke to me from across a

cluttered desk. "It's my understanding that if you hadn't administered CPR as quickly as you did, a man would have died."

"Actually, when I got to him I thought he was already dead. Looked to me like he had stopped breathing. Anyway, he was my cell partner and I just did what I'd seen 'em do on TV. How is he?"

"He had a major stroke, but he's gonna make it," said the chief deputy, "thanks to you."

"I'm glad to hear that," I told him.

"Well, we appreciate it and I'm sure that his family does. I'd like to do something to reward you. How about I allow you a special contact visit?"

"I appreciate the offer," I said, "but I don't have anybody willing to come see me."

During the next couple weeks I suffered my own depression, and even though I continued to work out the exercise did little to relieve my hopelessness. I considered the gravity of my situation. I would more than likely be convicted of the Mobile bank robbery and sentenced to life without parole under Alabama's habitual offender laws. That, combined with the existing Mississippi sentence, would leave me with little to lose, so I decided to take a calculated risk. And if that risk didn't work out exactly as I planned, then the worst that would happen would be months in solitary confinement, which was preferable to the chaos, constant noise, and bickering I found living in the general population.

The next day, when we went to the recreation yard, I removed a twenty-pound, four-foot-long steel bar from the Universal weight machine. Hiding it in my pant leg and walking stiff legged as if I had injured my leg, I smuggled it into the pod.

In my cell I hid the steel bar under the edge of my mattress until that afternoon. While most of my fellow prisoners were watching TV and the guard in the cubicle was listening to a ball game on a radio headset, I concealed the steel bar in a blanket and carried it downstairs to the shower, the only blind spot in the dayroom. Turning the hot water on in all the shower stalls to create a wall of steam, I folded the blanket and placed it carefully against the concrete wall, holding it in place with my knee. Swinging the steel bar like a battering ram, I hit the blanket as hard as I could, knocking a hole the size of a baseball in the wall. I then furiously attacked the wall, hitting it again and again, each time removing a chunk of concrete. When I stopped, I had removed two concrete blocks and had a hole large enough to crawl through.

My plan was simple but risky: I intended to climb inside the space between the two separate concrete walls and make my way through the ceiling, where I would then pry open a thin sheet of steel, knock a hole in three inches of concrete plus roofing material, and gain access to the roof. From the roof, I would climb over a ten-foot fence topped with razor wire.

During my climb upward, I grabbed a bundle of live electrical wires, shocking me and causing me to bang my knee on a jagged piece of concrete. I lost my balance and fell six feet to the wet shower floor.

Just as I got to my feet, I heard over the intercom, "Count time! Everybody in your cells for count time!" I quickly hid the blanket and steel bar in the hole and limped to my cell, hoping that by some miracle of negligence the guards wouldn't see the gaping hole in the shower wall.

Watching from my open cell door, I saw the first guard walk past the shower, not seeing anything out of the ordinary, but the second was more observant. He walked into the shower, then

rushed back out again, keying his radio and frantically waving at the first guard.

Certain that someone would point me out as the culprit that had busted the hole in the shower wall, I sat down on my bunk to wait. Fifteen minutes later my cell door opened and four guards rushed in. They pinned me against the wall, searched and handcuffed me, then took me to the chief deputy's office. His attitude was quite different from a few weeks earlier.

"What the hell are you trying to do, Bridges?" asked the chief deputy.

"What do you mean?" I asked.

"You know damn well what I mean! That hole you just knocked in the wall of my new jail!" I didn't respond. He continued. "There's no use denying it. We got more than one witness. And we found that steel bar you used. I'll tell you what. I'm gonna ask the D.A. to charge you with attempted escape and destruction of county property. You're gonna get more time and have to pay to have that wall repaired."

"Chief, I don't care about the extra time. I'm facin' more than I can serve now!" I shouted. "And guess what—I ain't got no money!"

"Well then, let's see how much you care about being locked in the hole!" he shouted back.

I was taken to another room, strip-searched thoroughly, bound again in handcuffs and leg-irons, and hustled into the back of a patrol car. Driven to the old jail, I was put in a six-by-eight-foot cell that, judging by the large rivets on the heavy door, must've been built in the twenties. The cell had a twelve-foot ceiling and there were no lights or windows. It was essentially a steel tomb, the only air and light coming from a thin slit in the tray slot in the door.

In the dark I lay down on a thin, torn, stinking cotton mattress spread on a steel bunk, a small smile of satisfaction on

266

my face. *Maybe I didn't get away*, I thought, *but at least I've found some peace and quiet.*

I've loved the peace and security of dark confined places since I was young. I clearly remember the old dresser and mirror in Aunt Dolly's room and how I often crawled into the small empty space in the middle, pulling the chair in after. I would sit for what seemed like hours. But my favorite place was the laundry closet in the bathroom of our duplex in Trade Alley.

My mother and I were so close that even at an early age I was able to understand her pain and suffering simply by studying her expressions, particularly her eyes. I noticed that her pain usually arrived in one of two ways: it either came fast, leaping and rushing like an electrical charge and shocking her, or it came slow, oozing like hot molten lava down the face of a crater, burning her slowly head to foot.

When I would see her grimacing in pain, I'd walk down the short hall to the bathroom, open the trapdoor to the laundry closet, climb inside, and wrap myself in dirty clothes. I loved the sour sweaty smell; it was familiar and comforting. And I loved the silent safe darkness. I'd burrow to the bottom like a mole, hugging my knees to my chest and listening to the rhythm of my heart. It would beat quickly at first, then more slowly as I continued to stare into the void.

Tears would flow, each fragile globule containing microscopic universes inhabited by sad and lonely creatures. Each an expert in absorbing pain. I would then brace myself against the sides of the laundry bin, inhale quickly and deeply—once, twice, three times—until my sobbing jerked to a sudden stop and only a pulsating quiet remained.

In my young mind, I was helping my mother by sharing her pain.

I had nothing—no soap, no toothbrush or toothpaste, and, worst of all, no toilet paper. When I relieved myself, I had to wipe with a section of torn t-shirt that I would then wash out as best I could and hang on the sink to dry.

After about ten days, one afternoon the tray slot opened unexpectantly and a guard joked, "Hey, Bridges, you still in there?"

I stepped to the tray slot and the guard handed me a sheet of paper.

"What's this?" I asked.

"Read it and find out," he said, slamming the tray slot closed.

"Hey, how about a roll of toilet paper!" I yelled, banging on the steel door with my fists. He didn't respond. I sat on the floor next to the tray slot so that I could catch the least bit of light and read, "You are hereby recognized for … ."

"I'll be damned," I said. "It's a commendation for helping to save George's life, signed by the sheriff himself and stamped with an official gold seal. Damn."

Later that evening, sitting on the toilet, I reached behind me for the t-shirt rag to wipe my ass but abruptly changed my mind. I smiled, then reached over and picked up the commendation.

Chapter 28

After a couple of weeks, living conditions in the isolation cell improved. I was given soap, toothpaste, a toothbrush, and toilet paper. I was even allowed what seemed like luxuries—a pen, paper, and books.

I went to trial several months later and was convicted of the 1987 Mobile bank robbery. As expected, I was charged as a habitual offender and sentenced to life without parole.

A few days after sentencing, the local newspaper, the *Mobile Press-Register*, published an article about me, and a couple days after that I was sent to Holman prison to serve my time. There, while being processed, the guard in receiving told me that all new prisoners with sentences of life without parole were required to serve a ninety-day observation period in segregation prior to being released to population. He then escorted me to a cell in segregation, located next door to death row.

As we walked the first thing I noticed was the smell. It was a rank combination of rat shit, spoiled food, urine, body odor, and pine oil. I gasped and the guard noticed.

"Don't worry, you get used to it," he said.

The second thing I noticed was the ankle-deep trash in the hall that ran the length of the cellblock. And then I saw the roaches, dozens of them, cleaning the last bits of meat and grizzle from the chicken bones, mixed in with other trash. (I later found out that Holman served chicken every Sunday and that the prisoners in segregation protested their isolation by throwing the bones on the floor, where they remained until cleaned up.) In most places, roaches scamper when humans approach, but not at Holman. They were so bold they just ambled to the side to let us pass, then continued feeding.

My new cell was about the same length as the isolation cell in Mobile but more narrow. Being an average-sized man, I could stand in the middle of the cell and touch the opposite walls with the tips of the fingers of my outstretched arms. Concrete formed the cell on three sides. The front was steel bars floor to ceiling, covered over with a strong steel mesh. The sliding door was operated electronically by a guard in an unseen cubicle. Built into the door, waist high, was a narrow tray slot. Bolted to the wall was a steel bunk that took up most of the floor space. Near the foot of the bunk, attached to the floor and back wall, was a stainless steel toilet with a sink above.

I lay down and fell asleep but was awakened a couple hours later when I felt something crawling lightly across my chest. I sat up. It was a roach! I flicked it off and when it hit the floor I squashed it with my shoe, then wiped the remains off with a wad of toilet paper. When I stood to throw the toilet paper in the toilet, I noticed roaches everywhere; a couple raced around the sink as if at a roller rink.

I lay back down and thought of Angola and what had happened to me there ten years earlier. One morning I had awakened, feeling considerable pain and movement in my left ear. *I've gone insane*, I told myself. *So this is what it feels like.*

Getting out of bed, I leaned my head to the left and slapped the right side several times with my right hand. Out popped a roach. It hit the floor and scampered away before I could recover enough to chase it.

With the stub of a pencil that I kept in a Styrofoam cup next to my toothbrush wrapped in cellophane, I drew a calendar on the grayish-green wall next to the toilet. Every morning after breakfast and before going back to sleep I studied the calendar, noting the time on my watch, then marking a diagonal line through the date.

270

Then one morning I noticed that some of the diagonal lines were drawn in a hurried and haphazard fashion, while others were drawn with the very neat and deliberate hand of an architect. It was then that I realized that it was possible to look back at the calendar and decipher my mood or state of mind at the beginning of a particular day by simply studying the way I had drawn that morning's diagonal line. Wanting my state of mind to always be "neat and deliberate," not just on some days, I started using the straight edge of a piece of cardboard to draw my diagonal lines.

One morning a couple weeks later, while standing at my calendar admiring the perfectly drawn lines, I felt despair instead of pleasure when I realized that I had now destroyed my ability to interpret my true state of mind, so I quit marking the calendar altogether.

It was just as well that I gave up on the calendar because a couple weeks later U.S. marshals showed up to transport me to Portland, Oregon, to face bank robbery charges. I hoped that somewhere between Alabama and Oregon I'd get a chance to escape.

Put in a van along with four other federal prisoners, I was driven north. That night we were dropped off at the Federal Correctional Institution near Talladega, Alabama, and because of my history of escape I was put in an isolation cell, where I lived for the next three weeks.

Then, along with one other prisoner, I was taken to an airfield and put on a small jet bound for Oklahoma. Again, because I was considered an escape risk my wrists were tightly handcuffed, then covered with a locked, black plastic box, making it impossible to move my wrists. The box was then locked to a chain wrapped around my waist. It was painful, making the twelve-hour ordeal the most uncomfortable in memory. For further security, one of the marshals wrapped a

heavy ten-foot chain around and around my chest and locked it to the seat.

"What if the plane crashes and catches fire?" I asked the marshal. "I'll burn up before you can get all these chains off me!"

"Well, if we crash I doubt any of us will survive, but if we do, all I gotta do is find this seat and I'll find you." He laughed.

I deplaned that night at FCI El Reno in Oklahoma. It had been twenty years since last I'd been there during diesel therapy.

Three weeks later I was put on a large federal jet (similar to the one made popular by the movie *Con Air*) and sent to Tacoma, Washington. The next morning I was driven to Portland, Oregon. I went to court that afternoon. Assigned a lawyer, I pled not guilty to the August 1986 bank robbery.

Two months later I again met with my court-appointed lawyer, and after he showed me several very clear surveillance photos of me that were shot during the robbery, I conceded and agreed to plead guilty in exchange for an eighteen-year sentence to run concurrently with my Alabama sentence of life without parole.

The Portland conviction was my third and I now had sentences of life without parole in Alabama, fifteen years mandatory in Mississippi, and eighteen years in federal.

During the trip back, I spent six weeks in El Reno, three weeks in Talladega, and five weeks in the Atlanta federal prison.

I was in a one-man cell in C Block in Atlanta, an area used exclusively for those in transit. Allowed into the general prison population an hour or two every day, I'd sometimes go outside and play handball on Atlanta's infamous wall, but most of the time I cautiously walked around like a tourist in a prison museum.

While getting a haircut one afternoon I struck up a conversation with an inmate barber, and he told me that he had

been in Atlanta twenty years and was facing longer still. I told him of all the sentences I had, and he did something unusual, especially for two prisoners who didn't know each other: he slipped me a homemade handcuff key made from the metal barrel of a ballpoint pen. When I got back to my cell, I hid it in the insole of my shoe.

A couple weeks later, two U.S. marshals showed up to take me back to Holman. Shackled and handcuffed, I was put in a van with three other prisoners. In my shoe, I still had the homemade handcuff key and planned to use it should the opportunity present itself.

The opportunity came that evening when we stopped at a fast food restaurant southeast of Birmingham. While one marshal went inside to get the food, the other stood just outside the van's partially opened side doors.

All I gotta do, I told myself, *is get these leg-irons and handcuffs off, then hit those open doors like a linebacker. I should be able to get away before he recovers, and I doubt he'll leave the others unguarded to chase me.*

I fumbled in my shoe for the homemade handcuff key while the prisoner next to me watched. When I looked over at him, he looked away. I knew he was scared. Hell, I was scared. When I found the key, I looked through the crack in the doors to make sure the marshal wasn't watching. Satisfied, I inserted the key in the leg-irons. It wouldn't turn, so I pressed down hard and twisted, breaking the tip of the key off inside the keyhole.

I remember feeling relief rather than disappointment; I had been that scared. And now that I think back, I'm not sure that I didn't break that key on purpose just to "save face" with myself.

We arrived at Holman after midnight. While one marshal stayed with the van, the other escorted me through the prison's back gate.

In receiving, when the marshal inserted his key into the leg-irons, he found it plugged. The guard tried his key. It wouldn't work either.

"Looks like it's plugged up with something," the guard told the marshal. He turned to me. "Bridges, you put something in this keyhole to plug it up?"

I said, "Don't blame me, the Feds got shitty equipment!"

"Right," said the guard. "You probably broke something off in 'em tryin' to get 'em open."

While the marshal and I waited, the guard walked to the tower near the back gate and brought back a large set of bolt cutters. He easily cut the leg-irons off.

Because of the incident with the leg-irons, I was told the next day that I'd have to spend an additional ninety days in segregation. I protested but didn't really mind. I was in no hurry to get to the general population.

Chapter 29

During the next couple of months to support myself, I drew pencil portraits from photos of the other prisoners' family members. Then one day the captain in charge of segregation passed by my cell and saw me drawing. He asked if I could paint, and when I told him that I had once worked as a sign painter he asked if I'd be willing to paint the seal of the Department of Corrections on the wall near the entrance to segregation. I agreed and was let out of my cell at night to work on the project. When I finished, it was understood that I would be allowed to keep the paint and brushes as payment.

A couple months later, released from segregation, I was sent to live in Holman's general population. There I continued to draw portraits, spending any extra money I made on additional art supplies. Soon I was able to afford to pay a prisoner that worked in the carpentry shop to make me a collapsible easel so that I would be able to paint in the space between my bed and the bed of the prisoner living next to me.

The prisoner that lived in the bed next to me was named Fred. He was from Huntsville, Alabama, and had been at Holman several years, also serving life without for robbery. Six-two and weighing about 210 pounds, Fred was easygoing, quiet, and had a good sense of humor. His only vice, as far as I knew, was his addiction to gambling. Fred would bet on anything, from NASCAR to football.

Always looking for a way out and preparing should I find one, I jogged an average twenty miles per week, plus lifted weights. But either I didn't look hard enough or Holman was just too secure because two years passed and I still had no viable escape plan.

Then one day, while lifting weights, I was approached by a prisoner I'd seen around but had never spoken to. He was a trustee and one of the few at Holman allowed to go outside the prison to work.

"Mind if I do a couple of sets with you?" asked the trustee.

"Sure," I said, "go ahead." I got up and gave him the bench.

About five minutes into the workout, he said, "I got something you might be interested in."

"What's that?"

He stepped closer and said in a low voice, "I got a pair of heavy-duty wire cutters for sale."

Ever cautious, I asked, "Now, just what makes you think I'd be interested in wire cutters?"

"Well, I see you out here running all the time, working out. I just thought you might be interested. But if I'm wrong ... just forget it." He turned to leave.

"Hold it!" I said. He stopped and turned back around to face me. "Those wire cutters you got—they strong enough to cut through these fences?"

"Like a hot knife through butter."

"Got any heat on them?"

"Now, that's the beauty of it," he said. "They didn't come from inside the prison but from outside. Brought them in myself. You see, I work outside every day, cuttin' grass and shit for the warden. Got these wire cutters from his toolshed out back his house. He don't never go out there. It'll probably be years before he misses them, maybe never."

"You gotta be shittin' me! You stole the warden's wire cutters!" I looked around to see if anybody had noticed my outburst. Nobody seemed to be paying us any attention.

"That's right," he laughed.

"How much?" I asked.

"Three cartons of named-brand smokes."

"Three cartons! Damn, that's pretty high."

"Might be, but you can't just go to the hardware store and buy 'em."

"I realize that, but not everybody wants 'em, either. I'll tell you what—I'll give you fifteen packs right now. Take it or leave it."

"You got the cigarettes close by?" he asked.

"In my locker."

"Deal," he said. "You get the smokes and I'll get the cutters."

Five minutes later I handed the trustee the cigarettes in a paper bag and he handed me the wire cutters hidden in a folded newspaper. I carried them inside and hid them under my mattress.

That evening, while most were in the chow hall, I carefully wrapped the wire cutters in plastic, put them in my waistband under my shirt, and walked outside. Sitting down next to the fence, where I could see the tower but the tower guard couldn't see what I was doing, I dug a hole six inches deep with a large metal spoon stolen from the kitchen and buried the wire cutters, marking the exact spot in my mind. I hurried to join the rest for supper.

Encouraged, I began to increase the number of miles I ran daily. One day, after a fifteen-mile run, my longest ever, a guard approached me while I was walking the track to cool down. He was one of the few at Holman I liked and we often talked when he stopped to admire one of my paintings. His name was Gary Hetzel.

"They sent me out here to get you," said Officer Hetzel.

"For what?"

"The warden wants to see you."

"What's he wanna see me for?" I couldn't help but wonder if something had happened to one of my sisters or my father in Lake Charles.

"I don't know—honest. I was just told to come get you and take you to his office."

We walked back to the dormitory, where Officer Hetzel waited while I took a quick shower and dressed. When we reached the grille gate beside the control center, Officer Hetzel handcuffed me and led me through to the warden's office across from Holman's visiting area. Officer Hetzel knocked and a voice behind the door said, "Come in."

The guard opened the door, stuck his head inside, and said, "Warden, I got Bridges for you."

"Bring him in," said the warden.

It was a large paneled office. Warden Jones, a tall, slim man in his early fifties, looked up at me. He leaned back in his large plush office chair and propped his Western boots on his heavy ornate desk. An angry scowl on his face, he got to the point.

"I know that when you city boys get sent up here to Holman you look around and the first thing you think is, 'What a bunch of damn rednecks they got working there.' But you're wrong, mister. You're dead wrong. Here at Holman we know how to teach you city boys a thing or two. Yes sir, and you'll find out!" He paused. "They tell me you're getting ready," continued the warden.

"Warden, I don't know what you are talking about," I said.

"Oh, you *know* what I'm talking about, all right! You know damn well what I'm talking about! Out there running all day! I know you ain't training for the Olympics, so that leaves only one thing! You don't know what I'm talking about! Humph!"

The warden looked down at his desk and shook his head. In a quieter voice he said, "What I oughta do is have my guards take your ass outside that fence and shoot you down like a dog—

278

leave you lyin' in the mud. Be done with you." He looked up, waiting for my reaction.

A chill crawled up my spine. I had heard the rumors and had read the newspaper articles about the mysterious graves found in Southern prisons. I didn't doubt the warden was serious. Still, I couldn't stop myself saying, "But, Warden, it ain't rained in weeks."

The warden leapt to his feet, his face beet-red. Fearful, I stepped back, bumping into Officer Hetzel. The warden kicked his heavy chair and sent it banging into the wall, rattling the numerous diplomas and plaques hanging there. Pointing his finger at me, he gasped, "Get him outta here! Lock his fuckin' ass up right now!"

Once again I found myself in a roach-infested closet for the incorrigible, but I didn't really mind. I lay back on my bunk, luxuriating in the quiet and solitude after almost two years living in a chaotic and crowded dormitory, content that I had a secret no one knew about.

I'll just hang out here for a couple of months, I told myself, *stay in shape. Then once I'm sent back to population, I'll slip out onto the recreation yard one foggy night, dig up my wire cutters, and cut through the fences. Then it's goodbye asshole warden, goodbye Holman, and hello world! I'm back!*

A month later, a guard came to my cell. "Put on some clothes," he said. "The warden wants to see you."

"Well, I don't wanna see *him*," I said. "Tell him I ain't home."

The guard didn't see the humor. "No, you tell him 'cause you're gonna see him even if I have to get on this radio here and get some help! Now get dressed!"

I got dressed.

Handcuffed, I again stood in front of the warden's ornate desk. Drilling me with his eyes, he said in a quiet measured voice, "I want them damn wire cutters."

I was shocked. *How the hell does he know about the wire cutters?* I asked myself, trying not to show the fear I felt. "Warden, I don't know what you're talking about," I said, the words sounding false. "I've been locked up a month. How am I supposed to know about some damn wire cutters?"

"Bridges, I'm tired of hearing your shit. I know you got 'em and I know who you bought 'em from. I can even tell you how much you paid for 'em—fifteen packs of cigarettes. Yeah, that's right, that trustee sold 'em to you told on you." He looked at me, a self-satisfied smile on his face. "Now, where's my damn wire cutters!"

"I don't know where you're gettin' your information from, Warden, but it's bogus. I ain't got no cutters."

The warden spread his hands in conciliation. In a quiet voice he said, "I know you got 'em hid somewhere. Now, tell me where they are and I'll let you out of segregation. I'll give you your choice of beds in population. I'll let you have your art supplies and I'll even help you sell your paintings. I got more connections than you realize. Now, where are they?"

I couldn't believe what I was hearing. It all just sounded too good to be true, and the maxim "If it sounds too good to be true, it usually is" popped into my head. *If he just hadn't thrown in the part about helping me sell my paintings, I might have gone for it.*

I looked down at my feet and said in a quiet voice, "Look, Warden, I don't know nothin' about no wire cutters and I'm tired. Just let me go back to my cell."

"You're tired?!" He pounded the desk with his fists, furious, causing his stapler to jump off his desk and land on the floor. He kicked it. He screamed, "He's tired! Ya hear that! Get his fuckin' ass outta here! Get him outta my sight!" The guard

pushed me out the door, and just before it shut I heard the warden yell, "Your ass is gonna rot in that cell!"

The talk throughout the prison finally made it to segregation, and while pacing the floor that evening I overheard one prisoner tell another, obviously not realizing that they were talking about me, "Man, when I went to the infirmary I heard they got the whole prison locked down because somebody stole a pair of wire cutters from the warden's toolshed. They say the warden's pissed and he's gonna keep the prison locked down until he gets 'em back, that he don't care if it's Christmas or not. Right now he's got a whole team of guards out searching the recreation yard with metal detectors."

In the middle of the night two guards came to my cell and roughly awakened me. They made me strip naked, then put handcuffs and leg-irons on me. Still naked, I was taken downstairs to the basement in receiving and locked in one of the three isolation cells there. The isolation cells in receiving were even smaller than those in segregation and they had no windows. Naked, I shivered, sitting on my concrete bed while listening to two guards talking just outside the solid steel door.

"Now that we got him down here in the dungeon, we oughta beat his ass," said one of the guards. "If you hold him, I believe I can make him come up with them wire cutters in about two minutes."

Sitting in the cold and dark, totally isolated, I told myself, *This is gettin' dangerous now. It would be so easy for the warden to have me killed. I better be careful how far I take this.*

That evening I was given clothes, a roll of toilet paper, and two cheese sandwiches on stale bread. I ate one of the sandwiches and saved the other, not knowing how regularly I'd be fed.

Later I heard a *whoosh* and a rattling of the vent above the toilet. Standing on the toilet, I reached up and felt heat blasting

from the vent. *Hallelujah! I got clothes, food, and now heat! Things are looking up!* I congratulated myself for hanging in there.

But the heat just kept coming, getting hotter and hotter. Soon I felt like a turkey in an oven. I stripped off my clothes. When I pushed the button on the sink to get a drink of water, nothing happened. I then tried to flush the toilet. Nothing. The water had been turned off. I climbed back up on the toilet and plugged the heating vent as best I could with small wads of toilet paper.

The heat assault lasted all night, and at noon the next day the heat was reduced to normal and the water turned back on. Three times a day the guards changed shifts, and during each shift at least one guard threatened me, trying to get me to tell him where I had hidden the warden's wire cutters. I didn't budge.

Then someone came up with a totally new tactic. The door to the cell next to me slammed shut. A guard banged on my cell door with his baton. "Hey, Bridges! I know it gets lonely down here, so I brought you some company for the holidays!" He laughed as he walked away.

A couple of minutes later I heard a voice coming from inside the vent. "Troy! Troy! Can you hear me?"

I stood on the toilet and spoke into the vent. "Yeah, I hear you. Who is it?"

"It's Fred!" said the voice.

"Fred! What the hell you doin' here!"

"Man, the warden had me locked up 'cause I wouldn't tell him where you got them wire cutters hid! You know I don't know nothin' about no wire cutters and I told him, but he don't believe me so he locked me up!"

"Sorry you got caught up in this!" I shouted back.

"No big deal! This ain't my first time in lockup! I just hate I'm gonna miss all them football games on TV. You know that

282

son of a bitch took all the TVs out of the dorms too, plus he stopped handin' out the Christmas packages sent from home!"

"Shit, I didn't know that!"

"Yeah, he said Holman wasn't having Christmas this year until he gets his wire cutters back!"

"What's everybody in population think of that?" I asked.

"Man, they're about to riot and tear up some shit! And I ain't gonna lie to ya; you ain't the most popular dude at Holman. They blame you for everything! But I don't! I understand! And they know better than to say anything about you to me 'cause they know you and me are tight!"

I now understood the new game the warden was playing. Since I had not responded to his threats and promises, he intended to punish the entire prison and blame it on me, making me the Grinch who stole Christmas. *I gotta give it to him,* I smiled to myself. *He's certainly teaching this city boy a thing or two, just like he said.*

The next morning when the guard came around, I told him where I had hidden the wire cutters. He was as pleased as if I'd given him an early Christmas present (and I suppose I had). By noon, the heavy cloud that had hung over Holman lifted and everything was sunshine. The warden's wire cutters were found, the lockdown lifted, the TVs turned on, and Christmas saved.

Fred was released and sent back to his dorm in time to place a bet on a football game that afternoon. I was given a large breakfast the next morning before being wrapped in chains, put in a van, and driven north to Donaldson prison.

Chapter 30

December 1992

It rained continuously during the drive north. I tried to sleep but the prisoners next to me talked the entire trip, making it difficult.

"Man, I hope they drop me off at St. Clair," said the prisoner to my right. "Ain't no way I wanna go to Donaldson. That place ain't nothin' but a throwaway camp."

"What the hell's a throwaway camp?" asked the prisoner to my left.

"It's where they send you when they just wanna get rid of ya," said the prisoner to my right. "You know, like when you give 'em a lot of trouble. They just throw you away like a sack of garbage."

"So Donaldson's a throwaway camp?"

"Hell yeah."

"Where is it?"

"Just outside Birmingham. Near the town of Bessemer."

The mention of the name Bessemer jarred loose an old memory. I was eight years old, living in Trade Alley and out of school for the summer. Bored, I repeatedly begged my father to let me go with him on one of his out-of-state runs for F.M. and he repeatedly refused. My mother intervened and he reluctantly agreed.

We left early the next morning for Bessemer, Alabama, to pick up hundreds of bags of fertilizer to bring back to Shelby. I was excited and felt like a grown-up when I climbed into the cab of F.M.'s truck. Immediately I crawled onto the narrow bed above and behind the seats and from that vantage point watched the changing landscape through the small side windows.

When we got to Bessemer later that day, we went straight to the fertilizer plant where our flatbed trailer was loaded with bag after bag of fertilizer. I helped my father cover the fertilizer with a heavy tarp and we immediately headed back to Shelby, my father driving fast as if late for an appointment.

Late that night we stopped at a large truck stop in Georgia. Inside the restaurant everyone seemed to know my father and they asked about my grandfather, F.M. Our waitress, a pretty, slender woman with long dark hair, asked my name. She told me that hers was Janey.

After we ate my father gave me a handful of nickels and directed me to a pinball machine, telling me to stay there and not move until he returned. That wasn't hard to do. I was so fascinated by the machine's dazzling lights and sounds that I barely looked up until my last nickel was gone.

I don't know how much time passed but it seemed like only minutes, although I'm sure it was much longer. When I ran out of money I hung around the machine and watched others play until my father showed up. Our waitress, Janey, now wearing different clothes, was with him.

While my father drove I once again crawled into the sleeper, where the hum of the big tires on the asphalt quickly sang me to sleep. We got home around noon and my father went straight to bed.

While he was sleeping, my mother sat me in a chair at the small table in the kitchen and grilled me for information. She wanted to know every detail about our trip. When I got to the part about the friendly waitress named Janey and how my father had left me alone to play the pinball machine, my mother's demeanor changed. She ran into the bedroom and beat my father awake with her fists, screaming, "You cheatin' son of a bitch! I knew it! Janey! Who's Janey, Chuck? Don't deny it. Rickey told me all about her!"

They fought until my father finally dressed and left. My mother left soon after.

My father never took me with him again.

That afternoon we stopped first at St. Clair prison to drop off the other prisoners, and I alone was taken to Donaldson, about fifteen miles northwest.

At the end of a hilly, winding road, deep in mining country, sat Donaldson prison. Built in a huge bowl carved out by strip miners, the prison was surrounded by hills thickly wooded with maple, oak, and pine. It was a beautiful location except for the three ugly fences topped with razor wire that marked the prison's perimeters. Two of the fences were twelve feet tall and the third was a ten-foot-high voltage electric fence. Six guard towers, strategically positioned and manned twenty-four hours a day by guards armed not only with shotguns but AR15 automatic weapons, were part of the reason that no one had ever successfully escaped Donaldson.

Originally named West Jefferson after the county where it's located, it was renamed in 1991 after a mentally ill prisoner in segregation, trying to stab another inmate, accidentally killed a guard named William E. Donaldson.

Statistically, Donaldson was the most violent prison in the state, and appropriately the street address was 100 Warrior Lane. It was home to seventeen hundred prisoners. Six hundred lived in cellblocks, stacked three to a cell, and were seldom allowed outside, creating a great deal of tension, and another six hundred lived in dormitories in an area called the south side. The rest, perhaps five hundred, lived in segregation cells.

Because of my behavior at Holman, I was escorted through the back gate, processed, and sent to a cell in segregation.

The cells were larger than those at Holman and were constructed of concrete blocks on all sides, with a heavy steel

door on a sliding rail. The bed was a four-foot-wide slab of concrete that ran the length of the cell. Above the bed was a long, narrow window covered in plated steel. It had a small opening at the top, a few inches wide, and covered over with heavy steel mesh. The mesh was so clogged with dirt and grime that only a minimum amount of fresh air and sunlight was able to get through. A stainless steel toilet and sink stood against the far wall.

As usual, in the door was a tray slot but this one was slightly larger than the one at Holman. It was actually large enough to allow the more sociable—or more disturbed—prisoners enough room to twist their heads to the side and squeeze them through the tray slot where they could then look around and talk or argue with other "heads."

Carrying my mattress and an old army blanket in my cuffed hands, I was escorted to my cellblock. The door opened and I stepped into the small dayroom, stood for a moment, and looked around to see one of the strangest sights I'd ever seen: six heads, four on the bottom tier and two on the top, were staring at me like demented jack-in-the-boxes.

One head yelled, "Hey, man, where you from?"

Another said, "Got anything to smoke? I'm dying for a cigarette."

"Don't start begging the man already," said a shaggy old head with gray whiskers. "You got any coffee?" he then asked, a crazed look in his eyes.

I didn't respond. I knew better. I quietly went to my cell. The door slid shut and I backed to the tray slot so that the guard could remove my handcuffs.

Every morning at 6:00 A.M. two guards went from cell to cell and confiscated the blankets and mattresses. They were returned every evening at 6:00 P.M. Those that refused to give up their blankets and mattresses were beaten.

We were served only two cold meals a day and allowed outside for an hour, two to three times a week. On those days, we were allowed a six-minute shower. The exercise cages were similar to those at Holman, with one major difference: chunks of baseball- and football-size concrete had been cemented to the floor of the cages to prevent anyone lying down or even pacing without difficulty.

Donaldson had a large population of mentally ill prisoners, and most lived in special units in segregation called "the doghouse." It took me several days to realize that I had been sent to one of these special units, compliments of the warden at Holman.

Several in the doghouse urinated in cups or defecated in paper bags and threw it on anyone that came near their cell. Usually it was one inmate splashing another after an argument, but occasionally a guard would also get splashed. Whenever this happened, four to five guards dressed in full riot gear would rush into the cell and beat the prisoner unconscious. They would then take him to the infirmary where he would be shot full of psychotropics and returned to his cell. He would refrain from splashing for two to three weeks, then resume throwing urine and feces as if nothing had happened.

When it was quiet at night, which was rare but did happen occasionally, mice would come out looking for food, and the prisoner in the cell next to me would catch them with a simple but effective trap. After attaching a long string to the leather loop on the back of his brogan, he would place the boot on the floor and then a paper bag upside down, with the edge propped on the boot. He would then place a scrap of food under the bag, hold the string, and wait. When a mouse crept under the bag to get at the food, he would simply jerk the string and pull the boot to him, causing the paper bag to fall on the mouse. He would usually keep the mouse for several days, often tying a long leash

to the mouse's tail so that he could lie in bed and control the rodent's movements. When he got bored—and he always did—he would then flush the mouse down the toilet and a few days later catch another.

It may have been the constant noise in the doghouse or the nervous energy of those housed there, but for the first time ever I experienced anxiety attacks. Just the sound of steel banging on steel or keys rattling in locks affected me like fingernails scraping on a blackboard. And I hated the expectation that accompanied the sounds, the conflicting thoughts of hope or fear: *Are they coming to let me out or to shake me down?*

But what really tested my sanity were the sounds of the constant bickering and, often, unintelligible ranting. Every night at 9:00 P.M., prior to pill call, someone on the top tier howled like a wolf. And voices thick with paranoia echoed throughout the cellblock day and night.

I really didn't know how to deal with these new feelings but didn't want to ask for medication. I had seen far too many walking around like zombies, slobbering on themselves, their eyes vacant as if they had just undergone a lobotomy.

My past actions had cast me adrift as surely as if I had been on a raft in the middle of the Pacific Ocean. Totally alone, I had no one to write or telephone or talk to. And in the doghouse I was in a prison within a prison, surrounded by men perhaps worse off but at least as desperate. I had three sentences in three different jurisdictions and had been told that I would never get out.

Clad in underwear and carrying a towel, washcloth, and a bar of soap in my cuffed hands, one morning I was escorted to the shower, only thirty feet from my cell. There the guard removed my handcuffs and stood close by.

"Okay, Bridges," he said, "you got six minutes." He set the timer on his watch.

Quickly I adjusted the water and soaped all over, enjoying the hot shower, one of the few pleasures in the doghouse. Just a few minutes later the guard said, "Okay, time's up. Turn it off and get out."

I dried quickly, put on underwear, and offered my wrists. The guard snapped the handcuffs on me. On the short walk back to my cell, I noticed a thick paperback book on the floor against the wall, partially covered with trash. It had a long dark-brown cigarette burn on the cover. Always looking for something to read, I stopped.

"Let's go, keep moving," said the guard.

"Can I get this book?" I asked.

"Yeah, go ahead."

Switching my towel, washcloth, and soap to my left hand, I squatted over the book and grabbed it with my thumb and two fingers. The book firmly clenched in my cuffed hands, I entered my cell and dropped it on my mattress. The heavy door slid shut and the guard removed my handcuffs.

Later, sitting on my bed, I thumbed through the book. It was entitled *We're All Doing Time*, by Bo Lozoff. It was fascinating, unlike anything I'd ever read. When I got to the section on meditation techniques, I stopped thumbing and started reading.

Chapter 31

In the doghouse, memories were like photos of past failures and disappointments. Unbidden, they appeared jumbled and out of order as if printed on giant flash cards shuffled then held up one at a time for me to review: Here I was at eleven, selling peanuts at the Battery in Charleston. Then as an eighteen-year-old Marine, cold and disillusioned, trying to thumb a ride in a swirling snowstorm. An instant later, I'd see myself in a baggy orange jumpsuit, standing expressionless before a judge, or as a small boy in ragged jeans, selling newspapers at a busy intersection in Miami.

Whenever I found myself living too long in the past and experiencing the inevitable sadness that came with it, I learned to trick my mind by closing my eyes and fantasizing of a glorious future instead, one in which all my hopes and dreams were realized. But, unfortunately, while the sadness that came from living in the past often lasted for hours—sometimes days—the joy that came from living in the future was unsustainable and short-lived, as if it were easier to be unhappy than happy.

The meditation techniques that I learned reading *We're All Doing Time* revealed a third option: living in the present.

At first, I could only meditate for fifteen minutes before being totally overwhelmed by painful memories. I often ended my meditation session with tears in my eyes. But as time passed and I was able to sit for longer and longer periods of time, meditation left me calm and contented.

I didn't realize it at the time, but I was undergoing a process of purification. Meditation was helping me to uncover and heal layers of painful childhood trauma. I also didn't realize that this healing process would take years and thousands of hours of

"sitting," but I *did* realize that finally I had found what felt like the right path for me.

I had envied those prisoners I'd seen in prayer groups or alone on their knees at their bunks. I had read the Bible, had taken the study courses, had gone to church regularly, and had prayed, but I had never been able to give myself completely to conventional religion the way I'd seen others do. Every time that I came close to letting go and joining the ranks of the righteous, I'd see those same (saved) men violently arguing over scripture or even what to watch on TV and would pull back.

One day I was taken outside and put in a cage next to a small, older prisoner with wild white hair and white stubble on his face. He was barefoot and leaning on a cane, staring into the woods beyond the tall fences.

"What's going on?" I asked the old man, but either he didn't hear me or ignored me, so I stepped closer to the fence that separated us. "Last week when I was out here, I saw a whole family of turkeys on that ridge over there, under them oak trees," I said, "probably eating acorns."

He turned his head and looked at me. "Humph!" he said loudly. "Got a cigarette?"

"Nah," I said. "Quit a couple months ago. Ever been turkey huntin'?"

"I ain't interested in no damn turkeys!" shouted the old man. "Humph!" he said, turning his back on me.

"Sorry, old-timer," I said. "No offense." I turned my back.

The old man wasn't standing at the fence appreciating the beauty of nature. To do that he would've had to live in the present, and he hated everything about the present and felt he had no future. He had learned to live in the past where his memories were the only thing left him. Yet even accessing his memories was getting harder and harder to do because the older

and weaker he got and the longer he spent in prison, the more his memories faded.

The guard interrupted the old man's reverie. "Okay, time to go."

The old man wheeled on the guard. "I ain't had my hour!" he shouted.

"Well, according to my watch," said the guard, "you been here an hour and five minutes."

"That's a lie! You need another watch!"

"Now, come on, Jack" pleaded the guard. "You do this every time you go on walk. You've done had five extra minutes."

"Y'all always cheatin' me, that's why. I know I didn't get no hour."

"Look, let's go!" shouted the guard, losing his patience. "Don't make me come in there and get you!"

"Sumbitch!" yelled the old prisoner. "Sumbitch! I know I didn't get my time!" Finally, he gave up and walked out of the cage.

A couple of days after I saw the old prisoner in the exercise cage, I had a dream. In that dream, I had a simple but important realization, one that would help me begin to change my life. Awakening suddenly, I jumped to my feet. As soon as they hit the floor, I said out loud, "What goes around comes around!"

Pacing the small cell, excited, I tried to recall the dream I'd just had. In the backyard of Pawpaw and Granny's house on Gardner Street, I stood in front of a large wicker basket ten feet tall. Leaning against the basket was a ladder. Slowly I climbed the ladder and looked inside; what I saw were baseball-sized rocks. I was disappointed. I didn't want rocks. I wanted gold. Then I realized *if day after day all I put in this basket are rocks, then of course all I can expect to see when I look in the basket are rocks.*

Continuing to pace the cell, I realized that the reason my life had been so full of negativity, anger, and despair was not because of what had been done to me but rather what I had done to myself. The world hadn't been out to get me. I had been out to get the world. I had filled my basket with rocks.

After studying many religions during my long years of incarceration, I further realized that the truth of "what goes around comes around" was universal. The Bible says we reap what we sow. The Koran says not one of us is a true believer until we want for our brother what we want for ourselves. And Karma, which often seems to be the thread that holds everything together or causes it to unravel, states that we must suffer or enjoy the consequences of our actions, if not in this life then surely in the next.

We're all connected, I told myself. *That's why I should be concerned about my brother's welfare. What I do to him, I do to me. And what I think of him, what I want for him, how I treat him is either the rock or gold that I put into the basket that represents my life.*

The dream reminded me of what I already knew but hadn't been able to admit: My life had been a disaster so far and it was time to change. I was finally tired of all the negativity and despair. I wanted something clean and new and untainted. I wanted something better. I wanted some of the good experiences that I had seen others having.

I made a decision, perhaps born of selfishness, but nonetheless I intended to follow through, if only for twenty-four hours. *For the next twenty-four hours, I'm going to try my hardest to give love, respect, and understanding to everybody I come in contact with, no matter the situation,* I told myself, *no matter how difficult. If it's true that what we put out we get back, then I'm gonna put out good, even if only for one day. I want gold in my basket instead of rocks.*

A few hours later, when the guard opened the tray slot to pass in a tray of grits, gravy, and biscuit, I bent down so that I

could make eye contact through the open slot. "Thank you," I said. "I appreciate it."

The guard, befuddled by my change in attitude, said, "Yeah, sure. Okay, Bridges. Whatever." He closed the tray slot.

Thirty minutes later, when the same guard opened the tray slot to get my empty tray, he said, "Here."

I looked down, and sitting on the edge of the tray slot was a paper towel wrapped around something. I picked it up and unwrapped the paper towel. Inside were two biscuits. I couldn't believe it. I stared at the biscuits as if I'd been given a two-inch-thick steak.

"Thank you," I said, a big smile on my face. *I can't believe this,* I told myself. *This kindness stuff really works.*

A little later I beat on the wall to get the attention of the mouse wrangler in the cell next to me. I traded him the biscuits for one hand-rolled cigarette and a match. After wrapping the cigarette and match in a piece of paper, I put the paper in my waistband and waited for the guard to take me on the walk. I wasn't sure if I'd see the little old man again but was prepared if I did.

Sure enough, I was again put in a cage next to the little old white-haired man the guard had called Jack. He was doing exactly the same thing he had done the last time that I'd seen him—standing and staring beyond the fences. I approached him but this time knew better than to talk about turkeys.

"What's up, old-timer?" I said.

He turned to look at me, resentful at being interrupted. "Humph!" he mumbled. "Got a cigarette?"

"As a matter fact, I do," I said, smiling. "Plus, I got a match." I showed him the match and cigarette.

"Can I get the short on it?" he asked, a glimmer of hope in his tired old eyes.

"Nope," I said. His face fell. "You can have it all. It's all yours!"

The old prisoner flashed impish smile. It was pure gold and would fit nicely into the new basket I was filling.

Chapter 32

I continued to meditate twice a day, often for as long as an hour, and about two months later I was released from the doghouse and sent to the south side. I was ambivalent about my release. On the one hand I looked forward to freedom of movement and fresh air and sunshine. And I was excited about jogging and working out and having a larger choice of books to read. But on the other, I was afraid that I would miss the solitude and that my meditation practice would suffer. I was also concerned about the negative influences of once again living in a chaotic, crowded, and violent population and doubted whether I'd be able to stay on the new path I'd chosen.

The south side was four open-bay dormitories under one large metal roof. Each dormitory was separated by a concrete block wall and housed one hundred thirty prisoners in a space originally built for fifty.

One of the best things about the south side was the freedom of movement. The doors to the dormitories were never locked and we were allowed outside day or night.

One of the worst things was the lack of privacy. The beds were double bunked and close together. There were no curtains or partitions concealing either the showers or the toilets, which were located in the very center of the dormitories. One could stand a few feet inside the front door and see or speak to someone taking a shower or sitting on the toilet. Only eighteen inches separating them, there were only four toilets and one long urinal to service one hundred thirty prisoners and it was rare, especially during the day, to find one empty for any length of time.

Most on the south side didn't seem to mind the lack of privacy, even when relieving themselves. In fact, some viewed their time on the toilet as a social occasion, a time for gossip and small talk. But after enjoying the privacy of a cell for months, the last thing I wanted to do was carry on a conversation while sitting on the toilet.

After making my bed I grabbed a roll of toilet paper and headed for an empty toilet. Squeezing my way between beds, I was moving along at a fast walk when suddenly I was cut off by a man sprinting like a halfback. By the time that I reached the toilets he had already dropped his pants and sat down.

"Sorry. When you gotta go, you gotta go," he said.

"I know, that's right," I said, shaking my head in embarrassment.

Slowly I walked back to my bed and lay down but kept my eye on the toilet area. Ten minutes later two men got off their toilets at the same time. I stood slowly, determined to regain my lost dignity, looked around and lazily stretched my arms, giving anyone a full fifteen seconds to make their move. When no one did, I casually strolled over to one of the empty toilets and sat down.

Two minutes later a large man walked up and sat down on the toilet next to me. He looked over.

"Need a shit partner?" he asked, smiling.

I didn't answer but now felt so self-conscious all I could do was pass gas. After pulling up my pants, I walked over to the sink and washed my hands. *Hell*, I thought, *I coulda saved myself a lot of frustration and just stepped outside to do that!*

My first morning living on the south side I got up at 4:00 A.M. It was dark and quiet. The dormitory was bathed in red night-lights. Most of the one hundred thirty men were asleep,

but two sat on a wooden bench in the TV area talking, their hand-rolled cigarettes flaring like fireflies in the dark.

I watched Jack, the old man I'd given the cigarette in segregation, now in population himself, prowl the dorm, using his cane like a metal detector. Whenever he came across a cigarette butt he stopped, picked it up, and examined it carefully. If it passed inspection, he put it in a small, round snuff can he carried.

After placing my folded blanket on the concrete floor in the space between my bed and the bed next to me, I sat down to meditate. Thirty minutes later, while I was making my bed, the old prisoner who had been picking up butts and I locked eyes across the sleeping dormitory. He limped over and sat down on my footlocker.

"I seen you sittin' on the floor," he said.

"Yeah, I was meditating," I said.

"What's that?"

"It's just sittin' still and watchin' your breath," I told him. "Makes me feel calm and peaceful."

"Well, that's a damn fool thing to do," said the old prisoner. "You looked like you was doin' some of that X-rated prayin' them magic people in the movies do."

"Ain't nothin' magic about it. Like I said, it just makes me feel good."

"Well, a cigarette makes me feel good."

"I understand," I said. "How about a cup of coffee, that make you feel good too?"

"Yeah," he smiled, "but I ain't got nothin' to trade you for it."

"Ain't askin' for nothin'. It's just a cup of coffee."

The next morning after meditation I found a biscuit wrapped in toilet paper sitting on the locker at the foot of my bed. When I looked around I saw the old man watching me. I

held up the biscuit to show him that I had found it. He waved, then got up and limped over. Without a word, he held out his stained coffee cup and I put a heaping spoon of instant coffee in it.

Every morning thereafter the old prisoner came by for a cup of coffee. Sometimes he quietly left and sometimes he stayed to talk. Also every morning, he left some small payment on my footlocker: a plastic container of sugar-free jelly, half a roll of toilet paper, two Band-Aids, half a pencil, a couple of rubber bands, or two aspirin. Once I even found a blue-black crow's feather.

When I got to Donaldson, there was only one self-help class available—a twelve-week course called Transactional Analysis. Sanctioned by Donaldson's psychologist, it was taught by a dynamic inmate named Rick Smith. Rick had already been in prison fifteen years by the time we met, serving life without parole for murder. He was self-educated and charismatic, with a sharp wit and a great sense of humor. Rick had been teaching Transactional Analysis for five years.

After I graduated Transactional Analysis, Rick and I became close friends. We both loved to work out and shared an interest in meditation and occult literature.

I asked for and got a job in the prison library. To work there I had to complete a short course in bibliography, taught by a Department of Corrections librarian who drove to Donaldson from Montgomery to train three of us. I was assigned as the librarian responsible for selecting and delivering books to those in segregation and on death row.

In six months, I had gone from living in the doghouse and hoping for a book to read to delivering books to the doghouse for others to read, and I knew the importance of a book to someone in isolation. I took the job seriously.

One morning a man named Michael NiCastro asked me to teach him how to meditate. A smart, handsome man, forty years old, he had been in prison twenty years, serving a life sentence for murder. He told me that he had actually meditated before but wanted to know more so I gave him the book *We're All Doing Time*. He loved it and even started writing the author, Bo Lozoff.

Michael soon joined me at 4:00 every morning and a couple weeks later Rick Smith, my Transactional Analysis instructor, also joined us.

Chapter 33

In the fall of 1994 I wrote a letter to Unity South Church in Birmingham, a church that I knew used meditation as part of their service. In my letter, I told a little about myself and our small meditation group and asked if anyone there would be willing to correspond with me.

It was during this period that I came across two books that greatly influenced me: *The Spectrum of Consciousness,* by Ken Wilber, and *The Body of Time: And the Energies of Being,* by Bruce Thomas.

Two weeks after I wrote Unity South Church, I received a letter from Jacqueline Dicie. I don't remember exactly what she said but I do remember the subject. It was a lighthearted discussion regarding the differences between the "smaller" self (ego) and the "larger" self (God). I was thankful for the books I'd been reading, especially *The Spectrum of Consciousness.* I thought, *If I want to continue to correspond with Ms. Dicie, I better study harder. This is one smart lady.*

Many years later I asked Jacqueline Dicie to write her version of how we met and, if possible, her reaction to my initial letter. This is what she wrote:

"I was going home, that was clear. I had spent two years [in San Francisco] fooling around with posers and my mother was getting old. My fifteen-year-old son had decided he was dropping out of the fancy alternative school I had moved to the West Coast to put him in, and my lover had played one too many high-class mind games to take up any more of my precious time. I was done. Weirdly, that week this random woman on Market Street had come up to me and told me that I had moved to the Bay Area to be with someone that didn't seem to have time for me (yeah, that was the sophisticate, right up until I said I was

leaving) but that I was going to find what I needed back home in Alabama and could she have money to buy milk for her baby.

"I wept the whole two-thousand-mile drive home.

"Back in Birmingham my son went into a black funk, took up residence in my mother's concrete basement, and slept. We worried. I found a small church with a metaphysics teacher I credited with saving my sanity. She was fabulous at unpacking thoughts.

"A few months into training with the teacher, she posed the question, If you knew Jesus was coming again next month, what would you do? To someone who still identified herself as a Catholic, no matter my in-and-out status with the Church, this was a question that deserved thought. I thought of my good-hearted but dysfunctional parents who had loved me the best way they knew and therefore raised me in relentless insanity. I thought of my subsequent sicko relationships and my marriage that had produced a darling boy unable to function in the world but smart enough to fool mental health professionals I had dragged him to over the years. I thought of the must be millions who are raised with insanity but not love. If I was damn lucky not to be dead, considering the massive self-destructive hole I was still trying to claw my way out of, what in the world happens to them?

"So I replied, 'I'd find people who are in prison but who are open to what we're learning here and I'd share it with them.' Those words just came out of my mouth.

"After the service, one of the board members sought me out. 'Funny you should say that,' she said. 'We got this letter in the mail last week and I really didn't know what to do with it.'

"It was an extended letter from an inmate in the most maximum-security state prison located thirty miles on the outskirts of town. He explained that he was an artist—photo of him with one of his paintings included—and that he had been

303

meditating for some time. Ours was the only church that advertised meditation in the yellow pages, he said, and the only other brands of spirituality offered him were Native Americanism and Islam. He asked if someone at the church would be willing to carry on a correspondence with him? He needed to bounce some ideas around and hear fresh ones. He posed a lot of theories but hadn't found all that he needed.

"In the photo he sent I saw the most intense eyes a human being could bear to look into. He stood in front of a painting, his paintbrush poised as if the camera had caught him just before he had made a stroke. The painting was of an old hobo and his dog by the boxcar they may have just exited. You could see the long suffering of the old man and the tender affection he shared with his pup. The whole effect was unbearable.

"I wondered how the hell someone with that degree of intelligence and sensitivity had gotten himself in prison. What was his crime? How long was he in for?

"'Okay,' I said. 'I'll take this off your hands.'"

Chapter 34

Early one morning after meditation, I was sitting on my bed reading when I heard the prisoner next to me say, "The shakedown squad's here."

"Where?" I asked.

"They just finished a shaking down in 3 Block, then sure as hell they're headed this way."

"Well, I really ain't got no serious contraband," I said, "but still I hate to lose what little I got. But what I really hate is the way they treat us. Seems to me they've gotten worse over the years."

"Yeah, I hate it too," said the prisoner. "Look, I gotta go warn a couple other dudes."

The word spread quickly. All around me men scurried about like ants, looking for a place to hide their contraband. Most of the contraband didn't amount to much—small things, like an extra pillow or blanket or sheet, perhaps some food from the chow hall. Those who had the serious contraband, like drugs or weapons or cash money, had long ago found their hiding places and could now just sit back and ride out the shakedown.

The shakedown squad was officially called the Correctional Emergency Response Team, or simply CERT. It was primarily a group organized to deal with riots and escapes but since those events rarely occurred, CERT sharpened their skills by periodically terrorizing the inmate population.

Most of the CERT members were young, in their twenties or early thirties, and were physically fit. Ex-soldiers not long returned from the Middle East, where many had worked as military police and guards at the area's most notorious prisons, they had learned the art of intimidation and torture. Bringing

these skills home, they adapted them for use in America's prisons.

We heard them before we saw them, the sound of their heavy boots rhythmically pounding the blacktop ominous. The experienced prisoners rushed to get on their beds, while the inexperienced foolishly lingered.

It never fails—in every living area there is always at least one prisoner who hasn't learned to be wary of CERT. Usually he is young and new to prison and eager to show how tough he is, with no idea that he is playing right into the hands of CERT, who are always on the lookout for someone to make an example of.

The front door flung open and a squat, muscular, bald-headed Black man wearing chevrons stepped inside. He looked around, then shouted, "I want every swingin' dick on your bed right now! You will lay facedown, hands locked behind your head, legs crossed at the ankles! Now move!"

The sergeant then stepped to the side, and in rushed twenty guards, all dressed in black. They carried two-foot-long batons.

An inexperienced prisoner was talking on the phone. He had been warned a few minutes earlier that CERT was on the way and had snapped, "I don't care who's on the way, I'm talkin' to my wife. They'll have to wait till I'm finished."

The first two guards through the door headed straight for the prisoner on the telephone. The first to reach him slapped the telephone out of his hand, causing him to stumble. Shocked, he yelled, "Hey, man! I was talking to my ... ," but before he could finish the second guard jabbed him in the solar plexus with his baton. The prisoner gasped, doubled over, and dropped to his knees.

The first guard said to the prisoner, "Don't ever call me 'man'!" He kicked the prisoner in the upper back and the man

landed on his face. The guard knelt beside him. "Now, stay where you are. Lock your hands behind your head. Cross your ankles. Don't you dare move or you're gonna have a really bad day."

I too had dealt with CERT (called by different names in different prisons) and quite honestly was scared of their sanctioned violence. So when they appeared on the scene, I kept my head down and tried not to be noticed. I knew what to expect. They would yell and scream, kick over trash barrels, slap a couple of people around, shake down, confiscate, and scatter property, then move on to another area of the prison while we cleaned up and tried to put our lives back together.

I also knew, because I had overheard several of them talking one day—and this may be the most cruel aspect of all—that they viewed it all as fun, usually getting together after a shakedown to drink a few beers and laugh about their acts of cruelty.

Chapter 35

Michael, Rick, and I sat talking after meditation one morning. "What do you guys think about having a weekly meditation group?" I asked.

"We could try," said Rick.

"I'm game," said Michael. "Dudes ask me about meditation all the time, so I know there's a lot of interest in it."

"I think it's a good idea," said Rick, "but if we're gonna hold a weekly group, then we need a quiet place. I think people will feel self-conscious sitting on the floor in a crowded dormitory, especially during the day when everybody's up and moving around. And here's another problem—suppose a lot of people show up? Where we gonna put 'em?"

"We can control the number of people that show up," I said. "We'll just find some floor space, then figure out how many we can accommodate."

"I still say people are gonna feel self-conscious sitting on the floor in front of everybody," said Rick. "I know I did the first couple of times I meditated in the dorm."

"Funny thing," said Michael. "It never bothered me. If most people can run around and yell and scream and nobody says nothin' to 'em, then they sure ain't got no right to say something to me for just sittin' down and being quiet."

"I actually like the idea of sittin' on the floor meditatin' in the dormitory," I said. "I feel like it sends a positive message and will somehow affect the consciousness of everybody in the dorm."

"Maybe it will," said Rick.

"Okay, let's give it a try then," I said. "How about in the middle of the week?"

"There's nothing going on Wednesday night," said Michael.

"Okay then. How about Wednesday night?" I said. "Say, about 7:00, a couple of hours before they count?"

"Sounds good to me," said Rick. "I'll talk to some people."

"Me too," said Michael.

"Okay then. We're set for Wednesday at 7:00," I said.

Wednesday night twelve men showed up for our first meditation group. It was a diverse group. Among them was the imam of the Shiite Muslims, the chaplain's clerk, the prisoner who controlled all the gambling inside the prison, and two gang leaders. All were highly respected within the prison and had lots of power and influence, automatically giving our meditation group credibility.

My bed was next to the window and about two feet from the wall. We moved it into the walk space, giving us an area of about four-by-ten feet in which to meditate.

Most brought blankets and pillows. We settled into an irregular circle, face-to-face, knees touching front and sides. After explaining the importance of learning to quiet the mind by focusing on the breath, I led the group in a popular relaxation exercise that lasted about five minutes. Rick spoke for a few minutes about the benefits of meditation, then we began our inward journey.

Just a few minutes into our meditation, a wrestling match took place a couple of beds away. Then a domino slammed a steel table, sounding like a high-powered rifle, making me jump and sending a tingling sensation from the top of my head to my feet. I got lost in the sounds and sensations and my thoughts. Then I remembered to forget.

I returned to my breath. Breathing in. Breathing out. I visualized each man's face and position in our circle. In and out, I saw each bathed in a golden light. I felt myself sinking deeper and deeper, touching the silence within. The basketball game

that had been blaring on the television when we first sat down had now faded to an unintelligible murmur. Someone yelled, and the sound seemed to burst forth from the mouth of a tunnel miles away.

In and out. Again I let it all go. Deeper and deeper, the silence now comforting, the group's combined energy electrifying.

The alarm on my wristwatch beeped; the world was calling. Twenty-five minutes had passed. I opened my eyes and saw tranquility shining on most faces. A few were smiling. The dorm seemed much quieter. Those prisoners standing nearby our group now whispered, showing a new respect. The men in the group sat quietly for a moment, just looking at each other. Then as if on cue several started talking, describing their experience. Others quietly gathered their pillows and blankets, excused themselves, and left the circle.

Jacqueline's amazing intelligence, courage, and compassion challenged and invigorated me, giving me hope. We wrote two or three letters a week for the next few months, and mail call became one of the most important parts of my day.

I found out that Jacqueline was two years younger than me, college educated, and had been a professional musician and singer before becoming a registered nurse. In my last letter I had asked her to send me a photo and also if she would be willing to come visit in the future. Anxiously, I awaited her reply.

Her reply arrived a week later. When I opened the letter, a black-and-white photo fell out. It was of a beautiful Middle Eastern woman with long, curly black hair. She was strumming a guitar and singing. Her head thrown back, she had a joyous smile on her face. Jacqueline said in her letter that she was willing to come visit.

310

I couldn't believe my good fortune. I remembered the doghouse and the gold nugget dream. I was finally having some of the good experiences I'd seen others having.

When I walked through the doorway that led to Donaldson's visiting area, I recognized Jacqueline immediately. She was sitting at a small square table, looking around the large room, her hands peacefully folded. I walked over. She stood.

"I'm Troy," I said.

"Jacqueline," she responded. "It's nice to see you in person."

We embraced, then sat down facing each other. "Thank you for coming," I said.

"I'm glad to finally meet you face-to-face."

"Did you have any trouble finding the prison?" I asked, slightly nervous.

"No, your directions were easy to follow."

After talking a short while, we meditated using a technique Jacqueline suggested.

About twenty minutes later we opened our eyes at almost the same time. Jacqueline's eyes shined with a deep calm. I felt peaceful.

"In one of your letters, you wrote about the need for prison reform in this country. Tell me more," said Jacqueline.

"There's not only a need for prison reform but also sentencing reform. The problem began in the early eighties when America gave up tryin' to rehabilitate prisoners and instead encouraged states to pass habitual offender laws," I said. "At the same time, funding for the mentally ill was cut, leaving them with no place to go for treatment. Thousands ended up in state and federal prisons.

"Prisoners sentenced under the new 'three strikes laws' were sentenced to life—and even life without parole—for stealing as

little as a carton of cigarettes. I know, because I've talked to those men, have read their paperwork.

"Prisons filled to overflowing; thousands came in, but few got out. More prisons were built. And these prisons were usually located in depressed and rural counties where unemployment was high. The prisons produced jobs for the locals and created spin-off businesses. The building and maintenance of prisons became big business and everybody, from construction workers to senators, rushed to get a piece of the pie."

"When I was driving out here, I wondered why they had built Donaldson in West Jefferson County. I knew that this county had one of the highest rates of unemployment in Alabama and suffered extreme poverty, because I used to come out here to treat patients when I worked as a hospice nurse," said Jacqueline.

"Well, you can believe that Donaldson prison has had an impact on this county's economy," I said. "Did you know that because of the habitual offender laws, Donaldson has the highest percentage of inmates serving life without parole in the state? Almost 30 percent. Plus, Donaldson has the largest population of mentally ill prisoners in the state. It's no wonder that we have more incidents of violence than any other prison. There are almost no self-help programs—only one that I know of and it's taught by an inmate, my friend Rick Smith."

"You told me about that course in one of your letters. Transactional Analysis, isn't it?"

"Yes, and my friend is a great teacher. I doubt anyone in the free world could do as good, but still there should be more programs to help those who want help. As it stands now, many will leave prison just as ignorant and perhaps more violent than when they arrived. Most will reoffend, only adding to the overcrowding."

"That's sad," said Jacqueline.

"It is. And, of course, overcrowding causes an increase in violence as more prisoners compete for fewer resources. And the administration, rather than push for reform, tries to stop the increase in violence with violence. They've created these paramilitary squads that are freely allowed to abuse, torture, and terrorize prisoners. Treat a dog like that and you won't stop it from bitin'; it'll only get more vicious. Education and discipline, that's the answer," I said.

"I agree," said Jacqueline. "Trying to stop violence with violence is never the answer. I believe that Gandhi once said, 'An eye for an eye only makes the whole world blind.'"

"I remember readin' that," I said. "But look, I've talked enough about what's wrong in my world. Tell me about what's goin' on in yours."

"It pales by comparison," said Jacqueline.

"Well, it's relative," I said. "What's important to you *is* important."

I was amazed when Jacqueline told me about some of the community activities in which she worked as a volunteer, and I wanted to ask her *why* she volunteered but didn't want to appear callous or ignorant. Then she told me herself. "As you know, I was raised a Catholic and have always believed that it was my duty to serve others, especially the poor."

I thought of some of the volunteers that came to Donaldson and wondered if they felt the same.

Regarding that first visit, years later Jacqueline wrote, "You were an artist, and I wrote music. You considered yourself a kind of New Age Buddhist, and I considered myself a Catholic, even though I went to this little off-the-grid church. You were searching for a deeper relationship with the Divine or whatever you called God. Okay, I bit. After the stream of egregious idiots I had dealt with in what passed for the 'free world,' let's see what

you got. Could you call me? Guess so. (Nice voice, friendly and masculine. Charming drawl. Quick on the uptake. Pleasantly goofy. That was a plus.) Would I possibly come visit you, you asked.

"Hmmm …

"Even though I was forty-four and had been on my own for years, I told my mother that I was going to a special yoga class at a nearby state park for about five hours. I just couldn't see telling an eighty-four-year-old Middle Eastern mother who worried for a living, especially about her beloved daughter and grandson, that I was visiting a man in the most maximum-security prison in the state and that we were going to talk about God.

"Visiting a prison in the greatest country on earth is an enlightening experience most people could care less about. Lots of things should be said, very specific things. But after visiting state prisons regularly for over two decades now, I can make it excruciatingly simple: State Departments of Corrections in the USA, reflective of our general population, are too intellectually lazy to put much thought into rehabilitating the psychologically wounded; they would just rather endlessly punish and abuse them. In this way, they are more like Satan than Jesus.

"Most people in prison are not narcissistic sociopaths. They may have serious behavioral problems for one reason or another—childhood neglect or abuse ('no raising,' as my father would say) or maybe an addiction that's against the law (not unlike sex, food, and alcohol). Maybe they got into a bad crowd in their adolescence because they were trying to survive and made a fatal mistake. Maybe they're mentally ill.

"Many have absolutely no violence in their history. Yet they're subjected to daily abuse by violent inmates and prison guards. They are not given adequate health care or decent food. They aren't given a chance to earn even $.25 an hour for their

prison jobs and therefore are unable to build the savings that will give them a chance at survival when released. (The prison gives them $10 and a bus ticket.)

"Old prisoners are forgotten and left to die in filth pits, and we call it justice. We consider ourselves self-righteous in comparison, like the Pharisee and the Publican. We are complacent about all this. And we probably call ourselves Christian.

"Which is why the man I was about to meet was so extraordinary. He had hit a brick wall the last time he had been sent to the hole, wondering why in the hell his life was so hard, why he never got a break. Always the maximum punishment for the smallest infractions.

"Then, in the hole he had a symbolic dream. In that dream he realized that the reason the basket that represented his life contained only rocks was because that was all he had put into it. Yet he wanted gold in that basket instead. So the next morning he decided to try a secret experiment without telling anyone his intentions: he began to treat everyone with kindness, patience, and respect—guards and inmates, no matter how they treated him. Slowly his life began to change but he continued looking for gold to put in his basket.

"Troy told me that he had done everything that he could think of to get close to God. He said that he meditated twice a day and tried to give back patience and kindness for abuse, except when it was dangerous to do so; he said that some in prison see kindness as weakness and will try to take advantage. He told me that he read books on metaphysics and spirituality every day but still felt that something was missing. He said that he wasn't as close to God as he wanted to be, then asked what I did to get closer to God.

"I told him that as a Catholic, the way I get close to God is service to the poor. And that I didn't know any poorer population than the one he had right in front of him."

Chapter 36

Our weekly meditation group continued to meet every Wednesday night at 7:00, and once, after meditation, Rick again suggested that we try to find a private place for our weekly group. Most liked the idea and I wasn't opposed to it, although I still didn't mind meditating openly in the crowded dormitory.

"I'll talk to the psychologist," said Rick, "see if we can use the therapy room once a week."

The next day Rick said, "I talked to Dr. Cavanaugh and he liked the idea of a meditation group but said that we'd have to come up with a self-help course that included meditation before he could let us use the therapy room."

When Rick brought me the news, I said matter-of-factly, "Well, I guess we'll just have to find a self-help course that includes meditation." Then I gave the idea no more thought.

The next day, while working in the library, the officer there handed me a box of books. "These were sent to us from the Department of Corrections in Montgomery," he said. "See what they are, catalog them, and put them on the shelf."

Inside the box I found twenty paperback books entitled *Houses of Healing: A Prisoner's Guide to Inner Power and Freedom*. I read the introduction. It was a course of study in emotional awareness/emotional healing, with sections on forgiveness, anger, stress management, and so much more.

I read that the course was currently being taught in Massachusetts prisons by the author, Robin Casarjian, along with several volunteers of her Lionheart Foundation, and that it was a twelve-week course. But what I found really interesting was that each session began with a short period of meditation. I couldn't believe that without even trying, I had found a self-help course that taught meditation.

This discovery was momentous, but I wouldn't know until years later that I had discovered a course that would help thousands of prisoners reach a new level of understanding and would help me personally heal persistent pockets of pain lingering since childhood. I had also discovered a course that would teach me the value of service to others.

That night I went to bed, amazed and satisfied—amazed that the universe had heard Donaldson's cry for help, and satisfied that I was continually being enriched in ways that I never could have imagined. I was indeed replacing rocks with gold.

The next day I dropped by Dr. Cavanaugh's office, handed him the *Houses of Healing* book, and explained how I had found it. He agreed to read through the book and give me his opinion.

The following day the psychologist told me that he thought *Houses of Healing* was a good course of study and asked who would facilitate the course. I thought about it for a moment, then told him that since the course was twelve weekly sessions and there were twelve in our group, it only seemed natural that each man should have the opportunity to facilitate a lesson. He thought that a good idea and agreed to sit in on our classes.

When I got back to the library, I wrote Robin Casarjian, the author of *Houses of Healing,* and told her about our weekly meditation group, how I had found her book, and that we intended to facilitate her course at Donaldson.

Two weeks later I received a gracious letter from her. She told me that she was sending me, free of charge, a training manual and cassette tapes. We scheduled the first Houses of Healing class for the first week in July 1995.

Jacqueline was all that I desired in a mate, but when she didn't come back to see me until six weeks after our first visit, I began to fear that somehow I had scared her off.

Again, years later here's what she wrote: "'What did I do to scare you off?' you asked, incredulous that I wasn't coming back the very next week! 'Are you kidding?' I thought. Let me count the ways. First of all, you were attractive to me and that's always unsettling, more so considering my recent history. Besides your physicality and your spiritual search, which you expressed so simply and directly (I wasn't concerned with being duped in that regard; I knew your sincerity would reveal itself in time. You would either put your life behind your words—or not. I was prepared to wait), you radiated an easy confidence, with a warm wit that was disarming. Unless you're a master charlatan, that kind of self-assurance and lightheartedness seemed uncharacteristic for someone in your situation. And you had a sentence of life without parole. I still remember the moment you told me. We were outside on the patio attached to the visiting room. My heart went thud on the concrete.

"A nonviolent victim of the 'three strikes laws' of the 1980s, you shared the same fate of serial murderers and rapists and the guy you told me about whose third felony was to steal a $50 bicycle. And yet the crime rate had not decreased whatsoever. Brilliant.

"'Don't worry,' you assured me. 'Alabama's got to change the law soon. The prisons are overcrowding and they can't afford to keep us forever. I'm just lucky not to have violence in my history, in or out of prison. The nonviolent will be first to go. Three to five years tops and I'll be out of here.'

"Made sense, but making sense can be dangerous in Alabama. Don't expect the general population to always be willing to reason. They're too beaten down and fearful. Behold our politicians. Among a veritable smorgasbord of

ultraconservative policies, they haven't raised taxes in forever, yet everyone wonders why our infrastructure is crumbling, our teachers have impossible jobs, and our health-care system is a sham. And by the way, we expect people to be able to live on nothing.

"Now, I'm an Alabamian by birth. Born and bred. Love my state. It's beautiful. In some ways it's ahead by being behind. (We still have a lot of undeveloped land, praise the Lord!) The language is colorful, the musical heritage rich, and the people are salt of the earth. So I was convinced the laws would easily change.

"And therein lay our struggle. In years to come, I would give to you more than had ever been given to you before and much more than I imagined I could because your actions proved to merit every good gift. I would fight for you with all the passion of a heart opened bare by love because your courage and grace came to own me. And I would tell any other man with whom I came into contact that I would never desert you, whatever our relationship would be, because you deserved something you'd never had and wanted desperately—a family that stuck with you to the death. I'd had it. I could give it. I willed myself to give it.

"But at that moment, I was honestly prepared to face the possibility of living the rest of my life alone. For that reason, part of my heart held back. Your heart, however, was on a mission to survive."

Chapter 37

After leaving the dormitory for the therapy room, a guard stopped me at the gate. "Stay behind the fence," he told me. "The south side's temporarily locked down." He didn't explain why but I soon understood when, a few minutes later, two guards escorted a pale middle-aged man, bound in handcuffs, a belly chain, and leg-irons, past.

"Man, look at how pale that dude is. Looks like a vampire," said a prisoner to the man standing next to him. "One thing's for sure," he continued, "they ain't gettin' much sunshine up there on death row."

"His due date's close," said another. "They're takin' him to Holman to get his fry on."

"Holman?"

"Yeah, that's where the electric chair is; Yellow Mama, they call it."

"Poor son of a bitch," said the first prisoner.

"He's probably ready to go and get it over with," said the second.

We stood at the gate and silently watched the condemned man shuffle to the back gate where he was locked inside a white prison van for the drive south to meet his fate.

The guard then flung open the gate. "South side's open!" he yelled.

I walked through, then up the hall to the therapy room.

It was agreed that each member of our meditation group would facilitate one of the twelve-week lessons in the course Houses of Healing. I had agreed to facilitate the first lesson, along with a short introduction. I was nervous, having had little experience in public speaking and none facilitating a self-help

course, but I was prepared, having read the entire book and training manual.

Standing behind a short podium, I looked at my fellow prisoners and the psychologist, sitting in a semicircle of chairs. Nervously shuffling my notes, I took a deep breath and said, "Welcome to the course Houses of Healing. I hope you've all read the introduction and the material in the first lesson. If you have, you'll know that Houses of Healing is not just a course in emotional awareness and emotional healing but so much more.

"What do the words 'emotional awareness' mean? I must admit that when I first read them, I had no idea. Can anyone tell me?" I looked around.

Omar Rahman, leader of the Shiite Muslims, raised his hand. "Seems to me that 'emotional awareness' just means being aware of how you're feeling," said Omar.

"It's straightforward and simple," I said. "When you're emotionally aware, you're aware of your emotions. You're emotionally literate. We know that when someone is literate, that means they have learned to read and write. So when a person is emotionally literate, that means they've learned to read their emotions.

"What is the advantage of learning to read your emotions?" I asked.

Michael NiCastro raised his hand. "Well, according to what I've read so far, when we learn to read our emotions or identify our feelings, then we're better able to express and manage them."

"Exactly," I said. "And this leads to better impulse control and increases our self-awareness and self-understanding. If we don't learn self-control, then the people and events around us will control us and we will be little more than puppets controlled by people and events and our own impulses and passions.

"Houses of Healing will not only teach you how to recognize and manage your feelings but will help you discover who you really are. One of the biggest problems we have in the world today is that of mistaken identity. Most of us don't know who we really are and certainly haven't discovered our true purpose in life.

"As you all know, one of the tools we'll be using in this course is meditation. I know that all of you are familiar with meditation, but some people, when they hear the word 'meditation,' get an image of a man with a foot-long beard sitting in a mountain cave, staring into space twenty-four hours a day. Some people believe that meditation is against their religion, although all major religions have some form of meditation. Some believe that it's a mystical practice connected with devil worship. Actually, it's none of these.

"Meditation is simply a way of learning to connect with what Houses of Healing calls the 'larger self.' And we'll talk more about the 'larger self' in a moment.

"As you know, you don't need to associate with any religious cult or become a mystic to meditate. If you're an atheist or a Baptist, you can benefit from meditation. I've read that some call meditation simply a form of self-hypnosis and I can understand why." I glanced at the psychologist who, just a week earlier, had expressed that same belief.

"But, according to Jack Kornfield, a meditation teacher and author with a PhD in clinical psychology, meditation is not self-hypnosis but de-hypnosis in that the techniques are mental disciplines that allow you to calm, focus, and examine the mind. It's a deconditioning process of slowing down and observing our usually very active thoughts, perceptions, reactions, and feelings—a letting go of our desires, prejudices, conditionings, and instincts. Meditation is practicing being clear and alert."

Rick Smith raised his hand. "So, according to Kornfield, most in society are living in a hypnotic state brought about by their daily activities and lifelong conditioning."

"That's my understanding," I said.

Our first Houses of Healing course went so well that Dr. Cavanaugh asked if I would facilitate another with men from the general population.

To help recruit a new group, he printed a flyer taken from the Houses of Healing training manual and posted it in all the open living areas. The response was good, and in just a couple of weeks we had twenty men signed up. Dr. Cavanaugh again agreed to attend the introductory lesson to help give the course credibility, then after that he left me on my own.

As soon as I stood before my new group of students, I knew that teaching wouldn't be the same as sharing the lessons with our meditation group, who were experienced meditators and open to change. The new class was mostly Black and young and affiliated with one of several gangs thriving at Donaldson. And they weren't in attendance because they wanted to change; they were after a certificate of completion to show to the parole board.

I also knew that I had four strikes against me from the beginning: I was white. I was over forty. I wasn't associated with any gang. And I was a prisoner trying to teach other prisoners.

But I also knew that I had a few things in my favor too. First of all, I had experienced a genuine conversion and I believed in the material in Houses of Healing. Secondly, I came from a background similar to that of many of my students and so could speak honestly about childhood abuse and poverty.

I could also speak about crime and its effect (on the criminal *and* the victim) because I had been an experienced criminal. And I could talk about the need for prison reform because I had been

in some of the worst prisons in America and knew what changes were needed most.

Chapter 38

Most first-time prisoners, after suffering the trauma of arrest, conviction, and sentencing, are malleable when they arrive at prison to begin serving their time. Because they are so easily influenced in the beginning, prisoners need an environment that is peaceful and positive rather than the normally hostile and negative environment most first-timers experience. This doesn't mean an environment that lacks discipline (discipline is necessary for change) but rather an environment that promotes education and self-help instead of ignorance and violence.

When I was arrested for the first time—in 1967 outside Meridian, Mississippi—and taken to the jail in Meridian, I had no idea what to expect. I was totally ignorant of life inside jail or prison. Put in a cell with a negative and sadistic man named Trigger, a man who had already been to prison twice and was headed back again, I was paired with the worst role model a young first-timer could have had. Unfortunately, this happens far too often in America, a place where young people, even those who have broken the law, are still our most cherished resource. Yet with little thought, these first-timers are thrown like lambs to wolves, creating career criminals that become wolves themselves and now prey on a society that spends billions apprehending, convicting, and incarcerating them.

In 1998, when Donaldson's administration initiated two important projects—the development of a therapeutic community (commonly referred to as a drug dorm) and an honor community (a safe environment set aside for prisoners desiring change)—members of our original meditation group rushed in to help. Rick Smith and Omar Rahman agreed to live

in the drug dorm as tutors, while I, along with new Houses of Healing co-facilitator Benjamin Oryang, moved into the honor community to help. There we were privileged to help write the basic rules and regulations governing those living there and to serve as the first inmate council.

We knew that if the honor community was to succeed, those living there would have to be held to a strict set of standards. Not only were they expected to maintain good behavior, but they were also required to work a certain number of hours maintaining the community and attending self-help classes (some taught by free-world volunteers). And those that didn't have a high school diploma were required to attend GED classes.

In exchange for maintaining good behavior and participating in the honor community, residents were assured a safe place to live and given incentives. Many were recommended for a transfer to a lower-level security facility and granted parole when eligible.

The honor community was self-governing, with an inmate council and an oversight committee consisting of the chaplain, the psychologist, and the captain in charge of prison security.

Until I took the course and read the book *Houses of Healing*, particularly the section on healing the inner child, I never realized just how much the trauma I had suffered as a child had influenced my adult life. Following the advice in *Houses of Healing*, I wrote a series of letters to and about my inner child, particularly reliving my early life in Trade Alley. I shared those letters with Robin Casarjian, who shared them with Houses of Healing volunteer, author, therapist, and cultural anthropologist Dr. Jenny Phillips. Dr. Phillips then wrote me a letter, the beginning of a lifelong correspondence and friendship.

I sent her various writings and she wrote back, encouraging me to continue writing. I trusted her when she told me that what I had written had merit. After all, she was a highly educated writer herself and had been exposed to great literature all her life. Her grandfather was Maxwell Perkins, often celebrated as America's greatest editor. He worked at Scribner's in New York in the thirties, helping to shape the careers of Ernest Hemingway, F. Scott Fitzgerald, Thomas Wolfe, and many others.

My father came to visit. I hadn't seen him since 1983 in Tampa. This wasn't his first attempt to visit me in an Alabama prison. He had come to visit me in 1991 at Holman but I didn't get to see him. After arriving by bus from Lake Charles on Friday night, he had checked into a motel only a mile from the prison but never slept in the bed. Instead, he spent the entire night gambling and drinking at a nearby Indian casino. Consequently, the next morning he arrived drunk at the prison and was denied entrance.

But this time, thanks to Jacqueline, who picked him up at his motel in Birmingham and drove him to the prison, he arrived sober if a little shaky. My father hadn't changed much since the last time I'd seen him in Tampa. He was still slim and dressed the same—a Western-style shirt, Levi's, and Western boots. But instead of an artificial eye (he later told me that he had cracked it), he now wore a black eye patch.

Seeing my father after so many years, and now in front of Jacqueline, I felt awkward and embarrassed. My father had always been a quiet man, except when drunk; then he became a braggart and a loudmouth. But now, sober, he was quiet, allowing me to dominate the conversation. Full of enthusiasm, I talked about the classes I was teaching and the books I had

read, trying to impress my father more than Jacqueline (who was well aware of my small accomplishments).

Patiently he listened and didn't say a word until I started talking about a book I'd just read describing the possibility of the existence of alternate dimensions. Then with just one short sentence he brought me back to *this* dimension, triggering past pain.

"Damn, Rickey!" he interrupted. "There ain't no other di-men-shuns!"

All the pain and frustration and suffering I had endured as a child came rushing back and I lashed out as I'd always done. "What the hell do you know!" I yelled. "You're just … ."

Then I remembered what I had been teaching in Houses of Healing about self-control and anger and forgiveness. I stopped, took a deep breath, looked at my father. *Why is he here?* I asked myself. *He's here because he wants what we all want. He wants love and understanding in his increasingly lonely world.* And then I no longer saw my father sitting across from me, but I saw a little boy picking up cigarette butts at the cotton mill in Shelby, a little boy on the playground at school, a patch covering his eye, surrounded by children yelling and taunting, "One-eye! One-eye!"

I hung my head, pondering the staggering amount of pain and humiliation my father must have suffered as a child, and silently I forgave him for anything he may have done to me when I was a child. Quietly I said, "Dad." He looked at me. "Please forgive me. I'm sorry that I lost my temper."

I waited. He didn't respond.

"You're probably right. I just get carried away talking about some of the books I've read. I understand that most are just pure speculation on the part of the authors."

My father still didn't respond, and there was an awkward silence.

Jacqueline broke the silence. "During the drive over here, your father told me about this scooter he has. What did you call it, Mr. Bridges?" Jacqueline turned to my father.

"A Vespa," he said. "It's a Vespa."

"Oh yeah, I've heard of those," I said. "Seen them on TV. How fast does it go?"

The tension between us melted like a bag of ice put in a hot oven. We joked and laughed the rest of the visit, which passed too quickly.

When it was time to go we all stood. My father extended his hand, but I ignored it and stepped toward him. In that short step a deep chasm was crossed. We hugged for the first time ever.

"I love you, Dad," I said. "I hope you'll forgive me for anything I've ever done to hurt you."

"I love you too, Rickey," said my father for the first time. "I know I ain't never done right by you. I hope you'll forgive me too."

I'll always cherish that moment, for it was to be the last time we'd ever see each other. But we corresponded and talked on the phone until he died a few years later of lung disease.

Chapter 39

The beginning of the year 2000 brought many changes. Donaldson prison, after years of being seen in a negative light and thought of as the number one throwaway camp in the state, was beginning to be seen as a positive place to do time and was enjoying state and even national recognition for the programs and numerous self-help courses now available. Donaldson's therapeutic community and honor community had become models for other prisons throughout the state. And a new mental health unit was being built.

I too enjoyed several small successes. Robin Casarjian, *Houses of Healing* author and my friend of several years, came to Donaldson to observe one of my classes and to facilitate the introductory lesson of Houses of Healing in the therapeutic community. An essay I wrote, entitled "Another Gold Nugget" (about the epiphany I had in the doghouse), was published in the best-selling book *Chicken Soup for the Prisoner's Soul,* and I was asked to contribute a few pages to the book *Radical Acts of Love* by Susan Skog. I was featured in the premiere edition of *Prison Living Magazine.*

Dr. Jenny Phillips, along with Robin Casarjian and nationally known artist Loring Coleman, arranged an exhibit of my paintings at the Concord Art Association. I sold several paintings and received a favorable review in the *Boston Globe.*

Years later Jacqueline wrote, "The administration was so impressed to have a national figure like Robin Casarjian come to their little backwater prison that they didn't know what to think. When she arrived, she was taken everywhere but to the Houses of Healing classes taught by Troy. But to her credit, she just flat told them that she had come to Donaldson to watch Troy teach

and if they wouldn't allow her to do that she would turn right around and fly back to Boston. They relented.

"Robin was touched by Troy's teaching methods, unique from the free-world folks that usually taught the course. Earlier, when she had sent Boston therapist and cultural anthropologist Dr. Jenny Phillips to test Troy's students, the data showed that his students had the same results as students taught by professionals; their IQ rose as they learned to identify and manage their emotions. The results were published in the *American Journal of Forensic Psychiatry* and the *American Journal of Forensic Psychology*.

"I was spellbound watching this man go like a house afire. He will tell you to this day that he only accomplished all this because of my continued support and encouragement. But I've never seen anyone else respond to my love and attention that way. It was like, you give him a crumb and he'll bake a cake. A man in the free world might spend $100 to take you out on the town, but Troy would give a hundred hours of his time doing things for others that no one else would care to imagine.

"Troy developed other courses at Donaldson using Houses of Healing principles. A couple of the courses were used statewide as a requirement for inmates trying to qualify for parole (all the while he himself ineligible for parole). He helped write the rules for the honor community, a safe living area created for inmates desiring to change. He painted beautiful murals on the walls so that his fellow prisoners didn't have to focus on the filth in which they had to live.

"I could go on but I digress and, anyway, who would believe it. I wouldn't have, had I not been there. Against my will I was beginning to have serious feelings."

Also in 2000, the Alabama Legislature finally realized that the Habitual Felony Offender Act (in existence almost twenty

332

years) was not working as intended. More and more prisoners were coming into the system and fewer and fewer were getting out, packing Alabama's prisons. As overcrowding increased and prisoners competed for space, violence increased. As violence increased, fewer correctional officers stayed on to risk their lives, resulting in a shortage of officers.

An inmate named Kirby contested the habitual offender law in the Alabama Supreme Court and won, prompting lawmakers to take a closer look. The Kirby bill was passed, an amendment giving sentencing judges the authority to reduce habitual sentences if felons met certain criteria.

This was hopeful news for thousands of prisoners who had been told that they would never get out of prison. With financial help from Jacqueline and friends in Massachusetts and Vermont, I hired a lawyer and filed for a sentence reduction under what was now called the Kirby bill.

Granted a hearing a few months later, I was transported to the Mobile County jail (the same jail that I had tried to escape from twelve years earlier) to await a hearing.

Chapter 40

Even though I met the criteria set forth in the Kirby bill, my motion for a sentence reduction was denied, and after seventy days in the Mobile County jail, I was sent back to Donaldson.

A couple weeks later my father died of lung cancer. Knowing that because of the length of my sentence I wouldn't be allowed to attend his memorial service in Lake Charles, Jacqueline volunteered to go in my place. She drove all the way to Lake Charles, attended my father's memorial service, played the harp and sang, then drove back to Birmingham. Her attendance was one of the most beautiful, self-sacrificing gifts I'd ever been given.

In 2002, after visiting each other for over eight years, Jacqueline and I were married in the prison chapel. It was one of the happiest moments of my life.

Dr. Jenny Phillips, who managed a mental health department at a Massachusetts clinic, and I continued to correspond. She encouraged me to keep writing and sent me books. I encouraged her to try meditation. She did and enjoyed it so much that she took a ten-day course called Vipassana (Insight) Meditation. She sent me a video of a very successful vipassana meditation group in a prison in India and I showed it to my Houses of Healing classes.

For the next two years Dr. Phillips worked tirelessly to get permission from the Alabama Department of Corrections to bring vipassana to Donaldson. She finally succeeded, and for the first time ever a ten-day meditation retreat was held in a maximum security prison in the U.S.

For ten days, twenty of us (several from our original meditation group), along with three free-world meditation

teachers, lived in the prison's gym, where we observed total silence while receiving instruction in the ancient art of vipassana meditation.

Dr. Phillips brought in a film crew and made an award-winning documentary of the experience, entitled *The Dhamma Brothers*. She later wrote two books related to vipassana at Donaldson prison.

In 2005, again with the financial support of devoted friends, Jacqueline and I hired another lawyer and again filed a motion asking for a sentence reduction. I was transported to Mobile for a hearing in Judge Johnston's court. Again I was denied and again I appealed to the Alabama Supreme Court. I was denied there as well.

In 2008 Donaldson got a new warden. His name was Gary Hetzel. It just so happened that the new warden was the same man who, as a young officer at Holman sixteen years earlier, had escorted me to Warden Jones's office during the incident involving the stolen wire cutters.

During Warden Hetzel's first year he created an important and much-needed hospice program to care for Donaldson's terminally ill prisoners. I heard about it and volunteered to be a part of it. Warden Hetzel told me that the reason he had created the program was to ensure that all terminally ill prisoners (and their numbers were increasing) would be allowed to die with dignity, regardless of the nature of their crime.

In a short training program I learned that my job would be primarily that of companion. I would wash the patient, talk to him, feed him, write letters for him, read to him, and, of course, alert the nurses should some medical complications arise.

When I volunteered to work in the hospice program, I had no idea it would become so personal. Two of the terminally ill patients I cared for had been in our original meditation group

and were graduates of the first Houses of Healing class. One had actually been my first teacher at Donaldson—Rick Smith. The other I had known even longer—Omar Rahman, whom I had met when I was in segregation in Holman prison.

Over the years I had worked out with both Rick and Omar, and it was extremely difficult to watch what had been two healthy men only a few short months earlier deteriorate into helpless invalids. And even though both were very frail toward the end, they were also very courageous and seldom complained.

I stayed with the hospice program for about a year and a half, then left to concentrate on developing a prison newsletter for Warden Hetzel and to spend more time writing and painting.

Warden Hetzel assigned me as the institutional artist and allowed me a small storage room to use as a studio/office. Besides creating a newsletter, I was responsible for repainting all the signs throughout the prison as well as numerous murals. I relished the solitude the studio gave me and loved the work. I also continued to teach Houses of Healing classes in the therapy room and now in the honor dorm, plus a class in problem solving. I taught a weekly art class in the newly opened mental health unit.

In 2013 our friend and lawyer J.T. Simonetti spent a great deal of time preparing a brief, again asking for a sentence reduction under the Kirby bill. We were granted a hearing date and thought it prudent to hire a well-known Mobile lawyer, Jackie Brown, to represent us in court. This time I opted not to go to Mobile for the hearing. Instead, Jacqueline, along with Robin Casarjian, who flew down from Boston, went to Mobile to speak on my behalf.

While waiting for the judge's decision, the legislature, claiming that the Kirby bill had clogged up the court system, rescinded the bill, leaving hundreds of habitual offenders in a

hopeless situation. But because I had applied to the court before it was rescinded, I was one of the few allowed one last chance to apply for a sentence reduction. It was all or nothing.

On February 6, 2014, my final hearing was held in Mobile, presided over by Judge Johnston, the same judge that had ruled against me almost ten years earlier. Later Jacqueline told me that Judge Johnston was so impressed with author Robin Casarjian and the fact that even though after being denied a sentence reduction in 2005 I had gone back to Donaldson and accomplished more than ever the past ten years, that on May 13, 2014, he reduced my sentence to life, making me eligible for parole. I couldn't believe it. After twenty-six years with a sentence of life without parole hanging over my head, I now had a chance to be released on parole.

It took another year for the parole board to set a date for a hearing. While waiting, I continued as before.

Jacqueline hired yet another lawyer, this one in Mississippi, to find out if the twenty-seven-year-old detainer against me was still valid. We wanted to take care of it before meeting the parole board. The attorney contacted an assistant D.A. in Sunflower County (where the 1988 escape charges from Parchman would have been filed), and the assistant D.A. sent a letter to the new warden of Donaldson, Cheryl Price. The letter read:

"Regarding: *State of Mississippi vs. Rickey Troy Bridges*

"Dear Ms. Price:

"In reference to the above matter, I understand that your office has a detainer from this office against Mr. Bridges. Please be advised that this office will not exercise that detainer from your jurisdiction and hereby request that such detainer be dismissed.

"Should you have any questions, please contact my office."

We were overjoyed when we got that letter but soon found out that the MDOC wouldn't honor the assistant D.A.'s letter.

We hired yet another Mississippi lawyer, Tim Moore, to find a solution to the problem of the detainer. He was unable to do so.

With no satisfactory solution to the Mississippi detainer, a parole hearing was scheduled in Montgomery for July 30, 2015. Again Robin Casarjian flew down from Boston to attend the hearing with Jacqueline.

Jacqueline wrote of the experience, "We approached Troy's parole hearing without a legitimate prayer. Having frantically tried to resolve the Mississippi detainer problem ever since Troy's life without had been reduced—hiring one lawyer, then another, watching thousands of dollars fly out the door—I had finally met defeat after ten months. It seemed like the more we dug into the process, the louder the faceless cruelty of the opportunistic justice-system machine hissed.

"The first lawyer took $5,000 to get a buddy of his to write a note saying the assistant D.A. in Sunflower County was not interested in prosecuting a nonviolent sixty-seven-year-old man that had served thirty years. Sounded good. We bought it!

"The only problem was that the Mississippi Department of Corrections refused to drop the detainer without a judge's order, or if not, as one official put it, 'Mr. Bridges will finish out his time with us!' Seemed to me that he was frothing at the mouth to have a new soul to torture. Fifteen more years would make him eighty-one when I came to get him, provided both of us were still alive. Over forty years of incarceration for never physically hurting a living soul. I hired yet another Mississippi lawyer.

"The second lawyer, Tim Moore, worked like a demon, first to locate the detainer (Surprise! It came from Forrest County, not Sunflower) and then to try to get someone from the MDOC, or a judge, to work with him. It was an exercise in head banging, but he did honest work and it helped my soul. But we still didn't get the relief we sought.

"The morning I was to drive to Montgomery for the parole hearing, Tim called to ask if there was anything his office could possibly do to help us. I asked if he was a praying man.

"Driving I-65 south from Birmingham to Montgomery at seventy-plus miles an hour while suffering an overwhelming sense of despair was not safe. After experiencing a miraculously sweet victory in Mobile, it was weird to think that after twenty-three years together, all our effort had come to this one hearing.

"The first question the parole board representative asked was, 'What about this detainer in Mississippi?' I reached in my purse and handed him the letter from the Sunflower County assistant district attorney. He read the letter, looked up, and said, 'Well, that takes care of that. Parole granted.'

"The parole board representative also told me that because Troy had been locked up for so many years, he'd have to spend six months in a transition center before being released on parole.

"And so it came to be that the Alabama Board of Pardons and Paroles, which never paroles anyone to a detainer, paroled Troy based on a letter obtained from an assistant D.A. in the wrong county.

"Despite the inconsistencies and the Mississippi Department of Corrections' refusal to recognize the letter, the Alabama Board of Pardons and Paroles gave Troy a chance to one day live free. We thought it a miracle."

Chapter 41

August 2015, a week before Labor Day, I walked through the back gate of Donaldson prison for the last time and got in a white prison van for the two-hour drive to Kilby prison in Montgomery to await assignment to a transition center. Wearing only handcuffs, it was the first time in twenty-eight years that I had been allowed "outside" without handcuffs attached to a locked belly chain and leg-irons. I didn't feel exactly free, but I did feel freer than I had felt in a long time.

Kilby, the oldest prison in the state, is the designated processing center for all male inmates entering prison in Alabama. It is also a stopover for those going to and from court. The last time I had been to Kilby was in 1989, when I was first committed to prison in Alabama. Then, because I had life without, I had lived segregated in a one-man cell for six weeks before being sent to Holman prison to do my time. But now, because my sentence had been reduced to life, I was being sent to live in one of the dormitories in population until space in the transition center was available.

After living in Donaldson for so many years I'd gotten to know most of the older guards, and although we weren't exactly friends there was a level of trust and respect between us. Because of that I'd forgotten how rude, obnoxious, and even cruel some prison guards can be. While being processed into Kilby, I was reminded.

While sitting on a bench in the infirmary waiting for the nurse to take my vital signs, I thought of a question that seemed important at the time. I stood and walked over to a guard sitting near the exit. When I was within a few feet (a normal distance in which to communicate), he suddenly reached out and jabbed the edge of the clipboard he held into my solar plexus, stopping me

340

still, momentarily taking my breath, and shocking me. In all my years in prison I had never had that done to me.

"Stop right there!" shouted the guard. "Don't you ever walk up on me like that again!"

I forgot the question, turned, walked back to the bench, and sat down.

After my examination in the infirmary I was sent to receiving, where I was given a mattress, sheets, a blanket, and directions to my living area. I walked down a long, narrow hall of tile and brick until I came to an area with a large "K" crudely painted over the barred door. The guard inside the cube saw me and pushed a button, causing a grille gate to slide open. I stepped inside, stopped, and looked down. I was standing on broken floor tiles in half an inch of water, the seeping sewerage covering the soles of my shoes. Then I noticed the clamor: the blaring of a television, the shouting, the slamming of dominoes on steel tables, and men wrestling while others yelled encouragements.

The dormitory was long, narrow, and dimly lit, with row after row of double bunks. I found my bunk—a bottom bed near the TV—and flopped my mattress onto it. Immediately I began to make up my bed. While doing so, I glanced around. It appeared that the dormitory would accommodate about two hundred men and was presently three-quarters full with the usual majority, mostly Black men in their twenties and thirties, although I did see a couple of men that appeared to be in their mid-fifties. But I didn't notice anyone as old as me or see anyone familiar.

I wasn't the only one looking around. While I was evaluating the situation, I was being evaluated by more than one pair of eyes, which was normal when entering a new prison. You are watched and measured, most asking the same questions, "Is he weak or strong? Friend or foe?"

The dormitory was without supervision of any kind. The only time a guard entered was to shake down or count. At times, particularly on Friday and Saturday nights, I felt I was sleeping inside a saloon in an 1860s cow town full of cowboys whooping it up after a long cattle drive. From my bed I watched men fight, gamble, smoke drugs (particularly a new menace called Spice), and engage in sex.

It had been a long time since I had lived in such a dirty, dismal, and depressing environment, and I felt genuinely shocked after having lived so many years in Donaldson's clean and well-ordered honor community, where the men may not have been perfect but they were continually trying to improve themselves and their living conditions. The men I saw around me now didn't seem to care about their living conditions or improving themselves. They didn't even know that they should care.

The dorm to which I had been assigned was a transit dorm, and soon I ran into several former Houses of Healing students. For the first time, now in their element, I realized how closely aligned many were with prison gangs, a few even ranking gang members with considerable power and influence. Again Karma favored me. Because of my teacher/student relationship with these men, and perhaps because of my age, I was treated with deference, even respect, and didn't have to endure the testing of younger or even first-time older prisoners. And for that I was thankful.

After a couple of weeks a guard walked into the dormitory one day and told me to report to social services. Immediately I felt a sense of foreboding. I feared that somehow this unusual summons had to do with the Mississippi detainer, and so I took with me a copy of the letter from the Sunflower County district attorney's office.

Inside social services I was shown to the office of the director of classifications. There she told me that Mississippi had lodged a detainer against me. She asked if I'd be willing to sign extradition papers. Of course I said no, then handed her my copy of the letter from Sunflower County. She read it, then handed it back.

"I understand why you thought the detainer had been dropped," she said, "but apparently they've reissued it. Do you still refuse to sign extradition?"

"Yes, I do," I said, then left, returning to my living area.

That night I called Jacqueline and told her what happened.

Unexpectantly, very early the next morning, along with several others waiting to go to the transition center, I was sent to the infirmary to have blood drawn, standard procedure for those leaving prison. I clung to the thin hope that when the group left later that morning for the transition center, I'd be allowed to go with them.

All hope was lost when a short time later a guard entered the dorm and called out the names of those leaving for the transition center. Disappointed, I prepared a space on the floor next to my bed, sat down, and tried to meditate.

A few hours later I was escorted to the warden's office. There the warden, a tall, stern Black woman in her late forties, said, "I have some extradition papers for you to sign."

"Respectfully, Warden," I said, "I'd like to talk to my lawyer before I sign anything."

"Well, you'll either sign these papers or we're gonna take your parole away from you. You may not be aware of it, but Alabama doesn't parole inmates to detainers."

I was silent for a moment. *I'm in a tight spot*, I told myself. *If I don't sign the papers, I'll be stuck in an Alabama prison with a life sentence, and every time I go up for parole I'll be denied because of the*

Mississippi detainer. It'll be the same as having a life without parole again. I made a tough decision.

"All right, Warden, I'll sign, but only if I get to keep my parole status in Alabama. That way, hopefully, I can go back to Mississippi, get this matter cleared up, and then come back to Alabama a free man on parole." And what I didn't say but thought was, *If I sign, there's also the possibility that Mississippi won't come and get me.*

The warden agreed and I signed the extradition papers. Afterward, I returned to the dorm, lay down on my bunk, and thought about my predicament. I knew that Mississippi had thirty working days in which to come and get me or Alabama would have to release me. I also knew that all I could do now was count the days and hang on to another very thin hope.

I telephoned Jacqueline and gave her the news. We waited.

Chapter 42

October 12, 2015

Lying on my bunk in the noisy dormitory, I inserted earplugs, adjusted my sleeping mask, rolled over, and tried to sleep. But my thoughts had their own agenda and they created their own noise, causing me to toss and turn and remind myself, *Tomorrow's the deadline. It's Day Thirty. I'll either be released on parole or Mississippi will come get me to serve another fifteen years. Don't think about it. Just relax. Go to sleep and just get the day over with.*

Finally, I fell asleep, only to be awakened a few hours later by a disturbing dream that I tried to remember but couldn't. Frustrated, I sat up and looked at my watch. It was 3:10 A.M. *May as well get up*, I told myself. *If Mississippi's comin', they'll probably be early, around 4:00 or 5:00.*

After making a cup of coffee, I sat on my bunk and glanced at my watch every few minutes, conflicted. I wanted time to speed up so that I could quickly learn my fate, and at the same time I wanted it to slow down, afraid of what I might learn.

I felt a tiny spark of hope when Mississippi didn't show up at 5:00, and when they didn't show up at 6:00 that tiny spark flamed. At 7:00 hope blazed inside, and I allowed myself to dream of freedom after almost thirty years in prison. I imagined how happy my wife and friends would be after working so hard for so long to help me gain my freedom.

At 7:15 a guard entered the dorm. He stood and looked around, then headed toward my bed. *This has to be good news. Surely Mississippi won't show up this late*, I told myself.

"Bridges?" asked the guard.

"Yeah, I'm Bridges," I said.

"Pack up and go to receiving."

"Am I being released?"

"I don't know," said the guard. "They don't tell me nothin'—just to pack you up and take you to receiving."

In receiving, I was directed to a holding cell with benches all around. I glanced at my watch. It was 7:40. I thought of my wife, who had sent me the watch six years earlier, and recalled last night's telephone conversation.

We had talked about our immediate plans should I be released in the morning but had deliberately ignored the possibility that Mississippi might try to extradite me.

Then, right before we hung up, I said, "Look, I don't want to be negative—you know how much I believe in positive thinkin'—but I feel like I have to say something about Mississippi. If they do show up tomorrow, and I don't think they will, but if they do, don't worry about me. I know you'll be disappointed. I will too. But don't worry about me. I'll be okay and I'll stay strong and do what I have to do. We'll figure it out. Always have."

At 8:05 two guards dressed in black cargo pants, black shirts, and boots and gloves entered receiving. When they walked past where I sat and I saw the Mississippi Department of Corrections seal on the back of their shirts, my heart sank.

My greatest fear realized, I had no further doubt about my future. Fear quickly turned to anger. *Dammit,* I told myself. *Well, at least I can quit foolin' myself! Fifteen more years in prison! How in the hell am I gonna make fifteen more years! And what about my wife? What about her! This is gonna be harder on her than on me.*

I remembered the last words I spoke to my wife and asked myself, *Am I being strong like I promised her I would be? Or am I acting like a spoiled child? This is nothing more than karma. Why can't I show real strength like the Indian leader Gandhi? What was it he said to his wife when the British came to take him back to prison? "I've been on many journeys. This is just another journey."*

Now, that's real strength, a strength that comes from a place few people ever reach, and I'm no exception. I'll never reach that place. I'm no one special. I'm not enlightened like Gandhi. I'm just a convicted bank robber that escaped from a Mississippi prison twenty-eight years ago and now has to pay for it.

I watched closely as the two Mississippi guards conferred with the Alabama guard. When the three turned and looked in my direction, my stomach rolled.

"Bridges!" shouted the Alabama guard. "Over here! Bring all your personal property!"

I took a deep breath, picked up my laundry bag, and walked toward the three guards. I reminded myself how important it was to maintain self-control, no matter what happened. *I may not be Gandhi,* I told myself, *but I think I can at least be polite, even if I don't feel like it.*

When I got to the counter where they all stood, I said in a pleasant voice, "Well, I guess you guys are here from Mississippi to get *me.*"

"Put all your shit on the counter," said the younger of the two guards. It was obvious he wasn't buying what I was trying to sell.

After I had placed everything on the counter, the older of the two guards, who looked like the late singer James Brown, said, "All you can take with you is a Bible and your legal material."

I couldn't believe what I'd just heard. "Well, what about all my hygiene stuff? You know—toothbrush, toothpaste, a razor, deodorant, soap, stuff like that?"

"Just a Bible and legal material, that's all. Just like when you went to county jail."

"It's been a long time since I went to a county jail, but last I remember I could have everything on this counter."

"Times change. Now it's just a Bible and legal material."

347

I looked at the small mountain of my personal possessions on the counter: soap, shampoo, deodorant, toothpaste, toothbrush, dental floss, two knit caps, radio, headphones, batteries, shower shoes, thermal underwear, boxers, t-shirts, writing paper, envelopes, stamps, pens, pencils, paper, peanut butter, cereal, coffee, tea, mixed nuts, crackers, noodles, and more. I watched the younger guard sweep it all into a large trash barrel, leaving only a few books and an expandable legal file nine by twelve inches and at least four inches thick. Inside were a few photos and legal letters and my most valuable possession: a daily journal and a four-hundred-page handwritten manuscript that I'd been working on for years.

Hoping to slip the journal and manuscript past as legal documents, I pushed the heavy file forward, "Legal material," I lied.

The two guards pounced on the expandable file like hungry wolves that now had something they could finally sink their teeth into.

The older grabbed the legal letters, while the younger grabbed the journal and manuscript. After reading the legal letters, the older guard said, "You can't have these. They don't have nothin' to do with Mississippi; this is all Alabama stuff."

"Of course it is," I said. "I've been in prison in Alabama twenty-eight years. But it's still legal material."

The guard paused for a moment, then said, "Tell you what, you can either have the letters or the envelopes, but you can't have both." He smiled. "Your choice."

I paused to consider. "I'll take the letters," I said.

"Now, that's a good choice," he said in a parent-to-child tone of voice.

Meanwhile, the younger guard, who hadn't even been born when I came to prison, had been quietly reading my manuscript. He looked up.

"This ain't legal material. This is some kinda book."

"Well, thank you," I said.

"It's nothin' but bullshit! You think you're so smart! I'll tell you what, Slick, you can't have it."

He pushed the manuscript and daily journal to the far side of the counter. Then, as if afraid that I might lunge across the counter for it, he picked it up, turned, then purposely walked around the counter and dumped it all in the large trash barrel.

"Well, so much for my first critical review," I said, determined to make light of one of the most painful experiences in my life. The guard didn't say a word; he just stared at me, the fire of hatred in his eyes.

I picked up the self-help book *Houses of Healing*. "What about *this* book?" I asked the older, more patient guard. "I don't have a Bible."

"No," he said.

I picked up the book *We're All Doing Time*. "How about this one? It's kinda like a Bible for prisoners."

"If it's not a real Bible, you can't have it," said the older guard.

When I picked up a booklet on meditation, the younger guard snatched it out of my hands and threw it at the trash barrel.

"Don't you get it! You must be retarded! A *Bible* and *legal material*—that's all!"

I ignored him and picked up the only thing left on the counter: a frayed, brown corduroy eyeglass case that I'd had for ten years.

"Can I at least have my reading glasses?" I asked the older guard.

"You can have the glasses but not the case," he said.

"Thanks."

I smiled at the younger guard, enjoying my small victory.

"Okay, let's go to the shower area," said the older guard. "We gotta shake you down."

When I turned, the younger guard noticed my watch for the first time. "You can't have that watch," he said, reaching out his hand.

I unbuckled the watch, but instead of handing it to him I turned to a nearby trustee sweeping the floor.

"Hey, you want a watch?"

"Well, sure," he said, startled by the unexpected gift.

"Enjoy it," I said. "It's a good watch."

"Let's go," said the younger guard, shoving me.

In the shower area, I stripped naked and was carefully searched. I was then handed a pair of dark-blue work pants and a green polo shirt. I put on the free-world clothes, the first I'd worn in decades, then sat down on a bench. When I reached for my socks and shoes, the younger guard blocked me with his body and used his foot to push my socks and shoes out of reach.

"No socks. No shoes," he said.

"You gotta be jokin'!" I said. "You expect me to go barefoot?"

"Do I look like I'm jokin', smart-ass? No socks! No shoes! Now, get down on your knees so I can put these leg-irons on you."

I did as I was told and the guard fastened leg-irons on my bare ankles.

"Stand up!" he said.

He then wrapped a chain around my waist and secured it with a small padlock. To the belly chain he attached handcuffs, then tightened the cuffs onto my wrists until they were uncomfortable.

"These cuffs are too tight," I complained.

"Get used to 'em," said the younger guard.

The older guard in front and the younger behind, we stepped outside and slowly moved toward the back gate, a hundred yards away.

The blacktop, running from the rear of receiving to the back gate, was covered in loose gravel and was wet and muddy from a recent rain. With every step, the leg-irons dug into my ankles and the gravel into the bottom of my feet. Whenever I paused, the younger guard shoved me with his elbow, causing me to stumble.

By the time we reached a small gatehouse directly under the gun tower, I could barely walk. The Alabama guard in charge of the gatehouse looked at my muddy feet and asked, "What happened to his shoes?"

"I took 'em," said the younger guard. "That's the way we do it in Mississippi."

"Well, that may be the way you do it in Mississippi, but *this is Alabama*, and when a man leaves an Alabama prison, he leaves wearing shoes." He turned to a nearby trustee. "Go get this man some shoes."

I tried not to smile but silently cheered. *All right, Alabama!*

When the trustee returned with an old pair of brogans, the younger guard took his anger out on me.

"Face the wall!" he yelled. "And get on your knees!"

I did as told and the guard removed the leg-irons. He then threw the boots at me. "Now, put these fuckin' boots on!"

I put on the boots, then without being told got on my knees again and faced the wall. The guard reattached the leg-irons.

"Get your ass up!" shouted the younger guard. I stood. "Don't look at me! Put your nose on that wall and don't move an inch!" He then got real close and spoke quietly into my ear. "We can make this trip easy or tough, it's up to you."

"I don't want no problem," I mumbled to the wall.

"Damn straight you don't!" he now yelled. "Not with me you don't! Don't say another word between here and Mississippi or I'm gonna stop the van and stomp a mudhole in your ass! Got it?"

I didn't answer, but I *did* get it. Our battle of wits had escalated; we were now moving closer to a physical confrontation and I certainly didn't want any part of it. It was time to surrender.

For the next ten minutes I quietly stood facing the wall while the guards completed their paperwork. I was then escorted through the back gate and into a large white van sitting in the parking lot.

Five minutes into our drive, the older guard pulled onto the shoulder and stopped. The younger guard got out and opened the sliding side door. He stuck his head inside. I thought, *Is this where I get a mudhole stomped in my ass?*

"Take them fuckin' boots off and give 'em here."

Relieved, I quietly removed the brogans and slid them toward the guard. He grabbed them, turned, and threw them one at a time into a gully that ran alongside the highway.

We continued down a winding, two-lane blacktop, passing patches of thick woods, farms, and beautifully cultivated fields. I stared out the window but refused to see the beauty. I was as sad as I'd ever been in my life.

Eventually we came to a small town, and just on the other side of the courthouse square we stopped at a fast food restaurant. The younger guard went inside while the older stayed in the van with me. Ten minutes later, the guard returned with two large bags of food. He gave one to the older guard and kept one for himself.

The smell was sweet torture, and I immediately started salivating like one of Pavlov's dogs. It was then I realized that I was not only hungry but thirsty, and that I also needed to use

the restroom. Afraid to say anything, I stared out the window and pretended that two guards weren't enjoying a picnic just a few feet away.

They pretended that I didn't exist too.

"How's your chicken?" asked the younger guard.

"Man, it's good," said the older, smacking his lips. "Nice and crispy, just the way I like it. How's your burger?"

"It's good, but I shoulda got fries instead of onion rings. This fried apple pie's good, though. Shoulda got two of 'em."

When they finished eating, we hit the road again.

Again I stared out the window, seeing sights I hadn't seen in decades, and again I was unable to appreciate the beauty all around me. I turned away and bitterly asked myself, *Why stare out the window at what you can't have? Looking only leads to dreaming and dreaming to despair. You're just making yourself even more miserable.*

Still, mile after mile I stared out the window, wallowing in self-pity and viewing the world through an ugly, gray filter, so disillusioned and miserable that I felt I was drowning in my own despair.

I remembered my life before prison—the selfish years of poor choices and the moments of instant gratification that had eventually led to my self-destruction.

I remembered the last thirty years in prison, especially the last twenty-five when I had committed to change, taking numerous self-help courses and reading book after book, hoping to improve my life. I remembered twenty-five years of self-reflection and daily meditation.

And yet, even though all that training had taught me what to do, I forgot it all as soon as my first big test came about and reverted to my old ways, lashing out and blaming everyone for the very problems *I* had created.

I knew that the only way that I could save myself from certain self-destruction now was to take responsibility for my present predicament and change my perspective.

Ever since Mississippi showed up this morning, you've played the part of the mistreated prisoner, I told myself. *It's as if your misery was so deep that it hypnotized you into assuming a totally different personality, and that's not who you really are now. That's just a false identity that you've created to help you cope with your anger and disappointment.*

If you've been mistreated by the guards, it's because you've provoked them with your childish behavior, and they've just responded in kind.

You've got to snap out of it! This is a chance to see differently, to respond differently. Change your perspective and you'll change your reality.

I leaned back and closed my eyes. Breathing deeply in and out, I used the hum of the van's tires on the blacktop as my mantra. Soon I was relaxed and totally at peace.

A short while later I opened my eyes and looked out the window. The sun was shining brightly, the sky a beautiful light blue. *This is just another journey,* I thought. *Just another journey.*

A sign flashed by; it read, You Are Leaving Alabama. A moment later, I read another: Welcome to Mississippi. The Magnolia State.

At 12:15 we arrived at Central Mississippi Correctional Facility, the state's processing center for prisoners.

Epilogue

I've spent hundreds of hours reconstructing this manuscript after it was destroyed during my extradition to Mississippi.

In 2000 I wrote an essay, entitled "Another Gold Nugget," describing a life-changing experience I had in 1993 while in solitary confinement. It was published in the popular book *Chicken Soup for the Prisoner's Soul.* I had no idea just how prophetic this paragraph would be: "We often do terrible things, such as commit an unlawful act or treat someone cruelly, and later think we have gotten away with it, that we won't have to suffer the consequences of our actions. It may take fifty years for the effect to catch up with the cause, but be ready, it's coming!"

And it did!

I've now been in prison in Mississippi five years and have ten more to serve. My release date is March 6, 2030.

During the last five years my lawyers have filed two separate motions seeking my release and I've had two hearings, years apart. The judge has denied both. Presently, we're appealing to the Mississippi Supreme Court.

When I first started writing *Spiral,* I blamed my parents' transgressions and weaknesses for the terrible turn my life had taken. But after years of reflection and rewrites, I realized just how minor their infractions were compared to my own major crimes and began to take responsibility.

Still, I continued to ask these questions: Were the lives of my mother and father wasted? Has my own life been wasted? Then one day I came across a comment by author and teacher Marianne Williamson that said there are no wasted lives, there are only lessons that we have chosen not to take advantage of at this time.

It was such an intoxicating idea, one free of guilt or blame and filled with possibilities, not least of all a second chance at life.

If it's true that life is a large classroom where we are assigned certain lessons at birth, then it's also true that we are endowed with free will (but not wisdom) and may later in life choose our own lessons.

And after a life of blame and complaint and dissatisfaction, one spent running and hiding and avoiding, one of the biggest lessons I've learned is the difference between giving up and surrender: When you give up, you're planted where you fall. When you surrender, you grow where you're planted.

—R. Troy Bridges
South Mississippi Correctional Institution
June 2020

R. Troy Bridges has spent over forty years in some of America's most brutal prisons. In 1993, while in an isolation cell, he had an epiphany that led to a complete change in perspective. This revelation was later written as the short story, Another Gold Nugget, and published in the book, Chicken Soup for the Prisoner's Soul.

In 1994, he started a meditation group in the maximum-security prison, Donaldson, and later, with the help and support of the Lionheart Foundation, facilitated a self-help course based on the book, Houses of Healing. Over the next ten years he taught hundreds of prisoners how to meditate.

In 1998, he was interviewed in Susan Skog's book, Radical Acts of Love, and that same year featured in the magazine, Prison Living.

He is an award-winning artist whose work has been favorably reviewed in the Boston Globe. During the twenty-one years he spent in Donaldson Prison, he helped create a faith-based program called the Honor Dorm that became the model for prisons throughout the state of Alabama. He also helped bring to Donaldson a ten-day meditation retreat called Vipassana—the first ever in a maximum security prison in the United States.

His work as an illustrator and artist for the award-winning prison magazine, The Angolite, has recently been included in the newly-created collection of the Smithsonian National Museum of African-American History and Culture in Washington, D.C.

Judged a nonviolent offender on the thirteenth of May, 2014, by Mobile County Court Judge, Joseph S. Johnston, he has been in prison since 1987 and will be released in 2030.

This is his first book.

X

Prologue

After my mother's suicide attempt, she was sent to the state asylum at Morganton. My sisters Dianne, now ten, and Tonda, two, were taken in by relatives, and my father and I moved to Trade Alley.

Trade Alley was made up of eight dilapidated frame duplexes randomly placed in a low-lying area surrounded by hills. Built in the early 1930s, it was an attempt by the town of Shelby, North Carolina, to provide cheap housing for the white poor and served as a buffer between the town's middle class and a small but growing population of Black people in an area called shantytown. Few of Shelby's respectable citizens ever went to Trade Alley unless it was to hire a laborer or to collect a debt. And they almost never went to shantytown unless it was to buy bootlegged whiskey or to arrest someone.

But our family was different. We often went there. I went to shoot marbles in shantytown's dusty alleys, while my mother went to buy bootlegged whiskey and hide from my father. My father went there to search for my mother.

Most of what I knew of my family's history I learned from my mother during her more lucid moments. When we were alone, we talked for hours. And according to her, even the circumstances surrounding my birth involved fraud and deception. It was almost as if at the moment of my birth I had been enrolled in a school for future criminals.

This practice led to the writing of letters to that child and became the basis for this book. I am forever grateful for Robin's friendship over the years. Without her help, I would never have had my prison sentence reduced or have had the courage to write this memoir.

—R.T.B.

Introduction

Written over a twenty-year period, this book is more than just about childhood abuse, true crime, or prison (where I've spent more than forty years); it is also about hope, forgiveness, change, and the power of love to transform.

Once, asked by Ruth Porter, friend, author, publisher, and mentor, how I had been able to remember my past in such detail, I replied that after spending so many years in isolation without access to books or pencils or paper, I discovered I could count my fingers and toes only so many times before I had to face my past, particularly my childhood. Eventually I had to ask myself, "How did I get here?"

Of course, everything written here is not exactly as it happened. How could it be? But it is as truthful as my memory could make it. I have changed most of the names, but I have tried to give an honest account of the brutality and violence and racism that prisoners encounter in their everyday lives. Some of the language is shocking but it is not exaggerated. It's what I hear every day. I could have left it out but I wanted to tell my story truly.

It was also in isolation (after another failed escape attempt) that I discovered meditation. Meditation not only quieted my mind and gave me new insight, but infused my memories with energy, giving them new clarity.

Later, finally released to the general prison population, I started a meditation group that led to the discovery of a course in emotional healing based on the book *Houses of Healing* by teacher and author Robin Casarjian. Participating in this course (and later helping to facilitate it for over ten years) taught me how to use meditation and visualization to help heal the wounded inner child that lives inside many of us and is responsible for many of the harmful choices we make as adults.

Author, age 12, Charleston Harbor, South Carolina

Acknowledgments

Robin Casarjian's course and book *Houses of Healing* lit the fire that became *Spiral*, but Ruth Porter, author, friend, and mentor, fanned the flames that moved this twenty-year project to completion.

I thank my sisters Dianne Beddingfield and Tonda Leger, who have shared many of these childhood experiences and have been the guardians of most of the photos, many of them taken by Dianne, used in this book.

Sita Lozoff of the Human Kindness Foundation and publisher of the book *We're All Doing Time* has been as constant as the North Star and has shone as brightly in my life, always there with material support and words of love, support, and wisdom.

I thank attorney J.T. Simonetti for his encouragement, advice, and friendship.

Most of all I thank my loving wife Jacqueline Dicie, who for twenty-six years has supported me emotionally and financially, often denying her own needs so that I could have the best legal representation available. She has never failed me. Her strength and compassion continue to amaze me. By example she taught me the value of service to others, the importance of family, and how to love unconditionally.

In loving memory of Peggy King and
Jenny Phillips,
whose encouragement and support
made this book possible.

SPIRAL: MURDER, MADNESS, AND MEDITATION
Published in the United States of America

BAR NOTHING BOOKS, LLC
100 State St.
Suite 351, Capitol Plaza, Box 3
Montpelier, VT 05602
802-223-7086
info@barnothingbooks.com
SAN 256-615X

Spiral:
Murder, Madness, and Meditation

R. Troy Bridges

Bar Nothing Books

Foreword

For so much of my life, I lived in fear. What if we run out of money? What if we come up short? What if we don't have enough? Like many people I know, I allowed my inner financial fears to talk me into delaying a life of generosity. One day, when we are debt free, or have plenty extra, or make more money, then I'll start to give bigger.

My internal faithless whispers might have actually won out. There was only one problem: God had a different plan for me. And I suspect he might have a different plan for you too.

The closer I got to God, the more his Word challenged my self-centered, fear-filled view of money and possessions. Many of us are tempted to let money claim the dominant spot in our hearts. When you think about it, money promises what only God can provide. Money promises security, happiness, and significance. If you have enough money, you will be secure, you can buy what you want, and people will admire, love, and respect you. The truth is, only God can provide what money falsely promises to give. That's probably why Jesus said plainly, "You cannot serve both God and Money" (Matt. 6:24; Luke 16:13).

People often say, "You can't out-give God!" As a pastor, I preached this truth many times. After years of talking about it, I decided to actually live it. After many months of praying, the leaders of our church decided to give away everything we could to serve other churches. For absolutely no charge, we'd give our sermons, transcripts, videos, curriculum, and more.

I clearly remember all my reservations. Not only would I be giving away lots of potential personal income, but our giving would cost our church hundreds of thousands of dollars. Could we afford it? Could we sustain it? Would God really provide as we gave?

Looking back, that decision is hands-down the best decision we've made in the history of our church. I never dreamed how much it would help churches, what God would do in my heart, and how God would provide for us with supernatural measures. Who would have thought we could give resources to over ninety thousand churches worldwide—literally millions of free resources? I never dreamed that hundreds of churches would one day use our video teaching to show to their churches every weekend. Most of all, I'm thankful to God that he has provided every resource necessary for us to give away well over fifty million YouVersion Bible apps to people around the world.

Now when I say, "You can't out-give God," I don't just believe it; I've lived it. I know beyond a shadow of a doubt, generosity is not only a Christian virtue, but it is one of the best evidences of the Spirit's transformational work in a person's life. Generosity involves turning away from yourself and toward another person to meet his or her needs. It shows that you've shifted from a mindset of needing to be served to serving others. It demonstrates that you are committed to helping others to the point that you're willing to sacrifice to make that happen.

And as God blesses us, we grow to realize that all his blessings are not for us. As we allow his goodness to flow through us, he will often provide even more for us to give. Instead of raising our standard of living, we can raise our standard of giving. We can live to give. And we can give to live.

That's why I'm so thankful for Stan Toler's amazing book. In it, you will find both inspiration and practical principles for shifting from a self-focused lifestyle to one that is generous and giving. What makes this book really powerful is that it's written by a man who lives by its principles. Stan Toler gives to live. He sacrificially gives his time to serve leaders and gives financially to provide for people and ministries worldwide. Being generous is not something he does. Generous is who he is.

One of the best witnesses a person can give to the truth and reality of the redemption found in Christ is a transformed life. By absorbing and practicing the principles in this book, not only will your life be changed, but you will play a part in others' lives being changed as well.

You give so others can live.

—CRAIG GROESCHEL, founding pastor of Lifechurch.tv
and best-selling author of *It*, *The Christian Atheist*, and *Weird*

Acknowledgements

Special thanks to Don Cady, Kevin Scott, Craig Bubeck, Rachael Stevenson, and the entire WPH team. You have been a delight to partner with on this project. Also, I extend gratitude to my church treasurer Dad, William Aaron Toler (deceased), and to my step-father Jack Hollingsworth, who also served as a church treasurer, for forming and motivating a giving attitude in my life as well as the lives of my minister brothers Terry and Mark. Finally, much appreciation to my friend and brother Larry Wilson for his creative insights and editorial assistance on this project.

Introduction

a new way to live!

In 1978 I heard Dr. Chuck Millhuff preach a message that he titled "Giving Living." The message was life impacting. In fact, I invited Chuck to come and share his message at every church I pastored from that time forward. While this book in no way copies his great message, the title was indeed inspired by the best message on giving that I have ever heard. This book describes a new way of living from what most of us are used to. Simply put, it is a lifestyle of abundance, generosity, and openness to others: We need to give to live.

John Wesley's advice on personal finances has been summed up as: "Earn all you can, save all you can, give all you can."[1] It is great advice, but generosity does not come naturally to most of us. Perhaps the strategy of most Christians today is to "Earn all you can, can all you get, sit on the lid!"

Many good Christians find it difficult to practice generosity. We are trained by the society we live in to be the exact opposite of generous. We are conditioned by an endless stream of marketing and advertising to focus on obtaining all the stuff we can and to amass as much material wealth as we possibly can. The saying "He who dies with the most toys wins" is one that we are all familiar with. That is unfortunate because generosity is the first law of economics in God's kingdom. When we are generous with what we have, we honor God, impact others, and receive a blessing in the process.

In this book, we'll identify some of the major obstacles to developing a giving lifestyle, and you will discover that it is possible to have a complete change of heart in the area of generosity and personal stewardship.

This book will motivate and equip readers to practice a lifestyle of generosity. You will—

* understand the biblical principle of generosity;
* learn to trust God with your personal finances;
* discover practical ways to practice a lifestyle of generosity;
* realize the impact your giving can make upon the world; and
* experience the blessing that comes from giving to others.

God doesn't intend for us to be trapped by the standards of this world; he has given us a new way!

Giving Is More Rewarding Than Consuming

Brethren, join in following my example, and observe those who walk according to the pattern you have in us. For many walk, of whom I often told you, and now tell you even weeping, *that they are* enemies of the cross of Christ, whose end is destruction, whose god is *their* appetite, and *whose* glory is in their shame, who set their minds on earthly things. For our citizenship is in heaven, from which also we eagerly wait for a Savior, the Lord Jesus Christ; who will transform the body of our humble state into conformity with the body of His glory, by the exertion of the power that He has even to subject all things to Himself. (Phil. 3:17–21 NASB)

August H. Francke was a German preacher who, in the latter part of the seventeenth century founded an orphanage to care for the homeless children of Halle. He told of a time when he desperately needed funds to carry on his work and found help from an unexpected source:

In 1698, I sent a ducat (nine shillings and sixpence) to a very poor woman, whom afflictions and trials had awakened to see the importance of her soul. She sent me word "that the ducat had been delivered to her at a time when she much needed it, and that she had intreated the Lord to reward our poor with many ducats." Soon after a benevolent person offered me one single and twelve double ducats; and, on the same day, a friend from Sweden sent me two ducats: these again were immediately followed by five and twenty sent by post from some person unknown; and by a further twenty presented to the charity by an eminent person. About the same time, Prince Lewis of Wirtemburgh died at Eisenach, and bequeathed us five hundred golden ducats, deposited in a bag, and inscribed "For the Hospital at Halle"—I now remembered the prayer of the pious woman who "intreated the Lord to reward our poor with many ducats."[2]

Whether or not we receive such remarkable and indisputable compensation for our generosity, we can be grateful knowing that we have been delivered from the futility of chasing things and given the privilege of meeting others' needs.

Blessing Doesn't Come from Recognition

Charles Spurgeon and his wife would sell the eggs their chickens laid; but they refused to give them away, even to close relatives. As a result, some people thought of the Spurgeon family as greedy and grasping. "They accepted the criticisms without defending themselves, and only after Mrs. Spurgeon died was the full story revealed. All the profits from the sale of their eggs went to support two elderly widows. Because the Spurgeons were unwilling to let their left hand know what their right hand was doing (Matt. 6:3), they endured the attacks in silence."[3]

When our most important priority is not our happiness but the happiness of others, we understand the essence of kingdom living.

I love the story of Samuel Hearne, an eighteenth-century explorer who travelled to the Coppermine River in the Northwest territories of Canada. Hearne tells how a group of natives tricked and "plundered me and my companions of almost every useful article we had, among which was my gun . . . till at last nothing was left but the empty bag, which they permitted me to keep." The next day, Hearne wrote, "as the above ravagers had materially lightened my load, by taking everything from me . . . this part of my journey was the easiest and most pleasant of any I had experienced since my leaving the fort." The devastating loss of Hearne's supplies meant nothing more to him than easing the load.[4]

How we respond to losing some of our resources for God's work depends on whether we are on the move or waiting for our last stand. For Christians on the move, everything is for temporary use; all of our resources are borrowed. We have our minds on heavenly things. We are waiting for a Savior from heaven. That Savior is, of course, Jesus Christ.

Jesus discussed this idea in Luke 12:33 when he said, "Sell your possessions and give to charity; make yourselves money belts which do not wear out, an unfailing treasure in heaven, where no thief comes near nor moth destroys" (NASB). As a citizen of the kingdom, you no longer view your possessions only in terms of how they benefit you, but how they may benefit others.

It's an Exciting Adventure

A man once came to Peter Marshall, former chaplain of the Unites States Senate, with a concern about tithing. "I have a problem," he said. "I have been tithing for some time. It wasn't too bad when I was making $20,000 a year; I could afford to give up $2,000. But now that I am making $500,000, there is no way I can afford to give away $50,000 a year."

Peter Marshall reflected on this wealthy man's dilemma but gave no advice. He simply said, "Yes, sir. I see that you have a problem. I think we ought to pray about it. Is that all right?"

The man agreed, so Dr. Marshall bowed his head and prayed, "Dear Lord, this man has a problem, and I pray that you will help him. Please reduce his salary back to the place where he can afford to tithe."[5]

We may laugh at the wealthy man whom Dr. Marshall so kindly put in his place; but when you think about it, tithing is rather ridiculous. No one in his or her right mind would simply give away $50,000 a year. It doesn't make sense. That's a lot of money, even for someone who is rich. Imagine if this gentleman invested his $50,000 every year instead of giving it to the church. With compound interest, he could retire fifteen years later as a multimillionaire! Asking him to tithe the whole $50,000 per year is actually requiring him to give up more than just that amount, which is significant enough—it's asking him to give up the investment money he could have earned with it too. Is that even fair of God to ask someone to give more than 10 percent?

God's way doesn't always seem best. Sometimes we may wonder if God is a bit too far removed from life here on earth to understand what is realistic for us. God may seem like the CEO of a big company who gives a rousing talk to all the employees about how their hard work and extra hours are making such a difference—without having any idea of what it's like to be a single parent with demanding kids or to have ailing parents who need constant care or to have a second job to pay the bills. He just doesn't know what he's asking. Or God may remind us of parents who told us to be nice to the weird kid—without realizing that meant we would get beat up. They just didn't know what they were asking. Or God may remind us of a spouse who wants to have a big vacation added to the budget without decreasing spending or increasing earnings. He or she just doesn't get it.

Is God's tithing plan a little out of touch—maybe nice in theory, but highly impractical or even impossible?

To answer that question we must have a broader understanding of what God is like; we have to go beyond the question of tithing. We have to ask: Who is God and how does he relate to us?

God certainly is removed from us. We are not even microscopic specks in the vast universe he created. He stands outside of time, beyond the laws of gravity, and without limitation. He is holy, perfect, and almighty. He is too big for us, too mysterious for us, and too holy for us to even look at him: So how are we supposed to draw near to him? And the more apt question is: How he can possibly understand us?

Philip Yancey tells a story about keeping a saltwater aquarium. Management of a marine aquarium, he discovered, was no easy task. He had to run a portable chemical laboratory to monitor the nitrate levels and the ammonia content. He pumped in vitamins, antibiotics, sulfa drugs, and enough enzymes to make a rock grow. He filtered the water through glass fibers and charcoal and exposed it to ultraviolet light.

You would think, in view of all the energy expended on their behalf, that his fish would at least be grateful. Not so. Every time Yancey's shadow loomed above the tank, they dove for cover into the nearest shell. They showed him one emotion only: fear.

Although Yancey opened the lid and dropped in food on a regular schedule, three times a day, they responded to each visit as a sure sign of his designs to torture them. He could not convince them of his true concern. To his fish, Yancey was a deity. He was too large for them, his actions too incomprehensible. His acts of mercy they saw as cruelty; his attempts at healing they viewed as destruction.

Yancey began to see that changing their perceptions would require a form of incarnation. He would have to become a fish and speak to them in a language they could understand.[6]

We're like fish to God. He knows what's best for us, and he loves us. That's why he incarnated himself. He is too big for us to understand or to believe that he understands us, so he came down from heaven in the form of a human being—as a helpless baby—to speak our language. He wants us to trust him, not to scatter like fish in an aquarium when he draws near.

God's command to tithe our income feels like an intrusion— just as Yancey's tank cleaning must have felt like an intrusion to the fish. We may not see how tithing helps us or how not tithing hurts us. It comes down to trust. When God's shadow looms above our aquarium as we're paying our bills and managing our budgets, are we going to hide in a shell or swim joyfully up to the surface with our tithe in hand? Do we trust him enough? "'For I know the plans I have for you,' declares the LORD, 'plans to prosper you and not to harm you, plans to give you hope and a future'" (Jer. 29:11).

It may not make sense to you to give away $50,000 a year, or even $50 a year. But it makes sense to God. And his way really is better than ours. Are you ready to begin the adventure of a lifetime, a life marked by abundance, possibility, and blessing? Your own Give to Live life awaits!

PART 1

God's Secret to a Successful Life

Let's identify the key theological principles that form the foundation for a giving lifestyle—stewardship, trust, blessing, and love. You will discover that God created us to find our greatest joy in loving him and others. This will enable you to make a conceptual change from putting yourself first to putting others first.

What's Mine Is Yours

understanding stewardship

Key Insight
God owns everything and allows you
to manage his wealth.

In the early morning hours of September 8, 1860, a ship called the *Augusta* raced out of control through the tumultuous waters of Lake Michigan. Before the captain could shout out the order, the 129-foot schooner smashed into the side of the crowded passenger steamer, *The Lady Elgin*, which was on its way back to Milwaukee after a night of dinner and dancing in Chicago.

As *The Lady Elgin* foundered seven miles off the coast of Illinois and slowly broke apart, guests from the steamboat chopped off doors and pieces of the deck to float on. Luckily, the water temperature of Lake Michigan in September was at its warmest. It was still frigid,

> Give thanks to the LORD, for he is good; his love endures forever. Who can proclaim the mighty acts of the LORD or fully declare his praise?
> —Psalm 106:1–2

but a virtual hot bath compared to the below freezing temperatures of late fall and winter. An estimated five hundred survivors were afloat on pieces of *The Lady* or treading water as dawn approached.

At daybreak, students from Northwestern University's lifesaving squad gathered on the shore and began to rescue the people out of the water who had floated into the shallows. One brave student, Edward W. Spencer, swam out deep into the waters a total of seventeen times, saving people each time. After his seventeenth trip into the deepest parts of the water, fatigue and delirium set in and he was taken back to the university where he lay sick in bed for several months. Edward Spencer's health revived, and after he graduated from school he moved to California where he died at the age of eighty-one. A local newspaper reported a tragic fact of this story in his obituary—not one of the people he rescued ever visited Edward to thank him. Not one out of seventeen ever showed him gratitude over a sixty-year period.[1]

Ingratitude has plagued the human race since the time of Adam and Eve. Ingratitude toward the salvation of a loving God, offered free of charge via painful sacrifice, seems to be of the worst kind. We are prone to make our needs known. We cry out to God for help, for rescue from the miry pit. But how often do we voice our gratitude? How often do we say, "Thank you"?

In the opening verses of Psalm 106, David offered helpful advice about proper thanksgiving: "Give thanks to the LORD, for he is good; his love endures forever. Who can proclaim the mighty acts of the LORD or fully declare his praise?" (vv. 1–2). In these short stanzas, David gave us the what, why, and wow of giving thanks to the Lord. As we walk through these three facets, open your hearts in honesty before the Lord. Ask the Holy Spirit to measure and weigh your gratitude.

The What: Give Thanks to the Lord

The statement is simple. The command is clear. Give thanks to the Lord. The psalmist offered no alternative option or prerequisite requirements. He did not say to give thanks to the Lord if you feel like it or think you have a good reason. Give thanks to the Lord. This is what you are to do. At all times, in all circumstances. David was taking for granted your reverence for Almighty God. He made this command, this request, on the foundation of a theology that knows that God is the supreme being of the universe and worthy of our unending praise and thanksgiving. David knew that God is the source of all goodness, of all blessings.

David later gave reasons why we should give thanks to the Lord, but I love that he began with the straightforward action of what we are supposed to do as followers of God. And this prompting from David applies to all areas of our lives. We are to praise God for the material blessings and the spiritual ones, the big and the small, the seen and the hidden.

In order to give thanks for these many blessings, though, we must recognize that we are blessed! Many of our prayers include the phrases "bless me," "bless us," or "bless them," and it is good to request the blessings of God. But let us not forget or forget to recognize that we are already blessed beyond our wildest imaginations—and that all these blessings come from God.

As Christians we have been saved by grace through faith, being rescued from eternal death and damnation. We were born with hearts bent away from God and headed down a path that led straight to hell. But God, in his mercy and love, reached down and lifted us from the grip of sin and washed us white as snow. Praise the Lord! Give thanks to the Lord. We are blessed to be more than conquerors when it comes to sickness, disease, and death. Praise the Lord! As Christians we are blessed to be a part of the body of Christ. We are blessed to be in service to a kind and benevolent Master. Give thanks to the Lord!

Many of us who live in the United States are blessed materially. It is a materially wealthy nation. Where do you think our good fortune has come from? The American dream makes it seem as if our wealth comes from our determination, hard work, and free-spirited entrepreneurship (and all these things are good), but God is the true source. He is the one to be praised and thanked.

When you look at the global picture, the wealth of America comes into focus. The wealth of even our poorest neighborhoods becomes evident. Did you know that a "poor" college student making $8,000 a year working in a coffee house is in the seventieth percentile of worldwide wealth? That means that college student is richer than 70 percent of the rest of the world. I know that the cost of living is different and a lot of other factors work in here, but many of us need a global economy lesson.

I would like to bring a bit of caution here on the subject of material blessings. God cares for our needs, just as he cares for the flowers of the field and the birds of the air, but the subject of material blessings can get unclear in a hurry. Some things we consider blessings are actually distractions. The very things we praise God for distract us from serving him, reading his Word, and growing in relationship with him. When we give thanks to God for material blessings, let us keep the proper perspective. Let us praise him for food, shelter, and family. You can even praise him for high-speed Internet and satellite TV; just don't get distracted by them. Never lose sight of God.

The simple command of David begs us to go beyond blessings, though, and beyond circumstances and feelings to a place of continual thankfulness. He wanted us to understand that even in our darkest hours we have reason to give thanks to God. As this psalm reveals to us the why of our thankfulness, the attention is taken off of us and places it solely on the goodness of God.

The Why: For He Is Good

Give thanks to the Lord. Why? Because he is good. His goodness ultimately translates itself into blessings for us and good actions toward us, but the focus is on the fact that God, in his very being, is good. David praised the goodness of God countless times in other psalms. "I will sing to the LORD, for he has been good to me" (Ps. 13:16). "According to your love remember me, for you are good, O LORD" (Ps. 25:7). "How great is your goodness, which you have stored up for those who fear you, which you bestow in the sight of men on those who take refuge in you" (Ps. 31:19). Beyond what God does for us, he is good. Beyond our present happenings, the Lord is good.

A. W. Tozer had this to say in his wonderful book *The Knowledge of the Holy* about the goodness of God: "The goodness of God is that which disposes Him to be kind, cordial, benevolent, and full of good will toward men. He is tenderhearted and of quick sympathy. . . . By His nature He is inclined to bestow blessedness and He takes holy pleasure in the happiness of His people."[2] He takes pleasure, holy pleasure, in blessing us. His blessings toward us flow from his goodness. They go hand in hand. This is why David told us to praise him without reservation.

To better understand David's heart and the heart of this message, we must also understand the cultural context in which this phrase was used and how it applies to us today. David was writing

28

this song in a religious climate that was filled with many gods. The Israelites were surrounded and often seduced by the gods of the nations around them. But the gods that were preached and worshiped in foreign temples were gods of malice and anger. People worshiped them and offered them sacrifices to appease them, not because they were worthy of praise in the sense that God, Yahweh, is worthy of praise.

It's as if David were saying, "Give thanks to the Lord because he is good. He is not like the false gods Baal or Molech, who threaten you with anger and retribution. They care nothing for you. They show you no compassion. But God, he is good. He cares for you." We should praise God because he is not like the other gods. His very nature is good. And because he cannot act contrary to his nature, he does what is good on our behalf.

This is in sharp contrast not only with the foreign gods during the time of David, but also with every great mythology. The Greek gods especially were no better than the Greeks who served them. They lied to each other. They were unfaithful in their relationships. They envied each other. And they treated their subjects with contempt and only used them for their own profit. They never blessed those who worshiped them. They never sacrificed themselves for the good of the common man.

Imagine if the Lord were not good. Imagine how cold the world would be if God acted maliciously toward us and only used us for his own gain. But praise be to God; he is good! He treats us with compassion and grace. David knew this and praised him for it—without knowing the full story of the gospel. Think if David would have seen Jesus die for the sins of the world. Think how great his command for thanksgiving would have been then.

We must not confuse God's goodness with a lack of justice here. God is no softy when it comes to sin. Just because he is good does not mean that he is unjust. His justice flows from his goodness. In other words, because he is good, he must be fair and just. But he judges from a pure heart, from a heart of true love. He is not envious or proud.

It would be easy to stop here at God's goodness. But God's infinite goodness isn't even the best part yet. Earlier I mentioned Edward Spencer, the Northwestern student who saved all of those people out of Lake Michigan. We can consider him good, right? I mean, that was a pretty good thing he did. In fact, if he had gone out into the water only once to save someone's life, we would consider him a hero. But he went back into the water again and again and again. Seventeen times. This is the wow of David's song.

The Wow: His Love Endures Forever

God is not only good and worthy of our praise and thanksgiving; his love for us endures forever. It is a concept that the human mind can barely wrap itself around: a love that endures. For us, even the best of us, love is conditional many times. I will love you as long as you are nice to me and love me back. I will love my football team as long as it keeps winning. Human love is controlled by human emotions that ebb and flow with life's changing tides. God's love is constant and unstoppable. C. S. Lewis said simply, "Though our feelings come and go, His love for us does not."[3] Like young Edward, God enters the water time after time to save us, even when we turn our backs on him and swim the other direction.

God's love endures when all else fails. This is the icing on the cake. David's whole thought was leading up to this point: God's love endures forever. For this we should be truly thankful. We would all be lost if it were not for this profound truth. It's amazing and awesome to think that God is good, and he loves us with a love that will never cease.

He loves us with a love that is pure. Think of the famous description of love that Paul gave in the thirteenth chapter of 1 Corinthians. You probably hear this passage most at weddings, reminding spouses how it is that they are to love one another. "Love is patient, love is kind. It does not envy, it does not boast, it is not proud. It is not rude, it is not self-seeking, it is not easily angered, it keeps no record of wrongs. Love does not delight in evil but rejoices with the truth. It always protects, always trusts, always hopes, always perseveres" (1 Cor. 13:4–7). This is God's love for us, an ideal love from the ideal lover.

In the second verse of Psalm 106, David asked a question: "Who can proclaim the mighty acts of the LORD or fully declare his praise?" The answer is a resounding *everyone*. We all have reason enough to give thanks to the Lord. We all have been infinitely blessed by God. We are all in debt to his goodness and can respond in no other reasonable way than to give him incessant praise and thanks.

As you go through your day, week, and year, remember the formula for thanksgiving that David so cleverly gave us in the lyrics of his psalm. Remember to give thanks to God. Give thanks to him in the morning, at noontime, and in the evening. Give thanks to him in silent prayer and joyful proclamations. Give thanks to him because he is good. Hold onto the goodness of God this week. When you are feeling low or like God doesn't notice you, remember that he is good. His very nature compels him to pour blessing after blessing upon you.

And best of all, remember that God's love for you endures forever. His love cannot be contained. It will never end. Give thanks to the Lord!

Takeaway

Because I know that God has dominion over the earth,
I will use my resources wisely.

Count on Me!

learning to trust

Key Insight
You can trust God to provide.

In his book *Holy Sweat*, Tim Hansel tells about an experience he had with his son Zac. One day the two of them were out in the country, climbing on some cliffs. Tim heard his small son yell, "Hey Dad! Catch me!" He turned around to see Zac joyfully jumping off a rock straight at him. The boy had jumped even before he yelled, "Hey Dad!" The dad became a circus act, catching his son in midair then falling to the ground. After catching his breath, the anxious dad asked in exasperation, "Zac! Can you give me one good reason why you did that?"

> But Jacob replied, "I will not let you go unless you bless me." The man asked him, "What is your name?" "Jacob," he answered. Then the man said, "Your name will no longer be Jacob, but Israel, because you have struggled with God and with men and have overcome." . . . Then he blessed him there.
> —Genesis 32:26–29

The boy responded with remarkable calmness: "Sure . . . because you're my Dad."[1]

Wouldn't it be great to have that kind of confidence in your heavenly Father? Here's the good news. You can! God is trustworthy and we can have full confidence in him.

There are few things I enjoy more than a candle-lighting service, especially on Christmas Eve. There's something about watching that candle glow fill the entire room that is very moving. It's amazing, too, that it all starts with one tiny flame. From one candle, the light is passed on until the whole room is aglow.

Did you ever wonder why the original flame doesn't get smaller? How is it possible that you can take a candle flame, give away some of its light, and repeat the process several times, yet the original candle continues to burn just as brightly?

Here's why. The flame doesn't diminish when you share it; it spreads. When you give your flame away, you have more light, not less.

Many people think that when you share a blessing, you lose half of it. Even many of God's people think that when you share something good with other people, you will lose in the process. In reality, sharing a blessing is like sharing the flame on a candle; it spreads the light. When you share the good things God has given, you increase the blessing. It never diminishes one bit.

We have a God who delights in blessing his people; generous in every way. He is like that initial flame in the candle-lighting service. From him, all good comes. And he blesses us so that we can in turn bless others.

God Can Give All We Need

When my kids used to ask me for Christmas presents, they always knew that they might not get what they were after. I enjoy giving, but my kids knew they wouldn't get everything on their list. They knew I could give them any particular present. And that's the kind of confidence we can have when we come to God. Whatever we request, we know that he can do it.

In Genesis 32, Jacob wrestled with a man. He was strong and held his own in the fight. When the man asked Jacob to let him go, he refused unless the man would bless him. Jacob had no doubt that the man could bless him. The question was whether he would.

According to Genesis 32:29, the man did bless Jacob. What did it mean for the man to bless Jacob and how did Jacob know he had been blessed? The night of the wrestling match, Jacob recognized that the man was not an ordinary man, but an angel of the Lord. That's why Jacob gave the place a new name: Peniel, which means "face of God." He realized he'd come face-to-face with God.

It might seem odd to be wrestling with an angel of the Lord—or, as many scholars suggest, struggling with God himself—but remember where Jacob was. This was an important night in Jacob's life. He was preparing to face his brother Esau, who had threatened to kill him. Jacob knew that in order for him to return to his homeland, he'd have to settle things with Esau. He knew he needed strength beyond himself to face the brother he had wronged and cheated. That's why Jacob was so desperate to have God's blessing. He needed the help!

Have you ever felt that way? You have come to a place in your life where you know you just can't make it on your own.

Maybe it's financial trouble or illness. Maybe it's a problem in your marriage or family. You come to a place where all you can do is hang on tight and cry out, "Lord, please help me now!" That's where Jacob was.

But listen: God has promised that he will bless us with good things. Whatever we need, we know that we can come to him with confidence that he can provide it. What are some of the blessings God has given us?

Think about your own life for a minute. Think about all the good things that God has already given to you. Think of the evidence of God's blessing in your life. Think of how you have seen his touch in your world.

God Is Trustworthy

Over the years, I have met some people who were hard to trust. Once someone has violated that trust, it makes it hard to trust that person again. I'm sure that you have met people who you can't trust.

But there are people that I know I can trust with my life. It wouldn't matter what the situation was, if they gave me their word, I would believe them with no questions asked. They are absolutely reliable.

That's the way God is. He is completely dependable, and you can always trust him.

Abraham had been following the Lord faithfully ever since God called him out of the land of Ur. We're not sure how many years had passed since God first spoke to Abraham in Genesis 12 until he spoke to him again in Genesis 15, but by then, he had been learning to trust the Lord for some time. When God spoke to him again, Abraham asked God about the promises he had made to him and his descendants.

Abraham was now an older man, somewhere between seventy-five and eighty-six years old. He knew that his wife Sarah could no longer bear children, and the couple was childless. If I were Abraham, I'd have been wondering, "What is God up to? How in the world can he keep his promise now?" Abraham was beginning to think about who would inherit his property when he died. He identified a servant, Eliezer of Damascus, as the one who stood next in line for his estate (Gen. 15:2). He didn't think that was what God had intended in his promise, so he raised the question.

In other words, Abraham was trying to believe God, but he was having a moment of doubt.

Has that ever happened to you? You really want to trust God, but you're just not sure you can. Maybe that happens when someone you love becomes ill. You want to believe that God is good, but can you really trust him? Maybe that happens when you find yourself in financial need. You want to believe that God will provide for your every need, but can you trust him?

God has given us his word that he is faithful. The Bible has many examples of people who experienced God's faithfulness to them. Adam and Eve, Noah, Abraham, Jacob, Joseph, Esther, Joshua, Ruth, and Samuel are a few who found God to be faithful to his word. The psalmist David said, "The LORD is faithful to all his promises and loving toward all he has made" (Ps. 145:13). When we have moments of doubts, we can read about or remember those to whom God has proven himself. We can know that as he proved trustworthy to them, he will also be worthy of our trust. He won't fail us. We have his word on it, and we can trust him.

One pastor shared the following story:

Some years ago, a pastor in Romania was arrested by the police because of his Christian activities. When he was arrested and taken to jail, the jailer taunted him about his belief in God.

Rubbing his stomach, the jailer said, "Can your God take good care of you like the state takes care of me?" Our pastor reassured the jailer that his God could take care of him. "Oh! So you think your God can take care of you as well as the state takes care of me?" The pastor said yes. "OK," the jailer said. "I will give you only water for the next four days and we will see how well your God takes care of you."

The pastor was taken to a cell, and the door was locked. He began to pray very earnestly and fervently to God for his protection and needs. He told God that he was his servant and he did not know how God would provide for his needs, but he knew that God would take care of him. As he was praying, he heard a cat meow. When he opened his eyes, he saw a cat just outside the cell with a slice of bread in its mouth. He reached through the cell and took the bread from the cat's mouth.

Next he took and broke off the piece the cat had in its mouth and ate the rest of the bread. Each morning and evening for the following four days at the same time, the cat came bringing a slice of bread in its mouth.

On the fourth day, the jailer returned expecting to find a hungry man. "Well," the jailer said, "Look at how well the state has taken care of me, and how has your God taken care of you?"

"Oh!" the pastor replied, rubbing his stomach, "God has taken good care of me also." The jailer, being curious, asked how that was done. "Well," the pastor said, "twice a day God sent a cat with a piece of bread in its mouth for me."

As he was speaking, the cat meowed and as the jailer looked down, he saw the cat with the bread in its mouth. "That is my house cat bringing my bread from my table," said the surprised jailer. "Yes, surely your God did take care of you."[2]

God may not send a cat to feed you, but you can be sure that God keeps his word. Time after time, he has proven that what he has said, he will do.

Are you willing to believe that today—and everyday?

Acting in Trust

It's one thing to know that God is reliable; it's another thing to actually trust him. That's the difference between faith and action. At some point, you and I will have to take that step of faith, putting our complete confidence in God.

Abraham believed God, but he had trouble trusting him. As a result, he got himself into some rather trying situations. Once when he and Sarah went to Egypt, Abraham was afraid Pharaoh would kill him so he could take Sarah as his wife. So Abraham told Sarah to say he was her brother (Gen. 12:10–20). This was not totally untrue, since they were in fact half brother and sister. But it was deceitful, and they needed the Lord's intervention to get them out of the mess they were in. Oh, and once wasn't enough. They did the same thing later in Gerar (Gen. 20). That time, too, God straightened out the problem they created.

Perhaps more critical to Abraham's trust in God was Abraham's decision to father a child with Hagar. Sarah suggested it, and Abraham acted on her suggestion (Gen. 16). They had somehow rationalized that this was the way God would keep his promise of children to them. After it was done, God came again to Abraham to renew his promise that Abraham and Sarah would have a son. The Lord said that he would bless the son of Hagar and he'd be the father of twelve tribes, but the unique covenant people would come through Sarah's son (Gen. 17).

God honored his promises to Abraham. He also honored Abraham's faith and helped him grow in his confidence of God. Abraham's faith in God is noted throughout the Bible. Genesis 15:6 says, "Abraham believed the LORD, and he credited it to him as righteousness." This verse is quoted in four other places (Rom. 4:3, 9; Gal. 3:6; James 2:23), and in each instance, Abraham's faith is cited as a model of the kind of faith you and I can have.

Abraham was living in the difficult position between receiving God's promise and having it fulfilled. He understood the promise but was having trouble putting that faith into action.

If you are going to trust God totally, you must come to the point of acting on what you believe. You must not only believe that God provides; you must act as if God is going to take care of you. You must not only believe that there is a heaven; you must live as if heaven is your home.

Lean Your Whole Weight upon Him

The story is told of missionary John Paton who found a unique way to communicate the necessity of trusting in God:

Three months after arriving on the island of Tanna, Paton's young wife died, followed by their five-week-old son. For three more years, Paton labored alone among the hostile islanders, ignoring their threats, and seeking to make Christ known to them before escaping with his life. Later he returned and spent fifteen years on another island.

Paton was working one day in his home on the translation of John's gospel, puzzling over John's favorite expression . . . "to believe in" or "to trust in" Jesus Christ—a phrase that occurs first in John 1:12. "How can I translate it?" Paton wondered. The islanders were cannibals; nobody trusted anybody else. There was no word for *trust* in their language.

His native servant came in. "What am I doing?" Paton asked him. "Sitting at your desk," the man replied. Paton then raised both feet off the floor and sat back on his chair. "What am I doing now?" In reply, Paton's servant used a verb that means "to lean your whole weight upon." That's the phrase Paton used throughout John's gospel to translate "believe in."[3]

We need to put our whole weight upon God. He can hold us. He wants to hold us. He will hold us if we lean our whole weight on him in total trust. Because he is trustworthy, we can rely on him. Do you believe God is trustworthy? Are you willing to lean your whole weight on him? Will you let him carry you and all the concerns of life that you have? Isaiah 50:10 calls a person to "trust in the name of the LORD and rely on his God." Are you ready to lay all you are in his hands and rely on him?

Exercise Trust

Just as Abraham had to make a conscious decision to trust God, we must also choose to trust him. We'll find that some days it is easier to trust than others, but even when moments of doubt come, we can still choose to trust God.

Here's a gentle way to remind ourselves that trusting in God is fundamental to every aspect of our lives. The story has been told of a woman and her husband who were invited to spend the weekend at the husband's employer's home. She was nervous about the weekend. The boss was wealthy with a fine home on the waterway and cars costing more than her house. The first day and evening went well, and she was delighted to have this rare glimpse into how the very wealthy live.

The husband's employer was quite generous as a host and took them to the finest restaurants. She knew she would never have the opportunity to indulge in this kind of extravagance again and was enjoying herself immensely.

As the three of them were about to enter an exclusive restaurant that evening, the boss was walking slightly ahead of her and her husband. He stopped suddenly, looking down on the pavement for a long, silent moment. The lady wondered if she was supposed to pass him. There was nothing on the ground except a single darkened penny that someone had dropped and a few cigarette butts.

Still silent, the man reached down and picked up the penny. He held it up and smiled, then put it in his pocket as if he had found a great treasure. How absurd! What need did this man have for a single penny? Why would he even take the time to stop and pick it up?

Throughout dinner, the entire scene nagged at her. Finally, she could stand it no longer. She casually mentioned that her daughter once had a coin collection and asked if the penny he had found had been of some value. A smile crept across the man's face as he reached into his pocket for the penny and held it out for her to see. She had seen many pennies before! What was the point of this?

"Look at it," he said. "Read what it says." She read the words "United States of America."

"No, not that; read further."

"One cent?"

"No, keep reading."

"In God we trust?"

"Yes!"

"And?"

"And if I trust in God, the name of God is holy, even on a coin. Whenever I find a coin, I see that inscription. It is written on every single United States coin, but we never seem to notice it. If God drops a message right in front of me telling me to trust him, who am I to pass it by?"

Are you willing to trust God today with everything in your life? With your finances? With your family? With your health? With your career? With your future?

Perhaps today you will want to do an exercise of trust. Imagine yourself in a large room, and you are there with God. All your interests, possessions, family, friends, resources, and things of personal value are around you. Take each person or thing and place it into God's hands. Trust him with your most prized possessions. Trust him with your most valued relationships. Give him everything you have and are. If you find you're having trouble giving him something, spend some time praying about it. He is trustworthy. You can rely on him.

I like the way the poet expressed it:

Trust Him when dark doubts assail thee,
Trust Him when thy strength is small,
Trust Him when to simply trust Him
Seems the hardest thing of all.
Trust Him; He is ever faithful;
Trust Him, for His will is best;
Trust Him, for the heart of Jesus
Is the only place of rest.[4]

Takeaway
Because I trust God to provide for me,
I have the confidence to share with others.

3

The Blessing Principle

learning to give as well as receive

Key Insight
We are blessed to be a blessing.

"God does not give us everything we want, but he always gives us everything we need."

Perhaps you've heard that saying before. Often we use it when we are telling someone about something we want but can't get. It is almost always meant to be an encouragement, but the truth is, it does not always feel that way. The reason why it sometimes feels more like a burden than a precious promise is because we are so accustomed, as twenty-first-century Americans, to get

For this reason I bow my knees before the Father, from whom every family in heaven and on earth derives its name, that He would grant you, according to the riches of His glory, to be strengthened with power through His Spirit in the inner man, so that Christ may dwell in your hearts through faith; and that you, being rooted and grounded in love, may be able to comprehend with all the saints what is the breadth and length and height and depth, and to know the love of Christ which surpasses knowledge, that you may be filled up to all the fullness of God.
—Ephesians 3:14–19 NASB

whatever we want whenever we want it. Society teaches that no one is more important than me, and if there is something that I feel I must have to be happy, then I should get it. That is the exact opposite of what the Bible tells us.

While society tells us we should have everything we want, Paul told us God gives us everything we need and more. Paul was encouraging us to recognize and experience God's abundance. But God's abundance doesn't necessarily come in the way we would expect.

Glorious Riches

We can trust God to supply our needs because he is rich. He has unlimited resources; Paul described them as "glorious riches" (Eph. 3:16). Some of us may hear that phrase and think of massive piles of money. You might think of an old cartoon where a character literally swims through stacks of money and gold coins.

God's riches are altogether different. While he certainly owns the cattle on a thousand hills, Paul had something else in mind. To understand what Paul was referring to, we need only flip back to Ephesians 2. In verses 4–5 Paul said, "Because of his great love for us, God, who is rich in mercy, made us alive with Christ." God's riches include his mercy. In verse 7 of the same chapter, Paul used another term to describe God's riches. He said, "In order that in the coming ages he might show the incomparable riches of his grace, expressed in his kindness to us in Christ Jesus." We can trust in God's provision for our needs because he is rich. He is rich in mercy and grace.

46 There is another reason why we can trust that God's provision is enough for our needs—God loves us. If you have children, you

know the joy that comes with presenting your own children a present. The expression of delight that comes over children's faces as they receive something they want or need is one every parent enjoys. In the Sermon on the Mount, Jesus said whenever our children ask for something good, we don't hesitate to give it. He went on to say that, "If you then, being evil, know how to give good gifts to your children, how much more will your Father who is in heaven give what is good to those who ask Him!" (Matt. 7:11 NASB).

We can know that God's resources are sufficient for our needs because he loves us and he loves to give us exactly what we need. Paul said that part of his prayer for believers was that we would grasp "the breadth and length and height and depth, and to know the love of Christ" (Eph. 3:18–19 NASB). God's love for us in Christ Jesus is so large that Paul knew we would have trouble comprehending it. Yet out of that great love, God has promised to bless us and provide for us out of the riches of his mercy and grace.

Hymn writer Frederick M. Lehman summed up the love of God for us in a hymn titled "The Love of God." A portion of the song reads:

The love of God is greater far
Than tongue or pen can ever tell;
It goes beyond the highest star,
And reaches to the lowest hell;
The guilty pair, bowed down with care,
God gave His Son to win;
His erring child He reconciled,
And pardoned from his sin.
Oh, love of God, how rich and pure!

How measureless and strong!
It shall forevermore endure—
The saints' and angels' song.
Could we with ink the ocean fill,
And were the skies of parchment made,
Were every stalk on earth a quill,
And every man a scribe by trade;
To write the love of God above,
Would drain the ocean dry;
Nor could the scroll contain the whole,
Though stretched from sky to sky.[1]

God will provide for all our needs out of his abundant resources
because he loves us.

God Gives Us Enough

The dictionary defines satisfaction as fulfillment, gratification, and contentment.[2] The act of being satisfied in God is a state
of mind. It is something that we have to work at.

Part of the reason we find it so difficult to be satisfied with
God's provision is because we have unreal expectations of what
God should provide for us. We may expect that the moment we
become a Christian life will become easy for us or that we will
have wealth, good health, and high public regard. When we don't
receive those things, we become disillusioned.

The apostle Paul had something to say to us about this as well.
Paul gave his life for the spread of the gospel. An educated man,
he sacrificed all that he could have achieved in order that he
might be able to travel and preach. In fact, Paul said that all he

had gained—his education, status, and public regard—was rubbish to him. He understood that there was something more important than all of those things. In Philippians 4, Paul shared the secret to being content with what we have been given. He said, "I know how to be brought low, and I know how to abound. In any and every circumstance, I have learned the secret of facing plenty and hunger, abundance and need. I can do all things through him who strengthens me" (paraphrase).

Paul was familiar with having very little. In the midst of those times, he realized that the secret to being satisfied with what God had given him was the power of Christ living inside him. This passage brings us full circle. We said earlier that God has an abundance of riches from which to bless us. That abundance is experienced through Jesus Christ. Paul said that the same power God uses to bless us out of his abundance also strengthens us to be satisfied with everything that he gives us. What an amazing blessing!

Paul had more to say about our satisfaction in God in Ephesians 3:19. Here he said that part of his prayer for us is that we will be "filled to the measure of all the fullness of God." Two times in that one verse he used variations on the word *full*. We can be satisfied with what God has given us because he seeks to give us not just enough, but an abundance of his blessing. When we have a proper expectation of God's provision for us, we can truly experience what it means to be filled with God's provision. Benjamin Franklin said, "Content makes poor men rich; discontent makes rich men poor."[3] When we learn to be content with what God has given us, we will realize that there is no satisfaction like the fullness God can provide.

We don't always know the way that it will come, but we can always be sure that God will provide us with exactly what we need. | 49
If each of us were to take inventory of our lives, we would quickly

realize that God has always given us exactly what we need, exactly when we need it. In a society that encourages us to look to ourselves to provide, Paul told us that it is God alone who can provide everything we need for our lives, and we should be thankful to him.

I am reminded of the words of the psalmist in Psalm 46. He wrote that God has been proven to be "an ever-present help in trouble" (46:1). God has repeatedly shown that he will provide all we need for life. We can trust him. His resources are sufficient for all our needs. We must learn to be satisfied with what God has given us and to be continually thankful.

The first American Thanksgiving didn't occur in 1621 when a group of Pilgrims shared a feast with a group of friendly Indians. The first recorded Thanksgiving took place in Virginia more than eleven years earlier, and it wasn't a feast. The winter of 1610 at Jamestown had reduced a group of 409 settlers to a mere sixty. The survivors prayed for help without knowing when or how it might come. When help arrived in the form of a ship filled with food and supplies from England, a prayer meeting was held to give thanks to God.[4]

God's provision may not come in the way we think or how we expect, but it always comes. Pray that God will help us to see his provision for us, to be fully satisfied, and to always be thankful.

Faithfulness

"But while Joseph was there in the prison, the LORD was with him; he showed him kindness and granted him favor in the eyes of the prison warden" (Gen. 39:20–21).

Thankfulness is important, but it's only the beginning. Being thankful for what God has given us should inspire us to be faithful to use his blessings to bless others. The idea of faithfulness has suffered in our generation. We more often hear stories of betrayal or unfaithfulness than we do of those who are faithful, especially when it comes to marital faithfulness. According to a Gallup poll, 73 percent of Americans under age forty-five believe that life spent with the same partner is both unusual and unnecessary.[5] In another Gallup poll, 89 percent of people currently going through a divorce sited a family history of divorce as being a contributing factor to the ending of their marriage.[6] From that report, we can deduce that when we model unfaithfulness, we influence others who follow us.

The good news is that when we model faithfulness, we influence others to be faithful! When we observe people who are faithful, whether in marriage or in their walk with God, we are encouraged to be faithful, too.

You and I make choices every day. And every choice we make means not choosing something else. If I'm going to get up and go to work, that means I must choose not to sleep in. If you choose to study and do your homework, that means choosing not to watch TV.

Sometimes there are obstacles to the choices we make. If you want to complete a college education, it'll cost you something in time and money. If you want to be successful in your business, you'll have to beat the competition. It's not always easy to follow through on your choices.

It's the same with being faithful. Faithfulness is a choice, and it's one you'll have to stick with. Think about Joseph (Gen. 37–50). He was Jacob's favored son. Because of that, his brothers envied him. The short version of Joseph's story is that he told his brothers about dreams he'd had where they bowed down to him. That infuriated them, and when they had the opportunity, they decided to get rid of him. First, they planned to kill him, but instead they sold him into slavery.

Joseph's buyers took him to Egypt and sold him to Potiphar, the captain of the guard. Potiphar soon saw that Joseph was successful in whatever he did. The Scriptures say that it was because the Lord was with Joseph that he was successful. As Potiphar benefited from Joseph's work and God's blessing, he gave Joseph more and more responsibility.

Potiphar's wife noticed Joseph and made advances toward him. Joseph's response is critical for us to hear today. He said, "How then could I do such a wicked thing and sin against God?" (Gen. 39:9). His words were reflected in David's psalm of repentance, "Against you, you only, have I sinned and done what is evil in your sight" (Ps. 51:4). When we're unfaithful to other people, we're unfaithful to God. Who knows how tempting it may have been for Joseph to give in to the offers of Potiphar's wife? What we do know is that he made the difficult choice to remain faithful to Potiphar and to God.

Joseph made the choice to be faithful. And he stuck with that choice.

Gladys Aylward, missionary to China more than fifty years ago, was forced to flee when the Japanese invaded Yangcheng. But she could not leave her work behind. With only one assistant, she led more than a hundred orphans over the mountains toward free China.

During Gladys's harrowing journey out of war-torn Yangcheng, she grappled with despair as never before. After passing a sleepless night, she faced the morning with no hope of reaching safety. A thirteen-year-old girl in the group reminded her of the much-loved story of Moses and the Israelites crossing the Red Sea.

"But I am not Moses," Gladys cried in desperation.

"Of course you aren't," the girl said. "But Jehovah is still God!"[7]

Regardless of how great the temptation is for us to be unfaithful in our lives, God is still God.

What is the choice that you are facing right now? Maybe you're struggling to be faithful. You're facing a difficult time, and it isn't easy. But faithfulness means sticking with the choice you made. Maybe you're struggling financially. You've made a commitment to tithe your income, but there are challenges. Remember that while times may be tough, God is still God.

God will not abandon us to a situation or setting for us to succeed or fail alone. He will help us make the best choices if we ask him for help. Is that a habit of your life? Do you seek to do the things God wants you to? Do you strive to be faithful in your service to God as you serve others?

Be Faithful with Your Gifts

Let's get back to the story of Joseph. Do you realize that even though Joseph made the right choice to be faithful to God, he still suffered injustice? Potiphar's wife falsely accused him, and her husband put Joseph into prison. When you consider how the favored son became a slave in prison, you might expect him to throw up his hands in frustration and say it wasn't worth the effort. That's not the way the story goes, though. Joseph continued to be faithful to God even though his circumstances were bleak. He used his skills to benefit the prison as he had used them in Potiphar's house. Joseph was faithful in honoring the Lord, and the Lord showed him favor. Joseph later said that though his brothers meant him ill, God used him to bless others (Gen. 50:20). He seemed to recognize God's favor even through the unpleasant experiences of his life.

God will bless us as we give faithfully to him. When we refer to giving to the Lord, we often think of finances first. Let's think of finances later. Did you know that there are other ways we can be faithful in giving to the Lord? Think for a moment about your time. Are you faithful in giving your time to God? Do you allow him to help you set priorities in how you use your time each day? Do you offer and give time to serve others through the church or in your community? What about your talents? What gifts has God given you that you can use faithfully? Have you—or will you—commit them to God's use? How about the ways you can touch others in a unique way? Are you being faithful to give yourself to God in that way? Once you've looked at all the other areas where you can be faithful, examine your use of money. Is the way you spend and give in line with the rest of your life? Are your priorities of giving evidence of your faithful service to God?

Years ago, I heard Waldo Weaning say that there are three levels of giving:

1. You have to (law);
2. You ought to (obligation); and
3. You want to (grace).[8]

If you haven't yet reached the place where you want to give your time, talent, treasure, touch, and yourself in faithful service to God, will you ask God to help you get there?

Once there was a talent show at a local hall. The first contestant played a saxophone solo. It was so brilliant that the audience cheered wildly and gave him a standing ovation. . . . Shortly after he walked off the stage, a prominent individual in the music industry offered the player a recording contract, and a chance to play with some of his jazz heroes.

The second contestant read a poem she wrote. The words and the way she read them moved some people to tears. When she was done, the audience cheered enthusiastically. Shortly after she walked off the stage, she was offered a position writing poetry for the local newspaper and an opportunity to publish her work.

The third contestant walked out to the stage carrying a guitar. "Well," he stammered, "I had thought I would play this guitar my father gave me. But since there are other players so much better than me, I didn't put anything together."

The crowd fell silent. Shortly after he walked off the stage, his father seized the guitar and gave it to the saxophone player saying, "Take this and use it so that others may hear the music this instrument makes."[9]

I don't know about you, but there are times when I've felt like that third contestant. Perhaps you are feeling like you have a talent for something, but you're not sure if you are talented enough. Have you ever thought about where your talents come from?

God knows our potential better than we do! He gives us an abundance of talents because he loves us enough to trust us with them. It is up to us to use those talents.

When you use your gifts for God's glory, he will reward you. You may not see that now. You may not be able to see any way that good could result from it. Like Joseph sitting in prison, you just can't see the end of the story. But God is faithful. If you are faithful in serving him, he will be faithful in rewarding you.

Be Faithful in Blessing Others

George Washington Truett was a preacher in Dallas for forty-seven years. He once visited a wealthy West Texas rancher and had dinner in his huge ranch home. After dinner, the rancher took Truett up to a veranda on top of his house and lit a big cigar. The sun was setting, and if you've ever been to west Texas, you know you can see a long way out there. The man pointed to the south toward some oil rigs and said, "I own everything in that direction as far as you can see." He pointed east toward some cotton fields and said, "And I own everything in that direction, too." He pointed north toward a huge herd of cattle and bragged, "And, preacher, I own everything as far as you can see in that direction." He turned to the west, and said, "And I own everything you can see in that direction, except the sun, of course."

Truett turned to the man and pointed straight up the sky and said, "And how much do you own in that direction?"[10]

What are you good at? What are the things you do well, perhaps better than others? What are your gifts and talents?

Now here's a second question. Why are you good at those things? Why is it that God has given you the ability to sing or teach or make money or lead or create? I'll tell you why? God has given you those gifts for a purpose, and that purpose is to bless others.

Joseph was blessed with gifts and talents that allowed him to be a blessing to the people in Egypt. He continued to prove himself trustworthy, and God showed him favor, even in prison.

We have a false idea that there are greater or better gifts and talents. The reality is that God knows each of us and gives us the things that we can most effectively use in his service. Whether it's cleaning the restrooms or preaching the sermon, we each have a responsibility to use the gifts, graces, and talents God has entrusted to us.

After a classroom discussion on spiritual gifts, a young man asked the professor:

"Is my gift prophecy or exhortation?"

Knowing him very well, [the teacher] was careful as [he] responded, "I don't think either one is your gift. But if I have ever known someone who has the gift of helps, you're it. You're sensitive to the needs of other people and always ready to help."

A look of disappointment came over [the young man's] face. "I knew it!" he responded. Struggling with a low self-image, he was pursuing what he wrongly perceived to be a greater gift. You will never be fulfilled trying to become something you are not.[11]

God hasn't distributed gifts and talents equally, and for that reason alone, we can be assured that our sense of self-worth isn't based on what we do. Our self-acceptance comes from our identity in Christ and our growth in character. Show me someone who understands who he or she is as a child of God and whose character exemplifies the fruit of the Spirit, and I will show you someone with a healthy self-image.

God has given you gifts and talents, and they are not for your use alone. They are to be used to bless others. The greatest mistake you can make is to conclude that one gift is somehow better than another. In God's eyes, all are equal because they equally serve the body.

When God called Moses to lead the Hebrew people out of slavery, he asked Moses, "What is that in your hand?" (Ex. 4:2). He was ready to use Moses and the things he had. God asks each of us that same question today. What's in your hand? Do you know what your spiritual gifts are? Have you identified your talents? Are you willing to offer them in faithful service to God? Will you do it?

The benefits of your faithfulness may come to you in this life or you may not receive them here. You will have great reward in heaven when you hear God say, "Well done, good and faithful servant. Enter into your Master's rest." You'll only hear those words and receive lasting rewards if you've been faithful to keep God first in your life.

How much do you own in that direction?

Takeaway
I receive from God as I give to others.

The Generosity Factor

motivated by love

Key Insight
When we love God, we show love to others.

When John Lennon wrote his song "Imagine," he was envisioning a completely different world than the one he saw, a world filled with peace

> Carry each other's burdens, and in this way you will fulfill the law of Christ.
> —Galatians 6:2

and harmony. He imagined a world with no more war, murder, or poverty. Ironically and sadly, Lennon thought such a world could not have God. Lennon imagined a more peaceful, loving world to be one without God.[1]

I prefer to envision a world that is not unlike Lennon's utopia. But, of course, the key to the new world will not be the absence of God, rather the fullness of him and his Spirit. God exists. He is at work in the world and has been throughout history. We have experienced his love and grace. We have been changed into new creations by his hands. But imagine with me if you can a world where a unified body of Christ carries the burdens of one another. Imagine the peace and *shalom* that would fill the earth if each one of us shared the heavy load of this life. Pictures of poverty would not flood our televisions. Food pantries would spill over in abundance. The homeless would find shelter and the fatherless would find protection. Can you imagine?

Love for Your Community

Let's take a look at the world of insects to gain some insight on the subject of community. The book of Proverbs boasts of the wisdom of some of the smallest creatures on earth: ants (6:6; 30:25). When it comes to caring for one another's needs, ants get it. All summer, with no one giving orders and no boss handing out time cards, ants gather enough food that will last them all winter. And it's not every ant for himself. They gather as a team. They keep the food in common and share with all others equally. As a team, they are able to carry pieces of food hundreds of times bigger than they are individually.

Think of it this way: insects go hand in hand with terms like *swarms*, *hives*, and *nests*. Insects come in packs. They live together, work together, and if Walt Disney taught us anything, they even play together. Most insects' entire existence hinges on community. These communities provide the basic needs of life for every ant involved: food, shelter, and water.

Paul shared this same wisdom with us in Galatians 6:2, where he said simply, "Carry each other's burdens, and in this way you will fulfill the law of Christ." Paul wasn't revealing any mind-blowing theology here. He was stating the obvious. People who have been touched by the love of God should share that love and look after the needs of those around them. In one sentence, the apostle Paul gave us the blueprint for true Christian community. As we explore this concept, we are going to be looking at what carrying each other's burdens actually does for the body of Christ. I pray that God will soften our hearts to receive this simple yet profound message and empower us to take action.

Caring for One Another Lightens Everyone's Load

You've seen people walk with their heads held low. The heavy laden. The weary. Their hollow eyes sit on dark circles of unrest and worry. In fact, maybe you are one of the downtrodden. Paul wanted you to know that you are not alone. Paul wanted you to know that his idea of Christian community—more accurately, God's idea of Christian community—meets your needs and alleviates some of the weight of your burden. Burdens come in various sizes and shapes:

- unemployment,
- stacks of unpaid bills,
- empty cupboards,
- the death of a loved one,
- loneliness, or
- raising children as a single parent.

The list could be as long as you'd like. We have all carried burdens such as these, and we know the extreme force with which they push us down. Burdens can steal our joy and sap our strength.

God designed his body to be a community of burden bearers. The need for authentic relationships is woven deep into the DNA of mankind. The ability to share the task of carrying a burden is woven deep into the DNA of the church. The church, the body of our Lord Jesus Christ, is called by God to care for anyone in need. Just think, if we took this calling seriously and did it on a wide scale, our world would be changed forever. It is our responsibility to act on this calling. What if every believer gave Christ and the church 100 percent? Remember God has placed your church family together as one body so each member can care for one another.

There is a major theme running through the Bible, especially in the books of Leviticus, Deuteronomy, Jeremiah, and James. That theme is the care of the poor, widowed, and orphaned. In Leviticus 19:10, the Lord commanded the Israelites to not go over their fields twice so that the fallen grain would be left for the poor and the hungry. Numerous times in the book of Deuteronomy, God commanded the children of Israel to fight for the cause of the fatherless and the widowed.

Jeremiah 22:3 says, "This is what the LORD says: Do what is just and right. Rescue from the hand of his oppressor the one who has been robbed. Do no wrong or violence to the alien, the fatherless or the widow, and do not shed innocent blood in this place." And James 1:27 says it the best: "Religion that God our Father accepts as pure and faultless is this: to look after orphans and widows in their distress and to keep oneself from being polluted by the world."

I hope you are getting the picture by now. As we look at those words—*widow*, *orphan*, *poor*, *alien*—keep in mind what these verses are saying to us today. God is calling us to care for those in need. The widow and orphan have no one to look after them, no one to meet their needs. The poor and oppressed have no advocate except for the church.

You might be saying to yourself, "Well if I take care of everyone else's needs, who is going to take care of my needs? I can't do it all." That's exactly the point. You can't do it all, and if we all pitch in and start being the church God designed, the load will become lighter for everyone involved. If we love each other in this way, joy will not be crushed. Joy will thrive and grow in the hearts of the weary.

You Are Blessed to Be a Blessing

Jesus once said, "It is easier for a camel to go through the eye of a needle than for a rich man to enter the kingdom of God" (Matt. 19:24). If we're not as financially well off as we'd like to be, it's reassuring to interpret this in the most judgmental way possible. In truth, Jesus' words apply to everyone who is attached to their material blessings, even if they are quite impoverished. If we place our love for things over our love for others, we'll never enter God's kingdom; the rich, because they have so much stuff, are just more susceptible to its power.

When we have plenty, whether it's material wealth or other riches, it's easy to be happy. Maybe we have a good marriage and beautiful children. Maybe we have meaningful work and a gorgeous home. Maybe we even have a good relationship with God and know how treasured we are by him.

Maybe all this happiness is causing our scale to malfunction. We've been enjoying life so much that we're edging toward gluttony. Our blessing intake is not balanced with our blessing output. We're fat and happy.

I don't want to be fat and happy. I don't want to sit around and count my blessings when others are suffering. God blesses me so I can be a blessing to others. God didn't give Abraham a son so that old Abe could show off his family photo album to his friends. God gave Abraham a son so that all nations could be blessed through him. God didn't save Moses from certain death so that he could be a prince of Egypt. God intended for Moses to use his influence to save the Israelites. Jesus didn't appear to Paul on the road to Damascus so Paul could have a religious high. Jesus came to tell Paul to change his ways because he had an assignment.

We are blessed to be a blessing. God's love for you is equaled only by his love for others. He wants for us to enjoy the good things he has created and prepared for us, but only so much as our enjoyment pays forward the blessing to others.

Sometimes we don't even realize we have blessings to pay forward. I recently heard a father tell a story about his son. The youth had been to an amusement park, a water park, and out to dinner in one week's time. At the end of that week, he was stuck home for an evening and said, "I'm so bored! I never get to do anything!"

To be able to bless people with the good things we have, we must be aware of how blessed we are. What do you have that enriches your life? How might you use that blessing to bless others? John the Baptist said, "The man with two tunics should share with him who has none, and the one who has food should do the same" (Luke 3:11). What tunic can you give away? Perhaps you could open your home to the youth group for an evening or clear your pantry of overstocked food and donate it to a food bank.

Consider taking a small step and volunteering at a homeless shelter this week. You may be nervous, but just realize that these are type of people Jesus loved so madly. If he saw something in them, so can you.

There are times when it might be better for you to use your professional skills to benefit others rather than to advance your career. Could it be that you have saved a large amount of money and now God is calling you to use it to invest in others rather than another stock portfolio?

God didn't bless us so we can alienate ourselves from others, living in comfort and ease. Remember, fat and happy doesn't last forever. If we're not giving away as much of this joy as we can, we'll end up fat and miserable.

Stewardship is a natural result that flows out of a right heart. Love your neighbors as yourself. When you do, blessing them will be a natural result. A grandmother doesn't need to be told to lavish her grandson with love and affection. In the same way, we will automatically bless others when our hearts are full of the love of Christ.

Love for Our World

"But you will receive power when the Holy Spirit comes on you; and you will be my witnesses in Jerusalem, and in all Judea and Samaria, and to the ends of the earth" (Acts 1:8).

When Jesus taught us to pray what we call the Lord's Prayer, he gave us the essence of the kingdom. He said we should pray, "Thy kingdom come, Thy will be done in earth, as it is in heaven" (Matt. 6:10 KJV).

The disciples who first heard those words, along with many others in their day, thought of God's kingdom in political terms. They were tired of enemy nations oppressing them. After all, they were the chosen people of God. They wanted to throw off the shackles and be a powerful, independent nation. Yet when Jesus told them how to pray, he did not say anything about political power. He did not recommend overthrowing oppressive governments. He said to pray for the kingdom to come. And that means God's will being done on earth, even as his will is done in heaven. It is not a political kingdom; it is a spiritual kingdom.

Then just before he ascended back to heaven, Jesus gave this strong and compelling verse in the book of Acts. It is potent because it contains in a nutshell the power and program of the kingdom of God.

They certainly needed power. But how does one get power to accomplish spiritual things? Jesus did not say, "You will receive power when you finally get organized." He said, "You will receive power when the Holy Spirit comes on you" (Acts 1:8). Unless we are filled with the Holy Spirit, all our organization, tithing, and support of missions is just religious activity. He is our only source of real power. Anything else is a poor substitute.

Along with the power, we must follow the program. Jesus said the program of the church is to go and be his witnesses in the world. Jerusalem was home base. Judea was the province in which Jerusalem sat. Samaria was next door, a kind of half-Jewish region. The ends of the earth represent the whole world. So Jesus is saying that the program of the church is to be his witnesses first at home, but then to spread the good news across geographical boundaries as well as cultural and ethnic boundaries.

Jesus' Mission in the World Involves You

Jesus' gives this directive to be his witnesses first to the church, but it is also a directive to each individual. He actually makes a promise that those who receive the Holy Spirit will be his witnesses.

In a small village in Scotland, one of the town drunks was Sandy MacTavish. The local preacher had tried in vain to help Sandy, to get him off alcohol and "on the wagon." In a desperate effort to address the situation, he called a meeting of everyone in the town who had a problem with alcohol. He was pleased to see so many people, and especially to see Sandy MacTavish sitting in the back row. The pastor was so inspired that he preached an eloquent sermon, warning them of the dangers of alcohol to both body and soul.

At the end of the message, he sent a piece of paper around the group, asking everyone to sign it as a pledge to give up drinking. Everyone signed it and to his special delight, he noticed Sandy MacTavish signed it too. After the service, he could hardly wait to get home and tell his wife the good news. Coming into the house, he unrolled the sheet of paper and, sure enough, there at the bottom were the words: Witnessed by Sandy MacTavish. The drunk had not pledged to quit drinking; he only witnessed that the others had done so.[2]

That certainly is one kind of witness, but Jesus was talking about something else. Suppose you happen to be at the bank this week and just as you are about to step up to the next available teller, two men in ski masks walk in, holding loaded guns. In the next few moments, you witness a bank robbery.

After the thieves make their escape and the police come to investigate, they say, "Are there any witnesses?" Being the honest person you are, you say, "Yes, I saw the whole thing. I witnessed the robbery." That is a witness: someone who can testify about what he or she has seen or experienced.

Now, Jesus says, we are his witnesses, not to a bank robbery, but to the grace of God in our lives. And when the Holy Spirit comes into our lives, this he promises: we will be his witnesses. But perhaps someone is thinking: "It's just not my personality to be a witness."

It is not a matter of personality. Some people think that to be a good witness you must be outgoing and friendly and have an effervescent personality, a sort of super-salesman type of individual. We all need to be friendly, but there is no one personality type that is the perfect witness. God uses all personalities to accomplish his work. If you are naturally outgoing, you may find it easier to talk to people. But the most effective witnesses, regardless of personality, are those who have the power of the Holy Spirit in their lives and who can speak sincerely about what God has done for them.

It is not a matter of spiritual gifts. Others may think they are not gifted for witnessing. The Bible talks about the gift of evangelism, along with other spiritual gifts: the gifts of teaching, administration, serving, and so forth. If you have the gift of evangelism, witnessing will be easier and you will perhaps be more effective. But God has called each of us to be his witness. Even if we do not have the gift, we all must accept the role of a witness.

It is a matter of accepting the responsibility. If you witnessed the bank robbery I mentioned earlier, and if you heard one of the robbers call the other by name, wouldn't you feel a responsibility to give that information to the police? It was part of what you witnessed.

Witnessing is a matter of inner character. Because you are a person of integrity, you have been enlightened and you have friends and relatives who need the Savior. Your character and integrity say, "It is my responsibility to be a witness."

Jesus said, "Let your light shine before men, that they may see your good deeds and praise your Father in heaven" (Matt. 5:16).

You Can Support the Mission

You may not think you have the resources to support the mission, but you do! Follow these simple guidelines, and you may discover that you have more than enough to give.

Make Giving a Priority. Proverbs 3:9–10 says, "Honor the LORD with your wealth, with the firstfruits of your crops [or paycheck]; then your barns will be filled to overflowing, and your vats will brim over with new wine." If you repeat that act over and over, giving will become a habit.

Make Informed Choices about Giving. Don't give to any organization if you don't know something about their budgeting structure. How much do they spend on administration and fund-raising? How much actually reaches the intended recipient? The wisest thing is to give through the local church's missions and outreach ministry.

Make Your Giving a Private Matter. Jesus said, "So when you give to the needy, do not announce it with trumpets, as the hypocrites do in the synagogues and on the streets, to be honored by men. I tell you the truth, they have received their reward in full. But when you give to the needy, do not let your left hand know what your right hand is doing, so that your giving may be in secret. Then your Father, who sees what is done in secret, will reward you" (Matt. 6:2–4). Give as unto the Lord, not to be seen by others.

Make Giving a Celebration. Sometimes when we begin giving, we think about the sacrifice and we do not give joyfully. But as you continue to give, the feelings of joy will come. It is better to act your way into feeling than to try to feel your way into acting. The apostle Paul said, "Each man should give what he has decided in his heart to give, not reluctantly or under compulsion, for God loves a cheerful giver" (2 Cor. 9:7).

So what will you give to advance God's mission in the world? As you think and pray about this, ask God to help you step out in faith. Don't think just about what you can afford, but about what you can trust God to do through you in the coming year.

An old story in the form of a poem tells about six people who froze to death around a campfire because each one held on to the stick of wood he or she could have contributed to the fire's warmth. A woman in the group would not give up her stick of wood because there was a person of a different race in the circle. A rich man held onto his stick because he did not want to warm someone else who was obviously shiftless and lazy. A penniless man was there and would not surrender his stick of wood because of the rich man. Another refused to give up his wood because there was a person in the circle not of his religious belief. The black man held on to his stick as a way of getting even with the white people for what they had done to his race.

The fire slowly died, leaving them in the cold, because each one held onto the stick of wood for reasons each felt were justifiable. The story ends with the lines: "Six logs held fast in death's still hand was proof. They did not die from the cold without; they died from the cold within."[3]

This story reminds us that we should ask God to warm our hearts so that we will relinquish our grip on the resources that can cause his kingdom to flourish. Don't hold on too tightly.

God's Love for Us

Christ sacrificed his own rights so he could carry the burden of the sin of the world and nail it to the cross. Likewise, when we carry each other's burdens, pride is strangled and grace prevails. And when you unleash the Spirit of God, watch out! That's when things really start to happen. Those in need will have their needs met. Jobs will be found. The lonely will be blessed with companionship. The fatherless will be blanketed with love and protection. The hungry will go to bed with full stomachs. The body of Christ will be a unified, unstoppable force!

Do you remember Susan Boyle? She is the Scottish singer who came to international attention after she appeared on a

British talent show. When she appeared on the stage for the first time, the audience and judges appeared apprehensive and judgmental of her unpolished appearance. Upon finishing her song, she received a standing ovation from the live audience and unanimous praise from the judges.

Likewise, we often see the poor as unimportant and easy to overlook and would be shocked to discover they are real people with talents and passions just as we are. God doesn't overlook anyone. He knew Susan Boyle before she was famous, and he knows every homeless person who will never rise to fame. His love for every person he created is unconditional. He has a tenderness of heart especially for orphans and widows and gives instruction throughout the Old and New Testaments to provide for them. Jesus expects us to love the needy as he does, with hearts and hands.

The apostle Paul said, "And masters, treat your slaves in the same way. Do not threaten them, since you know that he who is both their Master and yours is in heaven, and there is no favoritism with him" (Eph. 6:9). This is not an implicit approval of slavery; it is a direct admonition to treat everyone fairly—to recognize that every person is equal in the eyes of God.

What does that mean? Should you give all your cash to a homeless man the next time he knocks on your window? Should you serve in the inner city as often as you feasibly can? Should you sell all your possessions and move to Africa to care for orphans? I'm not sure how the Holy Spirit will direct you, but there is one thing that is true for each of us: We can open our eyes to see real people who have great worth and dignity whenever we look into the eyes of the poor.

Have you ever walked through the first-class cabin in an airplane toward a middle seat in the back of the plane where you just know you'll be crammed between two people? The folks in first class have big comfy seats and a place to hang up their coats—plus the flight attendants are already serving them drinks. Later, when you're munching on stale pretzels, they'll be enjoying a hot meal; when you're feeling sweaty and smelly, they'll be wiping their hands and face with a hot towell served off a pretty silver tray with silver tongs.

You try to sneak glances at these people without them noticing. Who are they that they deserve this? You tell yourself that people should not be elitists. Sure, having the benefits they have would be great, but it's really so extravagant. Do they think they're better than everyone else just because they can pay to be set apart from the crowd? You see a woman who has had obvious plastic surgery and an older man whose suit is probably more expensive than your car, and you wonder how they can spend their money so frivolously. They probably don't even spend a cent on helping anyone else.

And so it goes. Whether jealousy or legalistic thinking drives your antagonism makes no difference; the lack of love is what matters.

As I said earlier, Jesus spoke the most harshly against those who would not care for the needs of the poor, but that doesn't mean he despised wealthy people; he despised injustice. Jesus loved all people; he didn't make distinctions between them based on social status or any other differential. He was opposed to neglecting the poor, but he wasn't against wealth. In fact, the women who provided for Jesus during his ministry were able to do so because they were wealthy. These women were some of the people nearest and dearest to our Lord.

The rest of the Bible reveals a consistent pattern. God's zeal for the poor matches his love for all types of people. He doesn't prefer a rich person over a poor person, or vice versa. Some of God's most beloved people were abundantly rich: Moses, Abraham, Job, and David, for example. It's not the class level that affects whether God loves us. We are his beloved children. "For God so loved the world that he gave his one and only Son, that whoever believes in him shall not perish but have eternal life" (John 3:16).

It's easy to be intimidated by or jealous of the rich. It's much harder to love them.

Loving the rich does not mean hanging around (hoping for benefits), saying whatever they want to hear. Loving them does not mean secretly adoring them; God has given them the same dignity he has given you. Loving them means seeing beyond their wealth to their humanity, just as Jesus did.

How do you do that? How do you love even those you have been jealous of? The same way you love the poor people you once disdained: You get to know them. You listen to their stories. You realize that they have the same basic needs as you, including the need to be loved and accepted. For sure, the issue is the balance between social redemption and spiritual redemption. Both are much needed in God's big world.

Takeaway
When I feel compassion for others, I will share
my time, talent, and treasure.

PART 2

The Giving Lifestyle

Now that you understand the biblical values of stewardship, generosity, and sharing, you probably want to develop a giving lifestyle. But how does one change a lifetime of behavior aimed at rewarding self and excluding others? Let's discover why consecration is the prerequisite for a lifestyle of generosity, then we will examine some realistic strategies for being generous with your talents, treasure, and time. This will enable you to make practical changes that will result in a lifestyle of generosity.

The Starting Point for Generosity

consecration

Key Insight
You can develop a lifestyle of generosity by
devoting yourself fully to God.

Remember Smarties, those bite-size, multicolored, chalklike, candies wrapped in clear plastic? They are perfect for sharing. Pastor Kevin Harney was not a huge fan of Smarties,

> But seek first his kingdom and his righteousness, and all these things will be given to you as well.
> —Matthew 6:33

but when he saw little Dustin come into church with a fresh roll, he just had to ask for one. Dustin peeled out a piece and handed it over with a smile. From then on, every time Dustin got a pack of Smarties, he took out the first one and set it aside for his pastor. Every Sunday morning before the worship service, Dustin would track Pastor Harney down at church and offer him a Smarty.

Sometimes Dustin would open a pack of Smarties during the week, but he would still save the first piece for his pastor.

By the time Sunday came, the Smarty was a little mangy and furry with lint, but Dustin never forgot to bring it. Kevin would thank the boy and put the candy in his pocket so he could "enjoy it later."

Dustin's mother viewed this ritual as a kind of tithing; out of ten pieces in a pack, Dustin gave the first tenth to his pastor. What Kevin saw was a little boy who loved to share and who understood the power of generosity.[1]

Generosity—is it something that only kids have and you grow out of it? Is it a personality thing; it's either in your DNA or it's not? Or can you develop a lifestyle of generosity; and if so, how?

It's true that some personalities are more inclined to generosity than others, and it's true that bad life experiences can teach you to grip tightly to what you have; but that's not the bottom line. Giving living is an issue of the heart, and the heart can be filled with whatever you choose to put in it.

Do you recognize the spiritual benefits of generosity and want to cultivate it in your life? Do you wish you had the faith to believe God would provide for you if you tithed and gave special offerings for missionaries, people in need, and worthy causes? Do you want to make a faith promise? Here's how: Consecrate yourself to God.

By concentrating on your needs and desires, you limit yourself to what you can achieve by your own means; you don't get anything more than what you can manage to pull into your grasp.

Realize That God Has More Resources

Listen to Jesus' words of wisdom on this subject:

> Do not worry about your life, what you will eat or drink; or about your body, what you will wear. Is not life more

important than food, and the body more important than clothes? Look at the birds of the air; they do not sow or reap or store away in barns, and yet your heavenly Father feeds them. Are you not much more valuable than they? Who of you by worrying can add a single hour to his life? And why do you worry about clothes? See how the lilies of the field grow. They do not labor or spin. Yet I tell you that not even Solomon in all his splendor was dressed like one of these. If that is how God clothes the grass of the field, which is here today and tomorrow is thrown into the fire, will he not much more clothe you, O you of little faith? So do not worry, saying, "What shall we eat?" or "What shall we drink?" or "What shall we wear?" For the pagans run after all these things, and your heavenly Father knows that you need them. (Matt. 6:25–32)

Sounds like another "Thou shall not," right? Thou shall not be a miser. One more thing to add to your list of things to feel guilty about.

Not quite. Because Jesus doesn't stop there. He gives the antidote to your tendency to worry, to pursue things that you believe will give you security. He said, "But seek first his kingdom and his righteousness, and all these things will be given to you as well" (Matt. 6:33).

Jesus isn't concerned about finding a way to get you all those things you think you need; not because he doesn't want you to have them, but because it's covered. The thing that consumes you and shapes your life—financial security—Jesus brushes aside with flit of his hand. It's like he's saying, "Oh that? Don't worry about it. I've got it covered. Look over here."

What is important enough to draw you away from what truthfully is an important endeavor—indeed, a mammoth task—of paying the bills and providing for the family? What is Jesus asking you to look at?

Consecrate yourself to the Lord. Experience his sanctifying presence. Seek first his kingdom—yes, first—before you worry about anything else. Jesus taught his disciples to pray for God's kingdom to come, for his will to be done; here he tells us to actively seek God's kingdom.

The word translated *kingdom* throughout the New Testament is the Greek word *basileia*, which denotes "sovereignty, royal power, [and] dominion."[2] We bring his kingdom on earth by making sovereign the things that matter to him, not our own agendas.

Scripture, especially in the gospel accounts of Jesus' life, but really throughout the Bible, reveals what God cares about: people. Broken people. More than anything else, our compassionate Father wants to restore us, to reconcile us to himself. The kind of kingdom he is establishing is one in which the broken are healed, in which the poor, weak, and despised are fed, empowered, and loved. It's simple then: Seeking his kingdom means feeding the poor, empowering the weak, and loving the unloved. Seeking his kingdom means looking for broken people and bringing them hope and healing.

Simple perhaps, but not easy. It takes great effort to free ourselves from our own selfish desires. But it is possible.

During John Wesley's life in the 1700s, Britain experienced rapid urbanization and the beginnings of industrialization. This caused the collapse of rural economies and problems in city centers, such as overcrowding, disease, crime, unemployment, debt, substance abuse, and even insanity.

Meanwhile, a small upper class spent large sums to distance itself, literally and figuratively, from the growing problems. This top 5 percent of the population controlled nearly one-third of the national income.

Wesley, part of the lower-middle class, interacted mostly with people who worked hard, owned little, and could never be certain of their financial future. But he eventually became so well-known as a preacher that he earned £1,400 per year—equivalent to more than $160,000 today. Still, he chose to live simply but comfortably on just £30 while giving the rest away. He donated nearly all of the £30,000 he earned in his lifetime. He said, "If I leave behind me £10 . . . you and all mankind [can] bear witness against me that I have lived and died a thief and a robber."[3]

Wesley had his eye on the kingdom, and his ministry is still impacting lives today. He gained so much for the Lord. Notice that all the other things he needed were given to him as well.

We can make a difference in the kingdom too if we quit putting our own agendas first. Studies show that if church members in the United States increased their giving to 10 percent of their income, there could be an additional $86 billion available for overseas missions. And according to researchers John and Sylvia Ronsvalle, founders of Empty Tomb Inc. in Champaign, Illinois, that amount of money would meet the most essential human needs around the world.

"Projects for clean water and sanitation, prenatal and infant/maternal care, basic education, immunizations, and long-term development efforts are among the activities that could help overcome the poverty conditions that now kill and maim so many children and adults," the Ronsvalles say.[4]

Do you want to cultivate a spirit of generosity? Look away from your own interests, and seek first his kingdom, consecrating yourself for him.

Rely on God's Riches, Not Your Ability

Even if all Christians contributed and united their efforts, overcoming poverty is a big mandate. Maybe it's more than big; maybe it's impossible. Honestly, saving the world is unrealistic; it's hard enough to get our own families fed and on the right track.

Wait a second, though. When Jesus said to seek first his kingdom, was he saying that you have to be responsible for the world, for eradicating poverty, for curing AIDS? No! You're just ambassadors for the kingdom; he's the King. He's the one responsible for saving the world. You don't have the power, resources, or ability to do it yourself. You have to rely on God's riches rather than your ability.

We think our great leadership skills, extensive education, bubbly personality, or whatever we have that we think is pretty good is what matters to God. But it's not. God takes whatever we offer him, even (or especially) our weaknesses and uses it to accomplish his purpose.

Two friends met after not seeing each other for a long time. One had gone to college and was now successful. The other hadn't gone to college and never had much ambition, yet he still seemed to be doing well.

The college graduate asked his friend, "How has everything been going with you?"

The less-educated man replied, "Well, one day, I opened my Bible at random and dropped my finger on a page. The word under my finger was *oil*. So I invested in oil, and boy, did the oil wells gush. Then I tried the same method again, and my finger stopped on the word *gold*.

So I invested in gold, and those mines really produced. Now I'm as rich as Rockefeller."

The college grad rushed to his hotel, grabbed a Gideon Bible, flipped it open, and dropped his finger on a page. When he opened his eyes, he saw that his finger rested on the words *Chapter Eleven*.[5]

God never follows any formula we may contrive. He works in different ways for different people. All we can do is have open hearts and open hands.

Take Briton Nordemeyer of Brandon, South Dakota, for example:

[At the age of eight, she] wanted to help the children who had lost everything during Hurricane Katrina. So when Briton's tooth fell out in the fall of 2005, she decided to donate the money she'd get from the tooth fairy to the Red Cross.

Instead of waiting for the tooth fairy to arrive, however, Briton mailed her tooth to the Red Cross. She included a letter explaining that the tooth fairy would render payment upon arrival.

When news about Briton's generosity reached the public, the Red Cross received a five-hundred-dollar donation from an anonymous donor who heard about Briton's tooth and wanted to help provide a fairy-tale ending.[6]

Briton didn't have the ability to provide even a small amount of money, but what she had she gave. Her gift was multiplied in a way she couldn't have anticipated.

It's our job to give; it's God's job to multiply our gifts.

Francis Chan puts it this way:

Remember that story where Jesus fed thousands of people with one boy's small lunch? In that story, according to Matthew, Jesus gave the loaves to His disciples and then the disciples passed them out to the crowd. Imagine if the disciples had simply held onto the food Jesus gave them, continually thanking Him for providing lunch for them. That would've been stupid when there was enough food to feed the thousands who were gathered and hungry.

But that is exactly what we do when we fail to give freely and joyfully. We are loaded down with too many good things, more than we could ever need, while others are desperate for a small loaf. The good things we cling to are more than money; we hoard our resources, our gifts, our time, our families, our friends. As we begin to practice regular giving, we see how ludicrous it is to hold on to the abundance God has given us and merely repeat the words *thank you*.[7]

God gives us good things so we can share them. When we share the little or the abundance that we have, God multiplies our gift. That's his job, not yours.

Offer Yourself as a Living Sacrifice

"Therefore, I urge you, brothers, in view of God's mercy, to offer your bodies as living sacrifices, holy and pleasing to God—this is your spiritual act of worship. Do not conform any longer to the pattern of this world, but be transformed by the renewing of your mind. Then you will be able to test and approve what God's will is—his good, pleasing and perfect will" (Rom. 12:1–2).

Who is the smartest person you know? Maybe you are. I know people who are in most ways reasonable and intelligent but do dumb things.

A friend of mine has a hearing problem and must wear a miniature hearing aid in each ear. One evening he was suffering from a bad headache. As he was going to bed, his wife laid out two pain tablets on his dresser and told him that if he had trouble sleeping he should get up and take the two tablets. During the night he woke up with his head hurting. He got up, took the two pain tablets, and went back to bed. When he got up in the morning, on top of his dresser he found one pain tablet and one hearing aide battery. During the night he had taken one pain tablet and one hearing aid battery for his headache.

Even intelligent people can do dumb things.

Nothing is as crazy as real life. A Seattle newspaper reported that a man attempted to siphon gasoline from a motor home parked on a street in the city. Police arrived at the scene to find an ill man curled up next to the motor home. A police spokesman said that the man admitted to trying to steal gasoline, but plugged his siphoning hose into the motor home's sewage tank by mistake.

I know people who are highly educated in a certain academic discipline but who struggle in other areas of their lives. They can decipher complex mathematic problems, but cannot remember where they left their car in the parking lot. While in college, I met one of my professors on the sidewalk. After a brief conversation, he asked which direction he was going when we met. When I told him, he said, "Oh, I guess I have already had lunch then." I guess if I had pointed him toward home, he would have gone back and eaten again!

You may consider yourself to be at least reasonably intelligent. But lest in your intelligence you miss it, let me tell you the smartest thing you can do.

One night after giving one of the greatest concerts of his brilliant career, the pianist Paderewski was greeted by an eager fan who said, "Oh, I'd give my life to be able to play like you do." Paderewski replied quietly, "I did."[8] Some things will never happen unless you are willing to give your life for them.

The smartest thing you can do is to lose your life so that you can find it, to give yourself to something great and bigger than yourself, and by doing so find yourself and find life. It is a principle of the kingdom: keep your life and you lose it; lose your life and you find it.

Paul said in Romans 12 that spiritual development involves giving yourself so completely to God that you are a "sacrifice." The New International Version says that offering your body as a living sacrifice "is your spiritual act of worship." It is a normal, reasonable response to God's mercy. The King James Version said that this sacrifice is "your reasonable service." The word *reasonable* means "rational" or "intelligent." Giving yourself completely to God as a sacrifice is a reasonable thing. It is intelligent. It is the smart thing to do.

Consecrating Your Life Is a Reasonable Action

Romans 12 begins with the word *therefore*. There are five times in the book where Paul proclaimed lofty theological, doctrinal truth and then made practical application. Each time, the transition is made by the word *therefore*. *Therefore* is like a hinge on a door that acts as the link between the wall and the door and enables the one to relate to the other. Here it holds together doctrinal principles and practical application.

Romans 12 begins with the phrase "Therefore . . . in view of God's mercy" (12:1). Consecration to God is reasonable when you take into view God's mercy. When we understand what we were before God came into our lives, it is only logical that we respond to his mercy by sacrificing ourselves to him. Beyond that, the preceding verse says: "For from him and through him and to him are all things. To him be glory forever" (11:36), followed by, "Therefore" (12:1). Consecration is reasonable because of what God has done. It is also reasonable because of who he is.

Why should you sacrifice yourself to God? Why is it smart? Because of him and through him and to him are all things. "From him" speaks of creation. All things have their origin in him. "Through him" speaks of continuation. All things continue their existence through him. He is the sustainer of life. He is the Lord of history. Your present existence is dependent upon him. "To him" speaks of completion or culmination. All things must ultimately relate back to God. The end of all things is found in him. When there is no relationship back to God, a part is always missing; life becomes mismanaged; a lack of purpose brings confusion; and ultimate fulfillment is lost.

It is possible for us to say that he is God in creation—all things are of him. We can say that he is God in continuation—all things are through him. Even then, we can still deny his place as God by not giving ourselves back to him. The unconsecrated life remains incomplete and God's purpose is not consummated.

God created you and sustains you, and only in consecrating yourself to him is his purpose in you made complete. Therefore, the smart thing to do is to give yourself totally to him.

Consecrating Your Life Is a Reasonable Response

Consecration is a response of an individual's will. No one else can consecrate you. It must be your response to the purpose of God in your life. This is something you have to do for yourself. As parents, we may dedicate (or consecrate) our children as a declaration that they belong to God and we intend to see that they grow up in the "nurture and admonition of the Lord" (Eph. 6:4 KJV). But the day will come when the consecration we made of them as parents must be matched by their own consecration. No one but you can surrender yourself to God. Consecration is a human response—a personal act.

Paul used an interesting word picture to describe consecration. We are to present our bodies as living sacrifices. *Present* is the technical term for the sacrifices and offerings presented by the priests under the laws of sacrifice given by God to Moses. The priest would carry his sacrifice—his offering—to the altar and place it facing the Most Holy Place, thus presenting it before the Lord. There it would be consecrated before God.

A Jewish person living in Paul's day would understand this word in terms of an act of giving to God—a giving that was total, complete—a giving of everything, even life. The last of the ten plagues in Egypt was the death of the firstborn son in every home that did not have the blood sprinkled on the doorposts. So when the Israelites left Egypt, the Lord said to Moses, "Consecrate [present] to me every firstborn male. The first offspring of every womb among the Israelites belongs to me" (Ex. 13:2). Luke 2:22, following the birth, circumcision, and naming of Jesus, says, "When the days of their purification according to the Law of Moses had been completed, Joseph and Mary took him to Jerusalem to present him to the Lord." The people who first read Paul's letter would understand this word in terms of a covenant act of sanctification, a declaration of belonging to God in a special, sacred way.

The word *presented* is also used in Acts 1:3 regarding the resurrection. "After [Christ's] suffering, he showed [presented] himself to these men and gave many convincing proofs that he was alive." Also in Acts 9:41, when Peter raised Dorcas from her deathbed, "He took her by the hand and helped her to her feet. Then he called the believers and the widows and presented her to them alive." In both of these occasions, someone stepped forth openly as evidence and proof, a living demonstration of what has happened: "Here I am. Look at me, and see what has happened."

Present is used another way in Romans 6:13: "Do not offer [present] the parts of your body to sin, as instruments of wickedness, but rather offer yourselves to God, as those who have been brought from death to life; and offer the parts of your body to him as instruments of righteousness." Here it means to surrender to a person or principle to be used for his purpose.

The life to which we are called includes a moment of crisis in which we are faced with a decision. It is a continuation of the decision we initially made to come to God for forgiveness of our sins through the atonement of Christ. It is a continuation of that decision, yet distinctly different. We first made a decision to receive. Having received, we must now make a decision to give. Having been forgiven, am I now willing to present myself to God:

- Like a sacrifice on an altar to be consumed in the holy flame?
- Like a declaration that I belong to God in a special, sanctified, made-holy way?

- Like evidence of the miracle of new life, I stand before God and the world and confess Jesus Christ to be Lord?

- Like a soldier surrendering his sword, I yield myself to God; I offer myself to be used as an instrument of righteousness?

Consecration is a "crisis" because it involves a definite act of my will. I cannot belong to myself and belong totally to God at the same time. I can't live half-on and half-off the altar. Sacrifices are intended to die. Only when I die to my self-centeredness can God cause me to be a living sacrifice.

Do you know the kind of crisis that involves sacrificing yourself completely to God? Have you made that presentation of yourself to him?

A young man sat in my office and said, "I would give my two arms to know God in a personal, warm experience." I told him that God didn't want his two arms. He wanted all of him. You don't present him with your talent and say, "Here I am God, lucky you. Put my talents to work where I can do some great thing for you." He will tell you, "Crawl up on this altar first where I can have all of you as a sacrifice, even your talent, then let's see what I can do with you." God cannot do great things with you until he has done a great work in you. Consecration moves self out of the way so God is free to do his great work in you.

As a special feature of a Veteran's Day ceremony, the people of Bradford, Pennsylvania, lit an eternal flame. A few hours later, police found some young people making use of the flame to toast marshmallows—marshmallow toasters at the eternal flame. The church often has people like that within it. They stop by to warm their hands and receive the goodies, staying on the outskirts, while God wants them to get into the flames.

Consecration is a response of our will to the will of God. It is a reasonable thing to do, but a response with which we struggle. Our struggle is usually because our focus is on what we may lose in surrender rather than on what we will gain.

Consecrating Your Life Produces Reasonable Results

Presenting is the human side of God's work of sanctification and holiness. God has chosen to give us the freedom to choose or reject his work in us. Our spiritual life depends on our response to what he offers, our surrender to his plan. The idea of surrender often clouds our view of the blessing that can only be experienced because of the surrender. Paul acknowledged the blessed life when he exclaimed: "Praise be to the God and Father of our Lord Jesus Christ, who has blessed us in the heavenly realms with every spiritual blessing in Christ. For he chose us in him before the creation of the world to be holy and blameless in his sight" (Eph. 1:3–4). God chose us. Now it is up to us to consecrate ourselves to him so he can bless us "with every spiritual blessing."

When we are completely consecrated to God, he makes us holy and acceptable. Our unconsecrated will causes us to be conformed to the world. When we sacrifice ourselves to God, he transforms us.

It is in the consecrated life that we discover how God's will is good, acceptable, and perfect. This can never happen until you are smart enough to lose yourself in God. Socrates said that the unexamined life was not worth living. If he fully understood life in Christ, he would have said that the un-presented life is not worth living. The surrendered life is the blessed life. It is the victorious life. It is the life that experiences God's good purposes.

To present yourself to God, you must withdraw yourself in some ways from other things. We can lose ourselves in our work, plans, fun, or interests. When we lose ourselves in anything other than God, we lose. What we find is that we have lost. When we lose ourselves in God, we find. We find God's fullness. We find ourselves. We find life.

Present yourself to God, as a sacrifice. Get rid of your excuses and reservations. Surrender your plans and self-interests. Lose yourself in God and find yourself transformed into a person who pleases him.

There are some things that will never come to you until you are willing to give yourself completely for them. The smartest thing you can ever do is to consecrate yourself—freely, fully to God. It is a reasonable response that brings wonderful results.

Takeaway
Consecrating my life fully to God
is the best thing I can do.

Using Your Talents

discover your hidden gifts

Key Insight
God has given you abilities, relationships, talents,
and time that you can use to bless others.

I heard recently about a rather strange gift. A farmer in Bulgaria, Mikhail Janko, claims he has a goat that can discern people's character. When he shows the goat pictures of people, the animal, by its behavior, will indicate a favorable or unfavorable impression. Apparently, the goat head-butts the pictures of unpleasant people but eats the pictures of pleasant people. Janko even used the goat to help him

> It was he who gave some to be apostles, some to be prophets, some to be evangelists, and some to be pastors and teachers, to prepare God's people for works of service, so that the body of Christ may be built up until we all reach unity in the faith and in the knowledge of the Son of God and become mature, attaining to the whole measure of the fullness of Christ.
> —Ephesians 4:11–13

choose prospective boyfriends for his four daughters. Perhaps some of you would like to have such a goat.

The psalmist prayed, "Give me discernment" (Ps. 119:125), but to the best of my knowledge, it had nothing to do with goats. Many of us would love to possess the gift of discernment. But whether God gives you that specific gift or not, he does want to give gifts to his people to make us effective in the work he has called us to do.

God Has Gifts for You

In Ephesians 4:11–13, we find four major gifts: apostle, prophet, evangelist, and pastor-teacher. We sometimes call these the equipping gifts because Paul clearly said such persons are to prepare or equip God's people for works of service.

The Greeks had two different words for *laypersons*. One word meant a person who was not knowledgeable in a specific field or was uneducated or inarticulate. We use this term when talking with the family physician. "Now, doctor, please say that in 'layman's terms,' because I did not understand you."

But that is not the word used in this passage or even in the New Testament. When Paul declared that God gives gifts to equip God's people for service, the term he used means the very people of God. So never say, "Oh, I'm just a layperson." If you ever hear someone say that, an appropriate response would be: "Wow! What an honor that you are just a person of God! What higher honor could you have?"

God intends for laypersons to be his people who minister to their communities in the name of the Lord Jesus Christ.

Now what God has called us to do—be his church in this world—he also equips us to do by giving us spiritual gifts, special abilities from the hand of God. In addition to the equipping gifts

92

in Ephesians, we find several other gifts in Romans 12 and 1 Corinthians 12. For instance, God gives some people the gift of leadership so they can direct the work of God. He gives others the gift of administration so they organize the work of the church. Others receive the gift of teaching and they have the extraordinary ability to communicate spiritual truth. Some possess gifts of mercy and service and they may do many things to meet the needs of people both in- and outside the church.

Every believer has at least one spiritual gift. Peter said, "Each one should use whatever gift he has received to serve others, faithfully administering God's grace in its various forms" (1 Pet. 4:10). At the same time, no believer has all the spiritual gifts.

We Need Each Other

Since each of us has at least one gift, and no one has all the gifts, we really need each other. God did not intend for anyone to be the champion of spiritual gifts to the exclusion of all others. Unfortunately, sometimes we develop a false hierarchy of gifts. In other words, we may think that certain gifts are superior to others. We may think those who have certain gifts are more spiritual than others. Yet God intends for each of us to use the gifts he has given us, because in this way we can help each other. And we really do need each other.

I once heard an ancient legend about a king who walked into his garden one day to find nearly everything withered and dying. He stopped and looked at the oak tree near the gate and found it was discouraged with life because it was not tall and beautiful as the pine. The pine tree was disillusioned because it could not grow sweet, delicious fruit like the pear tree. Yet the pear tree was dissatisfied because it did not have the fragrant aroma of the spruce tree. The king found that dismal mood spreading throughout the garden until he came to the pansy. Its face was bright with cheerfulness.

"Well, I am glad to find one happy countenance in the garden," he said.

"Your majesty," said the pansy, "I concluded that if you wanted a pear or oak tree here, you would have planted one. Instead you wanted a pansy, so I have decided to be the best and brightest flower I can be."

That's exactly the attitude each of us should take: to become the best and brightest person we can be for the sake of our King and for the sake of those around us. We don't all need to be oak, pine, or pear trees. And we certainly are not all going to be pansies. But we do need each other, the full variety of God's creativity within his body, the church.

A schoolteacher had been working with her class on the multiplication tables, teaching them to memorize and recite the various functions. She called upon Johnny to recite the nines. He stumbled along, not doing very well. When he finished, he said, "Teacher, I don't know the nines very well, but I'm a tiger when it comes to the sevens."

He acknowledged what a lot of us realize about ourselves: We're not good at everything, but we're tigers at other things. In the body of Christ, we don't all have to be great at everything because we have each other. What one lacks, another can provide. We need each other.

We Must Be Connected to One Another

Our Scripture passage implies we need to work together. God has not given us the gifts of the Spirit simply so each of us can become a star in our own little circle of influence. We will all be better if we work together.

The story goes that an elderly woman had made plans to travel abroad so she went to the post office to apply for a passport. At the time it was required to take an oath of loyalty to the United States. "Raise your right hand," the clerk instructed. The lady did as she was told.

"Do you swear to defend the Constitution of the United States against all its enemies, foreign and domestic?"

The woman hesitated, turned pale, leaned forward, and asked in a trembling voice, "Uh . . . all by myself?"

That would be a daunting task for any of us. No, we are not in this all by ourselves. We must become connected with each other so each of us will grow stronger and the work we do will be more effective.

On July 24, 2002, nine miners in western Pennsylvania became trapped 240 feet below the surface when they broke through into an abandoned adjacent mine that had collected millions of gallons of water. Rescue efforts began immediately but it was seventy-seven hours before all the miners got out safely. The thing that kept them alive was their decision to stay together and help each other.

The water kept rising, and the men became tired. Sometimes one person would feel weak and others would support him. They tied themselves together so that no one would float away or slip under the water. It was a team effort. They decided whether they lived or died, they would do it together.

An emergency like that almost forces people to make the decision to work together. In the church, we must make the deci-sion—whether we have a sense of urgency or not—to work together; to depend on each other; and to find comfort, courage, and strength from each other.

Mark Twain told about being disturbed at all the discord he saw among God's creatures. Trying to resolve the problem, he put a cat and dog in a cage with each other. Within an hour, he had taught them to be friends. An hour later he added a rabbit and taught them all how to get along with each other. Over the next several days, he added a fox, a goose, a squirrel, and some doves. Finally, he added a monkey, and in time they all became friends and lived together with affection.

Next he decided to take on a bigger problem and try his experiment with religious people. He put an Irish Catholic and a Scottish Presbyterian in a cage together. He added a Muslim, a Methodist, a Buddhist, and a Salvation Army Colonel. He stayed away for two days. When he came back to check the results, he discovered not a specimen remained alive.[1]

Now Mark Twain, who was no great friend of religion, wrote the story tongue-in-cheek, to be sure. But hopefully, it reminds us that in the body of Christ, for the sake of God and for his church, we not only get along but we work together. In so many ways, our survival depends on it, and if we are ever to make an impact on the world around us, it is absolutely essential.

Use What You Have to Help Others

If God gives us gifts—and he does—then he must intend for us to use them in ways that help others.

Years ago, Merv Griffin hosted a television show and one day he interviewed some body builders. As these men stood in front of the cameras, their muscles rippled and glistened. So Merv asked one of them, "What do you use all those muscles for?"

The guy struck one of those flex poses for which body builders are famous.

Merv asked again, "No, that isn't what I meant. What do you actually use those muscles for?"

The guy said, "Here I'll show you," and he turned and assumed a different flex pose.

Merv said, "You still don't understand what I'm getting at. What do you use those muscles for?"

And the guy posed again. He just didn't get it. The muscles were only for show. They apparently had no practical purpose.

That is not the case when it comes to the spiritual gifts God has given each one of us. He intends us to use our gifts to help others.

Helen Keller said, "Life is an exciting business, and most exciting when it is lived for others."[2] We understand that we may not be able to help everybody, but certainly, by God's help and grace, we can help somebody.

Queen Elizabeth, the Queen Mother, died in 2002 at the age of 102. On her eightieth birthday, the British expressed so much affection for her that it took many people by surprise. The British have been known to criticize members of the royal family, yet their attitude toward the Queen Mum, as they affectionately called her, was quite different. Many commentators believe this high regard was due to the Queen Mother's attitude toward her privileged position. She thought of her position as a platform of service, not just privilege. She was so committed to this attitude that during one twenty-five-year period, she did not miss a single engagement through illness.

While it is a great privilege to be a child of God and part of the church of God, we are saved not to be seen, for display, to be admired, or to fill a position, but to serve.

Gert Behanna was an unusual person. She ran through five husbands, was an alcoholic, attempted suicide, and then came to know Christ in her fifties. She began traveling around the country speaking to groups almost every day of the year and was responsible for thousands of people coming to know the Lord.

Bruce Larson talked to her one day and asked her what she had been doing. She said, "Well, I travel around a lot and I used to get so disgusted about the dirty restrooms in gas stations. To go into most of them, you've got to wear galoshes. Each time I used one, I complained to the Lord about how this servant of his was being treated. Then one day Jesus seemed to be saying to me, 'Gert, in as much as you've done it unto me . . .' I said, 'Lord, you mean you use these restrooms too?' When I realized he would be the next person who'd be coming into the gas station restroom after me, I knew I'd better do something about it. Now when I go into a messy restroom, I pick up all the towels and stuff them in the wastebasket. I take the towel and wipe off the mirror and the sink and the toilet seat. I leave the place looking as clean as possible and I say, 'Well, Lord there it is; I hope you enjoy it.'"[3]

It's an attitude of service that says, "I will use what I have to serve him and others."

One pastor told of an emergency call one day, urging him to come quickly. A little boy had been hit by a car. When he arrived, the boy had died. He did his best to comfort the grief-stricken mother. But he knew of another mother who had lost a son. He sent her over to see this young mother. Later the mother whose son had been hit by the car was talking to the pastor. She said, "You were great. You sympathized, but she empathized."

That pastor let someone with ability in that direction handle the situation more effectively than he ever could have done. You too have a spiritual gift that God can use to minister effectively to someone else. Use what you have.

God Has a Plan For You

The word of the LORD came to me, saying, "Before I formed you in the womb I knew you, before you were born I set

you apart; I appointed you as a prophet to the nations."
"Ah, Sovereign LORD," I said, "I do not know how to
speak; I am only a child." But the LORD said to me, "Do
not say, 'I am only a child.' You must go to everyone I
send you to and say whatever I command you. Do not be
afraid of them, for I am with you and will rescue you,"
declares the LORD. Then the LORD reached out his hand
and touched my mouth and said to me, "Now, I have put
my words in your mouth." (Jer. 1:4–9)

The owner of a hardware store in Watertown, New York, had
a problem. He had many items in his store that he could not sell.
A young boy who worked for the merchant had an idea. "Why
don't we put it all on a table out on the sidewalk and stick up a
sign that says, 'ten cents or less—take your choice!'"

The owner tried to put down the idea. He said, "People will
think because the merchandise is so cheap it's falling apart. They
won't buy it, not even for ten cents. (Of course, this was many
years ago when ten cents would have been a real bargain, but
not as ridiculous as it sounds to us today.)

The kid said, "The idea might work; it just might work." The
merchant finally agreed to try the idea.

So the boy set up a table and the items on the sidewalk, along
with his ten-cent sign. In no time, everything sold. The boy said,
"Let's do it again." But the boss said, "No, it won't work the
second time."

The kid got disgusted, quit his job, and started his own business, calling it a "five and ten cent store." Years later, he became
one of the most successful merchandisers in American history. His
name—F. W. Woolworth, whose stores became the forerunner of
stores like K-Mart and Walmart.[4]

God Calls Us to Serve Him

There are many people around even today who think, "It cannot be done." I have a feeling that at the beginning, Jeremiah was one of those people. We know God had a great plan for Jeremiah, but at first, the budding prophet was reluctant. He was not sure it would work, and perhaps God was calling the wrong person.

Jeremiah lived about six hundred years before Christ during a difficult period in the history of Judah. Years earlier, the golden kingdom of David and Solomon had split. By Jeremiah's time, the northern kingdom had already fallen to its enemy Assyria. Now Judah, the southern kingdom, tottered on the edge of disaster. The Babylonians were practically at the gates.

Jeremiah's name means "whom Jehovah hurls" or it can also mean "whom Jehovah exalts." Both ideas fit him, for he was thrust into a religious and political situation when his own personality would have preferred to stay in the background and avoid public appearance. Yet he was also exalted into the high position of God's spokesperson to Jerusalem and the nations.

We have some things in common with Jeremiah. For instance, Jeremiah said, "The word of the LORD came to me" (1:4). That phrase or its equivalent appears eight times in the first chapter. It keeps recurring through the book like a steady drumbeat. Jeremiah was a man with a message—God's message.

Before Jeremiah was born, God had this prophet in mind. Note these four statements God makes about Jeremiah in verse 5: "I formed you . . . I knew you . . . I set you apart . . . I appointed you as a prophet to the nations."

100 Jeremiah was not the only person whom God has known, formed, set apart, and appointed before birth. If the truth were

known, God has that same awareness of each of us. And he calls us to follow him. In Jeremiah's case, God called him to be a prophet. Few of us are called to be prophets, but that does not mean we are not called. If we could hear God speaking, he might be saying, "I have called you to be a teacher or a doctor or a salesperson or a homemaker." He might say, "I have called you to work in that factory or office or to attend that school. That's my call for you at this point in your life."

Someone defined a call as a strong inner impulse toward a particular course of action, especially when accompanied by conviction of divine influence. It isn't just preachers, prophets, missionaries, and ministers who are called. God calls each of us to follow him and to do the work he shows us to do.

Mother Teresa said, "By blood and origin I am Albanian. My citizenship is Indian. I am a Catholic nun. As to my calling, I belong to the whole world. As to my heart, I belong entirely to the heart of Jesus."[5]

Whatever your calling in life, I challenge you to be sure you surrender entirely to the heart of Jesus.

God apparently spoke to Jeremiah, either audibly or through a vision. I don't know how God will direct you. It may be through his Word. He does this often. It may be through the voice of his Spirit in your inner consciousness. It may be through your own personality and gifts and desires. But be conscious that just as God called Jeremiah, he calls us. He calls us first and foremost to follow him. As we are faithful to follow, he leads us in the specific way he wants us to go.

We May Be Reluctant to Accept God's Call

When God called, Jeremiah responded, "Ah, Sovereign LORD . . . I do not know how to speak; I am only a child" (1:6). The Lord cautioned Jeremiah not to say this. "Do not say, 'I am only a child.' You must go to everyone I send you to and say whatever I command you" (1:7).

Jeremiah was probably a young man when God called him. He was likely overwhelmed by the responsibility God was giving him. He may have really felt he was too young for the job.

Across the centuries, many others have made similar statements when faced with the call of God: "I am too young." "I am too old." "I am too poor." "I come from the wrong background." "I am too shy." "I don't have the talent for this." "I don't have anything to offer."

Many such statements rise out of feelings of inferiority and poor self-images. Maxwell Maltz said he believed 95 percent of people have some feelings of inferiority.[6] Why do we feel inadequate and ill-prepared for the work God calls us to do?

Past Failures

How many times have we thought, "I tried that before and failed. There's no point in trying again"? In that regard, I think about James Irwin, a pilot who was injured in a terrible plane crash. He experienced painful suffering, loss of memory, and various other problems. But Irwin refused to let that keep him down. He applied to the corps of astronauts and was rejected. He tried again and was rejected; tried again, rejected. Tried again . . . and became the eighth man to set foot on the moon. He refused to allow his past failures to limit him.

Upbringing

People sometimes blame their parents. I don't know any perfect parents; we have all made some mistakes. Unwittingly, parents sometimes encourage inferiority when they repeatedly criticize, shame, reject, and scold their children, especially when they rarely give praise, encouragement, compliments, and emotional support. Some unwise parents have even implied or stated openly that their children were a nuisance, stupid, or incompetent. So when children who are reared in such an atmosphere reach their teens and adulthood, they have the perfect excuse. They can say, "You see, I am the way I am because of the way my parents treated me."

The problem with giving in to the temptation to blame others is that we are creatures of choice. We can choose to live under the shadow of an unfortunate upbringing, or we can choose to work on overcoming those things.

Unrealistic Expectations

Some people set their goals so high that they invite failure. If a person sets a goal so high that he knows he cannot reach it, he can always say, "See, I knew I couldn't do it." He digs a deeper hole of inferiority in which to wallow. Sometimes we try to achieve the unrealistic expectations of others and again we experience defeat.

Faulty Theology

People often mistake inferiority for humility, and they confuse self-esteem with pride. The Bible encourages us to be humble and not to think of ourselves more highly than we ought. Some conscientious persons have read statements like: "There is no one righteous, not even one; there is no one who understands, no one who seeks God. All have turned away, they have together become worthless; there is no one who does good, not even one" (Rom. 3:10–12), and think that has to do with our self-worth. Such persons may say, "See, even the Bible says we are worthless. I'll never amount to anything."

But that passage of Scripture is showing how sin affects people when they let it dominate their lives. As Christians we are not supposed to be dominated by sin. When we say, "I am worthless, I don't have any talents, or if I do, I shouldn't say so; it wouldn't sound humble"—that isn't humility; it is an attitude of inferiority.

Humility is having a sane, sensible, honest, realistic estimate of yourself and your abilities. It means understanding that while you do have faults and have much room to grow, you also have talents and abilities to develop and use to your fullest potential with God's help!

The flip side of the coin is that sometimes people confuse pride and self-esteem. Pride is an exaggerated desire to win the notice or praise of others. It is an arrogant, haughty estimation of oneself in relation to others. Pride involves taking a superior position, disregarding the concerns, opinions, and desires of others.

Self-esteem means seeing ourselves as the Bible sees us. The Bible constantly affirms that human beings are valuable in God's sight. God created us in his own image with intellectual abilities, the capacity to communicate, the freedom to make choices, and the knowledge of right and wrong. The Christian view of self-esteem says that God sees us as persons of worth, significance, and value.

How to Overcome Reluctance

Think Positively

What did God tell Jeremiah? "Do not say, 'I am only a child'" (Jer. 1:7). We all need to reorganize our thinking about ourselves. We are not simply children in God's eyes, incapable of accomplishing worthwhile things for his kingdom. God formed us, as he did Jeremiah. He knew us before we were born, and he knows who we really are.

Someone once observed, "The man who thinks he can and the man who thinks he cannot are both right." So since we have a choice, let's choose to be positive.

I like what Edgar Guest said:

Somebody said that it couldn't be done,
But he with a chuckle replied
That maybe it couldn't, but he would be one
Who wouldn't say so till he'd tried.
So he buckled right in with the trace of a grin
On his face. If he worried he hid it.
He started to sing as he tackled the thing
That couldn't be done, and he did it.

Somebody scoffed: "Oh, you'll never do that;
At least no one ever has done it."
But he took off his coat and he took off his hat,
And the first thing we knew he'd begun it.
With a lift of his chin and a bit of a grin,
Without any doubting or quiddit,
He started to sing as he tackled the thing
That couldn't be done, and he did it.

There are thousands to tell you it cannot be done,
There are thousands to prophesy failure;
There are thousands to point out to you one by one
The dangers that wait to assail you.
But just buckle in with a bit of a grin,
Just take off your coat and go to it;
Just start in to sing as you tackle the thing
That "cannot be done," and you'll do it.[7]

Think positively about yourself and your abilities and especially about what God can do through you.

Take Responsibility

God told Jeremiah, "You must go to everyone I send you to and say whatever I command you" (1:7). Overwhelming feelings of inferiority cause us to avoid responsibility because we just "know" it cannot be done. But God encouraged Jeremiah not to be afraid of the people to whom he would send the prophet (1:8). He also assured Jeremiah that he would be with him. God provides the courage and strength to face whatever we have to face. He will help us do whatever we have to do. It is not a sin to think well of yourself, if that is a sane, sensible estimate of your abilities.

We *Can* Serve Effectively

Martin Luther King, Jr. was speaking about that very thing when he said, "Everybody can be great, because everybody can serve. You don't have to have a college degree to serve. You don't have to make your subject and verb agree to serve. You don't have to know about Plato and Aristotle to serve. You don't have to know Einstein's theory of relativity to serve. You don't have to know the second theory of thermodynamics in physics to serve. You only need a heart full of grace. A soul generated by love."[8] All of us can serve . . . and we can serve effectively, by his grace.

Who knows how much healthier all of us would be if we simply learned to use the gifts God has given us and serve others? Dr. Karl Menninger, the famous psychiatrist, was answering questions from the audience after giving a lecture. One man asked, "What would you advise a person to do if he felt a nervous breakdown coming on?"

Many of those present expected Menninger to reply, "Consult a psychiatrist." Instead he answered, "Lock up your house, go across the railroad tracks, find someone in need, and do something for them."[9] In other words, serve.

Benjamin Franklin was one of the greatest inventors in the history of our nation. Yet it was typical of Franklin to give his ideas away. In 1742 he invented a stove that would more efficiently heat a room instead of sending most of the warm air up the chimney. The governor of Pennsylvania offered to give him a monopoly patent. Not only did Franklin refuse this offer, he printed a pamphlet, giving complete instructions on how to build and operate such a stove, so that any good blacksmith could make one. A redesigned street lamp, the rubber catheter, and bifocal glasses are examples of other ideas he gave away, free of charge. He said, "As we enjoy great advantages from the inventions of others, we should be glad of an opportunity to serve others by any inventions of ours."[10]

You may never be an inventor like Franklin, but you can serve. God had a plan for Jeremiah and he has a plan for you and me.

Later in Jeremiah, God told the prophet, "Today I have made you a fortified city, an iron pillar and a bronze wall to stand against the whole land" (1:18). In other words, life would not be easy for Jeremiah, but God equipped him for it. The fortified city is a symbol of one who could not be easily conquered. An iron pillar could not be easily broken. And a bronze wall could not be penetrated. It was as if God were saying, "Jeremiah, whatever you face, I will make you a strong enough person to cope with it and to persevere."

In your life and mine, we face big challenges. The work of the kingdom is not always easy. But whatever God has called you to do, he will give you the gifts to do it effectively, and he will give you the strength to do it for as long as it takes.

Takeaway
I have what it takes to make a difference in the world!

How to Enjoy Giving Away Money

putting God first in your finances

Key Insight
When you put God first in your life,
you will be generous with others.

How much money would it take for you to feel you had a fortune? A $250 thousand? A million? Ten million? My guess is that not all of us would define a fortune in exactly the same way.

Several years ago, someone did research in which it was discovered that only 5 percent of Americans earning less than $15,000 a year believed they had achieved the American dream. I think that is understandable. Fifteen thousand dollars is not a great deal of money. So it makes sense that only

When the LORD brought back the captives to Zion, we were like men who dreamed. Our mouths were filled with laughter, our tongues with songs of joy. Then it was said among the nations, "The LORD has done great things for them." The LORD has done great things for us, and we are filled with joy. Restore our fortunes, O LORD, like streams in the Negev. Those who sow in tears will reap with songs of joy. He who goes out weeping, carrying seed to sow, will return with songs of joy, carrying sheaves with him.
—Psalm 126:1–6

5 percent of those people would feel that $15,000 constituted the American dream.

Yet the same research showed that of Americans who made more than $50,000 a year, the percentage who believed they had achieved the American dream was 6 percent. Imagine that! It's a difference of $35,000, but only one percentage point difference in happiness.

Now you might adjust the figures upward to account for inflation, but the point is that we all see it from our own perspective. Furthermore, the dollar amount required to make us feel we have achieved the American dream is probably somewhat more than what we have now!

Great Things

The people described in Psalm 126 had not lost only a fortune in money; they had lost nearly everything. Because the Babylonians had taken them into captivity, they lost their homeland, sacred religious sites, and livelihood—almost everything except their lives. When the Persians conquered the Babylonian empire, the Persian king released the Israelites to return to their homeland.

Psalm 126 celebrates that event. You can almost feel the hilarity that accompanied their return. They were "like men who dreamed." Their "mouths were filled with laughter" and their "tongues with songs of joy" (126:1–2). They almost had to pinch themselves to believe it was true.

The other nations, watching them stream back to their homeland, said, "The LORD has done great things for them" (126:2). The people of Israel said, "The LORD has done great things for us, and we are filled with joy" (126:3).

Interestingly, when the psalmist told about their deliverance from captivity, even though it came at the hands of the Persian monarch, he uttered not a word about the king of Persia. Instead it is "the LORD" who "brought back the captives to Zion" (126:1). That is our testimony as well, if we are honest.

God Has Done Great Things for Us

All of us have to say, "The Lord has done great things for us." Especially if you know the Lord and you are his child, you have to admit: If he never did another thing, we would still have to say, "He has done great things for us."

To experience forgiveness of sins is, in a spiritual sense, equivalent to being released from captivity. Paul told the Ephesians (and us), "You were dead in your transgressions and sins" but God "made us alive with Christ" (Eph. 2:1, 5). And he reminded the Colossians that God "has rescued us from the dominion of darkness and brought us into the kingdom of the Son he loves" (Col. 1:13).

Every redeemed person has a testimony. Although the details will differ, each one can say, "Before I met Christ, here's what my life was like . . . Then I met Jesus. And now, this is how my life has changed . . ."

Knowing God adds life, zest, and meaning to one's existence. I once heard of a man who explained his work in the sewers of Chicago this way: "I dig the ditch to get the money to buy the food to get the strength to dig the ditch."[1] Talk about a treadmill . . . and not a very attractive one at that! Yet that's the way many people live their lives.

It's no shame to work in the sewers. Somebody has to do it. But the point is: What adds meaning? Whether a person works in the sewers or in an immaculate office, what brings joy and contentment? We're saying that the Lord has done great things for us. That's our testimony! He has changed our lives forever for the better!

God Will Restore Our Fortunes

That phrase, "restore our fortunes" or some version of it, is repeated several times throughout the Old Testament. It nearly always refers to the people of Israel coming back from captivity. So in a sense, God had just done that. He had released them from their captivity and now they were back in the Promised Land. In a real way, their fortunes had been restored. So why would they now pray, "Restore our fortunes, O Lord" (Ps. 126:4)?

Although they were back in their homeland, it was a shambles. Their captors had destroyed the city of Jerusalem. They had destroyed the temple. They demolished other cities and towns and uprooted their vineyards. So although the people were back in their homeland, they faced an enormous task of rebuilding.

Perhaps this is why the psalmist spoke of sowing "in tears" (126:5) and going out "weeping" (126:6). On the one hand, they were delirious with joy; and on the other, they faced the sad, backbreaking work of starting over again.

Again, we can identify with these restored captives. Though delivered from our sinful past, we too face the task of rebuilding our lives. Like the captives, we would prefer that God restored our fortunes quickly "like streams in the Negev" (126:4). In the dry, desert region of the Negev in southern Israel, a downpour could suddenly fill the wadis, gullies, and watercourses. That kind of sudden restoration is what we all prefer. Our prayer might be, "O Lord, restore my fortune like a flood, a flash flood, filling up all my empty places with your overwhelming blessings."

Yet we know that in God's providence, rebuilding often takes time like a ripening crop. This is why the psalmist strongly asserted that those who patiently "sow in tears" will eventually "reap with songs of joy" (126:5). So our prayer might be, "Lord, if my fortune can't be restored like a flash flood, at least let it be restored with the certainty of harvest that follows planting, of reaping that follows sowing."

As we think about rebuilding our fortunes personally, this is a good opportunity to talk about the importance of developing good financial habits. Actually, some of this may happen automatically. When people come to Christ, they often change many things for the better, including their spending habits. Instead of spending their money on bad habits that cause one's fortune to trickle down the drain, they become more responsible. They take better care of their families. Their priorities change as they grow in Christ and begin to understand the things that are important to the kingdom.

The story has been told that a man who had recently become a believer encountered an old friend, who had not yet made a commitment to Christ, but who had a better knowledge of the Bible than the new believer. The unbeliever began peppering him with questions.

"Where was Jesus born?" he asked.

The man did not know.

"Where did he grow up?"

The new believer shrugged.

"Do you know where Jesus turned the water into wine?"

The poor fellow finally said, "No, I must confess that I'm so new to the faith that I don't know very much about the Bible yet. But this is what I do know: God has been turning alcohol into clothing and food and furniture at our house because my life has been so completely changed."[2]

New priorities will change our patterns of spending and some-times that alone is a great step toward restoring our fortunes.

So, with hope, we pray for God to restore our fortunes, know-ing full well that we may have to do a lot of work to cooperate with his program for us.

After the Great Chicago Fire in 1871, residents saw this notice on the blackened ruins of a shop that had once flourished: "Everything lost, except wife, children and hope! Business resumes as usual tomorrow morning!"[3]

God Will Bring a Harvest of Blessings

Dudley lived in a small town in West Virginia. On his seventy-fifth birthday, a local pilot offered to take him for an airplane ride. For about thirty minutes, they flew over the small town and he treated Dudley to a perspective on his community he had never seen before. When they landed, one of the man's friends asked how he enjoyed the flight and inquired, "Were you scared, Dudley?" He hesitated a moment and said, "Well, no, but I never put my full weight down."[4]

Such hesitation, such lack of confidence, will never work if you are in the sowing and reaping business. A farmer has to put his whole effort into it and sow the seed with the confidence that a harvest will result. Just as the farmer has to sow the seed with confidence, we must take the steps toward restoring our fortunes with confidence.

Confidence in God Involves Trust. Someone observed that trust involves letting go and knowing that God will catch you. The wise man said, "Trust in the LORD with all your heart and lean not on your own understanding; in all your ways acknowl-edge him, and he will make your paths straight" (Prov. 3:5–6).

Billy Graham said, "Our lives must be consistent with the slogan on our coins, 'In God We Trust' . . . There's little point in talking about corporate or national dealing with the problem if we don't come to grips with it individually ourselves.... You must choose, even this day, whom you will serve. Will it be God or money?"[5]

In determining how much we will give to God's work through the church, people are sometimes hesitant to give the percentage they know they should give because they're always wondering, "Will I have enough left for other needs?" This is where we trust God and obey his directions. Acting confidently involves a spirit of trust.

Confidence in God Involves Commitment. Jesus told his followers, "Sell your possessions and give to the poor. Provide purses for yourselves that will not wear out, a treasure in heaven that will not be exhausted, where no thief comes near and no moth destroys. For where your treasure is, there your heart will be also" (Luke 12:33–34).

Purses that will not wear out. What an idea! He must be talking about a spiritual purse, because our physical wallets do deteriorate and we have to replace them. But think what it would mean to have God's blessings on your finances to the point that your wallet always has money in it!

Martin Luther said, "I have held many things in my hands, and I have lost them all; but whatever I have placed in God's hands, that I still possess."[6] That is like a purse that will not wear out and a treasure that will not be exhausted.

Luther also observed, "There are three conversions necessary: the conversion of the heart, mind and purse. Of these three, the conversion of the purse is most difficult."[7] Yet once we make that conversion, we can become a source of blessing to many.

Confidence in God Excludes Selfishness. John Wesley knew something of the peril of holding one's money too closely. He said, "When I have any money, I get rid of it quickly, lest it find a way into my heart."[8] Wesley could have become one of the wealthiest men in England. However, he continued to live on the same amount for his personal expenses, and as his income grew, he simply gave away larger and larger portions of his wealth. When we are less than fully generous with God, it hinders our ability to trust him. After all, if we withhold a portion of what we know belongs to him, why should we expect him to bless us with all the blessings he would like to give?

Israel's return from Babylonian captivity was tied to obedience. This had been true for centuries. Hundreds of years before the people of Israel went into captivity, God told them, "When all these blessings and curses I have set before you come upon you and you take them to heart wherever the LORD your God disperses you among the nations, and when you and your children return to the LORD your God and obey him with all your heart and with all your soul according to everything I command you today, then the LORD your God will restore your fortunes and have compassion on you and gather you again from all the nations where he scattered you" (Deut. 30:1–3).

What is God saying to you right now? Have you been obedient to him in terms of sowing the seeds of financial investment? Someone observed, "You can't take your money to heaven, but you can invest it for eternity." What kind of financial investments have you been making for the kingdom of God?

Perhaps you're thinking, "I am trying to have the confidence that God is going to restore my fortunes. But I'm just not there yet. What do I do?"

My best advice is to be faithful. Start where you are with as large a percentage as you can manage—stretching a bit by faith as you trust God to help you grow in this area of the stewardship of wealth. As Billy Graham points out, "Giving to God is a guaranteed investment with a certain return. Investment in God is a no-risk, always-profitable act that is not subject to the whims of the stock market or of economic uncertainties."[9]

The Duke of Wellington holds a place of honor in history as the person who defeated Napoleon at the battle of Waterloo in 1815. A recent biographer of the duke claims to have an advantage over all the other biographers who have written about him across the years. This biographer claims the advantage because he found an old account ledger that shows how the duke spent his money. That insight, claims the writer, gives us far better clues to what the duke thought was important than all the speeches he gave or the letters he wrote.

If someone wrote your biography, what would it say if all they had to guide them was your checkbook or your income tax return? What would it say you thought was important? What loyalties would it reveal? What priorities?

Everything we have comes from God's hand. We are stewards of all he has given us. Let's rise to the occasion and put our confidence in God. Embracing trust and exercising commitment, let's reject selfishness and move forward with hope. If we will walk in obedience to him, he will bring a harvest of blessings.

Great Church

"Everyone was filled with awe, and many wonders and miraculous signs were done by the apostles. All the believers were together and had everything in common. Selling their possessions and goods, they gave to anyone as he had need" (Acts 2:43–45).

I have a family portrait in my home. It is a collection of smiling, angelic faces, but the picture doesn't tell the whole story. We arrived at the studio about 7:00 p.m. The picture hanging in our living room, with all of the sweet little smiles, was taken about 8:58 p.m. It is a still shot, meaning you can look at it and it doesn't move—which is a good thing. It is a moment frozen in time that does not indicate all that went on before or during that moment. Getting each tired and hungry kid to hold still and smile at the same time is no small feat. You can't see my one hand trying to keep a little one from crawling off my knee while my other hand is twisted up in another's shirt trying to keep him corralled in place. The picture you see doesn't tell you everything about our family, but it's a pretty good representation.

I really like the picture we get of the church in Acts 2. It is a moment in the life of God's family frozen in time. It probably doesn't tell us everything that was going on. We don't see everything behind the scenes. But the portrait we get of the emerging church is something to cherish. The moment frozen in a picture becomes unfrozen and active in real time as the church functions as God's family in its contemporary context.

Acts 2 shows four core values that make up the portrait of the early church. These core values are transferable and become markers for a healthy church in any time or culture.

The Church Is in Tune with God

The God-centeredness of this church was evident in the first verses of the chapter as they gathered together in a room and waited until the Holy Spirit came upon them.

I don't wait well. If something is supposed to get done and those responsible are not getting it done, I have been known to step in and get it done myself. This is not good leadership, and I know it. But I want to see some action, and I want to see things get done.

This approach is too often transferred into church life. We want things done so we do them without regard to the plan, timing, or empowerment of God. Church life becomes self-centered rather than God-centered.

Knowledge is exploding at such a rate—more than two thousand pages a minute—that even Einstein couldn't keep up. In fact, if you read twenty-four hours a day, from age twenty-one to seventy, and retained all you read, you would be 1.5 million years behind when you finished. It seems impossible that we could really know God. But we can!

The church of Acts 2 came together and waited for God to act so they could join him with what he would do. They were together. Together is a great thing when God is in the center of the gathering. Being together can be dangerous when he is not. The reason for the church's togetherness was their commitment to God-centeredness.

Here's how the early church stayed in tune with God. They devoted themselves to:

- the apostles teaching about God;
- prayer and breaking of bread;
- praising God; and
- spending time at the temple every day.

The result of being God-centered was worship that was dynamic. God was present. Wonderful and miraculous things happened because of his presence. Everyone was filled with awe. They were aware of God. They were reverently engaged in worship.

Many wonders and miraculous signs were done by the apostles. It would be easy for strong personalities to take over as attention was drawn to their miracle-working power. This kind of activity can become intoxicating. It was critical that the apostles and the church be God-centered, not person-centered. It was critical that miracles not be the center of their activity, but that God be the center of their worship.

Worship is central to the activity of the church. God is central to worship in the church. A healthy church is marked by dynamic worship in which there is keen awareness of God and he is active in the activity of the church.

The Church Is in Touch with Others

When the church is in tune with God, it is going to be in touch with others. John Wesley said, "I want the whole Christ for my Saviour, the whole Bible for my book, the whole Church for my fellowship, and the whole world for my mission field."[10] That's a great portrait of the church.

People mattered to the Acts 2 church—both those who were inside and those who were outside. The togetherness that characterized their upper-room experience found its way into the fabric of what it meant to be a church. They were devoted to the truth that they shared, and they were devoted to each other.

The relationship they had with God enhanced the relationship they had with others. What a beautiful family portrait graces the walls of church history:

- They were devoted to the fellowship.
- All the believers were together.
- They gave to anyone as he had need.
- Their hearts were glad and sincere.

The needs of people were met in the fellowship—material, spiritual, emotional, and social.

The church is to be people focused. A few years ago, I was asked to go back to one of my first pastorates to speak. It was a church I pastored while in college. It was sad to see how much it had declined from the days when it was active and growing. At first I thought the small crowd was because they had announced that I was going to speak, but I found that the crowd was about the size usually expected. I sat on the platform with a key leader of the church who had been in the church all his life. I knew almost everyone there, with the exception of a young couple seated in the back. I asked the leader next to me the name of the couple and his reply was, "I don't know. They have been coming for a month or so, but I don't know who they are." I was surprised they had continued as long as they had.

A minister saw Robert Schuler's Hour of Power television service. He was impressed by the moment in worship when people turned to greet each other and speak to one another. This was totally foreign to their church's worship pattern. The minister felt that his church was a bit stuffy and that they should incorporate this time of friendliness. So one Sunday he announced that the following Sunday they were going to begin the custom. At the close of that same service, a gentleman turned to a lady behind him, smiled, and said, "Good morning." Shocked and upset by his boldness, she replied, "I beg your pardon. That friendliness business does not start until next Sunday."

Friendliness is not a program—it is to be the pattern of a vibrant fellowship of believers because the church is people focused.

Two great things dominated the devotion of the Acts 2 church—the apostles' teaching and "the fellowship." *Fellowship* is a great word. It embodies communion. It speaks of being in common, of sharing in a community where giving and receiving takes place at both a material and spiritual level. Fellowship is more than a cup of coffee and a piece of pie.

People need community fellowship. The church is a fellowship. Believers should share with each other at all levels of their lives. It's within this hallowed fellowship that they find connection with others and God.

The Church Gives Generously to God and Others

The great automaker Henry Ford was once asked to donate money for the construction of a new medical facility. The billionaire pledged to donate $5,000. The next day in the newspaper, the headline read, "Henry Ford contributes $50,000 to the local hospital." The irate Ford was on the phone immediately to complain to the fund-raiser that he had been misunderstood. The fund-raiser replied that they would print a retraction in the paper the following day to read, "Henry Ford reduces his donation by $45,000." Realizing the poor publicity that would result, the industrialist agreed to the $50,000 contribution in return for the following: That above the entrance to the hospital was to be carved the biblical inscription: "I came among you and you took me in."[11]

That's the attitude a lot of people have about giving to God and others. They think it's something like being ripped off or taken advantage of. But the true church—the church that is in tune with God and others—will give generously.

The Acts 2 church was mission driven. That mission is reflected in these verses. Their mission was to praise God and live so that people outside of the church would be influenced toward the Lord, be saved, and be assimilated into the family. The family picture is always changing as new members are added. They usually come as infants, who by their nature need a lot of attention and care by the old-timers. But because this is the mission of the church, there is a lot of rejoicing when a new one is added. It is sad when a church family has no new life reflected in its family picture. It won't be long before the picture will be tucked away in an attic or as a memory in a photo album somewhere—a family whose bloodline has ended. That happens when a church loses its commitment to mission: to praise God and influence others to join the family.

And they were willing to give generously to accomplish that mission. In fact, the church was so blessed, that people were willing to sell their possessions, giving whatever they had to further the kingdom of God and meet the needs of others. How were they willing to do that? Mother Theresa said, "If you give what you do not need, it isn't giving."[12] Maybe they realized that God would always meet their needs. So they could freely give what they had for others.

Here's the question for us to consider: Do we want churches that are truly in tune with God and in touch with others? Then we have to be giving. And this may sound too simple, but it is really true: A generous church is made up of generous people. If we are together going to be a generous body, then each of us must be willing to give generously. But for some of us, that doesn't come easily.

When you go to a doctor for your annual check-up, he or she will often begin to poke, prod, and press various places, all the while asking, "Does this hurt?" and "How about this?" If you cry out in pain, one of two things has happened. Either the doctor has pushed too hard, without the right sensitivity; or, more likely, there's something wrong, and the doctor will say, "We'd better do some more tests. It's not supposed to hurt there!" So it is when pastors preach on financial responsibility, and certain members cry out in discomfort, criticizing the message and the messenger. Either the pastor has pushed too hard, or perhaps there's something wrong. In that case, I say, "My friend, we're in need of the Great Physician because it's not supposed to hurt there."

If it hurts to be generous, then something is wrong. It means that we are either not in tune with God or in touch with each other. Generosity is not a painful thing. It is a delightful experience. When you are truly in tune with God, the natural response of your heart will be to give.

My friend Steve Doerr sends an e-mail newsletter out and reports on his work with Wycliffe Bible Translators. Recently the story of Sadie Sieker captured my attention. Sadie served for many years as a house-parent for missionaries' children in the Philippines. She loved books. Though she gladly loaned out some, others she treasured in a footlocker under her bed. Once, in the quiet of the night, Sadie heard a faint gnawing sound. After searching all around her room, she discovered that the noise was coming from her footlocker. When she opened it, she found nothing but an enormous pile of dust. All the books she had kept to herself had been lost to termites. What we give away, we keep. What we hoard, we lose.

Let's not lose the opportunity that has been given to us. This is our time. This is our moment to serve the Lord. We have been given great opportunities and tremendous resources. Let's use them to good advantage in serving the King. Let's keep ourselves in tune with God. Let's get in touch with the needs of other people. Let's give generously to God and others.

We can do it!

Takeaway

Tithing blesses God's kingdom people—and blesses me!

Welcoming Others

the lifestyle of hospitality

Key Insight
The giving lifestyle includes the biblical practice
of opening our lives to others.

Herb Gardner was a playwright whose most famous Broadway hit was *A Thousand Clowns*. He wrote other plays too and one that only lasted three weeks on Broadway was entitled, *The Goodbye People*. One scene in the play shows the lead character trying to get financial backing for his failing business from family and friends. He calls them on the telephone and as soon as they find out what he is after, one by one they back off, cool down, and say goodbye as quickly as possible.

Love must be sincere. Hate what is evil; cling to what is good. Be devoted to one another in brotherly love. Honor one another above yourselves. Never be lacking in zeal, but keep your spiritual fervor, serving the Lord. Be joyful in hope, patient in affliction, faithful in prayer. Share with God's people who are in need. Practice hospitality.
—Romans 12:9–13

He keeps hearing that "goodbye" from one after another and finally makes this observation: "At the end of the conversation, these sweethearts'll do a 'goodbye' for you—oh *boy*, its *beautiful!* 'Hello,' they don't do so good; and after 'Hello,' nervous and rotten . . . but 'Goodbye,' will they do a job for you on 'Goodbye'! 'Goodbye . . . keep in touch . . . so long. . . .' All of a sudden warm and personal and terrific . . . 'Goodbye to ya . . . we'll have lunch . . . see ya around . . .' All of a sudden it's happiness, it's sweetness, it's their best number, it's the goodbye people and they're feelin' terrific; they got through a whole phone call without promising anything."[1]

We are too often like the goodbye people. We are wary and cautious. We fend off people from our privacy. We don't want people to get too close. We have become the goodbye people, when what we really need is to become the hello people.

Tucked in among several practical instructions in Romans 12, the apostle Paul called us to become hello people. He said, "Share with God's people who are in need. Practice hospitality" (12:13).

Hundreds of years before Paul wrote these words, God commanded his chosen people to welcome the unchosen. Laws of that day protected the aliens who were living in Israel. God called upon his people to go above and beyond decent behavior to these outsiders and actually love the strangers in their midst (Deut. 10:19). Jesus also commanded his listeners to go an extra mile with someone like a Roman soldier, who would have been an uncomfortable stranger for Jewish people in that time (Matt. 5:41).

Now lest we think a stranger is only a foreigner, we should refine our definition a bit to fit the context of our church. A stranger may simply be someone you do not yet know. He or she might be someone from a different economic class or age group, someone with a disability different from yours, or even someone whose theological persuasion is a bit different from yours. For most of us, a stranger is probably someone whom we have not met and is in need of a friend.

I want to suggest some things that may help us grasp what Paul was teaching about practicing hospitality.

Practice Hospitality as a Lifestyle, not a Discipline

The Bible teaches us to be good stewards. God owns everything, but he gives us stewardship or control over many areas of life. We commonly associate stewardship with money, but he also gives us time, talents, and even influence. This area of influence directly relates to hospitality. In developing hospitality as a lifestyle, here is one thing to avoid: Don't confuse hospitality with entertaining. Someone has defined entertaining as: "Come to my house; admire my possessions; see the beautiful way the table is laid. Enjoy the scrumptious food that has taken me all week to prepare. See how perfectly neat and tidy and clean my house is. Come and listen to my views and thoughts."[2]

Inviting guests into your home can be pretty stressful unless you are gifted in that area. Some people seem to have a natural talent, or perhaps it is even a spiritual gift, of making others feel comfortable. I would guess that is not true for most people. But Paul said, "Practice hospitality" (Rom. 12:13). So what about those of us who do not have that gift? How do we practice hospitality?

Perhaps it will help if we break down the word *hospitality* and see that it comes from the same root as our words *hospital* and *hospice*. After all, should not the church resemble a hospital more than a country club? Is this not a place where people can find help, healing, and hope? This is a place to get bandaged up, not to be put on display.

| 127

The word *hospice* can mean "shelter." But for many, it has come to mean a place or a ministry that cares for people who are dying. People with terminal illnesses receive help from hospice. I have a feeling that more than we know people all around us are dying, not just from terminal illnesses, but from other things. People are dying on the inside. Some are dying to get connected. Some are dying to have a friend. Others are dying to be affirmed or dying to be touched, even if it is just eye contact. This is why people need the hospitality of the church; it's because they may feel they are dying inside and they need a place of shelter, hospitality, renewal, and hopefulness. We long for something else— friendship, meaningful connections, something deeper than a nod or an informal greeting.

Become a Person Whose Life Centers on Others

Someone asked Margaret Mead, the renowned anthropologist, to indicate the first sign of civilization in any culture. They expected her to suggest the first sign might be a clay pot or a fishhook or a grinding stone, or some other elementary symbol of civilization. Her surprising answer was, "A healed femur." The femur, as you know, is the leg bone above the knee. She explained that we never find evidence of a healed femur where the law of the jungle, survival of the fittest, reigns. A healed femur indicates that someone did an injured person's hunting and gathering for the weeks it took for the bone to heal. This evidence of compassion, she said, is the first sign of real civilization.

It appears that Paul was teaching us that such compassion should be part of the ministry of hospitality. Also, it stands as evidence of the true Christian spirit.

T. R. Glover said, "The Gospel of [Jesus Christ] began with friendship."[3] When you think about it, you can see it is true. Jesus did not go about simply teaching lofty theological concepts. He did not establish some great institution. He became friends with people, all kinds of people.

John Wooden, the great basketball coach, once said, "You can't live a perfect day without doing something for someone who will never be able to repay you."[4] That resonates with the proverb that teaches, "Do not withhold good from those who deserve it, when it is in your power to act" (Prov. 3:27).

Here's the point: Become a person whose life is centered on blessing others, whether they thank you or not. As William Kingman Brewster pointed out, "The fullness or emptiness of life will be measured by the extent to which a man feels that he has an impact on the lives of others."[5]

Look for Opportunities to Be Generous

The Scripture gives us a clear challenge—practice hospitality. It says in another place, "Do not forget to entertain strangers, for by so doing some people have entertained angels without knowing it" (Heb. 13:2).

Bruce Larson tells the story of a farmer named Worthy Taylor, who hired a young man named Jim to work for him one summer. Jim had many chores to do around the farm. He milked the cows and chopped the wood, among other things. He ate his meals with the family but slept in the hayloft out in the barn. Over the course of the summer, Jim fell in love with the farmer's daughter. He finally mustered the courage to ask the farmer for his daughter's hand in marriage. But Worthy Taylor refused young

129

Jim because he knew the young man did not have any money and did not appear to have bright prospects for the future. Jim packed his belongings and left.

Thirty-five years later, Worthy Taylor was doing quite well. He had prospered as a farmer and decided it was time to build a new barn. In the process of tearing down the old one, Taylor was looking at the rafters above the place where Jim had slept that summer, thirty-five years earlier. There on one of the rafters, Jim had written his entire name—James A. Garfield. That name meant something to Worthy Taylor because now James A. Garfield was president of the United States. Taylor had entertained a future president.[6]

We don't always know the investment we are making—for good or bad—when we give or withhold our hospitality. Yet we can look for opportunities to be generous.

Sometimes when we think of generosity, we think of those who are fabulously wealthy, and we know we can never achieve that level of giving. Some time ago, Bill Gates earmarked $1 billion over a twenty-year period to establish a charitable trust for health and education. While that is enormously commendable, probably none of us will ever be in a position to make a contribution of that magnitude.

Jesus did not say, "If you give $1 billion, you will not lose your reward." He said, "If anyone gives even a cup of cold water to one of these little ones because he is my disciple, I tell you the truth, he will certainly not lose his reward" (Matt. 10:42).

Who knows, but developing a generous spirit may actually make you a healthier, happier person. When John D. Rockefeller was fifty-three years old, he was probably the wealthiest man on earth at that time. But he was so focused on making money that it cost him his health. He had an income of $1 million a week, yet he lost all his hair and all he could eat was crackers and milk.

Then Rockefeller began using his wealth to help others. As he adopted a more generous lifestyle, his health improved. He began to sleep and eat normally and began to enjoy life in general. S. I. McMillen once referenced this story in a college chapel service and said, "Into the soul of John D. came refreshing streams of love and gratitude from those whom he was helping." His health changed so radically that he lived until he was ninety-eight.

That story bears out what Matthew Henry often said, "If the hand be shut, it is a sign the heart is hardened."[7] Open your hands and let God bless others through you.

An old legend has circulated about a monastery that fell on hard times. It used to be the center of much activity, with many young monks who actively did their work and a vibrant choir that sang in the chapel. Over time things changed. Only a few old monks remained and people no longer came there to be nourished by prayer.

An old rabbi came into the area and built a hut at the edge of the woods near the monastery property. No one ever spoke to him, but when they noticed he was around, word would circulate, "The rabbi walks in the woods."

The abbot of the monastery decided one day to visit the rabbi and bare his heart to him. Discouragement over the condition of the monastery was wearing him down and he was desperate to talk with someone about it. The rabbi welcomed the abbot with open arms and the two sat quietly together for awhile.

Finally the rabbi spoke. He said, "You and your brothers are serving God with heavy hearts and you have come to ask a teaching of me. I will give you a teaching, but you can only repeat it once. After that, no one must ever say it aloud again." The rabbi looked straight at the abbot and said, "The Messiah is among you."

The next morning the abbot called his monks together for a meeting. He told them he had received a teaching from the rabbi in the woods. Once he gave it to them, they were never to say it again. He told them, "The rabbi says that one of us is the Messiah."

Ripples of shock rolled through the group. What did this mean? The Messiah among us? Could it be old Brother John? No, he is too crotchety. Could it be Brother Thomas? No, he is too stubborn and set in his ways. Could I be the Messiah? What does this mean? They were deeply puzzled by the rabbi's teaching but no one ever mentioned it again.

Over time, something changed in the monastery. The monks began treating each other with reverence and kindness. They lived together as brothers again. Visitors to the monastery began sensing the change. Once more people began to flock to the monastery to be nourished by the prayers of the monks.

Is not this the spirit of hospitality—to treat each other as if the Messiah was among us? He is, after all. And he says, "I tell you the truth, whatever you did for one of the least of these brothers of mine, you did for me" (Matt. 25:40).

The ministry of hospitality. We need to make it a lifestyle in- and outside the church. We need to practice it by reaching out to others and finding ways to be generous. Why not begin today by greeting someone you don't know? Then continue with a conversation. Perhaps you can even share a meal with someone and get to know him or her better. Practice hospitality and give yourself away.

Takeaway
My life is enriched by the presence of others.

Experiencing God's Goodness

generosity and reward

Key Insight
The giving living lifestyle brings joy,
contentment, and peace.

Conservative Christians are serious about giving, according to a study from Syracuse University. "If you asked me, I would have expected to find that religious conservatives are stingy," said Arthur Brooks, who authored the study. "That's what we are told all the time." However, the study showed that conservative Christians give more than others in "every measurable way," from contributing money to donating blood.

Brooks identified four factors that seem to underlie conservative generosity: church attendance, two-parent families, a Protestant work ethic, and distaste for government social services. He further

> Give, and it will be given to you. A good measure, pressed down, shaken together and running over, will be poured into your lap. For with the measure you use, it will be measured to you.
> —Luke 6:38

noted that religious people are more likely to "behave in compassionate ways toward strangers." For example, they are much more likely to return extra change to a cashier when they are accidentally given too much.

This finding would be no surprise to sociologist Tony Campolo, who said, "The Religious Right, by conviction, is convinced that helping the poor is something that should be done individually or by the church."[1]

It's good to hear a positive report, isn't it? It's encouraging. It's motivating.

Want to hear some more good news? We give out of conviction, but that's not the end of story. Giving evokes a response from God, and the blessing is returned to us.

Thelma and Victor Hayes won more than $7 million in 2005 in Canada. When asked what the couple, who were then both eighty-nine years old, would do with the money, they said that at this stage of life they were unlikely to become "giddy high spenders." They planned to stay put in their retirement home. Victor Hayes planned to buy a Lincoln Town Car, but his wife simply wanted a new pair of nylons. Her response was widely reported as comical, if not foolish. How could someone win a fortune and change nothing but her nylons?[2]

In the same way, when we experience God at work we would be crazy not to change! And giving almost always produces a miracle: Perhaps he provides the funds for us to keep our faith promise commitment when we didn't think we'd even be able to pay our bills, or he gives us a glimpse of how someone's life was radically changed through our donation. Giving opens our eyes to see greatness of God, and suddenly spiritual resources we hadn't seen before are available to us.

We Are Blessed by Increased Faith

Shane Claiborne, who has taken the gospel beyond the streets of Philadelphia to the slums of Calcutta and war zones of Iraq, describes how God revealed himself through the homeless. He saw one woman in a crowd as she struggled to get a meal from one of the late-night food vans. When asked if the meals were really worth the fight, she said, "Oh yes, but I don't eat them myself. I get them for another homeless lady—an elderly woman around the corner who can't fight for a meal."

He saw a street kid get $20 panhandling outside of a store and then immediately run inside to share it with his friends. He saw a homeless man lay a pack of cigarettes in the offering plate because it was all he had. He met a blind street musician who was viciously abused by some young guys who would mock her, curse her, and one night even sprayed Lysol in her eyes as a practical joke. As Shane and his companions held her that night, someone said, "There are a lot of bad folks in the world, aren't there?"

She said, "Oh, but there are a lot of good ones too. And the bad ones make you, the good ones, seem even sweeter."

He met a little girl who was homeless and asked her what she wanted to do when she grew up. "I want to own a grocery store so I can give out food to all the hungry people."

Mother Teresa used to say, "In the poor we meet Jesus in his most distressing disguises." Shane knows just what she meant.[3]

Do you? Have you seen it? Have you given your time, money, resources, and heart to the people in your path who are in need—and have you met Jesus in the process? It's an experience no Christian should miss. It's a sweet time of connection with the divine, and it bolsters your faith long after the giving is over.

You don't have to go to the streets of Calcutta to give. Your impact can be in your own neighborhood and on your own family. A woman named Kate tells the story of a small, white envelope stuck among the branches of her Christmas tree. This tradition began ten years ago because her husband Mike hated Christmas—not the true meaning of Christmas, but the overspending, the frantic running around at the last minute, and the gifts given in desperation. Knowing he felt that way, Kate decided to do something different.

Their son Kevin was wrestling at the junior high school. Shortly before Christmas his team played a team sponsored by an inner-city church. These youngsters, dressed in sneakers so ragged that shoestrings seemed to be the only thing holding them together, were a sharp contrast to Kevin and his friends in their spiffy blue and gold uniforms and sparkling new wrestling shoes. As the match began, Kate was alarmed to see that the other team's boys were wrestling without headgear. It was a luxury they obviously could not afford.

Kevin's team ended up walloping them. As each boy got up from the mat, he swaggered in his tatters with false bravado, a kind of street pride that couldn't acknowledge defeat. Mike shook his head sadly. "I wish just one of them could have won," he said. "They have a lot of potential, but losing like this could take the heart right out of them."

That afternoon Kate went to a local sporting goods store and bought an assortment of wrestling headgear and shoes and sent them anonymously to the inner-city church. On Christmas Eve, she placed an envelope on the tree with a note telling Mike what she had done as her gift to him. His smile was the brightest thing that Christmas.

Each Christmas after that, Kate sent Mike's gift money to a different group—one year sending a group of youngsters with mental disabilities to a hockey game, another year giving a check to elderly brothers whose home had burned down the week before Christmas.

One devastating year, Kate and her boys lost Mike to cancer. When Christmas rolled around, Kate was so wrapped up in grief that she barely got the tree up. But on Christmas Eve she placed an envelope on the tree, and in the morning it was joined by three more. Each of their children had placed an envelope on the tree for their dad.[4]

Giving is sometimes the only joy we have. It strengthens not only our own faith, but others' as well.

We Are Blessed by Increased Resources

As if increased faith is not enough—and it is!—God also blesses us with increased resources when we live generously. Consider this true story:

St. Peter and St. Mary's Church in Stowmarket, England, needed repairs. So in December 2005, Reverend Michael Eden challenged his congregation to raise money with an application of the parable of the talents. He gave each of the ninety parishioners 10 pounds (about $18) and instructed them to [make some money for the church with it]. That's what the people did. One person bought baking ingredients and made over $750 selling cakes and scones. Another bought wool and earned $138 selling scarves. In the end, the church raised more than $9,200.[5]

That sounds like one of Jesus' parables, doesn't it? It hardly needs explanation; but if Jesus had told it, his disciples probably would have asked later what it meant. Maybe Jesus' answer would have been something like this: "The priest is like our heavenly Father; he gives us resources to manage wisely. We are to go forth and multiply."

It's a modern-day version of the parable of the talents, where the master gave each of his servants an amount of money. Some went out and spent it well, multiplying it; but one simply buried it in the ground out of fear of losing it altogether—and suffered the wrath of his master.

So is giving really the right idea? Can you imagine if that unfortunate servant had not just buried the money, but lost it altogether? If we just give away the money God entrusts to us, aren't we being irresponsible?

Notice what each of the servants did—in both the biblical and modern-day parables—they returned their earnings to their master. Everything we have is from God, and it is our responsibility to multiply his money and return it to him. And then he entrusts us with more. And he sends us out again, with more. And as we manage it wisely, he enables us to multiply it more, and to return that to him as well.

There's no doubt about it: giving back to God through tithing, sacrifices, and generosity to the poor really creates more.

We Are Blessed by Increased Potential

Generosity also releases our potential. Kevin Harney tells the story of a little boy who sat on the floor of the church nursery with red rubber ball in each arm and three Nerf balls clenched on the floor between his pudgy little knees. He was trying to protect all five from the other children in the nursery. The problem was, he could not hold all five at once, and the ball nearest to his feet was particularly vulnerable to being stolen. So whenever another child showed an interest in playing with one of the balls, the little boy snarled to make it clear these toys were not for sharing.

Now, Kevin knew he should have stepped in and made the little guy give up one or two of the balls, but he was too wrapped up in the drama. For about five minutes, this little guy growled, postured, and kept the other children away from the balls. Like a hyena hunched over the last scraps of a carcass, this snarling little boy was not in the mood for sharing. The other kids circled like vultures around the kill, looking for a way to jump in and snatch a ball without being attacked and bitten. Kevin did not know whether to laugh or cry as he watched.

Then it struck Kevin: this little boy was not having any fun. There was no cheer within ten yards of this kid. Not only was he unhappy, but all the other kids seemed sad as well. His selfishness created a black hole that sucked all of the joy out of that nursery. Furthermore, when church was over and his parents came to pick him up, the boy left the balls behind.[6]

What if that little boy hadn't been selfishly guarding the balls, but generously sharing them? He would have had fun! He would have played. And when it was time to go, he still would have left the balls behind, but he would have taken new friendships with him. We miss out on so much when we are selfish.

Self-absorbtion not only prevents us from enjoying good things, it keeps us captive. Consider Raynald III, a fourteenth-century duke in what is now Belgium, who was grossly overweight. His Latin nickname, Crassus, means "fat."

Raynald's younger brother Edward revolted against Raynald's rule. Edward captured Raynald but did not kill him. Instead, he built a room around Raynald in the Nieuwkerk castle and promised him he could regain his title and property when he left the room. This would not have been difficult for most people, since the room had several windows and a door of near-normal size, none of which were locked or barred. The problem was Raynald's size; to regain his freedom, he needed to lose weight.

Edward knew his older brother. Each day he sent a variety of delicious foods into the room. Instead of dieting his way out of prison, Raynald grew fatter. When Duke Edward was accused of cruelty, he had a ready answer: "My brother is not a prisoner. He may leave when he so wills." Raynald stayed in his room for ten years and wasn't released until after Edward died in battle. By then his health was so ruined that he died within a year—a prisoner of his own appetite.[7]

My friend Wayne Schmidt often says, "Saving without giving is hoarding." We have to quit hoarding! We have an abundance of good things to choose from, but we have to know how to say no. By gorging—through eating, spending, or any other gluttony—we prevent ourselves from receiving all that God has for us. Generosity—sharing the good things we have—opens doors for us in ways we can't imagine. Generosity isn't just sharing money, time, or resources; it is actively turning away from selfish ambitions and seeking ways for others to succeed. When we look outward, we inspire others and reach our full potential— achieving true greatness.

The Courage to Let Go

All of us tend to avoid pain. Sometimes, though, avoiding pain can lead to much greater suffering.

Consider the story of William "the Refrigerator" Perry. Perry was a colorful defensive lineman for the Chicago Bears when they won the Super Bowl in 1985. His nickname fit him well because he was big and wide. Perry was also a friendly man with a wide grin.

Unfortunately for his grin, though he was a mammoth man playing in the tough world of the football trenches, he apparently was afraid of the dentist—so afraid that he didn't go to the dentist for twenty years. He didn't go to the dentist even though his teeth and gums hurt terribly, even though his teeth began falling out. Eventually he had lost half of his teeth—some he pulled out himself!— and his gums suffered chronic infection. He was suffering!

Finally, as he neared age forty-five, Perry went to a dentist, who had to pull out all of his remaining teeth, insert screws in his jaw, and implant new teeth.[8]

Now there's a story every mother will tell her son when she tells him he has to go to the dentist or brush his teeth. But this is also a story for all who are afraid to adopt a spirit of generosity. It takes courage to let go. Just remember, it may hurt for a moment, but God will bless you more than you can imagine.

Takeaway
Generosity benefits me spiritually
as well as materially.

PART 3

The Impact of Giving Living

Now that you know more about *how* to be generous, you will learn what the impact of your generosity can be. Let's lift our vision to see God's purpose for the world—and you! You will discover a world of tremendous possibility. This will enable you to make tangible changes in your home, community, and world.

Seeing the World through God's Eyes

the power of vision

Key Insight
God has a vision to redeem the entire world,
and he has given us the resources to accomplish this.

The weather was a perfect 72 degrees and there wasn't a breath of wind — and yet the young couple couldn't seem to make any progress in moving their canoe across the lake. The others in their group were nearly to the other side, but Jennifer

> This, then, is how you should pray: "Our Father in heaven, hallowed be your name, your kingdom come, your will be done on earth as it is in heaven."
> —Matthew 6:9–10

and Chad weren't even close to half way. At first Jennifer hadn't minded their slow progress. She enjoyed having Chad all to herself. At times they would chat quietly; at other times they simply sat in silence or pointed out loons and other wildlife to each other.

But the further the distance grew between themselves and the others, the harder she paddled. The harder she paddled, the more aware she was of their struggle.

Jennifer couldn't help being a little mad. Chad was supposed to be the best paddler in the group, and she was certainly working as hard as she could. Clearly he was not doing his part.

She glanced back once to be sure he wasn't actually backstroking, but she couldn't tell. And he just winked at her. Jennifer turned back, dug her paddle into the water, and gave her full effort to moving forward. He wasn't taking it seriously, so she would have do it on her own.

But when she saw the first canoe reach the other side, she couldn't stand it anymore. "What's going on?" she said, turning around to face Chad. "Why aren't you doing anything?"

She saw his crestfallen face at the same moment she felt a thin rope under her fingers on the edge of the canoe. And then it hit her. Earlier that morning she had dropped anchor so she could fish without drifting away—and she never pulled it up.

It wasn't Chad's fault at all. It was hers.

We do that to God sometimes, don't we? We struggle to fight against the problems of this world without making any progress, and we wonder why God isn't doing anything.

Jesus taught us to pray for God's kingdom to come on earth as it is in heaven, but all too often if feels like God is not listening to this prayer. If that's the case for you, I want to encourage you to step back from your frantic efforts, hold off on your accusations, and let's see whether we've dropped an anchor that's holding us back from seeing the truth.

The Myth: God's Not Doing Anything

It's no wonder that any of us question whether God has abandoned us. This world is not always a pretty place. Our marriages and relationships struggle; our kids go astray; our jobs are not what we dreamed about; our finances are in shambles. Why won't God fix these things?

And beyond ourselves, people are dying of starvation around the world; tsunamis are devastating entire communities; and war ravages nations.

The issue that is probably most emotionally charged is that of human trafficking. Take Ruth Ada Kamara, for instance.

When Ruth was [eighteen] years old, she left her small, rural village in northern Sierra Leone to join an older female friend who had convinced Ruth to travel with her to Liberia for vacation. The women had been neighbors for three years, and Ruth was excited for the opportunity. The friend arranged Ruth's travel and documents, invited an old graying man to join them, and then disappeared. . . . Ruth had never been to Liberia before and was unfamiliar with the language and people. Not knowing the city, she did not know how to leave on her own. Furthermore, she had no money, travel documents, or even identification. [The man] raped Ruth, whipped her, and beat her . . . And that was just the beginning.

For more than two years, Ruth was trapped in a room without enough food or any way to communicate with the outside world. She was forced to serve as a sex slave to numerous men, and was tightly controlled by [her owner].[1]

Why won't God fix these things? If God won't save the innocent youth from being sold into sexual slavery, he's either heartless or impotent, isn't he?

The Bible doesn't directly answer all of our questions, but it does reveal who God is—and especially who God is in relationship to us. Many, many verses tell us directly that God is good and that he loves us. But the overarching story of Scripture makes that message all the more powerful: God created the world with humans as the pinnacle of his work; he gave us everything, including the freedom to return his love. We turned away from him over and over again, and he pursued us as many times. Ultimately he gave his Son to die on our behalf so that we would never have to be separated from him and all the good he has planned for us.

God cares.

The Bible also reveals God's power. He demands holiness. He hates the wicked and does not tolerate sin. He holds himself far above all of creation, and we simply cannot fathom his greatness. See what Job 38:1–18 says:

> Then the LORD answered Job out of the storm. He said: "Who is this that darkens my counsel with words without knowledge? Brace yourself like a man; I will question you, and you shall answer me. Where were you when I laid the earth's foundation? Tell me, if you understand. Who marked off its dimensions? Surely you know! Who stretched a measuring line across it? On what were its footings set, or who laid its cornerstone while the morning stars sang together and all the angels shouted for joy? Who shut up the sea behind doors when it burst forth from the womb, when I made the clouds its garment and wrapped it in thick darkness, when I fixed limits for it and set its doors and bars in place, when I said, 'This far you may come and no farther; here is where your proud waves halt'? Have you ever given orders to the morning, or shown the dawn its place, that it might take the earth by the edges and shake the

wicked out of it? The earth takes shape like clay under a seal; its features stand out like those of a garment. The wicked are denied their light, and their upraised arm is broken. Have you journeyed to the springs of the sea or walked in the recesses of the deep? Have the gates of death been shown to you? Have you seen the gates of the shadow of death? Have you comprehended the vast expanses of the earth? Tell me, if you know all this."

God can and does care. He sees the suffering of the world, and he is able to restore it.

You've probably seen him at work over and over again without even recognizing his hand. It is God who opens wombs to make new life; he captures people's hearts and transforms relationships; he heals broken bodies through divine intervention and enables us through natural means to heal. God is active in the world today.

Perhaps it is hard to see God at work because we pay attention only to the problems. We don't see that we've dropped anchor and are paddling in vain.

In my current role as a general superintendent in the Church of the Nazarene, I have the joy of being over the country of Africa. The church in Mozambique is growing so fast right now that there are not enough leaders to disciple all the new believers. "The harvest is plentiful, but the workers are few" (Matt. 9:37). People who had never heard the name of Jesus before are encountering him and responding in joy. Entire communities are giving their lives to Christ and then sharing the good news with others who carry on the good news to still more.

And Ruth is no exception. God was very much involved in | 147 her life. After two years in slavery, Ruth confided in a client who became sympathetic to her situation. The man paid for Ruth's freedom and brought her clothes. She married the man who saved her and they had a child together. The war in Liberia caused Ruth's family to flee to Sierra Leone, but Ruth's husband did not survive. The war spread into Sierra Leone, and Ruth and her child ended up in a refugee camp in Guinea. There she met Janet and turned her life over to Jesus.

God is not sitting on his hands. He is freeing the captives today just as he had in Bible times.

Do you trust him? Do you believe that he can and does care? How have you seen God at work in the world? If you can't think of anything, take some time this week to look around for the anchor you might have dropped that is preventing you from seeing his hand. Or maybe you need to get out of the boat and walk on the water—in other words, go to the places where he is at work rather than waiting for him to come to you.

The Truth: God Wants Us to Do His Will

If God cares and God can, why doesn't he? Why is there any evil in the world at all? Why does he save one victim from trafficking, but not another? These questions plague every Christian at some point in his or her walk with God, and there are no simple answers.

What we do know is that God has a plan, and that plan involves us. Even when Jesus walked the earth, he didn't do everything himself. When the disciples saw a crowd of hungry people and turned to Jesus for help, he said, "You feed them." Certainly it was by his power those few loaves and fishes turned into a meal for thousands, but it was the disciples who did the work.

Praying for God to let his kingdom come requires a radical kind of faith. What we're saying is that we want to be part of God's work in the world. With God working through us, people like Ruth are saved from sexual slavery. Through us starving children are fed. Through us lonely people are loved. Through us God's kingdom comes.

Considering how almighty our God is, his choice to use finite humans to minister in his big world may seem odd. Wouldn't it be easier for him to do it himself? I think God's desire to let us do the work is a gift to us. First of all, it is a sign that he has given us this world in full confidence of our ability to care for it. Obviously, he believes in us more than we believe in ourselves. But also, he knows that when we reach out to help others rather than getting caught up in self-centeredness, our lives are enriched. The old saying, "It is better to give than to receive," became a cliché only because it's true.

The true story I told about Ruth has another character who is easy to overlook: Janet, the woman who led Ruth to Christ. Janet, who is from the United States, chose to live her life in service to desperately needy people in another country. She was providing care to refugees who otherwise wouldn't have survived, and by so doing introduced them to Jesus. She was able to see first-hand how the love of Christ transformed lives over and over again. She experienced the thrill of being used by him to bring his kingdom here on earth.

One does not need to go to Africa to experience that. When you bring a meal to a hurting person; put your spouse's needs before your own; volunteer in your church or community; take time from your busy schedule to meet for lunch with a lonely, elderly person; or give a monetary gift—all of these things take the focus off yourself and free you to experience the joy of giving.

149

God wants us to do his will, and discovering his will is much easier than we make it out to be. Bringing his kingdom here on earth means caring for the poor and weak, being kind and gracious, loving others as we love ourselves, and giving God all the glory.

The Thrill: God Empowers Us to Change the World

If we find ourselves often grumbling about this world, perhaps we've dropped an anchor without realizing it. Here are some ways we prevent ourselves from working to make the world a better place:

- We get caught up in our own problems and don't have the time or emotional energy to help others.
- We become comfortable in our wealth or happiness and do not pursue awareness of the problems of others.
- We feel helpless and discouraged, certain that our small part won't make a difference.

To lift the anchor and become effective in bringing God's kingdom here on earth, we have to take the focus off ourselves. Certainly there are times when we are hurting and cannot be on the frontlines, but in time we have to allow God to bring us healing and restoration for our own good and the good of others. For sure, we are meant to enjoy the blessings God gives us, but we cannot forget that we are blessed to be a blessing. It's true, the problems of this world can be overwhelming, but we can be confident that God can and does care—and he'll use us to transform this world.

God empowers us, as imperfect as we are, to do his will. It's his way. He simply doesn't use the top-down approach, though his greatness is certainly far beyond us and he could. Scripture says that God chose the foolish things of the world to shame the wise, the weak things to shame the strong (1 Cor. 1:27). We really can pray, "Your kingdom come, your will be done" with the radical faith that will lead us to seeing it happen.

Ruth knows what it means to pray this prayer. Years after she had been saved both physically and spiritually, she was back to Sierra Leone to work at World Hope International. Janet, who knew nothing of Ruth's story, invited Ruth to become a public awareness officer for sex trafficking in her country, to stand up for the girls who were being stolen from their homes just as Ruth had been. Today, fifteen years after her escape, Ruth is influencing a nation as she empowers men and women to live free and safe lives.

Who knows how God will use you to bring his kingdom here on earth if you begin praying that prayer with radical faith? Will he turn your wounds and weakness into great strengths? Will he enrich your life by helping you use your blessings to bless others? Will he use you in huge, world-shattering ways; or will he lead you to small, daily acts of kindness that bring his kingdom into your home and community?

Now is the time to take the anchor out of the water and make a difference in the world.

When you look at the world, what do you see? Many people see chaos and disorder. Some see a personal playground. Others see both a world of great need and a world of nearly limitless resources. We need to learn to see the world not as the economists, pundits, or politicians see it, but as God does.

You will come to envision his purpose for yourself, and you will be motivated to use your time, talent, and treasure to create the future he has in mind for you—and for those around you. You will see a world of possibility!

Radical Living

A certain chapter of the Bible has been read and studied so frequently at women's events around the world that the character who emerges from these pages is known by everyone as the Proverbs 31 woman, a woman who is worth more than rubies: She loves her work and is busy from the wee hours of the morning until late at night, provides for her family with beauty and abundance, has people who work for her, is business savvy and profitable, is physically strong, generously cares for the poor, is married to a leader, has dignity and peace, is wise and loved, and fears the Lord. What a woman!

What a woman? What a person! It's not just women who can learn from her. All of us could hold her up as a model.

Having high expectations of ourselves may be intimidating, but it sure beats having low expectations. I'm glad that God doesn't think our being like the Proverbs 31 woman is out of reach. He wants the best for us, and he's made it possible for us to achieve that.

God Wants Us to Excel

How do we make sense of the Proverb 31 ultimate role model when so many other passages seem to promote weakness as the ultimate virtue. Passages like "Blessed are the meek" (Matt. 5:5), "The first will be last" (Matt. 20:16), and turn the other cheek (see Matt. 5:39; Luke 6:29) all say that strength is not the key to inheriting the kingdom of God. Humility is clearly a high value of Jesus who himself became a servant. We are to emulate him, to be humble.

Plenty of people have intentionally made themselves into doormats, thinking their calling as Christians is to be wimpy. In their attempt to be humble, they have lost their self-confidence; in their attempt to be unnoticed, they have become miserable failures.

Is that really what Scripture is calling us to do, though? Does God really want to beat us down, or to let others do it? As I have experienced him through Scripture and in my relationship with him, I have quite the opposite impression. God wants us to be "more than conquerors" (Rom. 8:37); to run to "win the prize" (Phil. 3:14); and to not be timid, but bold (2 Tim. 1:7). He gives us the strength to fly like eagles (Isa. 40:31), and he says we can do all things through him (Phil. 4:13).

We sometimes fear leadership or success because we know such selfish ambitions are prohibited in Scripture. And yet biblical characters like Esther's uncle Mordecai, a respected leader in a secular culture, are presented as heroes. Like the Proverbs 31 woman, Mordecai was strong, bold, successful, famous, wealthy—all the things we're told not to pursue.

Perhaps the pursuit of worldly success is exactly the problem, and the success itself is not actually significant. When we pursue glory, glory shall be our reward. When we pursue the purposes of God, any glory we get is simply incidental. We may or may not be famous and wealthy, but when we walk with God, we will certainly be strong and bold—and humble, because it is not ourselves we are promoting, but God.

God wants us to excel. The parable of the talents (Matt. 25:14–30) makes that abundantly clear. The master gave his servants money and expected them to manage it wisely, even turn a profit. Likewise, God has given us gifts, skills, and talents and he expects us to use them to further his kingdom. His anger will burn against those who waste what he has entrusted to them. He is counting on us to do his work. How can we "turn a profit" if we are scared of our own shadows? How can we draw people to Christ, defend the cause of the weak, and be caretakers of the earth if we don't use the gifts God has given us?

And we have been given gifts. We've been given different talents and different degrees of ability—exactly what we need to fulfill the mission God has given us. God wants us to use what he has given us to boldly pursue the mission he has in mind for us.

What is your talent? If you've been given much, much will be expected of you (Luke 12:48). Are you living up to God's expectations? Are you leading the people who are watching you along the path God has set for you? If you've been given little, are you using even that to the best of your ability? Are you joyfully serving and respecting the leaders God has placed over you? The day is coming when God will ask for an accounting of your life. He'll be looking for excellence, not excuses.

God Wants Us to Enjoy Good Things

So, God wants us to excel, but only for his benefit? Doesn't he want us to have any pleasure for ourselves? Does he want us to be wildly successful only so we can give away our hard-earned cash?

Seems like it. Jesus went so far as to say that "it is easier for a camel to go through the eye of a needle than for a rich man to enter the kingdom of God" (Matt. 19:24). The Bible calls the *love* of money "a root of all kinds of evil" (1 Tim. 6:10). That doesn't sound good.

Feeling guilty about the good things we have probably goes back to our childhood. Did your mom ever say something like, "Don't you know there are starving children in Africa?" We see coverage of poverty-stricken nations or maybe we've even been to one. When we see the shacks they live in, the lack of hygienic medical facilities, or the distance they have to walk to get water, it's hard to not be embarrassed about having four bathrooms and three cars.

But, like me, you probably enjoy having a place to live and driving a decent car and being able to pay for groceries—maybe eat out regularly. Is that so bad?

Poverty is certainly not what God envisions for us. Poverty is a result of the fall, something that breaks Jesus' heart. His command to us to provide for the poor clearly indicates that poverty is not an ideal situation. He made the world with an abundance of resources for us to enjoy and manage.

Just as we might look at our beautiful home, car, or other beloved possession and say, "I love that!" so God did after he created the world. "It is good," he said each day in admiration of his own work. God is the author and creator of beauty and order; he crammed this world full of good things; he made us the crown of creation, caretakers of the earth—surely God wants us to enjoy these good things. Even the role model he gave us in Proverbs 31 is a wealthy woman who enjoys beautiful, costly things.

God loves us and created us to be benefactors and even comanagers of his blessings. Unless God has called you to a lifestyle of poverty, having material blessing is not a sin. It's a blessing! Be grateful for your good gifts and enjoy them.

God Wants Us to Live within His Will

Not all of us have an abundance of material things. In fact, when we look around, it may seem that the people who have all the success, power, and money are not deserving people at all. The godly Proverbs 31 men and women are few and far between.

Scripture tells us not to be jealous of the wicked (Prov. 24:1). They may appear to have it altogether now, but God scoffs at them; they are like chaff that will be blown away in the wind (Ps. 1:4). God wants us to live within his will. He gives us a mission and purpose, and he also gives us talents to be able to accomplish that mission. In the parable of the talents, the servants' task was to take care of the master's property; likewise, God entrusts us to care for his world and the people in it. Our focus should be on accomplishing that mission; the talents are simply the tools with which to accomplish it.

The Proverbs 31 woman is wealthy and talented. Notice, however, that her hands are open. She is generous and hardworking. She is living in such a way that her wealth is an advantage to her, not a hindrance. The reason there are so many warnings about wealth in the Bible is because it can so easily morph from a blessing into a curse. Selfishness causes lack for others; gluttony and laziness spoil the pleasure of good things for self.

We don't have to be biblical characters to live like the Proverbs 31 woman. Even children are using their God-given talents to fulfill their mission.

Take Daniela Stransky, a thirteen-year-old girl who has a passion for riding horses. She has been riding since she was eight years old and loves to attend horse shows where it's not unusual for her to place in the events. Daniela and her family use their passion to help people in impoverished countries.

Daniela rides for the Step by Step Foundation, which provides basic necessities such as clean water and education for children in places like Haiti.

The Stranskys live in Miami, Florida, which is only about 150 miles from the impoverished country of Haiti. When Daniela learned about the difficulties children face there, she and her mother visited to see the conditions firsthand. "They have to share everything," Daniela said. "Poverty—they don't know what it means but they live it every day."

So far, the foundation has provided aid, money, and supplies to about twenty causes as Daniela has raised about $8,000 through riding competitions. Her mother, Liliane, hopes to expand the Step by Step Foundation to help kids in Africa and the Dominican Republic.[2]

Enjoy your good gifts, but do not neglect the mission God has for you.

The parable of the talents, the description of the model wife, and a myriad of other passages in the Bible all point to the same thing: God expects big things from you. He has a purpose for you, and he equips you to complete that purpose.

God's expectations may intimidate you or build your confidence. It's up to you how to respond. But if you want to fully enjoy the good gifts God has given you and if you want to make a difference in this world, I suggest you live up to it. Be all that you can be by using your gifts and talents to honor the Lord.

Takeaway
My generosity can have an impact on the world.

Christ's Hands and Feet

creating social transformation

Key Insight
God will use your generosity to bring peace
and justice to the world.

Transforming People

Forty years ago, a Philadelphia congregation watched as
three nine-year-old boys were baptized and joined the
church. Not long after, the church sold the building and
disbanded. One of those boys was Dr. Tony Campolo,
Christian sociologist at Eastern University, Pennsylvania.

> John answered, "The
> man with two tunics
> should share with him
> who has none, and
> the one who has food
> should do the same."
> —Luke 3:11

Dr. Campolo remembers, "Years
later when I was doing research in
the archives of our denomination, I
decided to look up the church report
for the year of my baptism. There was
my name and Dick White's—he is

now a missionary—and Bert Newman is a professor of theology at an African seminary."

Then Campolo read the church report for the year he joined the church. It said, "It has not been a good year for our church. We have lost twenty-seven members. Three joined, and they were only children."[1]

Fifty years ago a church in Columbus, Ohio, fed and clothed the Toler family at Christmas, and today all three brothers are ordained ministers. Don't forget, an act of kindness is never wasted.

Doing the work of the Lord may feel ineffective—and in fact we may never catch even a glimpse of what God is doing with our efforts. It may not feel like a good year. Perhaps you've paid your tithe and made a missions pledge and are faithfully giving, but now wonder whether it's making any difference.

You can be sure that your generosity is making a difference; God will not let your gift come back void.

Life to Those Who Lack Food and Shelter

A preacher and a barber were walking through city slums. "If God was as kind as you say, he wouldn't permit all this poverty, disease, and squalor," the barber said. "He wouldn't allow these poor street people to get addicted. I cannot believe in a God who permits these things."

The minister was silent until they met a man whose hair was hanging down his neck and had a half inch of stubble on his face.

"You can't be a good barber, or you wouldn't permit a man like this to continue living here without a haircut and a shave," the preacher said.

Indignant, the barber answered, "Why blame me for that man's condition? He has never come to my shop. If he had, I could've fixed him up and made him look like a gentleman!"

"Then don't blame God for allowing people to continue in their evil ways," the preacher said. "He invites them to come and be saved."[2]

It's true: God invites each person to turn to him and be saved, even the drunk on the park bench. Poverty may not be a choice, but living righteously always is; and even the most down-and-out person can live a godly life. It's not our responsibility to make others respond to God's love. Right?

True. But it is our responsibility to live godly lives ourselves, which includes giving to the poor. Besides, we may be the one God uses to extend his invitation to be saved.

On one level we know that giving to the poor shouldn't be a controversial subject; but the idea of handing a dollar to a homeless guy can get Christians dialoging for hours. How do we give responsibly so our hard-earned cash doesn't pay for a cheap bottle of wine? Should we give anything to people who are in bad situations because of their own poor choices? Aren't we just enabling them to continue living this way?

I'm not going to attempt to answer these questions—mainly because Jesus didn't ever seem to stop and consider whether someone deserved his help. In fact, he came for those who needed him most. In Mark 2:17, he said, "It is not the healthy who need a doctor, but the sick. I have not come to call the righteous, but sinners."

Don't think your way out of giving. In fact, keep your head out of it and let your heart lead.

On Friday nights, volunteers from Bridgetown Ministries help the homeless people gathered under the Burnside Bridge in Portland, Oregon. In addition to providing hot meals, shaves, and haircuts, some of the volunteers wash the homeless people's feet. Tom Krattenmaker, a writer for *USA Today*, was stunned when he saw that, calling it "one of the most audacious acts of compassion and humility [he had] ever witnessed."

This group of society's outcasts had their bare feet immersed in warm water, scrubbed, dried, powdered, and placed in clean socks. One man reported with a smile, "I can't find the words to describe how good that felt."

Krattenmaker later wrote, "Washing someone's feet is an act best performed while kneeling. Given the washer's position, and the unpleasant appearance and odor of a homeless person's feet, it's hard to imagine an act more humbling."

The leader of Bridgetown Ministries prepares volunteers for this ministry by saying, "When you go out there tonight, I want you to look for Jesus. You might see him in the eyes of a drunk person, a homeless person . . . we're just out there to love on people."[3]

Clarence Jordan, a philosopher-farmer in Americus, Georgia, was convinced that poor people living in dilapidated shacks could improve themselves with a little support. "They don't need charity," he said to Millard Fuller, who visited Jordan's church community, Koinonia Farm. "They need a way to help themselves."

Millard Fuller [at thirty years old and nearly a millionaire], was inspired by Jordan to begin what today is a worldwide organization to provide housing for the poor. Habitat for Humanity runs on what he calls "the theology of the hammer." The group raises money and recruits volunteers to renovate and build homes that are sold at cost. Mortgages are interest free to qualified recipients. Habitat now builds or renovates twelve houses every day.[4]

All our Lord asks us to do is open our eyes, see the need, and give a cup of cold water in his name.

Joseph Stowell tells the story of how one day, as he walked to work, he passed a *StreetWise* vendor. The Chicago-based newspaper *StreetWise* is sold by homeless people who collect a portion of the proceeds. It was a bitterly cold January morning, and he'd already stopped by Starbucks and paid more than a buck for a measly cup of coffee. Feeling noble, he struggled to find his wallet, reached in, and took out a dollar.

The homeless woman asked, "Do you really want the paper, or can I keep it to sell to someone else?"

"Keep the paper," he replied. Then he added, "How are you today?"

"I'm so cold," she said.

"I hope the sun comes out, it warms up, and you have a good day," he told her as he turned to go.

Joseph continued on, with the cup of coffee warming his hand. About half a block later, the conversation finally registered. He wrestled for a moment with what he should do, but he was late, so he kept walking. Ever since, he has regretted not giving her a cup of hot coffee in Christ's name.[5]

Your generosity makes a difference. Open your eyes and discover what you can do in Jesus' name.

Help to Those Who Suffer Violence and Injustice

Although the first Pilgrims established a peaceful relationship with the natives in America, the following generation struggled with bloody warfare. The war between Pilgrims and Indians, known as King Philip's War, began in 1675 and lasted fourteen months.

In March 1676, a group of nearly fifteen hundred Indians attacked the village of Rehoboth. Nathaniel Philbrick writes, "As the inhabitants watched from their garrisons, forty houses, thirty barns, and two mills went up in flames. Only one person was killed—a man who believed that as long as he continued reading the Bible, no harm would come to him. Refusing to abandon his home, he was found shot to death in his chair—the Bible still in his hands."[6]

Life isn't fair. We may do the right thing, even the spiritual thing, and things don't turn out the way we hope and we don't always get what we deserve.

This world is full of injustice and violence. Slavery may have ended, but racism still digs its claws into us. Children are sold into sexual slavery around the world, and even right here in the United States. The rich oppress the poor; the powerful take advantage of the weak. Can we even make a difference against such forces?

Money isn't everything, though. Generosity is giving of yourself in whatever form it is needed.

Ed Gilbreath is an African-American author and speaker. He tells a story of a time he was invited to lunch by a prominent white Christian leader. As they were sitting down to eat, all of a sudden the Christian leader started crying. He explained that God had blessed him—his children were healthy, and he was known throughout the country. But, he said, "I've had a hard time sleeping throughout the night."

Ed was wondering why the man was sharing this with him, but listened patiently.

The man said he had been to an annual conference on the other side of the country to discuss reconciliation and cross-cultural ministry. "Usually, when black leaders come into the meeting, we make them feel right at home and let them be part of the decision-making process," the man told Ed. "But to be honest with you, the decisions are made before your leaders ever get there. I'm used to hearing the jokes and the use of the N-word. But this time, when the jokes were going on and people were saying things, it didn't sound right to me."

The man was sobbing and asked Ed how he could get over his racism.

Ed was silent for a moment then asked him, "Do you like football?" The man seemed a little puzzled, but he said yes.

"I do, too," Ed told him. "I used to coach high school and college ball, and I have a lot of friends who play pro. I love a good game, and I love to cook out. So here's what we do: I need to get to know you, and you need to get to know me. Why don't you come over to my house? Bring your wife and meet my wife, and we'll just sit and talk and get to know each other. I'll barbecue some steaks, and let's start there."

The man said, "You want me to come to your house?"

"Yes," Ed said. "If you want me to sit here and clear your conscience for all you did, I can't do that. Friendship is not cheap. It takes time and commitment." Ed gave the man his home phone number and told him to give him a call.

Ed never heard from him again.[7]

Sometimes all we have to do is give a little time and effort to fight injustice. Are you ready to do that?

Hope to Those Who Are Lonely and Neglected

Once a month, a group of professionals armed with blow dryers, scissors, nail polish—and love—venture forth to serve those less fortunate than themselves.

Hairdressers in the Marketplace (HIM), a ministry of Willow Creek Community Church in suburban Chicago, offers monthly day of beauty sessions in which needy women receive free haircuts and manicures. HIM volunteers also go to nursing homes for the poor, homeless shelters, and facilities for the mentally disabled to provide free services.

Hairstylist Teresa Russo-Cox founded HIM in 1998. She says God gave her a vision for a group that not only communicates God's love and care to women in need but also reaches out to stylists. "That's what sets us apart from other ministries that offer haircuts to the poor," says Teresa. "We focus on evangelism to the beauty industry, which is filled with so much darkness. Its underlying message is all about external things—glamour and glitz. I want to bring the light of God's Word into our industry."

Some "clients" surprise the HIM volunteers. At one day of beauty event in 2006, teen girls going through drug and alcohol rehab told Melissa they hadn't ever had "sober" fun before. "They had never experienced that," Melissa says.

"I had no self-esteem," says Doreen, who was invited to a day of beauty after she and her two preschool children left her alcoholic, abusive husband. "That day gave me a boost on the outside, but it helped me on the inside too. I felt beautiful, special, and deserving."[8]

Your generosity brings hope to those who are lonely and neglected—and they come in all shapes and sizes. There are lonely people in the inner cities, in your place of work, and in your church. By giving of yourself, you connect with others, and bring them hope.

What can you give to the lonely and neglected? Friendship, of course. Respect. Care. Time. You can deliver food to the homebound, you can visit nursing homes, you can serve at a high-risk drop-in childcare center.

Jim Parker, a retired school superintendent, and his wife Linda, a teacher, give blood. The United States Red Cross has thirty-four blood-service regions across the country, and Jim and Linda made a seventeen-month tour visiting each one of them to donate blood. The Parkers estimate their donations will save 130 lives. They also hope to inspire others to give, thereby saving even more lives.[9]

What can you give?

D. A. Carson wrote, "People do not drift toward holiness. Apart from grace-driven effort, people do not gravitate toward godliness, prayer, obedience to Scripture, faith, and delight in the Lord. We drift toward compromise and call it tolerance; we drift toward disobedience and call it freedom; we drift toward superstition and call it faith. We cherish the indiscipline of lost self-control and call it relaxation; we slouch toward prayerlessness and delude ourselves into thinking we have escaped legalism; we slide toward godlessness and convince ourselves we have been liberated."[10]

Holiness is an intentional pursuit—and it's not just abstaining from destructive things; it is opening our eyes to see the needs of others.

Thomas Linacre was king's physician to Henry VII and Henry VIII of England, founder of the Royal College of Physicians, and friend of the great Renaissance thinkers Erasmus and Sir Thomas More. Late in his life, Linacre studied to be a priest and was given a copy of the Gospels to read for the first time. Linacre lived through the darkest of the church's dark hours under the papacy of Alexander VI, the Borgia pope whose bribery, corruption, incest, and murder plumbed new depths in the annals of Christian shame.

Reading the Gospels for himself, Linacre was amazed and troubled. "Either these are not the Gospels," he said, "or we are not Christians."[11]

Let's live up to our name. Let's be like Christ. Let's give.

Transforming World

Praise be to the God and Father of our Lord Jesus Christ, the Father of compassion and the God of all comfort, who comforts us in all our troubles, so that we can comfort those in any trouble with the comfort we ourselves have received from God. For just as the sufferings of Christ flow over into our lives, so also through Christ our comfort overflows. If we are distressed, it is for your comfort and salvation; if we are comforted, it is for your comfort, which produces in you patient endurance of the same sufferings we suffer. And our hope for you is firm, because we know that just as you share in our sufferings, so also you share in our comfort. (2 Cor. 1:3–7)

In 1975 a mighty tornado swept through Louisville, Kentucky. It tore across the Crescent Hill neighborhood where Southern Baptist Theological Seminary was located. Many professors' homes were damaged. Dr. Harold Songer tells how the backyard of his friend and fellow professor, Dr. Thomas Smothers, was particularly affected. Many majestic old trees fell, and the backyard looked barren following the storm. Songer continues to describe how the following spring, Smothers' backyard was awash with unexpected new growth. The same storm that destroyed the old vegetation had also spread seeds that would bring new growth.[12]

Living for over a quarter of a century in Oklahoma is a daily reminder of the fact that tornados are some of the most awesome, destructive, frightening, and fascinating forces of nature. Countless videos of brave Oklahoma storm chasers have often captured the violent force of these tornados. While it can be frightening to watch, it is also very difficult to look away. It is amazing to watch a tornado lift a home from its foundations or turn a semi-truck upside-down. When we think of tornados, the first thing we think of is the destruction they cause. I would be surprised if any of us ever think of a tornado and then comment, "A tornado is a very helpful, creative force of nature." That just isn't what we think of when tornados come to mind. Yet Timothy Keller, senior pastor of Redeemer Presbyterian Church in Manhattan, New York, once referred to God as a "spiritual tornado." He says that God never draws us into his whirlwind to bless us without then releasing us so that we may bless others.[13]

In 2 Corinthians 1:3–7, Paul essentially said the same. Paul concerned himself primarily with comfort in this passage, both his comfort and the comfort of his readers. The Greek root word for comfort appears no fewer than ten times in verses 3–7 alone. What is interesting is that Paul did not see comfort as merely a personal thing. He said several times that if he was comforted, it was so that others would benefit from it. What an amazing perspective! And it's one that we are going to look at in more detail. I hope that we will start to see the world through God's eyes and that we will stop focusing so much on ourselves and realize that God blesses us so that we may be a blessing to others. Ultimately we will see that, difficult as it may be to comprehend, God wants to use us to transform the world. Hopefully we will be motivated to use our time, talent, and treasures to make a difference in the world.

God Desires to Impact the World through You

You may have heard the story of two friends who met for dinner in a restaurant. Each requested filet of sole. After a few minutes the waiter came back with two pieces of fish, one large and one small, on the same platter. One of the men proceeded to serve his friend. Placing the small piece on a plate, he handed it across the table.

"Well, you certainly do have nerve!" exclaimed his friend.

"What's troubling you?" asked the other.

"Look what you've done!" he answered. "You've given me the little piece and kept the big one for yourself."

"How would you have done it?" the man asked.

His friend replied, "If I were serving, I would have given you the big piece."

"Well," replied the man, "I've got it, haven't I?" At this, they both laughed.

That story is obviously intended to be humorous, but there is an idea at the center of it that ought to be a little troubling for us. The man in the story was upset because he received the smaller piece of meat. Even though he protested that he would have given away the bigger piece, the fact is that he was primarily concerned about himself. I wonder how often we struggle with the same thing. It is very easy to live life as if we are the center of the universe. Each day is so full of opportunities to please ourselves that we have great difficulty finding time to serve anyone else.

In 2 Corinthians 1:4, Paul said that God "comforts us in all our troubles, so that we can comfort those in any trouble with the comfort we ourselves have received from God." Then in verse 7, Paul said, "Our hope for you is firm because we know that just as you share in our sufferings, so also you share in our comfort." Now without going any deeper into this passage, we could say that there is a lot of sharing going on here. Paul repeatedly spoke of us sharing in comfort and suffering. It's difficult to share anything when you are only concerned with yourself. Let's go deeper into this passage and see what Paul said about sharing so that we can better understand how God desires to impact the world through us.

At its heart, ministry is using the gifts, experiences, and abilities that God has given you to meet the needs of others. In this passage, Paul said that God comforts us so that we can comfort others. That's ministry. When we have experienced the comfort of God—the consolation, help, and encouragement of the God of comfort—we will be better equipped to comfort others. This idea is fascinating to me because we typically think of comfort as being in exactly the place we want to be. Whether it be in our own home or with our friends, comfort generally involves something we are familiar with and something that we prefer. Paul, however, said that even our comfort should be something that causes us to think of others. We should say to ourselves, "I have received comfort from God. How can I now use that to minister to someone else?" Are we getting the sense that God does what he does for us so that he can, in turn, use us to impact the world around us? We are simply not our own anymore. As Christians our lives take on new meanings. Even our very comfort is intended by God to be an opportunity for us to impact the world.

Paul also talked about Christians sharing in suffering. Remember what he said in verse 7: "Our hope for you is firm, because we know that just as you share in our sufferings, so also you share in our comfort." Paul was speaking about a particular hardship that he had just faced. He said that there was such a relation between him and the Corinthian believers that they shared in his suffering with him. We have to be aware of every situation in our lives because we never know when God is preparing us for an opportunity to impact the world. These opportunities can sometimes come in strange circumstances; whether it is in times of suffering or times of comfort.

We need to approach life with eyes wide open knowing that God wants to impact the world through us and never knowing when those opportunities may come.

John Wesley is widely known to have said, "I look upon the world as my parish." That is a great thought and one that we would do well to adopt. Our society is in desperate need of believers who are willing to sacrifice everything that is important to them so that they can put the needs of others first. Simply put, we need to be world Christians. We need to see the world around us. Instead of being bothered, frustrated, or outraged, we need to ask that God would help us to see the possibilities for transformation. What is so admirable about the apostle Paul is the way that he seized every opportunity set before him and used it as an opportunity to transform lives. One of the best examples of this is found in Acts 17 as he stood before the men of the Areopagus.

The men of the Areopagus liked to sit around and talk philosophy. They were especially interested in "new ideas." Any fresh concept that was coming down the pipeline was fodder for a spirited conversation. Paul noticed an altar dedicated to the worship of an "unknown god." Here was his response to this altar:

Men of Athens! I see that in every way you are very religious. For as I walked around and looked carefully at your objects of worship, I even found an altar with this inscription: TO AN UNKNOWN GOD. Now what you worship as something unknown I am going to proclaim to you. The God who made the world and everything in it is the Lord of heaven and earth and does not live in temples built by hands. And he is not served by human hands, as if he needed anything, because he himself gives all men life and breath and everything else. From one man he made every nation of men, that they should inhabit the whole earth; and he determined the times set for them and the exact places where they should live. God did this so that men would seek him and perhaps reach out for him and find him, though he is not far from each one of us. "For in him we live and move and have our being." As some of your own poets have said, "We are his offspring." (Acts 17:22–28)

Paul could have blasted the Athenian men for their godlessness. But Paul saw an opportunity for God to transform someone, and he did his best to seize it. This was Paul's way of life and he was wholly devoted to it. Remember earlier we saw that Paul was focused on comfort because he had just suffered a particular hardship. Instead of bemoaning that hardship however, he simply acknowledged that even the hardship was an opportunity to minister to someone. The world needs us to be that type of Christian—being focused on the needs of those around us and understanding that almost anything that happens to us can be used by God to transform others. This can be initially uncomfortable. Anything that causes us to get out of our comfort zone can cause anxiety, but we have to remember that this is why God called us out of our old lives.

The motor home has allowed us to put all the conveniences of home on wheels. Campers no longer needs to contend with sleeping in a sleeping bag, cooking over a fire, or hauling water from a stream. Now they can park a fully equipped home on a cement slab in the midst of a few pine trees and hook up to a water line, a sewer line, and electricity. One motor home I recently saw had a satellite dish attached on top. No more bother with dirt, no more smoke from the fire, and no more drudgery of walking to the stream. Now it is possible to go camping without even going outside. We buy a motor home with the hope of seeing new places and of getting out into the world. Yet we deck it out with the same furnishings as our living room. Thus, nothing really changes. We may drive to a new place and park ourselves in a place we've never been before, but the newness goes unnoticed because we've brought along our own familiar surroundings.

The adventure of new life in Christ begins when the comfortable patterns of the old life are left behind. God wants to use us to impact the world and we must become world Christians, seeing the possibilities for transformation all around us.

Make a Difference in the World

"Do not store up for yourselves treasures on earth, where moth and rust destroy, and where thieves break in and steal. But store up for yourselves treasures in heaven, where moth and rust do not destroy, and where thieves do not break in and steal. For where your treasure is, there your heart will be also" (Matt. 6:19–21).

The final step in the process is to use all that we have to make a difference in the world. We need to know that God wants to use us; we need to open our eyes so that we can see the possibilities; and then we need to act. The distinction that Jesus made in Matthew 6 is an important one. There he was talking about the difference between a focus on earthly and heavenly things. We have discussed what it means to focus on earthly things. This means that we concern ourselves more with wealth, power, and success. The reverse of that is to focus on heavenly things. This means we use all that we have to make a difference that will last.

Jesus said, "Where your treasure is, there your heart will be also." What is it that we treasure—that we value most of all? What Jesus is trying to get us to see—what Paul was trying to get us to see in 2 Corinthians—is that we need to strive to treasure the opportunity to meet the needs of others.

It has been reported that the body of David Livingstone was buried in his homeland of England, but his heart was buried in the Africa he loved. At the foot of a tall tree in a small African village, the natives dug a hole and placed in it the heart of this man whom they loved and respected. If your heart were to be buried in the place you loved most during life, where would it be? In your pocketbook? In an appropriate space down at the office? Where is your heart? We need to see the world around us and show—by our actions and with our heart—that we value the opportunities God gives us to impact the world.

I began *Give to Live* considering the overwhelming idea that God wants to use us to change the world. This can be frightening, particularly because the task seems so large and we seem so ill-equipped. Hopefully, God has spoken to you about what is required of all Christians to stop being self-centered and to start serving in his big world with our eyes wide open. The fact is that God's plan has always been to use ordinary people to impact the world. Perhaps we look at the stories of the great men and women of the Bible and think that those were unique circumstances and that we could never duplicate those great events. That may be true in one sense, but we have to remember that God uses people just like you and me who are simply willing to be used.

When you understand the grace and compassion of Jesus, you will be motivated to join his mission in the world. May we pray that God will do just that in us—that he will help us to see his glory and that like Isaiah, we will respond, "Here am I. Send me!" (Isa. 6:8). As you live, look around for opportunities to be used of God. Think in every situation, "Is this something that God is putting in front of me so that I can make a difference?" God wants to use us to transform the world; and with the power of Christ inside us, we can do it.

Takeaway
God wants me to provide food, shelter,
hope, and justice to others.

The Greatest Gift

bringing salvation to others

Key Insight
God will use your generosity to bring about
the salvation of the world.

But you will receive power when the Holy Spirit comes on you; and you will be my witnesses in Jerusalem, and in all Judea and Samaria, and to the ends of the earth.
—Acts 1:8

When you look out the window, what do you see? If you're like most people, you might see the sky, clouds, or moon. Some people are able to see more than that. Bill Hybels, in his book *Who You Are When No One's Looking*, relates the story of a boy who says much more.

It started like so many evenings. Mom and Dad at home and Jimmy playing after dinner. Mom and Dad were absorbed with jobs and did not notice the time. It was a full moon and some of the light seeped through the windows. Then Mom glanced at the clock. "Jimmy, it's time to go to bed. Go up now and I'll come and settle you later." Unlike usual, Jimmy went straight upstairs to his room. An hour or so later his mother came up to check if all was well, and to her astonishment found that her son was staring quietly out of his window at the moonlit scenery. "What are you doing, Jimmy?"

"I'm looking at the moon, Mommy."

"Well, it's time to go to bed now."

As one reluctant boy settled down, he said, "Mommy, you know one day I'm going to walk on the moon." Who could have known that the boy in whom the dream was planted that night would survive a near fatal motorbike crash which broke almost every bone in his body, and would bring to fruition this dream 32 years later when James Irwin stepped on the moon's surface, just one of the 12 representatives of the human race to have done so?"[1]

Some people are blessed with the ability to see things from a different perspective, and there is great power in that, for what we can see, we can believe in; and what we can believe in, we can achieve. That is the power of vision.

The Need for Salvation

Now let's turn that vision question away from the sky and toward the earth. When you look out at the world in which we live, what do you see? Again, if you are like most people, you might answer, "I see a huge world filled with people" or "I see incredible problems like crime, poverty, war, and disease." Jesus Christ looked out over that same world and saw a field of ripe grain, ready to be harvested. Where we see problems, he saw solutions. Where we see overwhelming need, he saw God's overwhelming supply. Where we see hopelessness, Jesus saw the hope of the world.

Today we're going to adjust our vision. We're going to look at life through a different set of glasses. We're going to begin seeing the world the way God sees it. And when we do, you will feel energized to join him in the marvelous mission to reach the world for Jesus Christ.

God Sees People in Need of a Savior

There is no question that we live in a world of need. Sometimes that fact is hidden from our view because we enjoy tremendous opportunities and privileges. Most of us have had opportunities for education, access to health care, favorable economic conditions, and—most important of all—the opportunity to hear the good news about Jesus Christ. Sometimes it is difficult for believers to imagine that most of the world does not know Christ, and millions of people have never even heard his name.

For example, consider the region of the world known as the 10/40 Window, that area between the tenth and fortieth parallels on the globe, roughly the region including northern Africa and southern Asia. Two-thirds of the world's population—more than 3.2 billion people—live in that region. Ninety-five percent of them are not evangelized. Many have never heard the gospel message even once. There are either no Christians or not enough of a Christian movement in many cultures in the 10/40 Window to carry out vibrant near-neighbor evangelism.

This is also one of the poorest regions on the globe. Eighty-five percent of those living in the 10/40 Window are the poorest of the world's poor.

Half of the world's least evangelized cities are in this window. The statistics of the numbers of non-Christians can seem overwhelming. In this area of the world alone, there are:

- 865 million unreached Muslims in 3,330 cultural subgroupings
- 550 million unreached Hindus in 1,660 cultural subgroups
- 150 million unreached Chinese in 830 groups
- 275 million unreached Buddhists in 900 groups[2]

If those people are to be reached with the good news about Jesus Christ, believers from other lands will have to go and deliver it to them, because there are no churches or Christian movements available to them where they are.

How aware of these needs would you say that you are? Do you see what God sees? Do you see a world filled with people who do not know Jesus Christ and are lost without him? Many of us fail to see this pressing need or fail to take any action on it. If you do not yet have God's vision for the world—that is, if you are not yet fully aware of the need that others have for salvation, I suggest that you can gain that vision by taking these simple steps.

Pray for Deeper Love. First, pray that God will give you a deeper love for other people. It is the love of others that helps us see their deepest need. When we care for people as deeply as Jesus cared for them, we will be moved with compassion as he was. Pray, asking God to fill your heart with a deeper love for others.

Go Where the Lost Are. Second, move out of your comfort zone and into the places where lost people are. Not surprisingly, most of us prefer to spend time among people who are like us.

Jesus, however, spent much of his time with people who were radically different from himself. Be observant as you go through you day. Engage in conversation people at your workplace who seem very different from you. Make it a point to see the people who are often unseen in our society—the poor, the homeless, the addicts.

When you see the world God sees and when you see people as he sees them, you will be moved with compassion as Jesus was. Pray that God will open your eyes to see other people—to really see them and their needs. Let your heart be filled with love for those who are lost.

God Sees Resources at Your Disposal

When we think about how much there is to do in the world, the task can seem overwhelming. It's a little like the fellow who moved from Alaska to California and shortly thereafter got a flat on one of his studded snow tires. The service-station attendant took a long look and then said, "Mister, I don't know how to tell you this, but you've got over a hundred nails in your tire!"

Sometimes we have a hard time seeing the solution because the problem is so large. Very often, the solution is right in front of us but we don't know it. We are a little like the disciples who brought a problem to Jesus—there was no food to feed more than five thousand people. All they had was a small meal intended for a boy, five loaves and two fishes. Jesus saw that lunch as the solution to a huge problem. He took it, blessed it, and fed the multitude (see Matt. 14:12–14; Mark 6:29–31; Luke 9:9–10; and John 6:1–3).

And remember when God called Moses to lead the Hebrew people from slavery in Egypt? Moses was filled with excuses. He could name a hundred reasons why he couldn't go and talk to

Pharaoh. He just didn't have the resources. But God asked a simple question: "What is that in your hand?" "It's a staff," Moses replied. God told him to throw it down, and it became a serpent—it was a display of God's power (see Ex. 4:1–3).

We hold that same power in our hands, so to speak, since God has released so many of his resources to us. We have what we need to get the job done; we just don't know it!

According to Ralph Winter of the William Carey Library: Americans give $700 million per year to mission agencies. However, they pay as much for pet food every fifty-two days. "A person must overeat by at least $1.50 worth of food per month to maintain one excess pound of flesh. Yet $1.50 per month is more than what 90 [percent] of all Christians in America give to missions. If the average missions supporter is only five pounds overweight, it means he spends (to his own hurt) at least five times as much as he gives for missions. If he were to choose simple food (as well as not overeat) he could give ten times as much as he does to missions and not modify his standard of living in any other way!"[3]

I've heard it said that 97 percent of the world has heard of Coca-Cola, 72 percent of the world has seen a can of Coca-Cola, and 51 percent has tasted Coca-Cola. Yet Coke has only been around since 1904. I think if God had given the task of world evangelization to the Coke company, we'd be done by now!

We have more resources than we think we have. How much money per year do you spend on some of these common items: ice cream, coffee, soft drinks, or chocolate? It's been reported that the average person consumes twelve pounds of chocolate per year. At the risk of sounding heretical, I wonder what resources we could mobilize to reach the world if we simply gave up chocolate!

And what difference could we make if we acted in concert, organizing our activities in our local churches? The Association of Church Missions Commissions once defined a mobilizing church as one in which 10 percent of the church's members are regularly and systematically praying for missions, 10 percent of the members are regularly and systematically sharing their faith, 10 percent of the church's budget is spent on cross-cultural outreach, 1 percent of the church's members are entering cross-cultural service, and the church is working to involve one neighbor church in missions.[4] Surely that would be an achievable goal for any congregation.

We can do a lot with what we have. Though our resources may seem small to us, God is faithful to bless our efforts as we respond to his call. What do you have that you can offer to the Lord's service? What portion of your time, talent, and treasure can you dedicate to reaching those whom Jesus loves? While we may look at the task and seem woefully inadequate, God's vision is greater. He sees the tremendous resources that are available to us as we answer his call. He sees that we have what we need to fulfill this great mission to reach the world.

God Sees the Impact Your Efforts Can Make

T. E. Lawrence, also known as Lawrence of Arabia, once said, "All men dream: but not equally. Those who dream by night in the dusty recesses of their minds wake in the day to find that it was vanity: but the dreamers of the day are dangerous men, for they may act their dreams with open eyes, to make it possible."[5] Seeing the world the way God sees it means seeing the impact we could make as we answer his call. You must begin to envision the possibilities.

You cannot achieve anything without vision. And when that vision begins to die, the mission dies too. It is critical to continually see the horizon—the next frontier to be reached.

Can you envision the impact that our efforts can have? Can you see the difference we can make? According to Randy Alcorn, every day the gospel is bearing fruit all around the world. Every day some 74,000 people come to faith in Christ. That's nearly one per second! The *Jesus* film has been shown in 228 countries, with 197,298,327 viewers indicating a commitment to Christ (with even more today). "In 1950, when China was closed to foreign missionaries, there were one million believers in the country. Today conservative estimates say there are well over [eighty] million. An average of 28,000 people become believers every day in the People's Republic of China. In A.D. 100 there were 360 non-Christians per true believer. Today the ratio is less than seven to every believer as the initiative of the Holy Spirit continues to outstrip our most optimistic plans! Throughout history the growth of the body of Christ has outdistanced the increase of world population."[6]

The gospel of Jesus Christ is already having an impact around the world. As we join God in his grand mission to reach the world, we will see that impact increase. Can you imagine the possibilities?

What would be the effect if we would each dedicate one hour per week to praying for the lost? What would be the effect if we would dedicate just 20 percent of our church's income to sending gospel messengers around the world? What would be the effect on global poverty, disease, or war, if we would bring one billion more people into a relationship with the Prince of Peace? How might your church, your community, your world be different if we work together to make known the name of Jesus?

Can you see it? Can you envision the impact of our work upon a needy world? Jesus could see it. That's why he was moved to say, "The harvest is plentiful, but the workers are few" (Matt. 9:37). When we see what Jesus sees, there will be more workers.

Without question, we are facing a huge task. There are more than six billion people on earth, and most of them do not know Jesus Christ. Every day, children go to bed hungry, deadly diseases such as AIDS claim the lives of thousands, and armed conflicts rage around the globe. If we were to look only at the problems in our world, it would certainly be discouraging.

Thankfully, we have been given a fresh vision of the world—we have been given a peek at the world through Jesus' eyes, and that is a vision of hope. It reminds me of the fellow who approached a little league baseball game one afternoon. He asked a boy in the dugout what the score was. The boy responded, "Eighteen to nothing—we're behind."

"Boy," said the spectator, "I'll bet you're discouraged."

"Why should I be discouraged?" replied the little boy. "We haven't even gotten up to bat yet!"

That's the powerful vision that Jesus had when he said, "The harvest is plentiful but the workers are few. Ask the Lord of the harvest, therefore, to send out workers into his harvest field" (Matt. 9:37–38). It's our turn at bat now. This is our time. This is our moment. This is our world, our need, our calling. God has called us to go forth and take the name of Jesus to every person and every place on the globe. We have the commission. We have the power of his Holy Spirit. We have the resources he has provided. Let's live up to the vision God has placed before us!

The Message of the Savior

The Spirit of the Sovereign LORD is on me, because the LORD has anointed me to preach good news to the poor. He has sent me to bind up the brokenhearted, to proclaim freedom for the captives and release from darkness for the prisoners, to proclaim the year of the LORD's favor and the day of vengeance of our God, to comfort all who mourn, and provide for those who grieve in Zion—to bestow on them a crown of beauty instead of ashes, the oil of gladness instead of mourning, and a garment of praise instead of a spirit of despair. (Isa. 61:1–3)

Isaiah wrote these words about seven hundred years before Jesus walked the earth. Jesus read the words from a scroll in a synagogue at Nazareth and told the worshipers that the words were fulfilled in their hearing that day. In other words, the Scripture referred to Jesus and his ministry.

In the Jewish synagogue, which was their place of worship, the order of service was fairly predictable. First someone would offer a prayer. Then came the reading of the Scriptures. Seven people from the congregation would read. As they read the Hebrew, someone would translate it into Aramaic or Greek for the sake of those who did not know the original language. First they would read a portion of the Law, that is, something from Genesis, Exodus, Leviticus, Numbers, or Deuteronomy. Then they would read from one of the prophets.

On the day Jesus showed up at the synagogue in Nazareth, the reading was from Isaiah. When someone handed him the scroll, he unrolled it, and found this passage in Isaiah 61.

Then came the teaching part of the service. In the synagogue, no one person gave the address all the time. Rather, the president of the synagogue would invite any distinguished person present to speak. That's how Jesus came to speak that day. His ministry had already begun to attract attention. Now here he was in his hometown, and the crowd wanted to hear what he had to say.

185

The custom was to stand while reading the Scripture and to sit while teaching it. So after reading, Jesus sat down. He told them the Scripture was being fulfilled before their very eyes that day. What a thrill that we get to share Jesus with others!

As we understand this passage, we begin to get some clues as to what Jesus was sent to do in our world.

Share the Good News

Nobody in all of history ever cared more about people than Jesus did. Wherever he went, crowds of poor people followed him. They wanted to hear him speak, see his miracles, and experience being in his presence.

Jesus loved them and they sensed it. Mark tells us, "The common people heard him gladly" (Mark 12:37 KJV).

What was the good news he preached to the poor? Was it the message: "Take heart. I am going to make all of you rich"? No. Jesus did not come particularly to make the poor people rich nor the rich people poor, in terms of material wealth. Poverty goes deeper than how much money you have. Wealth goes beyond what you have in the bank.

The poverty of sin is the worst kind. A life that is not in right relationship with God is a life of poverty. On the other hand, real wealth consists not in the abundance of the things a person may possess. Jesus asked, "What good is it for a man to gain the whole world, yet forfeit his soul?" (Mark 8:36).

Jesus himself is the pearl of great price. He gives eternal life, which is an asset of greater value than all else combined. If you have eternal life, then no matter how little you may possess otherwise, you are rich in the things of God. If you don't have eternal life, it doesn't matter how much money you have; you're poor in the things of God.

Bind Up the Brokenhearted

Luke translates it, "release the oppressed" (Luke 4:18); another translation says, "to set at liberty them that are bruised" (4:18 KJV). Greek scholars tell us the word *bruised* means "those who are shattered in fortune and broken in spirit."

Do you know anyone who is brokenhearted? Anyone whose fortunes have been shattered? Anyone who is broken in spirit? Do you know anyone who seems to have run out of hope?

A man sat next to a woman he did not know on an airplane. As they engaged in conversation, she told him about her husband who had suffered a near nervous breakdown. It seems the company for whom he had worked many years let him go because of a change of management. Not only that, her son's marriage had fallen apart after his wife had an affair with the next-door neighbor. Of course, their two small children would suffer as a result of that breakup. This lady was trying to be brave in spite of her difficulties, but it was obvious that she was bruised—she was crushed in spirit.

Jesus came to bind up the brokenhearted. He came to give liberty to the bruised and to release those who feel oppressed.

Proclaim Freedom for the Captives

Did Jesus come to release everyone who was behind bars? No. Actually, the word for "prisoners" means "prisoners of war."

Sin makes captives of people. It makes them prisoners of war. How do you become a prisoner of war? You might get caught behind enemy lines. Many people have intruded on Satan's territory. They thought they could participate in sin without suffering the consequences. But one day they woke up to discover they had been captured. They were prisoners of war. Sin had surrounded, bound, and trapped them.

But the beautiful message of Jesus is that he brings freedom to all people who will call on him for deliverance. The Scripture says, "If the Son sets you free, you will be free indeed" (John 8:36).

You do not have to be trapped in a web of sinful habits. Jesus has come to set us free.

Proclaim Release from Darkness

Luke's account says, "recovery of sight for the blind" (Luke 4:18). On various occasions, Jesus healed people who were blind. He touched their sightless eyes and they could see again. What a wonderful and merciful miracle that was.

Sadder than blind people who are unable to find their ways are those who are spiritually unable to see themselves as they are in sin or what they could become by the grace of God.

Satan wants to blind your vision as to what God can do for you. He does not want your eyes to become open to the truth; he wants us to stumble along through life because we can't see things in proper perspective.

Proclaim the Year of the Lord's Favor

This idea—the year of the Lord's favor—goes back to the book of Leviticus. God gave Moses instructions for Israel that said they were to observe a sabbatical year. In other words, every seventh year, they were to let the land lie fallow. They were not to sow grain. They were not to tend to their olive groves and vineyards. Whatever the land produced by itself was not to be harvested, but left for the public to use. The poor, slaves, and strangers could freely partake. In the sabbatical year, all who had borrowed money were not obligated to make payments on their debts. Every seventh year was to be a sabbatical year.

After seven sets of seven years, or forty-nine years, then the fiftieth year was to be a Year of Jubilee. It was like a sabbatical year but with even greater liberties. All land reverted back to its original family, free of all obligations in the Year of Jubilee. This meant that no family, tribe, or person could grow exorbitantly rich, nor could any family or person be doomed to perpetual poverty. All land was restored to its original owner every fifty years. In the Year of Jubilee, slaves were freed and debtors were absolved (see Lev. 25).

So when Jesus said, "[I] proclaim the year of the Lord's favor" (Luke 4:19), that phrase referred to the Year of Jubilee. Then he went on to say, "Today, this scripture is fulfilled in your hearing" (4:21), indicating that he was actually referring to something even better than Jubilee.

Jesus came to give us perpetual Jubilee. He says, "I don't just give your land rest from growing crops. I give your souls rest from the labor of sin. Not only are slaves freed, but I will free people from enslavement to sin and Satan. I will cancel the debt owed on account of sin for those who put their trust in me."

Do you know anyone who is poor? Then you can tell them how to be rich in Christ. Know anyone who is bound by sin? You can tell them how to be free in Christ. Know anyone who is spiritually blind? You can tell them how to have a new vision in Christ. Know anyone who is bruised and broken? You can give them new hope and help in Christ.

The author Rita Snowden tells about having tea one afternoon in a small town near Dover, England. As she sat there, she became aware of an unbelievably pleasant scent filling the air. When she asked the waiter where the scent was coming from, he told her it was from the people who were walking by. These people worked at a perfume factory down the street, and they were on their way home from work. All day long, the fragrance permeated their clothing and when they left the factory, they carried it with them.

That's what we as a church can be like when we are at our very best. As we worship, we should allow ourselves to be permeated with the love of Christ. Then as we go forth in the world, the fragrance of the Lord goes with us. As we come into contact with others, something of God's fragrance passes from us to them.[7]

Let's determine by God's grace that we will be the fragrance of Christ, sharing the good news with others.

Takeaway
Every person needs salvation through
faith in Jesus Christ, and I can help them find it.

Your New Life Starts Now!

keys to personal change

Key Insight
You can begin giving living today.

As a believer in Jesus Christ, you are both a new person and a member of a new community, the kingdom of God. Your life no longer functions according to the old rules where success was measured by how much you could earn, spend, and consume. Your life operates by different values now. In this kingdom, God provides for all your needs, people matter more than things, and the greatest contentment comes from serving others.

Your new life starts now!

All the believers were one in heart and mind. No one claimed that any of his possessions was his own, but they shared everything they had. With great power the apostles continued to testify to the resurrection of the Lord Jesus, and much grace was upon them all. There were no needy persons among them. For from time to time those who owned lands or houses sold them, brought the money from the sales and put it at the apostles' feet, and it was distributed to anyone as he had need.
—Acts 4:32–35

Change in Your Community

Lou Holtz, who coached football at Notre Dame and some other colleges and is a football analyst on television, told about watching a television program that examined why men died for their country. This program looked at the United States Marines, the French Foreign Legion, and the British Commandos. They said that men died for their country because of the love they had for their fellow man.

On the show, they interviewed a soldier who had been wounded in combat and was recovering in a hospital when he heard his unit was going back out on a dangerous mission. The soldier escaped from the hospital and went with them, only to be wounded again. When asked why he did it, he said that after you work and live with people, you soon realize your survival depends on one another.[1]

Whether we realize it or not, that applies to the church. Our survival depends on our sense of community. Where would we be without our mutual prayers, encouragement, and service to and with one another?

The early church understood and practiced this. Fresh from the hand of God and the creative power of the Holy Spirit on the day of Pentecost, they had no history to draw on as to how they should behave. The church had never existed before! So they didn't know any better than to respond positively to the leadership of the apostles and to the inner voice of the Holy Spirit in their hearts.

Consequently, they ministered in an extraordinary way to the tangible needs of others in their midst. They refused to claim that their possessions belonged only to them. They had the audacity to share what they had with those in need. They were so successful in this that there were actually "no needy persons among them" (Acts 4:34). If a need arose, someone who owned some property would sell it, bring the money to the apostles, and let it be distributed to those in need (2:45; 4:34–35). The church ministered with beautiful, magnanimous acts of Christian love and service that impress us even to this day. It was so impressive that Luke, when writing his history of the early church, said they were "one in heart and mind."

From the Greek word for heart we derive our English words *cardiac* and *cardiology*. But here it means more than the physical heart. It refers to the reason, emotions, and will. It covers the whole range of our mental and emotional activity. In other words, the believers thought and felt alike. They weren't carbon copies of one another; it just means they had a great unity and purpose. Their goals and desires so coincided with each other that Luke said they were "one in heart" (4:32).

He also said they were "one in . . . mind" (4:32). The Greek word for *mind* refers to the spiritual life of a person, the part of us that can be quickened and filled by the Holy Spirit. They served the same Christ, were filled with the same Spirit, and worshiped the same heavenly Father.

They also held their possessions loosely. This has prompted some people to think the early church practiced a sort of Christian communism, in which nobody held any private property, but everybody sold everything they had, brought the proceeds to the church, and shared and shared alike. But this is not what happened.

Luke went on to tell us about Barnabas who sold a field he owned and brought the money to the church. If everyone had done that, there would be no reason for singling out Barnabas. But here Luke cited him as one who gave generously to meet a need (4:36–37).

The point is: When a need arose, someone did what was necessary to meet the need and nobody had to suffer materially. So their behavior did not reflect Christian communism but Christian commitment. Communism would say, "What's yours is mine; I will take it." Christian commitment says, "What's mine is yours if you need it."

Beware of Individualism

Individualism holds within it three perils that can trip us up today and keep us from being the servants Christ has called us to be.

Independence

Independence is a concept we hold dear, and we need to be independent enough to stand on our own two feet. We do not want to be a burden on others, as long as we have the wherewithal to take care of ourselves. We certainly don't want to be like the fellow who ran a want ad in the newspaper that said: "Need co-author for a book on self-reliance." Isn't that a contradiction in terms? Yet perhaps even that is reminding us of how much we really do need each other.

A spirit of independence in the life of a Christian can be a terribly carnal, unspiritual trait when it is expressed in an attitude of "What's in it for me?" We can too easily adopt the idea that the world revolves around us. The Polish astronomer Copernicus studied the heavens and gradually came to the conclusion that the earth is not the center around which the universe revolves, but is rather a moving planet that itself revolves around the sun. This was a revolutionary idea in his day. And even in our day, some people are surprised to know the world does not revolve around their lives and interests.

194

Instead of asking, "What's in it for me?" we need to be the kind of people who ask, "What can I do for you?"

Indifference

This is another peril into which many people fall. It is expressed in the philosophy, "Who cares about anyone else?" At the heart of this peril is an attitude of self-centeredness. I heard Chuck Swindoll at a Promise Keepers event years ago ask, "What does the Lord do to help broaden my horizons and assist me in seeing how selfish I am? Very simple: He gives me four busy kids who step on shoes, wrinkle clothes, spill milk, lick car windows, and drop sticky candy on the carpet. Being unselfish in attitude strikes at the very core of our being. It means we are willing to forego our own comfort, our own preferences, our own schedule, and our own desires for another's benefit. And that brings us back to Christ."

We need to be the kind of people who care and share and openly meet the needs of others whenever possible.

Individuality

This third peril is a trap into which we can easily fall. We like to express our own identity, which is often appropriate. But when that expression fails to take into consideration the needs and concerns of others, it becomes a snare to us. Instead of looking out for others, we look out for *numero uno*.

When I was a college student, I got to hear the famed E. Stanley Jones, a veteran missionary to India speak. I will never forget one thing that he said: "Everywhere I go, I go along, and I spoil everything."

Someone once defined EGO as Edging God Out. Individualism not only edges God out, but it also edges others out and destroys a sense of community. Our challenge is to rise above a

195

self-absorbed existence and become the persons and the church God has called us to be.

Live with Others in Mind

This was the genius of the early church. They were a close-knit, loving, helpful community of faith and practice.

In order to become such a community, we need to get to know one another better. My friends, John Maxwell and Jim Dornan proposed three questions in their business seminars, dealing specifically with people we might try to mentor.

What Do You Cry About?

What moves people? What do they feel at their deepest levels? Do you know what they're passionate about? Someone has said the great men and women of history were great not for what they owned or earned, but for what they gave their lives to accomplish. As you get to know people around you, listen with your heart. You may discover the things for which others are willing to give themselves.

What Do You Sing About?

What gives people energy? What triggers their enthusiasm? Frank Irving Fletcher observed, "No man can deliver the goods if his heart is heavier than his load."[2] There is a big difference between the things that lift a person's heart and the things that weigh down a person. What lifts the spirits of your friends? What makes them sing?

What Do You Dream About?

Do you have any idea about people's ambitions? In their fondest imagination, how do they perceive their future? Wouldn't it be fascinating if we could read the blueprints of someone's future achievements? Wouldn't it be interesting to know what is on the drawing board of their vision? We might have that opportunity if we get to know something about their dreams, plans, and vision for the future.

Now why do we need to develop a sense of community? It's because one is too small a number to succeed. We need each other. The church is so much more effective—even we as individuals are more effective—when we work together as a community.

Find a Need and Fill It

This is where the rubber meets the road. This is where we discover great fulfillment as individuals and as a church—when we begin to find needs and fill them. As Henry Van Dyke said, "There is a loftier ambition than merely to stand high in the world. It is to stoop down and lift mankind a little higher."[3]

The amazing thing is that by helping others, we often help ourselves.

M. Scott Peck, the renowned psychologist and author, told of a woman patient who suffered from severe depression. One day when she had an appointment with him, she called to tell him her car had broken down. He offered to pick her up on the way to his office, but said he needed to make a hospital call first. If she would wait in the car while he made the call, they could have their appointment.

When they arrived at the hospital, he made another suggestion. He gave her the names of two other patients who were convalescing at that hospital and indicated they might enjoy a visit from her. They met again after an hour and a half, and she was on an emotional high. She told the doctor that visiting those people and cheering them up had actually lifted her own spirits. She was feeling wonderful.

Dr. Peck said, "Now we know how to cure you of your depression."

She responded, "You don't expect me to do that every day, do you?"[4]

That's our problem sometimes. We may too easily think that doing what Jesus calls us to do is burdensome, when in fact, it may be the very best thing for us. John Mason said, "When you help someone up a mountain, you'll find yourself close to the summit, too."[5]

There's an old Chinese proverb that recommends: "To be happy for an hour—take a nap. To be happy for a day—go fishing. To be happy for a month—get married. To be happy for a year—inherit a fortune. To be happy for a lifetime—help others."

Jean Nidetch is the founder of Weight Watchers, which has more than a million members in twenty-four countries. Someone asked her how she had been able to help so many people. Nidetch said when she was a teenager she regularly crossed a park and watched mothers chatting while their toddlers sat on swings with no one to push them. She said, "I'd give them a push. And you know what happens when you push a kid on a swing? Pretty soon he's pumping, doing it himself. That's what my role in life is—I'm there to give others a push."[6]

That's true for all of us. We're here to give each other a push, a little nudge in the right direction.

Perhaps you're thinking: I don't know where to start. I don't know who needs help. That's why we need to get to know one another better in this faith community. But I can tell you this for certain: everybody needs encouragement from time to time. Take an example from Winnie the Pooh. One day Pooh Bear is about to go for a walk in the Hundred Acre wood. It's about 11:30 in the morning. It is a fine time to go calling—just before lunch. So Pooh sets out across the stream, stepping on the stones, and when he gets right in the middle of the stream, he sits down on a warm stone to think about just where would be the best place of all to make a call. He says to himself, "I think I'll go see Tigger."

No, he dismisses that. Then he says, "Owl!" But he thinks, "No, Owl uses big words, hard-to-understand words."

At last his face brightens. "I know! I'll go see Rabbit. I like Rabbit. Rabbit uses encouraging words like 'How's about lunch?' and 'Help yourself, Pooh!' Yes, I think I'll go see Rabbit."

Don't you love to be around a person who is encouraging? Why don't you become such a person, an encourager of others, and you will have no trouble discovering people who need your help, your blessings, your encouragement.

Jesus said, "Whoever wants to become great among you must be your servant" (Matt. 20:26). Even Jesus himself "did not come to be served, but to serve, and to give his life as a ransom for many" (20:28).

We are not in this alone! We are part of a great community. We need to watch out for the perils of individualism because they can sidetrack us from being at our best in community. We also need to live with a greater sense of community as we get to know and appreciate each other better. But then as we realize how much we need each other, we will begin to find needs and fill them by the help and grace of God.

As a first step, why don't you ask yourself: Where can I best fit in my community of faith? How can I best serve? Then try to find someone within your church as well as neighborhood community whom you do not know, and make a conscious effort to get to know him or her.

What is our motive in all this? It has been said that Mother Teresa had a signal she greeted her sisters with: a raised hand, with all five fingers spread. It meant, "Do it all for Jesus." They would respond by raising their hands, with spread fingers, "We did it for Jesus."

We are not in this alone. You, Jesus, and I—we are in this together!

Takeaway
It is within my power to change.

Small Group Discussion Guide

The best way to learn from this book is with a group of friends. As you read together, you can discuss what you are learning, talk about how it impacts your life, and encourage one another to apply the concepts you discover. *Give to Live* isn't merely an idea—it's a lifestyle!

For each chapter of this book, four types of questions are provided:

- Tune In—A thought-provoking question or statement that will get your group focused on the big idea of the chapter.
- Explore—An opportunity to examine the key ideas of the chapter and dig deeper into their meaning.
- Engage—Challenging questions that will help you see the implications of these ideas for your life.
- Act—A bold challenge that will help you take the next step in developing a Give to Live life.

Each time you meet, remember to review a bit of what you have learned and allow your group members to share their experiences at developing a lifestyle of generosity.

Chapter 1
What's Mine Is Yours
understanding stewardship

Tune In

Everybody has a prized possession. What's yours?

Explore

What is the relationship between gratitude and generosity?

How do you know that God is completely trustworthy and good?

List some Bible passages that describe God's goodness or generosity.

Do you think most people do a good job of managing their money? Why or why not?

Engage

Make a short list of the blessings God has given to you. Share it with the group.

How do you feel about the concept that God owns everything, including your stuff?

Name some practical things you could do to remind yourself of God's blessings.

How would you explain the concept of stewardship to someone who had never heard it before?

What is your biggest problem area in your personal finances?

Act

This week, review your spending for the past month and ask, "How well am I managing the resources God has entrusted to me?"

Chapter 2
Count on Me!
learning to trust

Tune In

Fill in the blank: I find it easy to trust God, except when

_____.

Explore

Which passages of Scripture teach us that God will provide for our needs? Which ones are most meaningful to you? Why?

What is the difference between believing in God and trusting him? Which is harder to do? Why?

Why is it so difficult to trust God to provide for our needs?

Engage

Talk about a time when you had to trust God. How did you feel? What did you learn?

In what area of your life are you personally struggling to trust God?

Who have been some of your examples of trust in God—people in the Bible, from history, or your own life who have shown you how to practice faith?

What would help you overcome your personal hesitations about trusting God?

Act

Make a list of the blessings God has provided in your life and share it with a friend or family member. Ask them to do the same.

Chapter 3
The Blessing Principle
learning to give as well as receive

Tune In

What person has had the greatest impact on your life?

Explore

How would you state the principle of blessing in your own words?

How do you see the principle of blessing at work in Joseph's life?

List a few of God's blessings that are spiritual and material.

Why do you think God pours blessing into our lives?

Describe the relationship between our faithfulness and God's ongoing blessing.

Engage

Are you ever tempted to hoard money or resources? If so, why?

In what ways have you seen the principle of blessing at work in your life?

On a scale from one to ten—with ten being extremely generous and one being very stingy—how generous do you think you are? Do you think others would agree?

In what situations do you find it easy to be generous? Which types of situations are more difficult for you?

Name some practical steps you could take to develop the lifestyle of generosity?

Act

This week, give something away as a tangible expression of your belief that God provides.

Chapter 4
The Generosity Factor
motivated by love

Tune In

If you had the power to make one positive change in the world, what would it be?

Explore

Jesus spoke quite a bit about our need to love one another. Can you recall some of his teachings on this subject?

In what ways has God shown his love for us? For the world?

What are some practical ways we can demonstrate our love for others?

What are some of the practical benefits of loving others mentioned in this chapter?

Engage

Does loving other people come naturally to you? Why or why not?

List some of the people you find it easy to love. Whom do you have difficulty loving?

If Jesus could personally address your group, what do you think he would say about the subject of compassion?

Talk about a time when someone had compassion on you.

What practical steps could you take to gain a better understanding of the needs people in your community are facing?

Act

Identify a person or group of people whom you find it difficult to love, then learn more about them this week.

Chapter 5
The Starting Point for Generosity
consecration

Tune In

Name something you have more of when you give it away.

Explore

How would you define consecration? Sanctification?

What did the apostle Paul mean when he said that we are to be "living sacrifices" to God (see Rom. 12:1–2)?

Do you agree with the claim that giving our lives entirely to God is a reasonable thing to do? Why or why not?

What is the relationship between consecration and generosity?

Many people reserve one area of their lives, trying to keep it "secret" from God. Why do you think they do this?

Engage

What are some reasons people might give for not consecrating their lives to God? Have you ever had those objections?

Do you think you gain, lose, or remain the same when you consecrate your life to God? Why?

Is it possible to be partly consecrated or almost consecrated? Why or why not?

Have you consecrated your life to God? If not, why not do it now?

Act

Search your heart to see if there is anything you are holding back from God.

Chapter 6
Using Your Talents
discover your hidden gifts

Tune In

What is the best present you have ever received? Was it tangible or intangible?

Explore

What are some of the spiritual gifts God has given? (See Rom. 12, 1 Cor. 12, or Eph. 4 if you are not familiar with them.)

What are some other gifts God has given?

Why do you think God gives gifts to people?

List some reasons why people may be reluctant to use their gifts.

Engage

Do you know what gifts God has given you? If not, how might you discover them?

Have you ever felt that God was calling you to do something special in the world? Tell about that experience.

In what ways have you benefited from the gifts of others?

How do you feel about the prospect of using your gifts for others? Excited? Challenged? Eager? Afraid? Explain why.

Thinking about your family and community, what opportunities to serve do you see where you might make a difference?

Act

Make an inventory of your time, talent, and treasure, listing the gifts that God has given you to serve others.

Chapter 7
How to Enjoy Giving Away Money
putting God first in your finances

Tune In

If you could look into the future, would you do it?

Explore

Name some of the great things God has done in the past and has promised to do in the future.

What commands concerning generosity or giving has God given us in the Bible?

What is the relationship between obedience and generosity? Between obedience and faith?

How do you think God expects us to use our resources — as individuals and as a group? Is there a difference?

Why do you suppose most Christians do not tithe?

Engage

How are your financial priorities an expression of your personal values?

What is the biggest problem area in your personal finances?

Have you put God first in your personal finances? If so, describe that decision. If not, what causes your reluctance?

Act

Review your giving for the past year. Challenge yourself to step up one level in your commitment.

Chapter 8
Welcoming Others
the lifestyle of hospitality

Tune In

Do you prefer to be the host or guest of a party?

Explore

How would you define hospitality?

What biblical teachings or stories remind us of the need to show hospitality to others?

What are some contemporary situations in which people benefit from hospitality?

What are some signs that a person is either "open" or "closed" in his or her attitude toward welcoming others?

Engage

Do you think of yourself as being a hospitable person? Why or why not?

Are there some times at which—or some people with whom—you find it difficult to practice hospitality? Why?

Have you ever benefited from the welcome or hospitality of another person? Describe what happened.

What are some positive things that could result in your life from being open to others?

List some practical ways in which you could practice hospitality in your setting.

Act

Invite someone into your home this week.

Chapter 9
Experiencing God's Goodness
generosity and reward

Tune In

Tell about the latest shopping bargain you discovered.

Explore

Read Matthew 6:1–4 and Luke 6:38. What do you learn about reward from these texts?

This chapter listed three possible benefits of generosity. Describe how each of them could result from being generous.

Can you list other possible benefits that we receive when we practice generosity?

Engage

Have you experienced the connection between generosity and reward in your life? If so, describe it.

What is the connection between generosity and potential?

Name some reasons why people may hesitate to be generous. How would you answer those objections in light of the principle of reward?

In what ways have you seen a lack of generosity hinder the success of a person or organization?

What would you do today if God doubled your faith? Your resources? Your potential?

Act

This week, ask God to give you new opportunities to be generous—and new opportunities to grow.

Chapter 10
Seeing the World through God's Eyes
the power of vision

Tune In

Imagine that you are standing atop Willis Tower in Chicago. What do you see?

Explore

What is God doing in the world?

List some Bible passages that show us God's plan for the world.

It has been said that we (Christians) are God's Plan A for saving the world—and there is no Plan B. Do you agree with that statement? Why or why not?

Engage

When you look at the world, which do you see more of—problems or possibilities? What accounts for your answer?

What do you think God wants you to do with your life?

On a scale from one to ten, how satisfied are you that you are making an impact in the world?

What is your biggest hang-up or hesitation about joining God's mission to save the world?

Who or what inspires you most to catch God's vision for the world? Why?

Act

Make a list of the ministries you support in your local church as well as the various organizations to which you have contributed time or money this year. Choose one area where you will double your impact.

Chapter 11
Christ's Hands and Feet
creating social transformation

Tune In

Jesus once fasted for forty days. What is the longest you have gone without food? Describe your experience.

Explore

List some of the needs in the world that were mentioned in this chapter. Do you see these in your community?

Do you think that real transformation of communities is possible? Why or why not?

Some people have tangible needs such as food, shelter, or clothing. Others have intangible needs such as hope, fellowship, or justice. Which type of need do you think is more urgent?

List some organizations that are working to meet the needs of people. Tell what you know about them.

Engage

What do you feel when confronted with a person in need?

What do you see as the most pressing human need in your community? What makes you think so?

Of the three possible actions with regard to human need: relief, development, or justice, which appeals most to you? Why?

List some resources you have that could make an impact on the world.

Act

Commit yourself this week to taking the next step in meeting the needs of others.

Chapter 12
The Greatest Gift
bringing salvation to others

Tune In

Tell about how you came to know Jesus.

Explore

Do you agree that compassion for lost people is the starting point for evangelism?

What is God's vision for the world?

In your own words, what is the message of Jesus?

Do you agree that we already have the resources to complete the world mission? Why or why not? Have we accomplished it?

Engage

How much do you know about the unchurched people in your community? What could you do to find out more about them?

How important is giving to missions, outreach, and evangelism in your church? To you personally?

How would you respond to a person who thinks a church should spend all its resources to reach its own community?

What person, thing, or event most arouses your passion to reach the lost?

Act

Contact your pastor or a missionary whom your church supports this week and ask, "What do you most need in order to accomplish your mission?" Then seek to provide it.

Chapter 13
Your New Life Starts Now!
keys to personal change

Tune In

Is it difficult for you to make changes in your life? Why or Why not?

Explore

Do you agree or disagree that independence, indifference, and individuality are roadblocks to the a life of generosity. Why?

What is the connection between openness to others and a Give to Live life?

List some reasons why people procrastinate making positive changes in their lives. Which of those reasons might apply especially to beginning to live more generously?

Name some practical actions a person could take to begin practicing a lifestyle of generosity.

Engage

How strong is your sense of individualism?

What concepts in this study have been the most challenging to you personally? The most inspiring?

In what areas of your life do you see a need for change to practice a Give to Live life?

What is the next step for your personally in developing a lifestyle of generosity?

Act

Answer the question: "What will my life look like when I fully practice the principles of *Give to Live*?"

Notes

Introduction

1. This is a summary of advice given in John Wesley, "The Use of Money," in *The Works of John Wesley*, 3rd ed. (Kansas City, Mo.: Beacon Hill, 1979), L: 133. He said, "Having, First, gained all you can, and, Secondly, saved all you can, Then 'give all you can.'"

2. August Francke, *A Guide to the Reading and Study of the Holy Scriptures*, trans. William Jaques (London: D. Jaques, 1813), lv.

3. Craig Brian Larson, ed., "Giving" in *750 Engaging Illustrations for Preachers, Teachers, and Writers* (Grand Rapids, Mich.: Baker, 1993), 193.

4. Samuel Hearn and J. B. Tyrell, *A Journey from Prince of Wales's Fort in Hudson's Bay to the Northern Ocean* (Toronto: The Champlain Society, 1911), 96–98.

5. Kevin G. Harney, *Seismic Shifts: The Little Changes That Make a Big Difference in Your Life* (Grand Rapids, Mich.: Zondervan, 2005), 200.

6. Philip Yancey, *The Jesus I Never Knew* (Grand Rapids, Mich.: Zondervan, 1995), 38–39.

Chapter 1

1. See Brendon Baillod, "The Wreck of the Steamer Lady Elgin," Ship-wreck.com, accessed February 16, 2012, http://www.ship-wreck.com/ shipwreck/projects/elgin/; and Robert Cottrill, "Have I Done My Best for Jesus," WordwiseHymns.com, accessed February 16, 2012, http://wordwisehymns.com/2010/05/08/today-in-1689-christian-von-rosenroth-died/.

2. A. W. Tozer, *The Knowledge of the Holy* (New York: Harper Collins, 1961), 82.

3. C. S. Lewis, *Mere Christianity* (New York: MacMillan, 1952), 118.

Chapter 2

1. Tim Hansel, *Holy Sweat* (Waco, Tex.: Word, 1987), 46–47.

2. "The Cat," The Illustrator, accessed December 15, 2011, http://www.sermonillustrator.org/illustrator/sermon1/cat.htm.

3. "Trials of a Missionary," Bible.org, accessed December 15, 2011, http://bible.org/illustration/trials-missionary.

4. "Trust Him When Thy Wants Are Many," Hymnal.net, accessed January 27, 2012, http://www.hymnal.net/hymn.php/nt/647.

Chapter 3

1. Frederick M. Lehman, "The Love of God," 1917, accessed January 27, 2012, http://library.timelesstruths.org/music/The_Love_of_God.

2. "Satisfaction," Dictionary.com, accessed January 27, 2012, http://dictionary.reference.com/browse/satisfaction.

3. "Thoughts on the Business of Life," Forbes.com, accessed February 16, 2012, http://thoughts.forbes.com/thoughts/contentment-benjamin-franklin-content-makes-poor.

4. "First Thanksgiving," Bible.org, accessed February 14, 2012, http://bible.org/illustration/first-thanksgiving.

5. "Building Blocks for a Better Marriage," SermonCentral.com, accessed February 14, 2012, http://www.sermoncentral.com/sermons/building-blocks-for-a-better-marriage-james-kelley-sermon-on-family-38057.asp.

6. Ibid.

7. Jonathan G. Yandell, "Gladys Aylward," in *1001 Quotes, Illustrations, and Humorous Stories for Preachers, Teachers, and Writers*, ed. Edward K. Rowell (Grand Rapids, Mich.: Baker, 2008), 396.

8. Waldo Weaning, "Three Levels of Giving," Bible.org, accessed February 15, 2012, http://bible.org/illustration/three-levels-giving.

9. "The Talent Show," SermonIllustrator.org, accessed February 15, 2012, http://www.sermonillustrator.org/illustrator/sermon1a/talent show.htm.

10. Alan Smith, "How Much Do You Own in That Direction?" Thought for the Day, accessed February 17, 2012, http://tftd.faith site.com/content.asp?CID=19874.

11. Neil Anderson, "Using our Gifts and Talents," OnePlace.com, accessed February 15 2012, http://www.oneplace.com/devotionals/neil-andersons-daily-in-christ/using-our-gifts-and-talents-30631.html.

Chapter 4

1. Adapted from Dan Stires, "Caring for One Another," Sermon Central.com, accessed February 15, 2012, http://www.sermoncentral.com/sermons/caring-for-one-another-dan-stires-sermon-on-call-of-the-disciples-143285.asp.

2. "Thy Kingdom Come," SermonPlayer.com, accessed February 15, 2012, http://sermonplayer.com/c/eaglepointe/pdf/119812840_2534.pdf.

3. This oft-quoted poem is often attributed to James Patrick Kinney, but I have not been able to verify its source.

Chapter 5

1. Kevin G. Harney, *Seismic Shifts: The Little Changes That Make a Big Difference in Your Life* (Grand Rapids, Mich.: Zondervan, 2005), 188.

2. W. E. Vine, Merrill F. Unger, and William White, *Vine's Complete Expository Dictionary of Old and New Testament Words*, s.v. "kingdom" (Nashville: Thomas Nelson, 1985), 144.

3. Elesha Coffman, ed., *Christian History Newsletter*, November 30, 2001.

4. John L. Ronsvalle and Sylvia Ronsvalle, *The Poor Have Faces: Loving Your Neighbor in the 21st Century* (Grand Rapids, Mich.: Baker, 1992), 45, quoted in Craig L. Blomberg, *Preaching the Parables: From Responsible Interpretation to Powerful Proclamation* (Grand Rapids, Mich.: Baker, 2004), 51. See more statistics by the Ronsvalles at http://www.emptytomb.com.

5. Van Morris, "Random Guidance," in *1001 Illustrations that Connect: Compelling Stories, Stats, and News Items*, eds. Craig Brian Larson and Phyllis Ten Elshof (Grand Rapids, Mich.: Zondervan, 2008), Illustration 19.

6. Todd Hertz, "$500 Tooth Saves the Day," Ibid, Illustration 157.

7. Francis Chan, *Crazy Love: Overwhelmed by a Relentless God* (Colorado Springs: David C. Cook, 2008), 118–119.

8. Ted W. Engstrom, *The Essential Engstrom* (Colorado Springs: Authentic Publishing, 2007), 124.

Chapter 6

1. Roy B. Zuck, ed., "Conflict," in *The Speakers Quotebook* (Grand Rapids, Mich.: Kregel, 1997), 84.

2. "Helen Keller," BrainyQuote.com, accessed February 6, 2012, http://www.brainyquote.com/quotes/quotes/h/helen kelle121771.html.

3. Bruce Larson, *My Creator, My Friend: The Genesis of a Relationship* (Dallas, Tex.: Word, 1986), 76.

4. Brian Matherlee, "Because I Can or Because I'm Called," Sermon Central.com, accessed February 15, 2012, http://www.sermon central.com/sermons/because-i-can-or-because-im-called-brian-matherlee-sermon-on-gods-provisions-125074.asp?page=2.

5. "Mother Teresa," All Great Quotes, accessed February 6, 2012, http://www.allgreatquotes.com/mother_teresa_ quotes.shtml.

6. Maxwell Maltz, *Psycho-Cybernetics: A New Way to Get More Living Out of Life* (New York: Simon and Schuster, 1989), 55.

7. Edgar Guest, "It Couldn't Be Done," PoetryFoundation.org, accessed February 15, 2012, http://www.poetryfoundation.org/poem/173579.

8. Martin Luther King, Jr., "The Drum Major Instinct," Stanford.edu, accessed February 15, 2012, http://mlk-kpp01.stanford.edu/index.php/encyclopedia/documentsentry/doc_the_drum_major_instinct/.

9. Karl Menninger, "Wit and Wisdom from Dr. Karl," Menninger Clinic.com, accessed February 15, 2012, http://www.menninger clinic.com/about/early-history.htm.

10. "Benjamin Franklin's Inventions, Discoveries, and Improvements," USHistory.org, accessed February 16, 2012, http://www.us history.org/franklin/info/inventions.htm.

Chapter 7

1. Source unknown.

2. Source unknown.

3. John Maxwell, *Developing the Leaders Around You: How to Help Others Reach Their Full Potential* (Nashville: Thomas Nelson, 1995), 72.

4. John Casey, "Putting Your Weight Down," Preaching Today.com, accessed February 15, 2012, http://www.preaching today.com/illustrations/1998/april/2443.html.

5. Billy Graham, *Unto The Hills: A Daily Devotional* (Nashville: Thomas Nelson, 2010), June 16.

6. "Martin Luther," Thinkexist.com, accessed February 7, 2012, http://thinkexist.com/quotes/martin_luther.

7. Dave McFadden, "Being a Good Steward of My Treasure," Sermon Central.com, accessed February 15, 2012, http://www.sermoncentral.com/sermons/being-a-good-steward-of-my-treasure-dave-mcfadden-sermon-on-gifts-giving-101683.asp.

8. "John Wesley," Thinkexist.com, accessed February 7, 2012, http://thinkexist.com/quotation/when_i_have_money-i_get_rid_of_ it_quickly-lest_it/210228.html.

9. Graham, March 23.

10. "John Wesley," Daily Christian Quote, accessed February 7, 2012, http://dailychristianquote.com/dcq wesleyjohn.html.

11. "Henry Ford," Bible.org, accessed February 17, 2012, http://bible.org/ node/9911.

12. "Giving," Sermon Illustrations, accessed February 7, 2012, http://www.sermonillustrations.com/a-z/g/giving.htm.

Chapter 8

1. Herb Gardner, *The Collected Plays* (New York: Applause Books, 2001), 127.

2. Mary Barrett, "Hospitality: Our Contract with Jesus," Ministry Magazine.org, accessed February 16, 2012, http://www.ministry magazine.org/archive/1995/September/hospitality-our-contract-with-jesus.

3. T. R. Glover, *The Jesus of History* (n.p.: CreateSpace, 2011), 44.

4. John Wooden, BrainyQuote.com, accessed February 9, 2012, http://www.brainyquote.com/quotes/quotes/j/johnwooden106293.html.

5. "Weekend Roundup: Good Samaritan, News Opinions; Purple Weed & More," *The Nevada Herald*, April 4, 1976, http://news.google.com/newspapers?id=LZofAAAAIBAJ&sjid=Z9Q EAAAAIBAJ&pg=1426%2C156592.

6. Bruce Larson, *My Creator, My Friend: The Genesis of a Relationship* (Dallas, Tex.: Word, 1986), 101.

7. Matthew Henry, "Deuteronomy 15," in *Matthew Henry's Commentary on the Whole Bible* (n.p.: n.d.), http://www.ccel.org/ccel/ henry/mhc1.Deu.xvi.html.

Chapter 9

1. Sarah Eekhoff Zylstra, "Compassionate Conservatives," *Christianity Today* (February 2007), http://www.christianitytoday.com/ ct/2007/february/13.21.html.

2. John Beukema, "Lottery Winner Only Wants New Nylons," PreachingToday.com, accessed February 17, 2012, http://www.preaching today.com/illustrations/2006/november/9112706.html.

3. Shane Claiborne, *The Irresistible Revolution* (Grand Rapids, Mich.: Zondervan, 2006), 50.

4. "A Thoughtful Gift," Sermons.org, accessed February 15, 2012, http://www.sermons.org/xmasstories.html.

5. Author unknown, "Multiplying Talents," in *1001 Illustrations that Connect: Compelling Stories, Stats, and News Items*, eds. Craig Brian Larson and Phyllis Ten Elshof (Grand Rapids, Mich.: Zondervan, 2008), Illustration 44.

6. Kevin G. Harney, *Seismic Shifts: The Little Changes That Make a Big Difference in Your Life* (Grand Rapids, Mich.: Zondervan, 2005), 206.

7. Thomas B. Costain, *The Three Edwards* (Cutchogue, N.Y.: Buccaneer Books, 1962), 166–167.

8. "A Story with Some Teeth: Fridge Gets a New Smile," *Chicago Tribune*, December 20, 2007, http://articles.chicagotribune.com/2007-12-20/sports/0712190874_ 1_teeth-new-smile-procedure.

Chapter 10

1. Heather Gemmen Wilson, "Sex Trafficking," *Not the Worst Blog You'll Ever Read* (blog), December 11, 2006, http://www.this heather.com/2006/12/sex-trafficking.html.

2. Heather Sackett, "Horse Show Competitor Rides to Help Others," *Lake Placid News*, July 9, 2009, http://www.lakeplacidnews.com/page/content.detail/id/501317/Horse-Show-competitor-rides-to-help-others.html?showlayout=0.

Chapter 11

1. Marlene LeFever, "Looking Beyond Numbers," in *1001 Illustrations that Connect: Compelling Stories, Stats, and News Items*, eds. Craig Brian Larson and Phyllis Ten Elshof (Grand Rapids, Mich.: Zondervan, 2008), Illustration 49.

2. Brett Kays, "Blaming God for Evil," in *1001 Illustrations that Connect: Compelling Stories, Stats, and News Items*, eds. Craig Brian Larson and Phyllis Ten Elshof (Grand Rapids, Mich.: Zondervan, 2008), Illustration 222.

3. Tom Krattenmaker, "A Witness to What Faith Can Be," *USA Today*, December 18, 2006.

4. Ward Williams, "Jesus' Vacation," in *1001 Illustrations*, Illustration 297.

5. Joseph Stowell, "Called to Christ, Called to Compassion," in John Fuder, *A Heart for the City: Effective Ministries to the Urban Community* (Chicago: Moody, 1999), 42.

6. Nathaniel Philbrick, *Mayflower: A Story of Courage, Community, and War* (New York: Viking, 2006), 300.

7. Edward Gilbreath, *Reconciliation Blues: A Black Evangelical's Inside View of White Christianity* (Downers Grove, Ill.: InterVarsity, 2006), 101–103.

8. Keri Wyatt Kent, "Pampered with a Purpose," *Today's Christian Woman*, November/December 2006.

9. Keith Jordan, "Giving of Themselves," *Reader's Digest*, November 2005.

10. D. A. Carson, *For the Love of God: A Daily Companion for Discovering the Treasures of God's Word*, vol. 2 (Wheaton, Ill.: Crossway, 1999), January 23.

11. Os Guinness, *The Call: Finding and Fulfilling the Central Purpose of Your Life* (Nashville: Thomas Nelson, 2003), 104–105.

12. Harold Songer, "Abundance," e-steeple.com, accessed February 16, 2012, www.e-steeple.com/browse-by-topic/A/Abundance.html (site discontinued).

13. Timothy Keller, "The Cost of Mission," October 30, 1994, mp3, http://sermons2.redeemer.com/sermons/cost-mission.

Chapter 12

1. Bill Hybels, *Who You Are When No One's Looking: Choosing Consistency, Resisting Compromise* (Downers Gove, Ill.: InterVarsity, 1987), 35.

2. "10/40 Window: Do you need to be stirred to action?" Southern Nazarene University, accessed February 25, 2012, http://home.snu.edu/~hculbert/1040.htm.

3. Ralph Winter, "Missions Movement: War-Time Lifestyle," Christian History, accessed February 16, 2012, http://www.christianity today.com/ch/1987/issue14/1430.html.

4. Association of Church Missions Commissions, newsletter, fall 1989, 1. The ACMC became to a ministry of pioneers in 2007 and then was retired in 2011 after thirty-five years of service.

5. T. E. Lawrence, Thinkexist.com, accessed February 9, 2012, http://thinkexist.com/quotation/those_who_dream_by_night-in_the_dusty_recesses_of/9428.html.

6. Randy Alcorn, "World Evangelism Statistics, and Missions Giving" (blog), July 17, 2008, http://www.epm.org/blog/2008/Jul/17/world-evangelism-statistics-and-missions-giving.

7. Tony Campolo, *Let Me Tell You a Story* (Nashville: Thomas Nelson, 2000), 164–165.

Chapter 13

1. John Maxwell, *Developing the Leaders Around You: How to Help Others Reach Their Full Potential* (Nashville: Thomas Nelson, 1995), 131–132.

2. Frank Irving Fletcher, "Thoughts on the Business of Life," Forbes.com, accessed February 10, 2012, http://thoughts.forbes.com/thoughts/heart-frank-irving-fletcher-no-man-can.

3. Henry Van Dyke, BrainyQuote.com, accessed February 10, 2012, http://www.brainyquote.com/quotes/quotes/h/henryvandy145354.html.

4. Tony Campolo, *Let Me Tell You a Story* (Nashville: Thomas Nelson, 2000), 91.

5. John Mason, *Know Your Limits—Then Ignore Them* (Tulsa, Okla.: Insight, 1999), 91.

6. Irene Sax, "Encouragement," Sermon Illustrations, accessed February 10, 2012, http://www.sermonillustrations.com/a-z/e/encouragement/htm.